The Good H

The Good Hotel Guide 2008

Great Britain & Ireland

Editors:
Desmond Balmer
and Adam Raphael

Editor in Chief:
Caroline Raphael

Founding Editor:
Hilary Rubinstein

Contributing Editors:
Bill Bennett
Nicola Davies
Peter Hines

The Good Hotel Guide Ltd

Please send reports on hotels to
The Good Hotel Guide
50 Addison Avenue, London W11 4QP
or (if posted in UK)
Freepost PAM 2931, London W11 4BR
Tel/fax: 020-7602 4182
Email: Goodhotel@aol.com
or Goodhotel@btinternet.com
Website: www.goodhotelguide.com

The Good Hotel Guide Ltd

This edition first published in 2007 by
The Good Hotel Guide Ltd

1 3 5 7 9 10 8 6 4 2

Design: Mick Keates
Production: Hugh Allan
Text editor: Daphne Trotter
Managing editor: Alison Wormleighton
Computer consultant: Gwyn Evans

A CIP catalogue record for this book may be found in the British Library.

ISBN-10: 0-9549404-2-3
ISBN-13: 978-0-9549404-2-3

Typeset from authors' disks by
MATS Typesetters, Southend-on-Sea, Essex
Printed and bound in Great Britain by
Cromwell Press, Trowbridge

Contents

The truly independent guide

This is the leading independent guide to hotels in Great Britain and Ireland. Hotels cannot buy their entry as they do in most rival guides. No money changes hands, and the editors and inspectors do not accept free hospitality on their anonymous visits to hotels. The only vested interest is that of the reader seeking impartial advice to find a good hotel.

Our hotels are as independent as we are. Most are small, family owned and family run. They are places of character where the owners and their staff spend time looking after their guests, rather than reporting to an area manager. We look for a warm welcome, with flexible service. We like hotels where early-departing guests are offered breakfast before the kitchen officially opens, and arriving visitors are given a cup of tea and home-made cake. We don't like rules which are written for the convenience of the hotel, not the guest.

We recognise that one size doesn't fit all: each traveller has individual requirements. This explains the diversity of choice in our selection. An entry for a grand country house might be followed by one for a simple B&B. We describe some of our favourite places as guest houses; they may not have the full range of facilities, but the welcome will be warm. Our B&Bs, never with fewer than three bedrooms, often provide a better breakfast than some five-star hotels. We include some chain hotels, especially in the larger cities; each one will have met our criteria of high standards of service.

Our readers play a crucial role by reporting on existing entries as well as recommending new discoveries. Reader reports, written on the forms to be found at the back of the book or sent by email, bring our entries to life, and give the *Guide* a unique 'word-of-mouth' quality. Many correspondents join our Readers' Club (see page 59). The editors make a balanced judgment based on these reports, backed where necessary by an anonymous inspection.

Annual updates give the *Guide* an added edge. We drop a hotel if there has been a change of owner unless reports after the change are positive, if this year's reports are negative, or in rare cases where there has been no feedback. About 80 hotels fall by the wayside every year; a similar number are introduced, often interesting new discoveries.

Introduction

At a time when British hotels have become the most expensive in Europe, an independent guide which separates the outstanding from the run of the mill is crucial. This year, the average price paid for a hotel room in the UK jumped to £98, a rise of 17 per cent. Bath is the most expensive city for hotels in Britain (£114), even higher than London (£107). At these prices, a visitor cannot afford to make a mistake.

Fast-rising property prices, increasing council taxes, and the highest level of VAT in Europe put British hotels at a disadvantage compared with their European counterparts. But many are also weighed down by a large bank loan, and some suffer from a get-rich-quick mentality. Whatever the reason, and there are many, including the high level of the pound, high British hotel prices are damaging our tourist industry. Currently many British hotels are simply not competitive with their Continental European counterparts.

Reluctantly this year, we have abandoned the 'Budget' label that we formerly used to identify hotels which charge £35 per person or less for bed and breakfast. Only a few now meet this criterion, and some of those that do feel that the term itself is open to misunderstanding. Rosemary Reeves, owner of one of the *Guide*'s best-loved guest houses, *The Grey Cottage* at Leonard Stanley, sent us a comment from one of her visitors: '"Budget" indicates basic, cheap and often nasty, which you are certainly not.'

You don't have to look far to find the reason for this shift of meaning. The low-cost airlines have created a climate where travel has become a commodity. In the 21st century, the consumer identifies the 'budget' label with low levels of service as well as low cost: find your own seat, carry your own baggage; want something extra, you pay for it. In contrast, the *Guide* has always sought places which provide high levels of service. That is why we have dropped the 'Budget' label. We have, however, introduced a new 'Value' category in our Hotelfinder chapter: we identify ten of the hotels which we think give especial value within their price range. There are many others scattered throughout the pages of the *Guide*.

Why are British hotels so distrustful of children?

'I have been buying your guide as the essential prerequisite for decent weekends away and holidays for years, but have recently become distinctly unwelcome at many of the suggested hotels, and barely tolerated at most others.' A mother's lament this year about a 'problem' that is all too familiar: she has a two-year-old daughter and a baby on the way. 'The fact that we have children does not mean that we have lowered our standards or want to stay at expensive child-only ghettoes,' she writes. 'We would like to go on staying at the kind of small, personal hotel that we have always enjoyed.'

It is sad that we still find it easier to compile a list of dog-friendly hotels than to identify places which make a point of welcoming children. One hotelier wrote to tell us that he was no longer 'able to serve children's high tea'. He explained: 'We are very happy to see children here, but experience shows that British children under ten years old are generally not happy in the dining room of an evening.' But how do children learn how to behave in hotels and restaurants if they are not given the experience?

No fewer than 137 hotels in this edition of the *Guide* impose some form of age restriction on child guests. A further 37 enforce an age limit on children in their restaurant in the evening. Many of these are outstanding hotels, and we would not wish to exclude them for this discrimination. On the positive side, we highlight hotels with a child-friendly policy in our entries; and we are particularly pleased to receive reports from parents on such places. Take for example, *Pen-y-Gwryd*, Nant Gwynant, where, one reader told us, the owners, Brian and Jane Pullee, hold a 'touching ceremony' for youthful visitors who have climbed to the top of Snowdon. 'Mrs Pullee celebrates their achievement with a tiny speech, and rewards the young climbers with a badge.'

The isolation of children is peculiarly British (one of our writers recalls that the only time he encountered child restrictions in France was at a hotel owned by a British couple). The reader who raised the issue wants to support the British tourist industry, but worries that she will be driven abroad by prevailing attitudes. Memories of childhood holidays often shape our choice of destination as an adult. Hotels which discriminate against children are missing a business opportunity this year, and for years to come. The Pullees' successors may well be welcoming the children of this season's young climbers.

Could do better

A senior *Guide* inspector, not in the first flush of youth, arrived at the *Old Bridge Hotel*, Huntington. 'Your room is up there,' said the young receptionist, pointing a finger vaguely skywards. Minutes later she watched as our grey-haired, female inspector lugged a heavy suitcase up two flights of steps. A regular correspondent wrote of another hotel: 'A healthy young man appeared, we registered, and he gave us keys, telling us that our rooms were on the first floor and pointing at a staircase. He presumably thought my 86-year-old mother enjoyed carrying her cases up stairs, through stiff fire doors and along narrow corridors.'

A poor welcome is one of the most frequent complaints made by *Guide* correspondents. Another is the unhelpfulness often encountered by potential visitors when they telephone to make a reservation. 'Why do hotels not realise how important first impressions are?' one reader remarked. A reply by a linguistically challenged member of staff or a telephone answering machine is not a good start, nor is being made to wait in a series of digital queues.

Muzak

The presence of this aural curse is another cause of frequent complaint. Why should it be imposed on visitors who would prefer peace and quiet? Many of our readers, particularly musicians, hate muzak. We suspect that it is often played to keep the staff, rather than the guests, happy. We asked every hotel included in this volume whether or not they play piped music, and we give details in the rubrics.

Old warhorses stay the course

'What's new this year?' is a question we are often asked. And we share the excitement of the quest for the new. This year, the *Guide* has 73 new entries, many of them interesting discoveries. We say full marks to those newcomers who know how to attract attention in the new media age. It would be wrong, however, to forget those places that manage the even more difficult task of maintaining high standards year after year. This is where the *Guide* comes into its own, as our entries are updated every year by readers and inspectors who provide fresh reports on old favourites.

Kit Chapman, owner of *The Castle at Taunton*, wrote to us this year: 'It really irritates me to see all those industry awards featuring "best newcomer" prizes. What happens? Said newcomer operates for a year or two and then sells up or goes awol. It's time someone invented an "old warhorse" award for sheer endurance in striving to maintain standards in an increasingly difficult business world.'

The *Guide* has long recognised some fine old warhorses in our annual *César* awards. *The Castle at Taunton* won theirs as long ago as 1987. Four other early *César* winners deserve special mention for having had an entry in every edition of the *Guide*: *Rothay Manor*, Ambleside; *Lastingham*

Grange, Lastingham; *Currarevagh House,* Oughterard; and *Ballymaloe House,* Shanagarry. We salute our long-serving hoteliers alongside the bright-eyed newcomers.

Thank you

Finally, we thank our many loyal readers and our team of inspectors for their illuminating reports without which this guide would not exist. Please write to us whenever you stay at a hotel, whether or not it is in the *Guide.* Even just a few lines on our report form or by email are welcome, but we also love getting letters full of detail and anecdote. They make this guide what it is – an independent and reliable passport to the best of British and Irish hotels.

DESMOND BALMER AND ADAM RAPHAEL
July 2007

The 2008 César Awards

Our *César* awards, named after César Ritz, the most celebrated of all hoteliers, are the accolade that hoteliers most want to win. Every year we nominate ten places that stand out for their excellence. But our laurel wreaths are not given for grandeur. We champion independent hotels of all types, sizes and budgets. The following special places caught our eye this year. Each has a distinct character; what they have in common is an attitude to service that puts the customer first. Previous *César* winners, provided that they are still in the same hands and as good as ever, are indicated in the text by the symbol of a small laurel leaf.

London hotel of the year

The Capital

For more than 30 years, David Levin has maintained high standards at his grand hotel in miniature, an oasis of calm in busy Knightsbridge. The intimate restaurant is rightly regarded as one of the best in London.

Country hotel of the year

Hipping Hall, Cowan Bridge

At Andrew Wildsmith's stone manor house, the hotel and restaurant fire on all cylinders to provide a profoundly satisfying stay. A spectacular 15th-century Great Hall is a fitting setting for Jason Birkbeck's impressive modern cooking.

Gastropub of the year

The Lord Poulett Arms, Hinton St George

In a pretty Somerset village, Steve Hill and Michelle Paynton have renovated their 17th-century inn with flair. The bedrooms, with delightfully quirky touches, have real wow factor. Hideki Koike produces superior gastropub cooking in the bustling bar/restaurant.

Rural idyll of the year

Yalbury Cottage, Lower Bockhampton

The silence is palpable at Mark Collyer and Roy Fiddemont's chocolate box conversion of four thatched cottages in peaceful Hardy country. Everything demonstrates attention to the well-being of guests; Ben Streak's modern cooking is delicious.

Historic house of the year

Moccas Court, Moccas

At their family home, a magnificent Grade I listed Georgian house in lovely parkland by the River Wye, Ben and Mimi Chester-Master greet their guests with engaging informality. He cooks delicious dinners, served in a beautiful round room.

Restaurant-with-rooms of the year

West Stoke House, West Stoke

In glorious country on the edge of the South Downs, Rowland and Mary Leach run their former dower house with a charming touch of eccentricity. Richard Macadam, the manager, is supremely professional; the cooking of Darren Brown gets better and better.

Scottish guest house of the year

The Dower House, Muir of Ord

At their gabled *cottage-orné* in a beautiful Highland garden, Robyn and Mena Aitchison are warmly welcoming hosts. His gutsy modern British cooking is much liked; breakfasts are generous, and children are welcomed.

Green guest house of the year

Y Goeden Eirin, Dolydd

Trains are met, local transport is promoted, and recycling and composting policies are followed at John and Eluned Rowlands's small Welsh guest house near Caernarfon. Organic produce is used in the innovative cooking.

Welsh country house of the year

Plas Tan-Yr-Allt, Tremadog

Overlooking the Glaslyn estuary, this 19th-century villa is run on house-party lines by Michael Bewick and Nick Golding. They have decorated the bedrooms with great style. Dinner, around a huge refectory table, is a glorious, social affair.

Country house hotel of the year

Cashel House, Cashel Bay

The McEvilly family do everything right at their 19th-century manor house, a warm, lived-in place by a Connemara bay. Kay McEvilly runs the house in a relaxed but professional manner; the cooking of Arturo Amit and Arturo Tillo is much admired.

Hotelfinder

A visit to a hotel should be a special occasion. This section will help you find a good hotel that matches your mood, whether for romance or sport, or to entertain the children. Don't forget to turn to the full entry for the bigger picture.

DISCOVERIES

There are 73 new hotels in the *Guide* this year. Here are some of the most interesting finds

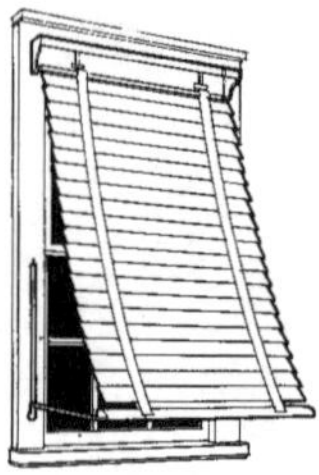

The Devonshire Arms at Beeley, Beeley

The Duke and Duchess of Devonshire have given a make-over to this old coaching inn on the Chatsworth estate, blending ancient and modern. A pub, not a hotel, it is 'good fun, perfect for a short break'. 'Dishes to suit most tastes' are served in the bright, modern brasserie.
Read more: page 104.

The Swan Hotel, Bradford-on-Avon

Renovated 'with sensitivity' in 2007, this listed hotel in a picture-perfect small town has exposed beams, polished wooden floors, modern-coloured walls and stylish furniture. Real ales in the bar, popular with locals. The cooking is 'unpretentious, fairly priced, good'. Breakfast had an 'excellent' buffet, 'delicious full English'. Bedrooms are 'simple, classy, light'.
Read more: page 123.

The Bull Hotel, Bridport

Richard and Nicola Cooper have created a 'lovely atmosphere' with their renovation of this listed coaching inn in the centre of a handsome market town. Bedrooms have 'all the right ingredients: antiques, ornate mirrors, supremely comfortable bed, spacious bathroom with powerful shower'. Chef Gerry Page uses seasonal local ingredients for his 'excellent' modern menus.
Read more: page 129.

The Trout at Tadpole Bridge, Buckland Marsh

Gareth and Helen Pugh, who earlier won a *César* at the *Painswick Hotel*, Painswick, have renovated this old Cotswolds pub with gardens that run down to the Thames. 'Dinners the strong point: fabulous bread basket, deliciously creamy garlic and potato soup, tender steak.' The bedrooms are 'pleasant, immaculate'.
Read more: page 137.

Parford Well, Chagford

Tim Daniel, for many years manager and co-owner of the elegant *Number 16* in London, runs this smart little B&B in a village in the Dartmoor national park. 'It is all a simple concept, but beautifully done; comfortable and tasteful.' The house, in a pretty walled garden,

has three 'immaculate' small bedrooms with 'everything you might possibly expect'.
Read more: page 145.

The Rectory Hotel, Crudwell

A new name, and a contemporary feel, have been given to this 16th-century former rectory in a Victorian walled garden by the church in a village near Malmesbury. 'A very pleasant place', it has a fine hall/sitting room with soft chairs and magazines, high-ceilinged bar/lounge, wooden-panelled dining room. The 'classic British' food is 'interesting, perfectly cooked'.
Read more: page 160.

The Gurnard's Head, Zennor

Charles and Edmund Inkin, owners of the popular *Felin Fach Griffin* in Wales, have overhauled a run-down building in a remote hamlet with 'beautiful sea views' near St Ives. It has been given 'lovely, up-to-date decor, light and airy' with a Mediterranean feel. Children of all ages are welcomed; so are dogs.
Read more: page 338.

Kilberry Inn, Kilberry

In a beautiful, remote setting on the Kintyre peninsula, this tiny red-roofed inn has been restored by Clare Johnson and David Wilson ('extremely likeable'). It is 'a haven of good food and wine plus some unusual beers'; a 'sensibly short menu' is served in two dining areas 'with plenty of character'. The 'stylish, modern bedrooms' are in adjacent buildings.
Read more: page 371.

Corsewall Lighthouse, Kirkcolm

Down a roughish track on a windy promontory north of Stranraer, this listed working lighthouse has been 'sympathetically' turned by Gordon Ward into a 'truly unique hotel'. Some smaller bedrooms are in the main building; suites are in separate buildings with panoramic views. The daily-changing five-course dinner is 'spot on for cooking and service'.
Read more: page 376.

Rhiwafallen, Llandwrog

'Thoroughly renovated to a high standard', this traditional granite farmhouse, near Caernarfon, is run as a restaurant-with-rooms by Kate and Rob John, who 'do almost everything themselves'. It is furnished in contemporary style, with an emphasis on natural materials. The food 'is a cut above the ordinary, genuine without unnecessary flourishes; one of the best meals we've eaten this decade', says an inspector.
Read more: page 428.

GREEN

Enjoy a guilt-free stay at these hotels and restaurants which take active measures to protect the environment

One Aldwych, London

Paper, plastic and cardboard are recycled, and long-life light bulbs are used at Gordon Campbell Gray's ultra-modern conversion of the old *Morning Post* offices, 'one of the UK's most eco-friendly hotels'. Bio-active bath products (with recyclable containers) are provided in the bathrooms. Organic ingredients are used in the two restaurants.
Read more: page 72.

The Old Rectory, Boscastle

'We aim to give you a luxurious stay without compromising our green credentials,' say Chris and Sally Searle, who run a B&B in an old rectory immortalised by Thomas Hardy. Their sustainable policy embraces growing their own produce, or buying locally; recycling all rubbish; supporting local tradespeople; and free collection of visitors who arrive by bus or train.
Read more: page 117.

The Chilgrove White Horse, Chilgrove

'We are lucky to live and work in a very old building (1765) in beautiful countryside. We want to share that with our guests now, and to leave it in a good state for generations to come,' write Charles and Carin Burton. They have a gold award from Green Tourism Business Scheme; a 14-point environmental policy is 'shared' with all new staff, and visitors.
Read more: page 149.

Bedruthan Steps Hotel, Mawgan Porth

'We care about the world we will pass on to our children,' say the owners of this north Cornish hotel who aim to make it 'as environmentally friendly as possible'. Guests are asked to help by recycling newspapers, magazines, cans and plastic bottles, using the bins provided; they are also offered a free 'real nappy kit'. 'Behind the scenes we reuse a wide variety of items.' Low-energy lighting has been installed.
Read more: page 231.

Milden Hall, Milden

Juliet and Christopher Hawkins promote 'the environmental benefits of sensitively farmed

Suffolk countryside and the real value of good local produce' at their listed 16th-century farmhouse. They promise to buy goods 'that are not over-packaged', to recycle and compost as much as possible, to be energy-efficient, and to 'minimise the use of the car'.
Read more: page 236.

Primrose Valley Hotel, St Ives

'We don't stand on a soapbox at breakfast,' say the eco-friendly owners of this Edwardian villa above the Blue Flag Porthminster Beach, 'but doing nothing is not an option.' Their website lists 50 things to do without a car, and an optional £1 charge on bills has raised more than £4,000 in two years for Cornish marine conservation initiatives.
Read more: page 280.

Innsacre Farmhouse, Shipton Gorge

'In a quiet way, we try to damage the environment as little as possible,' say Sydney and Jayne Davies, who are committed to local produce, organic where possible, at their 17th-century Dorset farmhouse. They promise: 'Injunctions in the rooms about waste and recycling are authentic rather than formulaic.' 'Hair shirts are entirely absent,' say visitors.
Read more: page 290.

Strattons, Swaffham

A discount of 10% on the B&B rate is given to visitors who arrive by public transport at Vanessa and Les Scott's Palladian-style villa ('a small but perfect hotel') in a Norfolk market town. The Scotts, long-time promoters of green awareness, rewrite their environmental policy annually; staff are encouraged to come up with new ideas.
Read more: page 300.

Argyll Hotel, Iona

On the 'spiritual' island of Iona, Daniel Morgan and Claire Bachellerie have a strong ecological ethos at their small hotel in a row of 19th-century houses. Most of their produce is organically home grown, local or Fairtrade. They are committed recyclers and users of environmentally friendly products. Corridor lights are dimmed in the evening.
Read more: page 370.

Y Goeden Eirin, Dolydd

Guests arriving by train are met at Bangor, and advice is given about the 'excellent local transport' at John and Eluned Rowlands's very green, very Welsh, small guest house near Caernarfon. They follow recycling and composting policies, serve locally sourced organic food, Fairtrade tea and coffee, and have installed solar panels.
Read more: page 421.

ROMANCE

Get in the mood for love by spiriting your chosen one away to one of these romantic hotels

Lovelady Shield, Alston

In three-acre gardens with the River Nent running through, this Cumbrian country hotel is loved for the silence and the unspoilt setting ('an oasis from modern life'). A romantic package includes a bouquet of flowers and champagne in the bedroom; Room 9 has a four-poster bed.

Read more: page 81.

Amberley Castle, Amberley

'Like a fairy tale, we were well looked after,' say visitors to this luxury hotel, a Grade I listed monument surrounded by a 60-foot wall and a dry moat, at the foot of the South Downs. The 'enchanting bedrooms' have an 'ambience of peace and silence'. Choose a room to match your taste; perhaps Pevensey, which has direct access to the battlements.

Read more: page 82.

Tor Cottage, Chillaton

A trug with sparkling wine, home-made truffles and fresh fruit is presented to arriving guests at Maureen Rowlatt's upmarket B&B in large wooded grounds in a secluded mid-Devon valley. Ask for Laughing Waters, a clapboard cabin by a stream, in a private corner of the garden: it has a log fire, a terrace, a hammock, and a gypsy caravan.

Read more: page 149.

Le Manoir aux Quat'Saisons, Great Milton

Ramond Blanc celebrates romance and provides 'luxury at a price' at his famous *domaine.* All bedrooms are individually designed: try Dovecot, on two levels, with a freestanding bath with glass surround and full-body water jets. Three menus to choose from in the conservatory restaurant (two *Michelin* stars), including the ten-course *menu découverte.*

Read more: page 184.

The Star Inn, Harome

Linger over dinner at this *Michelin*-starred North Yorkshire inn where 'delicious' modern cooking is served in an atmospheric bar and elegant dining room. Then stay in the lodge, a medieval longhouse, perhaps in Room 1, which has a bath at the

end of the bed, and a shower big enough for two; or Room 7, in the ground floor annexe, with its large spa bath 'for sociable bathing'.
Read more: page 187.

Lavenham Priory, Lavenham

An unusual and romantic B&B: there are five spacious bedchambers at this sympathetically restored 13th-century priory, later an Elizabethan merchant's house. There are sloping, beamed ceilings, an oak floor, unusual beds (four-poster, polonaise, sleigh). The suite has a ribboned four-poster, a slipper bath, and a private sitting room.
Read more: page 209.

Swinton Park, Masham

'A joy and delight,' say visitors to this creeper-clad 17th-century castle in huge landscaped grounds, now a luxury hotel with a spa. Sleep in the circular Turret suite with rooms on three floors linked by a steep curved staircase: there's a fabulous view from the shower room; and a freestanding rain bath on the top floor.
Read more: page 229.

The Old Railway Station, Petworth

'My surprised boyfriend was speechless,' said a reader who took him to this disused Victorian railway station which has been restored with flair. The biggest bedrooms are in the station building, but your beloved may prefer one of the 'well-designed' Pullman cars: they have 'particularly comfortable' beds.
Read more: page 258.

Isle of Eriska, Eriska

On a 300-acre private island ('a beautiful, peaceful location'), this Scottish baronial mansion is 'set apart from other hotels by outstanding service and attention to detail'. In the house, the tower room has a 'fantastic view, well worth climbing 54 stairs'; each of the spa suites in the grounds has a conservatory and private garden with hot tub.
Read more: page 359.

Ardanaiseig, Kilchrenan

Privacy is guaranteed at a suite in an old boat house on the shore of peaceful Loch Awe, in the grounds of this baronial mansion. Double-height windows open on to a deck above the water. The bedroom is on a mezzanine level; a balustrade allows uninterrupted views across the loch to Ben Lui.
Read more: page 371.

FAMILY

All too rare in Britain, these are places where parents can relax knowing that their children are welcomed

The Bull Hotel, Bridport

'We like children,' say Richard and Nicola Cooper, who have renovated this coaching inn in the centre of the handsome market town. Parents themselves, they have created family rooms to 'provide grown-up spaces for parents, with separate adjoining accommodation for the kids'.
Read more: page 129.

The Trout at Tadpole Bridge, Buckland Marsh

Gareth and Helen Pugh, also parents, have made their old Cotswold pub by a bridge on the Thames 'as child-friendly as possible'. They promise 'decent children's menus (no nuggets), games, toys, plenty of space outdoors'. They are a friendly couple; their staff are attentive.
Read more: page 137.

The Evesham Hotel, Evesham

'Our children had a really good time; they loved the swimming pool and play area,' say visitors to John and Sue Jenkinson's quirky hotel which has lots to keep younger guests happy. 'Fun things' in the garden include a trampoline and slides; there's an indoor swimming pool, a junior *à la carte* menu, and a games room. The Alice in Wonderland suite is particularly popular with families.
Read more: page 168.

Moonfleet Manor, Fleet

'Our five-year-old daughter made loads of friends and loved every minute,' says a returning visitor to this sprawling Georgian manor house (part of the Luxury Family Hotels Group) behind the Fleet lagoon. It has 'excellent' facilities for children of all ages, including a swimming pool, computer games, ping-pong, indoor tennis and a supervised nursery. Parents can pack as many offspring as they can tolerate into their bedroom.
Read more: page 173.

Fritton House, Fritton

There is much for children to do on the Somerleyton estate of the Hon. Hugh Crossley, who has turned this old inn into a contemporary hotel. There are rowing boats and pedaloes on a lake; assault courses and aerial

slides at an adventure playground; giant board games and slides; and a model farmyard.
Read more: page 176.

Seaview Hotel & Restaurant, Seaview

'Children are welcomed, not merely tolerated', at this small hotel/restaurant in a seaside village on the Isle of Wight. Much to do on the island: beaches with rock pools abound; access to a local sports club, with swimming pool, tennis, etc. The very young have high tea at 5 pm.
Read more: page 288.

Calcot Manor, Tetbury

A large family party (three years old to 70) found 'something for everyone' at this child-friendly conversion of a 14th-century Cotswold farmhouse, cottages and outbuildings. It has baby-listening, an Ofsted-registered crèche, and a Playzone in a converted tithe barn. Suites have a bedroom for parents, and a sitting room with bunk beds or sofa beds for the young.
Read more: page 306.

Glenfinnan House, Glenfinnan

Children under 12 are accommodated free at this family-friendly, handsome, Victorian mansion on the shores of Loch Shiel. They have a playground, and special menus in the 'relaxed' dining room. Fans of the Harry Potter movies will recognise Glenfinnan Viaduct; you can also see Ben Nevis, and the monument on the spot where Bonnie Prince Charlie raised his standard.
Read more: page 363.

Porth Tocyn Hotel, Abersoch

'We have three young sons of our own; we reckon we know quite a bit about the joys and pitfalls of children in hotels,' say Nick and Louise Fletcher-Brewer, whose family has run this popular country hotel for five decades. 'Our children enjoyed their stay, making new friends and exploring the hotel and grounds,' say visitors. Parents can relax on sunbeds in the pretty garden while the children enjoy the many activities. Excellent beaches close by.
Read more: page 413.

The Druidstone, Broadhaven

In a 'stunning cliff-top position', this unusual place is 'a fantastic family-friendly establishment with bags of character'. The Bell family's 19th-century house is liked for the 'relaxed atmosphere plus real sense of comfort'. The hotel's own fisherman catches mackerel and sea bass before breakfast. The children's high tea 'is always interesting'.
Read more: page 416.

SEASIDE

Pack your buckets and spades and be ready to get sand in your shoes at these coastal places

Bedruthan Steps Hotel, Mawgan Porth

Above a large golden, sandy North Cornish beach with Atlantic waves for surfers, and sandy coves and rock pools for explorers, this purpose-built hotel is popular with families. There are countless activities for children. If they tire of the beach, they can enjoy 'fantastic play areas', indoor and outdoor swimming pools, children's clubs, and 'water fun sessions'. There are 'amazing sea views', coastal walks, and a spa.
Read more: page 231.

driftwood hotel, Portscatho

Above a quiet cove, in a 'peaceful, beautiful setting' in the Roseland peninsula, this contemporary hotel has superb sea views from most bedrooms. Steep steps through woodland lead down to a private beach; there is good walking on the coastal paths. The modern interiors with a 'simple white background and shades of blue' are in keeping with the seaside theme. A two-roomed Cabin on a hillside is 'tremendous fun'.
Read more: page 262.

St Martin's on the Isle, St Martin's

On a 'charming' small island (just 30 houses and a population of 100), this smart hotel was built in the 1980s to resemble a row of fishermen's cottages. It stands by a beach, and other sandy stretches can be found on the island. Many bedrooms face the sea; the best views are from the dining room on the first floor.
Read more: page 281.

Soar Mill Cove Hotel, Soar Mill Cove

In grounds that slope down to an isolated cove with a beautiful beach, framed by cliffs and regularly swept, this single-storey stone and slate building has a 'spectacular' setting. All around is National Trust land. Glorious views from the restaurant; sea-facing rooms, with patio, get the afternoon sun. Children are genuinely welcomed (high tea, high chairs, etc).
Read more: page 292.

The Wellington Hotel, Ventnor

Built into cliffs above a safe, sandy beach, this 'smart, stylish' hotel on the south side of the Isle of Wight has 'grandstand views of waves' which can be enjoyed from its balconies, terraces and large sun deck. It is a minute's walk to the 'safe and friendly' sands. All but two bedrooms face the sea.

'The only noise at night is the sound of the waves.'
Read more: page 317.

Kylesku Hotel, Kylesku

A former 17th-century coaching inn on the shoreline where lochs Glendhu and Glencoul meet in glorious north-west Sutherland. There are many magnificent beaches in the area; Oldshoremore beach, flanked by rocky cliffs, is recommended for a family picnic. Children are welcomed at the 'simple but comfortable inn'.
Read more: page 379.

Port Charlotte Hotel, Port Charlotte

On the water's edge of a pretty conservation village on the Isle of Islay, this small hotel is liked for its friendly staff. You can reach a sandy beach from the garden. There are lovely views across the water, and many deserted beaches elsewhere, on an island warmed by the Gulf Stream.
Read more: page 393.

Trefeddian Hotel, Aberdyfi

The Cave family's large Edwardian hotel on Cardigan Bay, stands above a 'fantastic' four-mile beach of golden sand (good for surfing, swimming, kite-flying, etc). 'Having brought my children, I'm now back with my grandchildren,' says one visitor. Even in busy half-

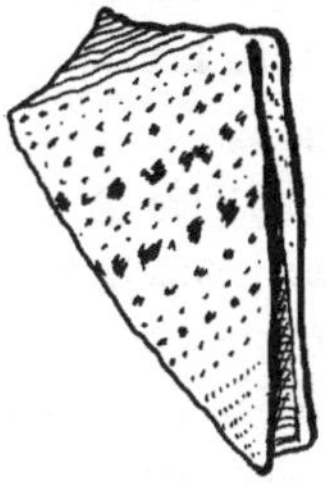

term weeks, the hotel 'absorbed all the children and kept cool'.
Read more: page 411.

The Druidstone, Broadhaven

A 'slightly rough-around-the-edge feel only adds to the welcome eccentricity' of this 'fantastic, family-friendly establishment', above 'a huge almost deserted beach'. 'Folk coming in from the beach do not want to worry about buckets of sand,' says the owner, Jane Bell.
Read more: page 416.

The White House, Herm

The only hotel on this beautiful, tiny, car-free island: on the approach by boat, visitors see a long stretch of sand that unfolds into three beaches. Over the hill is Shell Beach, rich in colour from tiny shells. 'Children are treated like VIPs.'
Read more: page 444.

GOURMET

Savour the pleasures of the table at these hotels and restaurants-with-rooms without having to drive home

Little Barwick House, Barwick

'A model small hotel,' says a visitor to Tim and Emma Ford's 'relaxed' restaurant-with-rooms, a Georgian dower house in quiet countryside, where 'cuisine comes first'. His cooking is 'delicious': 'mouth-watering appetisers' followed by 'delicious' modern dishes, eg, boned quail stuffed with a chicken and wild mushroom mousse. Well-spaced tables in an airy dining room. Stylishly arranged breakfasts.
Read more: page 94.

Fischer's Baslow Hall, Baslow

'Wonderful as ever', Max and Susan Fischer's restaurant-with-rooms is a Derbyshire manor house on the edge of the Chatsworth estate. Vegetables from the kitchen garden are used for the well-sourced modern cuisine. 'Excellent' tasting menu; 'good value' *menu du jour* with dishes like roast cod, herb crust, mussel and potato chowder.
Read more: page 96.

Simpsons, Birmingham

The atmosphere is relaxed at chef/*patron* Andreas Antona's listed Georgian mansion, a restaurant with four themed bedrooms, in a leafy suburb. With co-chef Luke Tipping, he serves classic French dishes (eg, pan-fried foie gras, lemon confit, dried apple, pain d'épice) in a series of dining rooms (in one you can watch the cooking through glass).
Read more: page 113.

Read's, Faversham

'Consistently excellent', Rona and David Pitchford's restaurant-with-rooms, in a handsome Georgian manor house in immaculate gardens, has 'a lovely atmosphere'. She is front-of-house, he the chef, serving classic seasonal dishes, eg, roasted breast of Gressingham duckling with glazed cherries, bok choi from the garden. Four vegetarian options are offered verbally each day.
Read more: page 172.

The Yorke Arms, Ramsgill-in-Nidderdale

'A magnificent restaurant, with beautifully maintained rooms and welcoming staff.' This year's praise for this creeper-clad old inn beside a village green of a North

Yorkshire village. The 'superb' cooking of Frances Atkins is highly praised: her dishes are 'classic with a modern touch', eg, Nidderdale lamb pie (faggots, braised lamb shank, horseradish lentils, boulangère potatoes). 'Miles away from any Yorkshire stereotype.'
Read more: page 266.

The Castle at Taunton, Taunton

Richard Guest is the fourth chef to be nurtured to a *Michelin* star by Kit and Louise Chapman at their elegant, castellated hotel. His modern British cooking is inventive, eg, fillet of beef with chips cooked in dripping, sauce Choron. Local producers are named on the menus. 'Very good' cheeseboard; 'excellent' wines. 'Helpful, caring' staff.
Read more: page 303.

The Stagg Inn, Titley

'This must be the most unpretentious and laid-back *Michelin*-starred establishment in Europe,' said inspectors of Steve and Nicola Reynolds's ancient inn in a small village in rolling Herefordshire countryside. 'A lovely place,' say visitors this year. The candlelit dinner is based on 'excellent local ingredients', eg, saddle of venison with horseradish gnocchi and kummel. 'All good value, as was the wine list.'
Read more: page 309.

Knockinaam Lodge, Portpatrick

Tony Pierce's cooking is much admired at this grey stone 19th-century hunting lodge, shielded by cliffs and thickly wooded hills. In the formal, candlelit dining room, he serves classic/modern Scottish dishes in 'small but satisfying portions', perhaps native salmon, potato water, paysanne of leek, red wine and star anise reduction. Vegetarians are well catered for.
Read more: page 393.

Plas Bodegroes, Pwllheli

'Restful, civilised and homely', Chris and Gunna Chown's restaurant-with-rooms, a Georgian house on the Lleyn peninsula, has a Scandinavian-inspired interior. In the 'gorgeous' dining room, his 'culinary wizardry' is 'superlative' (eg, rosemary kebab of mountain lamb with minted couscous). 'The staff are utterly charming.'
Read more: page 436.

Ballymaloe House, Shanagarry

At her family's hotel/restaurant and cookery school in an ivy-clad Georgian house east of Cork, the veteran Myrtle Allen ('what a star') still presides, 'carving for the magnificent Sunday buffet'. Jason Fahy's five-course dinner is served in five small dining rooms. 'You feel cherished.'
Read more: page 494.

GASTROPUBS

You can expect interesting cooking and a lively atmosphere in these revitalised old inns and pubs

The Drunken Duck Inn, Barngates

Named after ducks that drank from a leaking case, this Cumbrian inn has been renovated 'with a sure touch' by Stephanie Barton. The chef, Neil McCue, uses local ingredients, mainly organic, in his modern British cooking; perhaps confit drunken duck leg with forced rhubarb salad; spring lamb with celeriac ravioli.

Read more: page 93.

The Horse and Groom, Bourton-on-the-Hill

Tom and Will Greenstock run their Cotswold coaching inn as an informal dining pub. Tom is the 'engaging' front-of-house, Will the chef, serving 'just right' modern dishes from a blackboard menu beside the bar (popular with villagers). Try dishes like a 'meaty' crab cake; hake with a three-butter sauce; 'super side dishes including crispy chips, crunchy carrots and cabbage'.

Read more: page 119.

The Masons Arms, Branscombe

'A super place to stay', this popular 14th-century creeper-covered inn stands in the centre of an attractive National Trust village. The chef, Richard Reddaway, uses local ingredients for his English cooking in the busy bar (salmon, mussel, haddock and leek stew), and the restaurant (tian of West Country pork fillet).

Read more: page 128.

The Nobody Inn, Doddiscombsleigh

With inglenook fireplaces, antique settles and carriage lanterns, Nick Borst-Smith's 16th-century inn in a remote Devon hamlet is a haven for wine and whisky lovers (over 600 wines, 240 whiskies). 'The local ingredients, from cheeseboard to marmalade, were delicious.' The seasonal menu has interesting dishes, eg, local ostrich fillet with cranberry, gherkin and ox-tongue sauce.

Read more: page 163.

The Royal Oak, East Lavant

Nick and Lisa Sutherland's flint-stone Georgian inn, on the edge of the South Downs, is popular with locals as well as overnight guests,

who stay in six modern bedrooms in a converted barn. The restaurant, with a *carte* and blackboard specials, opens seven nights a week; the style is 'French, Mediterranean, new English', eg, terrine of ham hock; Thai baked sea bass and pak choi.
Read more: page 166.

The Museum Inn, Farnham

In a peaceful village on the Dorset/Wiltshire border, this part-thatched 17th-century inn combines a bright modern look with retained original features. Meals are served at wooden tables in the bar and, at weekends, in the *Shed* restaurant. Clive Jory is the new chef, serving modern dishes, eg, venison with butternut squash mash, honey-glazed parsnips and sour cherry jus.
Read more: page 171.

The Lord Poulett Arms, Hinton St George

A 'delightfully quirky' renovation of a 17th-century pub in a pretty village of stone houses and thatched roofs. The service is 'superb' in the busy bar/restaurant (with old oak and elm tables). The Japanese chef, Hideki Koike, uses local ingredients for his 'superior cooking'; perhaps baby spinach and pea soup; chowder of gurnard, conga eel and smoked bacon.
Read more: page 194.

Black Boys Inn, Hurley

A short walk from the River Thames, this 16th-century inn, with modern bedrooms at the back, was highly praised this year. In the dining room, which has polished oak floor, well-spaced tables, the food is 'reasonably priced, served with grace. We enjoyed crispy veal cheeks with creamed paysanne vegetables, fresh Salcombe crab, bewitching sauces.'
Read more: page 199.

The Felin Fach Griffin, Felin Fach

The 'evening buzz and welcoming bar' are enjoyed at this 'civilised' terracotta-coloured inn between the Brecon Beacons and the Black Mountains. The Dutch chef, Ricardo Van Ede, uses home-grown organic ingredients for his award-winning cooking: 'We drooled over scallops with morel and asparagus; probably our best risotto ever.'
Read more: page 422.

The Bell at Skenfrith, Skenfrith

In a peaceful setting beside an old stone bridge across the River Monmow, this 17th-century inn faces a ruined castle. The chef, David Hill, serves elaborate modern British dishes, eg, truffled leek soup; loin of halibut, basil and chorizo couscous.
Read more: page 437.

COUNTRY HOUSE

These bastions of old-fashioned service provide sumptuous bedrooms and plenty of pampering

Hartwell House, Aylesbury

In 90 acres of landscaped parkland, this stately home, with Jacobean front and Georgian rear, was for five years King Louis XVIII of France's court in exile. Magnificent public rooms 'flooded with light'. 'Nothing forbidding or gloomy'; antiques, 'to be used not just admired'. Jacket and tie no longer obligatory in dining rooms.
Read more: page 90.

Farlam Hall, Brampton

'A warm and welcoming hotel', this manorial house, approached up a sweeping drive, stands in a landscaped garden with a large ornamental lake. It has been run by the Quinion and Stevenson families, 'hands-on owners', since 1975. Public rooms are ornate, with patterned wallpaper, open fires; bedrooms are traditionally furnished.
Read more: page 126.

Gravetye Manor, East Grinstead

A creeper-covered Elizabethan manor standing amid woodland in grounds designed by William Robinson, pioneer of the English natural garden. The 'aroma of polish and pot-pourri' pervades the oak-panelled hall and staircase; there are leaded windows, open fires, antique furniture. Visitors like the 'personal touches' and 'genuine care and attention to detail'.
Read more: page 165.

Stock Hill House, Gillingham

'Pampering without pretension' is enjoyed at Peter and Nita Hauser's small luxury hotel, a Victorian building in landscaped, tree-lined grounds, with terraced lawns, herbaceous borders, and a small lake fed by a stream. There is a 'splendid formal lounge', and a 'cosy snug with log fire'. The bedrooms have antiques and curios. In the formal dining room, the 'delicious' cooking reflects the host's Austrian heritage.
Read more: page 178.

Hambleton Hall, Hambleton

'Exceptionally well run', Tim Hart's Victorian mansion has a 'memorable' setting on a peninsula jutting into Rutland Water. His wife, Stefa, designed the classic

interiors with Nina Campbell: fine fabrics, antiques, paintings, open fires. Four bedrooms, and the drawing room, have been refurbished 'with an identifiable *Hambleton* look'. The 'elegant' cooking of Aaron Patterson is a highlight.
Read more: page 186.

Hotel Endsleigh, Milton Abbot

In huge, 'glorious' grounds, this Victorian shooting and fishing lodge has been converted into a luxury hotel by Olga Polizzi; her 'charming' daughter, Alex, is the manager. 'A triumph of design, and an obvious labour of love', it has the atmosphere of 'a modern, comfortable country house'; everything 'exudes quality'. At night, candles provide much of the lighting.
Read more: page 236

Sharrow Bay, Ullswater

'Oozing a certain confidence', this famous country house hotel has a spectacular setting on Lake Ullswater. Now owned by von Essen Hotels, it is managed by Andrew King. Sitting rooms are 'beautifully furnished and decorated'; bedrooms, 'chintzy, cosy', 'exceptionally comfortable', with 'thoughtful provision of books and games'. The 'refined, classical' cooking of long-serving chef Colin Akrigg is admired.
Read more: page 315.

Gilpin Lodge, Windermere

'Quietly and understatedly perfect', John and Christine Cunliffe's Lakeland house is surrounded by moors, woodlands and 20-acre grounds. 'Helpful and hands-on owners', they run it informally (no reception area or bar). 'No weddings or conferences, just the art of relaxation,' they promise. The cooking of Chris Meredith is 'beautifully presented without being fussy'.
Read more: page 330.

Kinnaird, Dunkeld

Service is 'friendly without being overbearing' at this 'well-appointed' country house, a creeper-covered mansion on a vast Perthshire estate. It has family portraits, antiques, billiards; 'log fires seemingly ablaze in every room make this like a visit to a luxurious private home'. A chambermaid brings early morning tea to the bedroom on a tray.
Read more: page 352.

Castle Durrow, Durrow

'Space and elegance are married with quality furnishings and carefully chosen antiques' at this early 18th-century house which has been restored by Peter and Shelly Stokes. It stands in large grounds with manicured lawns, formal, herb, and vegetable gardens. Staff are 'pleasant and charming in the Irish way'.
Read more: page 472.

CITY CHIC

At these contemporary hotels you can expect high standards of service as well as cutting-edge urban style

One Aldwych, London

Gordon Campbell Gray's ultra-modern conversion of the Edwardian offices of the *Morning Post.* Muted tones, white pillars and a giant statue of an oarsman in the double-height lobby, with huge arched windows; trendy flower arrangements and a collection of 400 pieces of contemporary art displayed throughout. Even the smaller bedrooms are stylish. All rooms have the latest technology and an elegant granite bathroom.
Read more: page 72.

The rockwell, London

Architect Michael Squire and Tony Bartlett have converted two Victorian terrace houses on the Cromwell Road into a designer hotel. It has a bright facade with pea-green highlights; inside a modern decor, interesting wallpaper, patterns and colours. 'Exciting' mezzanine suites have a lounge and sleeping area down a curved staircase.
Read more: page 75.

The Zetter, London

In trendy Clerkenwell, this converted 19th-century warehouse has a striking contemporary decor. A glass entrance door leads to a white-walled lobby with a pink Murano chandelier. Bedrooms have bright colours; great lighting with a pink option; a patio with a panoramic view in roof studios. Good meals in the informal restaurant.
Read more: page 77.

drakes, Brighton

Andy Shearer's luxury design hotel is an expensive conversion of two 19th-century town houses on the seafront. Signage is discreet, just an etched opaque glass panel in the setting-down area. There's a touch of the orient about the style; the original central staircase has been given a contemporary twist. Bedrooms have bamboo wood floors, shutters. Some have a wet room, suites have a freestanding bath.
Read more: page 130.

Hotel du Vin Bristol, Bristol

The western outpost of this small chain of contemporary hotels is an imaginative conversion of old warehouses in the city centre. A glass canopy entrance opens to a reception desk beside a 100-foot chimney, and a sweeping steel and oak staircase. Some bedrooms are on two levels; all have the trademark bathroom with stand-alone bath, and powerful shower.
Read more: page 131.

42 The Calls, Leeds

The first boutique hotel outside London, this conversion of an old mill on the River Aire in the city centre retains its 'flair for design and decor'. It has hundreds of original paintings and drawings, bold fabrics, stylish public rooms. Bedrooms are 'fully kitted out for the business traveller', beds are 'supremely comfortable. Attractive weekend rates.
Read more: page 210.

Hart's Hotel, Nottingham

'A fine combination of modern design and good service', Tim Hart's purpose-built hotel, on the site of a medieval castle, has curved buttresses, lots of glass, limestone floors. It is liked for 'first-class service', 'comfortable' bedrooms (most have 'breathtaking' views), 'efficient' bathrooms. Interesting snacks, and wine and champagne by the glass in the 'crisp, bright' bar; excellent meals in the associated *Hart's* restaurant.
Read more: page 251.

Old Bank, Oxford

Jeremy Mogford displays his abundant collection of modern art in the public rooms and bedrooms of his striking hotel, an elegant conversion of three buildings, one a former bank, on the High. 'Stylish without being too cutting edge; modern but relaxing.' The old banking hall houses *Quod*, a lively bar and restaurant.
Read more: page 254.

Malmaison, Glasgow

A chic conversion of a former Greek Orthodox church in the city's financial district, with an 'unfussy' contemporary decor. There is a magnificent Art Nouveau staircase, and a champagne bar in the atrium. Bedrooms have bold colours and stripes, big beds, 'all the usual goodies'.
Read more: page 363.

The Clarence, Dublin

On Temple Bar, the city's lively cultural quarter on the south bank of the Liffey, this 19th-century warehouse has been restored with 'minimalist designer chic' by Bono and The Edge, of rock group U2. Wi-Fi Internet access in all public areas; modern bedrooms; upmarket toiletries in the bathroom. French/Irish cooking in the restaurant.
Read more: page 468.

GARDENS

Glorious gardens and beguiling landscapes make each of these hotels a destination in its own right

Lindeth Fell, Bowness-on-Windermere

In large grounds on a hill above Lake Windermere, Pat and Diana Kennedy's Edwardian house has 'superb views over the water'. The 'extensive, well-tended' gardens, filled with rhododendrons, azaleas and specimen trees, are best in spring and early summer, when open to the public. Lawns are laid for bowls and croquet.

Read more: page 121.

Hob Green, Markington

In 800-acre grounds with award-winning gardens, a farm, and woodlands, this 18th-century house, now a traditional hotel, has wide views across a valley. Walkways and paths lead through extensive herbaceous borders to feature lawns, a rockery. There's a large greenhouse and a walled kitchen garden.

Read more: page 228.

Meudon, Mawnan Smith

The Pilgrim family's traditional hotel stands at the head of a valley leading to a beach. It has a fine example of a Cornish 'hanging garden' (designed by Robert Were Fox *c.* 1800), with specimens from early RHS expeditions to the Yangtze and the Himalayas; rare shrubs, plants, trees. Giant Australian tree ferns were brought as ballast by packet ships to Falmouth, and thrown overboard in the bay.

Read more: page 233.

Millgate House, Richmond

Above the River Swale in the pretty town of Richmond, this 'spectacular Georgian town house' stands amid a much-admired sheltered walled garden. Meandering paths lead through luxuriant planting with an array of fragrant roses. Two of the bedrooms overlook the gardens, which are open to non-residents in summer.

Read more: page 269.

Stone House, Rushlake Green

'Everything is delightful' at Jane and Peter Dunn's 15th-century house (with 18th-century modifications) which stands in vast grounds in unspoilt rural Sussex. Guests are encouraged to enjoy the 'wonderful' five-and-a-half-acre garden, which has an ornamental lake, gazebos, a rose garden, a hundred-foot herbaceous border, a walled herb and a vegetable and fruit garden. A 'quintessentially English country experience'.

Read more: page 276.

Spread Eagle Inn, Stourton

A bonus of staying at this famous old inn is that it is in the middle of one of the great gardens of England, Stourhead (National Trust): 'you get free entry and can enjoy them after closing time'. The landscaped grounds, designed by Henry Hoare II in the 18th century, have classical temples and grottoes around a lake; a series of vistas; exotic trees in mature woodland.

Read more: page 297.

The Island Hotel, Tresco

The only hotel on this small private island which is famed for its subtropical 17-acre Abbey Gardens. The gardens' designer, Augustus Smith, built tall windbreaks and walled enclosures to allow species from 80 countries to flourish in terraces around the priory ruins. The hotter, drier terraces at the top suit South African and Australian plants; those at the bottom provide the humidity that favours flora from South America and New Zealand.

Read more: page 311

Rampsbeck, Watermillock

'You couldn't have a better setting' for this white-walled 18th-century country house on the shores of Lake Ullswater. It has spectacular views of lake and fells across 18-acre grounds, and it stands amid 'lovely gardens, with unusual

plants and well-tended lawns'. Many of the bedrooms have lake and garden views.

Read more: page 322.

Ladyburn, Maybole

An 'excellent retreat in a beautiful part of Scotland', Jane Hepburn's former dower house ('guests are treated as members of family') has large wild and formal gardens. Rhododendrons, bluebells, azaleas grow in spring. Guests may also walk in the grounds of the 'magnificent' neighbouring Kilkerran estate.

Read more: page 384.

Cashel House, Cashel Bay

In a sheltered bay on the lovely Connemara coast, the McEvilly family's 19th-century manor house has 'rambling gardens, full of surprises'. Kay McEvilly takes a keen interest in the gardens, which were planted by a previous owner, Jim O'Mara, parliamentarian and keen botanist. There are exotic flowering shrubs (many from Tibet), camellias and rare magnolias; woodland walks.

Read more: page 461

GOLF

Golfers and golf widows alike can enjoy these hotels, well placed for some of the best courses on these islands

Highbullen Hotel, Chittlehamholt

An 18-hole par-68 course winds its way around the wooded grounds of the Neil family's 'hotel, golf and country club'. Club selection is the key to a good round at this parkland course, which is protected by bunkers and water (especially on the par-3s); there are splendid views towards Exmoor and Dartmoor. For non-golfers there are three swimming pools, tennis and much else.
Read more: page 151.

Budock Vean, Mawnan Smith

On the south-facing bank of the Helford river, the attractive nine-hole parkland course at the Barlow family's traditional hotel is a good place to brush up your game. David Short runs three- and four-day golf schools, less intensive tuition breaks, and competition weeks for all handicaps, over five local courses.
Read more: page 232.

St Enodoc, Rock

On the Camel estuary, this contemporary hotel offers golf breaks at the adjacent St Enodoc links and other nearby courses. Don't miss the Church Course at St Enodoc, a fine traditional links designed by James Braid, with trademark undulating fairways, blind shots and firm greens. The course passes the sandy graveyard where John Betjeman is buried.
Read more: page 271.

2 Quail, Dornoch

Keen members of Royal Dornoch, Michael and Kerensa Carr describe their restaurant-with-rooms as 'undoubtedly the smallest golf hotel and restaurant in Scotland'. Golf has been played on these famous links since 1616; the course is popular with top American golfers preparing for the Open. The hospitality at *2 Quail* is 'outstanding'; Michael Carr's cooking is thought 'superb'.
Read more: page 351.

The Roxburghe Hotel & Golf Course, Heiton

In 200 acres of parkland in the grounds of the Duke of Roxburghe's castellated country house, this is the only championship course in the Scottish Borders.

The Duke, an avid golfer, commissioned Dave Thomas to build the course. From the elevated 14th tee, you can see a viaduct, and the River Teviot which hugs the left of the fairway.
Read more page 368.

Trefeddian Hotel, Aberdyfi

Guests at this large Edwardian hotel can get concessionary rates to play at the Aberdyfi links course, among the dunes of Cardigan Bay. The toughest test is the 12th, a par-3 to an elevated green with the sea to the right, and a steep bank to the left that kicks away anything other than the correct shot.
Read more page 411.

Stella Maris, Ballycastle

Golf memorabilia and photographs are on the walls of this converted 19th-century coastguard station in North Mayo. Terence McSweeney, who runs it with his wife, Frances Kelly, works for the US PGA in Florida in winter. He can guide golfers to the world-class links at Enniscrone and Carne and, further afield, Rosses Point and Westport.
Read more: page 453.

St Ernan's House, Donegal

On a wooded tidal island, this 'tranquil' and historic house is a few minutes' drive from the magnificent Donegal course at Murvagh. The fifth hole, known as the Valley of Tears, is a vicious 200-yard par-3, with high banks to the left of the hole, pot bunkers on the right. The reward, on the sixth tee, is a panorama of sea and hillside.
Read more: page 466.

Moy House, Lahinch

Antoin O'Looney's hotel overlooks Lahinch Bay, famous for its championship links created in 1927 by Dr Alister MacKenzie, one of the great golf course designers. Nature dictates the shape of the holes; fairways follow the dunes, and the greens follow the natural fall of the land.
Read more: page 482.

Admiralty Lodge, Miltown Malbay

Greg Norman's new course along the beach and dunes at Doonbeg is close to Pat O'Malley's Georgian country house on a flat stretch of the Clare coast. For a genuine links experience at a fraction of the cost (and no need for a handicap certificate), try the nine-hole Spanish Point just minutes away.
Read more: page 486.

FISHING

No need to cast around for the best beats; these hotels all have private access to rivers and lakes

The Arundell Arms, Lifton

A creeper-covered sporting hotel, run for 46 years by Anne Voss-Bark, an expert fly-fisher. She has 20 miles of fishing (salmon and brown trout in season) on the Tamar and its four tributaries, 'wild' rivers which rise on Dartmoor. There is a three-acre stocked lake with rainbow trout all year round. Fishing courses for all levels.

Read more: page 213.

The Peat Spade Inn, Longstock

Fly-fishing can be arranged at the chalk stream rivers near this old inn, which has been renovated by Lucy Townsend and Andy Clark. 'We also have access to a spring-fed private estate, perfect for beginners and improvers alike; a super fishing stalking water,' they say.

Read more: page 218.

The Sportsman's Arms, Wath-in-Nidderdale

Reached across an old packhorse bridge on the River Nidd, on which it has fishing rights, this unpretentious but smart Dales pub is popular with sporting visitors. The 'splendidly varied' clientele 'made a weekend fun'. The nearby Gouthwaite reservoir has wild brown trout.

Read more: page 323.

The Inn at Whitewell, Whitewell

In a lovely setting deep in the Forest of Bowland, this quirky inn has four rods on the Hodder for trout, sea-trout, and salmon in season. It has seven miles of river with 14 pools ('lots of interesting runs').

Read more: page 325.

Kinnaird, Dunkeld

The River Tay flows through the vast Perthshire estate of this creeper-covered mansion, a 'most well-appointed country house'. Guests may fish for salmon and trout on the Tay, and for trout in *Kinnaird*'s three lochs. Private ghillies and reserved beats for guests. Lunch can be served in one of the fishing huts. Good walking in the estate for those less interested in fishing.

Read more: page 352.

Gliffaes, Crickhowell

The trout- and salmon-laden River Usk runs through the large wooded grounds of this smart sporting hotel which owns a stretch of 2½ miles. Ghillies are available, and three-day fly-fishing courses for beginners are offered. The best bedrooms have a river view and balcony. Only fish from sustainable fisheries is served in the dining room.

Read more: page 419

Tynycornel, Talyllyn

In a 'most beautiful valley' on the shore of 222-acre Lake Talyllyn (which it owns) this white-fronted inn has been a fishing hostelry since 1800. 'A lot of money has been spent on it, and it looks good and works well,' says a visitor. The lake, which 'takes some beating' for fisherfolk, has one of the few remaining natural brown trout fisheries south of Scotland. Tuition, tackle, picnic lunches are available. There is a drying room and freezing facilities.

Read more: page 439.

Ballyvolane House, Castlelyons

Justin and Jenny Green 'typify the warmth for which the Irish are so well known' at their Georgian house in the Blackwater valley. They have four beats on a 24-mile stretch of the Blackwater, the best salmon fishing river in Ireland; these are available at all times in season, others can be arranged. When conditions on the river are impossible, there is fly fishing for rainbow trout on three lakes in the grounds.

Read more: page 464.

Newport House, Newport

On the estuary of the River Newport where it flows into Clew Bay, this Georgian mansion is run 'like a large private home' by Thelma and Kieran Thompson. They have eight miles of fishing on the River Newport, for spring salmon, grilse and sea trout; also fishing on Lough Beltra West, one of the few fisheries in Ireland where salmon can be fished from a boat. 'All our fish are wild,' they say.

Read more: page 488.

Currarevagh House, Oughterard

The Hodgson family's country house has a 'glorious setting of lake, lawns and woodland'. They have their own boats and ghillies on Lough Corrib, 'probably the best wild brown trout lake in Europe' (also pike, perch, and a small run of salmon from May to July). Fishing, usually from a drifting boat, is free (no licences or permits required). Good swimming and boating, too.

Read more: page 489.

WALKING

Your boots are meant for walking at these hotels which cater for serious ramblers and casual walkers alike

Biggin Hall, Biggin-by-Hartington

'Footpaths in all directions over beautiful countryside' lead from the grounds of this small hotel ('lovely, unfussy, simple') in the Peak District national park. One path starts at the side of the 17th-century stone house, which has antiques, mullioned windows, 'a marvellous fire in the living room'. Rooms in a barn conversion have an outdoor porch. Hearty cooking.
Read more: page 111.

The Leathes Head Hotel, Borrowdale

Popular with serious walkers and climbers, this Edwardian house, high up in wooded grounds outside Borrowdale, is run by Roy and Janice Smith who 'never cease to be available and are always friendly'. Daily-changing, 'quite ambitious', four-course dinner menu. The packed lunches are praised.
Read more: page 115.

Seatoller House, Borrowdale

Hikers and ramblers like this unpretentious guest house for its homely atmosphere, 'comfort, cuisine and warmth of welcome'. The 350-year-old building stands at the head of the beautiful Borrowdale valley, away from the main tourist areas. Traditional meals 'with a twist' taken at communal oak tables.
Read more: page 116.

Old Dungeon Ghyll, Great Langdale

In 'glorious scenery': at the head of the Great Langdale valley, this 300-year-old mountain hotel is owned by the National Trust; Neil and Jane Walmsley have managed it since 1984. It provides 'good value' for walkers, climbers and cyclists, 'a friendly welcome and decent grub'. Children welcomed.
Read more: page 183.

Underleigh House, Hope

Maps and packed lunches are provided for walks in the Peak District national park from Philip and Vivienne Taylor's barn and cottage conversion in the Hope valley. A 'delicious' breakfast is served around a large oak table in the flagstoned hall. 'Amazing value.'
Read more: page 196.

Heddon's Gate Hotel, Martinhoe

'Lovely, peaceful situation, superb walking,' say visitors to this small, old-fashioned hotel on steeply sloping grounds on the edge of Dartmoor. An 'excellent' afternoon tea (complimentary). Modern and traditional cooking in the dining room. Anne and Eddie Eyles are 'very friendly hosts'.
Read more: page 228.

Howtown Hotel, Ullswater

On the eastern shore of Lake Ullswater, Jacquie and son David Baldry's 'easy-going' guest house has fields and garden on one side, wooded hills on the other. 'Out on a limb, good for walkers,' say visitors. 'Traditional food; no surprises; generally good.' Generous breakfasts. Substantial picnics provided.
Read more: page 314.

Wasdale Head Inn, Wasdale Head

With a 'cosy, companionable atmosphere', this informal, three-gabled inn, seven miles up a dead-end road, with mountains on three sides, has long been popular with walkers and climbers. It has its own micro-brewery. The restaurant serves traditional dishes. 'Outstanding breakfast.' Packed lunches and cream teas available.
Read more: page 321.

The Airds Hotel, Port Appin

A folder in the bedroom details the walks near this old ferry inn, now run as a small luxury hotel by owners Shaun and Jenny McKivragan. 'Walking is perhaps the main pastime in the area,' they say. The Clach Thoull circular route around the loch starts here; nearby Glencoe has a range of trails. Paul Burns serves award-winning modern menus. 'Excellent' breakfasts and packed lunches.
Read more: page 392.

Pen-y-Gwryd Hotel, Nant Gwynant

'Oozing atmosphere', Brian and Jane Pullee's low-priced, 'mildly eccentric' inn at the foot of Mount Snowdon has long been popular with mountaineers. The bar is filled with climbing gear (this was the training base for Hillary's 1953 Everest expedition). There's a panelled lounge with log fire, and a 'natural' swimming pool in the garden. Substantial packed lunches.
Read more: page 432.

DOGS

No need to leave your best friend at home when visiting these hotels where dogs command special treatment

The Regent by the Lake, Ambleside

'A holiday for your dog to remember' is promised at Christine Hewitt's hotel opposite a slipway on Lake Windermere. Courtyard rooms allow dog owners to come and go as they please. 'We can prepare food for dogs the same as their owners; special requests and diets are no problem.'
Read more: page 83.

Corse Lawn House, Corse Lawn

Dogs can be exercised in fields within the extensive grounds of Baba Hine's 'unfussy, comfortable' listed Queen Anne building set back from the green and road in a village south-west of Tewkesbury. Bedrooms are 'like a spare room in someone's country house'; 'all requests are met with a smile'.
Read more: page 154.

Knocklayd, Dartmouth

Visiting dogs can sleep in the utility room or in the kitchen of Susan and Jonathan Cardale's large, rambling house at the highest point of Kingswear village. 'Very much a home; not for those who prefer a sanitised atmosphere', it is 'strongly recommended for dog lovers'. The Cardales have two elderly Labradors, Jack and Jessie, and Molly, a 'woolly little hearing dog for the deaf (retired)'.
Read more: page 161.

Overwater Hall, Ireby

Dogs are welcomed (no charge) at Adrian and Angela Hyde's castellated Georgian mansion in 18-acre grounds flanked by Skiddaw and surrounding fells. They may sit with their owners in the lounge (but not on chairs), and run about unleashed in the garden. Good walking from the door.
Read more: page 201.

Meaburn Hill Farmhouse, Maulds Meaburn

'We are dog-friendly,' say Annie Kindleysides and Brian Morris, owners of this 'blissfully relaxed' guest house in a 'peaceful and beautiful' village near Penrith. 'Even our dog was welcome to chill out in front of the fire,' says a visitor. Dogs are allowed in public rooms 'if acceptable to other guests'; there is a dog-walking area in the garden.
Read more: page 230.

Lydgate House, Postbridge

'Our dog was made very welcome,' say visitors this year to Peter and Cindy Farrington's unassuming late Victorian country house near the village's famous clapper bridge over the River Dart. The Farringtons have five cats, four dogs (not indoors) and two elderly sheep. Good walking on Dartmoor from the door.

Read more: page 263

The Boar's Head, Ripley

'Dogs are welcome providing they bring with them well-trained owners' at Sir Thomas and Lady Ingilby's old inn in a model village on their castle estate. Dogs are allowed (£10 charge) in two courtyard rooms, which may be smallish, but a 'turn-down Bono is placed in their basket, and water bowls are provided'.

Read more: page 269.

Prince Hall Hotel, Two Bridges

'Well-behaved dogs are very welcome at no extra charge,' say John and Anne Grove whose 18th-century house is in the middle of Dartmoor. 'The position is very special, facing south into a gentle valley.' You can walk from the grounds straight on to the moor. The Groves' dog, Bosun, a friendly black Labrador, welcomes visitors.

Read more: page 313.

Willowburn Hotel, Clachan Seil

Prospective canine guests receive a letter from the resident dogs and cat at Jan and Chris Wolfe's 'highly rated' small hotel on a little island on the shores of Clachan Sound. Sisko a 'food-guided' Labrador, Laren a 'non-stop play machine' collie, and Odo the cat explain the set-up to visiting dogs. The Wolfes are 'kind hosts'; the atmosphere is friendly.

Read more: page 348.

Rathmullan House, Rathmullan

A special room for dog lovers, 'complete with pooch's own bed', was included in a recent courtyard extension at the Wheeler family's handsome white mansion. It stands in a well-tended garden on a two-mile sandy beach on Lough Swilly, one of Donegal's finest. The informal country house is 'thoroughly well managed'.

Read more: page 491.

COTSWOLDS

Enjoy beautiful landscapes and explore towns and villages whose wealth was built on the wool trade

Bibury Court, Bibury

On the edge of the Cotswold village described by William Morris as 'the most beautiful in England', this old manor house stands in lovely grounds on the River Coln. It is 'full of character, a little faded, but this adds to the charm'. Some bedrooms have views of the gardens and a part-Saxon church. The 'very good' cooking of Antony Ely is praised again this year.

Read more: page 108.

Dial House, Bourton-on-the-Water

Set back from the touristy shops of a pretty if busy little town, popular with day-trippers and coach parties, this 17th-century house has a 'lovely atmosphere', beams, inglenook fireplaces, monk's chairs. The garden behind the house is 'a delightful retreat'.

Read more: page 120.

The Malt House, Broad Campden

'As good as ever', this 16th-century listed malt house in a small, honey-stoned village, is run as an upmarket B&B by Judi Wilkes, a 'warmly welcoming', 'perfectionist' hostess. Three of the bedrooms have their own entrance to the garden where teas and evening drinks are served in warm weather. From the gate you can walk on to the Cotswold Way.

Read more: page 132.

Burford House, Burford

Jane and Simon Henry's half-timbered, early 17th-century listed building stands on the steeply sloping high street of this attractive Cotswold town that runs down to the River Windrush. It is filled with family photos and souvenirs of foreign travel. The 'comfortable' bedrooms have a 'homely feel'.

Read more: page 138.

The Rectory Hotel, Crudwell

In a Victorian garden by the church in a village near Malmesbury, this 16th-century former rectory has been given a contemporary feel by new owners. It is 'a very pleasant place' with a fine hall/sitting room with soft chairs and magazines. A 'miscellany of furniture', and a new

king-size bed, in a 'spacious bedroom'; 'magnificent bathroom'. Peter Fairclough, the chef, who has stayed on, serves 'interesting, perfectly cooked' British classics.
Read more: page 160.

At the Sign of the Angel, Lacock

On the southern edge of the Cotswolds, this 'cosy and atmospheric' 15th-century half-timbered inn is the centrepiece of an ancient and pretty National Trust village. Rooms in the old house may be small but have 'bags of character'; four newer rooms are in a cottage 'through a garden and over a brook'.
Read more: page 203.

The Grey Cottage, Leonard Stanley

Guests arriving at Rosemary Reeves's little stone guest house near Stroud are greeted with biscuits and a choice of leaf teas. Bedrooms have 'wonderful touches', lots of goodies. The no-choice dinners are 'sumptuous'; bring your own bottle (no corkage charge). 'We felt really at home, except the breakfast was much better,' said visitors this year.
Read more: page 211.

Burleigh Court, Minchinhampton

Sir Clough Williams-Ellis designed the large gardens of this creeper-covered 18th-century stone manor house on a steep hill which overlooks the westernmost ridge of the Cotswolds. The owner, Louise Noble, 'is not content to rest on her laurels, and seems ever ready to improve the quality'. 'Staff were kindness itself.'
Read more: page 237.

The Redesdale Arms, Moreton-in-Marsh

'Warm with history', this old coaching inn, on the wide main street of this market town, has been welcoming travellers on the Fosse Way since the reign of Charles II. It has a 'pleasant, informal atmosphere', and 'courteous, cheerful' staff. Six new bedrooms are in a converted stable yard. The bar is popular with locals; the cooking is thought 'excellent'.
Read more: page 240.

Calcot Manor, Tetbury

Children are welcomed at Richard and Cathy Ball's hotel, a conversion of a 14th-century farmhouse, cottages and outbuildings. Mrs Ball runs a spa, which provides a retreat from younger guests, 'a real bonus in winter'. Michael Croft's modern cooking in the restaurant is thought 'excellent'; 'inexpensive good food' is enjoyed in the hotel's *Gumstool* pub.
Read more: page 306.

EAST ANGLIA

Whether you are seeking a seascape or a country hide-away, the *Guide* has a wide choice in Norfolk and Suffolk

The Wentworth, Aldeburgh

'Old-fashioned in the nicest sense', this family-run seaside hotel overlooks fishing huts and boats on Aldeburgh's shingle beach, with sea views from the best bedrooms. Chef Graham Reid serves 'generous', 'well-presented' dishes in the conservatory restaurant.
Read more: page 80.

The White Horse, Brancaster Staithe

'A successful blend of pub where locals drink, and excellent restaurant with good service and great views.' Cliff Nye's popular inn has a spectacular location, overlooking sea and salt marshes. The idiom is vernacular: bedrooms are light and spacious, 'with seasidey touches'. 'Delicious local fish dishes.' Children and dogs are welcomed.
Read more: page 127.

Byfords, Holt

On the main square of this enchanting Norfolk market town, this unusual establishment is a 'higgledy-piggledy world pleasure' combining a 'posh' B&B, café/bistro, restaurant and busy deli. 'Chic, clean rooms and attentive staff.' 'A must if you are in the area.'
Read more: page 195.

The Great House, Lavenham

An imposing part-Tudor, part-Georgian house on the market-place of the old wool town, run as a restaurant-with-rooms in professional French style by chef/*patron* Régis Crépy and his wife, Martine. Four of the five bedrooms are suites, with antiques, old beams, a marble bathroom. Classic French cooking is enjoyed in an oak-beamed dining room or a courtyard.
Read more: page 208.

Morston Hall, Morston

'Not a jot of pretension; a lovely atmosphere,' is a comment this year on this flint and brick Jacobean house in a designated

area of outstanding natural beauty on the north Norfolk coast. It is run as a restaurant-with-rooms by owners Tracy and Galton Blackiston. He has a *Michelin* star for his accomplished cooking on a four-course menu. 'Little touches' make the bedrooms 'special'.
Read more: page 241.

Beechwood, North Walsham

Lindsay Spalding and Don Birch are the 'caring proprietors' of this creeper-clad Georgian house (with Victorian character), once Agatha Christie's Norfolk hideaway. 'A very good hotel, well-trained staff, superb housekeeping.' Steven Norgate's modern cooking is thought 'excellent'. Guests travelling alone are 'especially welcome'.
Read more: page 248.

The Crown and Castle, Orford

In a peaceful Suffolk village, cookery writer Ruth Watson (Channel 5's 'hotel inspector') and her husband, David, run this red brick inn in 'slightly quirky style'. Bedrooms are 'stylish, well equipped'; those in the garden have been spruced up inside and out; each has a small terrace. In the restaurant, Ruth Watson and Max Dougal have a *Michelin Bib Gourmand* for their unfussy seasonal dishes.
Read more: page 253.

The Rose & Crown, Snettisham

'Very much a pub (a good one)', Jeannette and Anthony Goodrich's 14th-century village inn has twisting passages, hidden corners, low ceilings and old beams. Opposite the cricket pitch in a Norfolk village, it is popular with locals. Older bedrooms have been upgraded in the contemporary style of five newer rooms.
Read more: page 292.

Titchwell Manor, Titchwell

'Part Chelsea by the sea, but also popular with walkers and bird-watchers', the Snaith family's small hotel/restaurant (built as a farmhouse in 1890) faces dunes and salt marshes near Titchwell nature reserve. Public rooms have mosaic tiled floors, dark woodwork, Lloyd Loom furniture. In the conservatory dining room, seafood is a speciality.
Read more: page 308.

The Saracen's Head, Wolterton

'As always the welcome is warm' at Robert Dawson-Smith's popular 'lost inn' in a quiet rural setting in Norfolk. He may be 'resplendent in cravat, checked shirt and denim apron'. His cooking is thought 'wonderful'; up to ten choices for each course on a blackboard menu that changes for each meal.
Read more: page 334.

LAKE DISTRICT

In the magnificent setting of lakes and mountains, these are some of the *Guide*'s favourite hotels for a variety of budgets

Rothay Manor, Ambleside

With 'real country house style, but unpretentious', this 'very comfortable' hotel is run by brothers Nigel and Stephen Nixon: the family has been here for over 40 years. The ambience is 'professional but relaxed'. You can walk across fields to the head of Lake Windermere from the attractive grounds of the Georgian house. The traditional British/French cooking is admired.
Read more: page 84.

Fayrer Garden House Hotel, Bowness-on-Windermere

There are superb views of lake and mountain from Claire and Eric Wildsmith's Edwardian house in large grounds above Lake Windermere. 'We were pampered; staff were delightful; amenities very good,' says a visitor. Six bedrooms and the bar have been renovated this year.
Read more: page 121.

Lindeth Fell, Bowness-on-Windermere

Pat and Diana Kennedy's traditional hotel, on the hills above Lake Windermere, is 'unpretentious but gracious, with the right blend of formality and informality'. 'Stunning' views of the lake from the dining room and one lounge. Philip Taylor serves modern dishes on a daily-changing menu.
Read more: page 121.

The Cottage in the Wood, Braithwaite

On Whinlatter Pass, in the Lake District national park, this typical Lakeland inn is run by Liam and Kath Berney, 'welcoming and attentive' owners. 'A superb welcome,' said one visitor. The 'cosy' sitting room has an open fire, plants, magazines and books. Local suppliers are used for the meals' ingredients; breads, pasta and ice cream are home made.
Read more: page 125.

Aynsome Manor, Cartmel

'Staying here is like coming home,' say regular visitors to this traditional Lakeland hotel between fells and the sea in the Vale of Cartmel. Run for over 25 years by the Varley family ('excellent hoteliers'), it has views towards a Norman priory, meadowlands and woods.
Read more: page 142.

The Punch Bowl Inn, Crosthwaite

'A smartly informal hotel', Stephanie Barton's 300-year-old inn sits beside St Mary's church in the quiet Lyth valley. The bedrooms have original beams, large bed, flat-screen TV. In the low-ceilinged restaurant, Craig McMeekin serves 'hearty dishes with a modern twist'. There are two terraces for alfresco meals. The village post office operates from Reception.

Read more: page 159.

New House Farm, Lorton

In the beautiful Lorton/ Buttermere valley, on the north-west corner of the Lake District national park, Hazel Thompson runs her 'well-organised' country guest house 'almost single-handed'. The whitewashed 17th-century farmhouse has period features (oak beams, flagged floors). Traditional, no-choice meals are served. Marvellous views in all directions.

Read more: page 220.

Swinside Lodge, Newlands

'A haven of comfort', Eric and Irene Fell's Regency house stands at the foot of Cat Bells in a silent stretch of Derwentwater. They are 'attentive hosts, from the warm greeting to the personal farewell'. She welcomes guests with tea and cake; he 'is full of information about the area'. Chef Clive Imber's no-choice dinner mixes 'the rustic with the imaginative', ingredients 'local and fresh'.

Read more: page 246.

Rampsbeck, Watermillock

'You couldn't have a better setting', on the shores of Lake Ullswater, with spectacular views of lake and fells, for this white-fronted 18th-century house. Tom and Marion Gibb are 'hands-on owners'. The best bedrooms have lake views, and a balcony where the continental breakfast can be taken. The elegant lounges have large bay windows, high ceilings, elaborate mouldings.

Read more: page 322.

Holbeck Ghyll, Windermere

'As good as we remembered. If you like a country house feel, this is for you,' says a returning visitor to David and Patricia Nicholson's luxurious hotel. In large grounds that slope down to the water, it has 'wonderful' lake and mountain views. The public rooms have stained glass, open fires, wood panelling, antiques. Chef David McLaughlin earns a *Michelin* star for his refined cooking, served in two dining rooms.

Read more: page 331.

WEST COUNTRY

Dorset, Devon and Cornwall are hot spots for good *Guide* establishments

Blagdon Manor, Ashwater

In rolling country near Dartmoor ('perfect for a quiet stay'), Steve and Liz Morey's rambling manor house has fresh flowers, open fires, well-equipped bedrooms. She is a 'friendly' front-of-house; his cooking is 'stunning' (traditional 'with Mediterranean hints'). Breakfast, in a spacious conservatory, has exotic fruits, 'delicious porridge, perfect scrambled eggs'.
Read more: page 88.

The Bridge House, Beaminster

By a bridge in an attractive old town, Mark and Joanna Donovan's small hotel/restaurant is a former priest's house with thick walls, mullioned windows and old beams. The quietest rooms overlook a large walled garden. In a panelled dining room with conservatory extension, chef Linda Paget serves dishes 'rooted in Dorset produce'.
Read more: page 103.

The Henley, Bigbury-on-Sea

A favourite for 'food, location, relaxation', this small, unpretentious hotel stands on a cliff above the tidal Avon estuary. Bedrooms are 'spick and span'; some bathrooms are small, but all have fluffy towels. In the evening in the lounge, with Lloyd Loom chairs and wonderful views, Peta Scarterfield recites the short menu; the cooking of her husband, Martyn, is 'wonderful'.
Read more: page 110.

The Masons Arms, Branscombe

'A super place to stay', this popular creeper-covered inn is in the centre of a National Trust village. The owner, Colin Slaney, greets visitors warmly. All bedrooms (in the main building, in cottages behind the pub, and in the village) have been redecorated. Richard Reddaway's English cooking uses local ingredients wherever possible; a wide choice, large portions.
Read more: page 127.

Mill End Hotel, Chagford

With 'a homely feel rather than a smart country house look', Keith Green's white-walled former mill has a 'genuinely relaxing' atmosphere. There are large grounds to explore; the River Teign runs at the bottom of the garden. Christophe Ferraro's modern French cooking is 'as good as it gets'. Sympathetic modernisation is ongoing.
Read more: page 144.

Combe House, Gittisham

Ken and Ruth Hunt 'preside in an informal way' at their Elizabethan manor house on a vast country estate. Visitors are greeted by 'a roaring fire rather than a reception desk'. Grand public rooms have oak panelling, antiques, fresh flowers; bedrooms, 'unpretentious rather than sumptuous', have rich fabrics, 'extra touches'. Hadleigh Barrett's cooking is contemporary; producers are listed on the menus.
Read more: page 179.

Rosevine Hotel, Portscatho

Down a narrow road above a cove on the Roseland peninsula, Caroline and Chris Davidson's traditional, child-friendly hotel has a 'welcoming, relaxed atmosphere'; staff are 'charming and efficient'. Some bedrooms have a balcony overlooking the south-facing semi-tropical garden. Didier Beinaimé's cooking is 'enterprising and excellent'.
Read more: page 263.

Talland Bay Hotel, Talland-by-Looe

In a 'wonderful situation' in sub-tropical gardens, 150 feet above the bay, George and Mary Granville's hotel returns to the *Guide* this year after enthusiastic reports. The staff are 'courteous, efficient'; the modern cooking is 'outstanding'. The best bedrooms have 'smart draperies and great views'. 'Delicious' breakfasts.
Read more: page 302.

Prince Hall Hotel, Two Bridges

In a 'very special position', facing south over the gentle West Dart valley, John and Anne Grove's small hotel is 'blissfully quiet at night'. The 18th-century house is 'nicely proportioned, not over-fancy'. 'I was made to feel welcome; what a lovely place,' said a reader. The best bedrooms, like the lounge and bar, face the moor.
Read more: page 313.

The Nare, Veryan-in-Roseland

In gardens above a lovely bay in the Roseland peninsula ('an amazing location'), Toby Ashworth's unashamedly old-fashioned hotel is loved by a host of regular visitors: 'Brilliant, exceptional staff; we always get a welcome,' says a fan. In the dining room, dinner (jacket and tie preferred for men) is an event, with hors d'oeuvres and sweet trolleys.
Read more: page 318.

VALUE

Limit the damage to your wallet at each of these hotels which offer value in their own categories

The Victoria, London

Avoid central London prices by catching the train from Waterloo to Mortlake (25 minutes) to this lively gastropub in a leafy suburb. Two bedrooms are large; some may be 'compact, simple, even plain', but all are 'comfortable, warm, peaceful'. Modern European food is served in the bar and restaurant. B&B £54.25 per person (discounts sometimes available, or use your *Guide* voucher).
Read more: page 76.

Abbey House, Abbotsbury

'Marvellous value,' says a visitor to this guest house, a 15th-century building in a 'delightful' garden with wide lawns that slope down to a millpond and a Benedictine watermill. The owners, Jonathan and Maureen Cooke, 'run it impeccably, yet find time to chat'. B&B from £32.50 per person. Evening meals for house parties only.
Read more: page 80.

Lindeth Fell, Bowness-on-Windermere

'Incredibly good value, and without the pretension of many Lakeland hotels. Such a comfortable place.' Pat and Diana Kennedy's Edwardian house, on a hill above Lake Windermere, has superb views over the water. 'It is bliss to sit on the terrace while watching boats on the distant lake.' It is a traditional hotel, with 'just the right blend of formality and informality'. B&B from £45 per person; D,B&B from £70.
Read more: page 121.

The Nobody Inn, Doddiscombsleigh

Everybody's idea of what a Devon pub should be, in a remote hamlet, this 16th-century inn is noted for its exceptional wine list. It offers 'peaceful and comfortable accommodation, with a warm welcome. The food is consistently praised. Smaller bedrooms are 'fairly basic', but housekeeping is 'immaculate'. B&B from £25 per person.
Read more: page 163.

The Rosemary, Falmouth

'You feel special,' says a visitor to Suzanne and Geoff Warring's ten-room B&B near the Coastal Path, in a quiet residential road. 'Welcoming, clean and comfortable', it has a small bar and a pretty garden

with a sun deck. 'Each bedroom is excellent'; a 'great' breakfast. B&B from £31 per person.
Read more: page 171.

Underleigh House, Hope

Recommended for its 'unobtrusive hospitality' and 'amazing value', this extended barn and cottage conversion is run as a B&B by Philip and Vivienne Taylor. 'Everything one could want' is provided in the bedrooms. Drinks are served on the terrace. A huge and 'delicious' breakfast is taken around a large oak table. B&B from £35 per person.
Read more: page 196.

The Redesdale Arms, Moreton-in-Marsh

Popular with locals, this centuries-old coaching inn, on the wide main street of an attractive market town, offers 'good value' for the Cotswolds and 'a pleasant, informal atmosphere'; 'friendly' manager, Robert Smith, and 'courteous'. staff. B&B from £32.50 (mid-week offer).
Read more: page 240.

Bealach House, Duror

'We loved it.' Jim and Hilary McFadyen's small guest house, once a shepherd's croft then a farmhouse, stands up a forestry track in the north-west Highlands, surrounded by woods and mountains (much wildlife). Bedrooms, not large, are warmly furnished, 'immaculate'. The cooking is thought 'superb'. B&B from £40 per person. Set dinner £25.
Read more: page 355.

Gladstone House, Kirkcudbright

In a 'pleasant little town', Gordon and Hilary Cowan's Georgian town house is much liked as 'a value-for-money guest house'. The light, elegant building is 'beautifully decorated'; a 'fine' drawing room takes up much of the first floor. Guests can use the secluded garden. 'Delicious' evening meals (by arrangement, £19.50); 'excellent' breakfasts. B&B from £32 per person.
Read more: page 377.

The Mill, Dunfanaghy

Overlooking a lake outside a small coastal village in north-west Donegal, Susan and Derek Alcorn's restaurant-with-rooms delivers 'remarkable value'. She is a 'vivacious' hostess, welcoming visitors with 'pleasing informality'. Dinner is 'the main event': tables must be booked far in advance to enjoy the host's cooking of 'wonderful local ingredients'. B&B €47.50. Set dinner €40.
Read more: page 469.

ACCESS

These hotels provide better-than-average facilities for visitors with impaired mobility or who depend on a wheelchair

For a full list of hotels in the *Guide* that provide accommodation for visitors in a wheelchair, see Disabled Facilities (overleaf).

One Aldwych, London

All public areas of Gordon Campbell Gray's luxury hotel, an ultra-modern conversion of the old *Morning Post*, are accessible by wide-entranced lifts. Six bedrooms, accessible by wheelchair, have an adapted bathroom. An induction loop is fitted in Reception; portable induction units are available in the two restaurants.
Read more: page 72.

Rothay Manor, Ambleside

Two bedrooms at the Nixon family's Lake District Georgian house are adapted for disabled visitors. One, on the ground floor next to Reception, has a fully equipped bathroom. The other is a suite in an annexe: it has its own lounge, and paved access to the house, where there is full wheelchair access to the dining rooms and lounges.
Read more: page 84.

The Leathes Head Hotel, Borrowdale

Roy and Janice Smith's gabled Edwardian house, in wooded grounds outside Borrowdale, is popular with serious walkers and climbers; the 'less sprightly' are also catered for. Three ground-floor bedrooms can be accessed without steps; one has a square bathroom with a shower stand, lavatory frame, etc. 'Excellent' wheelchair access throughout the ground floor and gardens.
Read more: page 115.

Clow Beck House, Croft-on-Tees

The bedrooms at this 'fascinating and unusual' hotel on a working farm are in stone outbuildings. One, with its own reserved parking, is fully equipped for visitors in a wheelchair. There is ramped access on a paved pathway to the dining room. A disabled information pack is supplied on request.
Read more: page 157

Bedruthan Steps Hotel, Mawgan Porth

The three main floors of this large modern hotel, on a sloping site above a north Cornwall village, are accessible by lift. A suite on the ground floor is suitable for guests with limited mobility, and for those using a wheelchair. 'We are not able to make all areas totally accessible at the moment,' says the

hotel, which offers 'the help of our team' to overcome difficulties.
Read more: page 231.

The Rose & Crown, Snettisham

Two newer bedrooms, on the ground floor of this 'very relaxed' 14th-century inn, are adapted for guests with mobility problems. They are 'well appointed, smaller than some of the other rooms, but very comfortable'. One of the dining rooms is accessible from these bedrooms, but not all areas of the old building are fully accessible.
Read more: page 292.

New Lanark Mill, Lanark

Five of the 40 bedrooms at this converted cotton mill are equipped for disabled guests. They have grab rails and a wheel-in shower; panic buttons beside the beds. There are two lifts to every floor. The bar, lounge and restaurant are all accessible. The hotel is part of a World Heritage Site, owned and run by a conservation trust.
Read more: page 380.

Trefeddian Hotel, Aberdyfi

Disabled guests are 'marvellously catered for' at the Cave family's popular Edwardian building. A lift runs to all floors, and all bedrooms are on one level. No fully adapted bathroom, but some have a separate shower with a low lip. 'For many decades we have successfully looked after regular customers with various disabilities,' says Peter Cave, the managing director.
Read more: page 411.

Gliffaes, Crickhowell

'Don't do stairs, you can still do *Gliffaes*,' say Susie and James Suter of their smart sporting hotel on the banks of the River Usk. Unable to build a lift within the listed Italianate building, they added a ground-floor room in a cottage 30 yards from the hotel's access ramp; its bathroom is adapted for wheelchair users.
Read more: page 419.

Rayanne House, Holywood

Conor and Bernadette McClelland included a ground-floor bedroom equipped for disabled visitors in a recent extension to their guest house, a lovely old Victorian building in a small town on the Belfast Lough. He has won awards for his breakfasts with an array of interesting choices.
Read more: page 475.

DISABLED FACILITIES

Each of these hotels has at least one bedroom equipped for a visitor in a wheelchair

London

One Aldwych; **Zetter**.

England

Wentworth, Aldeburgh; **Rothay Manor**, Ambleside; **Callow Hall**, Ashbourne; **du Vin Birmingham**, Birmingham; **Leathes Head**, Borrowdale; **Millstream**, Bosham; **White Horse**, Brancaster Staithe; **drakes**, Brighton; **du Vin Brighton**, Brighton; **du Vin Bristol**, Bristol; **Frogg Manor**, Broxton; **Brockencote Hall**, Chaddesley Corbett; **Chilgrove White Horse**, Chilgrove; **Beech House & Olive Branch**, Clipsham; **Treglos**, Constantine Bay; **Clow Beck House**, Croft-on-Tees; **Coach House at Crookham**, Crookham; **Evesham**, Evesham; **Fowey Hall**, Fowey; **du Vin Henley**, Henley; **Angel Inn**, Hetton; **Black Boys Inn**, Hurley; **Dashwood**, Kirtlington; **Northcote Manor**, Langho; **42 The Calls**, Leeds; **Lewtrenchard Manor**, Lewdown; **Healds**, Liversedge; **Cottage in the Wood**, Malvern Wells; **Bedruthan Steps**, Mawgan Porth; **Meudon**, Mawnan Smith; **Redesdale Arms**, Moreton-in-Marsh; **Cleeve House**, Mortehoe; **Chewton Glen**, New Milton; **Jesmond Dene House**, Newcastle upon Tyne; **Beechwood**, North Walsham; **Hart's**, Nottingham; **Old Bank**, Oxford; **Old Parsonage**, Oxford; **Old Railway Station**, Petworth; **Bourgoyne**, Reeth; **Rose & Crown**, Snettisham; **Royal**, Truro; **Nare**, Veryan-in-Roseland; **Windy Ridge**, Whitstable; **Old Vicarage**, Worfield; **Middlethorpe Hall**, York.

Scotland

Roman Camp, Callender; **Dornoch Castle**, Dornoch; **Three Chimneys and House Over-By**, Dunvegan; **Scotsman**, Edinburgh; **Ballathie House**, Kinclaven; **Corsewall Lighthouse**, Kirkcolm; **Lynnfield**, Kirkwall; **New Lanark Mill**, Lanark; **Plockton**, Plockton; **Cuillin Hills**, Portree; **Viewfield House**, Portree; **Wheatsheaf at Swinton**, Swinton; **Torridon**, Torridon.

Wales

Jolyon's, Cardiff; **Gliffaes**, Crickhowell; **Tyddyn Llan**, Llandrillo; **Bodysgallen Hall**, Llandudno.

Ireland

Dunbrody Country House, Arthurstown; **Stella Marris**, Ballycastle; **Seaview House**, Ballylickey; **Bushmills Inn**, Bushmills; **Rayanne House**, Holywood; **Aghadoe Heights**, Killarney; **Sheedy's**, Lisdoonvarna; **Rathmullan House**, Rathmullan.

TENNIS AND SWIMMING

Each of these hotels has a tennis court (T) and/or swimming pool (S)

London

One Aldwych (S).

England

Amberley Castle, Amberley (T); **Regent by the Lake**, Ambleside (S); **Hartwell House**, Aylesbury (T,S); **Bath Priory**, Bath (S); **Eagle House**, Bathford (T); **Park House**, Bepton (T,S); **West Coates**, Berwick-upon-Tweed (T,S); **Burgh Island**, Bigbury-on-Sea (T,S); **Blakeney**, Blakeney (S); **Woolley Grange**, Bradford-on-Avon (S); **Frogg Manor**, Broxton (T); **Brockencote Hall**, Chaddesley Corbett (T); **Tor Cottage**, Chillaton (S); **Highbullen**, Chittlehamholt (T,S); **Corse Lawn House**, Corse Lawn (T,S); **Cloth Hall Oast**, Cranbrook (S); **Rectory**, Crudwell (S); **Summer Lodge**, Evershot (T,S); **Evesham**, Evesham (S); **Moonfleet Manor**, Fleet (T,S); **Fowey Hall**, Fowey (S); **Stock Hill House**, Gillingham (T); **Hambleton Hall**, Hambleton (T,S); **Feversham Arms**, Helmsley (T,S); **Esseborne Manor**, Hurstbourne Tarrant (T); **Bindon Country House**, Langford Budville (T,S); **Bedruthan Steps**, Mawgan Porth (T,S); **Budock Vean**, Mawnan Smith (T,S); **Chewton Glen**, New Milton (T,S); **Penzance**, Penzance (S); **Rosevine**, Portscatho (S); **St Enodoc**, Rock (S); **Ennys**, St Hilary (T,S); **St Martin's on the Isle**, St Martin's (S); **Star Castle**, St Mary's (S); **Tides Reach**, Salcombe (S); **Seaham Hall**, Seaham (S); **Soar Mill Cove**, Soar Mill Cove (T,S); **Stoke Lodge**, Stoke Fleming (T,S); **Plumber Manor**, Sturminster (T); **Talland Bay**, Talland-by-Looe (S); **Calcot Manor**, Tetbury (T,S); **Old Rectory**, Thorpe St Andrew (S); **Nare**, Veryan-in-Roseland (T,S); **Island**, Tresco (T,S); **Holbeck Ghyll**, Windermere (T); **Middlethorpe Hall**, York (S).

Scotland

Kinloch House, Blairgowrie (S); **Kinnaird**, Dunkeld (T); **Greshornish House**, Edinbane (T); **Scotsman**, Edinburgh (S); **Isle of Eriska**, Eriska (T,S); **Greywalls**, Gullane (T); **Ardanaiseig**, Kilchrenan (T); **New Lanark Mill**, Lanark (S); **Kirroughtree House**, Newton Stewart (T); **Skirling House**, Skirling (T).

Wales

Trefeddian, Aberdyfi (T,S); **Port Tocyn**, Abersoch (T,S); **Glangrwyney Court**, Crickhowell

(continued overleaf)

(T); **Gliffaes**, Crickhowell (T); **Bodysgallen Hall and Spa**, Llandudno (T,S); **St Tudno**, Llandudno (S); **Lake**, Llangammarch Wells (T,S); **Llangoed Hall**, Llyswen (T); **Portmeirion**, Portmeirion (T,S).

Channel Islands

White House, Herm (T,S); **St Brelade's Bay**, St Brelade (T,S); **Longueville Manor**, St Saviour (T,S); **Petit Champ**, Sark (S).

Ireland

Dunraven Arms, Adare (S); **Cashel House**, Cashel Bay (T); **Castle Durrow**, Durrow (T); **Glin Castle**, Glin (T); **Marlfield House**, Gorey (T); **Shelburne Lodge**, Kenmare (T); **Aghadoe Heights**, Killarney (S); **Rosleague Manor**, Letterfrack (T); **Currarevagh House**, Oughterard (T); **Fort Royal**, Rathmullan (T); **Rathmullan House**, Rathmullan (T,S); **Coopershill**, Riverstown (T); **Ballymaloe House**, Shanagarry (T,S).

Join the *Good Hotel Guide* Readers' Club

Send us a review of your favourite hotel.

As a member of the club, you will be entitled to:

1. A pre-publication discount offer
2. Personal advice on hotels
3. Advice if you are in dispute with a hotel

The writers of the 12 best reviews will each win a free copy of the *Guide* and an invitation to our launch party.

Send your review via:

our website: www.goodhotelguide.com

or email: Goodhotel@aol.com or Goodhotel@btinternet.com

or fax: 020-7602 4182

or write to:

Good Hotel Guide
Freepost PAM 2931
London W11 4BR
(no stamp is needed in the UK)

or, from outside the UK:

Good Hotel Guide
50 Addison Avenue
London W11 4QP
England

How to use the *Good Hotel Guide*

Hotelfinder is for those looking for ideas: we suggest hotels to match your mood or interests, perhaps romance or sport, for a family or for gourmets. Ten hotels are highlighted in each of 20 categories, with a short profile and a cross-reference to the main entry.

Main entries carry our considered judgments, based on anonymous inspections and reader reports, of those hotels that we consider to be the best of their type. Hotels are listed alphabetically by country, under the name of the town or village. If you remember a hotel's name but not where it is, please consult the alphabetical hotel list at the end of the book.

Italic entries These short entries describe hotels which are worth considering, but for various reasons – lack of information, recent change of ownership, mixed reports – do not merit a full entry.

The Shortlist suggests alternatives, especially in areas where we have a limited choice. These short entries have not been subjected to the same rigorous tests as the main entries; standards may be variable.

The maps Each hotel's location is marked. A small house indicates a main entry, a triangle a Shortlist one. We give the map number and grid reference at the top of the hotel's entry.

Reading the entries

Information panels We give the number of bedrooms without detailing the type of room (the distinction between a single room and a small double for single use, a standard or a superior double, a junior or a senior suite varies widely between hotels). We give the geographical location, but not detailed driving directions. As with room types, these are best discussed with the hotel when booking; directions are often found on a hotel's website.

Prices We give each hotel's estimated prices for 2008, or the 2007 prices, which applied when the *Guide* went to press. The figures indicate the range from off-season to high season. A 'set lunch/dinner' can be no-choice or *table d'hôte.* The 'full alc' price is the cost per person of a three-course meal with a half bottle of wine; 'alc' indicates the price excluding wine. These figures cannot be guaranteed. *You should always check prices when booking.*

Symbols The label 'New' at the top of an entry identifies a hotel making its first appearance in the *Guide*, or one returning after an absence. We say 'Unsuitable for ♿' when a hotel tells us that it cannot accommodate wheelchair-users. We do not have the resources to inspect such facilities or to assess the even more complicated matter of facilities for the partially disabled. You will have to discuss such details directly with the hotel.

Names We give the names of the readers who have nominated or endorsed a hotel in brackets at the end of each entry. We do not name inspectors, correspondents who ask to remain anonymous, or those who have written critical reports.

Facilities We give an outline of the facilities offered by each hotel. We suggest that you check in advance if specific items (tea-making equipment, trouser press, sheets and blankets instead of a duvet) are important to you.

Changes We try to ensure that the details we provide are correct, but inevitably they are subject to change. Small hotels sometimes close at short notice off-season. Some change hands after we have gone to press.

Vouchers Hotels which join our voucher scheme (identified by a *V*) have agreed to give readers a discount of 25% off their normal bed-and-breakfast rate for one night only. You will be expected to pay the full price for other meals and all other services. *You should request a voucher reservation at the time of booking*, but a hotel may refuse to accept it at busy times. The six vouchers in the centre of the book are valid until the publication of the next edition of the *Guide*.

Traveller's tales These horror stories are taken from reports from readers. None of the hotels mentioned is included in the *Guide*, and the stories have *no connection* with the entry immediately above.

Report of the Year competition

Readers' contributions are the lifeblood of the *Good Hotel Guide.* Everyone who writes to the *Guide* is a potential winner of the Report of the Year competition. Each year a dozen correspondents are singled out for the helpfulness and generosity of their reports. They win a copy of the *Guide*, and an invitation to our annual launch party in October. The following generous readers are winners this year.

Avril Campbell of Aston Clinton
Sir Patrick Cormack of Stourbridge
AJ Gillingwater of London
Gill Holden of Keighley
Peter Jowitt of Hereford
Ann and Michael Maher of Blackburn
Joan and David Marston of Guiseley
Frances Rathbone of Llandrindod Wells
Richard and Catriona Smith of Cheltenham
Ann Walden of High Wycombe
Janet Walker of Malvern
Jelly Williams of Oxford

Hotel reports

The report forms at the end of the *Guide* may be used to endorse or criticise an existing entry or to nominate a hotel for inclusion in the *Guide*. But it is not essential that you use our forms or restrict yourself to the space available. Many readers email their reports to us.

All reports (*each on a separate piece of paper, please*) should include your name and address, the name and location of the hotel, and the date and length of your stay. Please nominate only places that you have visited in the past 12 months, unless friends tell you that standards have been maintained. Please be as specific as possible, and critical where appropriate, about the building, the public rooms and bedrooms, the meals, the service, the nightlife, the grounds.

If you describe the location as well as the hotel, particularly in less familiar regions, that is helpful. So are comments about worthwhile places to visit in the neighbourhood and, in the case of B&B hotels, recommendable restaurants.

We want the *Guide* to convey the special flavour of its hotels, and any details that you provide will give life to the description. We mind having to pass up a potentially attractive place because the report is too brief. Do not bother with prices and routine information about number of rooms and facilities; we get such details from the hotels. We want readers to supply information that is not accessible elsewhere. In the case of a new nomination, it helps if you include a brochure or mention a website.

Please never tell a hotel that you intend to file a report. Anonymity is essential to objectivity.

The 2009 edition of this volume will be written between mid-March and the end of May 2008, and published in early October 2008. Nominations should reach us not later than 15 May 2008. The latest date for comments on existing entries is 1 June 2008.

Please let us know if you would like us to send you more report forms. Our address for UK correspondents (no stamp needed) is: *Good Hotel Guide*, Freepost PAM 2931, London W11 4BR.

Reports can be faxed to us on 020-7602 4182, or emailed to Goodhotel@aol.com.

Reports posted outside the UK should be stamped normally and addressed to: *Good Hotel Guide*, 50 Addison Avenue, London W11 4QP, England.

British Isles maps

Map 1 South-West England
including the Channel Islands

Map 2 Southern England

Map 3 Wales and the Cotswolds

Map 4 The North of England and the Lake District

Map 5 Scotland

Map 6 Ireland

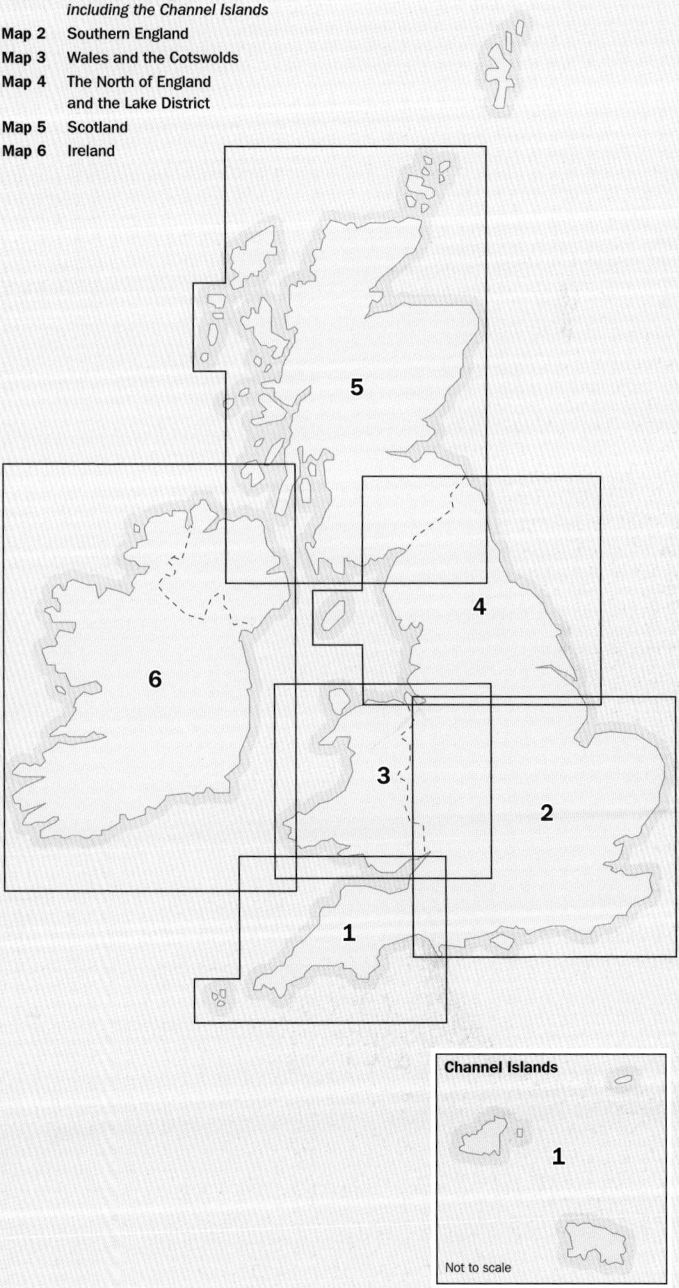

1 South-West England

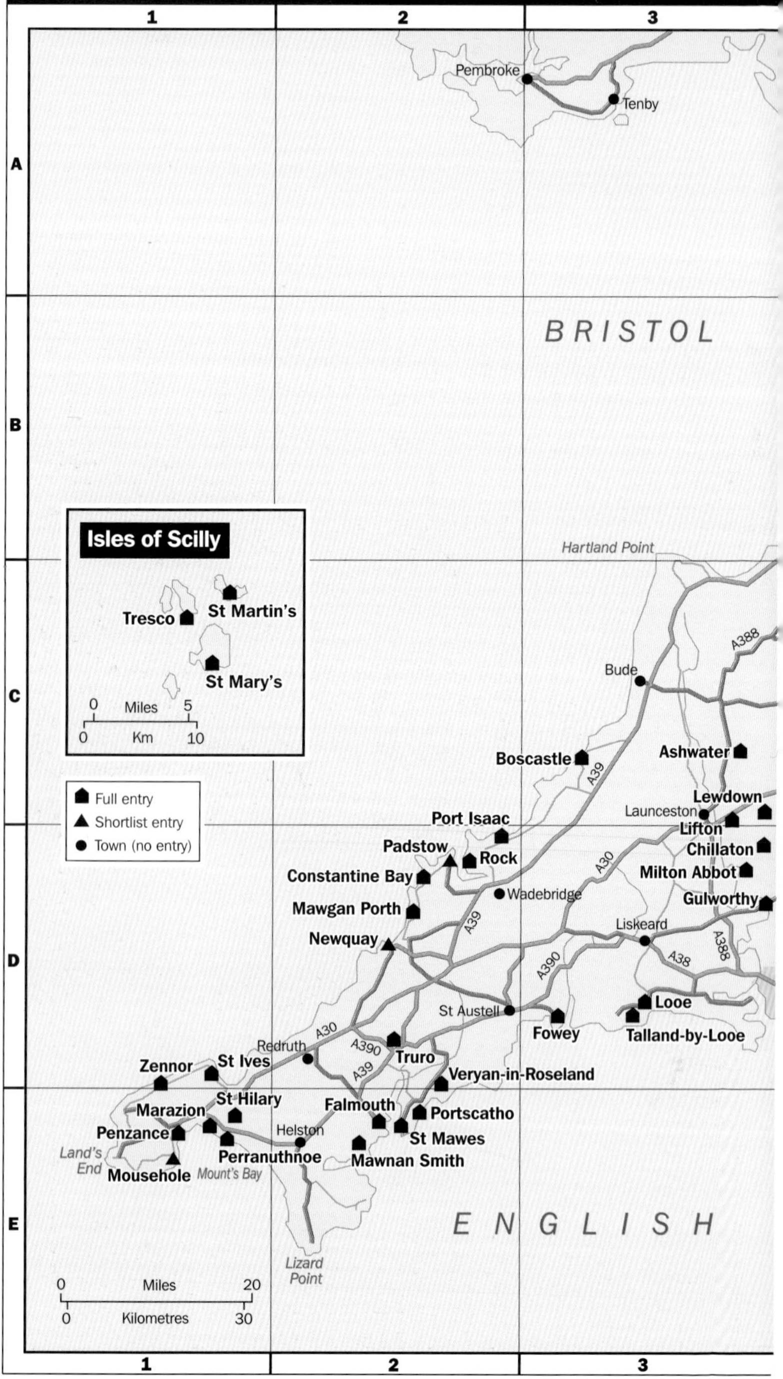

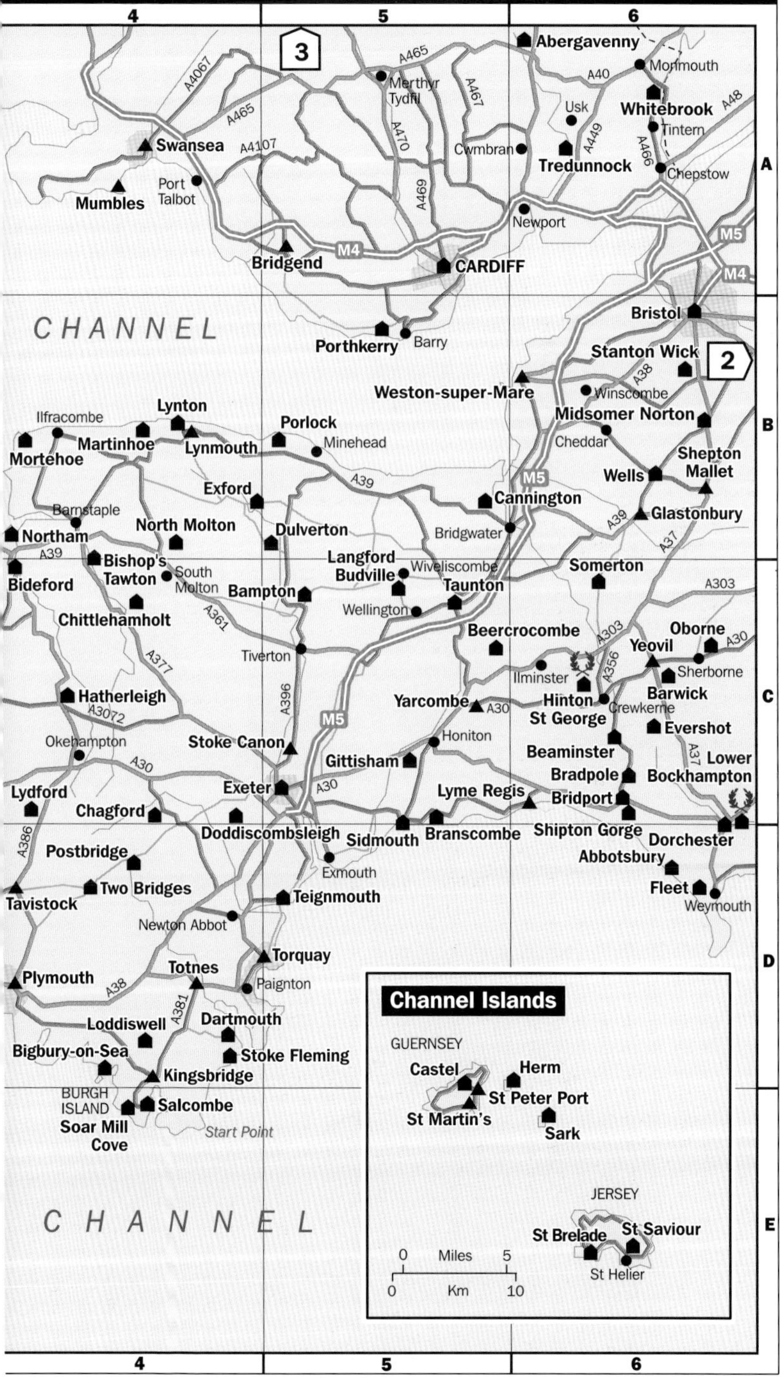
4
5
6
3
2
A
B
C
D
E
Abergavenny
Monmouth
A40
A465
A4067
Merthyr Tydfil
A467
Usk
Whitebrook
A48
A465
A4107
Swansea
A470
Cwmbran
Tredunnock
A449
A466
Tintern
Chepstow
Port Talbot
Mumbles
A469
Newport
M5
M4
Bridgend
CARDIFF
M4
Bristol
CHANNEL
Porthkerry
Barry
Stanton Wick
A38
Weston-super-Mare
Winscombe
Midsomer Norton
Lynton
Ilfracombe
Porlock
Martinhoe
Lynmouth
Minehead
Mortehoe
Cheddar
Shepton Mallet
Wells
A39
Exford
M5
Cannington
Barnstaple
Glastonbury
North Molton
Dulverton
Bridgwater
A39
Northam
A39
A37
Bishop's Tawton
Langford Budville
Wiveliscombe
Somerton
South Molton
Bideford
Bampton
Taunton
A303
Wellington
Chittlehamholt
A361
Beercrocombe
Oborne
A303
A30
Yeovil
A377
Tiverton
Ilminster
A356
Sherborne
Hatherleigh
A396
Barwick
A3072
Yarcombe
A30
Hinton St George
Crewkerne
M5
Evershot
Okehampton
Stoke Canon
Honiton
A37
Beaminster
Lower Bockhampton
A30
Gittisham
Bradpole
Exeter
A30
Lyme Regis
Lydford
Bridport
Chagford
Doddiscombsleigh
Sidmouth
Branscombe
Shipton Gorge
Dorchester
A386
Postbridge
Abbotsbury
Exmouth
Two Bridges
Teignmouth
Fleet
Tavistock
Weymouth
Newton Abbot
Torquay
Totnes
Plymouth
A38
Paignton
Channel Islands
A381
Dartmouth
Loddiswell
GUERNSEY
Bigbury-on-Sea
Stoke Fleming
Kingsbridge
Castel
Herm
BURGH ISLAND
Salcombe
St Peter Port
St Martin's
Soar Mill Cove
Start Point
Sark
JERSEY
CHANNEL
St Brelade
St Saviour
0
Miles
5
St Helier
0
Km
10
4
5
6

2 Southern England

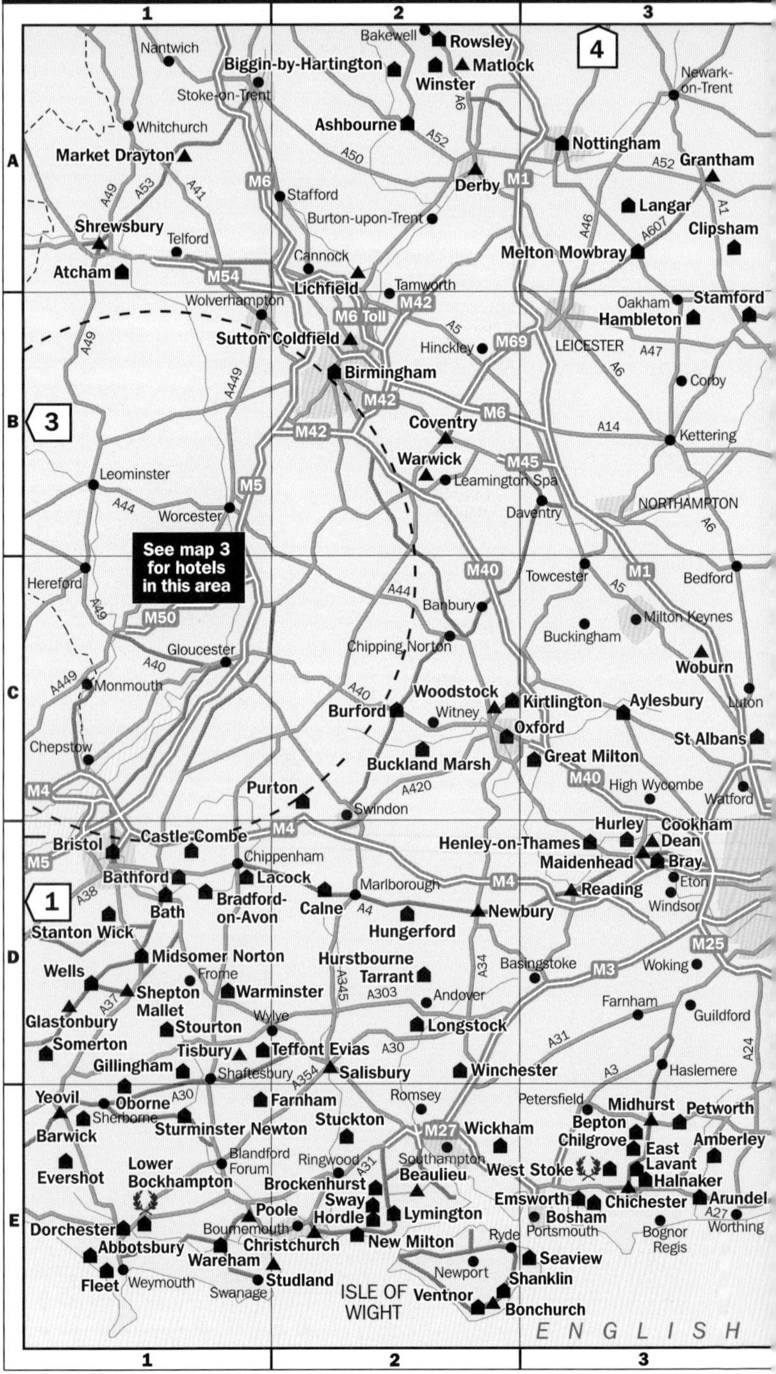

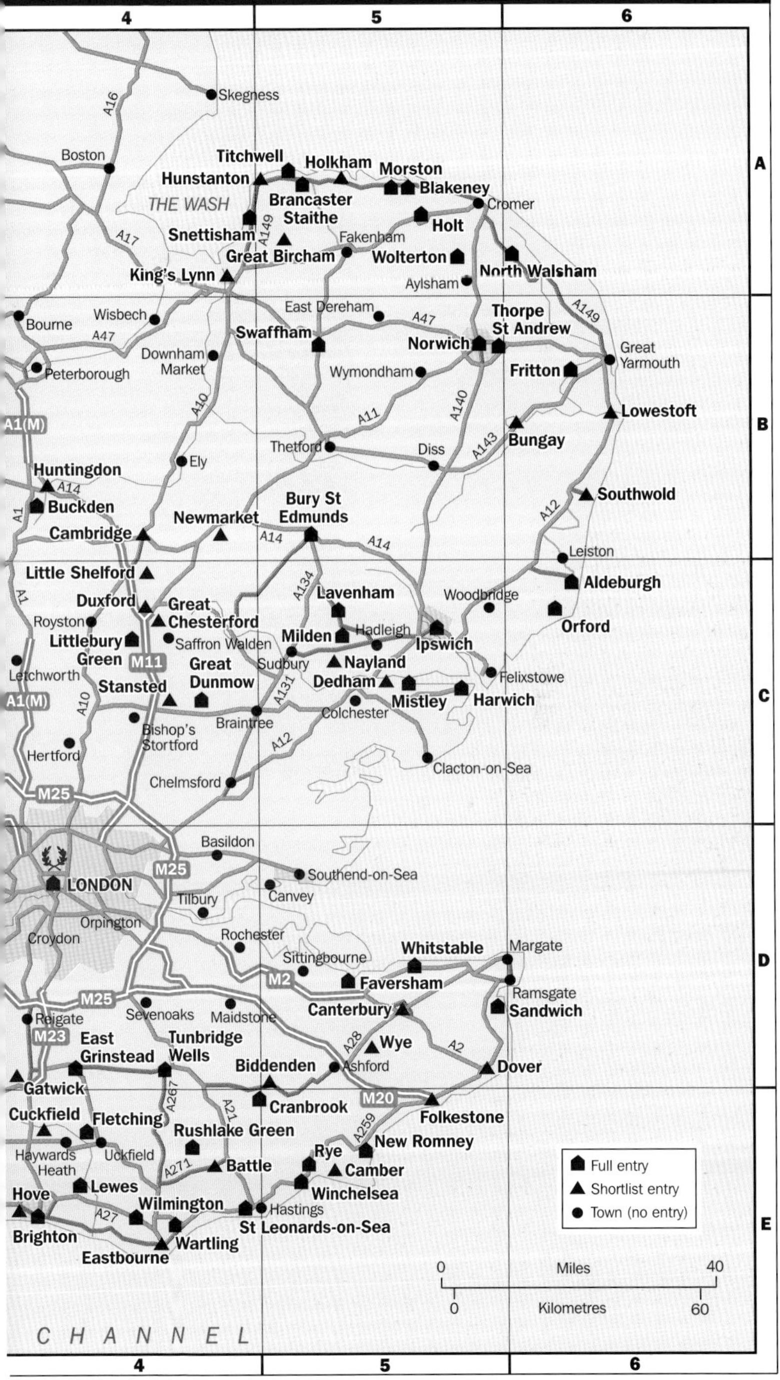
4
5
6
A
B
C
D
E
Skegness
A16
Boston
Titchwell
Holkham
Morston
Hunstanton
Blakeney
THE WASH
Brancaster Staithe
Cromer
A17
Holt
Snettisham
A149
Fakenham
Great Bircham
Wolterton
King's Lynn
North Walsham
Aylsham
Bourne
Wisbech
East Dereham
A47
Thorpe St Andrew
A149
A47
Swaffham
Downham Market
Norwich
Great Yarmouth
Peterborough
Wymondham
Fritton
A10
A140
A1(M)
A11
Lowestoft
Thetford
Diss
A143
Bungay
Ely
Huntingdon
A14
Buckden
Bury St Edmunds
Southwold
A1
Newmarket
A12
Cambridge
A14
A14
Leiston
Little Shelford
Aldeburgh
A134
A1
Lavenham
Woodbridge
Duxford
Great Chesterford
Royston
Orford
Littlebury Green
Milden
Hadleigh
Ipswich
Saffron Walden
Great Dunmow
Sudbury
Nayland
Letchworth
M11
Felixstowe
Dedham
Stansted
A131
Mistley
Harwich
A1(M)
A10
Colchester
Braintree
Bishop's Stortford
A12
Hertford
Clacton-on-Sea
Chelmsford
M25
Basildon
M25
Southend-on-Sea
LONDON
Tilbury
Canvey
Orpington
Croydon
Rochester
Margate
Whitstable
Sittingbourne
M2
Faversham
Ramsgate
M25
Sandwich
Canterbury
Sevenoaks
Maidstone
Reigate
M23
East Grinstead
Tunbridge Wells
A28
Wye
A2
Biddenden
Ashford
Dover
Gatwick
A267
M20
Cranbrook
Folkestone
A21
Cuckfield
Fletching
Rushlake Green
A259
New Romney
Rye
Haywards Heath
Uckfield
A271
Battle
Camber
Lewes
Winchelsea
Hove
Wilmington
Hastings
A27
St Leonards-on-Sea
Brighton
Wartling
Eastbourne
Full entry
Shortlist entry
Town (no entry)
0
Miles
40
0
Kilometres
60
C H A N N E L

3 Wales and the Cotswolds

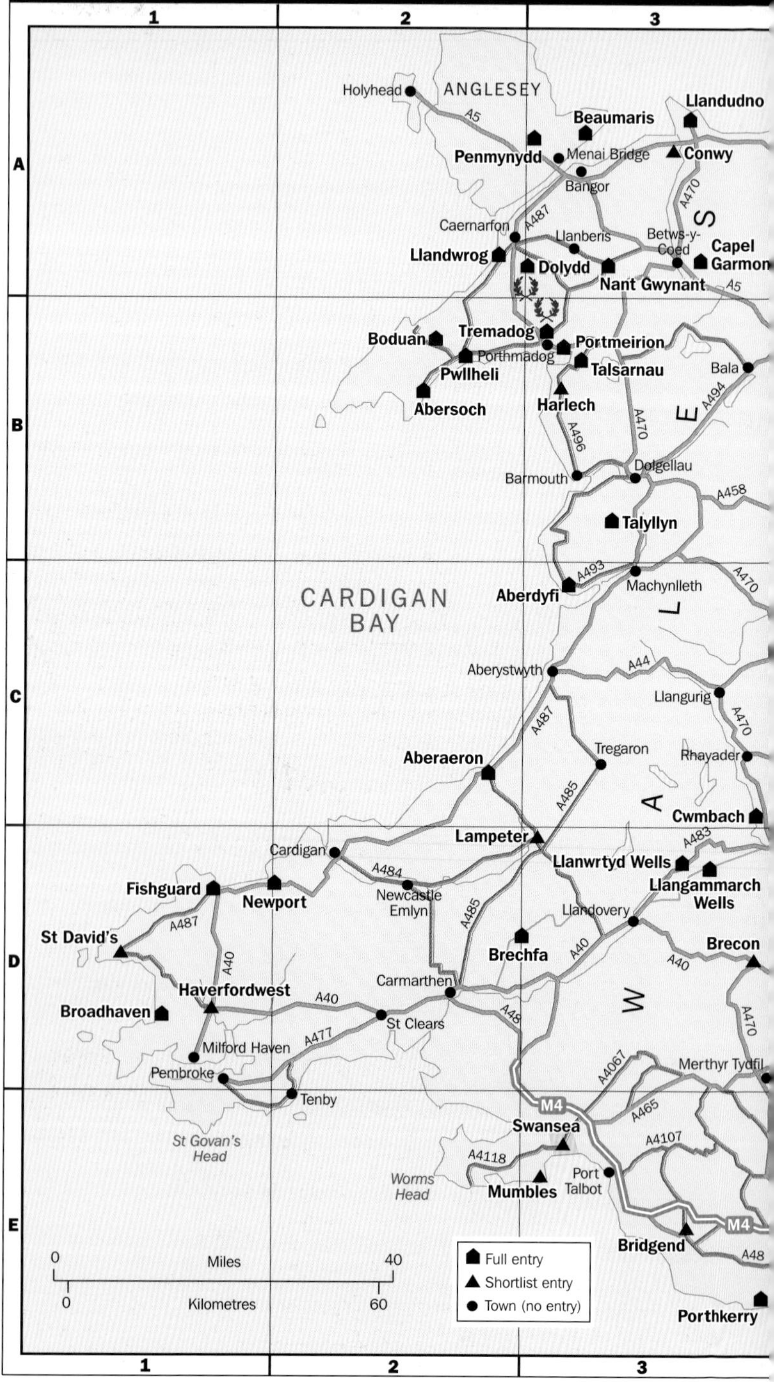

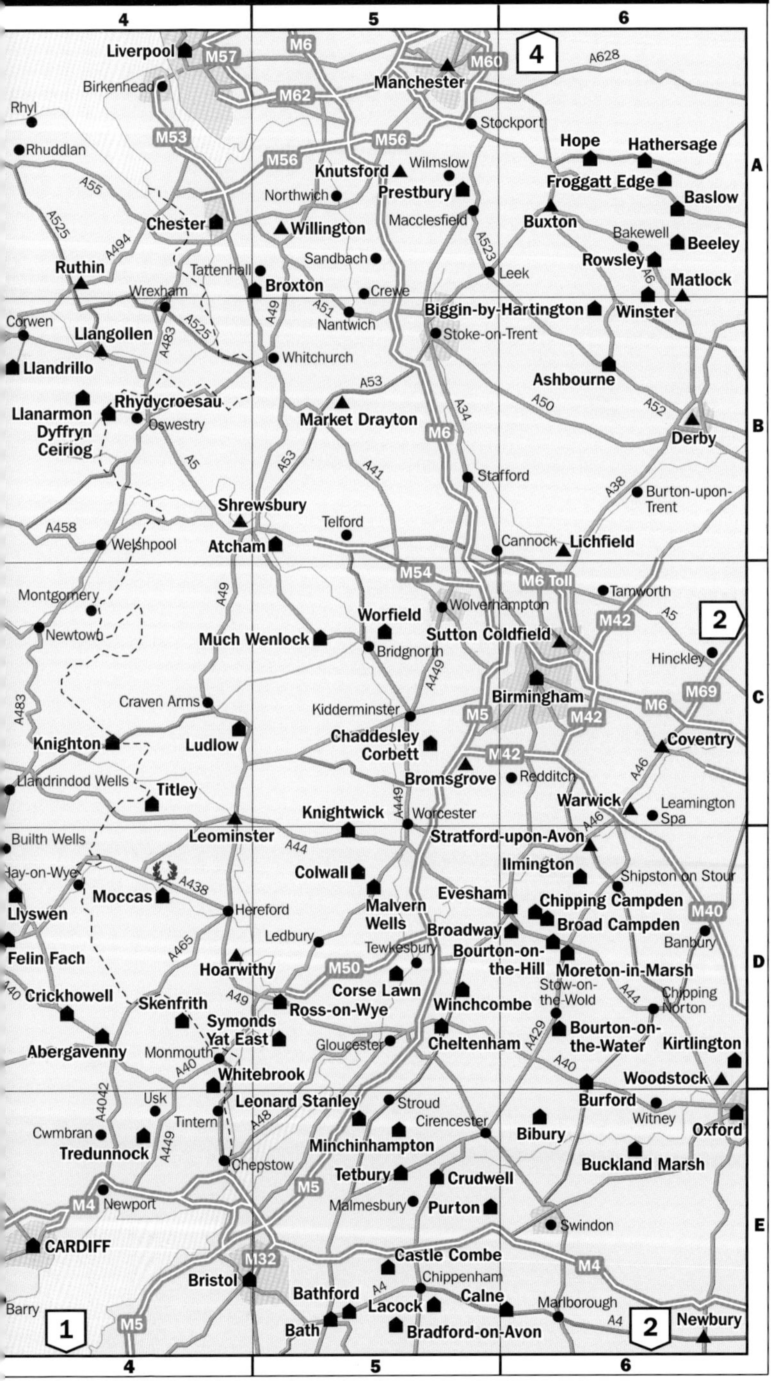
4
5
6
A
B
C
D
E
Liverpool
M57
M6
Manchester
M60
4
A628
Birkenhead
M62
Rhyl
Stockport
M53
M56
Rhuddlan
M56
Hope
Hathersage
Knutsford
Wilmslow
A55
Northwich
Prestbury
Froggatt Edge
Baslow
A525
Macclesfield
Buxton
Chester
Willington
A494
Bakewell
Beeley
A523
Sandbach
Rowsley
Ruthin
Tattenhall
Leek
A6
Matlock
Wrexham
Broxton
Crewe
A51
Nantwich
Biggin-by-Hartington
Winster
Corwen
Llangollen
A483
A525
A49
Stoke-on-Trent
Llandrillo
Whitchurch
A53
Ashbourne
Rhydycroesau
Llanarmon
Dyffryn
Ceiriog
Oswestry
Market Drayton
A34
A50
A52
M6
Derby
A5
A53
A41
Stafford
A38
Burton-upon-
Trent
Shrewsbury
Telford
A458
Welshpool
Atcham
Cannock
Lichfield
M54
M6 Toll
Tamworth
Montgomery
A49
Wolverhampton
A5
Worfield
M42
2
Newtown
Much Wenlock
Sutton Coldfield
Bridgnorth
Hinckley
A449
M69
Craven Arms
Birmingham
A483
Kidderminster
M5
M6
M42
Knighton
Ludlow
Chaddesley
Corbett
Coventry
M42
A46
Llandrindod Wells
Bromsgrove
Redditch
Titley
Warwick
Leamington
Spa
Knightwick
A449
Worcester
A46
Builth Wells
Leominster
A44
Stratford-upon-Avon
Hay-on-Wye
A438
Colwall
Ilmington
Shipston on Stour
Llyswen
Moccas
Hereford
Malvern
Wells
Evesham
Chipping Campden
M40
Broad Campden
Ledbury
Broadway
Banbury
Felin Fach
A465
Tewkesbury
Bourton-on-
the-Hill
Moreton-in-Marsh
Hoarwithy
M50
Stow-on-
the-Wold
A44
Chipping
Norton
Crickhowell
Skenfrith
A49
Corse Lawn
Winchcombe
Ross-on-Wye
Symonds
Yat East
A429
Bourton-on-
the-Water
Kirtlington
Abergavenny
Monmouth
Gloucester
Cheltenham
A40
A40
Whitebrook
Woodstock
A4042
Usk
Leonard Stanley
Stroud
Burford
Tintern
A48
Witney
Cwmbran
Cirencester
Bibury
Oxford
Tredunnock
A449
Minchinhampton
Buckland Marsh
Chepstow
Tetbury
Crudwell
M5
M4
Newport
Malmesbury
Purton
Swindon
CARDIFF
M32
Castle Combe
M4
Bristol
Chippenham
Barry
Bathford
A4
Lacock
Calne
Marlborough
A4
Newbury
1
M5
Bath
Bradford-on-Avon
2
4
5
6

4 The North of England and the Lake District

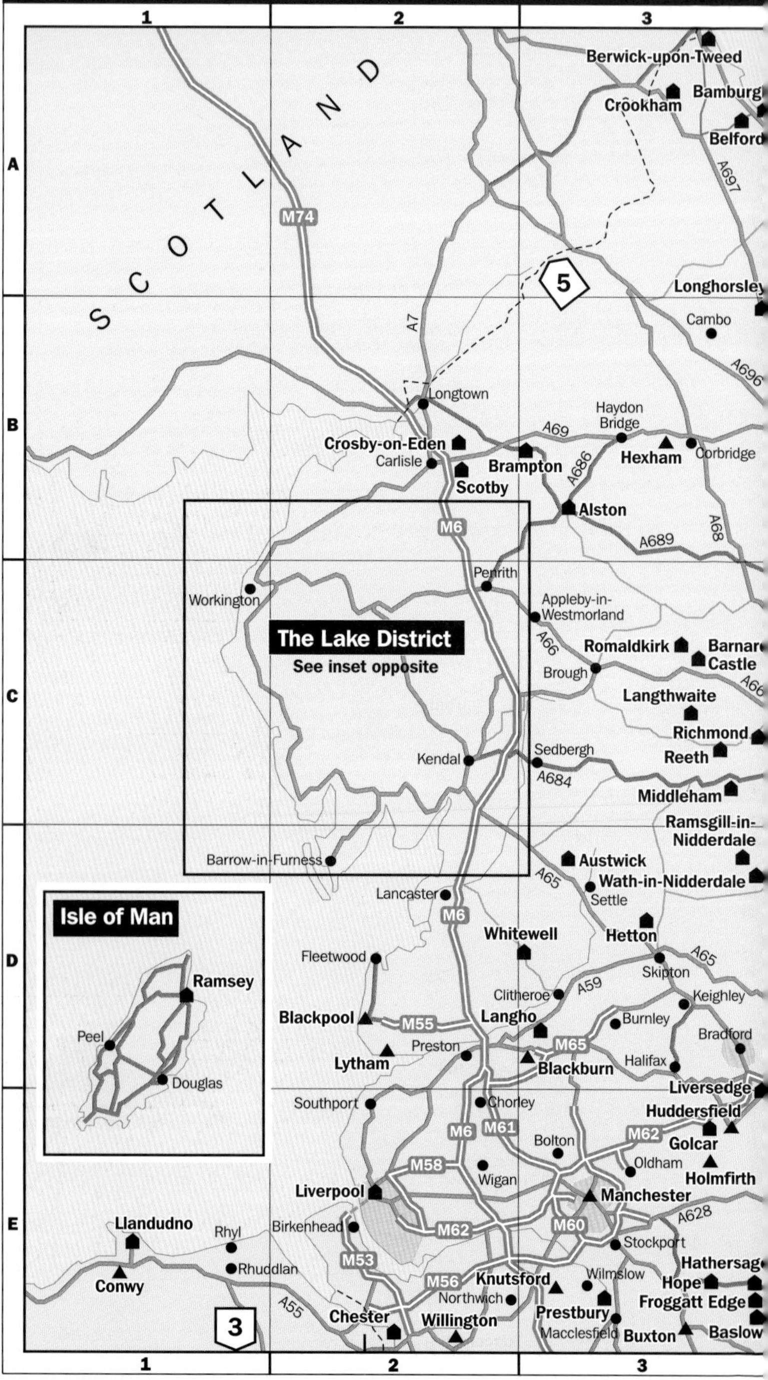

The North of England and the Lake District 4

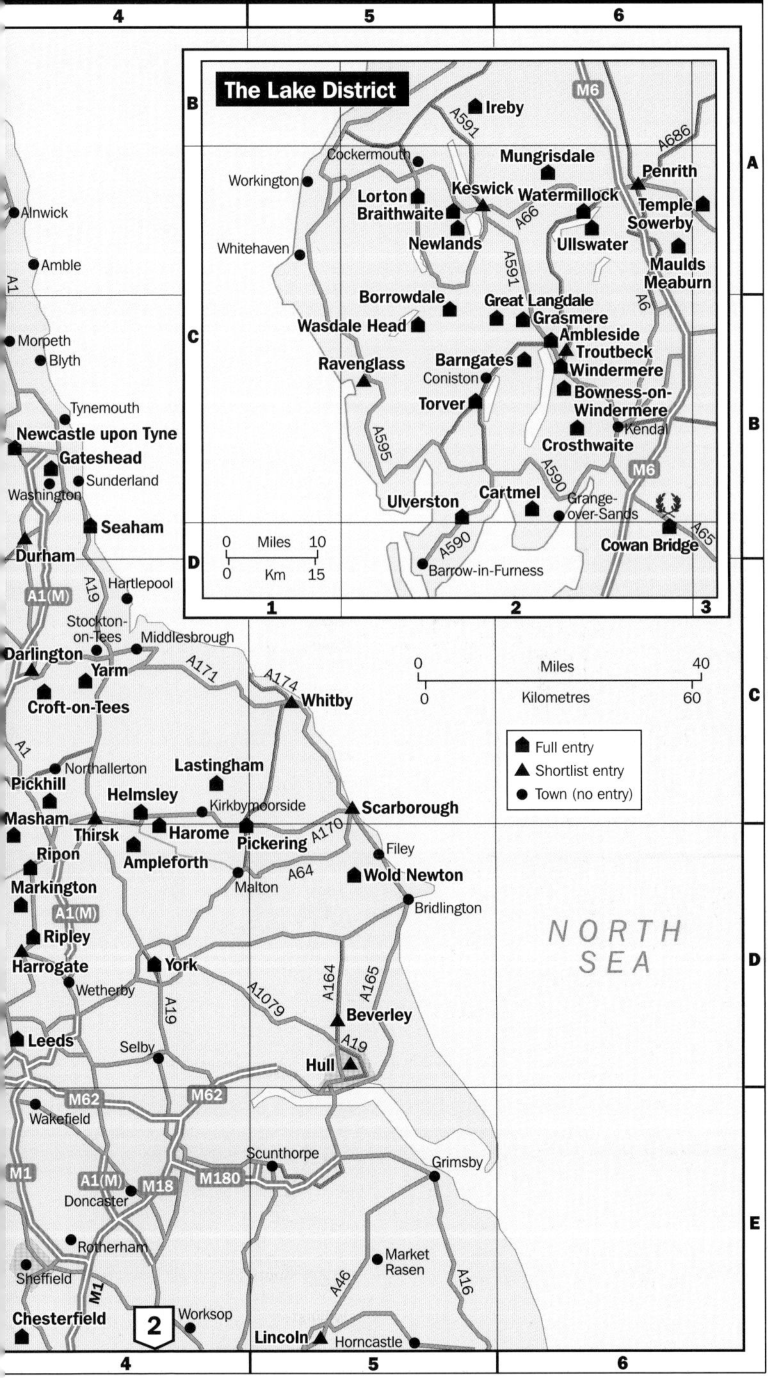

4
5
6
The Lake District
B
C
D
Ireby
A591
M6
A686
Cockermouth
Mungrisdale
Penrith
Workington
Keswick
Watermillock
Temple Sowerby
Lorton
Braithwaite
A66
Newlands
Ullswater
Whitehaven
A591
Maulds Meaburn
Borrowdale
Great Langdale
A6
Grasmere
Wasdale Head
Ambleside
Troutbeck
Ravenglass
Barngates
Windermere
Coniston
Bowness-on-Windermere
Torver
Kendal
A595
Crosthwaite
A590
M6
Ulverston
Cartmel
Grange-over-Sands
A65
Cowan Bridge
A590
Barrow-in-Furness
0 Miles 10
0 Km 15
1
2
3
A
B
C
D
E
Alnwick
Amble
A1
Morpeth
Blyth
Tynemouth
Newcastle upon Tyne
Gateshead
Sunderland
Washington
Seaham
Durham
A19
Hartlepool
A1(M)
Stockton-on-Tees
Middlesbrough
Darlington
Yarm
A171
A174
Whitby
Croft-on-Tees
0 Miles 40
0 Kilometres 60
Full entry
Shortlist entry
Town (no entry)
A1
Northallerton
Lastingham
Pickhill
Helmsley
Kirkbymoorside
Scarborough
Masham
Thirsk
Harome
Pickering
A170
Ripon
Ampleforth
Filey
A64
Malton
Wold Newton
Markington
Bridlington
A1(M)
Ripley
NORTH SEA
Harrogate
York
Wetherby
A164
A165
A1079
A19
Beverley
Leeds
Selby
A19
Hull
M62
M62
Wakefield
Scunthorpe
Grimsby
M1
A1(M)
M18
M180
Doncaster
Rotherham
Market Rasen
Sheffield
A46
A16
M1
Chesterfield
2
Worksop
Lincoln
Horncastle
4
5
6

5 Scotland

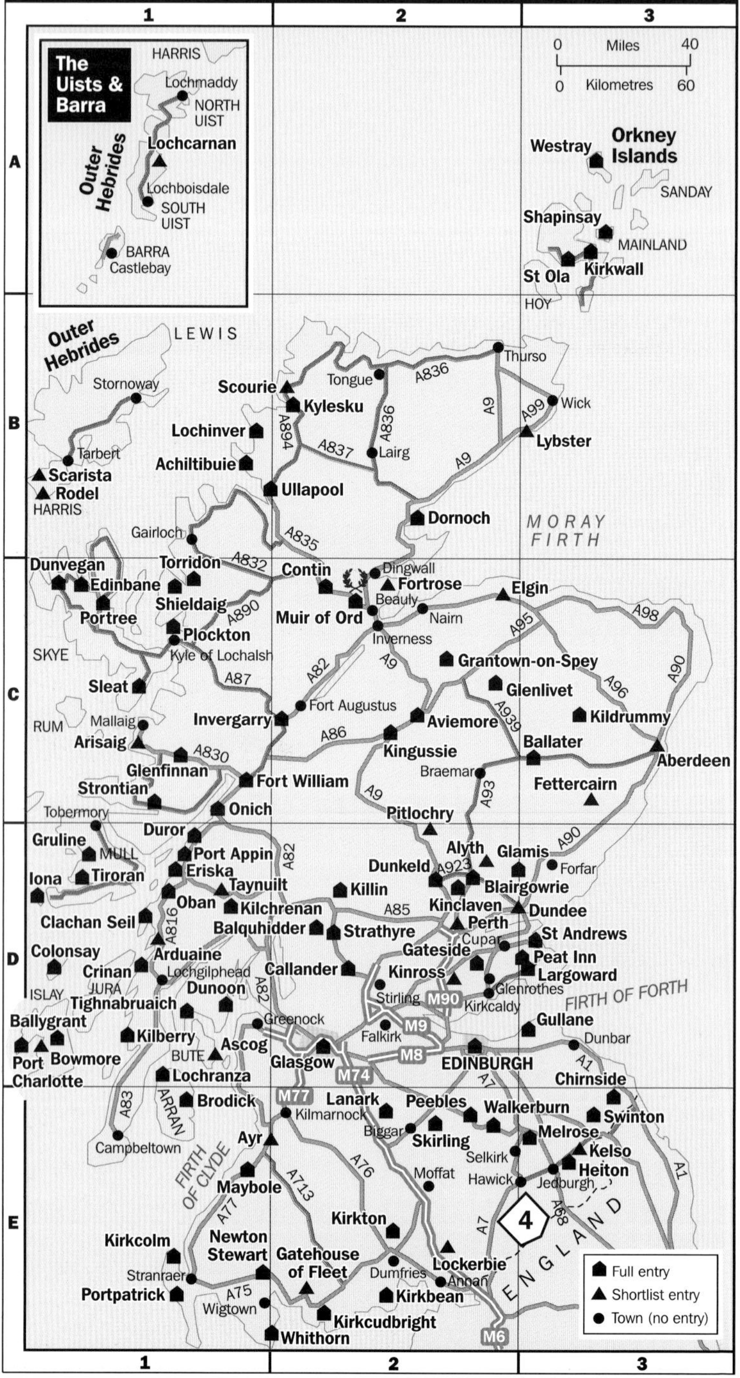
1
2
3
A
B
C
D
E
The Uists & Barra
Outer Hebrides
HARRIS
Lochmaddy
NORTH UIST
Lochcarnan
Lochboisdale
SOUTH UIST
BARRA
Castlebay
0 Miles 40
0 Kilometres 60
Orkney Islands
Westray
SANDAY
Shapinsay
MAINLAND
St Ola
Kirkwall
HOY
Outer Hebrides
LEWIS
Stornoway
Tarbert
Scarista
Rodel
HARRIS
Scourie
Kylesku
Tongue
A836
Thurso
Wick
A99
A9
Lybster
Lochinver
A894
A837
A836
Lairg
Achiltibuie
Ullapool
Dornoch
MORAY FIRTH
Gairloch
A835
Torridon
A832
Contin
Dingwall
Fortrose
Elgin
Dunvegan
Edinbane
Beauly
Nairn
A98
Portree
Shieldaig
A890
Muir of Ord
Inverness
A95
Plockton
Kyle of Lochalsh
A9
Grantown-on-Spey
SKYE
A82
A87
A90
Sleat
Glenlivet
A96
Fort Augustus
Kildrummy
RUM
Mallaig
Invergarry
Aviemore
A939
A86
Arisaig
Kingussie
Ballater
Aberdeen
A830
Glenfinnan
Braemar
Fort William
Fettercairn
Strontian
A9
A93
Tobermory
Onich
Pitlochry
Duror
Alyth
Glamis
A90
Gruline
MULL
Port Appin
A82
Dunkeld
A923
Forfar
Iona
Tiroran
Eriska
Blairgowrie
Taynuilt
Killin
Oban
Kilchrenan
A85
Kinclaven
Dundee
Clachan Seil
A816
Balquhidder
Strathyre
Perth
Cupar
St Andrews
Colonsay
Arduaine
Gateside
Peat Inn
Crinan
Lochgilphead
Callander
Kinross
Largoward
JURA
A82
Dunoon
Glenrothes
ISLAY
Tighnabruaich
Stirling
M90
Kirkcaldy
FIRTH OF FORTH
Ballygrant
Greenock
Falkirk
M9
Gullane
Kilberry
Ascog
Dunbar
Port Charlotte
Bowmore
BUTE
Glasgow
M8
EDINBURGH
A1
M74
A7
Chirnside
Lochranza
M77
Lanark
Peebles
Walkerburn
Swinton
A83
ARRAN
Brodick
Kilmarnock
Biggar
Skirling
Melrose
Ayr
Selkirk
Kelso
Campbeltown
FIRTH OF CLYDE
A76
Moffat
Hawick
Heiton
Jedburgh
A1
Maybole
A713
A77
A68
A7
4
ENGLAND
Kirkton
Kirkcolm
Newton Stewart
Gatehouse of Fleet
Lockerbie
Stranraer
Dumfries
Annan
Portpatrick
A75
Kirkbean
Wigtown
Kirkcudbright
M6
Whithorn
Full entry
Shortlist entry
Town (no entry)

Northern Ireland and the Republic of Ireland 6

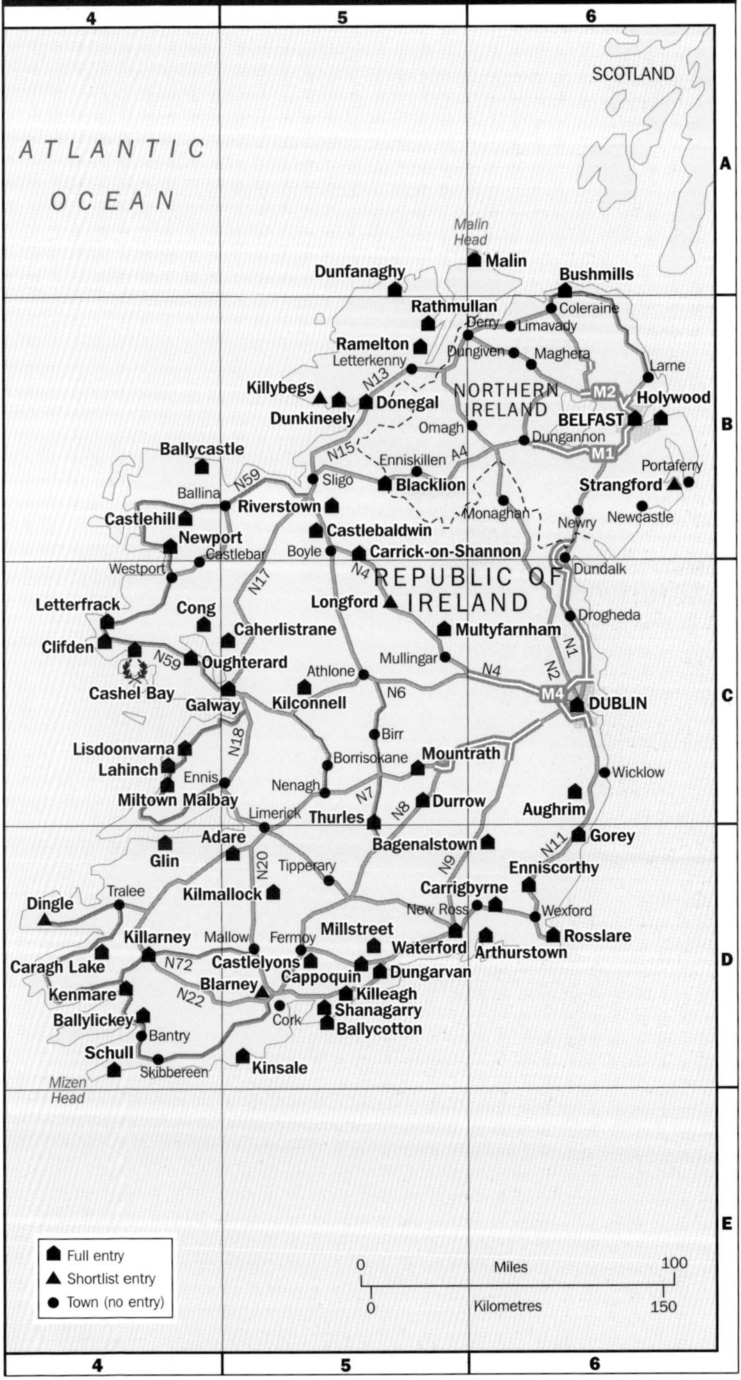

London

London may sometimes seem to be dominated by faceless, corporate hotels, but if you know where to look, you can still find places of personality and character of the type that the *Guide* celebrates. At these, the owners take a strong personal interest: the Goring family at *The Goring*; the Marler family at *Knightsbridge Green*; the Miller family at *Durrants*; Gordon Campbell Gray at *One Aldwych*; and the Levin family at *The Capital*, which receives a *César* award this year. 'If it were to close, I should have to stop visiting London,' said one reader.

The Capital, London

LONDON Map 2:D4

The Capital
22–24 Basil Street
London SW3 1AT

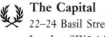

Tel 020-7589 5171
Fax 020-7225 0011
Email reservations@capitalhotel.co.uk
Website www.capitalhotel.co.uk

César award: London hotel of the year

'If it were to close, I should have to stop visiting London,' writes one fan of this 'wonderful *pied à terre*', which the Levin family have owned and run for 36 years. Henrik Muehle is manager. It stands on a busy little Knightsbridge street, but inside is 'an oasis of civilised calm'. Recent praise: 'From the moment of arrival (greeting and valet parking by the doorman), it's clear this will be good (and expensive) service.' 'Seriously high standards. Staff attentive without obsequiousness.' The decor is traditional, understated. Bedrooms have heavy fabrics, flowers, double glazing, air conditioning, marble bathroom; thick cotton sheets (no duvets). 'Every piece of furniture, work of art, and accoutrement has been specially commissioned,' says David Levin (his son, Joseph, is managing director of the Capital Group). In the intimate restaurant, with 'friendly, efficient' staff, Eric Chavot has two *Michelin* stars for dishes such as honey-roasted fillet of duck and macaroni gratin. 'Superb food; extensive wine list.' 'Good breakfasts', and 'afternoon tea was of impeccable country house standard'. Guests can also eat at the Levins' *Metro* brasserie, almost next door (the hotel above it, formerly *L'Hotel*, was due to reopen in August 2007, after a major refurbishment, as *The Levin*). A 'personal jogging partner' and a 'personal shopper' (Harrods and Harvey Nichols are near) can be provided. (*Peter Jowitt, and others*)

49 bedrooms. Central. (Underground: Knightsbridge.) Private car park (£5 an hour, £28 a day). Lift. Sitting room, bar (background music), restaurant; brasserie/bar nearby; 2 private dining rooms; business facilities. Only restaurant suitable for ♿. No smoking. No dogs. All major credit cards accepted. Room [2007]: single £210, double £285, suite £435. Breakfast £14–£18.50. Set lunch £29.50, dinner £55–£85. Christmas package.

Charlotte Street Hotel NEW
15 Charlotte Street
London W1T 1RJ

Tel 020-7806 2000
Fax 020-7806 2002
Email charlotte@firmdale.com
Website www.charlottestreethotel.com

'We spent two nights and liked it a lot,' says a long-time *Guide* contributor of this member of Tim and Kit Kemp's small Firmdale group (see also *The Pelham*). Just north of Soho, managed by Jakob Hansen, it has a 'Bloomsbury Set' decor. 'In an area densely populated with good restaurants', it has an 'elegant but not pompous' entrance hall and lobby, two 'comfortable, quite large' lounges 'in the spirit of Vanessa Bell and Duncan Grant'. They have artificial fires, sofas, newspapers and honour bar. Snacks are served here in the evening when it is nice 'to sit and wind down after the theatre' (many theatres are within walking distance). The bar/restaurant, *Oscar*, with open-plan kitchen, serves a short menu of dishes like rosemary-braised lamb shank; wild mushroom and winter truffle risotto. 'Our quiet, air-conditioned bedroom had sitting area, good storage, beautiful, well-heated bathroom. Staff exceedingly attentive and friendly. Excellent buffet breakfast' (fresh fruit, cereals, etc); cooked English. There is a 64-seat screening room. (*Wolfgang Stroebe*)

52 bedrooms. West End, N of Soho. (Underground: Goodge Street.) Restaurant closed on Sun noon–5 pm. Lift, ramps. Drawing room, library, bar/restaurant; 3 private dining/meeting rooms; screening room. No background music. Limited access for ♿. Smoking allowed in bedrooms. No dogs. All major credit cards accepted. Room [to 29 Feb 2008] (*excluding VAT*): single £210, double £240–£295, suite £350–£950. Breakfast £19. Set dinner Sun (including movie of the week; *excluding VAT and service*) £35. Full alc £45.

The Draycott

26 Cadogan Gardens
London SW3 2RP

Tel 020-7730 6466
Fax 020-7730 0236
Email info@draycotthotel.com
Website www.draycotthotel.com

'A cosy home-from-home', this 'delightful hotel' is composed of three Edwardian buildings in a quiet street near Sloane Square. Built by Lord Cadogan as part of the Cadogan estate, it is a member of the South African Mantis Collection and is managed by John Hanna. The bedrooms are named after authors and actors; some overlook a private garden square. The suites are spacious. Some double rooms have an adjacent single. A visitor in 2007 was upgraded from a single to a 'large, very pleasantly furnished room, with a good range of audio-visual toys. French windows gave access to the outside.' In the 'lovely' breakfast room there are 'excellent coffee, jams and pastries', but 'poor orange juice', and 'the cooked items bore little relation to what I had ordered from a charming, but linguistically challenged, waitress'. The lounges, with their paintings, open fire, flowers and chandeliers, are 'grand and attractive'. There is afternoon tea at 4 pm, champagne at 6. A full meal can be ordered from the 'imaginative' 24-hour room-service menu.

Children under 12 stay free. Seven steps to the building's front door make wheelchair access awkward. (*Peter Jowitt, and others*)

35 bedrooms. Central, behind Peter Jones store. NCP nearby. (Underground: Sloane Sq.) 2 lounges, library, breakfast room; private dining room. No background music. 1-acre garden. Unsuitable for ♿. Smoking allowed in 5 bedrooms. All major credit cards accepted. Room [2007] (*excluding VAT*): single £125–£135, double £176–£295, suite £309–£375. Breakfast £15.95–£19.95. Full alc (room service) £55.

Durrants
George Street
London W1H 5BJ

Tel 020-7935 8131
Fax 020-7487 3510
Email enquiries@durrantshotel.co.uk
Website www.durrantshotel.co.uk

Owned by the Miller family for nearly 90 years, this conversion of four terraced houses, with a Georgian facade, is well located in Marylebone, just north of Oxford Street, and near the Wallace Collection. Ian McIntosh is manager. It is proud of its 'quintessentially English' character (one reader wrote of a 'charmingly old-fashioned' ambience). It has small panelled lounges with leather settees and chairs; original paintings, prints and engravings; antique furniture. Guests tell us that they feel 'well looked after' by the staff ('from many different countries'). 'Their friendliness and efficiency is very noticeable.' Some bedrooms have been refurbished this year, and more renovation is planned. The larger rooms at the front may get some traffic noise; quieter rooms at the back might sometimes hear early-morning deliveries. 'My room had good lighting and a comfortable bed.' Some rooms have antiques; all have broadband Internet access. The restaurant serves 'generous portions' of international dishes. 'At breakfast there were good choices; service a little eccentric.' (*YH, and others*)

92 bedrooms. Some air conditioned. 7 on ground floor. Off Oxford Street. (Underground: Bond St, Baker St.) Restaurant closed for dinner 25 Dec. 2 lifts, ramp. 3 lounges/function rooms, bar, breakfast room, restaurant. No background music. No smoking. Guide dogs only. Amex, MasterCard, Visa accepted. Room [2007]: single from £120, double from £175, suite £340. Breakfast £11.50–£15.50. Full alc £45 (*excluding 'optional' 12½% service charge*).

> 'Set menu' indicates a fixed-price meal, with ample, limited or no choice. 'Full alc' is the hotel's estimated price per person of a three-course *à la carte* meal, with a half bottle of house wine. 'Alc' is the price of an *à la carte* meal excluding the cost of wine.

Egerton House NEW

17–19 Egerton Terrace
London SW3 2BX

Tel 020-7589 2412
Fax 020-7584 6540
Email bookeg@rchmail.com
Website www.egertonhousehotel.com

Following a major refurbishment by new owners, the Red Carnation group, in 2006, this Knightsbridge hotel returns to the *Guide* commended by visitors who were regulars under the previous regime. The 'warmly welcoming' Sandra Anido is still manager. 'Front desk impressive, all staff helpful, housekeeping spot on.' The conversion of two Victorian town houses overlooks two pretty, tree-lined garden squares. The bedrooms 'are attractive and outstandingly well equipped', but prices have risen steeply, and 'one doesn't get a lot of square footage for the money'. 'Our superior garden-facing room (£300) was peaceful, but we had occasionally to avoid collision when moving around.' At the evening turn-down, a scented candle is lit in the bathroom. The 'generous and good' breakfast, served in a pretty room, has a large buffet (fruit, ham, 'excellent' bread rolls, pastries and fresh orange juice) and traditional English. Afternoon tea is taken in the drawing room. The new bar, with its 'skilful, chatty' barman, Antonio (formerly of *Dukes Hotel*, St James's, and famed for his Martinis), 'has become a watering hole for neighbouring residents'. It provides sandwiches, salads, etc. Free Wi-Fi throughout. 'Many good restaurants nearby.' (*Kate and David Wooff*)

29 bedrooms. Some on ground floor. All air conditioned. Central. Valet parking. (Underground: Knightsbridge, South Kensington.) Lift. Drawing room, bar ('gentle classical/chill-out' background music), breakfast room; private dining/ meeting room. 24-hour butler service. No smoking. All major credit cards accepted. Room [2007] (*excluding VAT*): single £235, double £255–£395. Breakfast £17–£24.50.

The Goring

Beeston Place
Grosvenor Gardens
London SW1W 0JW

Tel 020-7396 9000
Fax 020-7834 4393
Email reception@goringhotel.co.uk
Website www.goringhotel.co.uk

César award in 1994

'Forever excellent, a really upmarket town hotel, now run by the fourth in the Goring line, Jeremy, who appears to have his father's mantle and enjoys the challenge.' An accolade this year for this traditional hotel, a few minutes' walk from Buckingham Palace and Victoria Station. David Morgan-Hewitt is managing director. Another returning visitor in 2007 found it still very good, 'though service was slow in the bar/lounge area'. The restaurant has been redesigned, to critical acclaim, by (Viscount) David Linley ('much brighter', and with quirky glass chandeliers which are lowered in the evening). Derek Quelch's traditional British seasonal cooking is always admired (eg, air-dried Cumbrian ham; steak and kidney pie with creamed potatoes). Breakfast has 'a mind-boggling selection of fruits'; 'the best kipper this fan of fish has tasted'. The 'clubby' bar has a light veranda facing the hotel's private garden (open to guests), and drinks and cream teas are served on a terrace in summer. Many bedrooms face the garden; some have a private terrace. Eccentric touches include large replica sheep which migrate between public rooms and bedrooms. (*Brian Pullee, Michael Forrest, and others*)

71 bedrooms. All air conditioned. Restaurant closed Sat lunch. Near Victoria Station (front rooms double glazed). Garage, mews parking. (Underground: Victoria.) Lift, ramps. Lounge bar (pianist in evening), terrace room, restaurant; function facilities. No background music. Free access to nearby health club. Civil wedding licence. Smoking allowed in all bedrooms. Guide dogs only. All major credit cards accepted. Room [2007] (*excluding VAT*): single £189–£295, double £199–£490, suite £319–£650. English breakfast £23. Bar meals. Set dinner £44; full alc £70. Weekend breaks. Christmas/New Year packages.

Hazlitt's
6 Frith Street
London W1D 3JA

Tel 020-7434 1771
Fax 020-7439 1524
Email reservations@hazlitts.co.uk
Website www.hazlittshotel.com

César award in 2002

In Soho, Peter McKay's stylish B&B hotel (managed by Fergal Crossan) is popular with people in film, fashion, music and publishing: writers who stay here leave signed copies of their books. Occupying three historic houses (no lift), it is named after the essayist who once lived here. The bedrooms are called after his friends (Jonathan Swift, Lady Frances Hewitt, etc). There are Victorian bathroom fittings (but modern plumbing), four-poster or half-tester beds in some rooms, plus air conditioning, Wi-Fi and flat-screen LCD television. Most rooms are light, though some at the back overlook an inner courtyard. The only public room is a small lounge. A continental breakfast is brought to the bedroom on a tray, and a simple room-service menu is available 11 am to 10.30 pm. Eight more bedrooms (including a rooftop suite with terrace) and a large sitting room, are due to open in an adjacent building in May 2008. More reports, please.

23 bedrooms. Soho (windows triple glazed; rear rooms quietest). NCP nearby. (Underground: Tottenham Court Rd, Leicester Sq.) Sitting room. No background music. 3 small courtyard gardens. Unsuitable for ♿. Smoking allowed in 7 bedrooms. All major credit cards accepted. Room [2007] (*excluding VAT*): single from £175, double from £205, suite from £300. Breakfast £9.75. Special breaks (Easter, bank holidays, etc).

Knightsbridge Green Hotel

159 Knightsbridge
London SW1X 7PD

Tel 020-7584 6274
Fax 020-7225 1635
Email reservations@thekghotel.com
Website www.thekghotel.co.uk

The Marler family's unpretentious B&B hotel has long been liked for its 'ideal location' (near Hyde Park, the South Kensington museums and the Knightsbridge shops) and 'good value' for London. Paul Fizia, the long-serving manager, heads a 'cheerful' staff. 'They made us very welcome,' say visitors this year. Signalled by a discreet canopy, the hotel has limited facilities (Reception is staffed from 7.30 am to 10.30 pm; porters are generally on duty between 7 am and 8 pm). Complimentary tea and coffee are available in a small lounge. Bedrooms vary in size; all have secondary double glazing, thick curtains, beverage tray, mineral water, biscuits and Wi-Fi Internet access (for which there is a charge). The spacious superior rooms on the upper floors have flat-screen TV. 'Our room had a vast double bed, comfortable chairs and a table.' Breakfast, from 7.30 am on weekdays, between 8 and 10 on Sunday, is delivered to the room: a choice of 'express', continental ('good coffee, orange juice, croissants and marmalade') or cooked (eggs, bacon and sausage). Following comments in the last year's *Guide*, Mr Fizia tells us, breakfast service has been upgraded: 'Our bread is now from Harrods.' (*Nikki Wild, Richard and Catriona Smith*)

28 bedrooms. All air conditioned. Knightsbridge. NCP nearby. (Underground: Knightsbridge.) Closed 24/25 Dec. Lift. Reception (background music), lounge; office (Internet access). Access to nearby health club. No smoking. No dogs. All major credit cards accepted. Room: single £115–£130, double £150–£175, suite £175–£205. Breakfast: express £5.50, continental £7, English £12.

****

Traveller's tale The new owner was an unpleasant, rheumy-eyed man who told us that we shouldn't have arrived before 4 pm, and that 'nobody expects to go into a hotel at 2 pm'. He then suggested that we went elsewhere. (*Hotel in Sussex*)

****

One Aldwych
1 Aldwych
London WC2B 4RH

Tel 020-7300 1000
Fax 020-7300 1001
Email reservations@onealdwych.com
Website www.onealdwych.com

César award in 2005

Opposite Waterloo Bridge, the Edwardian offices of the old *Morning Post* have been converted in ultra-modern style, by Gordon Campbell Gray, into 'one of the UK's most eco-friendly hotels'. Bathrooms have granite surfaces, 'green' toiletries, a 'vacuum-based waste water system'. Paper, plastic, cardboard are recycled; long-life light bulbs are used. Over 400 pieces of contemporary art are displayed throughout. The double-height lobby/bar has huge arched windows, a giant statue of an oarsman, 'trendy flower arrangements'. Visitors tell of 'impeccable service' from the young staff, led by manager Simon Hirst. Bedrooms have 'cutting edge technology': digital TV, modem sockets, etc. 'Luxurious beds; plump pillows. Huge windows looked over rooftops.' In the 'relaxed' *Indigo* restaurant, on a balcony, 'delicious meals' use organic ingredients. Classic European dishes are served in the more formal *Axis*, on the lower ground floor. The *Cinnamon Bar* provides soups, sandwiches, fruit juice cocktails, wine by the glass. Breakfast is continental, healthy or English. Keep-fit enthusiasts use the health club; personal trainers are available; two suites have a private gym. On weekdays, many clients are on business; at weekends there are reduced rates, and children are welcomed. *Dukes Hotel*, St James, is now under the same ownership and was being refurbished as we went to press (see Shortlist). More reports, please.

105 bedrooms. 6 adapted for ♿. All air conditioned. Strand (windows triple glazed). Valet parking. (Underground: Covent Garden, Charing Cross, Waterloo.) *Axis* closed Easter, Christmas, bank holidays. Lifts. 2 bars, 2 restaurants (*Axis* has background music Tues and Wed evenings); private dining rooms; function facilities, screening room; newsagent, florist; health club: 60-ft swimming pool, sauna, gym. Civil wedding licence. Smoking allowed in 46 bedrooms. Guide dogs only. All major credit cards accepted. Room [2007] (*excluding VAT*): double £185–£435, suite £575–£1,450. Breakfast £21.95. Set lunch/dinner (*Axis*) £22.50; full alc £55. Weekend breaks. 1-night bookings sometimes refused in high season.

When you make a booking you enter into a contract with a hotel. Most hotels explain their cancellation policies, which vary widely, in a letter of confirmation. You may lose your deposit or be charged at the full rate for the room if you cancel at short notice. A travel insurance policy can provide protection.

Parkes Hotel

41 Beaufort Gardens
London SW3 1PW

Tel 020-7581 9944
Fax 020-7581 1999
Email info@parkeshotel.com
Website www.parkeshotel.com

Three Victorian houses in a Knightsbridge cul-de-sac have been turned by Bertil Nygren into this much-admired boutique hotel. Guests are welcomed by a hand-written note from the manager, Susan Shaw; 'staff show the same attention to detail, making a point of learning your name, and using it'. Elegant bedrooms (fourteen are a suite with sitting room and kitchenette) are traditional. Some have a large balcony facing the leafy square. There are bold colours (rich red and saffron), chandeliers, tapestry curtains and sofas and oriental rugs, Wi-Fi, flat-screen plasma TV with movies on demand, and under-floor heating in the green marble bathroom; also a shoe-shine service and 24-hour front desk. The 'excellent' breakfast, continental or cooked ('fresh fruit; delicious poached eggs'), is served until 10.30 am. No restaurant, but 'a thoughtful information folder lists some excellent local restaurants which deliver'.

33 bedrooms. Some on ground floor. Knightsbridge (windows double glazed). Meter parking. (Underground: Knightsbridge.) Lobby, lounge, breakfast room; background music. Access to nearby health club. Unsuitable for ♿. No smoking. Dogs by arrangement. All major credit cards accepted. Room [2007] (*excluding VAT*) £199–£525. Breakfast from £12.50.

The Pelham

15 Cromwell Place
London SW7 2LA

Tel 020-7589 8288
Fax 020-7584 8444
Email pelham@firmdale.com
Website www.pelhamhotel.co.uk

The elegant public rooms at Tim and Kit Kemp's large, white, Victorian terraced building have wood panelling, antiques, china ornaments, log fires and elaborate flower arrangements. Well located (opposite South Kensington underground station), it also has 'competent concierge and desk staff'. The smallest bedrooms are in the eaves; larger rooms have big beds and antique furnishings; the spacious suites have high ceilings, original features. All rooms contain plasma TV screen, business facilities, and 24-hour room service. *Kemps*, the basement restaurant, is 'a good place for a reasonably priced lunch; and peaceful', says a reporter this year. It serves British dishes like beer-battered plaice, chips and tartare sauce; grilled Dover sole. Children are welcomed. Hyde Park is near; so are the Knightsbridge shops. More reports, please.

52 bedrooms. South Kensington, opposite tube station (windows double glazed). Meter parking; public car park nearby. Lift. Drawing room, library, bar, restaurant/bar; 3 private dining/meeting rooms. No background music. Gym. Access to nearby health club. Limited access for ♿. Smoking allowed in all bedrooms. No dogs. All major credit cards accepted. Room [to 29 Feb 2008] (*excluding VAT*): single £155–£170, double £175–£260, suite £450–£2,500. Breakfast £17.50. Set meal £12.95–£17.95; full alc £30.

The Portobello

22 Stanley Gardens
London W11 2NG

Tel 020-7727 2777
Fax 020-7792 9641
Email info@portobellohotel.co.uk
Website www.portobellohotel.co.uk

On a quiet Notting Hill street, this bohemian little hotel in a Victorian terrace is owned by Tim and Cathy Herring, with managing partner Johnny Ekperigin, and filled with gilt mirrors, military pictures, marble fireplaces, potted palms, Edwardiana, etc. It may seem 'a little shabby' now, but it has 'a happy atmosphere, quite un-London-like', say fans, and 'engaging' service. Themed 'special rooms' provide exotic accommodation: the Round Room has a large, freestanding Edwardian bathing machine and a round bed; the two Japanese water garden basement suites each have an oversized bath. The very small, cheaper 'cabins' have a tiny bathroom. A simple continental breakfast is included in the room rate; full English is available at extra cost, and the *à la carte* breakfast menu includes smoked salmon with scrambled eggs, champagne, fresh fruit, yogurt. The small basement restaurant/bar, open round the clock, also serves snacks. For more serious food, try *Julie's*, the restaurant/bar/café under the same ownership, in nearby Clarendon Cross: *The Portobello*'s residents get a discount. They may also use a nearby health club at reduced rates. Parking is awkward. Portobello Road, with its famous Saturday market, is close by. More reports, please.

24 bedrooms. Notting Hill. Meter parking. (Underground: Notting Hill Gate.) Closed 23–27 Dec. Lift. Foyer/lounge, restaurant. No background music. Access to nearby health club. Unsuitable for ♿. Smoking allowed in some bedrooms. Amex, MasterCard, Visa accepted. B&B [2007]: single £142, double £190, 'special' £242–£310. English breakfast £15. Full alc £30.

> If you dislike piped music, why not join Pipedown, the campaign for freedom from piped music? 1 The Row, Berwick St James, Salisbury SP3 4TP. *Tel* 01722-690622, www.pipedown.info.

The rockwell NEW

181 Cromwell Road
London SW5 0SF

Tel 020-7244 2000
Fax 020-7244 2001
Email enquiries@therockwell.com
Website www.therockwell.com

Two Victorian terrace houses have been turned 'with flair' by architect Michael Squire with Tony Bartlett into this designer hotel. 'Its bright facade with pea-green highlights stands out like a beacon on the busy Cromwell Road.' 'Very well run' with 'very friendly staff', it has 'well ventilated' bedrooms and, say inspectors, 'bright modern decor: interesting wallpaper, patterns and colour'. The 'fine, high-ceilinged' lounge has an open fire; the small bar opens on to a garden with plants in huge pots, where drinks and meals can be served. Spacious garden bedrooms have a patio; 'exciting' mezzanine suites have a lounge and sleeping area down a curved staircase. 'Our compact fourth-floor standard double made good use of space: built-in, light oak wardrobe, matching bedhead, minibar, flat-screen TV; well-lit bathroom with bathrobes and powerful shower. Double glazing kept out road noise. 24-hour room service.' In the restaurant, with 'palm-inspired' wallpaper, contemporary English dishes (eg, pork belly stuffed with prunes) are accompanied by a 'wide-ranging' wine list, and breakfast is served until 10 am: it has a buffet with 'the freshest of orange juice; home-made muesli; big jars of preserves' and various cooked dishes. 'Reasonable prices for central London.' (*TB, and others*)

40 bedrooms. All with shower. Some on ground floor. 1 mile W of West End; opposite Cromwell Hospital. (Underground: Earls Court.) Lift, ramps. Lobby, lounge, bar, restaurant; background music; conference room. Garden. No smoking. No dogs. Amex, MasterCard, Visa. Room: single £120, double £160, suite £200. Breakfast £9.50–£12.50. Set menu £25; full alc £30.

---

22 Jermyn Street

22 Jermyn Street
London SW1Y 6HL

Tel 020-7734 2353
Fax 020-7734 0750
Email office@22jermyn.com
Website www.22jermyn.com

César award in 1996

A rarity in London, Henry Togna's discreet and 'charming' town house hotel has been in his family for four generations. Tapestries hang in the panelled entrance hall. There are no public rooms in the Victorian building, but most of the accommodation is in well-equipped suites. Each has sofa and chairs, fridge/bar, multi-channel TV, DVD-player (popcorn comes free with movies from a library which has more than 100 titles), two direct-dial telephones, broadband and Wi-Fi Internet access. Room sizes vary from 'comfortable' to 'palatial', but 'all echo the same attention to detail'. 'Bedtime stories in leaflet form were on our pillows.' Some suites can be turned into two or three bedrooms. Children and pets are welcomed. Laurie Smith is the manager; the 'nice young' staff 'have a wealth of knowledge, and are well connected when it comes to booking tables or tickets'; visits are personalised, preferences remembered. Breakfast, brought to the room on a tray set with fresh flowers, includes fresh orange juice, cooked dishes *à la carte* (good porridge, eggs, etc). There is a wide-ranging room-service meal menu. Guests may use the sporting facilities at a nearby club, borrow a mountain bike, go jogging in St James's Park.

18 bedrooms. West End (St James's). Car park nearby. Valet parking (expensive). (Underground: Piccadilly Circus.) Air conditioning. 24-hour room service. Lift. Reception (background music); small conference facilities. Access to health club. Smoking allowed in some bedrooms. All major credit cards accepted. Room: double £220, suite £315–£350. Breakfast £13.20. Full alc £30–£45.

The Victoria

10 West Temple Sheen
London SW14 7RT

Tel 020-8876 4238
Fax 020-8878 3464
Email bookings@thevictoria.net
Website www.thevictoria.net

Just 25 minutes by train from Waterloo station, this unpretentious gastropub in leafy south-west London was preferred by recent visitors to 'any central hotel'. It is owned by Mark Chester with his business partner, the chef, Darren Archer. Their 'young, cheerful staff work hard to provide relaxed and attentive service'. The bedrooms are in an annexe at the back: two (No. 4 and No. 7) are large. All have free broadband Internet access, and Egyptian cotton bedlinen. 'Ours was compact, simple, perhaps even plain, but comfortable, warm and peaceful.' The atmosphere is 'lively' in the bar and the restaurant, where modern European dishes are served, eg, garlic soup with Parmesan; roast spring lamb with salad niçoise. 'First class, well presented and full of flavour.' Breakfast has fresh juices, 'DIY toast from good bread, home-made marmalade, tea in mugs (bag in)'. Parties and receptions are catered for in the conservatory. Service from the front desk was 'attentive; the lady who greeted us insisted on carrying my bag even though I was twice her size'. (*AA and CS, R and JH*)

7 bedrooms. 3 on ground floor. Near Richmond. Train: Mortlake (5 mins' walk) to Waterloo/Clapham Jct. Car park. Restaurant closed 4 days over Christmas. Ramp. Bar ('low-volume' background music), restaurant, conservatory. Garden: children's play area. Unsuitable for ♿. No smoking. No dogs. Amex, MasterCard, Visa accepted. B&B [2007] £54.25 per person. Set lunch £14.95; full alc £39.50. *V*

The Zetter

86–88 Clerkenwell Road
London EC1M 5RJ

Tel 020-7324 4444
Fax 020-7324 4445
Email info@thezetter.com
Website www.thezetter.com

Informally run by owners Mark Sainsbury and Michael Benyan, with manager Justin Pinchbeck, this converted 19th-century warehouse with contemporary decor 'lived up to expectations' in 2007: 'Comfortable bed, modern bathroom, easy parking at the weekend, excellent restaurant, proximity to Sadlers Wells.' 'Exceptionally friendly staff.' A glass door leads to a white-walled lobby with a pink Murano chandelier. Bedrooms are done in bright colours; there are duck-down duvets, raindance showers, free Wi-Fi connection. 'We were upgraded to a roof studio with patio and panoramic views.' A 'superior' room was 'small, a bit stark, but stylishly done. Great lighting, with a pink option; smart, if awkward, oblong granite basin.' Vending machines on each floor produce drinks, disposable cameras, champagne, etc. 'There is a good atmosphere' in the crescent-shaped restaurant; 'huge windows, tables well spaced'. An 'interesting menu (difficult to choose)' from chef Diego Jacquet. 'Starters included oysters; shrimps; delicious parsnip and apple soup. Very good John Dory; good puddings, too. Portions not too huge; reasonable prices.' On Sunday there is a brunch menu and a very short *carte.* Breakfast can be continental, classic English or *à la carte* (including porridge with apple compote; waffles with honey). *The Zetter* 'has an environmental conscience' (sustainable materials, energy-efficient technology). (*Max Lickfold, and others*)

59 bedrooms. 1 with ♿ access. In Clerkenwell, by St John's Sq. NCP garage, 5 mins' walk. (Underground: Farringdon.) 2 lifts, ramps. Cocktail bar, restaurant; 2 function/meeting rooms. No background music. Smoking allowed in 14 bedrooms. No dogs. Amex, MasterCard, Visa accepted. Room [2007] £150–£235, studio £264–£387.75. Breakfast £6.50–£16.50. Set dinner £18.50–£22.50; full alc £50. Weekend rates. Christmas/New Year packages.

See also SHORTLIST

ENGLAND

There is something for every taste in our selection of English hotels, which remains as broad as ever. Cool city hotels are listed alongside traditional country houses; fashionable dining pubs stand next to good-value guest houses. Some of our choices are distinctly un-hotel-like. Restaurants-with-rooms and simple (but affordable) B&Bs may not provide all the facilities of a full-service hotel, but they share the factor common to all our hotels: a warm welcome, and a sense of caring for the guest, created by a hands-on owner or manager.

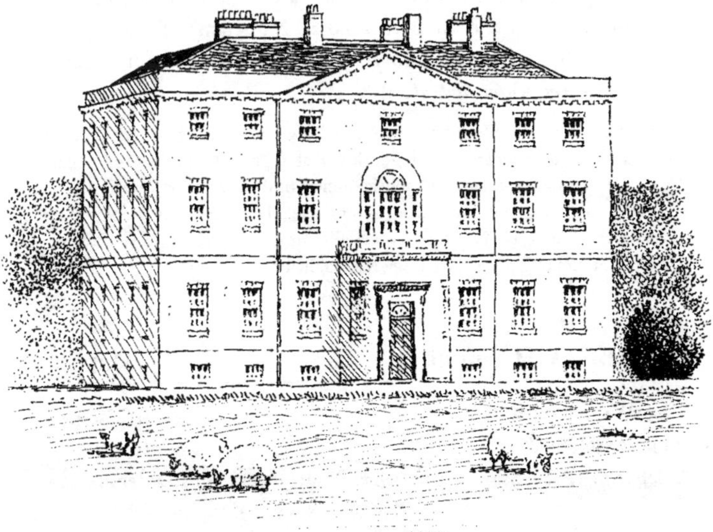

Moccas Court, Moccas

ABBOTSBURY Dorset Map 1:D6

Abbey House
Church Street
Abbotsbury DT3 4JJ

Tel 01305-871330
Fax 01305-871088
Email info@theabbeyhouse.co.uk
Website www.theabbeyhouse.co.uk

'Marvellous value for money' (one of this year's comments), this guest house is a 15th-century building on the site of an 11th-century abbey. Another visitor found it 'just as good as the *Guide* had indicated'. It has flagstone floors, panelled doors, original windows, 'cosy lounge with plenty of books'; 'lots of chintz and knick-knacks'. The 'friendly, attentive' owners, Jonathan and Maureen Cooke, 'run it impeccably, yet find time to chat'. The 'delightful' garden has flowerbeds, wide lawns that slope down to a millpond, and the only surviving Benedictine watermill in the country. Beyond is a huge, ancient tithe barn. Light alfresco lunches and cream teas are served in summer. The 'cottagey' bedrooms vary in size and style: one has a king-size brass bed; another an antique half-tester. Three have a new bed this year. Breakfasts, served with damask tablecloths, are 'very good'. Evening meals are available only for house parties (for which this is a 'brilliant venue'). *Abbey House* has a comprehensive list of local eating places, but most involve a drive. The village, 'a real find for a weekend away', is famed for its swannery (established by monks over 600 years ago), and its subtropical gardens. (*John Cutler, Guy Dehn, and others*)

5 bedrooms. Off B3157 halfway between Weymouth and Bridport. Tea room open for lunches midday Apr–Sept; closed at night, except for house parties. Reception (classical background music sometimes), lounge, breakfast/tea room. 1½-acre garden: stage for opera. Sea 15 mins' walk. Unsuitable for ♿. No smoking. No children under 12. No dogs. No credit cards. B&B [2007] £32.50–£40 per person. Christmas/New Year packages. 1-night bookings sometimes refused Sat.

ALDEBURGH Suffolk Map 2:C6

The Wentworth
Wentworth Road
Aldeburgh IP15 5BD

Tel 01728-452312
Fax 01728-454343
Email stay@wentworth-aldeburgh.co.uk
Website www.wentworth-aldeburgh.com

'Old-fashioned (in the nicest sense)', this traditional seaside hotel faces fishing huts and boats on Aldeburgh's shingle beach. Michael Pritt, 'much in evidence', is the third generation of his family in charge; his manager is the 'warm, pleasant' Jolyon Gough. 'Rooms and service very nice,' says a report this year. In the lounges are log fires, antiques, books, plants, fresh flowers and Russell Flint prints. Each bedroom has a copy of Kathleen Hale's *Orlando the Marmalade Cat* (her 'Owlbarrow' is Aldeburgh), and sea-facing rooms have binoculars. 'Our suite was well furnished, and had excellent views.' The annexe, *Darfield House*, has large rooms and a garden, but is not sea-facing. In the conservatory restaurant, the chef, Graham Reid, offers 'a good range of choices' of 'generous' dishes which are usually enjoyed (main courses like roast lamb with rosemary mash; confit of Blythburgh pork with spiced apple purée and red wine jus. Light lunches and cream teas are served under white parasols on a terrace. Dogs are welcomed. Musicians and actors often stay here during the Aldeburgh Festival. (*PD, and others*)

35 bedrooms. 7 in *Darfield House.* 5 on ground floor, 1 suitable for ♿. On seafront, 5 mins' walk from centre. Parking. Train: Saxmundham, 8 miles. Ramps. 2 lounges, bar, restaurant; private dining room; conference room. No background music. Small sunken terrace. Shingle beach 200 yds. No smoking. All major credit cards accepted. B&B [2007] £51–£107 per person. Set menus £17.50–£19.50. Weekend, midweek breaks; special events. Christmas/New Year packages. 1-night bookings refused Sat.

See also SHORTLIST

ALSTON Cumbria — Map 4:B3

Lovelady Shield
Nenthead Road
nr Alston CA9 3LF

Tel 01434-381203
Fax 01434-381515
Email enquiries@lovelady.co.uk
Website www.lovelady.co.uk

On the site of a 13th-century convent, Peter and Marie Haynes's white-fronted Georgian house, now a country hotel, stands in secluded grounds with the River Nent running through. It is liked for the silence: the unspoilt setting creates 'an oasis from modern life', and it is 'blissfully free from muzak'. 'A pleasing blend of elegance, simplicity and style,' is a comment this year. The two sitting rooms have been refurbished; one is a 'cosy library stuffed full of books and games for rainy days'. 'Our comfortable bedroom had plenty of storage space,' said one visitor, but another thought his 'luxury bedroom' was 'on the small side'. Early morning tea is brought to the room (for a charge), or tea-making equipment can be provided. Barrie Garton, chef for the past ten years, describes his style as 'British with continental excursions'. There is a daily-changing four-course *table d'hôte* menu. 'Food is excellent, the restaurant top-notch.' 'Excellent breakfast, and superb staff.' There is good walking from the door. (*Gareth Evans, Stephen Holman, and others*)

12 bedrooms. 2 miles E of Alston. 2 lounges, bar, restaurant. No background music. 3-acre grounds: river, fishing, croquet, woodland walks. Unsuitable for ♿. Civil wedding licence. No smoking. No children under 9 in restaurant for dinner. No dogs in public rooms. Amex, MasterCard, Visa accepted. B&B £80–£140 per person; D,B&B £100–£160. Reductions for 2/3 nights. Set dinner £40. Christmas/New Year packages. *V*

AMBERLEY West Sussex — Map 2:E3

Amberley Castle
Amberley
nr Arundel BN18 9LT

Tel 01798-831992
Fax 01798-831998
Email info@amberleycastle.co.uk
Website www.amberleycastle.co.uk

'Like a fairy tale; we were well looked after,' says a 2007 report on this luxury hotel (Relais & Châteaux) at the foot of the South Downs. 'Enchanting bedrooms, ambience of peace and silence. Staff, mostly young and foreign, engaging, eager to please.' Owned by Martin and Joy Cummings, managed by Oliver Smith, this Grade I listed monument, 900 years old, is surrounded by a 60-foot wall and dry moat, on a bend of the River Arun. The 'immaculate' grounds have 'lots of flowers', a putting course, a 'comfortably furnished' tree house. The main buildings, inside the battlements, include many bedrooms and suites (others are in the *Bishopric* in the moat, and a manor house; some have direct access to the battlements). Sizes vary greatly, but all rooms have antiques, fine fabrics, spa bath, flat-screen TV, DVD-player; 'fine china, fresh milk, fruit platter'. Fluffy toys abound. 'Housekeeping standards are high.' There is praise for James Dugan's modern European cooking: 'The dining experience was wonderful [men must wear jacket or tie]: fabulous canapés, double-cooked côte de boeuf, lovingly prepared; passion fruit soufflé exploded with flavour.' Breakfast has fresh orange juice, but 'indifferent toast, dishes kept hot under lamps, past their best when we got them; flavourless coffee'. Popular for weddings and functions. (*Matthew Caminer*)

19 bedrooms. 5 in *Bishopric*, outside walls. SW of village, 4 miles N of Arundel. Hall, 3 lounges, 2 restaurants; function facilities. No background music. 12-acre grounds: gardens, tennis, 18-hole putting course, croquet, ponds, wildlife. Helipad. Civil wedding licence. Unsuitable for ♿. No smoking. No children under 12.

Guide dogs only. All major credit cards accepted. Room [2007] £77.50–£197.50 per person; D,B&B (2 nights min.) £230–£497.50. Breakfast £16.50. Set lunch £20–£25, dinner £43–£50; full alc £69.50. Christmas/New Year packages. Min. 2-night booking weekends. Christmas/New Year packages.

AMBLESIDE Cumbria — Map 4: inset C2

The Regent by the Lake

Waterhead Bay
Ambleside LA22 0ES

Tel 015394-32254
Fax 015394-31474
Email info@regentlakes.co.uk
Website www.regentlakes.co.uk

'A super hotel. Good food and huge breakfasts,' says a visitor this year to Christine Hewitt's hotel which stands opposite a slipway on to Lake Windermere. Managed by her son Andrew, it offers flexible eating choices: a 'Dine around Ambleside' option gives guests deals at local restaurants; a picnic hamper in the bedroom is available for those wanting 'a cosy night in'. And breakfast, always liked ('you can order anything in any form'), is served until midday. In the split-level restaurant ('where the lighting could be brighter'), new chef John Mather offers a daily-changing dinner menu (main courses include slow-roast lamb on dauphinoise potato). One guest was initially served with 'meat too tough to eat', but it was 'immediately replaced by a dish of excellent tender beef with fresh vegetables'. Staff are 'all helpful'. The restaurant and lounges have a modern decor of pale browns and cream. Bedrooms, of all shapes and sizes, are designed to have 'a cottage feel'. Some have their own patio, and one has a view across Waterhead Bay and Lake Windermere. Dogs are welcomed. (*DRW Jervois, and others*)

30 bedrooms. 10 in courtyard, 5 in garden. 7 on ground floor. On A591, S of centre, at Waterhead Bay. Train: Windermere, 5 miles. Closed Christmas. Ramp. Lounge, sun lounge, bar, restaurant; background music at night; 50-ft heated swimming pool. Courtyard. ¼-acre garden. On Lake Windermere: sailing, waterskiing, fishing. No smoking. No dogs in public rooms. MasterCard, Visa accepted. B&B [2007] £60–£90 per person; D,B&B £70–£105. Set lunch £25. Special breaks. 1-night bookings sometimes refused Sat. *V*

The *V* sign at the end of an entry indicates a hotel that has agreed to take part in our Voucher scheme and to give *Guide* readers a 25% discount on their room rates for a one-night stay, subject to the conditions explained in *How to use the Good Hotel Guide*, and given on the back of the vouchers.

Rothay Manor
Rothay Bridge
Ambleside LA22 0EH

Tel 015394-33605
Fax 015394-33607
Email hotel@rothaymanor.co.uk
Website www.rothaymanor.co.uk

César award in 1992

'Truly civilised', this 'very comfortable' hotel stands near the head of Lake Windermere. Run by its owners, brothers Nigel and Stephen Nixon (the family has been here over 40 years), the white-fronted Regency house has been in every edition of the *Guide*. It is at the junction of several busy roads, but is surrounded by trees and attractive gardens. 'Traffic noise is unobtrusive by day, virtually non-existent at night.' Other comments: 'Real country house style, but unpretentious. Ambience professional but relaxed. Staff pleasant, efficient, a good mix of ages and nationalities.' 'Warm welcome. Luggage carried to our room. One of the proprietors is always around.' Bedrooms are 'well furnished' (many are large); quietest ones face the garden; four are in an annexe joined to the main building by a covered walkway. 'Sitting in the sun on our balcony was idyllic.' Children are welcomed (family rooms, special menus, cots, high chairs, etc). Chefs Colette Nixon and Jane Binns provide a daily-changing 'traditional British/French' menu with plenty of choice: 'Excellent fish; delicious rack of lamb.' Breakfasts have freshly squeezed orange juice, 'eggs perfectly cooked', 'very good toast and marmalade'. You can walk across fields to the lake. (*Margaret Box, Stephen and Pauline Glover*)

19 bedrooms. 2 in annexe, 20 yds. 2 suitable for ♿. ¼ mile SW of Ambleside. Open 25 Jan–3 Jan. Ramp. 2 lounges, bar, 2 dining rooms; meeting/conference facilities. No background music. 1-acre garden: croquet. Access to local leisure centre. No smoking. No dogs. All major credit cards accepted. B&B [2007] £67.50–£137.50 per person. Set menus £19–£41. Special breaks. Christmas/New Year packages. 1-night bookings refused Sat.

AMPLEFORTH North Yorkshire — Map 4:D4

Shallowdale House
West End, Ampleforth
nr York, YO62 4DY

Tel 01439-788325
Fax 01439-788885
Email stay@shallowdalehouse.co.uk
Website www.shallowdalehouse.co.uk

César award in 2005

'Recommended unreservedly for a relaxing break', Phillip Gill and Anton van der Horst's small guest house (now a Wolsey Lodge) stands on a sheltered south-facing slope of the Hambleton hills, on the edge of the North York Moors national park. 'An example of how a small hotel should be run,' is another comment. The 'welcoming' hosts ('they do work hard') serve 'complimentary tea and delicious cakes' to arriving guests. The architect-designed building (1963) has panoramic views of the surrounding countryside. The 'tastefully furnished' ground-floor drawing room has an open fire in winter. Two bedrooms are spacious; the third, slightly smaller, has a private bathroom across a corridor. 'Our large, airy room had French windows opening on to a small balcony (incredible views), and a dressing room (plenty of cupboard space).' Binoculars, torches and bathrobes are supplied. A four-course set dinner at 7.30 ('domestic eclectic' cooking) is served by arrangement (48 hours' notice), at separate candlelit tables: 'The food was superb, much of it sourced locally' (the main course could be duck breasts with braised endives and Marsala). Breakfast includes dry-cured bacon, Whitby kippers, home-made preserves. (*Mrs ME Hewson, Andrew Warren, Sue and Colin Raymond, and many others*)

3 bedrooms. W end of Ampleforth. Closed Christmas/New Year, occasionally at other times. Drawing room, sitting room, dining room. No background music. 2½-acre grounds. Unsuitable for ♿. No smoking. No children under 12. No dogs. MasterCard, Visa accepted. B&B: single £70–£80, double £87.50–£107.50. Set dinner £32.50. 1-night bookings sometimes refused weekends.

ARUNDEL West Sussex — Map 2:E3

Arundel House
11 High Street
Arundel BN18 9AD

Tel 01903-882136
Fax 01903-881179
Website www.arundelhouseonline.com

'Contemporary and comfortable', this bow-windowed 19th-century merchant's town house has been turned into a 'pleasing' restaurant-with-rooms by Luke Hackman (the chef) and Billy Lewis-Bowker. 'The loveliest hosts,' writes a visitor who stayed for a week in 2007. The decor is by Mr Lewis-Bowker's wife, Emma, whose paintings hang throughout. Meals are served in two 'attractive' rooms, one on each side of the entrance hall. The cooking is regularly praised: 'wild, local and seasonal' ingredients are used in the 'British-led, modern cuisine', eg, coarse pork rillette; rack of lamb with pine nut crust, creamy champ potatoes. 'A first-rate wine list that doesn't mug you.' No residents' lounge; bedrooms have flat-screen TV, free wireless Internet access and power shower. There is a choice between duvet and blankets (best specify when you book). 'Our room was well appointed, with all the latest fads in the bathroom.' One visitor thought breakfast 'a let-down: cereals in small packets, little pots of preserve, poor bread'. The house is on a short one-way system: no car park, but you can draw up outside to unload, and vouchers are given for the large, safe municipal car park opposite the castle entrance. (*Paula Antonini, Mike Hutton, and others*)

5 bedrooms. All with power shower. On High St. Municipal car park 200 yds. Closed 17–27 Feb, 19–29 Oct, 24–26 Dec. Restaurant (background music; closed Sun). Unsuitable for ♿. No smoking. No children under 16. Guide dogs only. Amex, MasterCard, Visa accepted. B&B £40–£80 per person. Set meal £25–£37. 1-night bookings refused bank holidays. *V*

The Town House

65 High Street
Arundel BN18 9AJ

Tel 01903-883847
Email enquiries@thetownhouse.co.uk
Website www.thetownhouse.co.uk

In their restaurant-with-rooms, in a Grade II listed Regency building opposite Arundel castle, owner/chef Lee Williams and his wife, Katie, are 'maintaining standards', says a returning visitor. 'A good experience. Food stunning, service charming,' say other guests. The dining room has an 'amazing' 16th-century carved Florentine ceiling, acquired in Italy by Lord Maltravers, son of an earl of Arundel (he once lived here). This year, 'delicious' shellfish soup was enjoyed; also partridge 'trimmed so that you don't end up fighting to get at the meat'. Of the bedrooms, 'Rosemary, on the second floor, decorated in beige and white, had a short lobby and an amazing amount of original intricate plasterwork and furniture mouldings. Plenty of wardrobe space, sash windows looking across the road to the castle. Adequate bathroom. Housekeeping faultless.' A suite has a four-poster bed and a balcony facing the castle walls. Breakfast is continental or 'full English with additions'. 'Excellent scrambled eggs and smoked salmon.' 'We try to create a relaxed clientele where children are welcomed,' write the Williamses. 'No dress code, and stuffiness is taboo.' Only 'downside': the background music. No lounge or grounds, so probably best for a short stay. (*RF, and others*)

4 bedrooms. On High St, next to 'Arundel Ghost Experience'. Municipal car park nearby. Closed 25 Dec, 2 weeks Jan, 2 weeks Oct. Restaurant (closed Sun/Mon; background CDs). Unsuitable for ♿. No smoking. No dogs. All major credit cards accepted. B&B double £85–£120. Set lunch £12.50–£16, dinner £22–£27.50. Off-season breaks. 1-night bookings sometimes refused weekends in high season. *V*

Report forms (Freepost in UK) are at the end of the *Guide.*

ASHBOURNE Derbyshire **Map 3:B6**

Callow Hall
Mappleton
Ashbourne DE6 2AA

Tel 01335-300900
Fax 01335-300512
Email enquiries@callowhall.co.uk
Website www.callowhall.co.uk

At the southern gateway to the Peak District national park, this Grade II listed Victorian house stands in large grounds, overlooking the Bentley Brook and the valley of the River Dove. The Spencer family owners, David, Dorothy, Anthony and Emma, admired for their 'warmth and professionalism', are continuing their programme of bedroom refurbishment, and flat-screen TVs are being installed to replace those previously criticised by a reader as 'old-fashioned'. The 'lovely old house' has 'beautifully furnished' public rooms, say fans. There are rugs on polished floors, stags' heads, large flower arrangements. Staff are 'always near if needed'. Mrs Spencer and her daughter run front-of-house; son Anthony and his father are in the kitchen. Butchery, curing and baking are done on site; salmon and bacon are home smoked. In the red-walled restaurant, the five-course dinner menu, with extensive choice, changes daily (main courses like breast of duck with Thai-style crushed sweet potato and confit duck). The bedrooms, up a wooden staircase, vary greatly: the larger ones are thought 'worth the extra money'; some others are 'small, with no view'. Children are welcomed. Functions are sometimes held, and one visitor found 'business people in evidence, so a certain amount of mobile phonery'. (*K and JC, and others*)

16 bedrooms. 2 on ground floor. 1 suitable for ♿. ¾ mile from Ashbourne, off A515 to Buxton. Train: Derby, 13 miles. Closed Christmas, 1 week early Feb. Restaurant closed for lunch except Sun. Lounge, bar, 3 dining rooms; function/conference facilities. No background music. 44-acre grounds: walled garden, woodland, farm, stables; river, fishing (tuition available). No smoking. Dogs by arrangement. Amex, MasterCard, Visa accepted. B&B [2007] £70–£125 per person. Set menu £44; full alc £44.50. Weekend/midweek breaks. *V*

****

Traveller's tale The service is pretentious and formal. When we arrived at the time I'd booked the table, we said that we wanted to go straight to the dining room. An effete young man barely out of his cot announced: 'We don't do things that way here,' and pushed us into the lounge to wait. His overbearing manner made us wonder what training, if any, he had received. I had to send a bottle of wine back three times before the correct one was finally produced. (*Hotel in Lancashire*)

****

ASHWATER Devon — Map 1:C3

Blagdon Manor
Ashwater EX21 5DF

Tel 01409-211224
Fax 01409-211634
Email stay@blagdon.com
Website www.blagdon.com

César award in 2006

'On our fourth visit to Liz and Steve Morey's country hotel I tried to find some faults. In the end I did – the weather!' 'Perfect for a quiet stay.' Two of many endorsements for this Grade II listed, rambling, 17th-century manor house. It looks across rolling countryside towards Dartmoor. Inside are many original features (oak beams, slate flagstones, etc). 'Friendly owners, roaring fires, attractive decor, stunning food,' is another comment. The setting is 'idyllic', 'deeply rural', midway between the north and south Devon coasts. 'Spotless' bedrooms vary in size and style: 'The best-equipped rooms I have seen. Those looking over the garden towards Dartmoor have the best views.' Fresh flowers and open fires are in the bar and lounge. Books, ornaments and striped fabrics abound. The dinner menu 'only changes every six weeks', but has six choices for each course, and supplementary dishes are offered to guests on a long stay. Some ingredients are home grown. Breakfast (with exotic fruits, 'delicious porridge, perfect scrambled eggs') and lunch are taken in a spacious conservatory. The Moreys have two 'gorgeous' chocolate Labradors and some cats. Guests' dogs are welcomed. (*GC, DF Clarke, Edwin Prince, Joanna Russell*)

7 bedrooms. 8 miles NE of Launceston. Closed New Year, 2 weeks Jan, 2 weeks Oct. Ramps. Lounge, library, bar, conservatory, restaurant; private dining room. No background music. 20-acre grounds: 3-acre gardens, croquet, giant chess, gazebo, pond. Sea 12 miles. Unsuitable for ♿. No smoking. No children under 12. No dogs in restaurant or conservatory. MasterCard, Visa accepted. B&B [2007] £62.50–£85 per person. Set dinner £35. 1-night bookings refused at Christmas. *V*

How to contact the *Guide*
By mail: From anywhere in the UK, write to Freepost PAM 2931, London W11 4BR (no stamp is needed)
From outside the UK: *Good Hotel Guide*, 50 Addison Avenue, London W11 4QP, England
By telephone or fax: 020-7602 4182
By email: Goodhotel@aol.com or Goodhotel@btinternet.com
Via our website: www.goodhotelguide.com

ATCHAM Shropshire Map 3:B5

The Mytton & Mermaid Hotel

Atcham, nr Shrewsbury
SY5 6QG

Tel 01743-761220
Fax 01743-761292
Email reception@myttonandmermaid.co.uk
Website www.myttonandmermaid.co.uk

On the banks of the River Severn, this early 18th-century Grade II listed building is named after Jack Mytton, an eccentric local squire who ended up in a debtors' prison. Its owners, Ann and Danny Ditella, provide 'service without pomp'. It was liked this year for the 'friendly, polite service'. Decor is a blend of 'modern and traditional'. The best bedrooms are in the main house (some have a 'Gothic' bed). 'Our comfortable room was enlivened by resident house martins.' 'Our large superior room had fab views.' Corridors and stairways have been refurbished this year, as have the ground-floor courtyard bedrooms (these are suitable for people with limited mobility). In the lounge, which faces garden and river, afternoon tea is served. The bar (open all day) has log fire and sofas. It serves meals, and holds a jazz evening every Sunday. In the candlelit restaurant, with antique oak tables and fresh flowers, the chef, Adrian Badland, offers interesting dishes like asparagus and goat's cheese terrine; char-grilled Gloucester old spot pork chop. There are menus for vegetarians and children. 'A little noisy: nearby busy road.' Attingham Park, a National Trust property in huge grounds, is opposite. (*CB, and others*)

16 bedrooms. 6 on ground floor, in courtyard. Also 4-bedroom cottage. 3 miles SE of Shrewsbury. Closed 25 Dec. Ramps. Riverside drawing room with TV, *Mad Jack's Bar* (background music all day), restaurant. 1-acre garden on River Severn (fishing rights). Civil wedding licence. No smoking. Dogs allowed in courtyard rooms. All major credit cards accepted. B&B £52.50–£80 per person. Set dinner £30.50; full alc £37.50. New Year's Eve package.

AUSTWICK North Yorkshire Map 4:D3

The Austwick Traddock

Austwick, via Lancaster
LA2 8BY

Tel 01524-251224
Fax 01524-251796
Email info@austwicktraddock.co.uk
Website www.austwicktraddock.co.uk

Informally run by owners Bruce and Jane Reynolds, this substantial Georgian house is in a 'lovely, tranquil' village in the Yorkshire Dales national park. 'It is cosy; the young staff (mostly American students) were friendly, welcoming, though sometimes inexperienced,' says a report this year. In winter there are log fires in the lounge. In summer, drinks are served on the deck facing the garden. The bedrooms are 'comfortably furnished in restrained country style' (patterned wallpaper, plain fitted carpets, 'fine country antiques'; also sherry and 'a profusion of good magazines'). A suite was 'beautiful, spacious'. 'Our small bathroom was well equipped, but lacked storage space.' The kitchen is certified as 100% organic by the Soil Association. Tom Eunson is the new chef: we would welcome reports on his cooking (main courses include haunch of wild venison with potato and beetroot gratin, parsnip purée and chocolate jus). 'We would return for the breakfast alone; the spread of fruit, the choice of cooked dishes, and the quality of ingredients, were the best we've encountered.' Children are welcomed; so are 'well-behaved pets'. Good walking from the door. (*Camelia Leveridge, and others*)

Note: This hotel went on the market as we went to press.

10 bedrooms. 3 miles NW of Settle. Train: Settle; bus. Large lounge, front lounge, bar, dining room, breakfast room; occasional background music; function facilities. 1-acre grounds: sun deck. Only public rooms accessible to ♿. No smoking. No dogs in public rooms. MasterCard, Visa accepted. B&B [2007] £70–£100 per person. Set menu £40. Activity breaks. Christmas/New Year packages. 1-night bookings refused Fri/Sat. *V*

AYLESBURY Buckinghamshire — Map 2:C3

Hartwell House
Oxford Road
nr Aylesbury HP17 8NR

Tel 01296-747444
Fax 01296-747450
Email info@hartwell-house.com
Website www.hartwell-house.com

César award in 1997

One of Britain's great stately homes, in a huge landscaped park, this luxury hotel is 'endorsed wholeheartedly' this year. Owned by Richard Broyd's Historic House Hotels (see also *Middlethorpe Hall*, York, *Bodysgallen Hall and Spa*, Llandudno), it is managed by the 'admirable', long-serving Jonathan Thompson. His staff are 'most welcoming', 'helpful without being intrusive'. 'There is nothing forbidding here,' said an earlier visitor. 'The ceilings are so high, the windows so tall and wide, that the place is full of light.' 'It feels lived in, we had a delightful time,' was another comment. The four drawing rooms are furnished with 'priceless antiques, there to be used, not just admired'; 'if there is a large jolly group in one, you can find another equally comfortable, and be quiet'. Bedrooms in the main house vary (some are large and grand).

Those in a converted stable block are 'attractively decorated' (some are split-level). The dress code for the candlelit dinner (served with silver and damask; a 'pleasant ambience') is 'smart, but jacket and tie not obligatory'. Chef Daniel Richardson's dishes include confit of monkfish tail and fennel soufflé with a champagne sauce. 'An excellent lunch after an exhausting morning of massage, swimming etc' is available in the spa's bar/buttery. (*Marilyn and Conrad Dehn, NC, and others*)

46 bedrooms. 16 in stable block. Some on ground floor. 2 miles W of Aylesbury. Lift, ramp. 4 drawing rooms, bar, 3 dining rooms, buttery; conference facilities; spa: 55-ft swimming pool, whirlpool, sauna, beauty salon, bar/buttery. No background music. Pianist in vestibule Fri/Sat evening. 90-acre grounds: tennis, croquet, lake (fishing), jogging track, woodlands. Civil wedding licence. No smoking. No children under 6. No dogs: public rooms, main house bedrooms. Amex, MasterCard, Visa accepted. B&B £145–£195 per person; D,B&B £190–£210. Cooked breakfast £6. Set lunch from £19.50; full alc £46. Christmas/New Year packages. *V* (Sun–Thurs)

BAMBURGH Northumberland — Map 4:A3

The Victoria Hotel NEW

Bamburgh NE69 7BP
Tel 01668-214431
Fax 01668-214404
Email enquiries@thevictoriahotelbamburgh.co.uk
Website www.thevictoriahotelbamburgh.co.uk

Opposite green of village with magnificent castle, on North Sea coast facing Farne Island: good-value hotel managed by Graham Young. 'Comfortable, if small, bedrooms; excellent dinner (pheasant; game pie); inexpensive wines.' Young children/babies welcomed (playroom, family accommodation, special menus). 29 bedrooms (some on ground floor). Closed 2 weeks Jan. 2 lounges, bar area (mirrors, pictures, board games, background music, extensive menu); smart brasserie with glass-domed ceiling; conference facilities. Civil wedding licence. No smoking. All major credit cards accepted. B&B £40–£85 per person; D,B&B £65–£110. Full alc £32. Group rates. Christmas/New Year packages.

****

Traveller's tale I have never stayed in such a bossy place. By the time we'd finished reading the house rules on the back of the confirmation letter, we felt nervous. Would we be told off for talking in the corridors? When we arrived, the receptionist showed us to our room and then delivered a ten-minute, unsmiling lecture on how to use a hotel. (*Hotel in Worcestershire*)

****

BAMPTON Devon — Map 1:C5

The Bark House

Oakfordbridge
nr Bampton EX16 9HZ

Tel 01398-351236
Email bark.house.hotel@btinternet.com
Website www.barkhouse.co.uk

César award in 2006

'Excels in every department; delicious food and impeccable service.' More praise in 2007 for Alastair Kameen's wisteria-covered 18th-century stone house, which he runs with Justine Hill as a 'simple but upmarket' guest house. They are 'immensely helpful'; 'the welcome and atmosphere are superb.' There are new soft furnishings in several bedrooms this year, and the bathrooms have been upgraded. Drinks are served, with generous canapés, in the candlelit dining room at 7 pm; dinner, cooked by Mr Kameen and served by Ms Hill at 7.30, is a set menu tailored to guests' wishes. 'Almost a bespoke service,' he says, 'based on a daily trip to the Bampton butchers.' The dishes are 'imaginative and beautifully cooked', eg, Thai-style monkfish curry. The short wine list is admired. Breakfasts are 'the best': the provenance of each ingredient is listed. Traffic noise could be a problem though a visitor this year reported: 'Road noise early and late, but it did not disturb this light sleeper during the night.' In a garden (on several levels) across the road, guests can look across the Exe valley to a wooded hillside. Bark House is on the market but no sale is imminent. (*Jonathan Brock, John RE Borron, Jill McLaren*)

5 bedrooms. 2-bedroom self-catering cottage. In hamlet 3 miles W of Bampton, on A396, 4 miles S of Dulverton. Open 'most of the year': occasional closures during quiet spells. Lounge, dining room (light classical background music in evening). 1½-acre garden: croquet. Cycling, horse riding, fishing, birdwatching nearby. Bedrooms unsuitable for ♿. No smoking. 'Children of considerate parents only; no "free-range" children.' No dogs in public rooms. No credit cards. B&B £47.50–£60 per person. Set dinner £31. Christmas/New Year packages. 1-night bookings occasionally refused.

BARNARD CASTLE Co. Durham — Map 4:C3

Homelands Guest House

85 Galgate
Barnard Castle DL12 8ES

Tel 01833-638757
Email enquiries@homelandsguesthouse.co.uk
Website www.homelandsguesthouse.co.uk

'As warm a welcome as you could wish' is given by Irene Williamson at her spacious Victorian town house B&B in a residential area of this

Teesdale market town. It stands on a road that is busy by day but quiet at night (windows are double glazed). The quietest bedroom, in the 'exquisitely tended' garden, is 'blissful'. Some rooms are 'compact', with a small shower room. The much-admired breakfast, served in a 'spotless' dining room, has cereals, fruit, etc, from a buffet; and 'a large choice of well-cooked dishes' including kippers, and scrambled egg with smoked bacon muffin. No evening meals, but advice is offered on local restaurants. Other comments: 'Lovely people. Could not do more for us.' 'Our favourite stop-over on journeys to the far north.' The Williamsons are planning to retire some time in 2008; you should check the position before booking. (*Gareth Evans, and others*)

5 bedrooms. 1 in garden. Central. No private parking. Closed Christmas/New Year. Lounge, breakfast room ('easy listening' background music). Garden. Unsuitable for ♿. No smoking. No children under 6. Guide dogs only. MasterCard, Visa accepted. B&B £30–£45 per person. 1-night bookings refused bank holidays.

BARNGATES Cumbria — Map 4: inset C2

The Drunken Duck Inn
Barngates, nr Ambleside
LA22 0NG

Tel 015394-36347
Fax 015394-36781
Email info@drunkenduckinn.co.uk
Website www.drunkenduckinn.co.uk

César award in 2006

'We thoroughly enjoyed our stay; the staff were kind and accommodating.' Praise this year from a regular *Guide* correspondent for this white-fronted inn (named after ducks that drank from a leaking cask). It has 'breathtaking' views of the surrounding fells. Stephanie Barton, the owner, whose 'sure touch with decor' earned praise from inspectors, has refurbished all the bedrooms. 'Ours, across the courtyard and beside the tarn, was comfortable; plenty of bathroom goodies and a constant supply of hot water.' The beamed Garden Room has floor-length windows and a large balcony. 'There are beautiful, wide wooden floorboards; interesting prints, cartoons and architectural engravings hang throughout.' 'Tea and scones in the lounge [included in the charge] were superb; luckily we were able to walk off one meal before it was time for the next.' The chef, Neil McCue, uses local ingredients, many of them organic, in his modern British cooking, eg, duck breast with apple, golden beetroot and port. In the lounge are squashy sofas, a stove, board games and a resident cat. Bar meals are served between noon and 4 pm.

A 'superb' breakfast has freshly squeezed juice, leaf tea, good toast and 'lavish cooked dishes'. The inn has its own fly-fishery and on-site brewery. Stephen Dodd is the manager. (*Sara Price, and others*)

16 bedrooms. 8 across small courtyard. Some on ground floor. 3 miles SW of Ambleside. Residents' lounge, bar, 3 dining rooms. No background music. 1-acre garden in 60-acre grounds. Fly-fishery 50 yds. No smoking. Dogs allowed in bar. Amex, MasterCard, Visa accepted. B&B [2007] £60–£112.50 per person. Full alc £45. Christmas/New Year packages.

BARWICK Somerset — Map 1:C6

Little Barwick House
Barwick, nr Yeovil
BA22 9TD

Tel 01935-423902
Fax 01935-420908
Email reservations@barwick7.fsnet.co.uk
Website www.littlebarwickhouse.co.uk

César award in 2002

'As good as ever,' say visitors returning in 2007 to Tim and Emma Ford's restaurant-with-rooms in a Georgian dower house in 'delightful countryside' near the Somerset/Dorset border. 'A model small hotel; we really enjoy coming back.' It has long been popular with readers who agree that 'cuisine comes first'. 'Tim's cooking is excellent'; his wife is the 'attentive front-of-house'. Visitors are welcomed with complimentary tea and 'fabulous' fruitcake. Bedrooms vary in size (some are small). 'Our large room had king-size bed, turned down during dinner; functional bathroom with good power shower.' 'Our high-ceilinged room was tastefully decorated; we liked the fresh milk and home-made shortbread.' 'An excellent three-night stay. What impressed us most was the absolute quiet.' A new boiler has been installed this year, and Room 4 given a power shower after a complaint last year. Tables are well spaced in the 'large, airy' dining room with conservatory extension. 'Mouth-watering appetisers' precede 'delicious' modern dishes like warm salad of pink roasted quail; Cornish brill with sun-dried tomato risotto. But a fish-eating (but not shellfish) vegetarian was disappointed one night to find nothing she could eat on the menu. The 'stylishly arranged' breakfast has fresh juices, fruit compote, 'melt-in-the-mouth croissants'. (*AJW and HM Harvey, CB, and others*)

6 bedrooms. ¾ mile outside Yeovil. Closed Christmas, 2 weeks Jan. Restaurant closed Sun evenings, midday on Mon and Tues. Ramp. 2 lounges, restaurant, conservatory. No background music. 3½-acre garden: terrace, pond, paddock. Unsuitable for ♿. No smoking. No children under 5. No dogs in public rooms. MasterCard, Visa accepted. B&B [2007] £69–£126 per person; D,B&B £84–£100.

Set dinner £37.95; full alc £40. 2-night breaks. 1-night bookings sometimes refused Fri/Sat.

BASLOW Derbyshire — Map 3:A6

The Cavendish
Church Lane
Baslow DE45 1SP

Tel 01246-582311
Fax 01246-582312
Email info@cavendish-hotel.net
Website www.cavendish-hotel.net

César award in 2002

On the edge of the Duke of Devonshire's Chatsworth estate, this traditional country hotel has many fans. 'An old favourite, going back more than 20 years,' one writes. 'Consistently good. Remarkably, the staff seem not to change,' adds a visitor on her seventh visit. 'Food and service extremely good. Rooms very clean, furnished to a high standard.' Also appreciated: 'Help with the luggage on arrival; a telephone call to the room after half an hour to make sure everything is in order.' The hotel stands on a busy road, but the bedrooms are at the back and are quiet at night. 'Our room had two large windows with views of Chatsworth park, large, comfortable bed, very good bathroom and shower.' Meals can be 'nearly formal' in the *Gallery* restaurant ('stunning, like a drawing room') or 'relaxed' in the conservatory *Garden Room.* Chef Chris Allison cooks modern dishes, eg, confit of rabbit rillettes; pan-roasted venison. Breakfast, served until midday and not included in the room price, is thought 'excellent', but one reader disliked 'every item being costed, down to the tea and toast'. Leasee Eric Marsh ('ever charming') has filled the hotel with a large collection of paintings. He owns *The George Hotel* in nearby Hathersage (*qv*): Philip Joseph manages both it and *The Cavendish.* (*Robert Ribeiro, Gill Holden, Padi Howard*)

24 bedrooms. On A619, in Chatsworth grounds. Restaurant closed 25 Dec to non-residents. Lounge, bar, 2 restaurants; 2 private dining rooms. No background music. ½-acre grounds: putting. River fishing nearby. Unsuitable for ♿. No smoking. No dogs. All major credit cards accepted. Room [2007]: single £116–£148, double £149–£187, suite £230. Breakfast alc from £14.90. Set menus £42 (*5% 'service levy' added to all accounts).* 1-night bookings sometimes refused weekends. Christmas/New Year packages. *V*

Please always send a report if you stay at a *Guide* hotel, even if it's only to endorse the existing entry.

Fischer's Baslow Hall
Calver Road
Baslow DE45 1RR

Tel 01246-583259
Fax 01246-583818
Email reservations@fischers-baslowhall.co.uk
Website www.fischers-baslowhall.co.uk

César award in 1998

Found 'wonderful as ever', with 'very engaging staff', Max and Susan Fischer's restaurant-with-rooms near the Chatsworth estate has gabled wings and mullioned windows. Though built in the style of a 17th-century Derbyshire manor house (wood panelling, beams, leaded casements), it dates from 1907. Residents must book for the elegant dining room where 'smart casual' dress is required. Max Fischer, chef/*patron*, and Rupert Rowley, head chef, have a *Michelin* star for dishes (served at well-spaced tables) like scallops with artichoke purée; roast rack and braised shoulder of lamb with pea tortellini. There is a standard dinner menu, a three-course *menu du jour*, and a 'Prestige' tasting menu (served to a whole table). 'Service was excellent, without being too formal. A quite small, homely operation. Our party of five all liked their chintzy rooms in the main house.' But some bedrooms in the main house may be 'a little cramped', with a small bathroom. The best rooms, in the *Garden House,* have a contemporary style and good bathroom, and are commended for 'peace and quiet'. 'The gardens are magnificent.' Freshly squeezed juice, a wide range of teas, and 'good fruit salad' appear at breakfast. The gastropub, *Rowley's Restaurant & Bar*, down the road, is under the same ownership. (*John Barnes, Peter Halliwell, Anne and Denis Tate*)

11 bedrooms. 5 in *Garden House.* Edge of village on A623. Closed 25/26 and 31 Dec. Restaurant closed to non-residents Sun night/Mon midday, 31 Dec midday. Lounge, bar, breakfast room, 3 dining rooms; function facilities. No background music. 5-acre grounds. Unsuitable for ♿. Civil wedding licence. No smoking. No children under 12 in restaurant after 7 pm. No dogs. Amex, MasterCard, Visa accepted. B&B: £70–£130 per person. English breakfast £9.50. Set dinner £45–£75. 1-night bookings refused at weekends in season.

****

Traveller's tale In the dining room, which could have done with some redecoration, a lady pianist banged out, without respite, very loud 'light' music on an upright piano. As we ate, one of the guests fainted and had to be carried out. I was callous enough to remark to my wife that at least he had escaped from the music. (*Hotel in Gloucestershire*)

****

BATH Somerset **Map 2:D1**

Apsley House

141 Newbridge Hill
Bath BA1 3PT

Tel 01225-336966
Fax 01225-425462
Email info@apsley-house.co.uk
Website www.apsley-house.co.uk

Guests in 2007 received a 'warm welcome' at Nicholas and Claire Potts's elegant Georgian house, a five-minute drive from the city centre. Built by the Duke of Wellington in 1830 as a country home for a mistress, and set in its own garden, it retains many period features and is furnished with fine antiques and paintings. There is a smart drawing room (with open fire and grand piano), and a small bar. Some bedrooms are large; two can be a family suite; one has an immense bathroom, a fireplace, and French windows opening on to the garden, where tables and chairs stand on the lawn. 'Our basement room had a door to the garden, up some steps, and was well furnished.' But another basement room was not liked this year. Breakfast is described as 'a feast', with marmalade served in a proper jar, 'none of those horrible little plastic containers'. Mrs Potts serves sandwich platters ('fresh and well presented') and light suppers by arrangement. (*PJK, and others*)

11 bedrooms. 1 on ground floor. 1 mile W of centre. Closed 23–27 Dec. Drawing room, bar, dining room; background radio (Classic FM) most of the time. ½-acre garden. Unsuitable for ♿. No smoking. No dogs. Amex, MasterCard, Visa accepted. B&B [2007]: £35–£140 per person. 1-night bookings refused Sat. ***V*** (not weekends)

The Bath Priory

Weston Road
Bath BA1 2XT

Tel 01225-331922
Fax 01225-448276
Email mail@thebathpriory.co.uk
Website www.thebathpriory.co.uk

'Beautiful and romantic', 'luxurious and well appointed', 'a warm and sincere welcome': recent comments on Andrew Brownsword's listed mansion, once owned by Bath Abbey. Built as a private residence in 1835, it stands in 'super' landscaped gardens (where one family this year 'enjoyed eating mulberries from two large trees'). The city centre is reached by a short walk through Royal Victoria Park. The drawing room and library have 'classic soft furnishings' in country house style, fresh flowers and log fires. Bedrooms (being redecorated this year) vary in size; 'premier deluxe' ones are 'seriously comfortable'; all have antiques and the latest technology (satellite TV, ISDN, voicemail, modem point, etc);

but some get traffic noise. The chef, Chris Horridge, has a *Michelin* star for his 'creative' cooking (eg, red mullet with avocado purée). 'The food was outstanding, as was the service.' 'Our children were not allowed in the restaurant for dinner, so we opted for the simple but good room-service menu.' 'Keen staff, mainly eastern European, some British.' There are good health and beauty facilities (see below). 'Very expensive, but good things do not come cheap.' Home-made jams appear at breakfast (which one visitor thought 'surprisingly mediocre'). (*Sue Kinder, Gilbert Hall, and others*)

31 bedrooms. Some in adjacent house. Some on ground floor. 1½ miles W of centre. Ramps. Library, drawing room, 2 dining rooms; private dining rooms; wine room; conference facilities. Spa: indoor heated swimming pool (30 by 15 ft), gym, sauna, beauty treatments. No background music. 4-acre grounds: heated swimming pool (35 by 15 ft), croquet. Civil wedding licence. No smoking. No children under 8 at dinner. Guide dogs only. All major credit cards accepted. B&B [2007] £122.50–£360 per person. Set dinner £55; full alc £79.50. Special breaks (romantic, pampering, etc). Gardening events. Christmas/New Year packages. 1-night bookings refused weekends.

County Hotel

18–19 Pulteney Road
Bath BA2 4EZ

Tel 01225-425003
Fax 01225-466493
Email reservations@county-hotel.co.uk
Website www.county-hotel.co.uk

'A wonderful place to stay.' Five minutes' walk from the centre, and with views over the cricket ground and Bath Abbey, this grey stone building near the Pulteney Bridge has 'a bonus for Bath': parking with a night-watchman. The owners, Maureen Kent, her son James (the manager) and her sister Sandra Masson, are 'friendly not fawning'; their mainly East European staff, says a visitor this year, are 'exceptionally helpful', and bedrooms are 'spotless and comfortable'. The decor is traditional, with flowery fabrics and heavy drapes. 'Our room was spacious, nicely furnished. Luxurious towelling robes. At night we liked watching the city light up.' Another visitor enjoyed watching balloon flights from her 'lovely room'. Tea, coffee and drinks can be served in the reading room, and private dining is available in the conservatory. 'Delicious sandwiches whenever we wanted them.' Breakfast (8–9 am on weekdays, 8–9.45 at weekends) has an 'extremely good buffet' plus full English (including dishes like mumbled eggs with Parma ham; local spinach with poached eggs and haddock) to order. The road is busy by day, but quiet at night. (*Mary and Rodney Milne-Day, Ann Bell*)

22 bedrooms. 5 mins' walk from centre. Station 1 mile. Car park. Closed Christmas/New Year. Bar area (background music), lounge/reading room, conservatory, breakfast room. Patio (seating). Unsuitable for ♿. No smoking. No children under 10. No dogs. All major credit cards accepted. B&B [2007] £50–£90 per person. Special breaks. 1-night bookings refused weekends. *V*

Harington's Hotel

8–10 Queen Street
Bath BA1 1HE

Tel 01225-461728
Fax 01225-444804
Email post@haringtonshotel.co.uk
Website www.haringtonshotel.co.uk

Near the abbey, Pump Room and main shopping areas, this small hotel is 'a haven of quiet in the centre of a busy city'. Owned by Melissa Pritchard and Peter O'Sullivan, it is composed of a group of 18th-century houses on a cobbled street. Other guests wrote of 'the fantastic location, lots of nice touches'. Some bedrooms are up a steep spiral staircase (no lift; listed building). One visitor said that the family bedroom 'though well decorated, is best for miniature people'. This year all bathrooms have been refurbished. The café/bar, open all day, serves meals until 8 pm; eg, goat's cheese and crispy bacon salad; braised lamb shank. There is free wireless broadband access, and guests may use the house laptop computer. Reserved parking is within five minutes' walk (you may stop on the double yellow lines outside the hotel for unloading). Two self-catering apartments are new this year. (*RL*)

13 bedrooms. Also 2 self-catering apartments. Central, near Queen Sq. Reserved parking with security cameras nearby. Closed 24–27 Dec. Coffee lounge, bar, restaurant; background music 7 am–12 pm. Small patio. Unsuitable for ♿. No smoking. No dogs. Amex, MasterCard, Visa accepted. B&B [2007]: £46–£123 per person. Full alc £34. New Year package (B&B only). 1-night bookings usually refused weekends.

Number 30 NEW

30 Crescent Gardens
Bath BA1 2NB

Tel/Fax 01225-337393
Email david.greenwood12@btinternet.com
Website www.numberthirty.com

A short walk from the main attractions, this 'light, airy' B&B, owned by David and Caroline Greenwood, was completely refurbished in 2007. Decor is in pastel colours (much blue and white). 'We were impressed,' one visitor wrote. Others talked of 'excellent hospitality' and 'attention to detail throughout'. 'Spotless room: crisp cotton sheets, blankets (we hate duvets but they are also available), flat-screen TV, CD-player, free Wi-Fi connection, natural toiletries from New Zealand.' Help is given with luggage, and restaurant reservations. Breakfast has an 'amazing range', including fresh fruit, fruit compote, loose-leaf tea, home-made muesli, organic toast, full English. 'A vegetarian option was a sumptuous English muffin spread with pesto and topped with avocado, tomato, mozzarella, and then grilled. All this, and home-made marmalade and hedgerow jam! Caroline gave good advice about sightseeing.' The on-site parking is a bonus. (*John Towler, G Dewsbery, Veronica Sharp*)

5 bedrooms. 1 designed for allergy sufferers. 5 mins' walk from centre. Parking. Closed Jan. Dining room. No background music. Patio garden. Unsuitable for ♿. No smoking. No children under 12. No dogs. MasterCard, Visa accepted. B&B: single £65–£80, double £72–£105. 1-night bookings refused weekends, particularly Sat. *V*

Paradise House

86–88 Holloway
Bath BA2 4PX

Tel 01225-317723
Fax 01225-482005
Email info@paradise-house.co.uk
Website www.paradise-house.co.uk

There are 'fabulous views' of the city from the secluded garden of David and Annie Lanz's listed Georgian house with Victorian extension. Backed by mature trees, it is on a quiet cul-de-sac on the ancient Fosse Way, overlooked only by the ancient Magdalen Chapel next door. This year there are new managers, Matthew Moy and Mella Shanahan. Most bedrooms are spacious and well appointed. 'Ours, on the ground floor, was compact, but the big bed had proper sheets and blankets. Furnished to a high standard (except for the captive hangers)' All bedrooms now have flat-screen TV with DVD-player, and there is Wi-Fi Internet access throughout. At the back of the house is a 'classic drawing room', with floor-to-ceiling arched windows. Here, drinks are served and newspapers supplied. Breakfast, taken in a bright room, and at busy times in the drawing room, too, has good cooked items (including Wiltshire bacon and sausages), 'proper toast', good tea and coffee. Continental breakfast can be served in the bedroom. No restaurant, but a list of recommended eating places, with sample menus, is provided. It's a seven-minute walk down a steep hill to the city centre (a little longer on the way back).

11 bedrooms. 4 on ground floor. Off Wells Rd, close to city centre. Closed 24/25 Dec. Drawing room with bar (classical background music all day), breakfast room. ½-acre garden. No smoking. No dogs. Amex, MasterCard, Visa accepted. B&B [2007] £65–£85 per person. 1-night bookings sometimes refused Sat.

The Queensberry
4–7 Russel Street
Bath BA1 2QF

Tel 01225-447928
Fax 01225-446065
Email reservations@thequeensberry.co.uk
Website www.thequeensberry.co.uk

Well located, in a quiet street just off the Circus and three minutes' walk from the Assembly Rooms, Laurence and Helen Beere's handsome small hotel is a conversion of four adjoining town houses designed by John Wood for the Marquis of Queensberry in 1771. The staff are 'welcoming and helpful', say visitors in 2007. Others liked the 'easy-going atmosphere'. A glass roof and white paint create a light feel, and 'a warren of stairs and corridors' leads to bedrooms of varying sizes. 'Our superior room was comfortable, though the grey colour scheme made it rather characterless.' All bedrooms will have been redecorated in contemporary style by early 2008. Four 'charming' terraced gardens, on different levels at the rear, are planted with shrubs, and there are 'good reception rooms'. In the 'very pleasant' *Olive Tree* restaurant, in three rooms in the basement ('a little dark'), Marc Salmon cooks in modern British style, eg, fillet of pork with glazed pig cheeks, squash and sage purée. Breakfast, 'an appetising affair' (which costs extra), is served here or in the bedrooms. 'The best rates are midweek (Sunday to Thursday),' writes the manager, Lauren McCann. (*Michael and Eithne Dandy, Sir James Spooner, Alec Frank*)

29 bedrooms. Some on ground floor. Restaurant closed Mon lunch. Close to Assembly Rooms. Lift. 2 drawing rooms, bar, restaurant (background music); meeting room. 4 linked courtyard gardens. Unsuitable for ♿. No smoking. Guide dogs only. Amex (2% handling charge), MasterCard, Visa accepted. Room [2007] £105–£425. Breakfast £10–£15. Full alc £45. 1-night bookings refused weekends. *V*

Tasburgh House
Warminster Road
Bath BA2 6SH

Tel 01225-425096
Fax 01225-463842
Email hotel@bathtasburgh.co.uk
Website www.bathtasburgh.co.uk

Set amid parkland and gardens above the city, Sue Keeling's red brick Victorian house is a five-minute bus ride away from the centre, or a short walk along the towpath of the Kennet and Avon canal. Inspectors admired the 'lovely grounds' and the views. The bedrooms, each named after an English author (Eliot, Dickens, etc), vary in size: some have a super king-size bed; all were recently renovated. Double glazing has been added to the family rooms at the front of the house (it stands on a busy road, 'but once inside, we didn't notice the traffic'). Mrs Keeling tells us she has removed 'the beverage trays with those awful UHT milk cartons and instant coffee'; instead, complimentary mineral water is provided and trays of fresh drinks are offered (for a charge). Breakfast, served in a conservatory, includes banana porridge with maple syrup, a wide range of cooked dishes, and a good selection of teas. Help is given with sightseeing and dinner reservations. Charlie, the parrot in Reception, provides entertainment. More reports, please.

12 bedrooms. 2 on ground floor. On A36 to Warminster, 1 mile E of centre. Closed Christmas. Drawing room, dining room; background radio/music all day; conservatory; terrace. 7-acre grounds: canal walks, mooring. Unsuitable for ♿. No smoking. No dogs. All major credit cards accepted. B&B £47.50–£70 per person. 1-night bookings refused Sat.

See also SHORTLIST

BATHFORD Somerset — Map 2:D1

Eagle House
Church Street
Bathford BA1 7RS

Tel 01225-859946
Fax 01225-859430
Email jonap@eagleho.demon.co.uk
Website www.eaglehouse.co.uk

Built by John Wood the Elder, this listed Georgian mansion has been run for 24 years as an informal and child-friendly B&B by its 'helpful owners', John and Rosamund Napier (it is their family home). In its large grounds are croquet lawn, grass tennis court, sandpit and tree house. There are toys and games in the drawing room. The Napiers are pet-friendly too: guests' dogs are welcome by arrangement. 'Old furniture (good, but not too smart) and family possessions are everywhere,' one guest wrote. 'A little charmer with a Jane Austen atmosphere,' said another. The handsome drawing room has a marble fireplace (log fires on winter evenings) and moulded ceiling. A curving wooden staircase leads up from the hall to some of the bedrooms; two others are in a cottage in the 'romantic' garden. All face the garden or surrounding countryside. Glasses and ice are provided for guests who bring their own drinks. Continental breakfast (freshly squeezed orange juice, yogurt, fruit, etc), served until 10 am, is included in the price; cooked breakfast costs extra. Bath city centre is easily reached from the village by regular buses. More reports, please.

8 bedrooms. 2 in cottage with sitting room, kitchen, walled garden. 3 miles E of Bath. Closed 10 Dec–8 Jan. Drawing room, breakfast room. No background music. 2-acre garden: tennis, croquet, sandpit, tree house, swings. Unsuitable for ♿. No smoking. MasterCard, Visa accepted. B&B [2007] £31–£68 per person. Cooked breakfast £4.80 extra. 1-night bookings often refused Sat, bank holidays. *V* (not weekends)

BATTLE East Sussex *See SHORTLIST* Map 2:E4

BEAMINSTER Dorset Map 1:C6

The Bridge House
Prout Bridge
Beaminster DT8 3AY

Tel 01308-862200
Fax 01308-863700
Email enquiries@bridge-house.co.uk
Website www.bridge-house.co.uk

'Comfortable, relaxed', and with 'very friendly staff'. In this attractive old town, Mark and Joanna Donovan's small hotel/restaurant (a former priest's house, said to date back to the 12th century) stands by a bridge. It has 'an original and pleasing interior', say visitors this year (thick walls, mullioned windows, old beams, open fires in inglenook fireplaces). It is backed by a large walled garden, which the quietest rooms overlook; front ones face a busy road. 'Our ground-floor room had three comfortable chairs and reasonable storage.' 'Ours was bright, well furnished, spacious.' Some small rooms and a family suite are in a coach house at the rear (baby-listening, cots, etc, provided). In the panelled dining room, with conservatory extension, chef Linda Paget serves dishes 'rooted in Dorset produce' ('our philosophy is "keep it simple" '), eg, Wyld Meadow lamb with cranberry sausage, herb mash and onion gravy. Breakfast and light lunches are taken in another conservatory; summer meals can be served in the garden. Tea is taken by a fire in winter. Nearby are Abbotsbury (with its famous swannery), the Jurassic Coast, Mapperton Garden, etc. (*Philip Quick, and others*)

13 bedrooms. 4 in coach house. 5 on ground floor. 100 yards from centre. Train: Crewkerne, 8 miles. Hall/reception, lounge, bar, 2 conservatories, restaurant; light background music at lunch and dinner. ¼-acre walled garden. Civil wedding licence. No smoking. No dogs in public rooms, or unattended in bedrooms. Amex, MasterCard, Visa accepted. B&B £58–£90 per person; D,B&B £81–£113. Set dinner £38.50. 2-night breaks. Winter discounts for returning guests. Christmas/ New Year packages. 1-night bookings refused weekends and peak season.

BEAULIEU Hampshire *See SHORTLIST* Map 2:E2

BEELEY Derbyshire Map 3:A6

The Devonshire Arms at Beeley NEW

Tel/Fax 01629-733259
Devonshire Square
Beeley, nr Matlock
DE4 2NR
Email enquiries@devonshirebeeley.co.uk
Website www.devonshirebeeley.co.uk

In 2006, this old coaching inn on the Chatsworth estate was given a make-over, blending ancient and modern, by its owners, the Duke and Duchess of Devonshire; Alan Hill is manager. Inspectors in 2007 reported: 'Good fun. Perfect for a short break, if you recognise that it's a pub, not a hotel.' The 'cosy' original bar area has undulating floors, heavy beams, low ceiling, tiny windows, stone fireplaces, but modern still-life paintings. The brasserie is contemporary: bright colours, large windows overlooking the village; modern round tables with cast iron legs, simply laid (white china, decent cutlery, good glass). 'We were welcomed by a charming young man and upgraded to the family suite, up a steepish staircase. Its bedroom was decorated in white and turquoise; the sitting room, with sofa bed, was very pink. Exquisite botanical watercolours by the duke's sister, Emma Tennant, but only one bedside light. Bathroom smallish, with narrow bath but excellent shower.' At dinner, 'the atmosphere was buzzing, staff were informally dressed, service was good-humoured, the meal well paced'. The menu 'had dishes to suit most tastes. Goat's cheese with endive salad beautifully presented; sea trout perfectly cooked; rice pudding with raisins and orange marmalade in generous portions. Excellent wines by the glass.' Breakfast 'could have been better (commercial juices, cereals but no fruit or yogurt)'.

4 bedrooms. 5 miles N of Matlock, off B6012. Small seating area, pub area, brasserie area ('easy listening' background music). No smoking. Amex, MasterCard, Visa accepted. B&B: double £145, family suite £165. Full alc £29. Christmas/New Year packages.

The terms printed in the *Guide* are only a rough indication of the size of the bill to be expected at the end of your stay. Always check the tariffs when booking.

BEERCROCOMBE Somerset — Map 1:C5

Frog Street Farm *Tel/Fax* 01823-480430
Beercrocombe, Taunton TA3 6AF

Veronica and Henry Cole's small 15th-century house in farmland between Taunton and Ilminster. Beamed ceilings, Jacobean panelling, inglenook fireplace. 'Absolute silence at night.' 'Warm welcome; good wholesome cooking.' Dinner, by arrangement (7 pm), generally at separate tables, but communal if guests choose. Bring your own wine. 3 bedrooms. 'Our double-aspect room was enormous, with equally large bathroom.' 2 lounges, dining room. No background music. Garden, trout stream. Unsuitable for ♿. Open Apr–Oct. No smoking. No children under 11. No dogs. No credit cards. B&B £35–£40 per person. 1-night bookings sometimes refused. No recent reports; we'd like some, please.

BELFORD Northumberland — Map 4:A3

Waren House *Tel* 01668-214581
Waren Mill, Belford *Fax* 01668-214484
NE70 7EE *Email* enquiries@warenhousehotel.co.uk
Website www.warenhousehotel.co.uk

'An excellent base from which to explore this area of outstanding natural beauty': this Georgian house stands in wooded grounds above the natural birdlife sanctuary of Budle Bay. Once owned by the third Lord Derwentwater, it is two miles from Bamburgh Castle and beach, and has good views towards Holy Island. Visitors this year 'had a bright and comfortable suite across the courtyard'. Only drawback: the lack of a shower in the bathrooms. The owners, Anita and Peter Laverack, have decorated with enthusiasm, 'cramming the reception area with antique dolls; bits and pieces on any vacant surface. The walls of every room are covered with old oil paintings, watercolours and antique mirrors.' The library has heavy leather chairs 'which swallow anyone so unwise as to sit in them'. Drinks and 'lovely' canapés are served in the drawing room from 6.30 pm and, in the long, narrow dining room, 'there was a different menu every night, local produce a highlight'. 'We enjoyed wholesome breakfasts, particularly the perfectly cooked Craster kippers.' (*G and SP, REC*)

13 bedrooms. 15 miles SE of Berwick-upon-Tweed. Drawing room, library, dining room. 6-acre garden. Golf nearby. No smoking. No children under 14. No dogs in public rooms. All major credit cards accepted. B&B £56.50–£135 per person; D,B&B (2 nights min.) £83.75–£164. Set dinner £32. Christmas/New Year packages. 1-night bookings sometimes refused weekends, public holidays.

BEPTON West Sussex Map 2:E3

Park House
Bepton, nr Midhurst
GU29 0JB

Tel 01730-819000
Fax 01730-819099
Email reservations@parkhousehotel.com
Website www.parkhousehotel.com

'The combination of tranquillity, first-rate staff, immaculate housekeeping and superb scenery made our stay memorable.' Praise from an inspector in 2007 for this 'exemplary' small country hotel in a sleepy village at the foot of the South Downs. Another guest liked the 'unfussy atmosphere'. The Victorian house, owned by the O'Brien family since 1948, is managed by Rebecca Crowe and James Coonon. 'The chatty receptionist greeted us at the front door, took us to our room, gave us a tour of the public areas. Downstairs is an unusually well-stocked honesty bar overlooking the terrace and fine garden. The huge drawing room has plenty of comfortable seating.' Dinner is taken in the formal dining room or in a conservatory where 'delicious starters' (fricassée of wild mushrooms; pork and apple balls in tomato sauce) and 'excellent desserts' were enjoyed. Main courses were thought 'bland'. No background music; good table linen. 'Our bedroom was large, elegantly furnished (some antique pieces), a two-seater settee under a bay window, a large, comfortable bed. Really good bathroom lighting. Turn-down service while we dined. Breakfast was perfect: a buffet, comprehensive choice of cooked dishes, no silly little pots of preserves.' There is a small converted barn for conferences and functions.

15 bedrooms. Some in 2 cottages. 1 on ground floor. 2½ miles SW of Midhurst. Lounge, bar, dining room, conservatory. No background music. 9-acre grounds: tennis, croquet, heated 40-ft swimming pool, pitch-and-putt golf. Civil wedding licence. No smoking. MasterCard, Visa accepted. B&B [2007] double £125–£290; D,B&B £100–£175 per person. Set dinner £31.95. Winter breaks.

BERWICK-UPON-TWEED Northumberland Map 4:A3

No. 1 Sallyport
1 Sallyport
Berwick-upon-Tweed TD15 1EZ

Tel/Fax 01289-308827
Email info@sallyport.co.uk
Website www.sallyport.co.uk

In a conservation area of this attractive town, this luxury B&B is a 17th-century Grade II listed town house on a cobbled lane once painted by LS Lowry. 'Lovely room, friendly service,' wrote one visitor. The 'effortlessly chic' owner, Elizabeth Middlemiss, 'knows when to leave you in peace', said another. There are polished wooden floors, contemporary works of art, goose-down duvets, plasma TVs and some 'funky' beds; also chocolates, magazines and flowers. A new loft suite, Manhattan, opened this year. Meals are taken at a communal table, by a large inglenook fireplace. The 'very good breakfast', which includes kippers, waffles and kedgeree, and Buck's Fizz on Sundays, is served until 10 am. An evening meal is available by arrangement on most evenings. 'Rustic French Provençal' dishes include courgette and basil soufflé; fillet of beef with an olive stuffing. Outdoor shoes are banned on the upper floors. (*RD, and others*)

6 bedrooms. Central. Garage, car park. Dining room. No background music. Patio. Unsuitable for ♿. No smoking. Diners, MasterCard, Visa accepted. B&B £65–£95 per person. Set dinner £38.50 (bring your own wine: £3 corkage). Christmas/New Year packages. 1-night bookings refused weekends.

West Coates *Tel/Fax* 01289-309666
30 Castle Terrace *Email* karenbrownwestcoates@yahoo.com
Berwick-upon-Tweed TD15 1NZ *Website* www.westcoates.co.uk

'Accomplished cook' Karen Brown, who runs a cookery school, welcomes guests to her Georgian house close to the centre of this historic border town. Set in an attractive, mature garden, it has a large indoor swimming pool and hot tub. One visitor wrote: 'It has beautifully furnished bedrooms, with everything one could want, including home-made cake on the hospitality tray each day. Wonderful breakfast (smoked salmon and scrambled eggs, porridge, yogurt, etc).' Mrs Brown uses local ingredients for her 'fabulous' no-choice three-course dinners, served by candlelight; dishes might include chicken with sherry and tarragon; baked peaches in Marsala sauce. And 'the Brown family are lovely, friendly people'. (*SK*)

3 bedrooms. 10 mins' walk from centre. Parking. Closed Christmas/New Year. Sitting/dining room (background music at mealtimes). 2½-acre garden: 40-ft indoor swimming pool; hot tub; croquet. Unsuitable for ♿. No smoking. No dogs. MasterCard, Visa accepted. B&B £50–£60 per person. Set dinner £35. Special breaks. ***V***

See also SHORTLIST

BEVERLEY East Yorkshire *See SHORTLIST* Map 4:D5

BIBURY Gloucestershire Map 3:E6

Bibury Court
Bibury
nr Cirencester GL7 5NT

Tel 01285-740337
Fax 01285-740660
Email info@biburycourt.com
Website www.biburycourt.com

In large grounds on the River Coln, this impressive manor house (part Tudor, mainly 17th-century), is on the edge of a Cotswold village described by William Morris as 'the most beautiful in England'. 'We really enjoyed out stay and could not fault the place,' say visitors this year. 'It is full of character; a little faded, but this adds to the charm.' Others praised the welcome, and the 'very good' cooking of the chef, Antony Ely (dishes like honey and thyme grilled quail with Parma ham; caramelised fillet of Scottish halibut with Fowey mussels). 'We liked the *amuse-bouche* that came with pre-dinner drinks. Desserts were excellent.' Meals are 'well served by the efficient young staff', in the small, 'rather dark' restaurant and the 'lovely' conservatory. 'We had a delightful, extra large bedroom with four-poster bed. The bathroom was more than adequate.' Some rooms have a 'huge' Victorian bath; some have views of the gardens and a part-Saxon church. Some rooms are small. 'At breakfast, our eggs were served to perfection, both scrambled and poached.' (*BA and PO, DM*)

18 bedrooms. 1 on ground floor. Village centre, behind church. Lounge, bar, restaurant, conservatory, billiard room. No background music. 7-acre grounds. On River Coln (fishing). Civil wedding licence. Unsuitable for ♿. Smoking allowed in 9 bedrooms. All major credit cards accepted. B&B £60–£125 per person; D,B&B £75–£150. Set dinner £35; full alc £45. Christmas/New Year packages. 1-night bookings sometimes refused weekends. *V*

BIDDENDEN Kent *See SHORTLIST* Map 2:D5

BIDEFORD Devon Map 1:C4

The Mount
Northdown Road
Bideford EX39 3LP

Tel 01237-473748
Fax 01237-373813
Email andrew@themountbideford.fsnet.co.uk
Website www.themountbideford.co.uk

Fronted by creepers and plants in pots, Andrew and Heather Laugharne's B&B is near the town centre and the quay where fishing boats unload their catches by the medieval bridge. The well-proportioned Georgian building, say visitors, is 'well run, spotless'; the Laugharnes are 'very friendly'. Inside are bright colours: red walls to the white-painted, winding staircase, pink in the lounge which has an open fire and a licence to sell alcohol, blue in the room where the 'excellent breakfasts' are served. 'The bedrooms are tastefully furnished, the beds are large and comfortable,' writes one of many fans. Guests have access to the pretty walled garden. Discounts are available at the Royal North Devon Golf Club. (*JR, and others*)

8 bedrooms. Some family. 1 on ground floor. 5 mins' walk from centre. Parking. Train: Barnstaple. Closed Christmas. Lounge, breakfast room; background music ('if I feel like it'). Walled garden. No smoking. No dogs. Amex, MasterCard, Visa accepted. B&B £30–£36 per person. 1-night bookings occasionally refused.

BIGBURY-ON-SEA Devon — Map 1:D4

Burgh Island Hotel NEW
Burgh Island
Bigbury-on-Sea TQ7 4BG

Tel 01548-810514
Fax 01548-810243
Email reception@burghisland.com
Website www.burghisland.com

'Not just a hotel, but a 1920s experience': Agatha Christie and Noël Coward were among 20th-century visitors to this Art Deco building on a private tidal island. At high tide, visitors are transported by a sea tractor (there is a secure car park on the mainland); at low tide they are brought in a four-wheel-drive vehicle. Tony Orchard and Deborah Clark, owners since 2001, have refurbished throughout, and added ten bedrooms (one room stands on stilts above the beach). 'Relaxed glamour' is the aim. 'Imaginative dressing up for dinner is strongly encouraged', and the dinners in the ballroom are praised (Conor Heneghan's cooking is 'modern British seasonal', eg, spiced lamb loin with root vegetable purée, spinach and pine nuts). 'Fabulous location; great atmosphere,' writes a returning visitor. 'Quiet, because non-residents are not admitted unless they have booked lunch or dinner. Excellent staff. The best seaside hotel that we know in the UK.' Accommodation is mainly in suites with a sea view: most have a balcony. Cream teas are taken in the Palm Court, 1920s cocktails in the Peacock Bar with its stained-glass dome. There is a natural swimming pool in the rocks below the hotel, and a private beach with water sports. The no-tipping policy is liked. The *Pilchard Inn* on the island is under the same ownership. (*Gilbert Hall*)

24 bedrooms. 5 miles S of Modbury, on island in Bigbury Bay. Private garages on mainland. Closed 2–18 Jan. Lift. Library, Captain's Cabin, 2 bars, 2 dining rooms; dinner/dance Wed and Sat; children's games room. On 26-acre island: natural sea swimming pool; beach, water sports; tennis; 14th-century inn. Civil wedding licence. No smoking. No children under 5; no under-12s in public rooms after 7 pm. No dogs. MasterCard, Visa accepted. D,B&B £177.50–£285 per person. Set dinner £55. Christmas/New Year packages.

The Henley

Folly Hill
Bigbury-on-Sea TQ7 4AR

Tel/Fax 01548-810240
Email thehenleyhotel@btconnect.com
Website www.thehenleyhotel.co.uk

César award in 2003

'Such charm. One of the best hotels we have ever stayed in.' 'Everything as good as before,' say visitors this year to Martyn and Petra Scarterfield's small, unpretentious hotel. An earlier comment: 'Still one of our favourites for food, location, relaxation.' On a cliff above the tidal Avon estuary, it was built as a holiday cottage in the early 20th century. The public rooms have dark red walls, well-polished old furniture, Lloyd Loom chairs. Books, magazines and binoculars are provided. Guests gather in the lounge at 7 pm for drinks and canapés before 'Martin's wonderful food', which 'owes much to the care taken in the preparation of each component': his wife recites the short menu (two choices for each course). Bedrooms are 'spick and span'; some bathrooms may be small, but all have 'fluffy towels'. At breakfast ('tasty and unhurried'), 'you are asked when you want toast. Good coffee and tea, replenished as you wish; excellent bacon and sausages.' The 'delightfully unfussy' garden, 'quite spectacularly precipitous', has 'many sheltered nooks with seating'. 'Our two dogs were made very welcome, and were joined on beach walks by the resident black Labrador, Kasper.' (*Brian and Kay Friend, Mrs CM Moore, S and JS*)

6 bedrooms. 5 miles S of Modbury. Open 16 Mar–29 Oct. 2 lounges, bar, conservatory dining room; background music. Small garden; steps to beach. Golf, sailing, fishing, Coastal Path nearby. Unsuitable for ♿. No smoking. No children. No dogs in public rooms. MasterCard, Visa accepted. B&B [2007] £47.50–£63 per person; D,B&B (4 nights or more) £75–£92. Light lunch available. Set dinner £30. Off-season reductions. 1-night bookings sometimes refused weekends.

> We asked hotels to quote their 2008 tariffs. Many hadn't yet fixed these rates as we went to press. Prices should always be checked on booking.

BIGGIN-BY-HARTINGTON Derbyshire Map 3:B6

Biggin Hall
Biggin-by-Hartington
Buxton SK17 0DH

Tel 01298-84451
Fax 01298-84681
Email enquiries@bigginhall.co.uk
Website www.bigginhall.co.uk

'A lovely, unfussy, simple place': this small hotel, high in the Peak District national park, is popular with walkers. Close by are 'footpaths in all directions over beautiful countryside'; one starts at the side of the house, and there are disused railway tracks which provide flat walking and cycling. 'Good value for money, a relaxing experience,' is another comment. The 17th-century Grade II* listed building has antiques, narrow mullioned windows. The public rooms are 'warm and inviting'; 'a marvellous fire in the sitting room' (it can get crowded when guests gather at 6.30 for pre-dinner drinks). The owner, James Moffett, is now 'semi-retired'; his manager is Steven Williams. One visitor liked his 'comfortable ground-floor room in a barn annexe', but another wrote of one that was 'very small, up steep stairs'. Other rooms, including the master suite (with beams and a four-poster), are in the main house. Dinner is served to everyone at 7 in the 'chintzy', small dining room. Mark Wilton's 'traditional English' cooking is hearty and generally thought 'well cooked', eg, honey-roasted ham with creamy Dijon sauce; apple and blackberry crumble with custard. Breakfast is now a 'comprehensive hot and cold buffet'. Packed lunches are available. (*Sally and Allan Saysell, Gwen Griffiths, David Preston, Virginia Murphy, and others*)

20 bedrooms. 12 in annexes. Some on ground floor. 8 miles N of Ashbourne. Sitting room, library, dining room (classical background music); meeting room. 7-acre grounds: croquet. River Dove 1½ miles. Unsuitable for ♿. No smoking. No children under 12. No dogs in main house. Amex, MasterCard, Visa accepted. B&B [2007] £37–£120 per person; D,B&B £50–£133. Set dinner £19.50. Christmas/New Year packages. 1-night bookings sometimes refused. *V*

BIRMINGHAM West Midlands Map 2:B2

Copperfield House
60 Upland Road, Selly Park
Birmingham B29 7JS

Tel 0121-472 8344
Fax 0121-415 5655
Email info@copperfieldhousehotel.fsnet.co.uk
Website www.copperfieldhousehotel.fsnet.co.uk

'Warm and comfortable', according to *Guide* readers, this red brick Victorian house stands quietly in a large garden in a suburb near the university. The owner (also the chef), Jeremy Thomas, is 'a mine of local information', his wife, Daphne, 'an excellent hostess'. 'Friendly staff made me feel at home,' was another comment. Some of the neat bedrooms have garden views, and those at the front have double glazing. All now have flat-screen TV and Wi-Fi Internet access. The lounge has an honour bar. The daily-changing dinner menu has a choice of four dishes for each course. Main courses include rack of lamb with mint gravy; lemon sole with lemon butter. Vegetarians are catered for. 'Delicious house wine' – the list is 'reasonably priced'. Breakfast has 'fresh juices and fruit, tasty full English'. More reports, please.

17 bedrooms. Some on ground floor. 2 miles SW of centre. Closed 24 Dec–2 Jan. Restaurant closed Sat/Sun. Ramp. Lounge, bar, restaurant; 'easy listening' background music. ½-acre garden. No smoking. No dogs in public rooms. Amex, MasterCard, Visa accepted. B&B [2007] £35–£82.50 per person. Set dinner £14.50–£17.50; full alc £27.50.

Hotel du Vin Birmingham

25 Church Street
Birmingham B3 2NR

Tel 0121-200 0600
Fax 0121-236 0889
Email info@birmingham.hotelduvin.com
Website www.hotelduvin.com

An artful conversion of Birmingham's red brick eye hospital, this ornate Victorian building has *trompe l'œil* stonework, a magnificent sweeping staircase and granite pillars. Mark Huntley is manager. The bedrooms, each sponsored by a wine producer, are on five floors around a central courtyard which has a retractable roof. Refurbished this year, they have a modern decor. There are large beds, Egyptian cotton sheets, good coffee and fresh milk. 'Bedlinen and towels were great, and changed daily; a superb power shower in my huge bathroom,' said one visitor. 'The staff, a mix of local, French and middle European, were friendly, efficient.' The *Bubble Lounge* has plump sofas and a choice of 50 champagnes; the basement bar has leather seating and jazz, and serves a large selection of rums and tequilas. A menu with a Mediterranean bias (eg, steak tartare; seared tuna Niçoise) is served in the 'relaxed' bistro, with its wooden floors and tables. The 'formidable' wine list, mainly French, 'has few bottles under £20', but it includes 'great delights'. 'Breakfasts, both continental and cooked, were substantial.' The spa is 'a bonus'. (*JC*)

66 bedrooms. 5 suitable for ♿. Central, near St Philip's Cathedral (quietest rooms face courtyard). Valet parking (£10 a night). Ramp, lift. Bistro, 2 bars ('chill-out' music in cellar bar at night); billiard room; spa; courtyard. Civil wedding licence. No smoking. No dogs in bars/bistro. Amex, MasterCard, Visa accepted. Room [2007] £140–£400. Breakfast £9.95–£13.50. Set menus £15.50–£17.50; full alc £40. Spa breaks. Christmas/New Year packages.

Simpsons
20 Highfield Road, Edgbaston
Birmingham B15 3DU

Tel 0121-454 3434
Fax 0121-454 3399
Email info@simpsonsrestaurant.co.uk
Website www.simpsonsrestaurant.co.uk

Chef/*patron* (and cookbook author) Andreas Antona has converted this listed Georgian mansion in a leafy suburb into a *Michelin*-starred restaurant with four themed bedrooms. Decor is a blend of Victorian and contemporary. 'It is superb,' said a visitor who arrived late and tired. 'Alison Antona greeted me and sent a glass of wine to my room; just what I needed. This set the tone for the rest of my stay.' The atmosphere is relaxed in a series of dining rooms (in one you can watch, through glass, the cooking). The menus (Luke Tipping is co-chef) are classical French, eg, duo of lamb, chop and pastilla, compote of aubergine, cumin sauce. The petits fours trolley is 'laden with treats like chocolate lollipops'. Children and vegetarians are catered for. Drinks are served in an orangery that faces the secluded garden; in summer you can dine alfresco. The best bedroom, French, has plaster mouldings, hand-painted cream and gold French furniture. Venetian has lots of velvet, reds and gold; Oriental is silk-lined, with dark lacquered furniture; Colonial, done in brown and beige, has dark wood furniture. Bathrooms are 'bright'. Breakfast is continental. (*KJ*)

4 bedrooms. 1 mile from centre. Closed Christmas/New Year, bank holidays. Restaurant closed Sun evening. Lounge, restaurant; private dining room; cookery school. No background music. Garden (alfresco dining). No smoking. Guide dogs only. Amex, MasterCard, Visa accepted. B&B [2007] £80–£112.50 per person. Set lunch £20; full alc £65.

See also SHORTLIST

BISHOP'S TAWTON Devon — Map 1:C4

Halmpstone Manor
Bishop's Tawton
nr Barnstaple EX32 0EA

Tel 01271-830321
Fax 01271-830826
Email charles@halmpstonemanor.co.uk
Website www.halmpstonemanor.co.uk

Standing in its own gardens off a country lane in this lovely part of north Devon, Charles and Jane Stanbury's manor house has links back to the 12th century. Views are 'magnificent, looking south towards Dartmoor where Hay Tor can be seen on the horizon'. 'The house is everything that a small country hotel should be; comfortable accommodation, good food and friendly proprietors.' It is 'beautifully furnished', and bedrooms have a four-poster or a coronet bed. 'Ours had a good-size bathroom; lots of extras, such as sherry, fruit and bottled water.' Help with luggage is offered to arriving guests to whom complimentary tea with cake is served in the recently refurbished lounge. There are log fires, deep sofas, 'flowers and family photos everywhere'. The four-course dinner (by arrangement only), served in a 'lovely wood-panelled room', is thought 'good – starters and sweets particularly'. No choice until dessert, but 'you are consulted at breakfast about likes and dislikes'. 'Splendid breakfasts, especially the porridge, made with plentiful cream.' You need a car to visit the nearby attractions, such as the magnificent beach and sand dunes at Saunton. (*Endorsed in 2007 by JS Waters*)

4 bedrooms. 4 miles SE of Barnstaple. Closed Christmas, New Year, Feb. Lounge, bar, dining room. No background music. ½-acre garden. Unsuitable for ♿. No smoking. No dogs: some bedrooms, some public rooms. MasterCard, Visa accepted. B&B [2007] £50–£70 per person. Set dinner £30. 1-night bookings refused bank holidays.

BLACKBURN Lancashire *See SHORTLIST* Map 4:D3

BLACKPOOL Lancashire *See SHORTLIST* Map 4:D2

BLAKENEY Norfolk Map 2:A5

The Blakeney Hotel

Blakeney
nr Holt NR25 7NE

Tel 01263-740797
Fax 01263-740795
Email reception@blakeney-hotel.co.uk
Website www.blakeney-hotel.co.uk

On the quay of this sailing and holiday village, Michael Stannard's large, traditional hotel is popular with families and, off-season, retired couples. One reader who 'will be returning' enjoyed talking to fellow guests who had visited annually for 30 years. Other comments: 'Suits its clientele.' 'Good as ever. Friendly, efficient service.' 'Dear old *Blakeney Hotel*. A wonderful week. Everything I complained about on my last visit had been corrected.' But there were criticisms too: 'Dining room windows needed cleaning. Parts of the building looked tired. Weak coffee.' 'Expensive for what is offered.' One couple complained of a 'poorly furnished' room. But a refurbished bedroom in the *Granary* annexe was thought 'very comfortable', and the traditional cooking, though 'not gastronomic', generally satisfies: 'roasted duck breasts; sirloin steaks; calf's liver'; 'prompt service'; 'fairly priced wines'. There are light lunches on weekdays; a choice of roasts on Sunday. 'Busy at the weekend with large family parties.' Public rooms have 'wonderful views' across the estuary and salt marshes to Blakeney Point. So do many bedrooms; others face the garden (some have a patio). 'All you could want for breakfast' (including local smoked kippers). The leisure facilities have had a facelift. (*WK Wood, Carol Jackson, MA, and others*)

64 bedrooms. 16 in *Granary* annexe opposite. Some on ground floor. On quay. Lift, ramps. Lounge, sun lounge, bar, restaurant; function facilities; indoor heated swimming pool (37 by 17 ft), spa bath, sauna, mini-gym; games room. No background music. ¼-acre garden: table tennis, swings. Sailing, fishing, water sports, golf, tennis nearby. No smoking. No dogs: public rooms, some bedrooms. All major credit cards accepted. B&B [2007] £77–£131 per person; D,B&B (min. 2 nights) £84–£144. Set dinner £25; full alc £45. Christmas/New Year packages. 1-night bookings usually refused Fri/Sat, bank holidays.

BONCHURCH Isle of Wight *See SHORTLIST* Map 2:E2

BORROWDALE Cumbria — Map 4: inset C2

The Leathes Head Hotel

Borrowdale
Keswick CA12 5UY

Tel 017687-77247
Fax 017687-77363
Email enq@leatheshead.co.uk
Website www.leatheshead.co.uk

High up in wooded grounds outside Borrowdale, this gabled Edwardian house is run as a traditional hotel by Roy and Janice Smith who 'never cease to be available and are always friendly'. It is popular with serious walkers and climbers. This year's praise: 'Efficient, personal, relaxing; good value for money.' 'A warm welcome, stunning food, a lovely location.' The house is furnished in keeping with its age; stained glass, old fireplaces and plasterwork retained. Tea and drinks (complimentary on arrival) are served in a sunroom with wicker armchairs. It is 'worth paying extra' for a double-aspect superior room: 'Ours was large, with sofa, coffee table and new plasma TV'; but another couple had a 'very small room'. Pre-dinner drinks are taken in the bar and lounge. 'We were impressed with the collection of gins, and the noteworthy wine list with sensible prices.' The chef, David Jackson, serves a daily-changing four-course menu with three choices for all except the fish course. The packed lunches are warmly recommended. Breakfast ranges from healthy to full English: 'Must be one of the best anywhere.' 'We saw red squirrels on the nut feeders.' Guests have access, for a small fee, to a nearby leisure club. (*Richard and Caroline Faircliff, CLH*)

12 bedrooms. 3 on ground floor. 1 suitable for ♿. 3½ miles S of Keswick. Open mid-Feb–end Nov. Ramp. Lounge, sun lounge, bar lounge, restaurant. No background music. 3-acre grounds: sun terrace, woodland. No smoking. No children under 9. No dogs. MasterCard, Visa accepted. D,B&B £70–£92 per person. Set dinner £31. 1-night bookings refused at weekends. *V*

Seatoller House

Borrowdale
Keswick CA12 5XN

Tel 017687-77218
Fax 017687-77189
Email seatollerhouse@btconnect.com
Website www.seatollerhouse.co.uk

'We run a traditional home from home, with a convivial atmosphere and communal dining,' say Daniel Potts and Lynne Moorehouse, managers of this unpretentious guest house. There are 'no such modern intrusions' as television and radio. At the head of the beautiful Borrowdale valley, the 350-year-old building, owned by a private company, The Lake Hunts Ltd, is popular with hikers and ramblers. Visitors like the homely atmosphere, the 'comfort, cuisine and warmth of welcome'. The sitting room has oak panelling, creaky floorboards, cosy chairs, cushioned window seats and a piano. Non-stop coffee is available in the tea bar (it can also be taken out in flasks); there is an honesty bar, and a self-help fridge. Lynne Moorehouse serves a no-choice, daily-changing menu at 7 pm; her style is traditional 'with a twist', eg, home-made smoked trout pâté; Aga-baked poussin with grapes in vermouth. On Tuesday, there is a light supper of soup, bread and cheese. Breakfast, between 8 and 8.30 am, is hearty. The simple bedrooms, redecorated this year, are warm in cold weather; all have private facilities, though six are not *en suite.* More reports, please.

10 bedrooms. 2 on ground floor. 1 in garden bungalow. All with shower. On B5289, 7 miles S of Keswick. Train: Penrith; regular buses. Open 9 Mar–24 Nov. Dining room closed midday. Lounge, library, tea bar, dining room; drying room. No background music. 1-acre grounds: beck. Unsuitable for ♿. No smoking. No children under 5 (unless full house booking). No dogs in public rooms.

MasterCard, Visa accepted. B&B £39–£53 per person; D,B&B £49–£63. Set dinner £18. Reductions for longer stays.

See also SHORTLIST

BOSCASTLE Cornwall — Map 1:C3

The Old Rectory
St Juliot, nr Boscastle
PL35 0BT

Tel/Fax 01840-250225
Email sally@stjuliot.com
Website www.stjuliot.com

Thomas Hardy, then an architect, met the rector's sister-in-law, Emma Gifford, here in March 1870 (he was working on the restoration of the church). They fell in love and were married in 1874. The rectory was later immortalised in Hardy's novel *A Pair of Blue Eyes*; the conservatory that he described still stands. Now this is the family home of the 'warmly welcoming' Chris and Sally Searle, who run it as a B&B. 'She is most welcoming in every way,' says a visitor in 2007. 'Breakfast is good.' Fairtrade tea and coffee, free-range chicken and duck eggs and locally produced bacon and sausage appear on the seasonal breakfast menu; also locally smoked salmon, mackerel and kipper, and 'the best produce we have in the garden', eg, peaches, figs, loganberries and gooseberries. All the bedrooms now have facilities *en suite.* Mr Hardy's, which has an antique carved double bed, is one of the three bedrooms in the house: it has a power shower. Emma's has a shower and the original thunderbox loo. The Rector's room has a whirlpool bath with shower, and a super-king-size bed. The fourth room, with a wood stove, bath and shower, is in stables, linked to the main house by the conservatory. The 'comfortable' guests' sitting room, with fireplace, faces over terrace and garden. (*Bobby Robson*)

4 bedrooms. 1 in stables (linked to house). 2 miles NE of Boscastle. Open mid-Feb–mid-Nov. Sitting room, breakfast room. No background music. 3-acre garden: croquet lawn, 'lookout'. Unsuitable for ♿. No smoking. No children under 12. Dogs allowed in stables room only (1 per visit; £6 per stay). MasterCard, Visa accepted. B&B [2007] £39–£57 per person. 1-night bookings sometimes refused weekends, bank holidays.

See also SHORTLIST

BOSHAM West Sussex Map 2:E3

The Millstream *Tel* 01243-573234
Bosham Lane *Fax* 01243-573459
Bosham, nr Chichester *Email* info@millstream-hotel.co.uk
PO18 8HL *Website* www.millstream-hotel.co.uk

In a pretty village on the West Sussex coast, this converted small manor house and 18th-century malt house cottage wins more plaudits this year: 'One of the nicest, most relaxed hotels we have ever stayed in.' 'Very welcoming, efficient service.' It is 'seriously pretty outside', with 'lovely' manicured gardens, the eponymous millstream and a gazebo. The long-serving, 'hands-on' general manager is Antony Wallace. Public rooms are pleasant and spacious. Bedrooms, with conventional decor, vary in size and all have 'thoughtful details' (ironing board, CD-player, flat-screen TV, etc). A wheelchair-dependent visitor found the Garden Room 'ideal, with wide doors and room to manoeuvre'. There is a new chef, James Fairchild-Dickson, whose modern British cooking was greatly admired by an inspector in 2007. 'Twice-cooked Roquefort soufflé was divine, as was wild bass with mustard seed and sorrel hollandaise. All bread is home made, ice creams too.' Those preferring traditional dishes 'have been appeased by the roast meat trolley, an imposing silver edifice bearing a rota of beef, lamb, pork and gammon'. Breakfast includes kippers, comb honey, fruit compotes. Bar lunches are available. Guests attending the Chichester theatre can have an early supper. (*Robert Ribeiro, Brian and Gwen Thomas, Dr JMR Irving, Zara Elliott, and others*)

35 bedrooms. 2 in cottage. 7 on ground floor, 1 suitable for ♿. 4 miles W of Chichester. Lounge (pianist Fri and Sat evenings), bar, restaurant; classical background music 10.30 am–10.30 pm; conference room. 1½-acre garden: stream, gazebo. Chichester Harbour (sailing, fishing) 300 yards. Civil wedding licence. No smoking. Guide dogs only. All major credit cards accepted. B&B [2007] £71–£106 per person; D,B&B (min. 2 nights) £83–£130. Set lunch £20, dinner £30. Christmas/New Year packages. 1-night bookings refused Sat.

****

Traveller's tale The owner was in evidence some of the time, but he did not seem to have his finger on the button. He hung around behind the bar doing nothing (and getting in the way of the young girl serving drinks) while we sat for five minutes without being asked if we wanted a drink or a menu. (*Hotel in Warwickshire*)

****

BOURTON-ON-THE-HILL Gloucestershire Map 3:D6

The Horse and Groom NEW

Bourton-on-the-Hill
nr Moreton-in-Marsh
GL56 9AQ

Tel/Fax 01386-700413
Email greenstocks@horseandgroom.info
Website www.horseandgroom.info

At the top of a hill in a honey-stone Cotswold village, this Georgian coaching inn was bought in July 2005 by brothers Tom and Will Greenstock, whose parents run the *Howard Arms*, Ilmington (*qv*). 'Engaging hosts', they run it as a dining pub; Tom is front-of-house, Will is the chef. 'This is just how an old inn should be done up; ancient beams, wooden floors and tables, sisal matting, and stools around the bar,' said an inspector. 'The mood is informal, and the modern cooking is just right.' Meals are chosen from a blackboard menu and can be taken in four seating areas, or alfresco. 'We sat in the garden with a splendid view down the valley. Fresh ingredients were beautifully presented: a large meaty crab cake; hake with a horseradish crust and a three-butter sauce; chicken wrapped in pancetta; super side dishes included crisp chips, crunchy carrots and cabbage. Terrific puddings.' Four of the five bedrooms have been refurbished in modern style; all are of good size and have a well-equipped bathroom, but light sleepers may hear traffic. 'Our room at the back was lovely and light with glazed doors opening on to the garden; well thought out with good storage space; a most comfortable bed. Excellent preserves, good toast, tea and coffee, and a generous helping of bacon at breakfast, but packaged juice.'

5 bedrooms. Village centre, 2 miles W of Moreton-in-Marsh. Closed 25 Dec, 31 Dec. Restaurant closed Sun eve, Mon lunch. Bar/restaurant. No background music. Garden. Unsuitable for ♿. No smoking. No dogs. MasterCard, Visa accepted. B&B £49–£70 per person; D,B&B (min. 2 nights) £72.50–£90. Full alc £33. 1-night bookings refused weekends.

****

Traveller's gripe Why do so many hotels fail to realise how important the first contact with a prospective guest is? The trainee receptionist left to cope on her own; the barman/chef/cleaner who answers the phone because Reception is unmanned; the person who, when asked about rooms, seems to have little knowledge of the hotel they are supposed to be representing. When a booking is made, how long it takes for confirmation to be sent, even by email.

****

BOURTON-ON-THE-WATER Gloucestershire — Map 3:D6

Dial House

High Street
Bourton-on-the-Water GL54 2AN

Tel 01451-822244
Fax 01451-810126
Email info@dialhousehotel.com
Website www.dialhousehotel.com

Said to be the oldest house in this pretty, if busy, Cotswold town on the River Windrush, this 17th-century building is set back from the street, 'removed from the bustle of day-trippers'. Owners Adrian and Jane Campbell-Howard aim for 'rural sophistication' in their small hotel. Inspectors wrote of 'lovely atmosphere: beams, inglenook fireplaces; a compatible mixture of modern tables and chairs and antique furniture', but 'intrusive background music'. Five rooms are in converted buildings to the side, overlooking the 'delightful' gardens. 'Ours had a huge bed; French grey trimmings; tea-making, fruit, mineral water; bright modern bathroom. Both rooms faced the car park but were quiet.' The best bedrooms, with antiques, are in the main house (one has an oak four-poster). Pre-dinner drinks, with canapés, are taken in the attractive bar, with log fire. A new head chef, Jamie Forman (designated a *Michelin* 'rising star' when he worked at Cotswold House, Chipping Campden, *qv*), arrived in May 2007. He 'has a very good relationship with local suppliers', we are told by the Campbell-Howards, self-avowed 'foodies'. The cooking style will be 'more traditional English', with some classic French elements. The 'first-rate breakfast', served at table, has fresh orange juice; porridge with whisky; 'superb bacon and sausage'. For computer buffs, there is 'access to state-of-the-art communications links'.

13 bedrooms. 5 in coach house. Town centre. Car park. Train: Kingham. Lounge, 2 dining rooms (background jazz/light music always). 1½-acre garden. No smoking. No children under 12. Dogs allowed in 1 bedroom; not in public rooms. All major credit cards accepted. B&B £40–£95 per person; D,B&B £55–£120. Full alc £40. Christmas/New Year packages. 1-night bookings refused weekends. *V*

How to contact the *Guide*
By mail: From anywhere in the UK, write to Freepost PAM 2931, London W11 4BR (no stamp is needed)
From outside the UK: *Good Hotel Guide*, 50 Addison Avenue, London W11 4QP, England
By telephone or fax: 020-7602 4182
By email: Goodhotel@aol.com or Goodhotel@btinternet.com
Via our website: www.goodhotelguide.com

BOWNESS-ON-WINDERMERE Cumbria

Map 4: inset C2

Fayrer Garden House Hotel

Lyth Valley Road
Bowness-on-Windermere
LA23 3JP

Tel 015394-88195
Fax 015394-45986
Email lakescene@fayrergarden.com
Website www.fayrergarden.com

Set in large grounds half a mile above Lake Windermere, Claire and Eric Wildsmith's former Edwardian 'gentleman's residence' has superb views of lake and mountain. One of the lounges, the dining room, the spacious terrace and some bedrooms face the water; other bedrooms have a garden view. A returning visitor this year reports: 'Food and accommodation as good as ever.' Other praise: 'We were pampered; staff were delightful; amenities very good. Our room was serviced with exemplary professionalism, though we never saw a cleaner.' Head chef, Eddie Wilkinson, serves a daily-changing menu of modern English dishes, using local produce wherever possible, eg, confit of Pooley Bridge chicken leg; loin of Grizedale venison. The Wildsmiths have continued with their refurbishment of the building; this year six bedrooms and the bar have been updated. (*Trevor Lee, DP*)

29 bedrooms. 5 in cottage. 7 on ground floor. 1 mile S of Bowness on A5074. Closed 2–18 Jan. 2 lounges, lounge bar (classical/pop background music), restaurant. 5-acre grounds. Civil wedding licence. No smoking. No children under 5. No dogs in public rooms. MasterCard, Visa accepted. D,B&B £53–£143 per person. Christmas/New Year packages. 1-night bookings sometimes refused Sat.

Lindeth Fell

Lyth Valley Road
Bowness-on-Windermere
LA23 3JP

Tel 015394-43286
Fax 015394-47455
Email kennedy@lindethfell.co.uk
Website www.lindethfell.co.uk

'Incredibly good value, and without the pretension of many Lakeland hotels. Such a comfortable place.' On a hill above Lake Windermere, Pat and Diana Kennedy's Edwardian house has 'superb views over the water'. Its garden, filled with rhododendrons, azaleas and specimen trees, is open to the public in spring and early summer. The hotel is traditional, 'with just the right blend of formality and informality', says a regular visitor. 'Mrs Kennedy made me and two young grandsons so welcome, and put us in a large, well-equipped family room, flowery but with every comfort.' Another room had 'large, comfortable bed; washbasin in the room, shower/WC *en suite*'. The single rooms are comfortable, too. 'Two drawing rooms ensure space for guests, and it is bliss to sit on the terrace eating delicious scones with jam and cream while watching boats on the distant lake.' There are patterned carpets, log fires, watercolours, bric-a-brac, books and magazines in public areas, patterned fabrics and wallpaper in the bedrooms. Chef Philip Taylor cooks in modern English style (eg, seared tuna steak with chilli and coriander salsa), and the four-course menu changes daily. Plenty of outdoors activities are available (see below). (*Dorothy Brining, RG*)

14 bedrooms. 1 on ground floor. 1 mile S of Bowness on A5074. Open 26 Jan–2 Jan. Ramp. Hall, 2 lounges, dispense bar, 3 dining rooms. No background music. 7-acre grounds: gardens, croquet, putting, bowls, tarn. Fishing permits. No smoking. No dogs. MasterCard, Visa accepted. B&B [2007] £45–£80 per person; D,B&B £70–£110. Set dinner £35. Christmas/New Year packages. 1-night bookings sometimes refused Sat. ***V***

Linthwaite House

Crook Road
Bowness-on-Windermere
LA23 3JA

Tel 015394-88600
Fax 015394-88601
Email stay@linthwaite.com
Website www.linthwaite.com

In 'beautiful surroundings, with very natural gardens', Mike Bevans's timbered, creeper-covered, white and stone house overlooks Lake Windermere. A reader who had a 'really enjoyable stay' with her family comments: 'Staff young, informal but professional. Decor a successful combination of traditional and contemporary.' 'Warm and welcoming' public rooms have oriental rugs, potted plants, cabin trunks and memorabilia. An enclosed veranda faces the lake. The bedrooms vary greatly: 'Our small suite was well furnished and equipped; good storage, firm mattress, good lighting.' Rooms 14 and 15 (each with king-size bed and lake views) are liked. 'New technology' includes 12-channel TV and a modem point. Refurbishment continues. Lunch can be taken on a terrace. At dinner, chef Simon Bolsover offers six choices for each of four courses ('all beautifully presented') on his modern menu (eg, seared halibut with hand-rolled gnocchi and langoustine espuma). 'Service, atmosphere and food all outstanding.' 'Excellent ingredients.' 'Our four-year-old son was made very welcome, and was served very good suppers in the bedroom. Good choice of cold and hot dishes at breakfast, and delicious scones at teatime.' Keith Floyd sometimes holds a cookery course here. Windermere Golf Club is 'just up the road'. (*Lydia Heah; also Gordon Hands*)

27 bedrooms. Some on ground floor. ¾ mile S of Bowness off B5284. Ramp. Lounge/bar, conservatory, 3 dining rooms; background music; function facilities. 14-acre grounds: croquet, tarn (fly-fishing). Civil wedding licence. No smoking. No children under 7 at dinner. Dogs allowed in grounds only (kennels), except guide dogs. Amex, MasterCard, Visa accepted. B&B [2007] £88–£164 per person; D,B&B £109–£184. Set dinner £47. Christmas/New Year/Easter packages. Cookery weekends. 1-night bookings refused weekends, bank holidays. *V*

See also SHORTLIST

BRADFORD-ON-AVON Wiltshire — Map 2:D1

The Swan Hotel NEW

1 Church Street
Bradford-on-Avon
BA15 1LN

Tel 01225-868686
Fax 01225-868681
Email theswan-hotel@btconnect.com
Website www.theswan-hotel.com

In early 2007, Stephen Ross, owner of the *Spread Eagle Inn*, Stourton (*qv*), completely renovated ('with sensitivity', say inspectors) this Grade II listed hotel in this 'picture-perfect' small town. 'Exposed beams and polished wooden floors (sloping and wonky in places) combine with modern-coloured walls and stylish furniture. The cosy lounge areas in front are charming; the gastropub at the back has wooden tables and chairs. The bar (popular with locals) stocks lots of real ales. The staff seemed really to care that we had a good stay. They welcomed us warmly and upgraded us to a lovely, simple, classy, light bedroom. Good bathroom. Bed a bit saggy. Useful information pack.' Some rooms might hear departing guests until closing time. Chef Tom Bridgeman serves English cooking, eg, lamb cutlets with asparagus and Jersey Royal potatoes. 'Unpretentious, fairly priced, good if unexciting. An unusually large number of wines by the glass, but bottle options were mostly pricey. Very good service: we were waited on by the chatty, friendly manager [Mark Heather], due to shortage of staff. Excellent breakfast: buffet with cereals, fruit, juices; thick-cut home-made bread, National Trust jams; cooked dishes included eggs Florentine, delicious full English. Newspapers on a side table. A great stay. Good value. They deserve to succeed.'

12 bedrooms. Town centre. Car park. 2 lounge areas, bar, dining room; background music. Terrace. Unsuitable for ♿. No smoking. No dogs. MasterCard, Visa accepted. B&B [2007] £47.50–£85. Full alc £30. 1-night bookings refused weekends.

Woolley Grange
Woolley Green
Bradford-on-Avon
BA15 1TX

Tel 01225-864705
Fax 01225-864059
Email info@woolleygrangehotel.co.uk
Website www.woolleygrangehotel.co.uk

'Just the right blend of luxury and informality for families with young children,' say visitors this year to this Jacobean stone manor house, set in big grounds on the edge of a medieval wool town. Part of the von Essen group's Luxury Family Hotels division, it is managed by Clare Hammond. 'Our small daughter loved it,' said an earlier guest. 'Beautiful house and grounds.' Guests pay by the room, sharing with as many children as they can tolerate. The very young are catered for in the Woolley Bears' Den; older children have the run of the Hen House (with games galore). Outside there is a plethora of sporting activities. Children take high tea, while their parents enjoy a candlelit dinner. The head chef, Paul Burrows, serves modern British dishes 'with a foreign influence', eg, rump of West Country lamb with a sweet potato fondant. (*Mrs Kris Henley, GH*)

26 bedrooms. 9 in courtyard, 3 in pavilion in grounds. 1 on ground floor. 1 mile NE of Bradford-on-Avon on B3105. Train: Bath/Bradford-on-Avon/Chippenham. Ramps. 2 lounges, TV room, 2 restaurants, dispense bar, conservatory; children's nursery, games rooms. No background music. 14-acre grounds: heated swimming pool (40 by 20 ft), badminton, croquet, trampoline, children's play area. Cycling, riding, golf, tennis, fishing, hot-air ballooning nearby. Civil wedding licence. No smoking. Dogs allowed in 3 bedrooms, not in restaurants. Amex, MasterCard, Visa accepted. B&B [2007]: double £170–£280, suite £260–£390; D,B&B £95–£230 per person. Light meals available. Full alc £38.50. Winter/7-night/midweek breaks. Gardening/cookery weeks for children. Christmas/New Year packages. 1-night bookings refused weekends.

BRADPOLE Dorset — Map 1:C6

Orchard Barn
Bradpole
nr Bridport DT6 4AR

Tel/Fax 01308-455655
Email enquiries@lodgeatorchardbarn.co.uk
Website www.lodgeatorchardbarn.co.uk

'Easily the nicest, most stylish B&B we have known,' write visitors to Nigel and Margaret Corbett's home on the site of an old Dorset farm (they live in a separate wing). 'Attention to our needs was exemplary,' said a correspondent who regularly visited the Corbetts when they ran the much-loved *Summer Lodge* at Evershot (*qv*). There are 'flowers everywhere', and a collection of cheese dishes. 'Nigel does front-of-house with zest.' The River Asker runs at the foot of the peaceful garden (you might spot a kingfisher or trout). 'The comfortable bedrooms are simple, but have fine linen, good lighting, free-range coat-hangers and individual temperature control.' Completion of the third bedroom is now due for 2008. 'Presentation, variety and quality of breakfast are outstanding.' Served in a room with log fire, or on a patio, it includes free-range eggs in many forms, local bacon and sausages, 'delicious, unusual yogurts', organic wholemeal toast, home-made marmalade and jams. A snack supper (soup, sandwiches, quiches and salads) can be served in the 'superb', large vaulted-ceiling lounge with its open fire and gallery. Many eating places are within a ten-minute drive. (*Suzanne and John Goodwin, Edwin Prince, Alan and Audrey Moulds*)

3 bedrooms. 1 on ground floor. Off A35, via Lee Lane, in village adjoining Bridport. Train: Dorchester; bus to Bridport. Lounge, dining room. No background music. ¾-acre garden: river. Sea 2 miles. Unsuitable for ♿. No smoking. Dogs allowed in public rooms subject to other guests' approval. Some credit cards to be accepted in 2008. B&B £47.50–£70. Snack supper £5–£12.50. 1-night bookings occasionally refused weekends.

BRAITHWAITE Cumbria — Map 4: inset C2

The Cottage in the Wood

Whinlatter Pass
Braithwaite CA12 5TW

Tel 017687-78409
Email relax@thecottageinthewood.co.uk
Website www.thecottageinthewood.co.uk

'Welcoming and attentive' hosts Liam and Kath Berney preside over this typical Lakeland inn. On Whinlatter Pass, in the Lake District national park and within England's only mountain forest, the 17th-century building looks down the valley to the Skiddaw mountain range. In the small garden, residents 'can take a drink or have a nap', says a visitor this year. Two bedrooms have a sleigh bed, and in 'what used to be our family attic' there is a roll-top bath and separate shower *en suite.* Other rooms are smaller. All bathrooms have been refurbished. The 'cosy' sitting room has an open fire, plants, walking magazines and books. Non-residents come to dine, attracted by the 'high quality and remarkably good value' of the cooking (a no-choice, daily-changing menu). 'We enjoyed home-cured gravadlax with beetroot purée; Galloway beef braised Burgundy style; exquisite tarte Tatin with thick cream, which my taste buds still remember. A short but interesting wine list, competitively priced.' Local suppliers are used. Breads, pasta and ice cream are home made. Breakfast includes fresh grapefruit, yogurts, fruit, and a Cumbrian cooked platter. (*Michael and Alison Garraway, and others*)

9 bedrooms. 1 on ground floor. 5 miles NW of Keswick. Feb–Dec. Restaurant closed midday, and Mon night. Lounge, bar, restaurant; background radio/CDs at mealtimes. 4½-acre grounds: terraced garden. No smoking. No children under 10. Dogs allowed in 1 designated bedroom; not in public rooms except bar. Diners, MasterCard, Visa accepted. B&B [2007] £35.50–£75 per person; D,B&B £58–£84.50. Set dinner £26–£30. Christmas/New Year packages. 1-night bookings sometimes refused peak weekends.

BRAMPTON Cumbria — Map 4:B3

Farlam Hall
Brampton CA8 2NG

Tel 01697-746234
Fax 01697-746683
Email farlam@relaischateaux.com
Website www.farlamhall.co.uk

César award in 2001

'As good as ever; well kept; hands-on owners.' 'Fun and friendly.' Returning visitors endorse this 'warm and welcoming' hotel (Relais & Châteaux), which has been owned and run by the Quinion and Stevenson families since 1975 (and has had an entry in the *Guide* since the first edition). Built in the late 16th century as a manorial house, the listed building was last transformed in 1860 for a coal baron and retains its Victorian character. Approached up a sweeping drive, it stands in an 'immaculate' landscaped garden, with a large ornamental lake, tall trees, a stream and a paddock. Ornate public rooms, with lots of knick-knacks and Victoriana ('perhaps a bit over the top'), have an open fire, patterned wallpaper and fresh flowers. Bedrooms are priced according to size (best ones have a whirlpool bath). 'Ours had traditional furnishings; good bed; plenty of reading matter.' Drinks are served in the lounge (no bar). In the dining room, Barry Quinion's 'competent English country house cooking' was found 'extremely good (we had half a lobster one night)'; other main courses might include breast of pheasant with a chicken mousseline; turbot on a couscous of vegetables. 'Not cheap, but good value.' (*Anne and Denis Tate, CN*)

12 bedrooms. 1 in stables. 2 on ground floor. On A689, 2½ miles SE of Brampton (*not* in Farlam village). Closed 24–30 Dec. Restaurant closed midday (light lunches for residents by arrangement). Ramps. 2 lounges, restaurant. No background music. 10-acre grounds: croquet lawn. Unsuitable for ♿. No smoking. No children under 5. No unattended dogs in bedrooms. Amex, MasterCard, Visa accepted. D,B&B [2007] £140–£175 per person. Set dinner £38.50–£40. 1-night bookings refused New Year. New Year package. *V*

BRANCASTER STAITHE Norfolk — Map 2:A5

The White Horse
Brancaster Staithe
PE31 8BY

Tel 01485-210262
Fax 01485-210930
Email reception@whitehorsebrancaster.co.uk
Website www.whitehorsebrancaster.co.uk

'A successful blend of pub where locals drink and excellent restaurant with good service and great views', Cliff Nye's Norfolk inn looks over sea and salt marshes. 'We have never been disappointed,' says a regular visitor. 'Fantastic; great for families,' say parents. Guests who felt 'a tinge of disappointment at the ordinariness' of the building were won over by 'the individual character and stylishness of the decor and furnishings'. The idiom is 'vernacular; wooden tables, unfrilly bedrooms, boards or neutral-coloured carpets under foot'. 'Our bright and comfortable room had seasidy touches: model boats and mounted sea shells.' The 'Room at the Top' (£15 supplement) has split-level facilities and a viewing balcony with telescope. The open-plan public area includes the bar (with sepia photographs, bar billiards, wall settles, modern unvarnished tables, 'all neat and tidy'), and an adjacent area with 'comfy' sofas and chairs. The restaurant, in a large conservatory, serves cooking in 'modern English style, with a traditional twist', by Nicholas Parker, who has worked for the Roux brothers. 'Delicious local fish dishes', eg, black bream, caramelised Jerusalem artichokes, fennel sauce. Children have their own menu. 'Our dogs were welcomed.' (*Conrad Barnard, G Potter, Richard Parish, Simon Rodway*)

15 bedrooms. 8 in annexe. 2 suitable for ♿. Centre of village just E of Brancaster. 2 lounge areas, public bar, conservatory restaurant, dining room; 'easy listening' background music 'at quiet times'. ½-acre garden. Harbour sailing. No smoking. Dogs allowed in annexe rooms and bar (£5 a night). Diners, MasterCard, Visa accepted. B&B [2007] £50–£75 per person. Full alc £32. Off-season breaks. Christmas/New Year packages.

BRANSCOMBE Devon — Map 1:C5

The Masons Arms
Branscombe EX12 3DJ

Tel 01297-680300
Fax 01297-680500
Email reception@masonsarms.co.uk
Website www.masonsarms.co.uk

In the centre of this National Trust village, this popular creeper-covered inn (Grade II listed) is 'a super place to stay, well worth its place in the *Guide*', say visitors this year. Another trusted correspondent praised the 'slick organisation: we were warmly greeted by Colin Slaney, the owner; a friendly receptionist checked us in'. Many bedrooms are in cottages (all of which have been redecorated) across the terrace behind the pub, well away from any noise from the bar. 'Our cottage room was first class: comfortable bed, easy chairs and table.' Other guests had 'a lovely room with exposed beams open to the eaves, windows on three sides, stable door opening to a tiny flower-filled balcony'. 'Blankets and sheets willingly supplied instead of a duvet.' Rooms in the main building (two more have been added this year) may hear some noise from the bar and kitchen. Richard Reddaway is the chef; his English cooking uses local ingredients whenever possible. 'There is a wide choice of dishes in both restaurant and bar. Portions are large.' 'Service was incredibly quick and efficient.' 'Breakfast was excellent.' 'The Christmas package doesn't impose seasonal "yo-ho-hos" on guests.' Booking is advised for both restaurant and pub. (*Andrew Wiltshire, BB*)

22 bedrooms. 14 in cottages. Village centre. Parking. Ramps. Lounge, 2 bars, 2 dining rooms. No background music. Large garden, terrace. Pebble beach ½ mile. Unsuitable for ♿. No smoking. Dogs allowed in bar, 3 bedrooms; not in restaurant. MasterCard, Visa accepted. B&B [2007] £40–£160 per person; D,B&B £67.50–£187.50. Set menu £27.50; full alc £37.50. Christmas/New Year packages. 1-night bookings refused weekends.

BRAY Berkshire — Map 2:D3

The Waterside Inn

Ferry Road
Bray SL6 2AT

Tel 01628-620691
Fax 01628-784710
Email reservations@waterside-inn.co.uk
Website www.waterside-inn.co.uk

A combination of an English riverside setting and French *haute cuisine*, Michel Roux's renowned restaurant-with-rooms (Relais & Châteaux), 35 years old in 2007, has held three *Michelin* stars for 22 years. Under the direction of M. Roux's son Alain, head chef Russell Holborn serves 'very professionally' prepared and cooked food in the 'opulent' restaurant. 'A cosseting dining experience.' 'Wine selection was superb.' At dinner, the *carte* has dishes like courgette flowers filled with wild mushrooms; langoustine soufflé scented with truffles. A five-course *menu exceptionnel* (to be ordered by the whole table) is available at £91 per person: its first course might be velouté de granny-smith et son tartare de noix de St-Jacques. Drinks can be taken in a summer house or on an electric launch. All bedrooms have linen sheets, Wi-Fi, flat-screen TV, flowers and access to a kitchenette. The two best rooms, La Terrasse and

La Tamise, open on to a terrace with 'stunning views of the river'. Breakfast, served after 8 am in the bedroom, is a large wicker tray with fresh orange juice, yogurt, croissants, etc; 'good coffee' and a newspaper. (*D and HA, and others*)

11 bedrooms. 3 in cottage, 30 yds. On Thames, 3 miles SE of Maidenhead. Closed 26 Dec–1 Feb, also bank holidays and Mon/Tues (except Tues evening June–Aug). Restaurant; private dining room (with drawing room and courtyard garden). Riverside terrace; launch for drinks/coffee. No background music. Unsuitable for ♿. Civil wedding licence. No smoking. No children under 12. Guide dogs only. All major credit cards accepted. B&B [2007] £90–£330 per person. Set 3-course lunch: Wed–Sat £44, Sun £56; full alc £130 (*excluding 'optional' 12½% service charge on meals*).

BRIDPORT Dorset — Map 1:C6

The Bull Hotel NEW

34 East Street
Bridport DT6 3LF

Tel 01308-422878
Fax 01308-426872
Email info@thebullhotel.co.uk
Website www.thebullhotel.co.uk

'Lovely atmosphere. Locals dropping in. Delicious food. An enjoyable stay.' In 2006, Richard and Nicola Cooper bought this Grade II listed coaching inn in the centre of this handsome market town. Renovation is almost complete. Bedrooms (on first and second floors) include Red (red walls, carved wood four-poster, roll-top claw-footed bath on a central platform); Silver (iron and brass bed); Gold (six-foot brass bed; tiny antique gilt sofa). 'Our room,' say inspectors in 2007, 'had all the right ingredients: antiques, ornate mirrors, supremely comfortable bed, spacious bathroom with powerful shower, but lighting not well thought out.' In the large, 'stylish yet informal' restaurant (with open fire), chef Gerry Page's 'excellent' modern menu uses seasonal ingredients, local when possible. 'Light, fluffy asparagus tart; large scallops with lemony sauce; chicken stuffed with ricotta. Our waiter was efficient; service otherwise a bit erratic. Breakfast had delicious mueslis; wonderful, creamy milk; real bread as toast.' Weekend brunch lasts until 3 pm. High teas, cocktails and real ales are served. In summer, meals are taken in the courtyard. The Coopers, parents themselves, 'do what we can to accommodate children of all ages' (cots, high chairs, toys, Sunday lunch crèche). In the huge first-floor Georgian ballroom (with minstrels' gallery), civil weddings, parties and conferences are held. Front bedrooms might hear local noise (particularly on market days).

13 bedrooms. Town centre. 14 miles W of Dorchester. Bar (background/live music), restaurant; snooker room; ballroom. Courtyard: bar, children's play area. Civil wedding licence. Unsuitable for ♿. No smoking. No dogs in bedrooms. Amex, MasterCard, Visa accepted. B&B [2007] £35–£125 per person. Full alc £30. 1-night bookings refused weekends. Christmas/New Year packages.

BRIGHTON East Sussex Map 2:E4

drakes
43/44 Marine Parade
Brighton BN2 1PE

Tel 01273-696934
Fax 01273-684805
Email info@drakesofbrighton.com
Website www.drakesofbrighton.com

Signage is discreet, an etched, opaque glass panel in the setting-down area, at Andy Shearer's luxury design hotel on the seafront near the marina. Two 19th-century town houses have been expensively converted, 'with a touch of the Orient'. 'Expensive, lovely rooms, though noisy on the front,' is this year's comment. 'Very comfortable beds, good linen; water everywhere in the wet room.' Some rooms have a freestanding bath, by a large window. An inspector had a 'smallish second-floor room up an attractive if steep hanging staircase (no lift); well designed, done in cream, shades of brown and natural wood, it had air conditioning, flat-screen TV, DVD-player, Internet access, etc. Excellent lighting; but not much storage space.' Most 'city view' rooms overlook the back gardens of houses. Hotel guests should reserve a table for the basement *Gingerman* restaurant, separately managed and popular locally. Ben McKellar's modern cooking is thought 'outstanding and reasonably priced', eg, rabbit leg stuffed with Agen prunes. 'Nice staff' too. Breakfast has fruit, yogurt, porridge, kippers, etc. There is 24-hour service in the ground-floor lounge bar. (*Jane Woollcott, and others*)

20 bedrooms. 2, on ground floor, suitable for ♿, but no ♿ access to restaurant. 3 miles from centre. Station 20 mins' walk. Parking arrangement with Marina, 1 mile. Ramp. Lounge/bar/reception, restaurant (separately owned); 'easy listening' background music all day; meeting room. Sea across road. No smoking. Guide dogs only. Amex, MasterCard, Visa accepted. Room [2007]: single £95–£125, double £120–£145, suite £155–£300. Breakfast £10–£12.50. Set dinner £35. 1-night bookings refused Sat. *V*

We ask for more reports on a hotel if we haven't received feedback from readers for some time. Please send an endorsement if you think a hotel should remain in the *Guide*.

Hotel du Vin Brighton
2–6 Ship Street
Brighton BN1 1AD

Tel 01273-718588
Fax 01273-718599
Email info@brighton.hotelduvin.com
Website www.hotelduvin.com

'The staff smile and are so helpful,' says a visitor on her sixth visit to this branch of the Hotel du Vin chain, a converted mock-Tudor building in a one-way street between the Lanes conservation area and the seafront. Lora Strizic is manager. Each bedroom is sponsored by a wine company: 'Ours was modern comfortable, well equipped.' 'Everything in the room works,' is one comment, though one reader had to 'descale a shower head myself'. A 'very impressive' suite has a 'huge bed and TV, and a shower big enough for a rugby team'. The fresh milk and CD-player are appreciated. The food and service in the busy restaurant 'were very good', though tables might be 'too close together'; the simple bistro menu has a French touch, eg, seared tuna and niçoise salad; confit duck leg with cauliflower purée. 'An enticing wine list.' Breakfast (which costs extra) has 'good fresh juice in large glasses'; buffet tables laden with cereals, fruit, etc; fresh toast and cooked dishes brought to the table. Cots and beds for children are supplied. Limited parking: telephone beforehand. (*Fredina Minshall, Michael and Eithne Dandy, and others*)

37 bedrooms. Some in courtyard. 2, on ground floor, suitable for ♿. 50 yds from beachfront. Lounge/bar ('easy listening' background music all day), bistro. No smoking. Dogs allowed in 5 bedrooms, not in public rooms. All major credit cards accepted. Room £155–£405. Breakfast £9.95–£13.50. Full alc £45. 1-night bookings refused weekends.

See also SHORTLIST

BRISTOL — Map 1:B6

Hotel du Vin Bristol NEW
The Sugar House
Narrow Lewins Mead
Bristol BS1 2NU

Tel 0117-925 5577
Fax 0117-925 1199
Email info@bristol.hotelduvin.com
Website www.hotelduvin.com

'An imaginative conversion of old warehouses, with trendy furnishings', this group of Grade II listed buildings in the city centre forms the Bristol branch of the Hotel du Vin chain. A glassed canopy entrance opens to a reception desk beside a 100-foot chimney. Spacious public areas have tables and potted plants, and a sweeping steel and oak staircase. Front bedrooms overlook a busy road but have thick curtains and double glazing; some rooms are on two levels. Visitors with a young child this year were upgraded to 'a massive room with plenty of space to tuck a cot into a dark corner; there was even a little baby pack of toiletries, spare bedding, etc. A large, very comfortable bed, massive bathroom.' A misunderstanding over baby-listening devices (which don't work in the building) was resolved by the 'helpful staff': a babysitter was provided free of charge 'while we enjoyed an excellent dinner' in the busy bistro (main courses like calf's liver and bacon with mashed potato; linguine with courgettes and slow-roast tomatoes). A high chair was provided 'without fuss' at breakfast. The hotel has a secure car park, but space is limited and cannot be reserved; other parking spaces are outside the building. Sunday jazz nights are held. (*Avril Campbell*)

40 bedrooms. City centre. Lift, ramp. Lounge, library/billiard room, 2 bars, bistro; 3 private dining rooms. No background music. Small courtyard. No smoking. All major credit cards accepted. Room [2007] £135–£350. Breakfast £9.95–£13.50. Full alc £40–£45.

See also SHORTLIST

BROAD CAMPDEN Gloucestershire — Map 3:D6

The Malt House
Broad Campden
nr Chipping Campden
GL55 6UU

Tel 01386-840295
Fax 01386-841334
Email info@malt-house.co.uk
Website www.malt-house.co.uk

'As good as ever,' reports an enthusiastic returning visitor to Judi Wilkes's 'delightful' Grade II listed malt house (with two adjacent cottages) in a small, honey-stone Cotswold village. 'Warmly welcoming', a 'perfectionist', she maintains the house with 'excellent taste' in a style appropriate to its age. The sitting rooms have low-beamed ceilings, log fires, antiques, *objets trouvés* and flowers. All the bedrooms overlook the garden; three have a private entrance. One room has a fireplace, one a small sitting room. 'Ours had good lighting, nice fabrics, a huge magnolia tree outside the window, fresh milk for tea-making, current magazines.' Breakfast is 'delicious': the freshly squeezed orange juice, fruit and home-made preserves are 'as satisfying as the cooked dishes'. In warm weather, teas (with home-made biscuits) and evening drinks are served in the summer house in the garden. Meals may be by arrangement, for groups of 12 or more, and house parties are catered for. Many good eating places are nearby and a map with recommendations is in each room. From the gate you can walk on to the Cotswold Way. (*BB, and others*)

7 bedrooms. 2 on ground floor. 1 mile S of Chipping Campden. Car park. Train: Moreton-in-Marsh, 5 miles. Closed Christmas. Ramp. 2 lounges, dining room. No background music. 3-acre garden: croquet, orchard, stream. Unsuitable for ♿. No smoking. Dogs allowed in 1 bedroom; not in public rooms. Amex, MasterCard, Visa accepted. B&B [2007] £66–£77.50 per person. Midweek winter breaks. 1-night bookings refused Apr–Nov weekends. *V*

BROADWAY Worcestershire — Map 3:D6

The Olive Branch NEW

78 High Street
Broadway WR12 7AJ
Tel 01386-853440
Fax 01386-859070
Email davidpam@theolivebranch-broadway.com
Website wwwtheolivebranch-broadway.com

In the centre of this lovely old Cotswold village, this 'super' Grade II listed 16th-century house was voted the best B&B in the UK in 2005. Its nominator agrees. Owners David and Pam Talboys, she writes, 'are the most welcoming and generous people. They work so hard and have thought of everything.' Arriving guests are helped with luggage, and given a glass of sherry in the 'cosy lounge' (wood floors, rugs, squashy sofas, books and magazines). 'Large vases of flowers, freshly picked from the garden, are in the lounge and dining room. Our bedroom was elegant and comfortable: king-size bed with plump pillows, mini-fridge, chocolates, teddy bear. Spotless shower room with lovely towels.' For breakfast (in a room with inglenook fireplace and original stone floor) there are home-made smoothies, fresh juices, home-made muesli. And 'David cooks an excellent English, with delicious herby mushrooms'. Guests may use the barbecue in the pretty walled garden. (*Ilse Evans*)

8 bedrooms. 1 on ground floor. Village centre. Parking. Lounge, breakfast room; background music. ¼-acre garden. No smoking. Dogs allowed in 1 bedroom only; not in public rooms. MasterCard, Visa accepted. B&B [2007] £37.50–£58 per person. 1-night bookings sometimes refused weekends Mar–Nov. *V*

****

Traveller's tale Dinner was accompanied by the full *1812 Overture*, bells and cannons included. Imagine what that did to the digestive system. (*Hotel in Essex*)

****

Russell's Restaurant
The Green, 20 High Street
Broadway WR12 7DT

Tel 01386-853555
Fax 01386-853964
Email info@russellsofbroadway.co.uk
Website www.russellsofbroadway.co.uk

César award in 2006

Named after Sir Gordon Russell, the Arts and Crafts furniture designer who once lived here, Barry Hancox and Andrew Riley's restaurant-with-rooms is a listed building which has been given a chic, modern look. 'A beautiful room, exciting and comfortable,' says a 2007 visitor. 'Stylish, with wonderful attention to detail,' was an earlier comment. Beams, inglenook fireplaces and the original oak staircase have been retained while modern gadgets and paintings have been added. 'Our room had a window seat with its own reading light; also a magnifying make-up mirror.' Some rooms face the village, but windows are double glazed, and 'all is quiet at night'. A supermarket car park is visible from the rear windows and patio. The L-shaped bistro-style restaurant has a comfortable sitting area and wooden tables with grey slate mats. Everyone agrees: 'Dinners were first class.' But an inspector found that 'lack of soundproofing made conversation difficult'. Matthew Laughton, head chef, serves a reasonably priced seasonal set menu at midday and from 6 to 7 pm; later, guests eat *à la carte.* Typical dishes: cream of wild garlic soup with poached duck egg; roast best end of Cornish lamb with Provençal vegetables. Waiting staff are 'smart in black top and trousers, and long black apron'. Breakfast was less satisfactory: 'Poor tea and brittle toast.' There is a 'parasol-covered patio with metal chairs and tables'. (*Tom Mann, MC, and others*)

7 bedrooms. 3 in annexe. 2 on ground floor. Village centre. Restaurant closed Sun night off-season. Ramp. Residents' lobby, bar, restaurant (background music); private dining room. Patio (heating; meal service). No smoking. No dogs in public rooms. Amex, MasterCard, Visa accepted. B&B [2007] £62.50–£162.50 per person. Set menus £18.95–£22.95; full alc £45. *V*

BROCKENHURST Hampshire — Map 2:E2

Thatched Cottage Hotel & Restaurant
16 Brookley Road, Brockenhurst
SO42 7RR

Tel 01590-623090
Fax 01590-623479
Email sales@thatchedcottage.co.uk
Website www.thatched-cottage.co.uk

A 'wonderfully picturesque' 400-year-old timber-framed thatched cottage in the New Forest national park is now this restaurant-with-rooms run by Martin and Michiyo Matysik (the chefs), and Martin's brother Mathias (front-of-house). There are low oak beams and 'at every turn, a profusion of dainty lace, flouncy fabrics, stencilled walls, dried flowers and antiques'. Bedrooms are named after blends of tea; three of them have an open-hearth gas fire. Assam Bop has a canopied double bed, Lord Earl Grey a four-poster. There is a two-bedroom suite in a cottage. 'Indulgent' afternoon teas are served, with sandwiches and cakes on a traditional three-tier stand. In fine weather it may be taken in the peaceful garden. The three- or five-course dinner menu includes dishes like corn-fed squab pigeon with pumpkin gnocchi and crisp pancetta. 'Cooking is refined, with great emphasis on presentation.' Breakfast, served until 11 am, has freshly squeezed orange juice, fresh-baked pastries and a choice of six cooked dishes. Well placed for station, village and forest walks. Some light sleepers might hear traffic at night. Cookery courses and wine tastings are held. More reports, please.

5 bedrooms. Some on ground floor. Near village centre. Restaurant closed Sun night, Mon. Lounge, restaurant. No background music. Small tea garden. No smoking. No children under 12. Dogs allowed in some bedrooms. MasterCard, Visa accepted. B&B £40–£90 per person. Set dinner £15–£60; full alc £50 (*'optional' 12½% gratuity charge added to meal prices*). 2 nights min. at weekends. Christmas/New Year packages. 1-night bookings refused Sat.

BROMSGROVE Worcestershire — Map 3:C5

See SHORTLIST

BROXTON Cheshire — Map 3:A5

Frogg Manor

Nantwich Road
Broxton, Chester CH3 9JH

Tel 01829-782629
Fax 01829-782459
Email info@froggmanorhotel.co.uk
Website www.froggmanorhotel.co.uk

César award in 1997

'A wonderful oasis from the mad, mad world,' says a visitor to John Sykes's Georgian manor house south of Chester, which is dedicated to 1930s/40s music and to frogs (there are hundreds – ceramic, straw, brass, etc). Other comments: 'A weird but enjoyable experience.' 'Nothing has changed; excellent as ever.' This year the 'mildly eccentric host' has added a 'bothy-type lodge' in a tree house to his collection of quirky bedrooms; it has a king-size bed and its own bathroom. In the main building, bedrooms are themed (Wellington, Sherlock Holmes, Nightingale, etc), and 'equipped with everything a guest could need, from spare tights to hair conditioner'. But one visitor thought 'housekeeping could be improved'. Public rooms are 'welcoming, with a hint of an Agatha Christie whodunnit'. Dinner, cooked by chef Sion Newton, is served between 7 and 10 pm in the conservatory dining room: 'Wonderful food, in a beautiful setting.' After-dinner coffee comes with chocolate frogs. Meals are accompanied by jazz classics; there is a small dance floor. Continental breakfast is included in the price; other breakfast dishes are *à la carte.* The large grounds, floodlit at night, have views across Cheshire to the Welsh mountains. (*Richard Hopkins, David H Ward, BD*)

8 bedrooms. 1 in tree house, 1 suitable for ♿. 10 miles SE of Chester. Closed 1 Jan. Ramp. Lounge, bar lounge, restaurant (1930s/40s background music); private dining room; conference/function facilities. 10-acre grounds: tennis. Civil wedding licence. No smoking in 3 bedrooms. Dogs allowed in 1 bedroom; not in public rooms. All major credit cards accepted. B&B [2007] £44–£165 per person. Alc breakfast from £5. Set menus £28.35–£39.90.

BUCKDEN Cambridgeshire — Map 2:B4

The George

High Street
Buckden PE19 5XA

Tel 01480-812300
Fax 01480-813920
Email mail@thegeorgebuckden.com
Website www.thegeorgebuckden.com

On the high street of a village near Huntingdon, this coaching inn has been 'discreetly enlarged' behind its Georgian facade. Owners since 2003, Annie, Richard and Becky Furbank, have created a 'fashionably stylish' decor of neutral colours (taupe, chocolate, grey-green). Their manager is Cynthia Schaeffer. 'Public spaces flow into one another, interrupted only by cylindrical pillars. Furnishings are well chosen, comfortable and eye-catching,' said recent visitors. The themed bedrooms, dedicated to Georges (Washington, Eliot, etc), are up a polished staircase. A standard room (Mallory, 'perhaps because of the climb') is 'smartly decorated', but has a 'slightly cramped' bathroom. Hanover (premiere) has blue walls, bed with brass bedhead. The busy brasserie, where breakfast, light lunch and dinner are served, has 'chic nightlight holders, quirky prints', wooden tables. The 'competent' chef, Haydn Laidlow, serves modern dishes like baked bream with saffron mash and basil pesto; steak can come with chips and ketchup. The wine list is well priced ('plenty in the £15–£16 range'). Waiters wear grey shirt and tie. Breakfast includes brown bread toast, croissants, fruit, cheese, etc, and any variation of a standard fry-up. 'Good coffee. Plenty of free newspapers.' Annie Furbank runs a smart clothing boutique next door.

12 bedrooms. Off A1, between Huntingdon and St Neots. Lift. Lounge, wine bar, brasserie; meeting room. No background music. Patios. No smoking. No dogs in public rooms. Amex, MasterCard, Visa accepted. B&B £50–£80 per person. Full alc £40. Christmas/New Year packages.

BUCKLAND MARSH Oxfordshire — Map 2:C2

The Trout at Tadpole Bridge NEW

Buckland Marsh
SN7 8RF

Tel 01367-870382
Fax 01367-870912
Email info@troutinn.co.uk
Website www.troutinn.co.uk

Gareth and Helen Pugh, who earlier won a *César* at the *Painswick Hotel* in Gloucestershire, in 2006 bought and renovated this old Cotswold pub. Parents themselves, they have made it 'as child-friendly as possible: decent children's menu (no nuggets), games, toys, plenty of space outdoors'. Chef Robert Ellis has stayed from the previous regime ('we take food seriously, but do not enjoy the label "gastropub"'). Inspectors write: 'Dinners the strong point. Fabulous bread basket; deliciously creamy garlic and potato soup; tender steak; really good vegetarian ratatouille feuilletté. The friendly owner came to each table to chat; he and the staff were all attentive. The bedrooms (all different) were very pleasant, immaculate, if slightly lacking individuality. Ours smelt lovely. Good points: flat-screen digital TV, quality toiletries. It was pretty well insulated, but we heard our next-door neighbours' dog whimpering when they left it alone. Breakfast had home-made bread again, a well-stocked sideboard, and the usual full English. The pub inside is very simple and combines contemporary colour schemes with traditional materials. Locals swelled the bar in the early evening. The half-board deal was good value.' Free Wi-Fi throughout. The garden slopes down to the fast-flowing Thames, by a bridge.

6 bedrooms. 3 in courtyard. 2 miles N of A420, halfway between Oxford and Swindon. Closed Christmas/New Year. Restaurant closed 3–6 pm daily, and Sun night in winter. Bar, dining area, breakfast area. 2-acre garden: river; moorings. Unsuitable for ♿. No smoking. Amex, MasterCard, Visa accepted. B&B [2007] £50–£70 per person. Full alc £34.50. 1-night bookings refused weekends May–Oct.

BUNGAY Suffolk *See SHORTLIST* Map 2:B6

BURFORD Oxfordshire Map 2:C2

Burford House
99 High Street
Burford OX18 4QA

Tel 01993-823151
Fax 01993-823240
Email stay@burfordhouse.co.uk
Website www.burfordhouse.co.uk

On the busy, steeply sloping high street of this attractive Cotswold town, Jane and Simon Henty's half-timbered, early 17th-century listed building is filled with family photos and souvenirs of foreign travel. It has two sitting rooms: one with a 'crackling fire, antiques, fresh flowers and expensive pieces of china'; the other has French doors opening on to the courtyard garden. The 'nicely decorated, comfortable bedrooms have a homely feel and a modern bathroom', say visitors in 2007. Three have a four-poster bed. Rooms at the front may be noisy 'as traffic rumbles up and down the hill', but those at the back are 'quiet enough'. Light lunches are served in the dining room from Monday to Saturday, eg, home-made soup; Provençal tart. Picnic lunches can be supplied. There is a 'short but interesting' wine list, and an honour bar. A 'nice' breakfast has a variety of fresh and cooked fruits, as well as the usual full English. 'The staff were friendly and helpful.' (*Michael and Eithne Dandy*)

8 bedrooms. 1 on ground floor. Central (2 rooms might hear traffic). Free car park nearby. Closed Christmas. Dining room closed evenings and Sun. Reception, 2 lounges (1 with honour bar), dining room. No background music. Courtyard garden. Unsuitable for ♿. Bicycles available. No smoking. No dogs. Amex, MasterCard, Visa accepted. B&B £75–£125 per person. 1-night bookings refused weekends. *V*

The more reports we receive, the more accurate the *Guide* becomes. Please don't hesitate to write again about an old favourite. New reports help us keep the *Guide* up to date.

BURY ST EDMUNDS Suffolk — Map 2:B5

Ounce House

Northgate Street
Bury St Edmunds IP33 1HP

Tel 01284-761779
Fax 01284-768315
Email enquiries@ouncehouse.co.uk
Website www.ouncehouse.co.uk

Liked for its feel of a family home, Simon and Jenny Pott's Victorian merchant's house stands at the high point of one of the finest residential streets in this attractive town. The 'chintzy' drawing room, filled with family photographs and knick-knacks, is 'nicely furnished, if a little cluttered'. A small library has games, videos and DVDs, and a small honesty bar. The individually decorated bedrooms are well equipped, 'perhaps a bit dated, but impeccably clean'. A front bedroom faces the busy road, but the others are quiet. 'Our room overlooked the garden, which has trees that successfully block out surrounding buildings. We slept with the windows open; the dawn chorus was impressive.' Breakfast, served communally around a large table, is 'traditional English, with good ingredients'. A three-course dinner can be similarly served, for four people or more (main courses like herb-crusted sea bass with dill sauce). Mrs Pott is 'a mine of information on local history'. More reports, please.

3 bedrooms. Central. Off-road parking. Drawing room, snug/bar/library, dining room. No background music. ¾-acre walled garden. Unsuitable for ♿. No smoking. No dogs. All major credit cards accepted. B&B £50–£85 per person. Set dinner (by arrangement: 4 or more) £30–£40. Weekend rates; reductions for 3 or more nights.

See also SHORTLIST

BUXTON Derbyshire *See SHORTLIST* — Map 3:A6

****

Traveller's tale At dinner, the soup was tasteless. For the first time in my life I sent back the main course (sea bass), as it was awful, and ordered the turbot instead. The manager came to the table and berated me. He said: 'The chef and I tasted it. There is nothing wrong with the dish. If you don't like it, it is your fault. You will be charged for it, and if you order the turbot, you will be charged for that, too.' (*Hotel in Scotland*)

****

CALNE Wiltshire — Map 2:D2

Chilvester Hill House
Calne SN11 0LP

Tel 01249-813981
Fax 01249-814217
Email gill.dilley@talk21.com
Website www.chilvesterhillhouse.co.uk

César award in 1992

'Superb; a lovely welcome and a cool bedroom on a hot weekend; informative and friendly hosts,' say visitors this year to this Victorian house. Built of Bath stone, and set well back from the A4, it is surrounded by fields with sheep. Earlier, our inspector was equally impressed: 'The charming owners, Gill and John Dilley, did everything possible to help us enjoy our stay.' There is a large drawing room with comfortable seating, magazines, books; a sitting room with a big TV. This and the pleasant dining room are papered with dramatic William Morris designs. The bedrooms are large, well furnished; 'ours had windows on two sides; the floral wallpaper was impressive, or startling, depending on taste.' Mrs Dilley serves a no-choice menu (likes and dislikes are discussed) by arrangement, around a long table, in dinner-party style. There is a 'short but comprehensive' wine list. No compulsion to dine in, and reservations can be made for local restaurants. Breakfast, 'a moveable feast, although most guests settle for something between 8 and 9 am', 'was good; fresh fruit, cereals, cooked English, home-made jams, strong coffee'. No brochure: Mrs Dilley sends a letter 'directed towards specific inquiries'. 'We are really the private country home of a professional family,' she says. (*Mick Fuchs, and others*)

3 bedrooms. ½ mile from Calne. Closed 7–10 days in autumn or spring. Drawing room, sitting room with TV, dining room. No background music. 2½-acre grounds (also 5 acres for sheep). Golf, riding locally. Unsuitable for ♿. Smoking discouraged in bedrooms. No children under 12. No dogs. Amex, MasterCard, Visa accepted. B&B [2007] £45–£70 per person. Packed/snack lunches. Set dinner (by arrangement) £20–£25. 1-night bookings 'very occasionally' refused.

CAMBER East Sussex *See SHORTLIST* — Map 2:E5

CAMBRIDGE Cambridgeshire *See SHORTLIST* — Map 2:B4

CANNINGTON Somerset — Map 1:B5

Blackmore Farm
Blackmore Lane
Cannington
nr Bridgwater TA5 2NE

Tel 01278-653442
Fax 01278-653427
Email dyerfarm@aol.com
Website www.dyerfarm.co.uk

'Ideal for holidays with children', Ann and Ian Dyer's B&B is a large 14th-century manor house on a working farm. A visitor in 2007 enthuses: 'Our family room, The Solar, comprised a large double bedroom, single bed in a closet leading off it, and *en suite* bathroom. My two-year-old daughter was provided with cot, bedding and breakfast at no extra charge. Hot milk in the morning no problem, provided by the ever-smiling Ann.' Period features retained include oak beams, stone archways, mullioned windows, medieval garderobes and a 'lovely little chapel'. Scattered about are old pewter pots, hay forks and 'nasty-looking man-traps'. Tea and 'delicious home-made cake' are served free to arriving guests; 'endless goodies' (fruit, biscuits, chocolates) are in the bedrooms. The West Room has the original roof trusses, an oak four-poster and views to the Quantock hills. The 'particularly good' breakfast, in the Great Hall (with coat of armour), is convivial: guests eat together at a long refectory table by a massive sandstone fireplace. 'Lots of local ingredients, very tasty.' 'At £70 for the night, cheaper than a Travel Inn on a weekday.' The *Maltshovel* pub nearby has a friendly atmosphere and serves 'pretty basic pub grub'. There are plenty of restaurants nearby. (*Avril Campbell, and others*)

6 bedrooms. 2 suitable for ♿. 3 miles NW of Bridgwater. Lounge/TV room, hall/breakfast room. No background music. 2-acre garden. Stream (coarse fishing). No smoking. No dogs. Amex, MasterCard, Visa accepted. B&B £35–£55 per person. 1-night bookings refused bank holiday weekends.

CANTERBURY Kent *See SHORTLIST* — Map 2:D5

****

Traveller's tale The room was sizeable and had a pleasant view, but it hadn't been thoroughly cleaned. When we decided to make coffee, we had first to wash the coffee cups. In the small bathroom, two floor tiles were unsecured, and the towel rail had been broken off and was lying on the floor. Towels and flannels were white round the edges but grey in the centre. (*Hotel in Dorset*)

****

CARTMEL Cumbria — Map 4: inset C2

Aynsome Manor
Cartmel
nr Grange-over-Sands
LA11 6HH

Tel 01539-536653
Fax 01539-536016
Email aynsomemanor@btconnect.com
Website www.aynsomemanorhotel.co.uk

César award in 1998

'Staying here is like coming home; we are greeted as old friends.' Praise again this year for this traditional Lakeland hotel which has been run by Christopher and Andrea Varley and his parents, Tony and Margaret, for over 25 years. Other comments: 'The high proportion of returning guests is confirmation that they are excellent hoteliers.' 'Christopher finds time to chat after dinner; Tony and Margaret are still around some of the time.' 'Full in mid-December: this says much about the hotel and the sensible pricing policy.' Standing between fells and the sea, in the Vale of Cartmel, *Aynsome* looks towards the Norman priory, meadowlands and woods. The bedrooms vary in size; some are suitable for a family, two are in a cottage with a lounge, across the cobbled courtyard. First-time visitors were 'very comfortable' in a smaller room at the top with 'a good view across rolling fields'. The dress code in the oak-panelled restaurant has been 'relaxed to smart and casual, less restrictive than jacket and tie'. Gordon Topp's daily-changing five-course dinner menu is 'of a high standard; family and waitresses charming'. 'An excellent place if you have dogs with you.' (*Christopher Beadle, CC Schofield, David Innes, and others*)

12 bedrooms. 2 in cottage (with lounge) across courtyard. ½ mile outside village. Closed 25/26 Dec, 2–28 Jan. Lunch served Sun only. Sun dinner for residents only. 2 lounges, bar, dining room. No background music. ½-acre garden. Unsuitable for ♿. No smoking. No children under 5 at dinner. No dogs in public rooms. Amex, MasterCard, Visa accepted. D,B&B £63–£94 per person. Set Sun lunch £16, dinner £23–£30. New Year breaks. 1-night bookings sometimes refused Sat, bank holidays. *V*

CASTLE COMBE Wiltshire — Map 2:D1

The Castle Inn
Castle Combe
Chippenham SN14 7HN

Tel 01249-783030
Fax 01249-782315
Email enquiries@castle-inn.info
Website www.castle-inn.info

In October 2006, Ann and Bill Cross bought this 'very pretty' inn in the market place of this much-photographed village. 'They run it well, Ann is a charming front-of-house, friendly, with just the right manner,' say visitors on a 'very agreeable' birthday outing in 2007. 'Cobbled together from several dwellings, some of them 12th-century', the building has 'fireside nooks, antiques and cosy corners, rambling corridors, different levels, low beams'. 'We were upgraded to a superior room. We slept well: the comfortable bed had cotton sheets and a duvet. The village is quiet at night. There is a small list of walks from the door.' Other rooms include one, 'spacious enough', with small doorway but high beamed ceiling, and another, 'richly draped in red and gold', and with a spa bath. In the elegant, green, candlelit dining room, the 'traditional English' dinner, eg, fillet of beef with mushroom cream sauce, cooked by Jamie Gemmel (who has stayed from the earlier regime), 'was beautifully cooked and came with plenty of vegetables, but our waiter, though efficient, slightly lacked warmth'. Bar meals include cod in beer batter; baguettes, etc. Breakfast, in the conservatory, includes 'good granary toast', smoked salmon with scrambled eggs. (*Karina Spero*)

11 bedrooms. Village centre. 7 miles NW of Chippenham. Closed 25 Dec. 2 lounges, bar, dining room; background music; breakfast room. Small courtyard garden. Unsuitable for ♿. No smoking. No dogs. Amex, MasterCard, Visa accepted. B&B [2007] £55–£125 per person. Full alc £25.

See also SHORTLIST

CHADDESLEY CORBETT Worcestershire Map 3:C5

Brockencote Hall
Chaddesley Corbett
nr Kidderminster DY10 4PY

Tel 01562-777876
Fax 01562-777872
Email info@brockencotehall.com
Website www.brockencotehall.com

'The friendliest hotel I've ever experienced,' says a fan (and regular *Guide* correspondent) in 2007 of Joseph and Alison Petitjean's luxury hotel. The late Victorian mansion stands in large landscaped grounds, with fine specimen trees, half-timbered Tudor dovecote, gatehouse and ornamental lake. One visitor reported a 'cool' welcome at a slack time, but there is otherwise praise for the service, mainly by 'Polish and French nationals in their twenties', and the 'good atmosphere'. 'The well-trained staff seem to enjoy their work.' 'We liked our bedroom, spacious and slightly eccentric.' 'Our superior room had a double-aspect view over the lawns. The four-poster bed was huge, and the bathroom had a shower cabinet and a good-sized bath.' The sitting rooms are 'very pretty'. Tables in the three-part restaurant are 'well spaced, each with a nice flower arrangement'. Didier Philipot has returned as head chef, and 'the food is sensational'. The *table d'hôte* dinner menu might include cream of lobster and langoustine bisque; supreme of corn-fed guineafowl with braised red cabbage. A six-course *dégustation* menu suggests a wine for each course, and there are separate menus for vegetarians and for children. (*Gordon Hands, and others*)

17 bedrooms. Some on ground floor, 1 suitable for ♿. 3 miles SE of Kidderminster. Restaurant closed Sat midday. Lift, ramp. Hall, 3 lounges, bar, conservatory, restaurant (3 rooms); soft background CDs; function facilities. 70-acre grounds: gardens, lake (fishing), croquet, tennis. Civil wedding licence. Smoking allowed in all bedrooms. No dogs. All major credit cards accepted. B&B £60–£120 per person; D,B&B £94.50–£154.50. Set dinner £36.50; full alc £55. Christmas/New Year packages. *V*

CHAGFORD Devon — Map 1:C4

Mill End Hotel

Sandy Park
nr Chagford TQ13 8JN

Tel 01647-432282
Fax 01647-433106
Email info@millendhotel.com
Website www.millendhotel.com

The River Teign flows by this white-walled former mill, which is being sympathetically modernised by owner Keith Green. A visitor this year praised the service and the food: 'The meal I had was as good as it gets.' There are large grounds to explore, and the park of Castle Drogo is adjacent. The lounges 'have a homely feel rather than a smart country house look, so the atmosphere is genuinely relaxing'. There are log fires on cold days. The bedrooms vary from a 'superb first-floor suite with large living room' to standard ones that face the road (there may be noise). Each of the three south-facing ground-floor rooms has a private patio. 'Our room was especially good, with masses of space and comfortable chairs.' But one visitor wrote that his bedroom 'needed new beds, and the television on the wall bracket should be consigned to the skip'. Mr Green says that refurbishment is ongoing. Non-residents and walkers frequent the bar, and the restaurant has a new chef, Christophe Ferraro, who specialises in 'modern French' dishes (eg, salmon fillet with a mussel and saffron broth). (*Andrew Wiltshire, BR, and others*)

14 bedrooms. 3 on ground floor. On A382, 2¼ miles NE of Chagford. 3 lounges, bar, restaurant. No background music. 15-acre grounds: river (fishing, bathing). No smoking. No children under 12 in restaurant at night. No dogs in public rooms. MasterCard, Visa accepted. B&B £95–£110 per person. Set dinner £35;

full alc £45. Christmas/New Year packages. 1-night bookings refused peak weekends. *V*

Parford Well NEW

Sandy Park
nr Chagford TQ13 8JW

Tel 01647-433353
Email tim@parfordwell.co.uk
Website www.parfordwell.co.uk

Tim Daniel, who for many years was manager and co-owner of the elegant *Number Sixteen*, London (see Shortlist), now runs this smart little B&B in a village in the Dartmoor national park (he lives in an adjoining small cottage). A *Guide* correspondent on his fifth visit wrote: 'Each time, something good gets better. It is all a simple concept, but beautifully done. Comfortable and tasteful.' Another returning visitor agrees: 'The most accommodating host.' Named after the village well, the house stands peacefully in a pretty walled garden overlooking meadows. It has a comfortable lounge with original paintings, fresh flowers, books and an open fire. 'No "Grand Hotel" offers such a varied breakfast, all cooked to order, nothing tinned, all fresh local produce.' It is normally served communally, round a farmhouse table, but guests wanting privacy may eat at a table for two across the hall, in a small room hung with luxurious drapes that once belonged to the Queen Mother. The 'immaculate' small bedrooms upstairs 'have everything you might possibly expect'. One has its bathroom across the hall. (*David Charlesworth, Keith Allison*)

3 bedrooms. 2 *en suite*, 1 with private bathroom. In hamlet 1 mile N of Chagford. Closed Christmas/New Year. Sitting room, 2 breakfast rooms. No background music. ¾-acre garden. Unsuitable for ♿. No smoking. No children under 8. No dogs. No credit cards. B&B £32.50–£50 per person. 1-night bookings sometimes refused in season.

CHELTENHAM Gloucestershire — Map 3:D5

Hotel Kandinsky

Bayshill Road, Montpellier
Cheltenham GL50 3AS

Tel 01242-527788
Fax 01242-226412
Email info@aliaskandinsky.com
Website www.aliashotels.com

In Cheltenham's fashionable Montpellier district, this listed white-fronted Regency mansion has a quirky decor, blending the classic with the contemporary. It is part of the small Alias group (see also Shortlist: *Hotel Barcelona*, Exeter, *Hotel Seattle*, Brighton). Maxine Silsby is now the manager. Readers like the young staff ('eager to please'), and the modern bedrooms (all have broadband Internet connection, and there is Wi-Fi access in the lobby). 'Our spacious room had a sparkling bathroom. First-class breakfast.' But a single was 'very small', with a poor outlook. The large bar has wooden floors, big sofas facing each other, lots of private areas. The 'enjoyable' *Café Paradiso* (open to non-residents; booking advised) is long and light, with Spanish chairs, polished wood tables close together, old wooden high stools, and a wood-fired pizza oven. 'Excellent lobster and salmon starter.' 'Delicious whole bream, baked in the oven and with a choice of dressings.' 'Decent, reasonably priced house wine.' Breakfast, which costs extra ('irritating as items mount up'), is buffet-led: 'Good yogurt, fruit, cheese, ham, bread and pastries.' The 1950s-style basement nightclub, *U-bahn*, attracts the local young. (*JH, GS, and others*)

48 bedrooms. Some on ground floor. ½ mile from centre. Free parking. Lift, ramps. Lounge, bar, restaurant, nightclub, cocktail bar; background music in public areas all day; free access to nearby gym and pool. No smoking. No dogs. All major credit cards accepted. Room [2007]: single £85, double £115, suite £140. Breakfast £8.95–£11.50. Full alc £35. Weekend D,B&B rates. Christmas/ New Year packages. 1-night bookings sometimes refused weekends.

Hotel on the Park

38 Evesham Road
Cheltenham GL52 2AH

Tel 01242-518898
Fax 01242-511526
Email stay@hotelonthepark.com
Website www.hotelonthepark.com

'Staff were unfailingly helpful, responding quickly and efficiently to any request,' says a visitor who this year stayed with her elderly mother at Darryl Gregory's elegant town house hotel. It stands opposite Pittville Park, near the centre of this Regency town. The public rooms have 'antiques, tasselled curtains, mirrors and ticking clocks and plenty of magazines'. The library and drawing room look through French windows over the courtyard garden, and the bar is thought 'particularly cosy'. Bedrooms are 'attractively furnished', and there are 'comfortable beds', but one reader found that 'water pressure and temperature in the ambitiously styled bathroom were variable'. Eight bathrooms have a spa bath. The road outside is busy, but front windows are double glazed. In the brasserie, *Parkers*, chef Wayne Sullivan serves modern dishes, eg, roasted belly of Gloucester Old Spot pork, chorizo risotto. The continental breakfast is thought 'somewhat bland', with packaged orange juice, 'flaccid toast, but delicious porridge'. Mr Gregory keeps a motor cruiser, available to guests, on the River Severn, six miles away.

12 bedrooms. On A435, 5 mins' walk from centre. Library, bar, brasserie; background music. Small courtyard garden. Unsuitable for ♿. No smoking. No children under 8. No dogs. All major credit cards accepted. Room: single £94.50–£108.50, double £129.50–£189.50, suite £159.50–£179.50. Breakfast £7.95–£11.95. Full alc £40.

See also SHORTLIST

CHESTER Cheshire — Map 3:A4

Green Bough
60 Hoole Road
Chester CH2 3NL

Tel 01244-326241
Fax 01244-326265
Email luxury@greenbough.co.uk
Website www.greenbough.co.uk

On a busy tree-lined street, Janice and Philip Martin's conversion of two Victorian town houses is a mile from Chester's historic centre (easily reached by bus). 'Unexpectedly sumptuous when you come in, but everyone was very friendly,' one couple wrote. Inspectors add: 'Welcome exemplary. A charming young receptionist explained everything in detail; the owner insisted on carrying our heavy suitcase.' Bedrooms vary. 'Our suite at the top faced the back and was quiet. It had a small sitting room, bedroom with medium-sized double bed, good bathroom. Large teddy on the bed, ducks in the bath. Free Wi-Fi. A card offered choice of pillows and type of bedding.' A 'large, light' deluxe room had 'antique brass bed, two armchairs, squashy sofa, luxurious fabrics'. There is a rooftop garden with water feature. Muzak plays all day in the lounge, where meal orders are taken. In the *Olive Tree* restaurant, Tim Seddon is head chef. 'One of the best dinners we've had in ages. Main courses, sea bass and monkfish, beautifully cooked, portions not too large.' Breakfast had 'a wonderful buffet of fruit compotes, salads, yogurt and comb honey. Cooked dishes OK, but orange juice not fresh.' (*S and JS, and others*)

15 bedrooms. 8 in lodge linked by 'feature bridge'. 1 mile from centre. Closed Christmas/New Year. Ramp. Lounge, champagne bar, 2 dining rooms; background music; banqueting room; theatre/conference room. Rooftop garden; small front garden. No smoking. No children under 13. Guide dogs only. All major credit cards accepted. B&B [2007] £87.50–£172.50 per person; D,B&B £95–£170. Set dinner £45. 1-night bookings refused during Chester races.

CHESTERFIELD Derbyshire Map 4:E4

Buckingham's Hotel NEW

85 Newbold Road, Newbold
Chesterfield S41 7PU
Tel 01246-201041
Fax 01246-550059
Email info@buckinghams-table.com
Website www.buckinghams-table.com

In a town famous for its church's twisted spire, Nick Buckingham (former head chef at *The Cavendish*, Baslow, *qv*) runs this unusual set-up with his wife, Tina, and children. Daughter Vicci is manager, son Will is co-chef. Two semi-detached Victorian town houses, in a residential area, have been painted dark green, and sympathetically converted into a small hotel with two restaurants. 'Warm welcome, attractive decor, well-stocked bar; our spacious bedroom was well equipped,' say inspectors. In *The Restaurant with One Table*, ten guests (a group or unconnected visitors) eat together off a 'surprise menu'. 'You give a list of likes and dislikes, and choose the level of meal, Bronze, Silver, Gold or Platinum' (the last one at £120 per person including wine). *Clowns* conservatory restaurant, open all day, has separate tables. The cooking ('spontaneous modern British') 'uses the best local ingredients'. Our inspectors ate 'very good' *amuse-gueule*; potato and thyme soup; venison roasted with pancetta. 'The meal was inventive. The atmosphere was fun, Nick whipped in and out of the kitchen, explaining the dishes. We could not fault the service. Portions are large.' There are 'stunning afternoon teas', award-winning breakfasts and Wi-Fi. And, says the brochure, 'children are more than welcomed'.

10 bedrooms. 1 mile NW of centre, on B6051. Limited parking. Closed Christmas/New Year. 2 lounges, bar, 2 restaurants; small conference facilities. No background music. Courtyard, garden. Only public rooms suitable for ♿. No smoking. Only guide dogs in public rooms. Amex, MasterCard, Visa accepted. B&B £50–£85 per person; D,B&B £75–£105. Set dinner £18.50–£120. *V*

CHICHESTER West Sussex *See SHORTLIST* Map 2:E3

****

Traveller's tale The hotel claims that there is wide choice on the menu, but the alternatives were roast pork, roast chicken or roast beef. When we asked for the wine list we were told: 'We have a bottle of Merlot.' It was the only red wine they had. (*Hotel in Middlesex*)

****

CHILGROVE West Sussex Map 2:E3

The Chilgrove White Horse
Chilgrove, nr Chichester
PO18 9HX

Tel 01243-535219
Fax 01243-535301
Email info@whitehorsechilgrove.co.uk
Website www.whitehorsechilgrove.co.uk

'Excellent hosts', Charles and Carin Burton, run their wisteria-clad 18th-century coaching inn as a restaurant-with-rooms with strong green credentials. 'A super place, with good staff,' says a visitor this year. The setting is splendid, in a prominent position on a winding country road, with the hills of the South Downs behind and heavily wooded countryside all around. The unpretentious bedrooms are in a modern extension at the rear. Each has its own entrance, allocated parking, and use of the secluded walled garden. There are now two 'champagne' rooms, 'large, with a good bathroom', which have a sofa, DVD, flat-screen TV and a fridge. Open log fires are in the large bar and in the restaurant lounge area. 'Delicious' modern dishes provided by chef Chris Richards include Chilgrove egg en cocotte, with wild mushrooms and truffle oil; Rother Valley organic lamb hotpot. The wine list, with 600 entries, 'is a joy'. Cooked breakfasts are available only for groups who book all the rooms and eat together. Other guests get a 'comprehensive' continental breakfast, brought to the room in a hamper. The Burtons have a Gold Award in the Green Tourism Business Scheme. (*Gordon Murray, and others*)

9 bedrooms. 1 suitable for ♿. 5 miles NW of Chichester. Closed Mon, New Year. Restaurant closed Sun night/Mon. Lounge area, bar area, restaurant (all only accessible during opening hours); background music; live piano Sat night. 1-acre grounds. No smoking. No dogs in restaurant/lounge area. MasterCard, Visa accepted. B&B [2007] £47.50–£95 per person. Full alc £45. 1-night stay Sat refused unless dining. Christmas package.

CHILLATON Devon Map 1:D3

Tor Cottage
Chillaton, nr Lifton
PL16 0JE

Tel 01822-860248
Fax 01822-860126
Email info@torcottage.co.uk
Website www.torcottage.co.uk

In large wooded grounds (ten more acres this year) in a secluded mid-Devon valley, Maureen Rowlatt's upmarket B&B is loved for its tranquillity and hospitality. 'In a class of its own for attention to detail, character, location and generosity of spirit,' says a visitor this year. 'Mrs Rowlatt greeted us warmly, gave us a drink while she explained the operation.' Guests are welcomed with a trug containing sparkling wine, home-made truffles and fresh fruit. Four bedrooms are in the garden; each has log fire, private terrace, fridge, CD-player. 'We were allocated Deco, a museum of Art Deco, with a cabinet full of collectibles to which many guests have contributed, and a splendid tiled fireplace. I couldn't fault any detail except perhaps poor reading lights, and smallish towels.' Laughing Waters is a bed-sitting room with Shaker furniture, its own gypsy caravan, a hammock and a barbecue. Breakfast, ordered the evening before, is taken in the conservatory or on a terrace. 'We asked for a modest portion of smoked salmon and scrambled eggs. I hate to think what a full portion must do to your figure.' Guests can swim in the outdoor pool until 11.30 am or at night (bring towels). (*HR*)

5 bedrooms. 4 in garden. ½ mile S of Chillaton. Open mid-Jan–mid-Dec. Do not arrive before 4 pm. Sitting room, large conservatory, breakfast room (background music). 28-acre grounds: 2-acre garden: heated swimming pool (40 by 15 ft), barbecue, stream, bridleway, walks. River, fishing ½ mile. Unsuitable for ♿. No smoking. No children under 14. Guide dogs only. MasterCard, Visa accepted. B&B (min. 2 nights) £70–£94 per person. Tray supper £24. Winter breaks (3 nights for 2); 7-night breaks.

CHIPPING CAMPDEN Gloucestershire — Map 3:D6

Cotswold House
The Square
Chipping Campden
GL55 6AN

Tel 01386-840330
Fax 01386-840310
Email reception@cotswoldhouse.com
Website www.cotswoldhouse.com

'As good as before; a fabulous hotel.' Visitors returning in 2007 still loved Ian and Christa Taylor's grand Regency house, on the square of this honey-stone Cotswold town. Its traditional facade fronts a striking modern interior: a magnificent central staircase spirals up to the roof; arched doors open on to the 'pretty, relaxing' paved rear garden with its fountain, roses, lavender and herbs. 'The Taylors are much in evidence, helpful and friendly as are the staff.' But one couple wrote of a 'cool' reception. The bedrooms, in the main building, the *Montrose House* wing and garden cottages, are 'chic, Italian-style dens, with deep, dark colours, huge, very comfortable bed, many stylish features'. 'Our junior suite was well appointed, lots of nice touches, coal-gas fire, wonderful bathroom.' Street-facing rooms can be noisy. Two restaurants: *Juliana's* has arched windows, modern paintings and a sophisticated menu; *Hicks'* serves a brasserie menu, snacks, breakfast, morning coffee, afternoon teas and a children's menu (the young are welcomed). John Sherry and Stewart

Lennox took over the kitchen in April 2007. 'Good breakfasts' include porridge with whisky and cream; scrambled egg with smoked salmon. *Cotswold House* and its sister, *Noel Arms*, were on the market as we went to press. (*Michael and Eithne Dandy, and others*)

29 bedrooms. Some in nearby buildings. Town centre. Lounge, bar, brasserie, restaurant, garden restaurant; 'modern' background music; conference/function facilities. 2-acre garden: terrace. Unsuitable for ♿. Civil wedding licence. No smoking. Dogs allowed in some bedrooms. Amex, MasterCard, Visa accepted. B&B £137.50–£262.50 per person; D,B&B £157.50–£272.50. Set dinner £49.50. Christmas/New Year packages. 1-night bookings refused Sat. *V*

CHITTLEHAMHOLT Devon — Map 1:C4

Highbullen Hotel

Chittlehamholt
Umberleigh EX37 9HD

Tel 01769-540561
Fax 01769-540492
Email info@highbullen.co.uk
Website www.highbullen.co.uk

The Neil family's 'hotel, golf and country club', on a huge estate in north Devon, offers an astonishing range of sporting pursuits, indoors and out. An 18-hole par 68 golf course winds its way round the grounds; there are four grass tennis courts, indoor bowls, aerobics, fishing, swimming (in three pools) and many other activities (see below). To repair any damage there is a fitness suite, health and beauty spa. *Guide* readers like the 'unspoilt views', 'friendly people', 'sheets and blankets, not duvets'. Colette Potter (née Neil) is the chef, and in the large restaurant the daily-changing three-course menu might include home-made cured salmon with pistachio dressing; roasted duck breast. The best bedrooms (some 'reached along numerous corridors and stairways') are in the original 19th-century Gothic mansion; many have good views. Most rooms are in cottages in the grounds: 'Basic but immaculate, and the comforts are there.' Breakfast, mainly self-service, has a large buffet (fruit, cereals, etc); cooked dishes cost extra. More reports, please.

40 bedrooms. 28 in cottages/converted farm buildings. Some on ground floor. ½ mile from village. Ramps. Lounge, library, 2 bars, restaurant; billiard room; games room; indoor 65-ft swimming pool, indoor bowls, steam room, sunbed, exercise room, table tennis, squash. 260-acre estate: woodland, garden, croquet, putting, 2 heated 15-ft swimming pools, 18-hole golf course, indoor/outdoor tennis; golf/tennis tuition; *Pavilion* sports complex: 65-ft swimming pool, beauty treatments, conference suite, dance suite; background music. 10 miles river fishing (ghillie available). Civil wedding licence. No smoking. No children under 8. No dogs. MasterCard, Visa accepted. B&B [2007] £63–£105 per person; D,B&B £83–£125. Bar lunches. Set dinner from £25; full alc £32. 1-night bookings sometimes refused.

CHRISTCHURCH Dorset *See SHORTLIST* Map 2:E2

CLIPSHAM Rutland Map 2:A3

Beech House & Olive Branch NEW

Main Street
Clipsham LE15 7SH

Tel 01780-410355
Fax 01780-410000
Email info@theolivebranchpub.com
Website www.theolivebranchpub.com

Opposite their *Michelin*-starred *Olive Branch* pub/restaurant in this village near Stamford, Sean Hope (chef) and Ben Jones, formerly of *Hambleton Hall* (*qv*), have opened some 'very attractive' bedrooms (say inspectors), in this honey-coloured Georgian house. Fronted by a lattice porch, it faces rolling fields. Its entrance hall is 'bright and cheerful': checked carpet on staircase, contemporary hunting prints. Bedrooms include Biscuit, Berry (ground floor), Apple, Aubergine (first floor), Chocolate (family room in annexe; also suitable for wheelchair users). Duvets on beds, but blankets and sheets available. 'Our room, Double Cream, had interesting antiques but a contemporary feel: bed with carved headboard; Victorian chairs and dressing table; Art Deco bedside lights (pretty but not practical). Stunning bathroom with two windows, claw-footed bath positioned so you get nice views while soaking, smart power shower.' The only public area is an upstairs landing with fridge, CDs, DVDs, magazines, books, local information. In the *Olive Branch* (stone-flagged and wooden floors, plain wooden tables, pews, open fire and 'rustic ambience'), the menu is 'interesting and good value'; the wine list 'short and amazingly reasonably priced'. 'Delicious bread; roast butternut soup; excellent char-grilled halibut, but fish and chips disappointed. Cheerful service by young local girls.' Breakfast, in the *Barn*, adjacent, includes fresh orange juice, boiled eggs with soldiers, smoothies, kippers.

6 bedrooms. 2 on ground floor. Family room (also suitable for ♿) in annexe. In village 7 miles NW of Stamford. Closed 26 Dec, 1 Jan. Ramps. Pub: dining room (background music: jazz/soul), breakfast room. Small front garden. No smoking. Dogs allowed in pub and ground-floor bedrooms (not unattended). MasterCard, Visa accepted. B&B [2007] £45–£150 per person. Full alc £37.75. 2-night breaks (10% reduction). 1-night bookings sometimes refused. *V*

Hotels do not pay to be included in the *Guide*.

COLWALL Worcestershire Map 3:D5

Colwall Park Hotel
Colwall, nr Malvern
WR13 6QG

Tel 01684-540000
Fax 01684-540847
Email hotel@colwall.com
Website www.colwall.com

'Very friendly and comfortable, with excellent cuisine,' writes a visitor this year to Iain and Sarah Nesbitt's traditional hotel. Built in 1905, the mock-Tudor building stands below the western slopes of the Malvern Hills (Elgar country). The bedrooms, redecorated this year, vary in size. Visitors on a 'good-value' gourmet break were upgraded to a 'huge room, with vast bed, sofa, chair and table, up-to-date glossy magazines; good-sized bathroom (shower over bath)'. A standard double 'had repro Edwardian furniture, large bed, lovely soft pillows'. Some bedrooms face the garden; some single rooms have only a shower; some attic rooms have limited head room. The *Lantern* bar, popular with locals, serves sandwiches, soups, and dishes like fish and chips; beef and mushroom pie. In the oak-panelled *Seasons* restaurant, James Garth's modern menu names the local suppliers, with emphasis on organic sources, and main courses include local venison with parsnip mash and juniper-scented red wine sauce. 'Faultless evening meals; home-baked breads sliced for you by a white-gloved waiter. All ingredients beautifully cooked, well presented.' Breakfast has a wide choice of continental options, and good cooked dishes. (*Ian Moore, and others*)

22 bedrooms. Halfway between Malvern and Ledbury on B4218. Train: Colwall. Ramp (bar and restaurant). 2 lounges (1 with TV), library, bar, restaurant (soft background blues/jazz at lunch and dinner); ballroom; business facilities. 2-acre garden: croquet, *boules*. Unsuitable for ♿. No smoking. No dogs: public rooms, most bedrooms. MasterCard, Visa accepted. B&B [2007] £60–£90 per person; D,B&B (min. 2 nights) £80–£120. Full alc £42.50. Gourmet breaks. Christmas/ New Year packages. 1-night bookings sometimes refused weekends. *V*

CONSTANTINE BAY Cornwall Map 1:D2

Treglos Hotel
Constantine Bay
Padstow PL28 8JH

Tel 01841-520727
Fax 01841-521163
Email stay@tregloshotel.com
Website www.tregloshotel.com

'An extremely enjoyable week; charming, efficient staff.' A returning visitor in 2007 endorses this traditional hotel. Set in landscaped gardens, it has fine views over the bay. The Barlow family has owned it for more than 40 years; Jim and Rose Barlow currently preside 'with skill'. There is a small indoor swimming pool and a spa. Fans love the old-fashioned values: early morning tea brought to the room (at a charge), nocturnal shoe cleaning, log fires. Chef Paul Becker's dinner menu has plenty of choice. 'No one should miss the shellfish bisque,' says a regular visitor. Main courses include roast pork with field mushrooms in thyme; chicken tikka masala. 'Wally, the *maitre d'*, rules the dining room in the most benevolent way.' The Barlows prefer men to wear jacket and tie in the evening, except during summer school holidays. The breakfast buffet has wide choice. Families are welcomed, but not children under seven in the restaurant after 6.30 pm. Bedrooms have light colour schemes. The garden has secluded sitting places and a children's play area. A wide sandy beach, popular with surfers, is ten minutes' walk away. The Barlows also own Merlin Golf and Country Club, ten minutes' drive. (*Juliet Sebag-Montefiore, Ian Dewey*)

42 bedrooms. Some on ground floor. 2 suitable for ♿. 3 miles W of Padstow. Train: Bodmin. Open 29 Feb–30 Nov. Lift, ramps. 2 lounges (pianist Mon and Thurs), bar, restaurant; children's den, snooker room; beauty treatments; indoor swimming pool (30 by 15 ft), whirlpool. 5-acre grounds: croquet, badminton, children's play area. Sandy beach 5 mins' walk. Golf club nearby. No smoking. No children under 7 in restaurant after 6.30 pm. No dogs in public rooms. MasterCard, Visa accepted. B&B [2007]: £57.10–£116.50 per person; D,B&B £72.60–£135. Set menu £28. Speciality weekends. ***V***

COOKHAM DEAN Berkshire — Map 2:D3

See SHORTLIST

CORSE LAWN Gloucestershire — Map 3:D5

Corse Lawn House

Corse Lawn GL19 4LZ

Tel 01452-780771
Fax 01452-780840
Email enquiries@corselawn.com
Website www.corselawn.com

César award in 2005

'All requests were met with a smile,' says a visitor this year to Baba Hine's red brick Queen Anne Grade II listed building. 'As good as ever' was another comment. Fronted by an ornamental pond (originally a coach wash) with ducks, it is set well back from the village green and a busy road. The bedrooms are liked: 'Like a spare room in someone's country house,' said an inspector. 'A useful information folder, no fussy notes about prohibitions, a small, quiet fridge with milk and water.'

Other guests add: 'Our ground-floor rooms were spacious, with well-appointed bathroom; plenty of space to relax.' Considerable redecoration has recently taken place. Mrs Hine has handed over the kitchen to Andrew Poole ('I love being out front after 30 years in the kitchen,' she says). His cooking is praised: 'I like their note that they use only sustainable fish: delicious gurnard; also excellent spinach tart and a wonderful crab mousse. No muzak, hurrah.' Nothing packaged at breakfast, which has 'delicious marmalade' and good cooked dishes. 'Smart casual' dress is required in the restaurant but jeans may be worn in the bistro, where light meals are available. Dogs are welcomed and may be exercised in adjacent fields. A small luxury spa is planned for spring 2008. (*Sara Price, Joanna Russell, and others*)

19 bedrooms. 5 on ground floor. 5 miles SW of Tewkesbury on B4211. Closed 24–26 Dec. Lounge, bar lounge, bistro/bar, restaurant; 2 conference/private dining rooms. No background music. 12-acre grounds: croquet, tennis, covered heated swimming pool (41 by 21 ft). Civil wedding licence. No smoking. All major credit cards accepted. B&B [2007] £72.50–£90 per person; D,B&B £97.50–£115. Set dinner £30.50; full alc £42.50. New Year package.

COVENTRY Warwickshire *See SHORTLIST* Map 2:B2

COWAN BRIDGE Lancashire Map 4:D2

Hipping Hall NEW

Cowan Bridge,
nr Kirkby Lonsdale LA6 2JJ

Tel 015242-71187
Email info@hippinghall.com
Website www.hippinghall.com

César award: Country hotel of the year

'The combination of hotel and restaurant both firing on all cylinders provides for a profoundly satisfying stay.' Inspectors in 2007 were greatly impressed by this conversion of a cluster of stone buildings in a village near Kirkby Lonsdale. 'Greeting by a pleasant young receptionist. Our large bedroom had white-painted walls and ceiling, no pictures, simple wooden bedside tables, big bed with duvet and quality bedlinen, flat-screen TV, CD-player; toiletries from the Royal Botanic Gardens at Kew. Absence of clutter; clean, neutral feel. Totally calm, despite slight traffic noise from nearby road. Tall sash windows overlooked the garden.' The sitting room, with 'large, comfortable sofas', paintings, patterned wallpaper, 'struck a more traditional note'. Meals are served in a 'spectacular' double-height 15th-century Great Hall, with beamed ceiling, minstrels' gallery, grand fireplace, big chandelier and halogen ceiling lights. 'A fitting setting for impressive food.' Chef Jason 'Bruno' Birkbeck's modern British dishes included ravioli of smoked salmon and langoustine; scallops, 'sweet and nutty', with cauliflower purée and caviar. 'Owner/manager Andrew Wildsmith took orders, dispensing advice, particularly on the interesting wine list. The German head waiter manages the dining room with efficiency and warmth.' Breakfast, 'too often an afterthought in British hotels', also supervised by the owner, had a 'fine choice of cooked dishes, leaf tea, fresh juices, rather good toast'.

9 bedrooms. 8 on ground floor. 2 miles SE of Kirkby Lonsdale, on A65. Closed 1–18 Jan. Ramps. Lounge, bar, restaurant; classical/modern background music. No smoking. No children under 12. Dogs allowed in Room 7 only. Amex, MasterCard, Visa accepted. B&B £72.50–£125 per person; D,B&B £97.50–£190. Full alc £45. Christmas package. 1-night bookings refused Sat.

CRANBROOK Kent — Map 2:E4

Cloth Hall Oast
Coursehorn Lane
Cranbrook TN17 3NR

Tel/Fax 01580-712220
Email clothhalloast@aol.com

'I have been taking guests now for 25 years, it's my life and I love it,' says Katherine Morgan, the 'ever-helpful' owner of this much-liked oast house in a lovely part of the Kentish Weald. 'A most attentive hostess; exceptionally high standards,' say fans. There are Persian rugs, 'beautiful porcelain and silverware and delicate paintings'. Sofas and armchairs face a deep carved stone fireplace in the elegant lounge where 'expanses of glass look over the garden'. Two bedrooms are in the oast house, the third is off a galleried landing. One room is triple-bedded. Bathrooms are 'state-of-the-art'. Mrs Morgan serves tea and cake to arriving visitors, and presides at the communal dinner. 'Relaxed evenings with imaginative home cooking.' No licence: bring your own wine. Mrs Morgan is a Cordon Bleu cook; dinners might include salmon en croûte; devilled lamb chops. 'Fine china, home-made jams and good coffee made breakfast a pleasure.' In the grounds are swimming pool ('heated – great!'), pergola and lily pond. The hostess is 'informative about local attractions' (Sissinghurst, Chartwell, Bodiam Castle, etc). (*JM, G and AE Crossley*)

3 bedrooms. 1 mile SE of Cranbrook. Closed Christmas. Sitting room, dining room. No background music. 5-acre garden: croquet, fishpond, heated 14 by 30-ft swimming pool. Unsuitable for ♿. No smoking. No dogs. No credit cards. B&B (*not VAT-rated*) £45–£60 per person. Evening meal £25. 1-night bookings sometimes refused Sat and bank holidays.

CROFT-ON-TEES Co. Durham — Map 4:C4

Clow Beck House
Monk End Farm
Croft-on-Tees
nr Darlington DL2 2SW

Tel 01325-721075
Fax 01325-720419
Email david@clowbeckhouse.co.uk
Website www.clowbeckhouse.co.uk

César award in 2007

'What a place! Peace and quiet; bedrooms with everything you need; you are greeted – and treated throughout – with friendly courtesy.' 'Five-star service at three-star prices.' Two of many enthusiastic reports on David and Heather Armstrong's unusual hotel. 'They have made a fine job of mixing B&B personality and hotel trimmings,' says another. The large, comfortable bedrooms are in stone-built outbuildings around a landscaped garden. Some have their own small garden. Free Wi-Fi is new this year. Decor is varied, sometimes flamboyant. 'My room, equipped for the disabled, had enough room to swing a cat, separate dressing room, towelling robes, coffee/tea, water, TV, CD-player (with discs).' 'Ours had sparkly chandeliers, carved wooden ceiling roses and bay window area like a proscenium arch.' The 'most attractive' large restaurant, on two levels, with beams, arched windows and tiled floor, leads to a terrace. David Armstrong serves 'good, huge rustic portions' of farmhouse food ('tasty soups; well-hung beef; delicious puddings and cheese'). 'Those with moderate appetite would do well to go for a starter and dessert, which will keep you going until it's time to tackle the huge breakfast.' Vegetarians are catered for. Children have their own menu. (*Stewart Lait, Conrad Barnard, Eric Hands*)

13 bedrooms. 12 in garden buildings. 1 suitable for ♿. 3 miles SE of Darlington, via unmade road (follow brown signs). Closed Christmas/New Year. Restaurant closed midday. Ramps. Lounge, restaurant (classical background music); small conference facilities. 2-acre grounds in 100-acre farm. No smoking. Guide dogs only. Amex, MasterCard, Visa accepted. B&B £65–£85 per person. Full alc £32–£37.

Traveller's tale Hotel staff hung around the small swimming pool, smoking. Many of them had a 'can't be bothered' attitude. When I asked where I could find garden chairs, they directed me to the back of a shed, where I found chairs covered in filth. Our room was large and light, but could have done with a revamp. Dead flies remained on the window sill throughout our visit. (*Hotel in Scotland*)

CROOKHAM Northumberland — Map 4:A3

The Coach House at Crookham
Crookham
Cornhill-on-Tweed
TD12 4TD

Tel 01890-820293
Fax 01890-820284
Email stay@coachhousecrookham.com
Website www.coachhousecrookham.com

'Very friendly' owners, Toby and Leona Rutter, run their listed 17th-century dower house, set back from the road near Flodden Field, with 'great dedication', say fans. They have completed a three-year refurbishment of the bedrooms; eight are *en suite* (the others each have a private bathroom). Most are in single-storey buildings linked by paved paths around a courtyard; several bathrooms have aids for disabled guests. The bigger rooms have large-screen TV and DVD/CD-player. Adjoining rooms are good for a family (children are welcomed, and so are dogs). 'My spacious room had fresh flowers, candles, views of fields and the Cheviot Hills.' The vaulted residents' lounge, with open fire, faces an orchard; drinks are taken here from an honesty bar before dinner at 7.30 pm, when generous portions of 'fresh, wholesome, tasty' food are served, eg, smoked sausage and pepperoni pancake; roast Aberdeen Angus with Yorkshire pudding. Breakfast 'is another happy experience' (a large selection of fruits, yogurt and cereals; 'the poached eggs easily passed my test'). Afternoon teas (free on the day of arrival) and drinks are taken in the former coach house, with its beamed ceiling and huge arched windows. (*V and AG, TL*)

11 bedrooms. 7 round courtyard. 3 suitable for ♿. On A697, 3 miles N of Milfield. Closed Christmas/New Year. Lounge, 2 dining rooms; terrace. No background music. Orchard. No smoking. No dogs: public rooms, main house bedrooms. MasterCard, Visa accepted. B&B £35–£48 per person. Set dinner £19.50.

CROSBY-ON-EDEN Cumbria — Map 4:B2

Crosby Lodge
High Crosby, Crosby-on-Eden
CA6 4QZ

Tel 01228-573618
Fax 01228-573428
Email enquiries@crosbylodge.co.uk
Website www.crosbylodge.co.uk

In partly wooded grounds overlooking parkland and the River Eden, this castellated, creeper-covered Grade II listed country house (1805) has been run for many years as a traditional hotel by Michael and Patricia Sedgwick. The chintzy decor is thought 'entirely appropriate to the feel of the place'. 'It lives up to your recommendation,' say visitors in 2007. 'Service was excellent and friendly. The food was good; care was given to a friend with special dietary requirements.' All the bedrooms are individually done; some face the park. 'Ours was comfortable, with stunning view; a bit old-fashioned (not unhappy with that),' said an earlier visitor. In the 'lovely' dining room (redecorated this year), fish is a speciality on the daily-changing four-course menu, eg, sea bream with lime and vegetable salsa. Breakfast has kippers, home-baked bread, home-made yogurt, silver teapots and bone china, and for lunch you could order haddock in beer batter. Fishing is available on the Eden. (*Clair and David Stevens, SM*)

11 bedrooms. 2 in stables (ramp), 1 on ground floor. 4½ miles NE of Carlisle, off A689. Open 12 Jan–24 Dec. Lounge/bar, restaurant; function facilities; background music on request. 4½-acre grounds: walled garden with gazebo. Civil wedding licence. No smoking. Dogs allowed in stable rooms, not in public rooms. Amex, MasterCard, Visa accepted. B&B £70–£95 per person; D,B&B £120–£145. Set dinner £40; full alc £65.

CROSTHWAITE Cumbria — Map 4: inset C2

The Punch Bowl Inn
Crosthwaite, Lyth Valley
LA8 8HR

Tel 01539-568237
Fax 01539-568875
Email info@the-punchbowl.co.uk
Website www.the-punchbowl.co.uk

In the quiet Lyth valley, this 300-year-old inn has been turned into a 'smartly informal hotel' by Paul Spencer and Stephanie Barton, owners of *The Drunken Duck Inn*, Barngates (*qv*). Jenny Sisson is now the manager. The welcome and the food were liked in 2007. The bedrooms, named after former vicars of Crosthwaite parish church, have original beams; there are large beds, flat-screen TVs. 'Our spacious, superior double room had a high ceiling, oversized sofa; subdued lighting from table lamps, adequate when supplemented by overhead spots; big bathroom with under-floor heating and claw-footed bath.' Complimentary tea and coffee can be delivered to the bedroom throughout the day. In the low-ceilinged restaurant, with smartly set tables, leather dining chairs, polished floorboards, chef Craig McMeekin serves a *carte* of 'hearty dishes with a modern twist', eg, slow-cooked shin of beef with mushroom gratin, red wine jus. The bar offers a 'good selection of brasserie dishes' in an informal atmosphere. There are two terraces for alfresco eating and drinking. Unusual breakfast dishes include potato and dill pancakes with quail's eggs and hollandaise sauce. 'Juice freshly squeezed; leaf tea.' The small lounge has deep leather sofas. The village post office is operated from Reception.

9 bedrooms. 5 miles W of Kendal, via A591. Lounge, 2 bar rooms, restaurant. No background music. 2 terraces. Unsuitable for ♿. No smoking. No dogs: restaurant, bedrooms. Amex, MasterCard, Visa accepted. B&B £55–£140 per person. Full alc £70–£90. Christmas/New Year packages.

CRUDWELL Wiltshire — Map 3:E5

The Rectory Hotel NEW

Crudwell, nr Malmesbury
SN16 9EP

Tel 01666-577194
Fax 01666-577853
Email info@therectoryhotel.com
Website www.therectoryhotel.com

New owners Julian Muggridge (antique dealer) and Jonathan Barry (ex-Hotel du Vin group) have given a 'contemporary feel' and a new name to this 16th-century ex-rectory (Peter Fairclough remains as chef). It stands in a Victorian walled garden by the church in a village near Malmesbury. Inspectors reported: 'A very pleasant place. Fine large hall/sitting room with soft chairs and magazines. A collection of ornamental glass well displayed in the high-ceilinged bar lounge, with its plastic side tables and glass-shelved alcoves. Our spacious bedroom had a miscellany of furniture but a brand-new king-size bed; sisal carpeting; a magnificent new bathroom.' The dining room, with the original 'lovely wooden panelling', faces a fish pond. The 'classic British' food was 'interesting, perfectly cooked. Surprising combinations of flavours. Slow-cooked beef in a horseradish sauce was rich and filling; tender calf's liver came with a first-class lyonnaise. Wine list rather expensive, but the Hollick Shiraz was a brilliant choice. At breakfast, the English platter was copious and tasty.' Meals are served bistro-style on bare wood tables. 'Pity about the paper napkins.' On a quiet Sunday night, the hotel 'was run fairly efficiently by the friendly young staff'.

12 bedrooms. 4 miles N of Malmesbury. Train: Kemble, 3 miles. Lounge, bar, dining room; background music. 3-acre garden: heated 65-ft swimming pool. Unsuitable for ♿. No smoking. No dogs in dining room. Amex, MasterCard, Visa accepted. B&B: double £105–£175, suite £135–£165. Full alc £32. Christmas package.

CUCKFIELD West Sussex *See SHORTLIST* Map 2:E4

DARLINGTON Co. Durham *See SHORTLIST* Map 4:C4

DARTMOUTH Devon Map 1:D4

Knocklayd
Redoubt Hill, Kingswear
Dartmouth TQ6 0DA

Tel/Fax 01803-752873
Email stay@knocklayd.com
Website www.knocklayd.com

'Strongly recommended for dog lovers', this small guest house stands at the highest point of Kingswear village. It has panoramic views over the estuary to Dartmouth, and up the river to Dittisham. The 'extremely hospitable' owner/managers, Susan and Jonathan Cardale, came to Kingswear from Culzean Castle in Ayrshire (where she managed the small hotel). They own an elderly Labrador, Jessie, and Molly, a 'woolly little hearing dog for the deaf' (retired). Visiting dogs can sleep in the 'doggie dormitory' (the utility room) or 'snuggle up to the Aga in the kitchen'. 'This is very much a home, not for those who prefer a sanitised atmosphere,' said the nominator. 'Our pretty and thoughtfully appointed room had wonderful views. Everything was stylish and of quality. The large double bed, extremely comfortable, was dressed with beautiful fabrics. Fluffy towels and hot water were abundant.' The 'five-star' breakfast, taken at a table with white linen and silverware, has 'delicious fruit, excellent coffee, full English, Vermont or continental, or a combination of the three'. Mrs Cardale, a Cordon Bleu cook, will provide an evening meal based on local fresh fish and meat. There is broadband Internet access. (*WA*)

3 bedrooms. 5 mins' walk from ferry to Dartmouth. Closed Christmas/New Year. Lounge, garden room, dining room. No background music. Garden. Rock beach 300 yds; sailing nearby. Unsuitable for ♿. No smoking. Children 'must be supervised'. MasterCard, Visa accepted. B&B [2007] £40–£50 per person. Set dinner £25–£30.

Nonsuch House
Church Hill, Kingswear
Dartmouth TQ6 0BX

Tel 01803-752829
Fax 01803-752357
Email enquiries@nonsuch-house.co.uk
Website www.nonsuch-house.co.uk

César award in 2000

'I have nothing but praise for it,' says a visitor to this Edwardian villa on the south-facing Kingswear side of the Dart estuary. It is run as an upmarket guest house by Kit and Penny Noble. They are 'perfect hosts', adds a report in 2007. 'Our second visit, even better than the first.' The informal approach is liked: 'No deposit required; a hand-written letter of confirmation.' Canary yellow walls, royal blue carpets, interesting ornaments and books enliven the building, and on fine days afternoon tea, with home-made cakes, is served under a parasol on the terrace, as boats go by. New this year: free Wi-Fi access for guests. Digital TV and CD-players were being introduced in the bedrooms as we went to press. Meals are served in a 'beautiful conservatory'. Breakfast has 'proper bread', fresh orange juice, home-made muesli. An 'excellent' dinner is available four nights a week; the blackboard menu depends on local produce, eg, scallops and bacon; Blackawton lamb with pistachio and Parmesan crust. Special needs are taken into account. No liquor licence – bring your own wine. When the dining room is closed, guests can take a ferry across the estuary to Dartmouth with its range of eating places (*Embankment* is recommended). (*Ilse Evans, Linda Lenahan*)

4 bedrooms. 5 mins' walk from ferry to Dartmouth. Dining room closed midday, and evenings of Tues, Wed and Sat. Ramps. Lounge, dining room/conservatory. No background music. ¼-acre garden: sun terrace. Rock beach 300 yds; sailing nearby; membership of local gym and spa. No smoking. No children under 10. No dogs. Diners, MasterCard, Visa accepted. B&B [2007] £47.50–£65 per person. Set dinner £30. 3-day off-season rates. Christmas/New Year packages. 1-night bookings sometimes refused weekends.

See also SHORTLIST

DEDHAM Essex *See SHORTLIST* — Map 2:C5

DERBY Derbyshire *See SHORTLIST* — Map 3:B6

Traveller's tale Our stay was a disaster. The first night we hardly slept owing to noise which was eventually identified as coming from a pump in the bar immediately below. A duty manager promised that 'the boss' would write to us shortly. Perhaps predictably, no such letter ever arrived. (*Hotel in Kent*)

DODDISCOMBSLEIGH Devon — Map 1:C4

The Nobody Inn
Doddiscombsleigh
nr Exeter EX6 7PS

Tel 01647-252394
Fax 01647-252978
Email info@nobodyinn.co.uk
Website www.nobodyinn.co.uk

In a remote Devon hamlet approached by narrow roads, Nick Borst-Smith's 16th-century inn is everyone's idea of what a traditional West Country inn should be, with the added advantage of a superb wine list. Managed by the owner's daughter, Clare Breading, it offers 'peaceful and comfortable accommodation, with a warm welcome', according to recent visitors. The food is consistently praised: 'The locally sourced ingredients, from cheese board to marmalade, were delicious.' The lounge has inglenook fireplaces, antique settles, carriage lanterns (no piped music or fruit machines). The bedrooms above the bar may be 'fairly basic', but housekeeping is 'immaculate'. The other rooms, in the annexe, *Town Barton*, were being redecorated in 2007, and their windows replaced. 'A flask of sherry was very welcome.' A continental breakfast is left in a fridge in *Town Barton*; an 'outstanding' cooked breakfast (£4 extra for *Town Barton* guests) is served at the inn. (*J and KO'M, and others*)

7 bedrooms. 3 (1 on ground floor) in *Town Barton* 150 yds. 6 miles SW of Exeter. Closed 25/26 Dec. Restaurant closed Sun night, Mon night. 2 bars, restaurant. No background music. 7-acre grounds: small garden, patio. Unsuitable for ♿. No smoking. No children under 14. No dogs. Amex, MasterCard, Visa accepted. B&B [2007] £25–£42.50 per person. Full alc £30.

DORCHESTER Dorset — Map 1:C6

The Casterbridge
49 High East Street
Dorchester DT1 1HU

Tel 01305-264043
Fax 01305-260884
Email reception@casterbridgehotel.co.uk
Website www.casterbridgehotel.co.uk

'The attention to small details' is praised this year at Stuart and Rita Turner's modest B&B hotel on the steep high street of Dorset's county town (model for Thomas Hardy's Casterbridge). Their family also owns *The Priory*, Wareham (*qv*). The welcome is friendly, the lounge area 'comfortable and spotlessly clean'. Street noise may be heard in four front bedrooms (no double glazing). 'When I mentioned that we had endured two dreadful nights of road noise, we were upgraded to a quiet room at the back. It was perhaps a little cluttered with old-fashioned furniture, but we like this.' There is good family accommodation, but some single rooms are tiny. Breakfast has a large buffet (cereals, muffins, fresh fruit of all kind, yogurt, etc), and 'top-quality bacon and sausages, good, yellow-yolked eggs'. 'Each day, our wish for hot toast for our marmalade was granted, a task which seems beyond the capabilities of many hotels.' No restaurant, but tea and coffee are available all day; guests may picnic ('cutlery and crockery provided') in the conservatory next to the breakfast room; and there are plenty of eating places nearby. Outings, guided walks and chauffeur-driven tours of local sights can be arranged. (*MJ Allsop, and others*)

15 bedrooms. 6 in annexe across courtyard. 3 on ground floor. On main street. Street parking close to hotel. 2 garages. Public car park nearby. Closed 24–26 Dec. Ramps. Lounge, bar/library, breakfast room, conservatory. No background music. Small patio garden. Smoking allowed in 1 bedroom. Guide dogs only. Amex, MasterCard accepted. B&B [2007] £49.50–£75 per person. 1-night bookings occasionally refused Sat in summer. *V*

DOVER Kent *See SHORTLIST* Map 2:D5

DULVERTON Somerset Map 1:B5

Ashwick House NEW

Ashwick, Dulverton
TA22 9QD

Tel 01398-323868
Email reservations@ashwickhouse.com
Website www.ashwickhouse.co.uk

A much-loved hotel on the southern edge of Exmoor returns to the *Guide* with 'engaging, enthusiastic' new owners (since January 2006), Bob and Barbara Clift; Dan Kings is their chef. In a 'beautiful moorland setting', this small Edwardian house stands in large grounds with a lake, mature trees and sweeping lawns. The Clifts have renovated, while keeping the Edwardian feel (original William Morris wallpaper and huge stained-glass windows in the 'splendid' galleried hall; wooden staircase and large landing). Visitors tell of 'such a warm welcome' (no formal Reception), 'comfortable lounge with nice sofas, oriental furniture and antiques', 'lovely, relaxed atmosphere'. Inspectors had a 'large, traditionally decorated bedroom with sitting area, overlooking manicured lawns' and, after 'superb canapés', an 'excellent dinner', including 'robust pheasant with pancetta, and pork tenderloin with mustard sauce'. Wines are fairly priced (many available by the glass). 'Breakfast included fresh orange juice, delicious fruit compote, good cooked dishes.' The dining room, decorated in white with touches of green, leads on to a panoramic terrace. In the garden there is a 'sculpture trail' of wood carvings from tree trunks. (*Zara Elliott, Anne McGhee, Mrs CJ South, and others*)

8 bedrooms. 3 miles NW of Dulverton. Reception hall, drawing room, library, dining room; background music. Terrace. 6-acre grounds: water gardens, woodland. Unsuitable for ♿. No smoking. No children under 10. Only guide dogs allowed indoors. MasterCard, Visa accepted. B&B [2007] £59–£90 per person. Full alc £25. Christmas/New Year packages. 3 nights for the price of 2 off-season. 1-night bookings sometimes refused weekends in season. *V*

DURHAM Co. Durham *See SHORTLIST* Map 4:B4

DUXFORD Cambridgeshire *See SHORTLIST* Map 2:C4

EAST GRINSTEAD West Sussex Map 2:D4

Gravetye Manor

Vowels Lane
East Grinstead RH19 4LJ

Tel 01342-810567
Fax 01342-810080
Email info@gravetyemanor.co.uk
Website www.gravetyemanor.co.uk

With an oak-panelled hall, drawing room and staircase, leaded windows, fires in public areas, antique furniture and the 'aroma of polish and potpourri', this is a classic country house hotel (Relais & Châteaux). The creeper-clad Elizabethan manor stands amid woodland in grounds (open only to hotel guests) designed by William Robinson, pioneer of the English natural garden. It is owned by Andrew Russell (manager) and Mark Raffan (head chef), who has a *Michelin* star for dishes like braised cheek of veal with roasted sweetbreads and cassoulet of beans with pancetta. There is a huge wine list. Bedrooms (the best are large) have fruit, magazines and books. Visitors tell of the 'personal touches, kindness and courtesy' and the 'genuine care and attention to detail'. The absence of background music is a bonus, so is the presence of Wi-Fi throughout (no charge). A good overnight stop before a flight from Gatwick. (*BWD, KS*)

18 bedrooms. 4 miles SW of East Grinstead. Restaurant closed Christmas night to non-residents. 3 lounges, bar, restaurant; private dining room. No background music. 30-acre grounds: gardens, croquet, trout lake (fishing). Only restaurant suitable for ♿. Civil wedding licence. No smoking. No children under 7, except babies. No dogs. Amex, MasterCard, Visa accepted. Room [2007]: single £110–£175, double £165–£225, suite £270–£335. Breakfast: continental £13, English alc. Set lunch £26, dinner £35; full alc £70. Off-season rates. New Year package. 1-night bookings refused Sat. *V*

EAST LAVANT West Sussex Map 2:E3

The Royal Oak
Pook Lane
East Lavant PO18 0AX

Tel 01243-527434
Email ro@thesussexpub.co.uk
Website www.thesussexpub.co.uk

'A lovely place to stay in all ways, position, accommodation, food and service,' says a visitor in 2007. 'Very good value.' Against a background of the South Downs, down a side road in an attractive small village, Nick and Lisa Sutherland's listed Georgian flint-stone inn has five modern bedrooms in a converted barn and cottage behind the restaurant; two 'serviced' two-bedroom, self-catering cottages opened this year. The bedrooms have 'pretty soft furnishings and nice touches': fresh flowers; flat-screen TV; CD- and DVD-player, discs and films. 'A soft but comfortable bed with big, soft pillows; excellent bathroom with underfloor heating and a strong shower.' Rooms in the barn have open beams. The restaurant, which has an *à la carte* menu (eg, twice-cooked confit of duck leg) supplemented by daily blackboard specials, is open seven days a week and is popular with locals and Chichester theatre-goers. 'Excellent food, good value.' Breakfast was in keeping, with melon, blueberries, banana and other fresh fruit. 'Cooked dishes well up to standard. Staff both efficient and friendly.' The front terrace is set with tables for dining alfresco, and has views of the countryside; a small garden is at the side. There is now a sister inn, *The Halfway Bridge*, at Petworth. (*Fredina Minshall, and others*)

5 bedrooms. 3 in adjacent barn and cottage. 2 self-catering cottages nearby. 2 miles N of Chichester. Bar/restaurant (background music). Terrace (outside meals), small garden. Unsuitable for ♿. No smoking. No dogs. Amex, MasterCard, Visa accepted. B&B [2007] £47.50–£80 per person. Full alc £35. Winter breaks. *V*

EASTBOURNE East Sussex *See SHORTLIST* Map 2:E4

> Hotels will often try to persuade you to stay for two nights at the weekend. Resist this pressure if you want to stay only one night.

EMSWORTH Hampshire — Map 2:E3

Restaurant 36 on the Quay
47 South Street
Emsworth PO10 7EG

Tel 01243-375592
Fax 01243-375593
Email 36@onthequay.plus.com
Website www.36onthequay.co.uk

On the quayside of an interesting little town, this attractive 17th-century building is run as a restaurant with rooms by its owners, Ramon (the chef) and Karen Farthing. A visitor this year whose arrival was clouded by a misunderstanding over a booking ('Karen ameliorated the situation with an apology and a half bottle of champagne') enjoyed a 'delicious' dinner. The restaurant has been refurbished this year; 'not a ruffle or lace in sight', says Mrs Farthing in response to an earlier *Guide* comment. The cooking ('modern British with a French influence') earns a *Michelin* star: 'We enjoyed our excellent meal; a little appetiser; fresh bread with seeds; foie gras with spiced apple Tatin; cannon of lamb with crispy sweetbreads. Good-sized table, good service.' Four bedrooms are above the restaurant. Nutmeg, though small, 'is tastefully decorated and furnished; nice touch: two large bottles of water'. Vanilla, pale yellow and cream, with low central beams, has a large sofa, 'comfortable, if narrow' bed, and view of the harbour. A 'superb' continental breakfast is served in the rooms or the reception area on the landing. 'Segments of pink grapefruit, peeled and sliced peaches; good coffee; hot brioche toast and croissants.' (*Carol Jackson, and others*)

5 bedrooms. 1 in cottage (with lounge) across road (can be let weekly). On harbour. Open late Jan–end Dec, except Christmas, Boxing Day, 1st week May. Restaurant closed Sun/Mon. Lounge area, bar area, restaurant (background music). Small patio. Only restaurant suitable for ♿. No smoking. Dogs by arrangement, in cottage only. MasterCard, Visa accepted. B&B £42.50–£70 per person. Set dinner £45.

EVERSHOT Dorset — Map 1:C6

Summer Lodge
9 Fore Street
Evershot DT2 0JR

Tel 01935-482000
Fax 01935-482040
Email summer@relaischateaux.com
Website www.summerlodgehotel.com

In a pretty Dorset village, this former dower house (designed in part by Thomas Hardy for the Earls of Ilchester) is run as a luxury hotel (Relais & Châteaux) by the Red Carnation group; Charles Lötter is the manager. Readers find the staff 'friendly and helpful'; 'names are remembered'. 'My favourite; pure perfection' is one comment. A visitor who has known

Summer Lodge for 30 years (mostly under the previous owners) said: 'Outstanding staff from all over the world. Welcome efficient. Log fires in the sitting rooms. Everything of high quality. In our bedroom a fire had been lit. Good bathroom. Good coat-hangers.' But some rooms are thought 'small for the price'. In the 'elegant dining room', which faces a walled garden, the 'excellent' chef, Steven Titmann, serves modern British dishes, eg, seared Cornish turbot with a braised ham and spring cabbage parcel. In the bedrooms are fine fabrics and CD/DVD-player. The spa has an 'excellent' swimming pool, aromatherapy and reflexology. Red Carnation also owns the less expensive *Acorn Inn* in the village, and the little local shop. A large deer park is nearby. (*EW, Jane Woollcott, and others*)

24 bedrooms. 9 in coach house and courtyard house. 4 in lane. Some on ground floor. 10 miles NW of Dorchester. Train: Yeovil/Dorchester (they will fetch). Ramps. Drawing room, lounge/bar (background music 11 am–12 pm), restaurant. Indoor swimming pool (25 by 13 ft). 4-acre grounds: garden; croquet, tennis. Civil wedding licence. Smoking allowed in 1 bedroom. No dogs: some bedrooms, drawing room, restaurant. All major credit cards accepted. B&B £105–£260 per person; D,B&B £155–£305. Full alc £70. Christmas/New Year packages. 1-night bookings refused weekends. *V*

EVESHAM Worcestershire — Map 3:D6

The Evesham Hotel
Cooper's Lane, off Waterside
Evesham
WR11 1DA

Tel 01386-765566
Fax 01386-765443
Freephone 0800-716969 (reservations only)
Email reception@eveshamhotel.com
Website www.eveshamhotel.com

César award in 1990

With themed bedrooms, 'fun things' for children to do, and a long-serving local staff, this quirky hotel has many fans, especially families. The owner, John Jenkinson, is a 'dominant presence', often dressed in red trousers, wearing 'ridiculous' ties, and proud of 'having the best loos in Britain'. Some guests find the joke mirrors in the downstairs cloakrooms 'tacky', 'but if you can cope with the eccentricity, your children will love it'. Mr Jenkinson's wife, Sue, designs the themed bedrooms: 'We were impressed by the research that went into the design of the Egyptian room,' say visitors this year, who appreciated the welcoming half bottle of wine and 'array of chilled drinks' (including fresh milk) in the bedroom fridge. Alice in Wonderland (a family suite) is among the beams at the top of the main house; South Pacific has a small aquarium under its basin. 'Our children had a really good time; they loved the swimming pool and the play area'; the garden has slides, a trampoline, etc. 'The highlight was the service we received at dinner; the house wine was excellent.' Lunch has a 50-dish buffet. Children are charged according to age and amount eaten. (*Frank G Millen, and others*)

40 bedrooms. 11 on ground floor. 2 suitable for ♿. 5 mins' walk from centre, across river. Parking. Closed 25–26 Dec. Lounges, bar, restaurant; function facilities; indoor swimming pool (15 by 36 ft). No background music. 2½-acre grounds: croquet, putting, swings, trampoline. Smoking allowed in 9 bedrooms. Only guide dogs allowed in public rooms. All major credit cards accepted. B&B: single £78–£91, double £129, suite £175. Full alc £34. New Year package. 1-night bookings sometimes refused weekends.

EXETER Devon — Map 1:C5

The Galley
41 Fore Street, Topsham
Exeter EX3 0HU

Tel 01392-876078
Fax 01392-876333
Email fish@galleyrestaurant.co.uk
Website www.galleyrestaurant.co.uk

Near the river and quay in Topsham, the historic port of Exeter, this quirky 'restaurant-and-spa-with-rooms' is co-owned by Paul Da-Costa-Greaves, a Master Chef of Great Britain, also 'a spiritual healer and alternative therapist', who runs his kitchen 'under the guidance of Zen'. 'The mix of informality, first-class service, cleanliness and excellent food is hard to beat,' says a regular guest. Another visitor thought 'the stay and the food were amazing; a healing session with Paul was lovely'. He and his partner, Mark Wright, offer jokey dinner menus: 'Teasing the palate' (eg, mango and prawns); 'Feeding the desire' (cumin-crusted gurnard on celeriac purée); 'Keeping the passion alive' (puddings with names like 'Take me', 'Seductress'). Local champagne is available by the glass. For lunch there is a *tapas* menu. The restaurant is decorated with ceramic fish, a huge blue octopus, fake seaweed. All bedrooms have river views, minibar, CD-player, etc. The Captain's Suite is in the main building, up steep stairs above the restaurant. The three other rooms are in a cottage nearby: these have exposed beams, slate floor, open log fire. Breakfast (including fruit, smoked salmon, yogurt) is left in the fridge in the room. There is complimentary broadband Internet access. (*HM Barnes, Urszula Zdunczyk*)

4 bedrooms. 3 in separate building. 2 miles from centre. Parking. Train: Exeter St Davids; bus. Closed Christmas/New Year. TV room, bar, restaurant ('easy listening' background music). 200-ft garden: spa, hot tub. Unsuitable for ♿. No smoking. No children under 12. Guide dogs only. MasterCard, Visa accepted. B&B £75–£125 per person. Set menus (2 courses) £28.50; full alc £45. *V*

St Olaves Hotel
Mary Arches Street
Exeter EX4 3AZ

Tel 01392-217736
Fax 01392-413054
Email info@olaves.co.uk
Website www.olaves.co.uk

Central, near cathedral: Grade I listed Georgian merchant's house in small street opposite Mary Arches car park. Owner is Carole Livingston, Sandra Murrin manages. New chef Rob Skuse serves 'modern European' dishes, with local ingredients, in bar and restaurant. 'Interesting building, friendly young staff, easy private parking.' 'Copious full breakfast,' say inspectors. Lounge, conservatory, bar/restaurant (background music at night). ½-acre walled garden. Civil wedding licence. No smoking. No dogs. MasterCard, Visa accepted. 14 bedrooms (some on ground floor): 'mine was a bit basic'; sound insulation may not always be perfect. B&B [2007] £47.50–£90 per person; D,B&B £67.50–£115. Set dinner £32.50; full alc £36.50. New Year package. *V*

See also SHORTLIST

EXFORD Somerset — Map 1:B4

The Crown
Exford
Exmoor National Park
TA24 7PP

Tel 01643-831554
Fax 01643-831665
Email info@crownhotelexmoor.co.uk
Website www.crownhotelexmoor.co.uk

'Warm feel; traditional atmosphere' at Chris Kirkbride, Sara and Dan Whittaker's sporting hotel (meeting place of local hunt) on green of picturesque village in Exmoor national park. 'Welcoming' public rooms have pictures of country pursuits. Large, rustic bar, popular with locals; cosy residents' bar. 'Expensive menu but competent cooking in restaurant; omnipresent muzak.' Tables and parasols in grounds; water garden; summer dining. 17 bedrooms: 'impressive, traditionally furnished; modern bathrooms'. Unsuitable for ♿. No smoking. No dogs in restaurant. MasterCard, Visa accepted. B&B £52.50–£67.50 per person; D,B&B £75–£90. Set menu £35. Christmas/New Year packages. More reports, please.

Italicised entries are for hotels on which we need more feedback – either because we are short of detailed or recent reports, or because we have had ambivalent or critical comments.

FALMOUTH Cornwall — Map 1:E2

The Rosemary NEW

22 Gyllyngvase Terrace
Falmouth TR11 4DL

Tel 01326-314669
Email therosemary@tiscali.co.uk
Website www.therosemary.co.uk

On a quiet residential road, a short walk from the centre and from a Blue Flag beach, Suzanne and Geoff Warring's white-walled, grey-roofed B&B is near the Coastal Path. 'Welcoming, clean and comfortable', it contains a collection of paintings by contemporary Cornish artists; there is Wi-Fi access throughout, a small bar, and a pretty south-facing garden with a sun deck. There are good sea views from here, the dining room and lounge. The Warrings, both Cornish, 'have extensive local knowledge' (excursions, eateries, etc) and 'offer excellent value for money'. There is a 'great' breakfast buffet, and the substantial, freshly cooked breakfasts are admired. 'You feel special,' says one fan. 'My request for blankets and sheets rather than duvet was immediately dealt with,' says another. 'Each bedroom is excellent,' adds another regular. For families there are adjoining rooms. (*Patricia Layzell, and others*)

10 bedrooms (4 allocated as 2-bedroom suites). 10 mins' walk from centre. Parking. Closed Nov–Jan. Lounge, bar, dining room. No background music. Small garden, sun deck. Unsuitable for ♿. No smoking. 'Well-behaved pets' by arrangement; not in dining room. MasterCard, Visa accepted. B&B [2007] £31–£41 per person; suite £108.50–£126 (for 2 adults and 2 children). 1-night bookings sometimes refused.

See also SHORTLIST

FARNHAM Dorset — Map 2:E1

The Museum Inn

Farnham, nr Blandford Forum
DT11 8DE

Tel 01725-516261
Fax 01725-516988
Email enquiries@museuminn.co.uk
Website www.museuminn.co.uk

César award in 2005

Built by 'the father of modern archaeology', General Augustus Lane Fox Pitt Rivers, to provide accommodation for his nearby museum (no longer open), this part-thatched 17th-century country pub is in a peaceful village on the Dorset/Wiltshire border. It has been given a bright, modern look by owners Mark Stephenson and Vicky Elliot, while retaining original features (inglenook fireplace, bread oven, flagstone floors). Meals are served at wooden tables in the bar (in three rooms) and, at weekends, in the pretty *Shed* restaurant (once the village hall). A new chef, Clive Jory, started in early 2007: we would welcome comments on the food. Main courses include venison loin with butternut squash mash, honey-glazed parsnips and sour cherry jus. The best bedrooms are in the main house: the General's Room has a four-poster, two balconies, a large model boat on a chest of drawers, big bathroom with two windows. Smaller, cheaper rooms are in the stables at the back. One couple were unhappy about maintenance and housekeeping in their spacious room, which 'detracted from an otherwise enjoyable visit'. Breakfast, with waitress service, has home-made preserves and good granary toast. Dogs are welcomed. Shooting parties are catered for in winter.

8 bedrooms. Some on ground floor. 4 in stable block. 7½ miles NE of Blandford Forum. Closed 25 Dec, evening of 31 Dec. Bar meals daily. Restaurant open Fri night/Sat/Sun midday. Ramps. Sitting room, bar (3 rooms), restaurant. No background music. Rear terrace, front garden. No smoking. No children under 8 as residents ('all ages welcome at lunch'). MasterCard, Visa accepted. B&B £47.50–£95 per person. Full alc £35. 10% service charge added to residents' meal costs. 1-night bookings sometimes refused weekends.

FAVERSHAM Kent — Map 2:D5

Read's

Macknade Manor
Canterbury Road
Faversham ME13 8XE

Tel 01795-535344
Fax 01795-591200
Email rona@reads.com
Website www.reads.com

César award in 2005

The 'lovely atmosphere and friendly, mainly young staff' are praised again this year at Rona and David Pitchford's 'consistently excellent' restaurant-with-rooms. She is front-of-house, he the *Michelin*-starred chef. The handsome Georgian manor house stands in immaculate gardens (lawns shaded by cedar, weeping willow and chestnut trees), near this historic market town. The walled kitchen garden provides herbs and vegetables for 'classic' seasonal dishes, eg, tortellini of ham hock and chives, pea cream sauce and mint oil. At least four vegetarian options are offered verbally each day. The menu is peppered with quotes, eg, 'Music with dinner is an insult to both the cook and the musician' (GK Chesterton). There are 'marvellous, soft upholstered chairs' in the candlelit restaurant. The 'fantastic' wine list includes some 'very expensive' bottles; but a 'Best Buys' section has many reasonably priced wines. 'Breakfast excellent too: you can have what you want.' The bedrooms are 'old-fashioned by design rather than default: rich, thick fabrics'. 'One of the most comfortable beds I've slept in.' Guests have access, on an honesty basis, to the Pantry, which has a fridge 'full of decent half bottles of wine', and tea/coffee-making kit. (*Tessa and Graham Spanton, and others*)

6 bedrooms. ½ mile SE of Faversham. Closed 25/26 Dec, 1st week Jan, 2 weeks Sept; restaurant open Tues–Sat. Sitting room/bar, restaurant; private dining room. No background music. 3-acre garden; terrace (outdoor dining). Unsuitable for ♿. Civil wedding licence. No smoking. No dogs. All major credit cards accepted. B&B £77.50–£185 per person; D,B&B £125–£230. Set lunch £23, dinner £48; full alc £57. Mid-week package.

FLEET Dorset — Map 1:D6

Moonfleet Manor

Fleet Road, Fleet
nr Weymouth DT3 4ED

Tel 01305-786948
Fax 01305-774395
Email info@moonfleetmanorhotel.co.uk
Website www.moonfleetmanorhotel.co.uk

'Excellent for families with small children', this sprawling Georgian manor house behind the Fleet lagoon and the Chesil Bank on the Dorset coast is part of von Essen's Luxury Family Hotels group. 'Our five-year-old daughter made loads of friends and enjoyed every minute,' says a returning visitor this year. 'The staff, mostly the same as last year, were particularly cheerful and friendly.' Lots of facilities for children of all ages: two indoor swimming pools, a den (where children can be left) with swings, slide, sandpit, etc; computer games, ping-pong, indoor tennis, supervised nursery, etc (see below). Some are in an 'extra-ordinarily large recreation building, very useful in rainy weather'. Strong currents rule out sea bathing, but there are good walks in either direction along the Coast Path. The large public rooms have a colonial feel. Bedrooms vary in size. Children sharing their parents' room stay free of charge; cots and Z-beds are available. There are special lunches for the young, and high tea at 5 pm. For adults, chef Tony Smith cooks modern dishes, eg, loin of venison with blackberries and carrots. Breakfast is a big buffet. (*GH*)

36 bedrooms. 6 in 2 annexes. 3 on ground floor. 7 miles W of Weymouth. Lift. 2 lounges with dispense bar, restaurant; meeting room; games room/nursery; disco; indoor 33-ft swimming pool, sauna, solarium, sunbed, aromatherapy; snooker. No background music. 5-acre grounds: children's play areas, tennis, bowls, squash, badminton, lagoon. Riding, golf, sailing nearby. No smoking. No dogs in public rooms. All major credit cards accepted. B&B [2007]: single £170, double £170–£260, suite £260–£310; D,B&B £80–£187.50 per person. Bar meals. Set menus £34; full alc £38. Christmas/New Year packages. 1-night bookings refused weekends, bank holidays.

FLETCHING East Sussex — Map 2:E4

The Griffin Inn

Fletching, nr Uckfield
TN22 3SS

Tel 01825-722890
Fax 01825-722810
Email info@thegriffininn.co.uk
Website www.thegriffininn.co.uk

In 'a beautiful setting, with fantastic views over the Downs' (although in the centre of a pretty village), the Pullan family's 'cosy' and popular 16th-century Grade II listed inn is liked for its 'oak-panelled warmth'. The 'charming' bedrooms have some unusual shapes; some are in the main building, others in a renovated coach house or the recently opened *Griffin House* next door. A room here was 'comfortable, with a king-size bed; the bathroom, though small, was pretty and functional'. Bar meals are generous, and Andrew Billings's cooking ('modern British with Mediterranean influences') in the restaurant is inventive, eg, fresh crab bruschetta with spring onion; local venison cobbler. The terrace has a wood-fired oven, where barbecues may be served. There is an 'unconventional but thoughtful' wine list. Home-made croissants appear at breakfast where service was 'variable': 'impressive and superbly cooked' for two mornings, 'very slow on our third morning; we might have been in a different hotel'. Children are welcomed: they can play in the large garden, and there is a 'healthy' children's menu. Four golf courses are nearby. (*Barbara Francis, and others*)

13 bedrooms. 4 in coach house, 5 in next-door house. 4 on ground floor. 3 miles NW of Uckfield. Closed 25 Dec. Restaurant closed Sun night (bar menu 7 pm–9 pm). 2 lounge bars (1 with TV), restaurant; live music at midday some Suns. No background music. Terrace. 1-acre garden. No smoking. Dogs allowed in bar only. All major credit cards accepted. B&B [2007] £47.50–£80 per person. Full alc £35–£36. 1-night bookings refused bank holidays. *V* (not Fri/Sat)

FOLKESTONE Kent *See SHORTLIST* — Map 2:E5

For details of the Voucher scheme see page 62.

FOWEY Cornwall **Map 1:D3**

Fowey Hall

Hanson Drive
Fowey PL23 1ET
Tel 01726-833866
Fax 01726-834100
Email info@foweyhall.com
Website www.luxuryfamilyhotels.com

Built for a Lord Mayor of London, this Victorian mansion stands in a large walled garden high above the Cornish sailing and fishing port. Part of the von Essen group's Luxury Family Hotels, it is managed by Nicolas Descotes. It is thought to have been the model for Kenneth Grahame's Toad Hall; some of the 'nicely furnished' bedrooms are named after characters in *The Wind in the Willows*. Parents may pack as many offspring as they can tolerate into their bedroom at no extra cost (they pay for meals only). There are baby-listening devices, and a baby-sitting service. Four rooms are interconnecting. Children under seven have a crèche; there is a games room, and lots of activities for older children. Adults can retreat to a child-free drawing room, and take dinner without children present in the wood-panelled main dining room, where the chef, Glynn Wellington, serves a monthly-changing menu (main courses like roast cod with garlic pomme purée, boudin noir and vanilla vermouth sauce). Families eat together in the *Palm Court* (soups, salads, seafood). More reports, please.

36 bedrooms. 8 in court annexe. Some on ground floor. 2 suitable for ♿. Top of town. Parking. Drawing room, library, billiard/meeting room, 2 restaurants (background music); crèche (supervised 10 am–6 pm), children's games room. 5-acre grounds: garden: covered heated swimming pool (42 by 16 ft), croquet, badminton, play area. Sea 10 mins' walk. Civil wedding licence. No smoking. No children under 12 in main restaurant. Dogs allowed in court rooms only, on lead in public rooms. Amex, MasterCard, Visa accepted. B&B [2007] £62.50–£170 per person. Set dinner £35. Off-season/last-minute offers (see website). Christmas/New Year packages. 1-night bookings sometimes refused weekends.

Old Quay House

28 Fore Street
Fowey PL23 1AQ
Tel 01726-833302
Fax 01726-833668
Email info@theoldquayhouse.com
Website www.theoldquayhouse.com

There are 'glorious views of harbour and estuary' from the rear terrace (where drinks, snacks and summer dinners are served) of Jane and Roy Carson's converted Victorian seamen's mission. 'An excellent little hotel,' says a visitor in 2007, 'but with a bit more attention to detail, it could be still better.' Inside, there is an 'eclectic collection of furnishings and ornaments' and 'lots of raffia'. Bedrooms are done in pale pastel shades. Seven have the estuary view. Some have a small balcony. 'Our room was spacious, light and comfortable, with two floor-to-ceiling corner windows facing the water, but soundproofing was inadequate and it lacked a coffee table.' There is an atmosphere of 'relaxed formality' in *Q*, the large restaurant with wooden floor, and white cloths and black napkins on dark brown tables. 'The raffia chairs were not comfortable, but the waiters were attentive and engaging.' Ben Bass serves cooking 'of a high standard'. 'First-class artichoke risotto and baked sea bass.' 'Breakfast has a good range of cereals and fruits, and the cooked menu was all that might be expected.' Thanks to Fowey's narrow streets, the nearest car park is at Caffa Mill, a short (flat) walk away. (*AW, and others*)

11 bedrooms. Central, on waterfront. Help given with parking. Open-plan lounge, bar, restaurant with seating area ('mellow' background music during meals). Waterside terrace. Unsuitable for ♿. Civil wedding licence. No smoking. No children under 12. No dogs. Amex, MasterCard, Visa accepted. B&B £62.50–£150 per person; D,B&B £92.50–£300. Set dinner £30; full alc £50. 1-night bookings refused weekends. Christmas/New Year packages. *V*

FRITTON Norfolk — Map 2:B6

Fritton House
Church Lane
Fritton NR31 9HA

Tel 01493-484008
Fax 01493-488355
Email frittonhouse@somerleyton.co.uk
Website www.frittonhouse.co.uk

On his family's Somerleyton estate, the Hon. Hugh Crossley has turned this 16th-century Grade II* listed inn, near a lake, into a contemporary hotel/restaurant. The setting (open farmland, mature trees, fields with sheep) 'is as attractive as the building', say visitors this year. 'Our bedroom, with double aspect, was beautifully furnished: comfortable king-size bed, modern, well-equipped bathroom. Strangely, no wardrobe, just three coat-hangers on a seat; we had to ask for a hairdryer.' Other guests wrote of a 'cheerful, lived-in feeling' and 'individual touches'; 'fresh flowers everywhere, interesting artwork; in the lounge, a large fireplace, comfy sofas, plentiful magazines and newspapers'. The manager, Sarah Winterton, is 'warmly welcoming'. In the cream-and-olive restaurant ('like a gastropub'), Alan Leech's cooking ('modern English with Eastern influences') is enjoyed by most visitors; comments on service vary from 'efficient' to 'unenthusiastic', and one guest's dinner was spoiled by 'noise of a football match from a large TV in the adjacent room'. 'Excellent breakfast.' 'There is plenty for children to do on the estate,' writes Hugh Crossley (it has a lake with rowing boats and pedalos) and the house is often busy with families. Somerleyton Hall and its gardens are open to the public. There are two Frittons in Norfolk: this one is on the Norfolk/Suffolk border.

9 bedrooms. 7 miles SW of Great Yarmouth, off A143. Train: Somerleyton. Lounge, bar, restaurant; private dining room; background music throughout, all day. 250-acre estate: formal gardens, lake, golf, walks. Unsuitable for ♿. Civil wedding licence. No smoking. No dogs in main restaurant. MasterCard, Visa accepted. B&B £70–£135 per person. Full alc £35. Christmas/New Year packages. *V*

FROGGATT EDGE Derbyshire — Map 3:A6

The Chequers Inn

Froggatt Edge
Hope Valley S32 3ZJ

Tel 01433-630231
Fax 01433-631072
Email info@chequers-froggatt.com
Website www.chequers-froggatt.com

'Great value', Jonathan and Joanne Tindall's 16th-century country inn stands below rugged Froggatt Edge (used for alpine training), amid some of the best scenery in the Peak District. 'We were welcomed in the afternoon when the pub was closed; the proprietor and staff were very helpful,' says a visitor this year. The bedrooms are simple, but thoughtfully furnished. One at the rear was 'quiet, well kept and cosy', with pine furniture, country-style decor; luxurious bathroom with roll-top bath. A front room had 'all the qualities we could want'; double-glazed windows, but 'noise from the main road was disturbing when we opened them on a hot summer night'. The food ('a cut above normal pub fare') is widely praised. Phil Ball's cooking is a 'mix between traditional and modern', eg, breast of duck with pumpkin mash; spiced beancake with tomato and coriander salad. Wines and dishes of the day are listed on blackboards; staff are 'smart, in black with dark green aprons'. Breakfast has a buffet followed by cooked dishes (including vegetarian sausages). 'Service first class; the owners are always around. An excellent place to stay as long as you don't expect hotel facilities such as a lounge.' (*Margaret Wall, HJ Martin Tucker, Gwyn Morgan*)

5 bedrooms. On A625, near Calver village. Closed 25 Dec. Bar, 2 eating areas; piped music everywhere all the time. Large garden, with seating. Unsuitable for ♿. No smoking. No dogs. Amex, MasterCard, Visa accepted. B&B £35–£47.50 per person. Full alc £34. 1-night bookings refused weekends.

GATESHEAD Tyne and Wear — Map 4:B4

Eslington Villa
8 Station Road, Low Fell
Gateshead NE9 6DR

Tel 0191-487 6017
Fax 0191-420 0667
Email home@eslingtonvilla.co.uk
Website www.eslingtonvilla.co.uk

'Within easy distance of the many attractions of the Gateshead area', Nick and Melanie Tulip's 19th-century villa (motto 'heritage with attitude') stands in a 'lovely', big garden (with rabbits), in a residential area. 'Excellent accommodation, friendly service,' says a visitor in 2007. Others 'loved the ambience and style'. Bedroom decor ranges from traditional, in the older part of the house (one room has a four-poster bed), to lighter, 'contemporary designer' in the extension. 'My room was plenty big enough.' In the airy restaurant, with its conservatory extension, chef Andy Moore serves a modern menu, eg, warm cured salmon with roasted tomatoes; lamb cooked two ways. The hotel attracts many diners, so the lounge gets full. 'Great food, if on the expensive side. Good smoked haddock risotto and tasty kippers for breakfast.' Wines are good value. 'Only disadvantage: the intrusive beat of the "music" at breakfast.' Seminars, private meetings and functions are often held. (*Tony Betts, Dorothy Brining, and others*)

18 bedrooms. 3, with separate entrance, on ground floor. 2 miles from centre. Closed 4 days at Christmas. Restaurant closed Sun night, bank holidays at midday. Ramp. Lounge/bar, conservatory, restaurant; background jazz throughout; conference/function facilities. 2-acre garden, patio. No smoking. No dogs. All major credit cards accepted. B&B £44.75–£79.50 per person. Set dinner £22; full alc £35. New Year package. *V*

GATWICK West Sussex *See SHORTLIST* — Map 2:D4

GILLINGHAM Dorset — Map 2:D1

Stock Hill House
Stock Hill
Gillingham SP8 5NR

Tel 01747-823626
Fax 01747-825628
Email reception@stockhillhouse.co.uk
Website www.stockhillhouse.co.uk

'We have not been swamped by the spa tidal wave that is washing over many similar establishments,' say Peter and Nita Hauser, owners of this small luxury hotel (refurbishment continues this year). They regularly win praise: 'We were very satisfied. Good staff, well trained.' 'Really excellent. Pampering without being pretentious.' The Victorian building sits in landscaped, tree-lined grounds with terraced lawns, herbaceous borders, a small lake (lots of wildlife). There are two guest lounges, one 'splendid and formal', the other 'cosy' with log fire. The bedrooms, with a mix of antiques and curios, 'differ tremendously in size and facilities; the rates reflect this'. 'Ours was spotless; excellent bed, plenty of room, two comfortable chairs.' In the dining room, 'tables are spaced to permit conversations with neighbours but far apart enough if you choose to be unsociable'. Food, wines and settings are of a high standard; 'attention to detail throughout.' Service is formal. Mrs Hauser is a solicitous hostess; her husband's cooking reflects his Austrian origins, 'especially the desserts' (eg, Malakoff Torte auf Beerensaft). Main courses include pork tenderloin with mustard seed, brandy and cream, Bohemian bread dumpling. 'Well-behaved children are welcome.' (*Anne and Denis Tate, Diane Moss, and others*)

8 bedrooms. 3 in coach house. On B3081, 1½ miles W of Gillingham. Closed Mon lunch. Ramp. 2 lounges, restaurant, breakfast room; private dining room. No background music. 11-acre grounds: tennis, croquet; small lake. Unsuitable for ♿. No smoking. No children under 7. No dogs (kennels nearby). MasterCard, Visa accepted. D,B&B £120–£165 per person. Set lunch £27, dinner £39. Christmas/New Year packages. 1-night bookings sometimes refused.

GITTISHAM Devon — Map 1:C5

Combe House
Gittisham
nr Honiton EX14 3AD

Tel 01404-540400
Fax 01404-46004
Email stay@thishotel.com
Website www.thishotel.com

César award in 2007

'Welcomed by the sight of a roaring fire rather than a reception desk, we felt at home from the start,' say visitors in 2007 to Ruth and Ken Hunt's extended Grade I listed Elizabethan manor house. It stands up a mile-long drive, in a vast estate where 'Arab horses prance in pastures'. The greeting is 'convivial': 'Ken and Ruth preside in an informal way; their staff are friendly, attentive.' Grand public rooms have carved oak panelling, antiques, fresh flowers, 18th-century portraits. Bedrooms have antiques and rich fabrics, and are serviced at night. 'Unpretentious rather than sumptuous,' said a reporter. One couple, unhappy with the grouting in their bathroom, were 'upgraded to the Linen Suite (the former laundry room), with huge lounge with original features, six-foot circular copper bath in the bathroom'. Another guest liked 'the extra touches; sofa, magazines, fruit, etc'. But a room at the back 'needed renovation'. The contemporary cooking of Hadleigh Barrett is generally liked: 'Top-quality local ingredients' (the producers are listed), but there might be 'a paucity of vegetables'. Breakfast, served until 10 am, has 'the best toast, from three types of home-baked bread, thickly cut and served hot when requested'. Children are welcomed. (*W Watkins, Michael and Maureen Heath, Robert Ribeiro, and others*)

16 bedrooms. 2 miles SW of Honiton; take A375 towards Sidmouth. Closed 2 weeks in Jan. Ramp. Sitting room, Great Hall, bar (classical background music), restaurant; private dining rooms. 10-acre garden in 3,500-acre estate. Helipad. Coast 9 miles. Only public rooms suitable for ♿. Civil wedding licence. No smoking. No dogs in some bedrooms. MasterCard, Visa accepted. B&B [2007] £84–£167.50 per person; D,B&B (min. 2 nights) £117.50–£207. Set menus £27–£42. Midweek and seasonal breaks. Christmas/New Year packages. Fri, Sat min. 2-night bookings most weekends.

GLASTONBURY Somerset *See SHORTLIST* Map 1:B6

GOLCAR West Yorkshire Map 4:E3

The Weavers Shed
Knowl Road, Golcar
Huddersfield HD7 4AN

Tel 01484-654284
Fax 01484-650980
Email info@weaversshed.co.uk
Website www.weaversshed.co.uk

In a converted 18th-century cloth-finishing mill, deep in a Pennine valley, this restaurant-with-rooms is run by chef/*patron* Stephen Jackson with his wife, the 'warmly welcoming' Tracy. They 'take immense pride in their work'. 'It takes real detective work to discover this haven of peace,' says a returning visitor. The slightly sombre stone exterior 'fails to convey the warmth and style to be found inside'. The bedrooms, each named after a local textile mill, are in the former mill-owner's house next door, above the restaurant's lounge (there is direct access from the main building). 'Plenty of free goodies, including a decanter of sherry, but why only one chair?' 'My large ground-floor room was in the shadow of a tree, but imaginatively lit with spotlights.' Stephen Jackson grows fruit, vegetables and herbs ('as organically as possible') in a kitchen garden in a neighbouring village. Eggs are supplied by the Jacksons' chickens and ducks. In the stone-floored, beamed dining room, 'food is of high quality;

tomato and duck egg custard; goat's cheese ravioli; local lamb, all perfectly (and promptly) served'. Breakfast included 'fresh juice, delicious scrambled egg and black pudding'. (*Robert Gower, Conrad Barnard, and others*)

5 bedrooms. 2 on ground floor. 4 miles SW of Huddersfield. Closed 2 weeks from Christmas. Restaurant closed Sat midday, Sun/Mon. Lounge/bar, restaurant; background jazz/light classical music; function/conference room. Garden. Unsuitable for ♿. No smoking. No dogs. All major credit cards accepted. B&B [2007] £45–£70 per person. Full alc £50.

GRANTHAM Lincolnshire *See SHORTLIST* Map 2:A3

GRASMERE Cumbria Map 4: inset C2

Rothay Garden Hotel NEW
Broadgate
Grasmere LA22 9RJ

Tel 015394-35334
Fax 015394-35723
Email stay@rothaygarden.com
Website www.rothaygarden.com

In a pretty riverside garden on the northern edge of this famous Lakeland village, this grey stone Victorian building is run by its 'accommodating owner', Christopher Carss. It has 'superb views' towards the fells. This year's comments: 'Our well-equipped bedroom opened on to the garden and the River Rothay. It had two large single beds, sofa, chocolates.' (Decor is traditional: patterned bedspreads and plain carpets; some rooms have a whirlpool bath.) 'Delightful, peaceful setting.' 'Ten out of ten for comfort.' 'Friendly staff.' 'An air of relaxed formality.' There is a 'cosy' cocktail bar with inglenook fireplace. In the candlelit conservatory restaurant, the chef, Andrew Burton, serves a four-course menu of 'well-presented' modern dishes, eg, pan-fried pollock with tomato and cheese crust and chive cream sauce. The price includes coffee, mints and fudge. In summer, white tables and chairs stand under parasols on the lawn. Guests have free access to a nearby leisure centre. Wordsworth's house, Dove Cottage, and Beatrix Potter's home at Near Sawrey are close by. (*Eileen Ward, Peter Warburton, and others*)

25 bedrooms. Some on ground floor. 1 for ♿ planned for 2008. On A591 on N edge of village. 2 lounges, bar, restaurant. No background music. 2-acre garden on river. Access to nearby leisure centre. No smoking. No children under 5 in restaurant at night. No dogs in public rooms. MasterCard, Visa accepted. B&B £50–£95 per person; D,B&B £75–£115. Set dinner £35. Special breaks all year. Christmas/New Year packages. 1-night bookings sometimes refused.

White Moss House
Rydal Water
Grasmere LA22 9SE

Tel 015394-35295
Fax 015394-35516
Email sue@whitemoss.com
Website www.whitemoss.com

Significant changes this year at Peter and Sue Dixon's much-liked grey stone creeper-covered house at the north end of Rydal Water. 'After 28 years of never having a day off; we are a two-person business', they have closed their restaurant (except for 'special weekends') and will offer room and breakfast only. 'We love *White Moss* and have no wish to sell,' they say. There are 'plenty of places to eat nearby'. House parties can also include dinner by arrangement. Drinks and wines are available; also advice on walks and information on Lakeland. 'The pose factor was zero; refreshing these days,' say regular correspondents. 'A very pleasant atmosphere.' The house was once bought by William Wordsworth for his son, Willie; you can trace the poet's steps around the lakes by following marked footpaths from the front door. A busy road is near but windows are double glazed, and there is little traffic at night. Two peaceful bedrooms are in *Brockstone*, the cottage up the hill. In the main house, the small bedrooms have a tiny bathroom and many extras (herbal bathsalts, fresh flowers, books, etc). Breakfast includes kippers and Cumberland sausages. (*Stephen and Pauline Glover*)

7 bedrooms. 2 in cottage (10 mins' drive or footpath). 1 mile S of Grasmere on A591. Open Feb–Nov. Lounge, restaurant; terrace. 1-acre garden/woodland. Unsuitable for ♿. No smoking. Dogs allowed in cottage. MasterCard, Visa accepted. B&B [2007] £39–£69 per person. Special breaks. 1-night bookings refused Sat at busy times. ***V***

GREAT BIRCHAM Norfolk *See SHORTLIST* Map 2:A5

GREAT CHESTERFORD Essex *See SHORTLIST* Map 2:C4

When you make a booking you enter into a contract with a hotel. Most hotels explain their cancellation policies, which vary widely, in a letter of confirmation. You may lose your deposit or be charged at the full rate for the room if you cancel at short notice. A travel insurance policy can provide protection.

GREAT DUNMOW Essex — Map 2:C4

Starr Restaurant with Rooms
Market Place
Great Dunmow
CM6 1AX

Tel 01371-874321
Fax 01371-876337
Email starrrestaurant@btinternet.com
Website www.the-starr.co.uk

On the market place of this little Essex town, this timber-framed 15th-century former inn is run by owners Terence and Louise George with a 'helpful European staff', says an inspector this year. 'The welcome was warm; luggage carried.' Inside all is 'smart and colourful'. The yellow-painted restaurant is in two parts, one with old beams stripped blond, the other in a bright conservatory extension. Neat bedrooms are in a converted stable block in the rear courtyard: 'Mine had green-patterned carpet, orangey checked bedspread, smart bathroom with a large bath and separate shower cubicle.' The best room has a four-poster bed and a freestanding Victorian bath. The Pine Room has 'his and hers hand basins set in marble – ideal for a romantic evening'. Chef Mark Pearson serves 'traditional/modern English dishes with a French accent', eg, canon of lamb and roasted kidneys with carrot purée and mustard velouté. 'Good, and well served, if pricey. Good choice of wines by the glass. Peaceful atmosphere (no muzak).' Breakfast includes freshly squeezed orange juice, fruit, a fry-up, 'good croissants'. A busy road runs alongside 'but it was quiet at night'. Stansted airport is 15 minutes' drive away.

8 bedrooms. In stable block. 2 on ground floor. Central (some traffic noise). Parking. Open 5 Jan–25 Dec. Restaurant closed Sun night. Bar/lounge, restaurant; 2 private dining rooms. No background music. Unsuitable for ♿. No smoking. No dogs. Diners, MasterCard, Visa accepted. All major credit cards accepted. B&B £60–£80 per person; D,B&B £92.50–£105. Set dinner £45. *V*

GREAT LANGDALE Cumbria — Map 4: inset C2

Old Dungeon Ghyll
Great Langdale
nr Ambleside LA22 9JY

Tel/Fax 015394 37272
Email olddungeonghyll1@btconnect.com
Website www.odg.co.uk

Remotely set in 'glorious scenery' at the head of Great Langdale valley, on the approach to Scafell Pike, this 300-year-old mountain hotel is owned by the National Trust. Neil and Jane Walmsley have run it since 1984, welcoming fell walkers, climbers and cyclists. They provide 'good value', a 'friendly welcome' and 'decent grub'. Fans love the unpretentiousness, the lack of TV and the absence of a mobile telephone signal (there is a payphone in the hall). The bedrooms, though modernised, retain 19th-century features (not all have facilities *en suite*). Carpets and wallpaper have a '1980s feel'. 'Our family room had a grand view through two windows, but rather old furniture. Shower and loo down the corridor.' Children are welcomed (they have their own menu). The 'light and airy' lounge has chintzy decor, a dresser with blue-and-white plates, board games, and an open fire in winter. The food is traditional English (steaks, etc). There is a quiet residents' bar. The public *Hikers' Bar* is lively on Saturday nights (a National Trust campsite is half a mile away): it serves 'a great range of beers', soups, sandwiches, sausages, etc; guests sit in old cattle stalls, or at tables in a courtyard.

13 bedrooms. NW of Ambleside by B5343. Closed 21–27 Dec. Residents' lounge, residents' bar, public bar (folk music 1st Wed of month, and 'when it happens'), dining room; drying room. No background music. Small garden. Unsuitable for ♿. No smoking. Amex, MasterCard, Visa accepted. B&B [2007] £50–£55 per person; D,B&B £70–£75. Set dinner £23. 1-night bookings refused weekends.

GREAT MILTON Oxfordshire — Map 2:C3

Le Manoir aux Quat'Saisons

Church Road
Great Milton OX44 7PD

Tel 01844-278881
Fax 01844-278847
Email lemanoir@blanc.co.uk
Website www.manoir.com

César award in 1985

'Luxury at a price' is provided at Raymond Blanc's famous *domaine* (Relais & Châteaux), co-owned with Orient Express Hotels. Readers recommend it for an 'occasional treat – well worth while'. The welcome begins in the car park, where a porter takes the car, and delivers luggage to the room. Many bedrooms are in garden buildings: 'Ours, Silk, traditionally decorated, had a four-poster bed, small patio with table and chairs; bowl of fruit and Madeira. The spacious bathroom had "his and hers" basins.' A room in the main house was 'beautifully furnished in the style of the building; two easy chairs *and* a settee made it relaxing'. In the famous conservatory restaurant (two *Michelin* stars), M. Blanc has restructured his menus. You can choose between a short *carte* (three choices for each course), a lunchtime *menu du jour* ('most enjoyable'), a five-course *Les Classiques* of 'best-loved' dishes, or a ten-course *menu découverte.* 'We enjoyed the *carte*: memorable starter of ceviche of sea scallops and tuna with shaved fennel salad; melt-in-the-mouth milk-fed Pyrenean lamb. Superb fresh-baked breads at dinner and breakfast.' 'The setting is peaceful', and the grounds, with 17th-century pond and organic kitchen garden, are 'beautifully designed'. (*John and Jane Holland, and others*)

32 bedrooms. 23 in garden buildings. Some on ground floor. 8 miles SE of Oxford. 2 lounges, champagne bar; 'relaxing' background music all day; restaurant; private dining room; cookery school. 27-acre grounds: gardens, croquet, lake. Civil wedding licence. Smoking allowed in all bedrooms. No dogs in house (free kennels). All major credit cards accepted. B&B ('French breakfast') [2007]: double £380–£645, suite £620–£940. Cooked breakfast £25. Set lunch £45, *Les Classiques* £95, *menu découverte* £110; full alc £110. Midweek breaks; residential cookery courses. Christmas/New Year packages.

GULWORTHY Devon — Map 1:D3

The Horn of Plenty

Gulworthy
nr Tavistock PL19 8JD

Tel 01822-832528
Fax 01822-834390
Email enquiries@thehornofplenty.co.uk
Website www.thehornofplenty.co.uk

Amid gardens and orchards in a 'beautiful area' near Tavistock, this wisteria-covered stone Georgian house has 'stunning views' of the Tamar valley. A 'lovely, friendly' place (a recent comment), it is run as a restaurant-with-rooms by the chef, Peter Gorton ('one of Devon's finest'), who owns it with Paul and Andie Roston. In the L-shaped restaurant, refurbished this year, he serves international dishes, eg, brill with creamy jasmine rice, coriander broth; venison with spiced pear, gratin potatoes and a port sauce. On Monday evening there is a shorter, reduced-price 'Pot Luck' menu. There are lots of fresh flowers, and a log fire in the drawing room. The most expensive bedrooms are in the main house. Others, each with a balcony (where breakfast can be served) and a small bathroom, are in a converted coach house. Cookery courses and weddings are held. (*A and DT*)

10 bedrooms. 6 in stables (20 yds). 4 on ground floor. 3 miles SW of Tavistock. Closed 24–26 Dec. Restaurant closed Mon midday. Drawing room, lounge/restaurant (classical background music); library/private dining/meeting room. 5-acre grounds. Civil wedding licence. No smoking. No children under 7 at dinner. Dogs allowed in garden rooms only; not in public rooms. Amex, MasterCard, Visa accepted. B&B £80–£265 per person. Set lunch £26.50, dinner £45. New Year package. *V*

All our inspections are paid for, and carried out anonymously.

HALNAKER West Sussex — Map 2:E3

The Old Store

Stane Street, Halnaker, nr Chichester
PO18 0QL

Tel 01243-531977
Email theoldstore4@aol.com
Website www.theoldstoreguesthouse.com

'Strongly endorsed' in 2007, by visitors who used the *Guide* to find a B&B near Chichester, this unpretentious guest house adjoins the Goodwood estate. The owners, Patrick and Heather Birchenough, are 'model hosts and a delight to talk to (he lent us his OS map)'. The 18th-century Grade II listed red brick and flint house was once the village store and bakery. Inside are beamed ceilings, and a small lounge and breakfast room downstairs. Some bedrooms look across fields to Chichester cathedral, some are suitable for a family. 'Mine, attractive, spotless, had mineral water, tea-maker, fresh milk in Thermos flask, biscuits and chocolate.' A 'perfect' breakfast had 'hot toast served in folded linen', free-range eggs, local sausages, etc. The Birchenoughs are 'helpful about places to eat and details of walks'; they offer a laundry service and will make a packed lunch. A half-hourly bus service to Chichester passes the door. 'Traffic begins early on the busy road.' Plenty of interesting sightseeing: Arundel, Petworth, Uppark, Fishbourne Roman palace, etc, and a footpath leads to walks through woods to the South Downs. The village name is pronounced 'Hannaka'. (*Colonel AJW and Mrs HM Harvey, and others*)

7 bedrooms. 1 on ground floor. 4 miles NE of Chichester. Open Mar–Dec; closed Christmas. Lounge, breakfast room. No background music. ¼-acre garden, with seating. Unsuitable for ♿. No smoking. Guide dogs only. MasterCard, Visa accepted. B&B [2007] £32.50–£45 per person (higher for Goodwood 'Festival of Speed' and 'Revival' meetings). 1-night bookings sometimes refused weekends.

HAMBLETON Rutland — Map 2:B3

Hambleton Hall

Hambleton
Oakham LE15 8TH

Tel 01572-756991
Fax 01572-724721
Email hotel@hambletonhall.com
Website www.hambletonhall.com

César award in 1985

'Wonderful, exceptionally well run. We loved it.' Praise in 2007 from trusted *Guide* reporters for Tim and Stefa Hart's Victorian mansion, 'memorably set' on a peninsula jutting into Rutland Water. Returning visitors, 'welcomed like long-lost friends', were 'intoxicated as ever by the setting and old-world charm'. Stefa Hart designed the classic interiors (fine fabrics, antiques, good paintings, open fires) with Nina Campbell. Four bedrooms, and the drawing room, have been refurbished 'with an identifiable *Hambleton* look'. The best bedrooms face Rutland Water (seen through a screen of mature trees). The Croquet Pavilion suite is good for a family: one couple commented on the 'enlightened attitude to children'. Some rooms are smaller. 'Our Blue room had great views over the gardens.' The seasonal cooking of Aaron Patterson (*Michelin* star) 'is a highlight; beautifully balanced portions; intense flavour'. 'Elegant cooking with a liking for "assiettes" (we encountered one of tomato, one of beetroot), foams and the like. Restaurant service first class.' Continental breakfast, included in the price, is 'generous: a cornucopia of fruits and cereals; hot toast and croissants just when you want them'. 'Just one disappointment: an anonymous farewell.' Tim Hart also owns *Hart's Hotel*, Nottingham (*qv*). (*David and Kate Wooff, M Sachak-Patwa*)

17 bedrooms. One 2-bedroomed suite in pavilion. 3 miles SE of Oakham. Train: Peterborough/Kettering/Oakham (branch line); helipad. Lift, ramps. Hall, drawing room, 2 bars, restaurant; 2 private dining rooms; small conference facilities. No background music. 17-acre grounds: swimming pool (heated May–Sept), tennis, cycling; lake: fishing, windsurfing, sailing. Civil wedding licence. No smoking. Only children 'of a grown-up age' in restaurant, except at breakfast. No dogs: public rooms; unattended in bedrooms. All major credit cards accepted. B&B £100–£300 per person. English breakfast £14.50. Set menus £40–£50; full alc £100. Winter rates. Christmas/New Year packages. 1-night bookings refused Sat.

HAROME North Yorkshire — Map 4:D4

The Star Inn
Harome, nr Helmsley
YO62 5JE

Tel 01439-770397
Fax 01439-771833
Email starinn@btopenworld.com
Website www.thestaratharome.co.uk

César award in 2004

A gastropub with 'separate accommodation in various forms', this medieval cruck-framed longhouse has a *Michelin* star for 'modern original cooking heavy with Yorkshire influences'. It is served in the low-ceilinged, 'atmospheric', if dark, bar and the 'elegant' small dining room (tables close together). Typical dishes: deep-fried Scarborough woof with scallops; a celebration of Yorkshire rhubarb. Coffee is taken in the beamed loft. In warm weather, meals are served in the garden, fragrant with herbs and lavender. 'The food is delicious, and the owners [Andrew and Jacquie Pern] are charming,' says a visitor in 2007, 'but it can get very crowded.' The bedrooms are in *Cross House Lodge*, opposite, a converted stone farm building, and *Black Eagle Cottage*, a few minutes' walk away. A three-bedroom detached farmhouse, five minutes' walk from the inn, has been added this year. All rooms have TV, CD- and DVD-player, home-made biscuits, fruit, fudge. Room 1 has a shower for two, Room 2 a spa bath. Decor is 'a mix of rustic and modern'. 'Our large beamed room had a big bed and a full-size snooker table.' Continental breakfast is served in the bedroom or round a huge table in the *Wheelhouse*. Andrew Pern also serves light lunches and snacks in his restaurant in the walled garden at nearby Scampston Hall. (*JR, P and LB, WKW*)

14 bedrooms. 8 in *Cross House Lodge* opposite, others in separate buildings. 3 on ground floor. Village centre. Closed 25/26 Dec, 1 Jan. Restaurant closed Mon. 2 lounges, coffee loft, bar, breakfast room, restaurant; private dining room; varied background music. 2-acre garden: small heated swimming pool. Civil wedding licence. No smoking. No dogs. MasterCard, Visa accepted. B&B £70–£115 per person. Full alc £55.

The Pheasant NEW

Harome, nr Helmsley
YO62 5JG

Tel 01439-771241
Fax 01439-771744
Email reservations@thepheasanthotel.com
Website www.thepheasanthotel.com

Owned by the Binks family, this old inn, formerly the village smithy, two cottages and a shop, 'makes a pleasant alternative to the busy *Star Inn* close by', says its nominator in 2007. 'The outlook is very pleasant. We arrived tired, and late due to horrendous traffic, on a winter's evening. We were welcomed in an unhurried way, and the dinner was quite excellent.' The cooking is traditional (eg, roast sirloin of local beef with Yorkshire pudding; apple pie with cream). The conservatory dining room is 'very attractive', and the bedrooms are 'spacious, if quite simple'. They face south or south-west; some overlook the village pond and millstream, the others the courtyard and walled garden. The thatched *Holly Cottage*, with two sitting rooms and two bedrooms, down a quiet lane, has a large garden and a courtyard. The inn has a small oak-beamed bar with log fire, and a kidney-shaped indoor swimming pool. The large drawing room and dining room open on to a stone-flagged terrace that faces the stream. Reduced green fees are available at the 18-hole golf course at Kirkbymoorside. (*Joanna Russell*)

12 bedrooms. 1 on ground floor. 2-bedroomed cottage 350 yds. Village centre. 3 miles SE of Helmsley. Closed Christmas/New Year. Restaurant closed Mon in winter. Sitting room, bar, dining room, conservatory. No background music. Indoor swimming pool. Courtyard. 1-acre garden. Golf, riding, fishing nearby. No smoking. No children under 7. No dogs: public rooms; unaccompanied in bedrooms. MasterCard, Visa accepted. B&B £60–£70 per person; D,B&B £82–£85. Set menu £25. 1-night bookings usually refused Sat.

HARROGATE North Yorkshire *See SHORTLIST* Map 4:D4

HARWICH Essex Map 2:C5

The Pier at Harwich

The Quay
Harwich CO12 3HH

Tel 01255-241212
Fax 01255-551922
Email pier@milsomhotels.com
Website www.milsomhotels.com

Built in 1864 to accommodate passengers leaving for the Continent, these two buildings, owned by Paul Milsom (managed by Nick Chambers), stand on the lively quay in old Harwich. The two popular restaurants, and most bedrooms, are in the larger building; other rooms, and the beamed lounge, are in a former pub. In the first-floor *Harbourside* restaurant, with its 'minimalist' decor and polished pewter champagne bar, chef Chris Oakley specialises in seafood, eg, lobster bisque; roast monkfish in pancetta. 'Very fresh ingredients, well cooked.' Downstairs, the informal *Ha'Penny Bistro* (named after the original entry fee to the pier) serves brasserie-type food. Many dishes can be ordered in an 'ample' or a 'generous' portion. Bedrooms vary: 'Ours, smart and comfortable, had a fine view. A good stay in every way.' But some rooms are smaller, with a less than beautiful outlook. Breakfast includes freshly squeezed juice, 'wonderful thick slices of ham and cheese'. 'Management much in evidence. Service competent *and* friendly.' In summer, tables and chairs stand on the front terrace (surrounded by potted plants). The Milsom family also own *Le Talbooth* restaurant in Dedham and two sister hotels: *milsoms*, a 'stylish gastropub with rooms', and *Maison Talbooth* (see Shortlist), which will close between October 2007 and April 2008 for major alterations. (*LW, THB*)

14 bedrooms. 7 in annexe. 1 on ground floor. On quay. Ramps. Lounge (in annexe), restaurant, bistro; background music all day. Small front terrace. Civil wedding licence. No smoking. Guide dogs only. Amex, MasterCard, Visa accepted. B&B [2007] £48.75–£86.25 per person. Set lunch £18–£24; full alc £50. Winter breaks. Christmas package. *V*

Make sure the hotel has included VAT in the prices it quotes.

HATHERLEIGH Devon — Map 1:C4

Pressland Country House
Hatherleigh, nr Okehampton
EX20 3LW

Tel 01837-810871
Email accom@presslandhouse.co.uk
Website www.presslandhouse.co.uk

'Great value, a delight', this large, refurbished Victorian manor house stands in a landscaped garden with 'glorious' views across fields to Dartmoor. It is 'very comfortable, absolutely everything thought of', say visitors. One couple 'felt like favourite guests, though this was our first visit'. Fresh fruit, flowers, magazines and 'nice toiletries' are in the 'spotless' bedrooms (two, on the ground floor, have their own entrance). There is a large drawing room with log fire, and a library/bar. Owner Graham Giles 'is front man, who greets and advises, serves meals'; his wife, Gill, is a 'superb cook'. The dinner menu changes daily, and has three choices, which may include roasted peppers Piedmontese; lemon-grilled lamb. 'Local produce, beautifully cooked and presented.' Vegetarian meals are a speciality. Breakfast has a wide choice of cooked dishes, including devilled kidneys; poached smoked haddock. There are sun loungers and outdoor furniture in the garden. Barbecues can be arranged in fine weather, and wedding receptions and large parties can be held in a marquee. Local attractions include RHS Rosemoor, Castle Drogo and the Lydford Gorge. (*G and LJ*)

6 bedrooms. 2, on ground floor, in garden annexe. 2 miles S of Hatherleigh. Open mid-Mar–mid-Nov. Lounge, bar, dining room; background music at mealtimes. 1¾-acre garden. Croquet lawn. Walking, riding, fishing nearby. Unsuitable for ♿. No smoking. No children under 12. Guide dogs only. MasterCard, Visa accepted. B&B [2007] £32.50–£77 per person; D,B&B (min. 2 nights) £58.50–£108. Set dinner £26. Reductions for longer stays. 1-night bookings refused weekends in season, bank holidays.

HATHERSAGE Derbyshire — Map 3:A6

The George Hotel
Main Road
Hathersage S32 1BB

Tel 01433-650436
Fax 01433-650099
Email info@george-hotel.net
Website www.george-hotel.net

Owned by Eric Marsh, tenant of *The Cavendish* at nearby Baslow (*qv*), and managed by Philip Joseph who works at both, this 600-year-old grey stone Peak District inn is now a comfortable hotel (Best Western). Charlotte Brontë is thought to have stayed here while writing *Jane Eyre,* and to have based some characters on village residents. The 'lovely' sitting rooms have original stone walls, oak beams, open fires, much antique furniture and original paintings, but a visitor in 2007 reported some evidence of 'wear and tear'. Bedrooms are 'thoughtfully equipped'; the least expensive front ones have double glazing but may get some road noise. 'Always ask for a back room,' said one regular visitor. In the contemporary restaurant, with 'nice glass, china and cutlery', chef Ben Handley serves modern dishes, eg, herb-stuffed slow-roasted pork belly. 'Food is still good; the "Early Bird" menu is excellent value: sea bass with masses of fresh asparagus; creamy sweetbreads with a crisp herb crust and a stunning salad. Delightful service from charming young staff. A good range of wines by the glass.' Breakfast, served until 11 am, includes 'a large selection of fruits, cereals, etc, and a massive grill'. Snacks and 'generous' sandwiches are served at lunchtime in the lounge. (*Padi Howard, and others*)

22 bedrooms. In village centre. Private parking. Lounge/bar, restaurant (background jazz); 2 function rooms. Courtyard. Only restaurant accessible for ♿. Civil wedding licence. No smoking. No dogs. All major credit cards accepted. B&B [2007] £58–£147 per person. Full alc £43. Special breaks. Christmas/New Year packages. 1-night bookings occasionally refused weekends. *V*

HELMSLEY North Yorkshire — Map 4:C4

The Feversham Arms
1 High Street
Helmsley YO62 5AG

Tel 01439-770766
Fax 01439-770346
Email info@fevershamarmshotel.com
Website www.fevershamarmshotel.com

Simon Rhatigan's former coaching inn stands on the main street of this 'attractive town with interesting shops'. It is praised for the 'excellent service, and relaxed and friendly ambience' this year by visitors, but they were less happy with their 'small superior room which had little storage and a cramped bathroom; the owner accepted our criticism with grace, and our stay was otherwise comfortable'. The bedrooms vary greatly: earlier guests liked theirs, 'tricked out in pale blue and burgundy; wonderful bed, excellent pillows, cloud-like duvet'. Fittings include 'cutting-edge' TV, DVD-player and PlayStation. For families, some rooms have a sofa bed and some are interconnecting. Five poolside suites have been added this year. There are 'relaxing' sitting areas, a high-roofed conservatory restaurant, a swimming pool, a tennis court in the sloping grounds, and a little garden, facing the church, where tea and drinks are served. The chef, Simon Kelly, offers 'very good locally sourced dishes of high quality', such as corn-fed

Goosnargh duck breast, with endive and gooseberry tian. 'Wonderful cheeseboard.' (*CL, and others*)

24 bedrooms. 4 in garden. 4 on ground floor. Central. Parking. Ramp. 2 lounges, bar, conservatory restaurant (classical background music); private dining room. Terrace (outside dining). 1-acre garden: heated swimming pool, tennis. Civil wedding licence. No smoking. Amex, MasterCard. B&B [2007] £70–£182.50 per person. Set dinner £32; full alc £55. Christmas/New Year packages. 1-night bookings sometimes refused Sat.

See also SHORTLIST

HENLEY-ON-THAMES Oxfordshire — Map 2:D3

Hotel du Vin Henley-on-Thames

New Street
Henley-on-Thames
RG9 2BP

Tel 01491-848400
Fax 01491-848401
Email info@henley.hotelduvin.com
Website www.hotelduvin.com

'Excellent, as one expects from the group,' says a visitor to this branch of the Hotel du Vin chain, a 'brilliant' conversion of the former Brakspear's Brewery. A series of buildings grouped around a courtyard, it has airy interiors, arched windows, white walls, cast-iron beams and sisal flooring. James Nichols is manager. An earlier comment: 'Friendly, efficient staff; valet car parking, a boon in a crowded town; and in the room a powerful shower, comfortable bed, fresh milk in a fridge.' The bedrooms, each sponsored by a wine house, have a plasma-screen TV, huge bed, deluxe bedding, good lighting. Ruinart has a bathroom up steep stairs, and a terrace with an alfresco hot tub. Children are welcomed: 'baby kits' are provided free of charge, and there is a listening system. The dimly lit bistro and bar are 'full of atmosphere'. In addition to the standard Mediterranean bistro fare, the chef, Matt Green-Armytage, has devised a 'land, sea, local' menu of dishes using ingredients produced by ethical and traditional methods, eg, Family Farm Shop-cured ham; char-grilled Appleton lamb's liver with courgette and tomato fondue. In summer, there is a barbecue. (*Patricia Darby, and others*)

43 bedrooms. 2 suitable for ♿. Central (the 3 front rooms might hear traffic). 50 yds from river. Trains from London/Reading. Limited car parking. Valet parking. Bar (background music all day), bistro; billiard room; 3 private dining rooms; conference/function facilities. Courtyard: cigar shack. Civil wedding licence. No dogs in bistro. All major credit cards accepted. Room [2007] £135–£425. Breakfast £9.95–£13.50. Full alc £35–£40. New Year package.

THE GOOD HOTEL GUIDE 2008

Use this voucher to claim a 25% discount off the normal price for bed and breakfast at hotels with a *V* sign at the end of their entry. **You must request a voucher discount at the time of booking and present this voucher on arrival. Further details and conditions overleaf.** Valid to 2nd October 2008.

THE GOOD HOTEL GUIDE 2008

Use this voucher to claim a 25% discount off the normal price for bed and breakfast at hotels with a *V* sign at the end of their entry. **You must request a voucher discount at the time of booking and present this voucher on arrival. Further details and conditions overleaf.** Valid to 2nd October 2008.

THE GOOD HOTEL GUIDE 2008

Use this voucher to claim a 25% discount off the normal price for bed and breakfast at hotels with a *V* sign at the end of their entry. **You must request a voucher discount at the time of booking and present this voucher on arrival. Further details and conditions overleaf.** Valid to 2nd October 2008.

THE GOOD HOTEL GUIDE 2008

Use this voucher to claim a 25% discount off the normal price for bed and breakfast at hotels with a *V* sign at the end of their entry. **You must request a voucher discount at the time of booking and present this voucher on arrival. Further details and conditions overleaf.** Valid to 2nd October 2008.

THE GOOD HOTEL GUIDE 2008

Use this voucher to claim a 25% discount off the normal price for bed and breakfast at hotels with a *V* sign at the end of their entry. **You must request a voucher discount at the time of booking and present this voucher on arrival. Further details and conditions overleaf.** Valid to 2nd October 2008.

THE GOOD HOTEL GUIDE 2008

Use this voucher to claim a 25% discount off the normal price for bed and breakfast at hotels with a *V* sign at the end of their entry. **You must request a voucher discount at the time of booking and present this voucher on arrival. Further details and conditions overleaf.** Valid to 2nd October 2008.

CONDITIONS

1. Hotels with a *V* have agreed to give readers a discount of 25% off their normal bed-and-breakfast rate.
2. One voucher is good for a single-night stay only, at the discounted rate for yourself alone or for you and a partner sharing a double room.
3. Hotels may decline to accept a voucher reservation if they expect to be fully booked at the full room price.

CONDITIONS

1. Hotels with a *V* have agreed to give readers a discount of 25% off their normal bed-and-breakfast rate.
2. One voucher is good for a single-night stay only, at the discounted rate for yourself alone or for you and a partner sharing a double room.
3. Hotels may decline to accept a voucher reservation if they expect to be fully booked at the full room price.

CONDITIONS

1. Hotels with a *V* have agreed to give readers a discount of 25% off their normal bed-and-breakfast rate.
2. One voucher is good for a single-night stay only, at the discounted rate for yourself alone or for you and a partner sharing a double room.
3. Hotels may decline to accept a voucher reservation if they expect to be fully booked at the full room price.

CONDITIONS

1. Hotels with a *V* have agreed to give readers a discount of 25% off their normal bed-and-breakfast rate.
2. One voucher is good for a single-night stay only, at the discounted rate for yourself alone or for you and a partner sharing a double room.
3. Hotels may decline to accept a voucher reservation if they expect to be fully booked at the full room price.

CONDITIONS

1. Hotels with a *V* have agreed to give readers a discount of 25% off their normal bed-and-breakfast rate.
2. One voucher is good for a single-night stay only, at the discounted rate for yourself alone or for you and a partner sharing a double room.
3. Hotels may decline to accept a voucher reservation if they expect to be fully booked at the full room price.

CONDITIONS

1. Hotels with a *V* have agreed to give readers a discount of 25% off their normal bed-and-breakfast rate.
2. One voucher is good for a single-night stay only, at the discounted rate for yourself alone or for you and a partner sharing a double room.
3. Hotels may decline to accept a voucher reservation if they expect to be fully booked at the full room price.

The Red Lion
Hart Street
Henley-on-Thames
RG9 2AR

Tel 01491-572161
Fax 01491-410039
Email reservations@redlionhenley.co.uk
Website www.redlionhenley.co.uk

The 'comfortable rooms and exceptionally well-trained staff' are praised by a regular visitor to this creeper-clad 16th-century red brick inn which overlooks the Royal Regatta course. It changed hands in spring 2007, but the manager, Richard Vowell, who 'continues to produce the goods, even when the hotel is bursting at the seams', is staying on, and refurbishment is planned (some of the decor is now 'quite dated'). Public areas have antique panelling and furniture, paintings and prints; there are flagstones, an open fire, leather chairs and rowing memorabilia in the small bar, where light meals can be served. Some bedrooms overlook the river; others a pretty church and its graveyard; double glazing mitigates the sound of traffic from a busy bridge close by. In the restaurant, chef Stéphane Pasquier serves food 'which is always good, sometimes outstanding (faultless fish soup with rouille)' and 'by no means expensive'. Another plus point: 'In a town where the local powers are dottier about parking than most, it has a decent-sized car park which is locked at night; no charge.' (*Peter Jowitt*)

26 bedrooms. By Henley bridge (windows double glazed). Trains from London/Reading. Large car park. Ramp. Bar, restaurant; 'easy listening' background music; conference/function facilities. On river: boat hire (picnics arranged). Unsuitable for ♿. Smoking allowed in all bedrooms. No dogs. Amex, MasterCard, Visa accepted. Room [2007]: single £115–£125, double £145–£165; D,B&B £99.50 per person. Breakfast £9.50–£13.50. Set lunch £16.50; full alc £37.45. Special offers on website. ***V***

HETTON North Yorkshire — Map 4:D3

The Angel Inn
Hetton, nr Skipton
BD23 6LT

Tel 01756-730263
Fax 01756-730363
Email info@angelhetton.co.uk
Website www.angelhetton.co.uk

In 1983, this old coaching inn in the Yorkshire Dales was opened by Denis and Juliet Watkins as a 'fine-dining pub'; more recently, five bedrooms were created in a converted barn across the road. Andrew Holmes is now manager. 'Our room and facilities were excellent,' say visitors this year. A series of panelled and beamed rooms leads off the bar, which has nooks and crannies and cosy alcoves. In the restaurant, chef Bruce Elsworth, known for his support of local producers, serves modern English dishes, eg, home-made black pudding; roasted Goosnargh duck breast. The bar/brasserie has its own menu with blackboard specials. In summer, meals may be taken on a flagged forecourt overlooking Cracoe Fell. Breakfast, served until 10 am, has 'very good' fresh juices, big bowls of cereals and fresh fruit, and an 'immense' Yorkshire platter. Most visitors continue to enjoy their visit, but one *Guide* reader this year was disappointed with the food and service, 'maybe an off day'. We would welcome more reports.

5 bedrooms. In barn across road. 1 suitable for ♿. Off B6265, 5 miles N of Skipton. Car park. Closed Christmas Day, New Year's Day, 1 week in Jan. Bar (3 rooms), bar/brasserie, restaurant (2 rooms); wine shop. No background music. Terrace (outside dining). Civil wedding licence. No smoking. No dogs in public rooms. Amex, MasterCard, Visa accepted. B&B [2007] £65–£155 per person. Set lunch (Sun) £23.50, dinner (Sat) £35; full alc £37.50. New Year package. *V* (Mon–Thurs)

HEXHAM Northumberland *See SHORTLIST* Map 4:B3

HINTON ST GEORGE Somerset Map 1:C6

The Lord Poulett Arms NEW *Tel* 01460-73149
High Street *Email* steveandmichelle@lordpoulettarms.com
Hinton St George *Website* www.lordpoulettarms.com
TA17 8SE

Cesar award: Gastropub of the year

'Delightfully quirky; the building is a joy': inspectors' verdict on Steve Hill and Michelle Paynton's restaurant/pub-with-rooms in a pretty and quiet village of stone houses and thatched roofs. Recently renovated, it has floors of bare flag or boards, tables of old oak or elm, antique chairs, open fires. 'Our room (No. 1) had considerable wow factor. Big bed with massive carved headboard; huge old wooden wardrobe; old-fashioned bath (with an optional screen) by the window; loo in what was probably once a large old cupboard. This eccentric arrangement will not please everyone but it preserves the integrity of the 17th-century room. We thought it great fun.' The information pack includes a section on 'how to spend your time without a television'. 'The staff couldn't have been more helpful,' was another comment. In the kitchen, Japanese chef Hideki Koike, using local ingredients, produces 'superior gastropub cooking'. Our inspectors' meal, accompanied by a warm loaf of bread, included curried parsnip soup; 'nicely spiced chicken with sticky rice'; dark chocolate and hazelnut tart. 'Superb service from staff dressed in black; a good, buzzy atmosphere.' The 'excellent' breakfast, served until 9 am, includes fresh juices, fruit compote, leaf tea, thick toasted home-made bread. Behind the building is a 'French-style' garden with a *boules* piste edged by lavender; beyond are fruit trees and wild flowers. Summer visitors may dine alfresco. In the 'bustling, informal' bar, 'dogs sleep on the hearth and interesting local conversations can be overheard'. (*Emma Lambert, Ian Malone, and others*)

4 bedrooms. Village centre. 2 miles NW of Crewkerne. Check-in 12 noon–3 pm, 6.30–11 pm. Bar, restaurant, private dining room. No background music. 1-acre grounds. Unsuitable for ♿. No smoking. No dogs in bedrooms. MasterCard, Visa accepted. B&B £44–£59 per person. Full alc £30.

HOARWITHY Herefordshire *See SHORTLIST* Map 3:D4

HOLKHAM Norfolk *See SHORTLIST* Map 2:A5

HOLMFIRTH West Yorkshire *See SHORTLIST* Map 4:E3

HOLT Norfolk Map 2:A5

Byfords
1–3 Shirehall Plain
Holt NR25 6BG

Tel 01263-711400
Fax 01263-714815
Email queries@byfords.org.uk
Website www.byfords.org.uk

'Chic, clean rooms and attentive staff. A must if you are in the area.' This year's praise for this unusual establishment on the main square of this enchanting Norfolk town. The owners, Iain and Clair Wilson, describe their Grade II listed flint-fronted building as 'a higgledy-piggledy world of pleasure', combining 'posh B&B', a café/bistro, a restaurant and busy deli. A room 'facing a flower-filled courtyard' was liked: 'It had the largest high-tech TV/DVD/radio I have come across in any hotel, movable, so viewable from sofa or bed; dimmers on all lights; tea-making equipment with fresh milk, delicious home-made shortbread.' The café serves breakfasts, but residents have their own breakfast room where the meal was 'as generous and posh as the accommodation: jugs of freshly made fruit juices, excellent coffee, home-baked bread and pastries, cooked dishes including kedgeree and kippers'. In the conservatory restaurant, with its open kitchen, traditional dishes 'with a twist' are served, eg, a Morston mussel selection; hotchpotch of local game. Visitors are given a comprehensive handbook of information on the area. (*G Potter*)

9 bedrooms. Some on ground floor. Also self-catering accommodation. Central. Restaurant closed 25 Dec. Private, secure car park. Ramps. 5 internal eating areas, 1 external; conservatory; background jazz; deli. Unsuitable for ♿. Beach 4 miles. No smoking. No dogs. MasterCard, Visa accepted. B&B [2007] £60–£95 per person; D,B&B £75–£110. Full alc £25. Christmas/New Year packages. 1-night bookings refused Sat.

HOPE Derbyshire — Map 3:A6

Underleigh House
off Edale Road
Hope S33 6RF

Tel 01433-621372
Fax 01433-621324
Email info@underleighhouse.co.uk
Website www.underleighhouse.co.uk

An extended barn and cottage conversion in the Hope valley, dating from the late 19th century, is now an 'excellent' B&B owned by Philip and Vivienne Taylor, who provide 'unobtrusive hospitality' and offer 'amazing value'. Our inspectors found much to praise: 'Vivienne Taylor greeted us by name and offered us tea with delicious lemon cake. She is delightful, warm, with a giggle.' A small bedroom had 'lots of patterns, views on both sides of fields with sheep, everything one could want, even bathrobes (nice lightweight ones); small bathroom with a bath; a comprehensive information pack'. This year, the Thornhill Suite has been refurbished, and given a new bathroom, bed and soft furnishings. The 'delicious' breakfast, served round a large oak table in the flagstoned hall, has won awards. The huge menu includes jugs of orange juice, eight types of home-made jam, own-recipe muesli, fresh and dried fruits from the buffet; porridge and croissants from the Aga; the 'Full Works' traditional cooked breakfast. The Taylors serve drinks in a large lounge (no muzak) with a log fire, or on a terrace. Maps and packed lunches are provided for walks in the Peak District national park from the door. (*Frances Rathbone, and others*)

6 bedrooms. 2 on ground floor. 1 mile N of Hope. Train: Hope; bus from Sheffield. Closed Christmas/New Year, most of Jan. Lounge, breakfast room. No background music. ⅓-acre garden. Unsuitable for ♿. No smoking. No children under 12. Dogs allowed in ground-floor bedrooms by arrangement. MasterCard, Visa accepted (*both 3% surcharge*). B&B [2007] £35–£55 per person. 3-night rates. 1-night bookings refused Fri/Sat.

HORDLE Hampshire Map 2:E2

The Mill at Gordleton
Silver Street
Hordle, nr Lymington
SO41 6DJ

Tel 01590-682219
Fax 01590-683073
Email info@themillatgordleton.co.uk
Website www.themillatgordleton.co.uk

On the edge of the New Forest, this 17th-century mill is now a 'pleasant pub-cum-restaurant' owned by Elizabeth Cottingham and managed by Teresa Seabright. Visitors in 2007 wrote of a warm welcome. 'Staff uniformly friendly and efficient. Housekeeping of a high standard. The weekday calm impressed. Our room, furnished in artistic fawn and blue, had a large, comfortable bed and a nice terrace where we sat in the sun. A very modern bathroom with an intricate shower; we would have liked a stool.' Outside are terraces where ducks and geese sometimes wander, and 'beautifully sculpted' gardens by a stream. A busy road is near but, said earlier visitors, 'Our mini-suite was well positioned and insulated, so there was no trace of noise.' In the bustling restaurant, which faces the stream, the cooking of chefs Karl Wiggins and David Baker ('English with a contemporary twist') was found 'excellent, particularly the duck breast with raspberries; generous helping of tender venison; good vege tarian risotto. Home-made bread; home-made ice creams, all magnificently served.' There is a vegetarian dish of the day. The good wine list has a wide price range. A useful base for visiting Beaulieu, Buckler's Hard, the Isle of Wight, etc. (*Sir William and Lady Reid*)

7 bedrooms. 4 miles W of Lymington. Closed 25 Dec. Restaurant closed Sun night, 26 Dec night, 1 Jan night. Lounge, 2 bars, restaurant; background music; conference room. 3-acre grounds on river (fishing rights). Only restaurant suitable for ♿. No smoking. Dogs allowed in small bar. Amex, MasterCard, Visa accepted. B&B [2007] £62.50–£85 per person. Set lunch £12.50–£15.50, (Sun) £19.90; full alc £40–£45. 1-night bookings sometimes refused bank holidays.

HOVE East Sussex *See SHORTLIST* Map 2:E4

Report forms (Freepost in UK) are at the end of the *Guide.*

HUDDERSFIELD West Yorkshire *See SHORTLIST* — Map 4:E3

HULL East Yorkshire *See SHORTLIST* — Map 4:D5

HUNGERFORD Berkshire — Map 2:D2

The Bear NEW

41 Charnham Street
Hungerford RG17 0EL

Tel 01488-682512
Fax 01488-684357
Email info@thebearhotelhungerford.co.uk
Website www.thebearhotelhungerford.co.uk

Historic inn, once owned by Henry VIII, in town centre: bought in 2005 by a group of investors; ground floor and most bedrooms given contemporary look. 'Air of attractive tranquillity.' Manager Colin Heaney leads 'welcoming, efficient' staff. 41 'stylishly comfortable' bedrooms: custom-designed furniture, flat-screen TV (movies on demand), Wi-Fi. Front rooms face busy A4; quietest ones, and restaurant, face River Dunn. Chef Phillip Wild serves much-admired modern European cooking; 'excellent' light meals available. Weddings, functions, etc, held. Good advance booked/weekend rates. Car park. Small lounge, snug, bar area, restaurant (closed Sun night, bank holidays, except 25/26 Dec); background jazz; private dining room; courtyard (meal/drinks service); meeting facilities; civil wedding licence. Riverside terrace, small lawn area, island. Unsuitable for ♿*. No smoking. Amex, MasterCard, Visa accepted. Room [2007]: single £120, double from £135, suite £190. Breakfast £9.95–£12.95. Full alc £39.50. Weekend rates. New Year package.* *V*

HUNSTANTON Norfolk *See SHORTLIST* — Map 2:A5

HUNTINGDON Cambridgeshire *See SHORTLIST* — Map 2:B4

> If you are recommending a B&B and know of a good restaurant nearby, please mention it in your report.

HURLEY Berkshire — Map 2:D3

Black Boys Inn
Henley Road, Hurley
nr Maidenhead
SL6 6NQ

Tel 01628-824212
Email info@blackboysinn.co.uk
Website www.blackboysinn.co.uk

Visitors whose 'passion is food' have high praise for the cooking of Simon Bonwick, 'a rare talent', at this 16th-century inn a short walk from the River Thames. Accommodation, too, is praised: owners Adrian and Helen Bannister have added modern bedrooms at the back in converted stables. 'Ours was immaculate, with a trad and fad effect; massive bed, thick fabric blinds, crisp bedding, chic colours, discreet details (cotton buds, toothbrushes, magazines); great power shower.' Another room had vaulted ceiling with original heavy beams, 'very pretty green-walled bathroom'. A 'lively but fairly small' bar is separated from the dining room by a wood-burning stove. 'Polished oak floor. Tables well spaced, simply laid (plain white china, good glassware); comfortable Gothic-style chairs; paintings and ornaments representing ducks.' The food (*Michelin Bib Gourmand*) is 'reasonably priced, served with grace. We enjoyed crispy veal cheeks with creamed paysanne vegetables; fresh Salcombe crab; bewitching sauces.' 'Good wines by the glass. Staff young, well informed, smartly turned out.' Breakfast has 'quality sausages, bacon and eggs; memorable black pudding', and fresh orange juice is now served, following last year's *Guide* comment. The inn faces a busy road: some traffic noise is inevitable. (*Catherine Ogden, and others*)

8 bedrooms. 1 suitable for ♿. 4 miles W of Maidenhead on A4130. Parking. Closed 24 Dec–2 Jan. Restaurant closed Mon. Small bar area, restaurant; classical background music; meeting room. 1½-acre grounds. No smoking. No children under 12. No dogs. Diners, MasterCard, Visa accepted. B&B [2007] double £75–£95. Full alc £33.

HURSTBOURNE TARRANT Hampshire — Map 2:D2

Esseborne Manor
Hurstbourne Tarrant, nr Andover
SP11 0ER

Tel 01264-736444
Fax 01264-736725
Email esseborne@aol.com
Website www.esseborne-manor.co.uk

Off a busy road, but approached up a long drive flanked by fields with sheep grazing, this small Victorian house has been sympathetically extended by its owners, Lucilla and Mark Hamilton. A *Guide* inspector thought it a 'stylish, unstuffy' hotel, providing a 'family-run atmosphere and efficient service'. Eleven bedrooms are in the main house (some have a spa bath, some a four-poster). The six rooms in the extension around a courtyard are good for a family (children are welcomed, though there are no special facilities for them). Three small rooms are in cottages. 'We were upgraded to a massive suite with canopy bed and private patio. Good technology. Good lighting (apart from bedside lights). But we weren't keen on the opaque glass loo door in the huge bathroom.' In the traditionally decorated dining room (red-patterned wallpaper, blue carpet, big windows), the cooking of Bosnian chef Steven Ratic is 'conventional' ('what our clients prefer'). The Menu du Vin is recommended ('good value'): sea bass with asparagus; filet of pork with celeriac purée; 'nice home-baked rolls. Breakfast buffet a little uninspiring: boring toast, but good cooked dishes.' Weddings (marquee on the lawn) and meetings are catered for.

20 bedrooms. 6 in courtyard, 3 in cottages. On A343, midway between Andover and Newbury. Closed 26 Dec–3 Jan. 2 lounges, bar, restaurant; function room. No background music. 3-acre grounds: formal gardens, tennis, croquet. Arrangements with nearby golf club and fitness centre. Civil wedding licence. Smoking allowed in 10 bedrooms. No dogs in public rooms. All major credit cards accepted. B&B [2007]: single £98–£110, double £125–£180, suite £240; D,B&B £92.50–£150 per person. *V*

ILMINGTON Warwickshire — Map 3:D6

The Howard Arms
Lower Green, Ilmington
nr Stratford-upon-Avon CV36 4LT

Tel/Fax 01608-682226
Email info@howardarms.com
Website www.howardarms.com

On the green of a pretty village south of Stratford-upon-Avon, Robert and Gill Greenstock's expanded 400-year-old stone pub is 'quintessentially English'. 'Very much a local', it has flagged floors, nooks for eating, and a log fireplace. The three bedrooms upstairs are 'cosy', with oak beams, antique furniture and prints, and comfy chairs, but 'modern lighting; spotless bathroom'. The 'first-class' food in the pub is a mixture of traditional and modern dishes, eg, salmon and shallot filo parcel; beef, ale and mustard pie. A larger room on a higher level has more formal dining, and is 'a lovely, light place for breakfast', which has 'delicious home-made bread toast', and fresh ground coffee. Summer meals can be taken in the pretty garden. Residents should not arrive between 3 and 6 pm (having arrived, they are given a key). Hidcote and Kiftsgate gardens, and Compton Verney Gallery, are nearby. The Greenstocks' sons, Will and Tom, run *The Horse and Groom* at Bourton-on-the-Hill (*qv*), nearby. *The Howard Arms* was on the market as we went to press; you should check the position before booking. (*Michael Blanchard*)

3 bedrooms. Green of village 4 miles NW of Shipston on Stour. Closed 25/31 Dec. Snug, 2 bars, dining bar. No background music. ½-acre garden. Unsuitable for ♿. No smoking. No children under 8 overnight. Guide dogs only. MasterCard, Visa accepted. B&B [2007] £60–£87.50 per person. Set Sun lunch £22.50; full alc £35. 2-night D,B&B breaks. 1-night bookings refused weekends.

IREBY Cumbria — Map 4: inset B2

Overwater Hall
Overwater, nr Ireby
CA7 1HH

Tel 017687-76566
Fax 017687-76921
Email welcome@overwaterhall.co.uk
Website www.overwaterhall.co.uk

In large grounds in an 'isolated part of the Lake District', flanked by Skiddaw and its surrounding fells, this castellated Grade II listed Georgian mansion is owned and run by Stephen Bore (the 'welcoming, gentle front-of-house') and Adrian and Angela Hyde. It was thought 'delightful' this year; 'recommended to anyone who wants to relax away from the bustle of more touristy areas'. The public rooms have a bold decor: 'audacious' wallpaper, contrasting panelling and lights. 'The bedroom we stayed in had magnificent views and was extremely comfortable.' Dogs are welcomed: no charge; they may sit with their owners in the lounge, and run about unleashed in the garden. Children are welcomed too. Adrian Hyde's 'smart menus' offer plenty of choice of modern dishes: much game, eg, wild pigeon on juniper creamed potatoes; rabbit saddle sautéed with Cumbrian air-dried ham. 'A well-balanced, well-proportioned meal. Tables elegantly laid.' Vegetarians are catered for. 'Smart casual' dress is expected of diners. Breakfast (served at table) is a 'full Cumbrian' affair. Good walking from the door; red squirrels, deer and woodpeckers can be seen, and ospreys nest nearby. (*Susan Chait, and others*)

11 bedrooms. 1 on ground floor. 2 miles NE of Bassenthwaite Lake. Drawing room, lounge, bar area, restaurant; background classical piano music at night. 18-acre grounds. Overwater tarn 1 mile. No smoking. No children under 5 in restaurant at night (high tea at 5.30 pm). MasterCard, Visa accepted. B&B £65–£180 per person; D,B&B £85–£220. Set dinner £40. 4-night breaks all year. Christmas/New Year packages. 1-night bookings refused Sat.

KESWICK Cumbria *See SHORTLIST* Map 4: inset C2

KING'S LYNN Norfolk *See SHORTLIST* Map 2:A4

KINGSBRIDGE Devon *See SHORTLIST* Map 1:D4

KIRTLINGTON Oxfordshire Map 2:C2

The Dashwood
South Green, Heyford Road
Kirtlington OX5 3HJ

Tel 01869-352707
Fax 01869-351432
Email info@thedashwood.co.uk
Website www.thedashwood.co.uk

In a quiet Oxfordshire village with pretty mellow stone cottages, this former pub has been converted into a contemporary restaurant-with-rooms by Martin and Ros Lewis. 'Splashes of colour from fabrics and paintings contrast well with the natural look of wood, leather, plain carpeting and stone,' said an inspector. In the informal bistro-style split-level restaurant, Marcel Taylor cooks in 'European style with Asian influences', eg, corn-fed duck breast, red pepper, shitake confit and udon noodles. 'Attentive service by attractive young people wearing black waistcoats.' Bedrooms have hand-made oak furniture, broadband Internet access, slimline TV; some are on a courtyard; one is in an attic. Breakfast until 10 am was 'limited; nice fresh fruit salad but no muesli or yogurt. Cooked food was fine, but no vegetarian dishes. Very nice croissants, but boring toast.' The main drawback: no guests' sitting room. 'But we had a pleasant stay, smart and unpretentious, if not a spoiling experience.'

12 bedrooms. 7 in barn. 3 on ground floor, 1 suitable for ♿. In village on A4095, 12 miles N of Oxford. Car park. Closed 1 week New Year, Sun evening 'if quiet'. Small bar area, restaurant; mixed background music all day. Small outside seating area. No smoking. No dogs. Amex, MasterCard, Visa accepted. B&B £55–£85 per person. Set lunch £12.50–£14.50; full alc £30. Christmas package.

Deadlines: nominations for the 2009 edition of this volume should reach us not later than 15 May 2008. Latest date for comments on existing entries: 1 June 2008.

KNIGHTWICK Worcestershire — Map 3:D5

The Talbot
Knightwick
WR6 5PH

Tel 01886-821235
Fax 01886-821060
Email info@the-talbot.co.uk
Website www.the-talbot.co.uk

'We are firmly rooted in the traditions and produce of the Teme valley,' say Annie and Wiz Clift, the sisters who own and manage this old coaching inn which stands peacefully on the banks of the River Teme in lovely Herefordshire/Worcestershire border countryside. 'This is the place to be if you want to enjoy a traditional inn with a strong huntin', shootin' and fishin' theme,' said a visitor on a winter evening when 'it was heaving with a large shooting party'. 'No smart country house hotel pretensions here.' The 'lively bar', which leads to a terrace, serves home-brewed ales. The breads, black pudding and pies are all home-made; vegetables are organically home grown; 'wild food is gleaned from hedgerows around'. The cooking is traditional, eg, hotpot of guineafowl. 'Our large bedroom had an ultra-modern power shower. Breakfast included some of the tastiest black pudding and bacon I have had. Special mention for the fireplaces: one had almost half a tree blazing in the hearth.' Fishing can be arranged. (*JH*)

11 bedrooms. On B4197, 7 miles W of Worcester. Parking. Closed 25 Dec evening. Ramp. Lounge bar, restaurant. No background music. Patio; riverside picnic area. Only restaurant suitable for ♿. Smoking allowed in 3 bedrooms. Dogs by arrangement, not in restaurant. MasterCard, Visa accepted. B&B £42–£50 per person; D,B&B £70. Set menu £30; full alc £38.50. New Year package.

KNUTSFORD Cheshire *See SHORTLIST* — Map 4:E3

LACOCK Wiltshire — Map 2:D1

At the Sign of the Angel
6 Church Street
Lacock, nr Chippenham SN15 2LB

Tel 01249-730230
Fax 01249-730527
Email angel@lacock.co.uk
Website www.lacock.co.uk

'Cosy and atmospheric', with oak panels, creaking doors, low ceilings and beams, Lorna and George Hardy's 15th-century half-timbered inn is in the centre of an ancient and picturesque National Trust village. 'We loved the old feel of the place,' say visitors this year. Rooms in the old house may be small, but 'ours was full of character, with huge four-poster bed and quality linen sheets'. There can be noise from the bar and the kitchens, and 'doors opening and closing with clunky wood latches'. 'Soundproofing may not be 21st century but this is an old building; our room was comfortable if cramped, which didn't matter as there is a spacious lounge and garden.' Four recently added bedrooms, with antique furnishings but modern bathroom, are in a cottage 'through the garden and over a brook'. In the medieval, candlelit dining rooms, guests enjoyed 'exceptionally fresh, seasonal, high-quality English cooking', eg, Stilton and walnut pâté; bangers and mash with onion gravy. 'The best summer pudding we have ever tasted.' 'The wine list was surprisingly good, and reasonably priced.' 'Breakfast a delight; an excellent range of tasty local produce; home-made bread, home-laid eggs, etc.' (*Steve Howard, RA Rosen, CG*)

10 bedrooms. 4 on ground floor. 4 in annexe. Village centre. Closed 23 Dec–31 Dec (open for dinner 31 Dec). Ramps. Lounge, bar, restaurant. No background music. Civil wedding licence. No smoking. No dogs in public rooms. All major credit cards accepted. B&B [2007] £52.50–£85 per person. Set menus £10–£15. New Year package.

LANGAR Nottinghamshire — Map 2:A3

Langar Hall
Langar NG13 9HG

Tel 01949-860559
Fax 01949-861045
Email info@langarhall.co.uk
Website www.langarhall.com

César award in 2000

'Like staying in someone's slightly down-at-heel country home,' says a visitor who enjoyed his visit to this honey-coloured Georgian house run in informal style by the 'hands-on' Imogen Skirving (her family have owned it since the mid-19th century). 'The eccentric owner, who takes orders at dinner, is charming.' The drawing room, with club fender and cheerful pictures, contributes to the 'family feel'; the small bar has high chairs, cartoons, photographs and prints. Family portraits line the stairs that lead up from the flagstoned hall to themed bedrooms. Bohemia, once an artist's studio, has rich fabrics, and poetry on the bathroom walls; Barristers is 'masculine, with painted panelling'; Agnews is a chalet in the garden. One couple wrote of a bathroom that was 'huge, but spartan'. The daily-changing menu uses local ingredients and fish from Scotland (eg, sirloin of beef, truffle mash; scallops, onion bhaji, apple dressing).

Light meals are served all day in a conservatory. The restaurant can be very busy at weekends. The grounds have gardens, canals, medieval fishponds, an adventure play area for children. Small dogs are accepted (£20), but their owners are asked to 'respect the sheep, hens, ducks, etc, around the house'. 'Lone travellers are made very welcome.' The adjacent church is 'unmissable'. (*John Chute, FS*)

12 bedrooms. 1 on ground floor. Also 1 garden chalet. 12 miles SE of Nottingham. Train: Grantham/Nottingham; link to Bingham, 3 miles. Sitting room, study, library, bar, garden room, restaurant; private dining room; small conference/function facilities. Classical background music 'on request only'. 20-acre grounds: gardens, children's play area, croquet, ponds; fishing. Unsuitable for ♿. Civil wedding licence. No smoking. Dogs by arrangement. MasterCard, Visa accepted. B&B [2007] £75–£110 per person. Set lunch £16, dinner £25–£39.50; full alc £40. (*Excluding 10% discretionary service charge.*) Mid-week offers. 1-night bookings refused for some bedrooms. *V*

LANGFORD BUDVILLE Somerset — Map 1:C5

Bindon Country House
Langford Budville
nr Wellington TA21 0RU

Tel 01823-400070
Fax 01823-400071
Email stay@bindon.com
Website www.bindon.com

In peaceful Somerset countryside, Lynn and Mark Jaffa's hotel (Pride of Britain) has 'the feel of hunting lodge rather than a grand country house', and a baroque Bavarian look. There are 'stunning' floor tiles in the hall, a fine panelled staircase under a stained-glass cupola; also 'heavily patterned carpets'. Inspectors in 2007 received a 'warm welcome; we had booked standard doubles with friends, but were upgraded to the two fine front rooms overlooking the lovely gardens. Both were light, with three large sash windows; large bathroom; slightly dated fabrics; big, comfortable bed.' Another room (a late booking) was 'adequate, not luxurious'. The wood-panelled library bar is lit with oil candles for pre-dinner drinks: 'Pleasant atmosphere, interesting canapés.' Chef Mike Davies's short set menu is praised. 'Portions well judged. Starters of sole in the lightest batter; a wonderful mushroom risotto; perfectly pink rump of lamb; tasty little extra courses; attentive service. Breakfast had a buffet of fruits, orange juice, cheeses, meats, cereals; good cooked dishes; a relaxed pace. A fresh pot of tea was brought and we were allowed to sit as long as we wanted.' There is Wellington memorabilia in the public rooms (the Iron Duke took his name from the nearby town). (*J Rochelle, and others*)

12 bedrooms. 1 on ground floor. 4 miles NW of Wellington. Only party bookings at Christmas/New Year. Hall (pianist on Sat), lounge, study, bar, restaurant (occasional classical background music); 2 conference rooms. 7-acre grounds: kitchen garden, rose garden, heated 30-ft swimming pool, tennis, croquet, *boules*; chapel; woodland. Coarse fishing 500 yds. Civil wedding licence. No smoking. No dogs in public rooms. All major credit cards accepted. B&B [2007] £57.50–£115 per person; D,B&B (min. 2 nights) £85–£135. Set dinner £35; full alc £49. Christmas/New Year packages. *V*

LANGHO Lancashire — Map 4:D3

Northcote Manor NEW

Northcote Road, Langho
nr Blackburn BB6 8BE

Tel 01254-240555
Fax 01254-246568
Email sales@northcotemanor.com
Website www.northcotemanor.com

Chef/*patron* Nigel Haworth and his business partner, Craig Bancroft, have been 20 years at their informal restaurant-with-rooms (*Michelin* star). It returns to the *Guide* after a major renovation. 'The public rooms,' say inspectors, 'have new carpets, but the beautiful wooden doors and windows, the brown leather armchairs and sofas in the sitting rooms, and original Edwardian features remain. Our "superior" bedroom, comfortable rather than stylish, had a magnificent Victorian wardrobe, large bed, *chaise longue*, games, magazines, CD-player, flat-screen TV, fridge; well-equipped, efficient bathroom. Gold wallpaper added to the sombre ambience, but the huge bay window, with view of fields, brought light and colour.' Most rooms are spacious. Some are up a handsome wooden staircase; others reached by 'a maze of corridors'. In the restaurant, 'window tables are the best'. The 'well-balanced' five-course tasting menu included 'refreshing' porridge of shrimps; 'tender, gamey' roebuck; cheeses 'in perfect condition'. Service was 'good-humoured, attentive'. Many ingredients are organically home-grown. The wine list has a 'fine selection of half bottles'. 'Generous breakfast: the usual cereals; traditional cooked dishes; cheerful waitresses.' The red brick building stands in wooded grounds with views of the Ribble valley, near the busy A59 (windows are double glazed). 'An attractive base in an unspoilt, uncrowded area.'

14 bedrooms. 4 on ground floor, 1 suitable for ♿. 4½ miles N of Blackburn, on A59. Closed 25 Dec, 1 Jan. Ramp. Lounge, drawing room, cocktail bar (background jazz), restaurant; private dining/meeting room. 2-acre garden. Civil wedding licence. No smoking. No dogs. Amex, MasterCard, Visa accepted. B&B £112.50–£195 per person. Set menus £50–£85; full alc £65. Gourmet breaks.

LANGTHWAITE North Yorkshire — Map 4:C3

The Charles Bathurst Inn
Langthwaite, Arkengarthdale
DL11 6EN

Tel 01748-884567
Fax 01748-884599
Email info@cbinn.co.uk
Website www.cbinn.co.uk

In a hamlet in wonderful walking country on the edge of the Pennine Way, this 18th-century inn was originally the home of Charles Bathurst, a land and mine owner. It has long been frequented by Arkengarthdale residents, who know it as the *CB*. Charles and Stacy Cody extensively renovated it when they bought it in 1996: local craftsmen using local wood and stone. There are open fires and antique pine furniture. 'We loved this lively place, warts and all,' say recent visitors. 'Our pleasant room had good views, but only one bedside table, and we disliked the soap dispenser. The cooking was excellent at breakfast and dinner.' The menu is written on a large mirror (it might include rabbit toad in the hole; Swale Hall rump of lamb with spicy ratatouille). Orders are taken at the bar. On busy days some meals are served in an annexe 'with uncomfortable bench seating'. Breakfast is 'hearty'. Packed lunches are provided. Water comes from the inn's own spring. Eleven bedrooms are in a new wing (built 1999): many have an open truss ceiling. For children there are special menus and a toy box. (*KH*)

19 bedrooms. 5 miles NW of Reeth. Closed Christmas. Ramps. Lounge, 2 bars, restaurant; pool room; background music all day. Small garden: children's play area. No smoking. No dogs. MasterCard, Visa accepted. B&B £40–£90 per person; D,B&B £52.50–£75. Alc dinner £30. 2- or 3-night rates. New Year package. 1-night bookings refused weekends.

LASTINGHAM North Yorkshire — Map 4:C4

Lastingham Grange
Lastingham YO62 6TH

Tel 01751-417345/402
Fax 01751-417358
Email reservations@lastinghamgrange.com
Website www.lastinghamgrange.com

César award in 1991

On the edge of the North Yorkshire Moors national park, this traditional country hotel is 'very well run' by Mrs Jane Wood with her sons, Bertie, the manager, and Tom. Their staff are 'watchful, attentive'. The converted 17th-century farmhouse, built around a courtyard, stands in extensive grounds in a historic village. It is 'as good as ever', say its greatest fans this year. Stone-walled, and built around a courtyard, it is 'not at all grand'. The decor is traditional: 'Floral carpet, floral tiles, floral shower curtain, floral wallpaper, "sitting Thai girl" prints; an open fire in the large lounge.' There is 'nothing fancy or pretentious' either about the cooking of Paul Cattaneo and Sandra Thurlow, eg, avocado vinaigrette; grilled fillet of plaice with lemon and parsley butter. The 'equally good' breakfast has 'delicious sausages; lots of cereals'. Rates include newspapers, morning coffee and afternoon tea. There is an adventure playground for children. From the garden you can walk straight out on to the moors. Good birdwatching and shooting. 'As usual we had a restful time, and met some interesting people.' (*Anne and Denis Tate*)

11 bedrooms. 5 miles NE of Kirkbymoorside. Open Mar–Dec; closed Christmas/New Year. Ramps. Hall, lounge, dining room; laundry facilities. No background music. 10-acre grounds: terrace, garden, adventure playground, croquet, *boules*. Limited assistance for ♿. No smoking. No dogs in public rooms. MasterCard, Visa accepted. B&B [2007] £55–£110 per person; D,B&B £75–£130. Picnic lunches/bar meals available. Set lunch £14.50, dinner £37.50. *V*

LAVENHAM Suffolk — Map 2:C5

The Great House

Market Place
Lavenham CO10 9QZ

Tel 01787-247431
Fax 01787-248007
Email info@greathouse.co.uk
Website www.greathouse.co.uk

Régis Crépy and his wife, Martine, have for many years run this restaurant-with-rooms in this peaceful medieval wool town. An imposing part-Tudor, part-Georgian house built by a local weaving family, it stands in a fine position overlooking the market square. 'It is very "correct" in the French sense,' said one reader, 'the welcome is cool in a professional rather than a glacial way; excellent quality and very good value.' Children are welcomed. Four of the five bedrooms are suites, with king-size bed, antiques, old beams, a marble bathroom; also sherry, freshly ground coffee and leaf tea on a tray, and fresh flowers. One has a Jacobean four-poster. This year there is a new bar/lounge area. Enrique Bilbault, chef for 15 years, serves classic French dishes, eg, terrine de foie gras mariné; carré d'agneau au romarin. They are served in the candlelit dining room, with its wooden floors and original inglenook fireplace, or, on warm evenings, in the quiet, enclosed courtyard: 'A real pleasure; unobtrusive service.' Light lunches are available from Tuesday to Saturday. 'An excellent, relaxed breakfast, again in the courtyard, with fresh orange juice, good croissanterie.' (*ML*)

5 bedrooms. By Market Cross, near Guildhall. Public car park. Open Feb–Dec. Restaurant closed Sun night, Mon, Tues midday. Lounge/bar, restaurant (French background music). ½-acre garden: patio, swings. Unsuitable for ♿. No smoking. No dogs in public rooms. MasterCard, Visa accepted. Room [2007]: single £65–£90, double £70–£165, suite £96–£165. Breakfast: continental £8.50, English £12.50. Set lunch £16.95, dinner £25.95; full alc £38–£45. Midweek breaks. 1-night bookings refused Sat.

Lavenham Priory

Water Street
Lavenham CO10 9RW

Tel 01787-247404
Fax 01787-248472
Email mail@lavenhampriory.co.uk
Website www.lavenhampriory.co.uk

'Everything has been well thought out' at this unusual and 'romantic' B&B. Sympathetically restored by Tim and Gilli Pitt, the lime-washed, half-timbered, Grade I listed medieval house was once a Benedictine priory, later an Elizabethan merchant's house. Guests have use of a 'snug' (with TV, videos and books) and the 13th-century Great Hall (with great beamed ceiling, huge inglenook fireplace, antique furniture and oak Jacobean staircase). Upstairs are mullioned windows and old oak floorboards. Visitors write of 'a lovely mixture of old-fashioned charm and modern comfort', and 'friendly, relaxed' hosts. The suite has a separate sitting room; the other five 'bedchambers' are spacious, with sloping, beamed ceilings, oak floor. There are unusual beds (four-poster, sleigh or polonaise), slipper baths and power showers. A communal breakfast is served around a large table in the 'stunning' Merchants Room. 'You squeeze your own orange juice, and make your own toast', and there are kippers, smoked haddock, scrambled eggs, three types of bread. Breakfast and drinks are served in the herb garden in summer. Help is given with booking in local restaurants.

6 bedrooms. Central (rear rooms quietest). Parking. Closed Christmas/New Year. Great Hall/sitting room, snug, breakfast room. No background music. 3-acre garden: medieval courtyard, herb garden. Unsuitable for ♿. No smoking. No children under 10. No dogs. MasterCard, Visa accepted. B&B [2007] £49–£85 per person. Discount for 2 nights or more. 1-night bookings refused Sat, some holidays.

Traveller's tale The food was OK if you like cream in every sauce and ridiculously vast portions (a whole loaf of bread with our starters). Good value, although I hate to think how many vegetables are wasted: my husband and I were given enough for a family of four at every meal. (*Hotel in Somerset*)

LEEDS West Yorkshire — Map 4:D4

42 The Calls

42 The Calls
Leeds LS2 7EW
Tel 0113-244 0099
Fax 0113-234 4100
Email hotel@42thecalls.co.uk
Website www.42thecalls.co.uk

In a quiet location overlooking the River Aire, this conversion of an old corn mill was the first boutique hotel outside London. It is owned by MBI International which has luxury hotels in Europe and the Middle East (see also *The Scotsman*, Edinburgh). Managed by Belinda Dawson, it remains a favourite choice because of the 'pleasant staff, central position and attractive weekend rates'. The 'flair is still there for design and decor'; there are 'hundreds of original paintings and drawings', bold fabrics, stylish public rooms. Bedrooms are 'fully kitted out for the business traveller' (Internet access, Wi-Fi, desks, etc). The handmade beds are 'supremely comfortable'; duvets have a 'high-quality cotton cover'; there is a trouser press, iron and ironing board in every room. Those rooms overlooking the canal are the quietest; some on the main road may be noisy. A wheelchair-user was pleased with the accessibility of his bedroom. A good continental breakfast can be brought to the room; *à la carte* breakfasts are served in the River Room. The independently run restaurant, *Brasserie 44*, has a *Michelin Bib Gourmand.* (*D and KW, and others*)

41 bedrooms. 1 suitable for ♿. Central, near Corn Exchange. Closed Christmas. Restaurant closed Sun, bank holidays. Lift. Lounge/bar, breakfast room (background radio), restaurant (independently run; background music); conference facilities. No smoking. No dogs in public rooms. All major credit cards accepted. Room [2007] £120–£395. Breakfast £14. Set lunch £13.50, dinner (early bird) £19.95; full alc £34.50. (*10% service charge added to meal price.*) Weekend breaks; special packages. 1-night bookings sometimes refused. *V*

See also SHORTLIST

LEOMINSTER Herefordshire — Map 3:C4

See SHORTLIST

> Smaller hotels, especially those in remote areas, may close at short notice off-season. Check before travelling that a hotel is open.

LEONARD STANLEY Gloucestershire — Map 3:E5

The Grey Cottage
Bath Road, Leonard Stanley
Stonehouse GL10 3LU

Tel/Fax 01453-822515
Website www.greycottage.ik.com

César award in 1999

'Our third visit. We felt really at home, except that the breakfast was much better.' Praise in 2007 for the 'effervescent' Rosemary Reeves's much-loved little stone Cotswolds guest house. Other comments: 'We were sent several pages of interesting/useful data in advance.' 'Wonderful welcome and help with luggage. We felt truly cosseted.' Arriving guests are greeted with leaf tea and biscuits. The spacious bedrooms have 'all the extras you could want; fresh fruit, bottled water, a tea and coffee tray with fresh milk in a Thermos flask; clothes brush, torch, etc, *and* a hand bell to summon Rosie in an emergency'. One room has its bathroom down a short hall. Dinner is by arrangement: no choice; preferences discussed at the time of booking. 'Beautifully presented, unfussy meals.' 'A memorable candlelit dinner: baked pork fillet in prosciutto; treacle tart with fresh raspberries and organic vanilla ice cream.' There is an honesty bar, and guests can bring their own wine (no corkage charge). Breakfast includes freshly squeezed orange juice, smoked salmon with scrambled eggs, home-made jams, loaves of home-made bread for DIY toasting. In the garden is a yew hedge planted in 1840. 'Noise from road just audible.' (*Count and Countess zu Dohna, Gordon Franklin, S and CR*)

3 bedrooms. 3 miles SW of Stroud. Closed Christmas, 'occasional holidays'. Advance booking essential. Sitting room with TV, conservatory, dining room. No background music. ¼-acre garden. Unsuitable for ♿. No smoking. No children under 13. No dogs. No credit cards. B&B £30–£55 per person; D,B&B £55–£80. Set dinner £25.

LEWDOWN Devon — Map 1:C3

Lewtrenchard Manor
Lewdown
nr Okehampton EX20 4PN

Tel 01566-783222
Fax 01566-783332
Email info@lewtrenchard.co.uk
Website www.lewtrenchard.co.uk

The long-serving Jason Hornbuckle now runs this romantic old stone house for the von Essen group as chef/*patron.* A visitor returning this year reports: 'Little has changed except that the very pleasant garden is much improved, and the cooking is noticeably better.' The house, once the ancestral home of the Revd Sabine Baring Gould who wrote 'Onward, Christian Soldiers', is a 'Victorian/Elizabethan fantasy': ornate plaster ceilings, oak panelling, stained glass, huge fireplaces, family portraits and antiques. The bedrooms are off a 'delightful' music gallery, reached by a fine wooden staircase: 'Our comfortable, well-furnished suite had king-size bed, and small sitting room. The bathroom, recently refurbished, was well laid out and equipped. Our dinners were tastefully served and well flavoured. A good range of options including fresh orange juice was on offer at breakfast. There were several hiccups: slow afternoon tea service, warm white wine, slightly chaotic service in the bar. We did not let them spoil our stay.' The 'idyllic' grounds have an avenue of copper beech and elm trees, a dovecote, sunken garden and lake with swans. Vegetables, salads and soft fruits are home grown in a renovated walled garden for the 'unfussy' cooking. (*AJ Ward, DF*)

14 bedrooms. 1 suitable for ♿. S of A30 Okehampton–Launceston. Nearest station Exeter St Davids (45 mins' drive). 2 lounges, bar, restaurant, 2 dining rooms (classical background music at lunch and dinner); function facilities. 12-acre garden. Civil wedding licence. No smoking. No children under 8 in restaurant after 7 pm (high tea provided). No dogs in restaurants. Amex, MasterCard, Visa accepted. B&B £57.50–£145 per person; D,B&B £100.50–£188. Full alc £52. Christmas/New Year packages. 2-night bookings preferred at weekends. *V*

LEWES East Sussex — Map 2:E4

Berkeley House — *Tel/Fax* 01273-476057
2 Albion Street — *Email* enquiries@berkeleyhouselewes.co.uk
Lewes BN7 2ND — *Website* www.berkeleyhouselewes.co.uk

'The owners took pains to make us welcome,' says a visitor in 2007 to Roy Patten and Steve Johnson's small B&B in this 'affluent' old town. 'Good value.' An earlier visitor wrote of the 'charming, knowledgeable and helpful hosts'. The late Georgian town house has 'an interesting history, nicely presented in pictures and prose'. The bedrooms are on the second and third floors (no lift). 'Ours were spotless, cosy and very quiet. My room looked over roofs to the South Downs [the roof terrace shares these views]. Traditional bedding, bottled water, alarm clock, etc.' The residents' lounge has 'a friendly cat and lots of material relating to nearby Glyndebourne. We enjoyed a glass or two of wine here, with local friends.' Drinks, tea and coffee are available 'at all reasonable times'. The 'comfortably furnished' breakfast room overlooks a small courtyard garden, and has a vast mirror, large oak dresser and flowers. The copious breakfast 'was excellent: fresh fruit, good cereals, delicious cooked dishes, plenty of tea and coffee. For dinner, they gave suggestions and made a booking for us. We were delighted with the Italian restaurant a few doors up the hill.' (*Trevor Lockwood*)

3 bedrooms. Town centre. Restricted street parking 8 am to 6 pm Mon–Sat (1-day vouchers for guests); also 1 parking space; public car park nearby. Lounge, breakfast room. No background music. Roof terrace. Unsuitable for ♿. No smoking. No children under 8. No dogs. All major credit cards accepted. B&B £35–£65 per person. 1-night bookings refused Sat in summer.

See also SHORTLIST

LICHFIELD Staffordshire *See SHORTLIST* Map 2:A2

LIFTON Devon Map 1:C3

The Arundell Arms
Lifton PL16 0AA

Tel 01566-784666
Fax 01566-784494
Email reservations@arundellarms.com
Website www.arundellarms.com

César award in 2006

Much loved by anglers, this creeper-covered sporting hotel has been run for 46 years by Anne Voss-Bark, herself an experienced fly-fisher. She has 20 miles of fishing on the Tamar and its four tributaries, and a three-acre stocked lake. Some hiccups of housekeeping were reported after the departure of the long-serving manager, Sally Hill, but visitors in 2007 report: 'A charming, helpful welcome. Our room was quiet and comfortable. Despite some caveats, we enjoyed our stay.' All the bedrooms have been redecorated. The best ones are in the extension at the rear; some of those in the main house hear traffic. Chef Steven Pidgeon cooks 'modern dishes with emphasis on local produce' (suppliers listed on the menu). 'Dinner was an event: most customers had made an old-fashioned effort to dress up. Service was exemplary, timing just right. Food excellent, full of flavour. Starter of scallops with lentils and tomato outstanding, if minuscule; carpaccio of beef full of flavour; puddings melted in the mouth, and we enjoyed the white

Sharpham wine from Devon.' Another visitor called the cuisine 'clever but not fussy'. 'Good bar meals.' But breakfast is still thought 'a hit and miss affair'. The terraced rear garden has seating for alfresco meals. (*Dennis and Janet Allom, and others*)

21 bedrooms. 4 on ground floor. Closed Christmas. ½ mile off A30, 3 miles E of Launceston (road-facing rooms double glazed). Ramp. Lounge, cocktail bar, public bar, 2 dining rooms; gentle classical background music; conference/meeting rooms; games room, skittle alley. ½-acre garden. 20 miles fishing rights on River Tamar and tributaries; 3-acre stocked lake, fishing school. Civil wedding licence. No smoking. All major credit cards accepted. B&B [2007] £80–£115 per person; D,B&B (min. 2 nights) £97.50–£120. Set menu £38; full alc £50. 2- to 6-night breaks all year. Off-season breaks: sporting, gourmet, etc. New Year package. *V*

LINCOLN Lincolnshire *See SHORTLIST* Map 4:E5

LITTLE SHELFORD Cambridgeshire *See SHORTLIST* Map 2:C4

LITTLEBURY GREEN Essex Map 2:C4

The Chaff House

Ash Grove Barns
Littlebury Green
nr Saffron Walden CB11 4XB

Tel/Fax 01763-836278
Mobile 07817-724448
Email dianaduke@btopenworld.com

In a rural village near the M11, this sympathetically converted barn, on a huge estate, 'offers a taste of country farmhouse living'. One bedroom (with exposed beams, sloping ceiling and huge bed) is in the *Chaff House* where the owner, Diana Duke, lives. Two other rooms are in an annexe which has a kitchen, so can be self-catering. 'No baths, but super power showers.' Guests can sit on the patio (with plants in tubs). An evening meal ('outstanding cooking,' said a regular visitor) is available, by arrangement, on weekdays. A sample menu: twice-baked cheese and herb soufflé with tomato coulis; duck breast in cherry sauce; pink grapefruit, orange and ginger caramel. Good local pubs include *Cricketers* at Clavering, run by Jamie Oliver's parents. Stansted airport and Cambridge are both about 30 minutes' drive away. (*CK*)

3 bedrooms. 2 in adjacent annexe (on ground floor). 4 miles W of Saffron Walden. Closed 25 Dec. Dining room closed midday, and Sat/Sun. Lounge, dining room. Kitchen for guests' use in annexe. No background music. In 900-acre estate: small courtyard garden with access to farmland. Unsuitable for ♿. No smoking. No children. No dogs. Diners, MasterCard, Visa accepted. B&B £32.50–£45 per person; D,B&B £57.50–£70. Set dinner £25. (*Not VAT-rated*)

LIVERPOOL Merseyside — Map 4:E2

Hope Street Hotel
40 Hope Street
Liverpool L1 9DA

Tel 0151-709 3000
Fax 0151-709 2454
Email sleep@hopestreethotel.co.uk
Website www.hopestreethotel.co.uk

On the road that links Liverpool's two cathedrals, this 19th-century carriage works in the style of a Venetian *palazzo* has been sympathetically converted by a local consortium into the city's first boutique hotel. Jane Farrelly is managing director. Her 'outstanding young staff' are thought 'warmly welcoming'. The decor is 'a fine example of well-executed minimalism'. Original iron columns, beams and exposed brickwork have been retained in public areas and bedrooms (all of the latter have been refurbished). The trendy bar, *The Residents' Lounge*, has leather sofas and pop music. The 'fine dining' restaurant ('one of Liverpool's best'), *The London Carriage Works*, has bare oak, yellow brickwork and dramatic floor-to-ceiling glass sculptures. Chef Paul Askew serves much-admired modern dishes (eg, grilled red mullet with courgette and basil purée and tomato sauce) on a seasonal menu. There is also a brasserie. Breakfast can be *à la carte*, continental or a 'super' cooked affair. Noise can be a problem: corridors have wooden floors, some covered in sea-grass matting, and soundproofing between rooms is not perfect. The area is the city's cultural centre (the Philharmonic Hall is opposite); it also has some of the city's hippest bars. More reports, please.

48 bedrooms. Opposite Philharmonic Hall. Lift, ramps. Lobby, reading room, bar (live music Fri/Sat), restaurant (closed Sat lunch, Sun evening, Mon), brasserie; background music. Smoking allowed on 1 floor; total ban from 1 Jan 2008. No dogs in public rooms. Amex, MasterCard, Visa accepted. Room [2007]: single/double £150–£225, suite £250–£375. Breakfast £15 (full English). Set dinner (restaurant) £43–£55; full alc (brasserie) £35. Website deals. New Year package. 1-night bookings sometimes refused.

See also SHORTLIST

LIVERSEDGE West Yorkshire — Map 4:D3

Healds Hall

Leeds Road
Liversedge WF15 6JA

Tel 01924-409112
Fax 01924-401895
Email enquire@healdshall.co.uk
Website www.healdshall.co.uk

The largest house in the Spen valley when it was built in 1764, Tom and Nora Harrington's inexpensive hotel stands up a hill, surrounded by a 'tightly packed housing estate', near an old industrial town. There is now free Wi-Fi access throughout the building, and bedroom refurbishment is ongoing. 'Our room, in the modern extension, was quiet and perfectly adequate,' says one reader, but others this year had a 'quite small' bedroom with a mattress that 'needed replacing'. The bar is 'very pleasant', and most visitors find the food in the popular restaurant 'very good, and good value', and the atmosphere 'upbeat and cheerful'. The *à la carte* menu includes grilled fillet of sea bass; roast loin of venison. But guests on a Sunday, when the restaurant is open to residents only, write 'we were the only ones there, and had to put up with noisy children running around'. 'Breakfast very satisfactory. Well-stocked buffet, good cooked platter. The lady of the house was much in evidence.' Private functions are often held, as are theme nights (eg, *tapas* evening, Mexican evening, paella night). (*Gareth Evans, and others*)

24 bedrooms. 2 on ground floor, suitable for ♿. Closed 1 Jan. Restaurant closed to non-residents Sat lunch, Sun night. On A62 Leeds–Huddersfield, 3 miles from M62. Parking. Bar with conservatory area, restaurant, bistro; background music; conference/function suite. 3-acre grounds: lawns, garden. Civil wedding licence. No smoking. No dogs: 23 bedrooms, public rooms. All major credit cards accepted. B&B [2007] £37.50–£63 per person; D,B&B £50–£76. Set lunch £8.50, Sun lunch £15.50; full alc £37. Special breaks. Christmas/New Year packages. *V*

LODDISWELL Devon — Map 1:D4

Hazelwood House

Loddiswell
nr Kingsbridge TQ7 4EB

Tel 01548-821232
Fax 01548-821318
Email info@hazelwoodhouse.com
Website www.hazelwoodhouse.com

In a 'brilliant setting' in a wooded Devon valley rich in wildlife, this 'lovely' Victorian house 'with a somewhat run-down feeling' has 'an ambience seldom achieved elsewhere', say visitors this year. 'We felt very happy there.' Owned by the 'charming' Jane Bowman, Gillian Kean and Anabel Farnell-Watson, it is 'wonderfully friendly' (guests on their own feel at ease). It won't suit everyone, but devotees love the 'spiritual quality', the 'informal but professional' hospitality, the 'very good' meals, largely based on local organic produce, and the 'comfort without frills'. Filled with simple furniture, antiques and paintings, and with log fires in the public rooms, the house stands in grounds that slope down to the River Avon. This year, the owners tell us, 'substantial work has been carried out so that it is not so crumbly'. Central heating has been added to the first floor and half the bedrooms now have facilities *en suite.* The best bedroom is spacious, but some rooms are small. The top-floor rooms are heated by electric fires. Cultural courses, concerts and weekends with entertainments (jazz, painting, story-telling, etc) are held. Children are welcomed. The sea is about six miles away. (*Simon Rodway, and others*)

14 bedrooms. 7 with facilities *en suite.* 4 self-catering cottages. 2 miles N of Loddiswell. Train: Totnes, 10 miles. Hall with piano, drawing room, study/TV room, dining room; music 'on request'; function/conference facilities. 67-acre grounds: river, boathouse; former chapel. Only restaurant suitable for ♿. Civil wedding licence. No smoking. Dogs by arrangement (on lead in public rooms). Diners, MasterCard, Visa accepted. B&B [2007] £35.25–£75.20 per person; D,B&B £52.87–£104.58. Set menus £14.10 (lunch)–£32.90 (dinner); full alc £45. Negotiable rates for groups. Christmas/New Year packages. *V*

LONGHORSLEY Northumberland — Map 4:B3

Thistleyhaugh NEW
Longhorsley, nr Morpeth
NE65 8RG

Tel 01665-570629
Email stay@thistleyhaugh.co.uk
Website www.thistleyhaugh.co.uk

Run by Enid Nelless, with daughters Zoe and Janice, this Georgian house stands by the River Coquet on 'very much a working farm':

Henry Nelless and his two sons rear beef and sheep, and keep geese, hens and ducks. 'Ideally situated for visiting the attractions, notably Alnwick garden,' say the nominators, 'but up a private road, well off the beaten track.' The 'spotless' bedrooms 'are decorated to a high standard', and you can choose between duvet and blankets. Each room has a small refrigerator with milk and bottled water; home-made biscuits are provided. Guests have the use of a 'large, comfortable' sitting room with open fire. An evening meal (you need to book it at breakfast) is served round a large oval table in a 'well-furnished period room'. Four courses, no choice, 'all superbly cooked from prime ingredients': home-made soups; roast local organic meat. Vegetarians are catered for, with advance notice. 'They are not licensed, but supply a bottle of wine for each couple.' Breakfast has 'a splendid choice of cereals, fruit and home-made preserves, and a cooked dish for each guest'. (*Joan and David Marston*)

5 bedrooms. 10 miles N of Morpeth, E of A697. Open Feb–Dec; closed Christmas/ New Year. Lounges, dining room; classical background music. 685-acre farm: garden with summer house. Fishing, shooting, golf, riding nearby. Unsuitable for ♿. No smoking. No dogs (kennels nearby). MasterCard, Visa accepted. B&B £37.50–£75 per person. Set dinner £20.

LONGSTOCK Hampshire Map 2:D2

The Peat Spade Inn NEW

Village Street
Longstock SO20 6DR

Tel 01264-810612
Fax 01264-811078
Email info@peatspadeinn.co.uk
Website www.peatspadeinn.co.uk

In a lovely village (with thatched houses, horses and a large Waitrose estate) in the Test valley, this old inn and 'rooming house' was bought in 2006 by Lucy Townsend (front-of-house) and Andy Clark (chef). They refurbished, encouraged by Robin Hutson, founder of the Hotel du Vin group, and aim to serve 'good British cooking in a distinctly pub setting'. Many visitors are fisherfolk. An expert reports: 'Excellent in every way. Well decorated. Food and atmosphere very good – unpretentious.' The 'rustic feel' is liked. Inspectors add: 'All you could wish for in a country pub: hands-on management, cheerful service, good, straightforward food, reasonable prices. Our charming room, up a flight of steps, was in the *Peat House*. It had steeply sloping ceiling, olive-green walls, pale carpet, fridge with fresh milk, modem point. Beautiful shower room (skylight, large cabinet, huge shower head).' In the three dining rooms, with wooden tables, 'we enjoyed beer-battered haddock with pea mousse; local sausages and mash; lemon and raspberry posset. Popular with locals, it was very busy at the weekend. Wines chosen with care; real ales stocked. Lucy came to chat as we ate.' Breakfast (no menu) includes eggs as you like, 'delicious fresh fruit salad, chunky toast'. There is a 'delightful rear patio'. (*Anne Voss-Bark, and others*)

6 bedrooms. Centre of village, 1 mile N of Stockbridge. Ample parking. Restaurant closed Sun night. Ramps. Lounge, bar, restaurant (background jazz); private dining room. Patio. No smoking. No children under 10 in bedrooms. No dogs in bedrooms. MasterCard, Visa accepted. B&B double/single £110. Set menu £25.

LOOE Cornwall — Map 1:D3

The Beach House
Marine Drive, Hannafore
Looe PL13 2DH
Tel 01503-262598
Fax 01503-262298
Email enquiries@thebeachhouselooe.com
Website www.thebeachhouselooe.com

With the South West Coastal Path running past its front gate, Rosie and David Reeve's B&B has panoramic views of Whitsand Bay and the coastline. White-walled and gabled, it is an easy walk from the town centre, and has direct access to the beach. Four bedrooms face the sea; rooms at the rear are 'decent sized' too. 'Our room, Fistral, the most expensive, was worth it for the view: its huge patio windows opened on to a balcony. The decor was subtle, in cream and gold, and extras made it more like a five-star hotel than a B&B.' Only one room, the twin-bedded Kynance, does not have facilities *en suite* (it has a shower room adjacent). The 'superb' breakfast room faces the sea. You make your choice the evening before, selecting a time which does not clash with other guests. 'Excellent: a buffet table with yogurt and juices; generous servings of full English; proper butter in glass dishes.' For meals, *Mawgans* is recommended. A non-refundable deposit of one night's tariff is required to confirm a booking. (*KP*)

5 bedrooms. ½ mile from Looe centre. Parking. Closed Christmas. Garden room, breakfast room (classical background music). Terrace; small garden. Beach opposite. Unsuitable for ♿. No smoking. No children under 16. No pets. MasterCard, Visa accepted. B&B [2007] £40–£60 per person. Min. 3-night booking July/Aug, public holidays.

See also SHORTLIST

LORTON Cumbria — Map 4: inset C2

New House Farm

Lorton
nr Cockermouth CA13 9UU
Tel 01900-85404
Fax 01900-85478
Email hazel@newhouse-farm.co.uk
Website www.newhouse-farm.co.uk

In the beautiful Lorton/Buttermere valley, Hazel Thompson's Grade II listed 17th-century, whitewashed farmhouse has long been liked by readers for its 'good atmosphere' and 'friendly welcome'. Period features include oak beams and rafters, flagged floors and stone open fireplaces. And there is also Wi-Fi. The small lounges have bright colours, comfortable seating, silver and antiques. There are 'marvellous views' in all directions. The bedrooms are all different; two (in a stable and old dairy) have a four-poster bed, another has a large double brass bed with airbath. Traditional food is served in large portions. The no-choice dinner might include cream of fennel soup; roast duckling; ginger pudding with butterscotch sauce. The short wine list has 'sensible, uninflated prices'. Breakfast includes fresh grapefruit, prunes, eggs and bacon, home-made marmalade. Lunches and teas are served in the café, in a converted barn. Pets are allowed the run of the grounds but not the public rooms; riders can bring their own horses. Traffic passes on the country road in front of the house, but the two rear bedrooms are 'perfectly quiet'. (*ALS*)

5 bedrooms. 1 in stable, 1 in old dairy. On B5289, 2 miles S of Lorton. 3 lounges, dining room. No background music. 17-acre grounds: garden, hot tub, streams, woods, field. Lake and river (safe bathing) 2 miles. Unsuitable for ♿. No smoking. No children under 6. No dogs in public rooms. MasterCard, Visa accepted. B&B £73–£120 per person. Packed lunch £7.50. Set dinner £22–£30. Christmas/New Year packages. 1-night bookings sometimes refused.

See also SHORTLIST

****

Traveller's tale We turned up at the appointed time to find the door locked. A lovely dog welcomed us from within, but no human came for some time. Eventually a woman appeared, but told us to wait in the hall; she disappeared, to talk on the phone for another five minutes. The hall had a fireplace but no flames. The dog was our only welcome. Our hostess returned, having finished her call, and showed us to our room. It was freezing. (*Hotel in Derbyshire*)

****

LOWER BOCKHAMPTON Dorset Map 1:C6

Yalbury Cottage NEW
Lower Bockhampton
nr Dorchester DT2 8PZ

Tel 01305-262382
Email yalburyemails@aol.com
Website www.yalburycottage.com

César award: Rural idyll of the year

In peaceful Hardy country, this conversion of four thatched cottages is warmly recommended by trusted correspondents in 2007. 'Think deluxe chocolate box. In the pretty garden, pansies drip out of baskets and urns, and fish laze in a little pond. Interiors are traditional, cosy, tasteful, with smart sofas, inglenook fireplaces, exposed beams (if over five and a half feet, you must mind your head), flowers, interesting books, excellent local information.' The owners, Mark Collyer and Roy Fiddemont, are 'thoroughly professional. Roy is the prototype "mine host", convivial but not over familiar. Everything demonstrates attention to the well-being of guests.' Bedrooms have 'modern traditional' wooden furniture. 'Ours was well lit, comfortable, simple but smart, with impeccable bathroom. Silence was palpable at night; to wake to birdsong and the clip-clop of horses on the road was a delight.' Pre-dinner drinks come with 'very good' *amuse-bouche*. As to Ben Streak's award-winning modern cooking: 'Everything was delicious. Starter of asparagus with cubed red mullet and foie gras; loin of lamb with root vegetables and spectacular tian of ratatouille; iced nougat parfait was indeed perfect. The small wine list was adequate if pricey.' Breakfast, 'delicious too', had 'noteworthy scrambled eggs with smoked salmon', local eggs, bacon and sausages, home-made croissants. (*Francine and Ian Walsh*)

8 bedrooms. 6 on ground floor. 2 miles E of Dorchester. Closed 2 weeks in Jan. Residents' lounge (discreet background music), restaurant. ¾-acre garden. No smoking. No dogs: some bedrooms, public rooms. MasterCard, Visa accepted. B&B £56–£70 per person. Set dinner £34. Min. weekend stay of 2 nights in high season. New Year package.

LOWESTOFT Suffolk *See SHORTLIST* Map 2:B6

When you make a booking you enter into a contract with a hotel. Most hotels explain their cancellation policies, which vary widely, in a letter of confirmation. You may lose your deposit or be charged at the full rate for the room if you cancel at short notice. A travel insurance policy can provide protection.

LUDLOW Shropshire Map 3:C4

Dinham Hall
Dinham, by the castle
Ludlow SY8 1EJ

Tel 01584-876464
Fax 01584-876019
Email info@dinhamhall.co.uk
Website www.dinhamhall.co.uk

Service, atmosphere and food are praised again in 2007 at this late 18th-century house, well placed for exploring the town. 'A very pleasant three-day stay.' Owned by Jean-Pierre Mifsud of *The Lake*, Llangammarch Wells, Wales (*qv*), the mellow stone building was once used by boarders at Ludlow grammar school: some rooms have initials carved by the boys, and school photographs are displayed in the lounge. The manager, James Garnett, 'makes you feel at home'. One returning guest experienced 'nothing but kindness and consideration'. Another wrote: 'Small and intimate. It has everything I look for in a hotel.' The ambience 'is in keeping with the beautiful old house; friendly conversation between guests gives ample evidence of this'. The walled garden and some bedrooms face the Teme valley and 'some lovely houses and gardens'. One suite ('comfortable, spacious') has a private terrace with fountain. Bedroom refurbishment continues. Former *sous-chef* Caitlin Proctor is now in charge of the kitchen and serves 'modern British cooking with Italian influences', eg, fillets of lemon sole with a pumpkin seed risotto and linguini of vegetables. 'Worth travelling for.' Breakfasts include 'fresh fruit, kippers, lashings of good toast'. (*Mrs G Smith, and others*)

13 bedrooms. 2 in cottage (30 yds). 1 on ground floor. Near castle. Parking. Ramp. 2 lounges, bar, restaurant; 2 private dining rooms. No background music. 1-acre walled garden. Unsuitable for ♿. Civil wedding licence. No smoking. No children under 8 at dinner. Dogs allowed in annexe rooms. All major credit cards accepted. B&B £70–£120 per person; D,B&B £90–£140. Set dinner £38.50. Christmas/New Year packages. *V*

Mr Underhill's
Dinham Weir
Ludlow SY8 1EH

Tel 01584-874431
Website www.mr-underhills.co.uk

César award in 2000

'Delightful staff.' 'The food was wonderful.' 'We love the setting.' 'It won't suit everyone, but if you go with the flow, you will be looked after with humour and affection.' Comments on Christopher and Judy Bradley's restaurant-with-rooms on the banks of the River Teme, below Ludlow Castle. He has a *Michelin* star; she runs front-of-house, with 'approachable formality'. Guests are told the proposed set menu (alternatives can be offered). 'Even after three nights of fairly rich eating, we enjoyed every mouthful,' says a long-term fan. 'Dinners are a marathon, but portions are adjusted to your appetite.' 'Service is smooth.' Other visitors 'enjoyed it enormously, but would have liked some choice'. Housekeeping 'might not always be perfect', and this is '*not* a hotel; you are asked not to arrive before 3.30 pm, and unless you have a suite, the bedrooms are too small to sit in for long'. The *Shed* suite, in the garden, is particularly liked; two other suites are in *Miller's House* opposite; the lower one, by the road, can be noisy. There is new accommodation in the *Old School*, nearby, for parties of up to six: 'A luxury bolthole where we encourage guests to look after themselves.' Breakfast has a choice of fresh fruit and yogurt or a cooked dish: 'excellent scrambled eggs'. (*SP, Padi Howard, and others*)

9 bedrooms. 3 in annexes. Below castle, on River Teme. Station ½ mile. Parking. Closed Christmas, 1 week in summer, 1 week in autumn. Restaurant closed Mon/Tues. Small lounge, restaurant; function facilities. No background music. ½-acre courtyard, riverside garden: fishing, swimming. Unsuitable for ♿. No smoking. No children 2 to 8. No dogs. MasterCard, Visa accepted. B&B £100–£150 per person. Set dinner £47–£52. New Year package. 1-night bookings often refused Sat.

See also SHORTLIST

LYDFORD Devon — Map 1:C4

The Dartmoor Inn

Moorside
Lydford, nr Okehampton
EX20 4AY

Tel 01822-820221
Fax 01822-820494
Email info@dartmoorinn.co.uk
Website www.dartmoorinn.com

César award in 2007

'The best place for food, friendliness and charm without chintz,' writes a visitor this year to Karen and Philip Burgess's small hotel on a busy road to the west of Dartmoor. Other praise: 'Charming and effortless service.' The inn is fitted out in 'charismatic style', with 'slightly distressed antique furniture'. 'We had a very spacious bedroom and bathroom, well furnished although the walls were a bit bare without pictures. A number or name on the door would have stopped me from walking into another guest's room.' Karen Burgess runs a 'rather fabulous' boutique in two of the ground-floor rooms; the others are dining areas, some formal, with wood-burning stove, others more casual. Praise continues for Philip Burgess and Andrew Honey's modern cooking, eg, watercress soup with nutmeg cream; casserole of sea fishes with saffron butter sauce. Coffee and florentines are taken by 'gently flaming logs in the bar'. Breakfast is 'breathtaking', with 'chocolate pots, fresh fruit, home-made breads and an incredible list of hot items'. 'It must be one of the best anywhere, and tables are laid with pristine damask cloths, real table napkins. This place shows care, flair, dedication and talent.' (*Andrya Prescott, Andrew Laugherne, David Stevens, and others*)

3 bedrooms. 6 miles from Tavistock on A386 to Okehampton. Train: Exeter/ Plymouth. Parking. Closed 25 Dec. 2 bars, restaurant. No background music. Jazz concerts, exhibitions. Small sunken garden. Unsuitable for ♿. No smoking. Not really suitable for small children. No dogs in bedrooms. Amex, MasterCard, Visa accepted. B&B [2007]: single £90, double £115. Full alc £30–£35. 1-night bookings sometimes refused bank holiday weekends.

LYME REGIS Dorset *See SHORTLIST* Map 1:C6

LYMINGTON Hampshire Map 2:E2

Britannia Guest House NEW *Tel* 01590-672091
Station Street *Email* enquiries@britannia-house.com
Lymington SO41 3BA *Website* www.britannia-house.com

Owner Tobias Feilke 'is a perfectionist', say admirers of this B&B, composed of two brick-built houses opposite each other. 'The location is excellent for those wanting to enjoy the lovely marina, cobbled streets and smart shops of Lymington,' wrote an inspector. In the older building, the decor is 'lush country house: heavy fabrics, chandeliers, etc, but characterful and homely'. The large upstairs sitting room, with wide views (harbour and marina), has 'a lovely ambience: decorated in dramatic blue and yellow, large, enveloping sofas, good lighting, plenty of books (lots in German), and magazines'. The bedrooms have plain walls, Berber carpets, patterned curtains, bedcovers and cushions. 'Our top-floor room was decent-sized, very pleasant, with adjacent romantic, spacious bathroom. Downstairs rooms are smaller, darker.' Three other rooms in a modern, quayside building are in more contemporary, plainer style: check fabrics, pine and painted furniture. In the large pine kitchen, 'Tobias cooks a good breakfast: delicious mushrooms, non-meat sausages for vegetarians'. This is served at a 'convivial' communal table. The station is close by. 'Noise from trains does not affect, but crack-of-dawn Monday rubbish collection might.' There is a 'pleasant little courtyard'. (*Malcolm Turner, and others*)

6 bedrooms. 5 mins' walk from High Street/quayside. Parking. Lounge, kitchen/ breakfast room. Courtyard garden. No background music. Unsuitable for ♿. No smoking. Children by arrangement only. No dogs. MasterCard, Visa accepted. B&B: single £50–£85, double £75–£85. 1-night bookings refused weekends.

See also SHORTLIST

LYNMOUTH Devon *See SHORTLIST* Map 1:B4

LYNTON Devon Map 1:B4

Lynton Cottage NEW
North Walk, Lynton
EX35 6ED

Tel 01598-752342
Fax 01598-754016
Email enquiries@lynton-cottage.co.uk
Website www.lynton-cottage.co.uk

There are 'stunning views' of the bay, Countisbury Hill and Watersmeet from this cliff-top building. A quartet of owners, Heather Biancardi (formerly the housekeeper), Allan Earl (the chef), Davie Mowlem and Bettina Earl, has run it since 2005. 'If, like me, you first look at the desserts on the menu,' writes its nominator, 'this is the hotel for you. All were first class; the coconut panna cotta left me feeling I was in heaven.' Main courses include Cornish mackerel with leek fondue and sweet potato. All bedrooms face the sea. 'The Bay Room, the best, is worth every penny for the amazing circular vista of the bay, let alone the furnishings.' Some rooms have a four-poster, some a small balcony. At breakfast, 'the American-style pancakes are delicious, but pride of place must go to the home-made bread'. Light lunches and cream teas are served (on the terrace in fine weather). Local art is displayed in the restaurant. You can walk down through the garden to the village, 600 feet below. (*Judy Waller*)

16 bedrooms. 1 on ground floor. Town centre. 14 miles NE of Barnstaple. Ample parking. Closed Christmas/New Year. Lounge, bar, restaurant; soft background CDs. Terrace. 2½-acre garden. Unsuitable for ♿. No smoking. Pets by prior arrangement, not in restaurant. MasterCard, Visa accepted. B&B [2007] £42–£78 per person; D,B&B £71.50–£107.50. Special breaks.

LYTHAM Lancashire *See SHORTLIST* Map 4:D2

MAIDENHEAD Berkshire *See SHORTLIST* Map 2:D3

MALVERN WELLS Worcestershire Map 3:D5

The Cottage in the Wood
Holywell Road
Malvern Wells
WR14 4LG

Tel 01684-575859
Fax 01684-560662
Email reception@cottageinthewood.co.uk
Website www.cottageinthewood.co.uk

Splendidly set, high on the wooded eastern slopes of the Malvern Hills, this traditional country hotel looks over 30 miles of the Severn vale, and is said to have 'the best view in England'. John and Sue Pattin, owners for 21 years, run it with son Dominic as chef, and son-in-law Nick Webb as manager. Visitors like the 'happy atmosphere', the comprehensive information guide, and the 'stunning walks from the door' (100 miles of tracks). Some rooms are in the Georgian main house; newer, larger ones are in the *Pinnacles* annexe: this suffered 'snagging problems' last year. They are 'now behind us', Mr Pattin writes, 'enough hot water to drown in, and peace from creaking floors'. All rooms have video and telephone with computer facility, Malvern water and home-made shortbread. Rooms with the view have binoculars. The public rooms have antiques, knick-knacks and panoramic views; there is free Wi-Fi. Half-board rates include three courses from the long *à la carte* menu, eg, crab cakes with ginger and lime tabbouleh; pot-roast pheasant with caramelised salsify. 'A very good meal,' is one comment. 'A sense of occasion,' is another. The Pattins are planning to increase the emphasis on local, fresh ingredients. More reports, please.

31 bedrooms. 4 in *Beech Cottage*, 70 yds. 19 (1 suitable for ♿) in *Pinnacles*, 100 yds. Off A449 to Ledbury, 3 miles S of Malvern. Train: Great Malvern. Lounge, bar, restaurant; function facilities. No background music. 7-acre grounds; terrace. Golf, squash nearby. Smoking allowed in 5 bedrooms. Dogs allowed in ground-floor bedrooms in *Pinnacles*; not in public rooms. Amex, MasterCard, Visa accepted. B&B [2007] £49.50–£109 per person; D,B&B (min. 2 nights) £75–£118. Full alc £45. Bargain breaks. Christmas/New Year packages. 1-night bookings sometimes refused. *V*

Hotels will often try to persuade you to stay for two nights at the weekend. Resist this pressure if you want to stay only one night.

MANCHESTER *See SHORTLIST* Map 4:E3

MARAZION Cornwall Map 1:E1

Mount Haven Hotel & Restaurant
Turnpike Road
Marazion TR17 0DQ

Tel 01736-710249
Fax 01736-711658
Email reception@mounthaven.co.uk
Website www.mounthaven.co.uk

From its vantage point overlooking St Michael's Mount, this 'bright and airy, contemporary hotel' is owned by Mike and Orange Trevillion and Tom Johnstone (front-of-house). 'It has an informal, relaxing atmosphere,' say visitors, and is 'run in a hands-on way'. Originally a coach house, much altered in 1970, it has been refurbished with silks from Mumbai, tapestries from Jaipur, modern paintings and pastel shades; incense burns. There are 'fresh flowers from local fields'. The terrace has decking, 'smart steel and slatted furniture'. Many bedrooms face Mount's Bay from a private balcony. Each of the two garden rooms has a patio. 'The food is first class and generous.' The cooking style of chef Julie Manley is 'modern British, with lots of seafood', eg, red mullet in a lime, ginger and garlic marinade with roast pepper dressing and couscous. A team of holistic therapists comes to give treatment to guests (Indian head massage, etc). (*MF, and others*)

18 bedrooms. Some on ground floor. 4 miles E of Penzance. Car park. Closed Jan, Christmas/New Year. Lounge/bar, restaurant; 'chill-out' music all day; healing room (holistic treatments). Sun terrace. ½-acre grounds. Rock/sand beaches 100 yds. Unsuitable for ♿. No smoking. Dogs allowed in public rooms only. MasterCard, Visa accepted. B&B [2007] £45–£90 per person; D,B&B £74–£115. Full alc £37.50. 3-night breaks spring/autumn. Min. 2 nights on bank holidays. *V*

MARKET DRAYTON Shropshire *See SHORTLIST* Map 3:B5

'Set menu' indicates a fixed-price meal, with ample, limited or no choice. 'Full alc' is the hotel's estimated price per person of a three-course *à la carte* meal, with a half bottle of house wine. 'Alc' is the price of an *à la carte* meal excluding the cost of wine.

MARKINGTON North Yorkshire — Map 4:D4

Hob Green

Markington
nr Harrogate HG3 3PJ

Tel 01423-770031
Fax 01423-771589
Email info@hobgreen.com
Website www.hobgreen.com

'Delightful. Warm welcome, offer of help with luggage. Every member of staff was kind and friendly.' 'Probably the best value of our trip. Lovely quiet location. Excellent for travellers with a dog.' 'Very pleasant restaurant.' Comments on this traditional hotel run for over 20 years by the Hutchinson family owners; Christopher Ashby is manager. The 18th-century house (with original panelling and moulding, antiques and curios) stands in huge grounds with award-winning gardens, farm and woodlands. The bedrooms, all different, have flowery fabrics and patterned wallpaper. 'Ours was pleasantly furnished and decorated, exceptionally well equipped; good lighting; wonderful views.' Two other couples were less keen: one found their room too cold in January; another had a 'very hot' room above the kitchen ('noisy fans ran all night'). Apart from one remark of 'over ambitious', Chris Taylor's cooking was enjoyed. 'Interesting without being too *nouvelle*; good variety of vegetables.' 'Lobster and prawn dish a real treat.' 'Wines sensibly priced. Good breakfast' (in summer it can be alfresco). Light lunches and teas are served. The terrace has wide views across the valley. 'Enjoyable walks in the grounds and the village.' Conferences and functions are catered for. Fountains Abbey is three miles away. (*PJK, David Innes, Elizabeth Russell, and others*)

12 bedrooms. 1 mile SW of Markington, 5 miles SW of Ripon. Hall, drawing room, sun lounge, restaurant. No background music. 800-acre grounds: 2½-acre garden, children's play area. Unsuitable for ♿. Civil wedding licence. No smoking. No dogs in public rooms. All major credit cards accepted. B&B [2007] £57.50–£95 per person; D, B&B (min. 2 nights) £77.50–£118. Set Sun lunch from £18.95, dinner from £26.50; full alc £39.50. 1-night bookings refused weekends.

MARTINHOE Devon — Map 1:B4

Heddon's Gate Hotel

Martinhoe, Parracombe
EX31 4PZ

Tel 01598-763481
Email hotel@heddonsgate.co.uk
Website www.heddonsgate.co.uk

Renamed *Heaven's Gate*, by a reader this year, Anne and Eddie Eyles's small hotel stands in steeply sloping grounds on the edge of Exmoor. 'Lovely, peaceful situation: superb walking. Very friendly hosts.' Other visitors warn: 'The excellent [complimentary] afternoon tea [home-made savouries, scones, cakes] can seriously damage your appetite for dinner.' The Eyleses have changed little since they bought the hotel in 2005, retaining the old-fashioned, 'mildly eccentric' decor, 'more comfortable than plush'. In the bar are stags' antlers and black leather furniture; in the lounge, tapestries on green walls, cases of china ornaments. Guests normally dine in. The daily-changing dinner menu (limited choice, served promptly at 8 pm) is 'modern and traditional' cooking, eg, smoked salmon roulade; roast breast and leg of guineafowl with Calvados sauce. The price includes coffee. Breakfast, not self-service, has freshly squeezed orange juice, eggs of all kinds, wholemeal toast. The bedrooms vary greatly (some are large). Some are named after their original use: Grandma's (Victorian-style); Nanny's (antique stained-glass windows); The Servants' Quarters (private sitting room). Beds are turned down at night. Good walks start from the door. (*Mrs C Leeming, Tim and Wendy Davey, Meri Lowry, Susan Lee, PE Carter*)

10 bedrooms. 6 miles W of Lynton. Train/coach: Barnstaple, 12 miles. Open mid-Mar–end Oct (or later, subject to demand), possibly Christmas/New Year. 2 reception halls, 2 lounges, library, bar, dining room. No background music. 2½-acre grounds. River, fishing, riding, pony trekking nearby. Sea ¾ mile. Unsuitable for ♿. No smoking. Children 'must be old enough to dine with parents at 8 pm'. No dogs unattended in bedrooms. MasterCard, Visa accepted. B&B [2007] £53–£80 per person; D,B&B £80–£107. Set dinner £31.50. Christmas/New Year packages subject to demand. 1-night bookings occasionally refused. *V*

MASHAM North Yorkshire — Map 4:D4

Swinton Park
Masham, nr Ripon
HG4 4JH

Tel 01765-680900
Fax 01765-680901
Email enquiries@swintonpark.com
Website www.swintonpark.com

A family home since the late 19th century, this creeper-clad, castellated 17th-century castle (Grade II* listed) sits in huge landscaped grounds with many activities (see below). Now a luxury hotel, owned by Mark and Felicity Cunliffe-Lister and managed by Andrew McPherson, it has large reception rooms (antique furniture, family portraits, mirrors, rugs on polished floors) and a spa. 'A joy and delight, staff were terrific,' say visitors in 2007. 'A wonderful stay,' was another comment. But weddings and functions might sometimes detract from private visits. The spacious bedrooms, all different, have Wi-Fi access. There are 'stunning views' from many, including the shower room in the circular three-floor Turret suite. 'The Wensleydale suite is one of the most spacious and comfortable we have ever experienced.' Four rooms have 'disabled-friendly fittings'. For children there are cots, high chairs, a special menu. In the restaurant, *Samuel's* (with gold-leaf ceiling, sumptuous decor, mahogany panelling, open fire), guests choose between chef Andy Burton's daily-changing three-course menu (main courses like Masham lamb three ways) and his eight-course tasting menu. Installation of a wood-chip boiler, which uses wood from the surrounding forests, has made the hotel 'carbon neutral'. (*Michael and Barbara Jennings, Jim and Fleur McClymont*)

30 bedrooms. 4 suitable for ♿. 1 mile SW of Masham. Lift, ramps. 3 lounges, library, bar, restaurant (classical background music); banqueting hall, private dining room (background jazz); spa; games room, snooker room, cinema; conference facilities. 200-acre grounds: grotto, orangery, deer park; 5 lakes: fishing (ghillies available), model boat racing; swings, play castle, bowls, croquet, cricket, 9-hole golf course, clay-pigeon shooting, riding, falconry, kite flying, etc. Civil wedding licence. No smoking. No dogs in public rooms. All major credit cards accepted. B&B [2007] £75–£175 per person. Set dinner £39–£48. Christmas/New Year packages. Cookery school. 1-night bookings refused some weekends. ***V***

MATLOCK Derbyshire *See SHORTLIST* Map 3:B6

MAULDS MEABURN Cumbria Map 4: inset C2

Meaburn Hill Farmhouse *Tel* 01931-715168
Maulds Meaburn, Penrith *Email* kindleysides@btinternet.com
CA10 3HN *Website* www.cumbria-bed-and-breakfast.co.uk

On the edge of the green of this village near Penrith, overlooking the River Lyvennet, Annie Kindleysides and Brian Morris run this 'blissfully relaxing' guest house. 'A perfect place to stay,' says one report. 'Excellent hosts, friendly, chatty, but never intrusive. If you want entertainment, don't go; if you hate dogs, don't go.' You can 'catch up on your reading', say the owners, 'or just listen to music in front of the fire in the library'. The old farmhouse (16th-century) is a 'comfortable home with knick-knacks everywhere', and oak beams. The bedrooms are up 14 steps. 'Ours had a cast iron bath in a corner. Bedside lighting might be a problem but the bifocal-wearing member of our party managed fine.' A two-course supper can be served by arrangement. The Aga-cooked dishes, 'Cumbrian with a fresh twist', use home-grown or locally sourced meat and vegetables. No wine licence: bring your own. At breakfast, eggs cooked to order are supplemented by 'delights like potato cakes, fish cakes, gorgeous vegetarian haggis'. Packed lunches can be supplied.

Afternoon tea can be served on the lawn. The only disturbance might be 'sound of stream and sheep on village green'. (*M and PJ*)

3 bedrooms. 1 mile N of Crosby Ravensworth. Open 2 Feb–2 Jan. Dining room closed Mon. Library/private dining room, dining room with TV/lounge area; background music during meals on request. 2-acre garden: tea/picnic area, dog-walking area. Unsuitable for ♿. No smoking. Dogs allowed in public rooms 'if acceptable to other guests'. No credit cards. B&B £40–£80 per person. Set dinner £15–£20. Christmas/New Year packages for groups, by negotiation. 1-night bookings sometimes refused.

MAWGAN PORTH Cornwall — Map 1:D2

Bedruthan Steps Hotel
Mawgan Porth
TR8 4BU

Tel 01637-860555
Fax 01637-860714
Email office@bedruthan.com
Website www.bedruthan.com

Above a golden, sandy North Cornwall beach this purpose-built hotel is owned by sisters Emma Stratton, Deborah Wakefield and Rebecca Whittington ('we are a bit quirky,' they write). Large (101 bedrooms) for the *Guide*, it earns its entry for its family-friendly nature (countless activities for children) and its green ethos. With its slate flooring, neutral browns and creams, lots of oak, it is 'reasonably glamorous'. It has an indoor adventure play area, an Ofsted-registered nursery, a soft play and ball pool for toddlers, a junior assault course and a teenagers' room. High teas, babysitters and nannies are available. There are also 'great facilities for parents', including a spa (redeveloped in 2007). A staff 'green team' meets monthly to discuss sustainable initiatives; visitors can join a quarterly clean-up of the beach. Accommodation ranges from 'villa suites', ideal for a family, to 'value rooms' (no view, let at a discount). A wheelchair-bound visitor was impressed by the kind treatment he received (the hotel is committed to be 'as accessible as possible to everyone'), and praised the cooking. Chef Adam Clark's *table d'hôte* menus are 'a mix of classic and contemporary', eg, Cornish mackerel escabeche; pork medallions with sherry vinegar sauce. (*Peter Fairgrieve*)

101 bedrooms. 9 adjacent. 1 suite suitable for ♿. 4 miles NE of Newquay. Closed 22–29 Dec. Lift. 2 lounges, 2 bars, 3 dining rooms (occasional background music); ballroom (live music 2/3 times a week); 4 children's clubs; spa: indoor swimming pool. 5-acre grounds: heated swimming pools, tennis, playing field. Civil wedding licence. No smoking. Guide dogs only. MasterCard, Visa accepted. B&B [2007] £68–£218 per person; D,B&B £80–£239. Set dinner £25.50. 10% discount to guests who arrive by public transport. Pre-Christmas package. New Year package. 1-night bookings refused high season, New Year.

MAWNAN SMITH Cornwall **Map 1:E2**

Budock Vean *Tel* 01326-252100
Helford Passage, Mawnan Smith *Fax* 01326-250892
nr Falmouth TR11 5LG *Email* relax@budockvean.co.uk
Website www.budockvean.co.uk

'Everything is right, starting with the hall porter's greeting,' says a regular visitor to Martin and Amanda Barlow's traditional hotel, a winner of a Green Tourism Gold Award. Other praise: 'The joy of arriving is knowing that you will not be let down.' In the grounds are a nine-hole golf course, hot tub and sauna, and a swimming pool in a building that opens on to a patio in summer and has a log fire in winter. The valley garden leads past terraced ponds and waterfalls to a secluded creek of the Helford River; a 32-foot Sunseeker takes guests on sea trips. 'From the sun lounge on the foreshore you can telephone for refreshments.' Well-equipped bedrooms (all have double glazing) lead off corridors enlivened by colourful prints. 'Flowers were in our good-sized room which looked over gardens and woods.' Men must wear jacket and tie after 7 pm in the bar and main restaurant. 'Mouth-watering' canapés come with pre-dinner drinks. Chef Darren Kelly serves 'a nightly feast of imaginative dishes'. 'Pan-fried local scallops with pancetta; wonderful roast fillet of venison from Bodmin.' Live music during dinner, 'but thankfully no background music'. Afternoon cream teas are served in the lounge. (*David Jervois, Tessa and Graham Spanton, Mary Woods*)

57 bedrooms. 4 self-catering cottages. 6 miles SW of Falmouth. Closed 2–25 Jan. Lift, ramps. 3 lounges, conservatory, 2 bars, restaurant (pianist/guitarist at night); snooker room. 65-acre grounds: covered swimming pool (45 by 27 ft), hot tub; health spa; country club: bar, restaurant, 9-hole golf course, tennis, croquet, archery, river frontage, water sports, boat trips. Unsuitable for ♿. Civil wedding licence. No smoking. No children under 7 on ground floor after 9 pm. No dogs: public rooms, some bedrooms. Diners (*2% surcharge*), MasterCard, Visa accepted. B&B [2007] £60–£143 per person; D,B&B £72–£155. Bar lunches. Set dinner £31.50; full alc £47. Christmas/New Year/Easter packages. Themed breaks. 1-night bookings refused weekends, except off-season.

****

Traveller's tale One girl seemed to be doing all the work: we saw no sign of the owners in this allegedly 'personally run' hotel. We got the feeling that they thought they were too important to be doing such mundane things as running a hotel. (*Hotel in Suffolk*)

****

Meudon
Mawnan Smith
nr Falmouth TR11 5HT

Tel 01326-250541
Fax 01326-250543
Email wecare@meudon.co.uk
Website www.meudon.co.uk

In wooded countryside on the south Cornish coast, this red brick building stands in a subtropical 'hanging garden', at the head of a valley that leads down to a beach. When it opened in 1966, it was Cornwall's most expensive hotel (£5 a night full board), say the owners, father and son Harry and Mark Pilgrim. 'Old-fashioned values' prevail (eg, nocturnal shoe cleaning), and many guests are returnees. One writes in 2007: 'We travelled 230 miles, well worth the effort for our annual visit.' Other praise: 'Our room was immaculate, serviced morning and evening.' 'Bright, clean decor. Thankfully no chintz.' All bedrooms have double-glazed windows. Suites have a patio or balcony; one has an adjoining room for children. The comfortable main lounge has a 'blazing fire', flowers and 'lovely views over the gardens'. Manager Shaun Davie 'runs an efficient, most likeable team'. A 'dress code of jacket and tie' is encouraged in the restaurant where chef Alan Webb uses local produce, including fresh fish from Newlyn, for his daily-changing menu, eg, grilled turbot with hollandaise sauce. 'The cooking is inspirational, and never repetitive.' *Meudon* is now developing environmentally friendly policies, we are told. (*Colonel AJW and Mrs HM Harvey, and others*)

29 bedrooms. 16 on ground floor. 2 suitable for ♿. Self-catering cottage. 4 miles SW of Falmouth. Car park. Train: Truro. Open 1 Feb–31 Dec. Lift, ramps. 3 lounges, bar, restaurant. No background music. 8-acre grounds: gardens, private beach; yacht. Golf, riding, windsurfing nearby. Smoking allowed in 4 bedrooms. No dogs in public rooms. All major credit cards accepted. B&B [2007] £70–£135 per person. Set dinner £29.50–£33; full alc £55. 3-day winter breaks. Christmas package.

MELTON MOWBRAY Leicestershire — Map 2:A3

Sysonby Knoll
Asfordby Road
Melton Mowbray LE13 0HP

Tel 01664-563563
Fax 01664-410364
Email reception@sysonby.com
Website www.sysonby.com

In a market town 'that seems to have kept its identity intact', this traditional hotel has been owned by one family since 1965; Jenny and Gavin Howling now run it. The original red brick Edwardian house has been extended as a quadrangle around a central courtyard. 'Good value; clean, well cared for,' say visitors this year. Returning guests, part of a large walking group, found 'standards still high'. The 'magic' garden, with manicured lawn in front, and trees on either side, leads to the River Eye, where guests may fish. The bedrooms vary greatly in size and shape: most face the courtyard; the two best rooms look over garden and river to cattle in fields. 'Our quiet room at the back had a slightly anonymous feel.' 'Our annexe room was very comfortable, but sound insulation between floors was poor.' The 'interesting' daily-changing *table d'hôte* menu has a choice of three dishes for the first two courses (eg, Belvoir mushrooms; escalope of pork with cider, apples and cream). There is an 'unusually large' dessert menu. Stalky, a miniature dachshund, is in attendance, and guests' dogs are welcomed. Children are not specifically catered for, 'but well-behaved children are welcome'; there is a family room. (*John and June Jennings, Mary Milne-Day, and others*)

30 bedrooms. 6 in annexe (30 yds). Some on ground floor. On A6006, ¾ mile from town centre. Closed Christmas/New Year. Unsuitable for ♿. Ramps. Reception/lounge, upstairs lounge, coffee lounge, bar, restaurant; function room; background music 'as appropriate'. 5-acre grounds on river: fishing. Smoking allowed in 20 bedrooms. All major credit cards accepted. B&B [2007] £39–£85 per person; D,B&B £55–£72. Set dinner £19; full alc £32. *V*

MIDDLEHAM North Yorkshire — Map 4:C3

Waterford House
19 Kirkgate
Middleham DL8 4PG

Tel 01969-622090
Fax 01969-624020
Email info@waterfordhousehotel.co.uk
Website www.waterfordhousehotel.co.uk

'Hospitality with a capital H.' 'Truly a special spot.' This year's accolades for Martin and Anne Cade's Grade II listed Georgian stone house. It overlooks the main square of this unspoilt little town, noted for its racehorses. 'We were made very welcome, as if we were family friends,' says another visitor. Guests enter through a paved garden filled with flowers in tubs. The interior is 'choc full of antiques, *objets d'art* and bric-a-brac'. The residents' lounge has a baby grand piano, log fire and huge pine dresser. 'My bedroom was spacious; the bath was huge.' 'Our four-poster room had lots of extras, including sherry, fresh fruit, chocolates, home-made biscuits.' Canapés are served in the drawing room before dinner, when Anne Cade's menu might include rillettes of duck; baked halibut with a herb and Chablis sauce. 'All the food was superb.' The 'impressive' breakfast includes 'a different fresh fruit concoction every day', good toast and croissants, huge choice of cooked dishes. 'Martin Cade spent time with me discussing the desired viscosity for the yolks of my boiled eggs. I received precisely what I requested.' The afternoon teas are praised, too. 'There is a wonderful springer spaniel in residence (outside).' Visits to the local stables can be arranged. (*Jon Hughes, John J Huber, CJR Thorne*)

5 bedrooms. Village centre. Closed Christmas/New Year. Restaurant closed Sun nights. Drawing room, TV room, restaurant. No background music. Walled garden, patio. Unsuitable for ♿. No smoking. No children under 12. No pets. MasterCard, Visa accepted. B&B [2007] £45–£75 per person. Set dinner £33.

MIDHURST Sussex *See SHORTLIST* Map 2:E3

MIDSOMER NORTON Somerset Map 2:D1

The Moody Goose at The Old Priory

Church Square
Midsomer Norton
nr Bath BA3 2HX

Tel 01761-416784
Fax 01761-417851
Email info@theoldpriory.co.uk
Website www.theoldpriory.co.uk

Guests this year received a warm welcome from proprietor/chef Stephen Shore on arrival at his restaurant-with-rooms. A 'good-looking' Grade II listed building, which dates in part to 1152, it stands by the church, in a peaceful walled garden. It has flagged floors, beams and old fireplaces. 'Artefacts and antiques line the hallway, requiring caution if you have bulky baggage.' The bedrooms are 'well decorated and fitted: mine had a comfortable four-poster bed; towelling robes and decent soaps in the bathroom. Only downside was the view into a neighbouring house.' Another report: 'We were upgraded to a family room on two floors, comfortable and quiet. Fresh milk provided for the complimentary tea tray with home-made biscuits.' All agree about the dinners: 'Very good indeed, a perfectly balanced meal; courteous staff in attendance. A comprehensive wine list.' The three-course set menu (three choices for each course) has modern dishes, eg, galantine of braised ham hock; braised shoulder of lamb with smoked garlic. Breakfast in the cheerful rear dining room was thought less good: 'Limited buffet, and cooked dishes centred on bacon and eggs.' But 'a good place; we will return'. (*Martin Arnold, Conrad Barnard*)

7 bedrooms. Closed Sun, Christmas, bank holidays, except Good Friday. 9 miles SW of Bath. 2 lounges, 2 dining rooms (classical background music at lunch and dinner); private dining/function room. ½-acre garden. Unsuitable for ♿. No smoking. No dogs. MasterCard, Visa accepted. B&B [2007] £52.50–£95 per person. Set menus £25; full alc £50.

MILDEN Suffolk — Map 2:C5

Milden Hall
Milden, nr Lavenham
CO10 9NY

Tel/Fax 01787-247235
Email hawkins@thehall-milden.co.uk
Website www.thehall-milden.co.uk

Amid wildflower meadows, hedged Suffolk countryside and a walled garden, this listed 16th-century hall farmhouse, 'rejigged in Georgian times', is run as an eco-friendly B&B by Juliet and Christopher Hawkins. They hold a Gold Award for Green Tourism in Suffolk, and manage their farm on sustainable principles. 'Sympathetic and cultured', they are keen conservationists and historians. 'What a place,' said one enthusiastic visitor. 'They gave a warm welcome on a cold autumn night. Our huge bedroom had an amazing array of antique prints and maps of Suffolk.' The three bedrooms share a spacious bathroom; and there is a second bathroom downstairs for busy times. The largest room is in Adam style; another is filled with artwork by Harry Becker, a local artist. The 'superb' breakfast has the farm's own free-range eggs, local bacon and sausages, and compote of home-grown fruit. 'Well-behaved' children are welcomed (toys, cots, nature trails, etc). Their visit might coincide with a 'farm fungus foray, dragonfly dawdle, or another wildlife event'. Wedding receptions and humanist weddings are sometimes held; groups can be catered for. (*MP*)

3 bedrooms. 3 miles SE of Lavenham. Front drive off B1115 between Little Waldingfield and Monks Eleigh. Sometimes closed Christmas/New Year. Hall/sitting/dining room. No background music. 3-acre garden; 500-acre farm. Tennis. Unsuitable for ♿. No smoking. No dogs. No credit cards. B&B £30–£40 per person.

MILTON ABBOT Devon — Map 1:D3

Hotel Endsleigh
Milton Abbot
nr Tavistock PL19 0PQ

Tel 01822-870000
Fax 01822-870578
Email mail@hotelendsleigh.com
Website www.hotelendsleigh.com

Built in 1813, for Georgina, Duchess of Devonshire, and once used as a shooting and fishing lodge by the Bedford family, this is now a luxury hotel. Owned by Olga Polizzi of *Hotel Tresanton*, St Mawes (*qv*), it is managed by her 'charming' daughter, Alex. Set in huge, 'glorious' grounds, it's 'a triumph of design, and an obvious labour of love', said a reader who liked the 'magnificent entrance hall', the atmosphere of 'a modern, comfortable country house', and the accommodation. 'Everything exuded quality.' Room 17 is the former gatekeeper's lodge at the top of the drive. Shay Cooper's Italian-influenced cooking, based on local ingredients, is served in two 'stunning wood-panelled rooms'. His daily-changing dinner menu might include Jerusalem artichoke risotto; rump of lamb, with spiced aubergine purée. At night, candles provide much of the lighting. Breakfast has 'everything you could ask for', and the afternoon teas are admired. The hotel owns seven rods on the River Tamar which flows through the grounds, and there are 'fantastic walks in the gardens with their streams and waterfalls (waterproofs and wellies provided)'. Picnics can be provided 'either in a rucksack, or a deluxe version in a hamper with a rug and cooler'. (*AK, and others*)

16 bedrooms. 1 on ground floor. 1 in lodge. 7 miles NW of Tavistock. Train/plane: Plymouth. Drawing room, library, card room, bar, 2 dining rooms. Terraces. No background music. 108-acre estate: fishing (ghillie available). Civil wedding licence. No smoking. No dogs in restaurant. Amex, MasterCard, Visa accepted. B&B [2007] £105–£210 per person; D,B&B £144–£249. Set lunch £30, dinner £39; full alc £55. Christmas/New Year packages. 1-night bookings refused weekends.

MINCHINHAMPTON Gloucestershire — Map 3:E5

Burleigh Court
Minchinhampton, nr Stroud
GL5 2PF

Tel 01453-883804
Fax 01453-886870
Email info@burleighcourthotel.co.uk
Website www.burleighcourthotel.co.uk

Owner Louise Noble 'is not content to rest on her laurels, and seems ever ready to improve the quality', say visitors this year to this creeper-covered 18th-century Cotswold stone manor house. 'Superb service. Good ambience.' 'Staff were kindness itself,' wrote others. On a steep hillside, the hotel overlooks the western-most ridge of the Cotswolds. Its large gardens, designed by Clough Williams-Ellis, have hidden pathways, terraces, ponds and a Victorian plunge pool. Light meals are served in the panelled bar lounge with its comfortable chairs and sofas. The formal dining room, painted warm cream, has chandeliers, flowers, white linen, good cutlery and glass. Adrian Jarrad, head chef, serves dishes like herb-roasted breast of corn-fed chicken with wild mushroom and leek fricassée. Most bedrooms are thought 'comfortable and attractive'. 'Ours was magnificent.' But one couple, in a suite in the Coach House, found its low ceilings 'claustrophobic'. Breakfast has fresh orange juice, fresh fruit and pastries, 'nicely cooked dishes'. Children sharing their parents' room are charged for meals only. (*B and P Orman, and others; also Eric Hinds*)

18 bedrooms. 7 in coach house. Some on ground floor. SE of Stroud, via A419 towards Cirencester. Closed 24–26 Dec. Ramps. Lounges, bar lounge, 2 dining rooms; classical background music. 4½-acre grounds: heated plunge pool, croquet. Civil wedding licence. No smoking. Dogs allowed in coach house bedrooms, not in public rooms. Diners, MasterCard, Visa accepted. B&B £62.50–£105 per person; D,B&B £60–£110. Set dinner £31. Full alc £39. 3-night breaks. New Year package. 1-night bookings sometimes refused. *V*

MISTLEY Essex — Map 2:C5

The Mistley Thorn — *Tel* 01206-392821
High Street — *Fax* 01206-390122
Mistley, nr Manningtree — *Email* info@mistleythorn.co.uk
CO11 1HE — *Website* www.mistleythorn.com

Built in 1723 on the site of an older pub, this inn was converted to a restaurant-with-rooms by Sherri Singleton (the chef), from California, and her husband, David McKay. Yellow-painted outside, it has panoramic views from some rooms down the Stour estuary. 'Inside,' our inspector reported, 'it has a seasidey freshness. Sage green panelling. Uncluttered bedrooms (No. 4, though not huge, felt spacious) have a decor of taupe and cream, large bed, two chairs, plenty of cupboard space, organic tea and coffee.' This year, three bathrooms have been updated, and all now have a double-ended bath and a shower. 'Wooden tables, basket-weave chairs and modern artwork enhance the busy restaurant.' Menus (*Michelin Bib Gourmand* for good food at reasonable prices) place an emphasis on seafood, and seasonal local produce, eg, Mersea Island rock oysters; seared wild bass fillet with salsa verde. A continental breakfast (fresh fruit, yogurt, sourdough toast) is included in the price; a generous cooked breakfast (£6.95) has free-range eggs and local bacon. Families are welcomed: there is a children's menu with 'not a turkey twizzler in sight'. Only a small sitting area for guests, 'but there is plenty to do outdoors in this interesting and attractive area'. Beth Chatto's garden is 15 minutes' drive away.

5 bedrooms. 9 miles W of Harwich. Closed 25 Dec. Small sitting area, bar, restaurant (soft background music). Unsuitable for ♿. No smoking. MasterCard, Visa accepted. B&B £40–£95 per person. Set lunch £11.95–£14.95; full alc £25–£27.95. Cookery courses. New Year package. 1-night bookings sometimes refused.

MOCCAS Herefordshire **Map 3:D4**

Moccas Court
Moccas, nr Hereford
HR2 9LH

Tel 01981-500019
Fax 01981-500095
Email info@moccas-court.co.uk
Website www.moccas-court.co.uk

César award: Historic house of the year

'Truly magical.' 'Memorable.' 'We felt like private guests in a stately home,' say visitors to Ben and Mimi Chester-Master's Grade I listed Georgian house ('must be one of the best Adam-designed buildings in private hands'), beautifully set by the River Wye, in a park designed by Capability Brown and Humphry Repton. Inspectors agreed: 'Ben is a descendant of Catherine Cornewall who built it, so this is a genuine family home. The owners are informal; we went immediately to first-name terms. Everything is in excellent shape: grounds in neat trim; house immaculate.' The stone-floored hall leads to a magnificent cantilevered staircase below a glass dome. 'Tea and pre-dinner drinks by the fire in the library hung with family portraits. A spacious first-floor room with big bed with drapes, mahogany furniture, long narrow bathroom with window and fast-flowing hot water. Upper rooms are smaller. Ben, a keen cook, passionate about local ingredients, serves dinner by arrangement (menu discussed in advance) at a round table in an exquisite circular room. Very good quail's eggs, avocado and tomato; scrummy roast pheasant.' Breakfast has hot croissants, good preserves and cooked dishes. Zulu, the black Labrador, will take guests for walks. The 12th-century church in the park has its original stained-glass windows. (*DCJ Howell, Felicity Chadwick-Histed, Tessa Harris, and many others*)

5 bedrooms. 10 miles W of Hereford. Open 1 Mar–15 Dec. Closed Sun. 2 lounges, music room, TV room, dining room. No background music. 100-acre grounds: river, fishing; church. Unsuitable for ♿. Civil wedding licence. No smoking. Children by arrangement. No dogs. Amex, MasterCard, Visa accepted. B&B: single £116–£156, double £145–£195. Set dinner £35. 1-night bookings occasionally refused.

****

Traveller's tale At dinner on our first night we found a long, black hair in my husband's starter. We asked for a new portion, which was provided, though the apologies weren't exactly effusive. Then I found another hair in the vegetables. Cowardice won, and I whisked it away before my husband saw it, because I couldn't face complaining again to our grim-faced waitress. (*Hotel in Devon*)

****

MORETON-IN-MARSH Gloucestershire Map 3:D6

The Redesdale Arms
High Street
Moreton-in-Marsh
GL56 0AW

Tel 01608-650308
Fax 01608-651843
Email info@redesdalearms.com
Website www.redesdalearms.com

On the wide main street of this attractive market town, this centuries-old coaching inn offers 'good value for the Cotswolds', say visitors this year. 'Warm with history', it has a 'pleasant, informal atmosphere'; the 'friendly manager', Robert Smith, leads a 'courteous' staff. Six new 'executive' rooms, in a converted stable yard, have been added in 2007: one is fully equipped for disabled visitors. These rooms, and ten in another annexe at the back, are the quietest. 'Our spacious first-floor suite had high sloping ceilings, neutral colours, a large sitting room, which opened on to a small roof terrace; real ground coffee with the tea-making facilities, complimentary sherry.' Front rooms have double-glazed windows, but there may be noise from the street when they are open in hot weather, and from the bar (popular with locals) below. The dinner menu comes with a specials list, perhaps monkfish and vine tomato kebabs; twice-cooked Gloucestershire Old Spot belly pork with chilli and ginger. 'Our room-service meal arrived promptly and was reasonably priced.' Breakfast is a buffet for both hot and cold dishes. A supplement of £20 is charged for early or late check-in. (*Virginia Murphy, JH, and others*)

24 bedrooms. 6 in stable yard, 10 in annexe. 11 on ground floor, 1 suitable for ♿. High Street by Redesdale Hall. Ramps. Lounge bar/reading room, public bar, 2 restaurants; 'computer-controlled' background music from 10 am. Heated open dining area. No smoking. No dogs in bedrooms. MasterCard, Visa accepted. B&B £32.50–£85 per person. Early/late check-in charge: £20. Full alc £29.50. Christmas/New Year packages. 1-night Sat bookings refused 1 Apr–1 Oct.

MORSTON Norfolk Map 2:A5

Morston Hall
Morston, Holt
NR25 7AA

Tel 01263-741041
Fax 01263-740419
Email reception@morstonhall.com
Website www.morstonhall.com

In a designated area of outstanding natural beauty on the north Norfolk coast, this flint and brick Jacobean house is run as a restaurant-with-rooms (*Michelin* star) by Tracy and Galton Blackiston (he is well known for his appearances on TV). 'Still as good as ever,' say visitors in 2007.

'Assistant chef Samantha Wegg keeps standards high when Galton is away.' Other comments: 'Very comfortable.' 'Lovely atmosphere. Not a jot of pretension. Our room in the eaves looked over the garden, and on to marshes and Morston Quay. Little touches made it special – bathsalts, fluffy bathrobes, checkers game, etc.' But some walls are thin, and there can be early noise from delivery vehicles. A pavilion, 'a short walk across the garden', was due to open as the *Guide* went to press: it will have six spacious suites, a sitting room and a garden terrace. The four-course dinner (7.30 for 8; no choice until pudding or cheese; menus discussed when you book) might include 'very good fish and excellent venison'. Vegetarians and special diets are catered for. Breakfasts have freshly squeezed orange juice, toasted home-made bread, local sausages, 'delicious smoked haddock'. For children there are high teas, toys, cots, etc. (*Anne and Denis Tate, DC Benfield, and others*)

7 bedrooms. 1 on ground floor. (6 in garden pavilion due to open autumn 2007.) 2 miles W of Blakeney. Open 1 Feb–1 Jan, except 25 Dec. Hall, lounge, conservatory, restaurant. No background music. 3½-acre garden: pond, croquet. Only restaurant suitable for ♿. No smoking. No dogs in public rooms (free kennels/£5 in room). All major credit cards accepted. D,B&B [2007] £140–£160 per person. Set dinner £48. New Year package. 1-night bookings refused Sat.

MORTEHOE Devon — Map 1:B4

The Cleeve House

North Morte Road
Mortehoe, nr Woolacombe
EX34 7ED

Tel 01271-870719
Email info@cleevehouse.co.uk
Website www.cleevehouse.co.uk

Recommended for its 'good value', this small, unpretentious hotel stands off the main road of a pretty village on a hill above Woolacombe. David and Anne Strobel are 'charming hosts', said a guest on her fourth visit. 'They immediately make you feel at home.' They serve 'home cooking of the highest standard', eg, chicken with cider, apples and cream; braised venison in red wine. 'Everything made on the premises,' they write. Breakfast can be continental or full English. The bedrooms, with their pine furniture, 'are fairly small, but have everything you might need'. Rear rooms have country views. There is a 'comfortable lounge'. You can walk on to the South West Coastal Path from the door; a flight of steps leads down to a pebbly cove; beaches are a mile away. (*CMM*)

6 bedrooms. 1, on ground floor, suitable for ♿. 4 miles W of Ilfracombe. Train/coach: Barnstaple. Open April–Sept. Restaurant closed Wed, and evenings 21 July–31 Aug. Ramp. Lounge, bar area, dining room. No background music.

½-acre garden: patio. Golf nearby. Woolacombe beach 1½ miles. No smoking. No children under 12. No dogs. MasterCard, Visa accepted. B&B £37–£57 per person; D,B&B £56–£76. Set menus £20. 1-night bookings sometimes refused Sat.

MOUSEHOLE Devon *See SHORTLIST* Map 1:E1

MUCH WENLOCK Shropshire Map 3:C5

The Raven
Much Wenlock
TF13 6EN

Tel 01952-727251
Fax 01952-728416
Email enquiry@ravenhotel.com
Website www.ravenhotel.com

Composed of a 17th-century coaching inn, 15th-century almshouses and a medieval hall, this white-fronted hotel is in a quiet street near the centre of this 'lovely little' market town. Reports this year are mixed: 'Fully deserves its *Guide* entry,' says a regular correspondent. 'As good as ever,' writes another. General manager/owner Kirk Heywood is praised: 'His enthusiasm is infectious.' The staff, mainly local and young, are described as 'uniformly helpful', 'anxious to please', but there are also comments about 'amateurish service'. The bedrooms vary. Some are reached from the plant-filled inner courtyard; one has a four-poster; the galleried suite is on two levels. Some rooms are found 'extremely comfortable'; 'nice and bright', but some may need renovation, and one room was 'too hot' in summer, another 'too cold' in winter. In the 'charming, rustic' restaurant, local produce is used by chef Steve Biggs, and herbs come from the *Raven*'s garden. 'Delicious dinner: the best chocolate pudding we have ever tasted.' 'Some of the food was quite exceptional: liver parfait canapé exploded with taste; imaginative medley of seasonal vegetables.' But 'the menu didn't alter over three nights'. A bar menu is also available. 'Breakfast was not bad, but not memorable.' (*Richard Baker, Joanna Russell, Matthew Caminer, LW, and others*)

14 bedrooms. 7 across courtyard. 100 yds from centre. Closed 25 Dec. Bar, 2 lounges, 2 dining rooms; classical background music. 1-acre grounds: courtyard; small herb garden. Unsuitable for ♿. No smoking. Guide dogs only. Amex, MasterCard, Visa accepted. B&B [2007] £60–£85 per person. Set lunch/dinner £23–£34. Special breaks. New Year package. ***V***

Make sure the hotel has included VAT in the prices it quotes.

MUNGRISDALE Cumbria — Map 4: inset C2

The Mill Hotel
Mungrisdale
Penrith CA11 0XR

Tel 017687-79659
Fax 017687-79155
Email quinlan@themillhotel.demon.co.uk
Website www.themillhotel.com

César award in 1993

In an unspoilt Lakeland village, against a background of crags and soft mountain slopes, this former mill cottage, built in 1651, retains millrace, waterfall and trout stream. Tucked away behind the *Mill Inn* pub (with which it shares an entrance), it is an unpretentious place, described by the 'very affable' owner, Richard Quinlan, as 'a comfortable family home'. This year, two bedrooms have been 'greatly improved', he writes. Some rooms are small, but all have 'thoughtful touches' (fruit, current magazines, etc). Two rooms in the old mill share a sitting room. There is a log fire in the beamed lounge, which has old furniture, pictures, fresh flowers, books and magazines. Here, guests take a drink before being called to dinner in succession. In a low-ceilinged, candlelit room ('with high-up windows'), they sit at separate tables, but Mr Quinlan 'likes fostering rapport among diners' while waiting at table. His wife, Eleanor, is the chef: her daily-changing three-course menu has limited choice (the main course could be pan-fried fillet of venison on roasted beetroot). 'Delicious bacon at breakfast.' An 'excellent stop-over on the way north'. As we went to press, the hotel was on the market, but an early sale is not anticipated. (*S and JS, and others*)

5 bedrooms. In village 2 miles N of A66 Penrith–Keswick. Open 1 Mar–31 Oct. 2 lounges, sun lounge, dining room (classical background music during dinner); drying room. Small cottage garden: millrace, waterfall, trout stream. Unsuitable for ♿. No smoking. Dogs by arrangement in bedrooms; not in public rooms. No credit cards. D,B&B £89–£95 per person. *V*

NAYLAND Suffolk *See SHORTLIST* — Map 2:C5

When you make a booking you enter into a contract with a hotel. Most hotels explain their cancellation policies, which vary widely, in a letter of confirmation. You may lose your deposit or be charged at the full rate for the room if you cancel at short notice. A travel insurance policy can provide protection.

NEW MILTON Hampshire — Map 2:E2

Chewton Glen
Christchurch Road
New Milton BH25 6QS

Tel 01425-275341
Fax 01425-272310
Email reservations@chewtonglen.com
Website www.chewtonglen.com

In large grounds with many outdoor activities (see below), this 'plush' red brick mansion, on the edge of the New Forest, near the sea, is now an upmarket hotel/country club (Relais & Châteaux). Privately owned, it is managed by Andrew Stembridge. He tells us that some bedrooms and suites have been refurbished, and the lounges were being given a 'fresh new look' as we went to press. Many visitors are there to use the award-winning spa with its 'beautiful' ozone-treated swimming pool, etc (see below). The international staff (many are Polish) are friendly, and fans like the 'lack of stuffiness, despite the luxury'. The welcome is warm (log fire in the entrance hall). Suites and bedrooms, some vast, are lavish. They combine antiques, contemporary textiles and technology like free Wi-Fi, and flat-screen TV with waterproof remote control in the bathroom. Recent visitors loved their suite, done in muted colours, and with a private terrace facing the garden. The daily-changing 'classic English seasonal menus' of chef Luke Matthews include dishes like monkfish nage with baby vegetables and champagne sauce; grilled Dover sole. Children under five are now welcomed in August. Conferences, weddings and functions are held. More reports, please.

58 bedrooms. 14 on ground floor. 1 suitable for ♿. On S edge of New Forest national park. Ramps. 3 lounges, bar, restaurant (pianist at dinner); function rooms; snooker room; health club: indoor tennis, 55-ft swimming pool, gym, beauty salon. 130-acre grounds: swimming pool, tennis, croquet, 9-hole par 3 golf course, lake, jogging course; helipad; bicycle hire. Beach, fishing, sailing, riding nearby. Chauffeur service. Civil wedding licence. No smoking. Children under 5 accepted in August. All major credit cards accepted. Room [2007]: single/double £295–£467, suite £572–£1,250. Breakfast £20. Set lunch from £24.50; full alc £75. Min. 2-night bookings at weekends. Various breaks. Christmas/New Year house parties.

NEW ROMNEY Kent — Map 2:E5

Romney Bay House
Coast Road, Littlestone
New Romney TN28 8QY

Tel 01797-364747
Fax 01797-367156

'A fascinating house: beautifully furnished, comfortable bedrooms.' Red-roofed and white-fronted, it was designed by Sir Clough Williams-Ellis of Portmeirion fame in the 1920s, for the American actress/journalist Hedda Hopper. Owned by Clinton and Lisa Lovell (he the 'excellent' chef, she front-of-house, 'so welcoming'), it is reached by a private road along the sea wall. Antiques, pictures and knick-knacks fill the house. The drawing room has 'charm and character'. At night, candles burn, and there is a log fire. 'Very good local produce' is used for the no-choice dinner, eg, Romney Marsh lamb with roasted endive and asparagus. 'Superb; portions just right.' 'First-rate after-dinner coffee included in the price.' The bedrooms have nearly floor-length windows with views of sea or golf course, plain carpet, light colours, four-poster or half-tester bed, armchairs. 'Lovely linen and towels.' All bathrooms have now been refitted. Breakfast is full English, or continental (cold meats, cheese, fruits, croissants, toast). Cream teas are served. 'A bonus: two beautiful, friendly, ginger-and-white cats.' 'Best not arrive on days when the dining room is closed, as you have to drive to New Romney for a meal, and the road is pitted with potholes.' (*Barbara Francis, Gill Holden, and others*)

10 bedrooms. 1½ miles from New Romney. Closed Christmas. Dining room closed midday, Sun/Mon/Thurs evenings. 2 lounges, bar, conservatory, dining room; small function facilities. No background music. 1-acre garden: croquet, *boules*. Opposite sea sand/pebble beach (safe bathing), fishing. Unsuitable for ♿. No smoking. No children under 14. No dogs. Amex, MasterCard, Visa accepted. B&B [2007] £42.50–£77.50 per person. Set dinner £39.50. (*Optional 5% service charge added to bills.*) New Year package. 1-night advance bookings refused weekends. *V*

NEWBURY Berkshire *See SHORTLIST* Map 2:D2

NEWCASTLE UPON TYNE Tyne and Wear Map 4:B4

Jesmond Dene House

Jesmond Dene Road
Newcastle upon Tyne
NE2 2EY

Tel 0191-212 3000
Fax 0191-212 3001
Email info@jesmonddenehouse.co.uk
Website www.jesmonddenehouse.co.uk

Once the home of a Victorian industrialist, this luxury hotel, owned by Terry Laybourne (Newcastle restaurateur) and Peter Candler, is in 'a wooded haven, but close to the city centre'. It has a wood-panelled Great Hall and two 'smart' lounges (one the former billiard room). Inspectors liked the 'charming location' and the combination of modern decor with retained Arts and Crafts interiors. 'Our spacious, restful bedroom, in fashionable "greige" colours, had all the comforts (Internet access, plasma-screen TV, specialist reading lights, etc).' Some rooms are high-ceilinged; others are 'cosy'. The spacious suites in the recently built *New House* have a sitting room. Some rooms face the Dene. Some have a fireplace. Bathrooms have under-floor heating. There are big beds, bold wallpapers. 'The welcome was warm. Restaurant staff were efficient and friendly.' There are two dining areas, one in the former music room (with delicate plasterwork), thc other in the 'light and leafy' oak-floored garden room. A new chef, Andrew Richardson, started in 2007: he serves 'straightforward' modern dishes, eg, three-cheese ravioli with fresh herbs; crispy pork belly with Bramley apple purée. The wine list 'is an interesting global selection'. Conferences are catered for. (*Mark and Patricia Jacques, and others*)

40 bedrooms. 8 in adjacent annexe. Some suitable for ♿. 5 mins' drive from centre via A167; Ilford Rd metro 10 mins' walk. Lift. 2 lounges, cocktail bar, restaurant; conference/function facilities; personal trainer; background jazz throughout public areas. 2-acre garden. Civil wedding licence. No smoking. Guide dogs only. All major credit cards accepted. Room [2007]: single/double £130–£150, suite £200–£235. Breakfast £13.50–£16. Full alc £60. Christmas/New Year packages. ***V***

See also SHORTLIST

NEWLANDS Cumbria — Map 4: inset C2

Swinside Lodge
Grange Road, Newlands
nr Keswick CA12 5UE

Tel 017687-72948
Fax 017687-73312
Email info@swinsidelodge-hotel.co.uk
Website www.swinsidelodge-hotel.co.uk

César award in 2007

'Small, quiet, friendly', 'a haven of comfort', Eric and Irene Fell's traditional Regency house stands at the foot of Cat Bells in a silent and scenic stretch of Derwentwater. They are 'attentive hosts, from the warm greeting to the personal farewell'. 'We were greeted by Irene with tea and home-baked cookies,' one visitor wrote. Bedrooms come in three sizes: 'Ours, with king-size bed, was large, airy, newly decorated. Textiles were tasteful, and there were all sorts of thoughtful extras.' There are 'crisp cotton sheets, fluffy white towels, good toiletries'. A smaller standard room was 'comfortable if a little cluttered'. Pre-dinner drinks come with 'delicious' canapés. In the dark red dining room, dinner is no-choice, preferences discussed on arrival. Clive Imber's modern cooking is widely admired: 'The menu mixed the rustic with the imaginative; ingredients were local and fresh.' Mr Fell 'is full of information about the area'. Breakfast has 'sensational' marmalade. Keen walkers 'came back soaking wet and muddy: our clothes were whisked away, dried and folded ready for the morning'. (*Helen Horlock, Katrina Halliday, Yvette Hales, Stephen and Jane Savery*)

7 bedrooms. 3 miles S of Keswick. Closed 2/3 weeks Jan. Dining room closed midday. 2 sitting rooms, dining room. No background music. 1-acre garden. Unsuitable for ♿. No smoking. No children under 12. No dogs. MasterCard, Visa accepted. B&B [2007] £68–£88 per person; D,B&B £88–£108. Set dinner £35. Special breaks. New Year package. *V*

NEWMARKET Suffolk *See SHORTLIST* Map 2:B4

NEWQUAY Cornwall *See SHORTLIST* Map 1:D2

NORTH MOLTON Devon Map 1:B4

Heasley House

Heasley Mill
North Molton EX36 3LE

Tel 01598-740213
Fax 01598-740677
Email enquiries@heasley-house.co.uk
Website www.heasley-house.co.uk

Fronting on to the tiny River Mole, this 'unassuming' Grade II listed Georgian dower house is at a crossroads on a minor country road in a hamlet on the southern edge of Exmoor national park. It was enjoyed again this year. 'We were made most welcome by the hospitable owners, Jan and Paul Gambrill, and offered tea and excellent fruit cake.' Inspectors add: 'We loved it for the little things that cost nothing.' Extensive renovations include a new restaurant lounge and reception area. In the restaurant, open to non-residents, Mr Gambrill, 'passionate about cooking', offers 'a range of choices exceptional for an establishment of this size', including Exmoor lamb with balsamic sauce; roast pork with mustard mash. 'A first-class dinner.' The wine list is 'very good, with modest mark-up'. Breakfast has freshly squeezed orange juice, home-made bread, 'really good porridge, super scrambled eggs and decent coffee'. Bedroom upgrading will be complete by early 2008. Freshly painted in pastel colours, all rooms will have *en suite* facilities with power shower. 'Our spacious bedroom was well furnished, wonderfully peaceful.' Downstairs are deep leather chairs, stripped wooden floors. Shooting parties come in winter. Dogs are 'positively welcomed'. (*Dennis R Wickett, JB, and others*)

8 bedrooms. Some family. 1 on ground floor. N of North Molton. Closed Feb. 2 lounges, bar (background music on request), restaurant. ¼-acre garden. Unsuitable for ♿. No smoking. No dogs in restaurant. MasterCard, Visa accepted. B&B [2007] £49–£75 per person. Set dinner £17.50–£21.50. New Year package for house parties. *V*

NORTH WALSHAM Norfolk — Map 2:A6

Beechwood
Cromer Road
North Walsham
NR28 0HD

Tel 01692-403231
Fax 01692-407284
Email enquiries@beechwood-hotel.co.uk
Website www.beechwood-hotel.co.uk

'A very good hotel; well-trained staff, caring proprietors, superb housekeeping.' High praise this year for this creeper-clad house, Georgian but 'with Victorian character'. Other comments: 'Superb welcome; excellent food.' 'Good value.' Owner/managers Lindsay Spalding and Don Birch 'did a superb job looking after us; they were never obtrusive, nor were their staff. The welcome from a young receptionist was the best ever. She took us on a tour while our cases were deposited in our ground-floor room in the new extension. It was spacious, with half-tester bed; fine, well-lit bathroom in black-and-white and chrome, with power shower and full-size slipper bath.' The cooking of Steven Norgate ('modern British with a Mediterranean influence') includes duo of sea bass and salmon on pea and prawn risotto. Breakfast has freshly squeezed juice, cereals galore, an 'artistic' buffet of sliced fruits: 'Faultless,' said one couple; another was less keen on the scrambled eggs. The 'lovely garden' has shrubs, a long lawn and sunken area. The dog-friendly environment is appreciated. Two Airedale terriers, Harry and Emily, appear at night, after their walk. Don Birch writes: 'We guarantee a restful stay because we don't take large groups, wedding parties or conferences. We try to make guests travelling alone especially welcome.' (*Ken and Mildred Edwards, Gwyn Morgan, Hilary and Bob Wade*)

17 bedrooms. Some on ground floor, 1 suitable for ♿. Near town centre. Closed Christmas. Restaurant closed midday Mon–Sat. 2 lounges, bar, restaurant; classical background music in evening. 1-acre garden: croquet. No smoking. No children under 10. MasterCard, Visa accepted. B&B £45–£80 per person; D,B&B £50–£102. Set lunch (Sun) £19, dinner £34. Winter/spring breaks (3 nights, including Sun, for the price of 2). New Year package. 1-night bookings sometimes refused. *V*

NORTHAM Devon — Map 1:B4

Yeoldon House
Durrant Lane
Northam, nr Bideford
EX39 2RL

Tel 01237-474400
Fax 01237-476618
Email yeoldonhouse@aol.com
Website www.yeoldonhousehotel.co.uk

'If only more hotels in the UK were like this,' say visitors in 2007, 'we would not go to France so much.' Set beside the River Torridge, the 'welcoming' 19th-century gabled house, Union flag flying, is 'very much a family concern', run by owners Jennifer and Brian Steele with sons Colin and Christopher. There are suitcases and teddy bears on the stairs, old stained glass and a large lounge. Bedrooms 'each have their own charm': one has a four-poster, another is split level, with its own balcony and lounge area. The popular Crow's Nest overlooks the estuary and has a battlemented balcony. The restaurant, also river-facing, is named after the famous chef, Alexis Soyer. Brian Steele 'takes pride in cooking and presenting good food in a relaxing atmosphere'. His 'chef's collection' dinner menu has a choice of five dishes for each course, eg: chargrilled Mediterranean vegetables, with toasted goat's cheese; guineafowl with caramelised orange and ginger stuffing. Wines are 'fairly priced'. Breakfast is traditional English or continental. Books and games are provided; donkeys graze in a meadow up the drive. Nearby are Rosemoor Garden and the delightful fishing town of Appledore. (*TJB Pellow*)

10 bedrooms. ½ mile N of Bideford. Closed Christmas. Restaurant closed midday and Sun evening. Lounge/bar, restaurant; classical background music at night. 2-acre grounds. Beach 5 mins' drive. Civil wedding licence. Unsuitable for ♿. No smoking. No dogs in restaurant. Amex, MasterCard accepted. B&B £55–£75 per person; D,B&B £77.50–£102.50. Set dinner £30. New Year package. *V*

The *V* sign at the end of an entry indicates a hotel that has agreed to take part in our Voucher scheme and to give *Guide* readers a 25% discount on their room rates for a one-night stay, subject to the conditions explained in *How to use the Good Hotel Guide*, and given on the back of the vouchers.

NORWICH Norfolk — Map 2:B5

By Appointment
25–29 St George's Street
Norwich NR3 1AB
Tel/Fax 01603-630730
Email puttii@tiscali.co.uk
Website www.byappointmentnorwich.co.uk

César award in 1999

In the historic centre, this 15th-century merchant's house is a restaurant-with-rooms liked for its theatrical style, 'warm welcome' and 'excellent food'. The owners, Timothy Brown and Robert Culyer, tell us that 'having continually fought technology because it did not fit with our quirkiness', they have now launched a website: each bedroom is described in detail. One has a roll-top bath, another a Victorian brass bed, another an open coal fire and double-ended bath. The house is entered through a tiny courtyard with a Della Robbia relief on the wall; inside are antiques and 'interesting/unusual pieces' (Edwardian wardrobes, hat boxes, old suitcases, etc). 'The clutter might not be to everyone's taste, but we could not fault the place,' is one comment. 'Not for the disabled or very tall.' In the four small dining rooms, dotted around the building, the menu is displayed on gilt-framed blackboards and read aloud, 'with aplomb', by Robert Culyer. The cooking is 'English with continental influences', eg, beef puff pastry parcels with a stroganoff sauce; poached fillet of sole with tiger prawns. 'Delicious and beautifully served.' There is a separate vegetarian menu. The admired breakfast has freshly squeezed juice, croissants, scrambled eggs with smoked salmon and wild mushrooms. (*P and JL, and others*)

5 bedrooms. Central; corner of St George's St and Colegate. Closed Christmas. Restaurant closed midday, and Sun and Mon evenings. 2 lounges, restaurant (jazz/classical background music at night; occasional live music). Unsuitable for ♿. No smoking. No children under 12. No dogs. MasterCard, Visa accepted. B&B £55–£85 per person. Full alc £42.90.

See also SHORTLIST

How to contact the *Guide*
By mail: From anywhere in the UK, write to Freepost PAM 2931, London W11 4BR (no stamp is needed)
From outside the UK: *Good Hotel Guide*, 50 Addison Avenue, London W11 4QP, England
By telephone or fax: 020-7602 4182
By email: Goodhotel@aol.com or Goodhotel@btinternet.com
Via our website: www.goodhotelguide.com

NOTTINGHAM Nottinghamshire — Map 2:A3

Hart's Hotel

Standard Hill, Park Row
Nottingham NG1 6FN

Tel 0115-988 1900
Fax 0115-947 7600
Email reception@hartshotel.co.uk
Website www.hartshotel.co.uk

César award in 2007

'A fine combination of modern design and good service', Tim Hart's purpose-built designer hotel is in a traffic-free cul-de-sac on the site of Nottingham's medieval castle. Inspectors were 'impressed by how well run it is': Paul Fearon is the manager; his staff are 'young, bright, enthusiastic'. Public areas are 'clean and light'. Bedrooms are 'well equipped, and naturally ventilated through louvred shutters, giving pleasant air quality without dryness or noise'. All have Internet access, voicemail, large TV, etc. 'Our superior double, though not large, had a stunning view through big windows over the city; dark wood, white walls, good linen; small, efficient bathroom; all in excellent taste. We were dismayed to be confronted by a duvet; blankets and sheets were swiftly provided.' The six garden rooms each have a private terrace. Lunch in the hotel's *Park Bar* 'was very good with attentive service'. 'Those requiring a *grande bouffe* are well served by *Hart's*', the adjacent restaurant in the former radiology department of Nottingham's general hospital (hotel residents must book). 'One of the best eating places in the area.' A reporter this year described it as the 'lifeblood' of the hotel ('bobby-dazzling bouillabaisse'). Newly refurbished, it has a 'spacious, sophisticated feel'. 'Breakfast the only let-down, obviously for businessmen in a hurry.' (*Peter Jowitt, Pat and Jeremy Temple, David and Kate Wooff, and others*)

32 bedrooms. 2 suitable for ♿. City centre. Restaurant closed 26 Dec and 1 Jan. Lift, ramps. Reception/lobby, bar (background music), restaurant (30 yds); conference/banqueting facilities; small exercise room. Small garden. Civil wedding licence. No smoking. No dogs: public rooms, or unaccompanied in bedrooms. Amex, MasterCard, Visa accepted. Room: £120–£260. Breakfast £8.50–£13.50. Set lunch £13.95, dinner (Sun–Thurs) £22.50; full alc £50. *V*

'Set menu' indicates a fixed-price meal, with ample, limited or no choice. 'Full alc' is the hotel's estimated price per person of a three-course *à la carte* meal, with a half bottle of house wine. 'Alc' is the price of an *à la carte* meal excluding the cost of wine.

Lace Market Hotel
29–31 High Pavement
Nottingham NG1 1HE

Tel 0115-852 3232
Fax 0115-852 3223
Email stay@lacemarkethotel.co.uk
Website www.lacemarkethotel.co.uk

Converted from four Georgian and Victorian town houses (one a former lace factory), this modern hotel faces the former Georgian law courts and the 14th-century church of St Mary the Virgin. Owner James Blick has a new manager this year, John Quero. The bedrooms have a smart, minimalist decor with strong colours and contemporary furniture. All rooms have air conditioning, DVD-player and wireless broadband. 'Superior' rooms are spacious. One couple was pleased to be upgraded to a split-level studio suite with fine views through huge sash windows. The 'classic bistro', *Merchants* (booking recommended), has a good brasserie menu, eg, smoked quail ravioli; roasted sirloin of Cornish beef with potato gratin. The hotel's 'gastropub', *Cock and Hoop*, which has a new kitchen this year, serves a short menu of salads, burgers, steak, etc. At breakfast the buffet has fresh orange juice, good pastries, 'delicious, treacly compotes'; 'mercifully no sign of butter in foil or sugar in paper wrapping'. Room service is 'prompt and accurate'. A warning: 'The discount arrangement with the local car park becomes invalid after 24 hours.' More reports, please.

42 bedrooms. City centre, opposite Galleries of Justice. Restaurant closed Sun/Mon (gastropub open). Lift. Reception (background music), bar (live music), brasserie, gastropub; lounge; private dining room; boardroom. Free use of nearby health club. Civil wedding licence. Unsuitable for ♿. No smoking. No children under 18 in bar. No dogs in public rooms (£15 a night in bedroom). Amex, MasterCard, Visa accepted. Room [2007]: single £95, double £119–£189, suite £239. Breakfast £14.95. Set lunch £14.95, dinner £29.50; full alc £50. Special offers.

See also SHORTLIST

OBORNE Dorset — Map 1:C6

The Grange at Oborne NEW
Oborne, nr Sherborne
DT9 4LA

Tel 01935-813463
Fax 01935-817464
Email reception@thegrange.co.uk
Website www.thegrangeatoborne.co.uk

Up a quiet lane, just off the A30, this 'pleasant country hotel' is well managed and has 'exceptionally good staff', says a visitor in late 2006. It is managed by Jennifer Mathews and her partner, Jon Fletcher. Her parents, Ken and Karenza, the owners, have extended the 200-year-old Portland stone former farmhouse. Some bedrooms are modern, some traditional; some have a patio and direct garden access; two have a balcony. 'Ours was large and nicely furnished, and faced the attractive garden. Traditional bedding, which we prefer, but the pillows were a bit hard. We later discovered that feather pillows could be provided. Corridors are newly carpeted. We thought the lounge decor a bit dated, and it was poorly lit.' Martin Barrett's cooking ('British with an emphasis on wholesome local produce') included good saddle of lamb and sea bass. 'To end, a dessert trolley, very popular with the guests. Wine list excellent, and fairly priced. Breakfast was fine, including a generous plateful of scrambled eggs and bacon. Best of all are the staff, mainly female, young and local, who have been exceptionally well trained.' (*Bill Bennett*)

18 bedrooms. 1 suitable for ♿. 2 miles NE of Sherborne by A30. Restaurant closed Sun night. 2 lounges, bar, restaurant; permanent 'easy listening' background music. ¾-acre garden. Civil wedding/partnership licence; function facilities. No smoking. Guide dogs only. All major credit cards accepted. B&B £52.50–£95 per person; D,B&B £79.50–£117. Set menus £26–£32. Hibernation breaks Oct–Mar. 1-night bookings refused Sat in summer. *V*

ORFORD Suffolk — Map 2:C6

The Crown and Castle

Orford, nr Woodbridge
IP12 2LJ

Tel 01394-450205
Email info@crownandcastle.co.uk
Website www.crownandcastle.co.uk

In a peaceful coastal village, this red brick inn, 16th-century in origin, much altered in 1896, is owned and run by cookery writer Ruth Watson (perhaps best known as Channel 5's 'hotel inspector') with her husband, David ('his repartee is appreciated'). Tim Sunderland is manager. *Guide* correspondents were enthusiastic this year: 'Everything we hoped for: good food, attentive young staff, comfortable room.' 'Slightly quirky style.' 'Our bedroom in the main house was comfortable, especially the king-size bed; views of sea from the bedroom and of castle from the bathroom, which was small but adequate, with good toiletries.' The 'excellent' spacious rooms in the garden have been 'spruced up' inside and out. The large bar lounge has a big chrome bar, and designer tables and chairs. In the 'attractive, bistro-style' *Trinity* restaurant, Ruth Watson and Max Dougal have a *Michelin Bib Gourmand* for 'unfussy' seasonal dishes like braised Suffolk lamb shank with its own juices and rosemary mash. 'Both dinner and breakfast were exceptional; prices reasonable; service superb.'

Light meals are available: they can be taken on the terrace in summer. Children are welcomed, 'but in limited numbers, and not in *Trinity* at dinner'. (*CJR Thorne, CL Hodgkin, Roger Viner, Kathleen Craddock*)

18 bedrooms. 10 (all on ground floor) in garden. 1 in courtyard. Market square. Closed 2nd week Jan. Lounge/bar, restaurant; private dining room. No background music. 1-acre garden. Unsuitable for ♿. No smoking. No children under 8 in restaurant at night. No dogs: some bedrooms, restaurant. MasterCard, Visa accepted. B&B £45–£95 per person; D,B&B £72.50–£130. Full alc £35. Special breaks. Christmas/New Year packages. 1-night bookings refused Sat.

OXFORD Oxfordshire — Map 2:C2

Old Bank
92–94 High Street
Oxford OX1 4BN

Tel 01865-799599
Fax 01865-799598
Email info@oldbank-hotel.co.uk
Website www.oldbank-hotel.co.uk

'A lovely, contemporary hotel where thought has been applied to "what guests want": firm, large beds, good bath products, Wi-Fi and, bliss, a quiet room when asked for.' A *Guide* hotelier's praise for Jeremy Mogford's elegant conversion of three buildings, one a former bank. Marie Jackson is manager. 'The location could hardly be bettered', opposite All Souls and St Mary's church, yet it is 'amazingly peaceful'. 'Public areas feel fresh, and look well cared for; the abundance of artwork is a delight.' 'Staff are bright and very helpful.' The decor is 'stylish without being too cutting-edge; mushroom cream and muted red colours, modern but relaxing'. 'Nicely finished' bedrooms have 'good facilities'. Most see the city's dreaming spires. 'Our attic room, very comfortable, had armchairs, a desk; pleasingly spacious bathroom with powerful shower, dressing gown, slippers.' The old banking hall houses *Quod*, a lively bar/restaurant, 'always busy': no reservations, though hotel residents have priority. The 'excellent' breakfast is served from 7 to 10.30 am ('my daughter loved the egg soldiers with a pot of marmite'). A brasserie-style lunch and dinner menu is available from 11.30 am (pizzas to slow-roasted lamb shanks). 'Good, if expensive.' (*Carin Burton, Sara Hollowell, Michael and Eithne Dandy, Richard and Tricia Bright*)

42 bedrooms. 1 suitable for ♿. Air conditioning. Central (windows facing High St double glazed). Access to rear car park. Lift. Residents' lounge/bar, bar/grill; 'relaxed' background music; dining terrace; 2 meeting/private dining rooms; conference centre planned. Small garden. No smoking. Guide dogs only. All major credit cards accepted. Room £80–£162.50 per person. Breakfast £10.95–£12.95. Full alc £30.

Old Parsonage
1 Banbury Road
Oxford OX2 6NN

Tel 01865-310210
Fax 01865-311262
Email reception@oldparsonage-hotel.co.uk
Website www.oldparsonage-hotel.co.uk

'We stayed over Christmas. It was wonderful. Terrific comfort and service; charming young staff.' Praise this year for this wisteria-covered 17th-century hotel also owned by Jeremy Mogford, managed by Marie Jackson, beside St Giles' church. Other comments: 'A perfect choice in Oxford; easily accessible; tons of charm.' 'Ambience of a small country house, though on a main road.' A massive oak door opens into the bar/restaurant (a popular meeting place for town and gown) with its year-round log fire ('such a nice room; busy but not overcrowded'). 'All very congenial, and diners seemed not to notice guests tramping through to get to their rooms.' A ground-floor bedroom was 'characterful and comfortable, more spacious than some of the first-floor rooms'. 'Our small room faced the car park. Reading lights abysmal (25 watts).' Chef Mark Bristow serves an all-day menu with reasonable choice, 'beautifully cooked and presented'. 'I was impressed to be offered a full menu well after 10 pm.' A 'very high tea' (wide range of sandwiches) is also available. 'Cooked breakfast full and satisfying' (continental may be less so). In fine weather, the 'pretty walled front terrace' is 'a chic spot for tea or a meal'. (*Antony Fletcher, Eric Siegel, Peter Jowitt, AW*)

30 bedrooms. 10 on ground floor. 1 suitable for ♿. NE end of St Giles'. Some traffic noise; windows double glazed. Small car park. Lounge, bar/restaurant (background music). Terrace (live jazz Fri). Roof garden, small walled garden. Civil wedding licence. No smoking. No dogs in restaurant. All major credit cards accepted. Room [2007]: single £140, double £160, suite £225. Breakfast £12–£14. Full alc £35. Christmas/New Year packages. 1-night bookings sometimes refused Sat.

See also SHORTLIST

PADSTOW Cornwall *See SHORTLIST* Map 1:D2

All our inspections are paid for, and carried out anonymously.

PENRITH Cumbria *See SHORTLIST* Map 4: inset C2

PENZANCE Cornwall Map 1:E1

The Abbey Hotel

Abbey Street
Penzance TR18 4AR

Tel 01736-366906
Fax 01736-351163
Email hotel@theabbeyonline.co.uk
Website www.theabbeyonline.co.uk

Dating from 1660, this small blue-painted B&B hotel is in a narrow street, high above the harbour and overlooking Mount's Bay. A listed building, it has a pretty Victorian garden, courtyard and period features. It was liked again this year for its ambience and decor. There are 'gorgeous fabrics and colour schemes, chintz sofas and chairs, elegant Greek statues, magnificent antiques, curios, fresh flower arrangements, lots of books'. 'The contents are fascinating and the architecture is entrancing,' an earlier visitor wrote. 'Our bedroom was charming, with a spectacular view,' was another comment. The lounge faces the garden, as do some bedrooms (others face the harbour). Attic rooms may be 'cramped'. Breakfast is served in an oak-panelled room. Thaddeus Cox has now joined his parents, Michael and Jean, as manager. There are plenty of places to eat in town, including the *Michelin*-starred *Abbey Restaurant* next door (not connected with the hotel). (*MC*)

6 bedrooms. Also 2 apartments in adjoining building. 300 yds from centre. Parking. Closed Dec–Feb, except for New Year. Drawing room, dining room. No background music. Small garden. Unsuitable for ♿. No smoking. No dogs in public rooms. Amex, MasterCard, Visa accepted. B&B [2007] £55–£100 per person. 1-night bookings refused bank holidays.

Hotel Penzance

Britons Hill
Penzance TR18 3AE

Tel 01736-363117
Fax 01736-350970
Email enquiries@hotelpenzance.com
Website www.hotelpenzance.com

A change of name, but not of ownership, this year, for the former *Mount Prospect Hotel*, in a quiet residential area near the harbour. Stephen and Yvonne Hill's 'very pleasant small hotel' looks over the harbour and the bay to St Michael's Mount. The attractive *Bay Restaurant* (with modern decor, sliding glass doors, well-spaced tables, local artwork and a bar) is popular with outside diners. Chef Ben Reeve offers modern European dishes with an emphasis on seafood, eg, grilled local sardines with steamed baby leeks. The provenance of ingredients (all from the West Country) is listed on the menu. A nine-course tasting menu is available. Recent comments: 'Our excellent bedroom had beautiful views. The furnishings were very good; the bathroom was well fitted.' 'Attractive curtains and bedspreads in bright modern colours.' 'Staff are friendly' (the manager is Andrew Griffiths). In the small subtropical garden there is a heated swimming pool. The heliport to the Isles of Scilly is five minutes' drive away. More reports, please.

24 bedrooms. 2 on ground floor. 10 mins' walk from train/bus station, off Cnyandour Cliff. Ramps. 2 lounges, conservatory, bar/restaurant; background jazz/'easy listening' music. ½-acre garden: terrace, heated swimming pool (30 by 15 ft). Rock beach, safe bathing nearby. No smoking. No dogs: some bedrooms, restaurant. Amex (*2½% surcharge*), MasterCard, Visa accepted. B&B £50–£80 per person; D,B&B £67.50–£107. Set menus £28; full alc £40. 1-night bookings sometimes refused bank holidays. Christmas/New Year packages. *V*

See also SHORTLIST

PERRANUTHNOE Cornwall — Map 1:E1

Ednovean Farm
Perranuthnoe, nr Penzance
TR20 9LZ

Tel 01736-711883
Email info@ednoveanfarm.co.uk
Website www.ednoveanfarm.co.uk

Amid beautiful Cornish countryside, Christine and Charles Taylor's B&B is a converted 17th-century granite barn below the brow of a hill in a quiet village above Mount's Bay. In front are sheltered courtyards; at the back, views across the bay to St Michael's Mount. Inside are Persian rugs, carved cats, antiques, and three bedrooms. The 'romantic' Pink Room has four-poster, exposed stone walls and an embroidered silk hanging. Blue (with French walnut bed and chandelier) and Apricot (cottage-style with iron sleigh bed) are in a separate wing; each has a private sea-facing terrace. All have a DVD-player (there is a collection of DVDs for guests to choose from). There are 'candles everywhere, bathrobes and aromatherapy oils'. Breakfast, at an oak refectory table in the beamed open-plan kitchen/dining room, includes muesli, stewed fruits, local breads, full English 'cooked in front of you'. Guests are given tea on arrival, and are offered complimentary sherry at night in the lounge, which has squashy sofas and embroidered silk wall hangings. In summer, you can sit in the Garden Room (its terrace has sea views). In the grounds are secluded corners, statues, an Italian garden, horses and chickens. A sandy beach is nearby. More reports, please.

3 bedrooms. Above village, 6 miles E of Penzance. Local bus 5 times a day. Closed Christmas/New Year, occasional other times. Lounge, Garden Room, breakfast room (classical background music). 1 acre garden. Unsuitable for ♿. No smoking. No children. No dogs. Amex, MasterCard, Visa accepted. B&B £50–£100 per person. 1-night bookings sometimes refused.

PETWORTH West Sussex — Map 2:E3

The Old Railway Station
Petworth GU28 0JF

Tel 01798-342346
Fax 01798-343066
Email info@old-station.co.uk
Website www.old-station.co.uk

An unusual and 'romantic' B&B, this Grade II* listed Victorian station on a disused railway line has been restored with flair. The biggest bedrooms (one up a spiral staircase and through a library) are in the station building. Most rooms are in Pullman cars (of the type used by the original Orient Express). The owners, Gudmund Olafsson (Icelandic) and Catherine Stormont, have redecorated the station house this year, adding a new reception area, and they were refurbishing the carriages as the *Guide* went to press. They are, inevitably, narrow but are 'beautifully restored, well designed, with comfortable bed and a surprising amount of furniture'. The former waiting room has a 20-foot vaulted ceiling, the original ticket office windows, and an open fire in winter. Large windows create 'a colonial feel'. Breakfast, served here or on the station platform, by waitresses in modified railway steward's uniforms, was enjoyed by inspectors: 'Fruit salad, scrambled eggs with delicious bacon, good coffee.' A champagne breakfast can be taken in the carriage. Menus of local eating places are in the information folders. The pretty garden has ancient trees, a sunken lawn where the railtracks were, and steep banks covered with shrubs.

8 bedrooms. 6 in Pullman carriages. 1 suitable for ♿. 1½ miles S of Petworth. Car park. Train: Pulborough. Closed 24–26 Dec. Lounge/bar/breakfast room (soft background classical CDs). 2-acre garden: platform/terrace. No smoking. No children under 10. No dogs. Amex, MasterCard, Visa accepted. B&B double £69–£160. 3-night winter midweek breaks. 1-night bookings refused weekends, holidays.

PICKERING North Yorkshire — Map 4:D4

The White Swan Inn
Market Place
Pickering YO18 7AA

Tel 01751-472288
Fax 01751-475554
Email welcome@white-swan.co.uk
Website www.white-swan.co.uk

Halfway up the hill in this 'pretty, friendly' market town, this former coaching inn has go-ahead owners, Victor and Marion Buchanan. This year they turned a barn into the Club Room, a residents' lounge, with open fire, complimentary tea/coffee, honesty bar, pool table, newspapers and magazines. Tim Fisher is manager. Reports are mostly favourable. 'A most enjoyable stay. Lovely old inn. Cosy public rooms.' Staff are 'charming, helpful'; 'polite even when pushed'. 'Attention to detail excellent.' 'No muzak.' The bedrooms, mostly smallish, done in white, ochre and beige, have TV, DVD-player, 'interesting pieces of furniture' (a walnut four-poster; a George III mahogany side table). The newer rooms are 'exceptionally good, and free of traffic noise', but one of the older rooms, at the top, was heartily disliked, and some visitors found prices high. In the restaurant ('candlelit, comfortable, relaxed') are flagstones, open fire, low ceiling and Gothic screens. Darren Clemmit's 'country cooking' uses meat from the 'unique', local Ginger Pig food producer. Main courses include slow-cooked shoulder of lamb; 'posh fish and chips'. There is a good-value set lunch, a snack menu and a children's menu. 'Excellent breakfast: fresh fruit, good toast, etc'; also full Yorkshire. (*Karina Spero, CB, and others*)

21 bedrooms. 9 in annexe. Central. Ramps to ground-floor facilities. Lounge, bar, Club Room, restaurant; private dining room; conference/meeting facilities. No background music. 1½-acre grounds. Small terrace (alfresco meals). Civil wedding licence. No smoking. No dogs in restaurant. Amex, MasterCard, Visa accepted. B&B [2007] £65–£145 per person; D,B&B £92.50–£175. Set lunch (Mon–Fri) £10–£12.95; full alc £45. Christmas/New Year packages. 1-night bookings sometimes refused weekends. *V*

PICKHILL North Yorkshire — Map 4:C4

The Nag's Head
Pickhill, nr Thirsk
YO7 4JG

Tel 01845-567391
Fax 01845-567212
Email enquiries@nagsheadpickhill.co.uk
Website www.nagsheadpickhill.co.uk

Popular with the racing fraternity, this busy country inn, in a Domesday-old village in Herriot country, is endorsed 'without reservation' by a visitor in 2007. It provides 'remarkable value for money', says a regular visitor. 'Small and relatively basic', it is 'very adequate for a short stay'. Edward and Janet Boynton, the 'welcoming owners', are in charge (their family have owned the inn for 30 years); service is 'helpful'. The bedrooms are comfortable and 'sensibly equipped'. An extensive menu is served in the bar and restaurant: dishes include game casserole; calf's liver and bacon: 'A delicious dinner. At breakfast my large fillet of haddock with poached egg was memorable.' The inn, says its website, 'is a feasting and meeting place for families, clubs and business people'. Children 'with one or two careful owners' are welcomed, and pets 'must be properly controlled'. (*Martin Wyatt, JH*)

16 bedrooms. 6 in annexe, 2 in cottage. 3 on ground floor. 5 miles SE of Leeming, 1 mile E of A1. Closed Christmas Day. Ramps. 2 bars, restaurant (background music); meeting facilities. Lawn: croquet, putting. No smoking. Dogs allowed in 2 bedrooms (not unattended). MasterCard, Visa accepted. B&B £40–£55 per person. Full alc £30. Weekend breaks. New Year package.

PLYMOUTH Devon *See SHORTLIST* — Map 1:D4

POOLE Dorset *See SHORTLIST* — Map 2:E1

PORLOCK Somerset — Map 1:B5

The Oaks
Porlock TA24 8ES

Tel 01643-862265
Fax 01643-863131
Email info@oakshotel.co.uk
Website www.oakshotel.co.uk

In an elevated position on the northern edge of Exmoor, this gabled Edwardian country house stands in pretty gardens, with wide lawns and oak trees, above the fishing village. It has 'great views' of Porlock and the Bristol Channel. Visitors this year wrote of a 'friendly welcome with tea and cakes' from the owners, Tim and Anne Riley. An earlier comment: 'Exceptionally quiet; an excellent dinner.' In the 'spotless' bedrooms, 'bedlinen is smooth and fresh, towels are thick and huge'; 'fresh fruit, milk and flowers every day'. The 'old-fashioned courtesy' is appreciated (help with luggage, etc). The main lounge has an open fire, chintzes, oil paintings and prints. In the restaurant, tables are arranged around the panoramic windows, so everyone can enjoy the view, and 'delightful sunsets accompany the evening meal'. Breakfasts (with home-made marmalade) and dinners (four courses) are 'well cooked with good choices'. The hostess 'has the lightest touch and uses the freshest ingredients' (eg, breast of local duckling with orange and brandy sauce; hot Somerset apple cake with clotted cream). A warning: 'The hotel's entrance is at a sharp angle of the main road.' (*Joy and Ron Driver, and others*)

8 bedrooms. ¼ mile from village. Open Apr–Nov, Christmas/New Year. 2 lounges, bar, restaurant (classical background music at night). 1-acre garden. Sea, pebble beach 1 mile. Unsuitable for ♿. No smoking. No children under 8. No dogs. MasterCard, Visa accepted. B&B £67.50–£95 per person; D,B&B (min. 2 nights) £92.50–£127.50. Set dinner £32.50. 1-night bookings sometimes refused. Christmas/New Year packages.

PORT ISAAC Cornwall — Map 1:D2

Port Gaverne Hotel
Port Gaverne
nr Port Isaac
PL29 3SQ

Tel 01208-880244
Freephone 0500 657867
Fax 01208-880151
Website www.english-inns.co.uk

'A simple, friendly place', Graham and Annabelle Sylvester's unpretentious inn is in a hamlet above a quiet cove north of the busy fishing village of Port Isaac. The bar, with its slate floors, wooden beams, local art work (for sale) and log fire, is popular with locals, and serves good food off a blackboard menu. 'We were given a pleasant welcome; Graham Sylvester wandered through with three black dogs. "Taking the girls to the beach," he said. The "girls" were back soon and sat under the tables.' Visitors' dogs are welcome, too ('ours was in pet heaven'). Not to all tastes: one visitor this year was unhappy, but another found it 'hard to find fault, a great pleasure'. The simple bedrooms are up steep stairs: 'Ours was presentable, and had a balcony.' Sound insulation may not be perfect. Ian Brodey's cooking is usually admired: 'Crab salad went down well; nicely pink duck, served at our request with sautéed potatoes.' 'Decent choice of house wines, a jug of water on the table.' Breakfast has a buffet for cereals, packaged juices; good cooked dishes brought to the table; good marmalade, pats of butter. (*John Tyrie, and others*)

15 bedrooms. ½ mile N of Port Isaac. Closed Christmas. Restaurant closed 3–31 Jan. Lounge, 2 bars, restaurant. No background music. Beer garden. Rock cove 60 yds; golf, fishing, surfing, sailing, riding nearby. Unsuitable for ♿. No smoking. No children under 7 in restaurant at night (room service supper available). No dogs: restaurant, some bedrooms. MasterCard, Visa accepted. B&B £42.50–£62.50 per person. Set dinner £27. New Year package.

PORTSCATHO Cornwall — Map 1:E2

driftwood hotel

Rosevine
nr Portscatho TR2 5EW

Tel 01872-580644
Fax 01872-580801
Email info@driftwoodhotel.co.uk
Website www.driftwoodhotel.co.uk

Above a quiet cove in the Roseland peninsula, Paul and Fiona Robinson's 'lovely small hotel' has a 'peaceful, beautiful setting'. 'The building and grounds are exceptional, as is the quality of the service and the general atmosphere,' says one visitor. The owners are 'so nice; we were relaxed, happy and very well cared for by the pleasant staff'. The design and interior decoration are contemporary, with 'simple white background and various shades of blue'. The public rooms are well thought-out, with rugs on bare floorboards, driftwood table lamps and mirrors; a log fire in the drawing room. 'One slight drawback; you have to walk through the dining room to reach some bedrooms.' Most of the bedrooms have the views. The two-roomed Cabin on the hillside (with sitting room and kitchenette) is thought 'tremendous fun'. The dining room is 'lovely, with many candles'. The chef, Chris Eden, serves modern European dishes, eg, saddle of lamb, pea shoots, feta, baby vegetables. 'Breakfasts were lavish and of high quality.' Steep steps through woodland lead down to the beach. The Eden Project and the Heligan Gardens are within a half-hour drive. (*TS, Conrad Barnard*)

15 bedrooms. 4 in courtyard. Also 2 in beach cabin (2 mins' walk). N side of Portscatho. Closed Christmas/New Year, Jan. 2 lounges, bar, restaurant (background jazz/classical music at night); children's games room. 7-acre grounds: terraced gardens, private beach, safe bathing. Unsuitable for ♿. No smoking. No dogs. Amex, MasterCard, Visa accepted. B&B £105–£165 per person; D,B&B (Nov–Mar) £95–£142.50. Set menu £39. 1-night bookings sometimes refused weekends.

Rosevine Hotel

Porthcurnick Beach, Rosevine
nr Portscatho TR2 5EW

Tel 01872-580206
Fax 01872-580230
Email info@rosevine.co.uk
Website www.rosevine.co.uk

Above a cove on the Roseland peninsula, Caroline and Chris Davidson's traditional child-friendly hotel is endorsed again this year. 'Welcoming, relaxed atmosphere; staff charming and efficient. Our dog even had his own private garden.' Earlier praise: 'Service and food were good.' 'We were warmly welcomed by the receptionist, who took us to our room and offered a complimentary cream tea.' Some rooms have a balcony overlooking the south-facing, 'very special' semi-tropical garden. Refurbishment continues this year; Wi-Fi is new. In the high-ceilinged dining room, chef Didier Bienaimé offers menus 'both enterprising and excellent', with generous portions. 'Superb fresh fish [eg, John Dory with a casserole of fennel and Pernod cream] and sumptuous puddings.' The vegetarian menu is thought 'outstanding'. Meals are served on a patio in fine weather. Menus are left in bedrooms in the afternoon; guests order by telephone. There is an 'adequate' swimming pool, a spa bath and a children's paddling pool. Loungers and parasols stand on the lawn. Close by is flat, safe Porthcurnick beach. Mrs Davidson's brother, Keith Makepeace, owns the *Soar Mill Cove Hotel*, Soar Mill Cove (*qv*), near Salcombe. (*Marion Stockley, and others*)

17 bedrooms. 6 in annexe across courtyard. Some on ground floor. Off A3078, N side of Portscatho. Open Feb–31 Dec. Ramps. Lounge, sun lounge, bar, restaurant (background music at night, pianist 2 nights a week); games room, children's playroom; indoor swimming pool (65 by 50 ft); laundry, drying room. 3-acre gardens: alfresco dining. No smoking. No dogs in public rooms. Amex, MasterCard, Visa accepted. B&B [2007] £70–£171 per person; D,B&B £106–£207. Set dinner £38; full alc £49. Themed breaks (gourmet, garden lovers, etc). Christmas package. *V*

POSTBRIDGE Devon — Map 1:D4

Lydgate House

Postbridge, Dartmoor
PL20 6TJ

Tel 01822-880209
Fax 01822-880202
Email lydgatehouse@email.com
Website www.lydgatehouse.co.uk

In Dartmoor national park, this unassuming late Victorian country house is reached by a private lane near the village's famous clapper bridge over the River Dart. 'A house-party atmosphere is felt on arrival,' say visitors this year, who appreciated the 'care, comfort and friendliness' given by the owners, Peter and Cindy Farrington. Other comments: 'Lovely position, excellent, unfussy food.' 'Wonderfully peaceful.' The Farringtons have five cats, four dogs (not indoors) and two elderly sheep. There are superb views from the sitting room, the conservatory dining room and most bedrooms. Two rooms have a small sitting room, two a sitting area. One correspondent commented on the plethora of 'twee cuddly toys; five teddy bears in my room'. Meals and cream teas are served to residents only. Guests choose, by about 6.30 pm, from a daily-changing dinner menu using locally sourced ingredients: eg, oven-roasted salmon with tomatoes and basil. 'Reasonably priced New World wines.' Breakfast has a wide choice of fruits and cereals from a central table; tasty cooked dishes ('I enjoyed smoked salmon with scrambled eggs'). 'Our dog was made very welcome', but children are not accepted. Good walking from the door. (*Mr and Mrs JJ Leary, AE Silver, Elizabeth Akenhead, Marilyn Frampton*)

7 bedrooms. 500 yds off B3212. Open Feb–Dec. Restaurant closed Mon night. Lounge with bar, snug, dining room. No background music. Terrace. 36-acre grounds: moorland, paddock, river (private access for guests; fishing, swimming). Unsuitable for ♿. No smoking. No children under 16. MasterCard, Visa accepted. B&B [2007] £50–£70 per person; D,B&B £78.50–£98.50. Full alc £34.50. 3-night rates. Christmas package.

PRESTBURY Cheshire — Map 3:A5

White House Manor
New Road
Prestbury SK10 4HP

Tel 01625-829376
Fax 01625-828627
Email info@thewhitehouse.uk.com
Website www.thewhitehouse.uk.com

On the edge of an affluent commuter village near Manchester, Ryland and Judith Wakeham's renovated manor house is noted for its unusual themed bedrooms. Crystal ('very superior', say visitors this year) has a chandelier, a locally crafted four-poster bed, a window seat and a hydrotherapy bath. The Millennium suite has a bed mounted on glass bricks, with lights underneath: 'There were home-made chocolates, fruit, a hidden TV and CD-player; lots of CDs. Silver lacquer was everywhere. The bathroom had stainless steel floor, loo and basin.' Glyndebourne has fine antiques and a sophisticated music system with a library of modern and classical music. A new ground-floor bedroom, Chantilly, opened in 2007: it has an antique ivory Bordeaux bed, its own secluded courtyard, and a 'fabulous bathroom with walk-in wet room and invigorating body jets'. All rooms have free Wi-Fi. Cooked breakfasts, including a 'full Cheshire', may be taken in the bedroom, the *Orangerie* (a new lounge/bar conservatory), or on a patio. 'Continental breakfast, served in the room, was good – croissants and muffins wrapped in a napkin.' Details are provided of the five eating places in the village. (*EJ and JG*)

12 bedrooms. 1 in coach house annexe. Edge of village on A538. Closed 25/26 Dec. Lounge, conservatory with honesty bar, breakfast room. No background music. ½-acre garden. Patio. Unsuitable for ♿. No smoking. No children under 10. No dogs. Amex, MasterCard, Visa accepted. Room: single £50–£80, double £110–£150. Breakfast £7.50–£11.50. Winter breaks.

PURTON Wiltshire — Map 3:E5

The Pear Tree at Purton

Church End
Purton, nr Swindon SN5 4ED

Tel 01793-772100
Fax 01793-772369
Email stay@peartreepurton.co.uk
Website www.peartreepurton.co.uk

Once a vicarage, Francis and Anne Young's Cotswold old stone hotel (Pride of Britain) stands on the edge of a Saxon village in the Vale of the White Horse. A visitor this year was 'very impressed, especially with the helpful, friendly staff' and 'good value'. Others wrote: 'Lovely hotel.' 'Excellent dinner, charmingly served.' 'Help with luggage' is appreciated. There are 'gorgeous gardens, comfortable lounges, and a pretty conservatory extension to the dining room'. In the bedrooms (each named after a village character), fresh flowers match the colour scheme: 'Ours was large, with excellent bed, ample storage, good furnishings, large decanter of sherry, mineral waters, biscuits and fresh fruit; a well-supplied bathroom.' One spacious ground-floor room has a private courtyard. Dinner, in the candlelit green-and-white restaurant, was 'most enjoyable; a wonderful Ribblesdale cheese salad with caramelised walnuts; excellent monkfish with Chinese-style vegetables; tender lamb; superb desserts'. 'Breakfast (no buffet, hurrah) one of the best we've had; good choice of freshly squeezed juices, good choice of fruits and cereals, super cooked items (smoked haddock with egg, kippers, etc).' Purton's old church is worth a visit. (*Jeanette Bloor, Becky Goldsmith, and others*)

17 bedrooms. Some on ground floor. 5 miles NW of Swindon. Closed 26–30 Dec. Restaurant closed Sat midday. Ramps. Lounge/bar, library, restaurant; function/conference facilities. No background music. 7½-acre grounds: croquet, pond, jogging route. Civil wedding licence. Smoking allowed in 3 bedrooms. No dogs unattended in bedrooms (sometimes allowed in public rooms, if quiet). All major credit cards accepted. B&B £60–£140 per person. Set dinner £34.50. Special breaks. *V*

RAMSEY Isle of Man — Map 4:D1

Hillcrest House

May Hill, Ramsey IM8 2HG

Tel 01624-817215
Email admin@hillcresthouse.co.uk
Website www.hillcresthouse.co.uk

The beautiful Isle of Man is self-governing and does not belong to the UK, so this small guest house owned by Aurea and Tony Greenhalgh is a maverick *Guide* entry. Comments this year: 'We were made to feel extremely welcome.' 'Warm and friendly.' 'Very caring, very comfortable.'

The bay-windowed Victorian building has marble fireplaces, wood panelling, moulded ceilings, period furniture, patchwork quilts, and an eclectic selection of pictures and books. Only three bedrooms; all have *en suite* facilities and a CD-player. Organic ingredients are used for the 'stunning' breakfasts which include freshly squeezed juices, home-made bread, leaf teas, Manx kippers, kedgeree, home-made breads and yogurts. Vegetarians are catered for. A simple evening meal is sometimes available in winter. The host is a qualified acupuncturist and can treat 'a wide range of conditions and ailments'. There are country walks in the area, along uncrowded lanes and footpaths; sandy beaches, an 18-hole golf course and ancient Celtic sites are nearby. (*Dr and Mrs Richard Gee, and others*)

3 bedrooms. ¼-mile walk from centre. Parking. Bus or tram from Douglas (10 miles) in summer. Closed 3 weeks Jan. Lounge, dining room; treatment room. No background music. Small front garden. Unsuitable for ♿. No smoking. No children under 10. No dogs. No credit cards. B&B [2007] £35–£38 per person. 1-night bookings refused in season.

RAMSGILL-IN-NIDDERDALE North Yorkshire — Map 4:D3

The Yorke Arms

Ramsgill-in-Nidderdale
nr Harrogate HG3 5RL

Tel 01423-755243
Fax 01423-755330
Email enquiries@yorke-arms.co.uk
Website www.yorke-arms.co.uk

César award in 2000

'Not just a restaurant-with-rooms, but a magnificent restaurant with beautifully maintained rooms and welcoming staff.' Praise this year for Bill and Frances Atkins's old inn beside Ramsgill village green. Cricket lovers found Mr Atkins (a Cambridge blue) an 'ideal host', and appreciated his wife's 'delicious food': she has a *Michelin* star, for dishes such as white truffle risotto; saddle of venison and sausage with sweet potato, cabbage and juniper. 'Miles away from any Yorkshire stereotype (no ladles of gravy covering voluminous Yorkshire puds). Bang-up-to-date bedrooms. Rarely have I seen such high-tech fittings and ultra-modern bathrooms, yet all within a traditional stone, ivy-clad building.' But one couple found their 'larger' room so small that 'we had to take it in turns to get dressed'. Breakfast, between 8 and 9 am, includes strong-cured bacon and home-made marmalade. The sitting areas have flagged floors, settles and wooden tables where walkers take a drink or a snack (bar lunches include home-made soup; gratin of scallops, spinach and bacon).

The restaurant has been redecorated this year. 'Staff were friendly and well trained – they actually looked you in the eye and smiled.' (*Jon Hughes, CJR Thorne, and others*)

14 bedrooms. Centre of village. Train: Harrogate. Sun dinner for residents only. Ramp. Lounge, bar, 2 dining rooms (classical background music); function facilities. 2-acre grounds. Unsuitable for ♿. No smoking. No children under 12. Dogs allowed in bar, 1 bedroom. Amex, MasterCard, Visa accepted. B&B [2007] £75–£120 per person; D,B&B £150–£190. Full alc £65–£70. Christmas/New Year packages.

RAVENGLASS Cumbria — Map 4: inset C2

See SHORTLIST

READING Berkshire *See SHORTLIST* — Map 2:D3

REETH North Yorkshire — Map 4:C3

The Burgoyne Hotel

On the Green
Reeth, nr Richmond
DL11 6SN

Tel/Fax 01748-884292
Email enquiries@theburgoyne.com
Website www.theburgoyne.co.uk

César award in 2002

Named after former residents, the Burgoyne Johnson family, this creeper-covered Grade II listed Regency house in the Yorkshire Dales national park has long been praised for its 'hospitality, comfort and food'. Derek Hickson is now running it on his own with his 'discreet, efficient' long-serving staff; sadly, co-owner Peter Carwardine died in June 2006. The building is traditionally furnished: there are antiques, an inglenook log fire, books and magazines in the spacious lounge. In the green-walled restaurant, chef Paul Salonga offers a daily-changing four-course dinner (with choice): 'traditional English with modern touches' (eg, veal escalope with lemon cream sauce). His cooking continues to be liked, though one couple wrote: 'The combination of richness and quantity made it an effort to complete all courses.' Wines are reasonably priced. Each bedroom (most are large) is named after a local hamlet, and many rooms face south over Swaledale; those at the back face the car park; three have their bathroom across a corridor. A suite is new this year. The breakfast menu has fresh fruit, Whitby kippers, eggs Benedict, as well as 'a huge mixed grill'. Maps and compasses are provided for walkers. (*PRJ, and others*)

9 bedrooms. 1 suitable for ♿. Village centre. Parking. Open 9 Feb–2 Jan. Restaurant closed midday. 2 lounges, dining room (jazz/classical background music 'when needed'). ½-acre garden. Trout fishing on River Swale. No smoking. No children under 10. No dogs: dining room, unattended in bedrooms. MasterCard, Visa accepted. B&B [2007] £53.25–£150 per person. Set dinner £31.50. Midweek, Christmas/New Year packages. 1-night bookings refused Sat in season.

RHYDYCROESAU Shropshire — Map 3:B4

Pen-y-Dyffryn

Rhydycroesau
Oswestry SY10 7JD

Tel 01691-653700
Fax 01978-211004
Email stay@peny.co.uk
Website www.peny.co.uk

César award in 2003

On the last hill in Shropshire, Miles and Audrey Hunter's listed Georgian rectory is just a hundred yards from the Welsh border. Long popular with readers, it earns fresh praise this year. The 'marvellous, caring, owners work really hard at keeping guests comfortable and happy', says one report. Other visitors found 'all their staff friendly and welcoming'. The Hunters tell us they have refurbished the restaurant and lounges, to give them 'a more contemporary feel without losing the informal ambience'. Bedrooms in the main house vary in size; the double-aspect Rector's Room is particularly liked. An 'airy, well-lit' coach house room, up steep steps, 'had small terrace, stone walls covered in clematis, lovely views'. The 'intelligent information folders' are mentioned. In the large dining room, chef David Morris presents a daily-changing menu with choice, using local ingredients where possible. 'Friends who joined us for dinner found the meal a revelation; especially enjoyable were a wood pigeon salad, and wonderfully tender veal.' Breakfast has DIY fresh juice, organic porridge, 'excellent full English'. Dogs are welcomed. Guests may fish for trout in pools in front of the house. Good walking from the door. (*Colin and Stephanie McFie, G Spalding, and others*)

12 bedrooms. 4, each with patio, in coach house. 1 on ground floor. 3 miles W of Oswestry off B4580. Train: Oswestry. 2 lounges, bar, restaurant; background music at night (classical/jazz/opera). 5-acre grounds: dog-walking area. Fishing, golf nearby. No smoking. No children under 3. No dogs in public rooms after 6 pm. MasterCard, Visa accepted. B&B £56–£86 per person; D,B&B £78–£104. Set dinner £35. Christmas/New Year packages. 1-night bookings sometimes refused weekends, bank holidays. ***V***

RICHMOND North Yorkshire — Map 4:C4

Millgate House NEW
Richmond DL10 4JN

Tel 01748-823571
Fax 01748-850701
Email oztim@millgatehouse.demon.co.uk
Website www.millgatehouse.com

Austin Lynch and Tim Culkin, two former English teachers, preside over this 'spectacular Georgian town house' and its award-winning garden. The building is 'beautifully and imaginatively furnished', say its nominators. Filled with antiques and an eclectic art collection, it has spacious bedrooms (some face the walled garden and the River Swale beyond), and 'large and luxurious' bathrooms. 'A vast range of choices for breakfast, served in the elegant dining room. Perfect croissants, top-notch cooked English. The delightful owners are hospitable in every way.' One double bed is 'so high you wonder how to get into it'. An evening meal is available for groups of 16 or more people; afterwards a magician can be produced. (*Elaine and Robert Smyth, and others*)

3 bedrooms. Also self-catering facilities for 12. Town centre. Parking. Hall, drawing room, dining room (occasional background music). Unsuitable for ♿. No smoking. No credit cards. B&B: single £65, double £85–£110. Set dinner £50. Christmas/New Year packages.

RIPLEY North Yorkshire — Map 4:D4

The Boar's Head
Ripley Castle Estate, Ripley
nr Harrogate HG3 3AY

Tel 01423-771888
Fax 01423-771509
Email reservations@boarsheadripley.co.uk
Website www.boarsheadripley.co.uk

César award in 1999

Sir Thomas and Lady Ingilby (his family has lived on the estate for 650 years) have revived with humour this old inn by the castle. It is liked by *Guide* readers for its 'combination of pub and country hotel, with the elegance of country house establishments, but without the stuffiness'. There is praise this year for the staff ('charming, helpful'), the 'excellent' food, and the manager, Steve Chesnutt, who 'has eyes everywhere and an easy manner'. 'Service is polite and personal; efficient, too, with excellent shoe cleaning.' The 'superior' bedrooms in *Birchwood House*, across a courtyard, have 'flowers, fresh fruit, bottled water, sherry; gigantic bed'. 'My pleasant single room was hot, but a fan was quickly provided.' Lounges have antique and period furniture, portraits and pictures from the castle's attics. 'Excellent food (carpaccio of venison with lavender dressing, and a fine fillet steak) and wine list made for two enjoyable visits.' Simpler meals and snacks are available in the bistro. Children and 'well-behaved dogs' are welcomed. Hotel guests have access to the castle's grounds. (*Joanna Russell, Robert Gower, Stephen Holman*)

25 bedrooms. 10 in courtyard. 6 in *Birchwood House* adjacent. Some on ground floor. 3 miles N of Harrogate. Ramps. 2 lounges, bar/bistro, restaurant. No background music. 150-acre estate (deer park, lake, fishing); 20-acre garden. Civil wedding licence (in castle). No smoking. Dogs allowed in 2 courtyard bedrooms, not in public rooms. All major credit cards accepted. B&B [2007] £62.50–£125 per person. Full alc: £40 restaurant, £20 bistro. Christmas/New Year packages.

RIPON North Yorkshire — Map 4:D4

The Old Deanery NEW

Minster Road
Ripon HG4 1QS
Tel 01765-600003
Fax 01765-600027
Email reception@theolddeanery.co.uk
Website www.theolddeanery.co.uk

Opposite the 'awe-inspiring' cathedral of this 'lovely place to visit', this 17th-century building has been stylishly modernised by owners Linda and Peter Whitehouse; Linda Mercer manages. Now a small hotel/restaurant/bar, it is enthusiastically nominated: 'We look for peaceful surroundings, good food, comfortable rooms with modern bathroom. It has all of these qualities. We were impressed.' The lounge has leather sofas, and a log fire on cold days. No lift: an 18th-century oak staircase leads up to the bedrooms. The six rooms on the first floor have original pine shutters and panelling, two have a Victorian slipper-style bath; two a four-poster. The 'characterful' second-floor rooms have a 'splendid' shower, old beams and sloping ceilings. All rooms have broadband Internet access, fresh fruit and bottled water. In the candlelit dining room, chef Barrie Higginbotham uses local ingredients in modern dishes like breast of duckling with caramelised cranberries. In summer, teas, drinks and meals are served in the garden. (*Michael Blanchard*)

11 bedrooms. Town centre. Parking. Closed Sun evening. Lounge, bar, restaurant; background music; conference facilities. 1-acre garden. Civil wedding licence. Unsuitable for ♿. No smoking. No dogs in public rooms. Amex, MasterCard, Visa accepted. B&B [2007] £55–£95 per person. Set menu £30; full alc £38. *V*

For details of the Voucher scheme see page 62.

ROCK Cornwall — Map 1:D2

St Enodoc
Rock, nr Wadebridge
PL27 6LA

Tel 01208-863394
Fax 01208-863970
Email info@enodoc-hotel.co.uk
Website www.enodoc-hotel.co.uk

On the Camel estuary, opposite Padstow, this popular family-friendly hotel has a 'super setting' in a cluster of houses on a hill overlooking the water. Inside, the decor is light, bright and colourful; public rooms have contemporary paintings and comfortable chairs, and there is a large, modern wood burner in one of the lounges. There are many facilities for children: baby-listening, a room with toys and videos, etc, and tea at 5.30 pm. The gym has been converted into a games room for older children, with table tennis and a PlayStation 2. Recent visitors liked their top-floor room: 'Well furnished, with outstanding view of the estuary.' The general manager is Victoria Hutton; the new head chef is former *sous-chef* Ian Carter. Meals are served at wooden tables in the large, split-level restaurant: it has panoramic views and a terrace for summer eating. Typical dishes: Thai fish cake with sweet chilli and coriander dressing; roast chicken breast with rösti and celeriac coleslaw. Bread is home made. There is a heated swimming pool in the small garden. The St Enodoc Golf Club is adjacent, and the small church in the sand where Sir John Betjeman is buried is nearby. (*WC, KJ*)

20 bedrooms. NW of Wadebridge. Open Feb–Jan, except Christmas. Ramps. 3 lounges (Classic FM in 1), bar/restaurant (soft contemporary background music); playroom, children's games room, sauna, billiards. ½-acre grounds: heated 40 by 20-ft swimming pool (May–Sept). Sandy beach, water sports, 3 mins' walk. Only restaurant suitable for ♿. No smoking. No dogs. Amex, MasterCard, Visa accepted. B&B [2007] £62.50–£192.50 per person. Full alc £45–£50. New Year package. Winter breaks. Golf breaks. 1-night bookings sometimes refused weekends. *V*

****

Traveller's tale After an exhausting and somewhat fraught day, we settled down in the beautiful and comfortable lounge, each with a large brandy, to be assailed by something which we presume was supposed to be an atmospheric/'easy listening' CD. We were the only people present, and there was nobody whom we could ask to turn it off. So we swallowed our drinks and went off to our bedroom, only to find that the 'music' was clearly audible there. (*Hotel in Kent*)

****

ROMALDKIRK Co. Durham — Map 4:C3

The Rose and Crown

Romaldkirk
nr Barnard Castle
DL12 9EB

Tel 01833-650213
Fax 01833-650828
Email hotel@rose-and-crown.co.uk
Website www.rose-and-crown.co.uk

César award in 2003

'Great pub, fantastic countryside, beautiful location.' 'Spotless, warm, friendly; excellent staff.' More praise in 2007 for Christopher and Alison Davy's 18th-century coaching inn. Opposite the village green (with stocks, pump and Norman church), it has log fires, panelling, old farming implements, gleaming brasses and fresh flowers. 'The yardstick by which I measure all other hotels,' adds one regular visitor. The 'hands-on owners work very hard', says another. Rooms vary in size; the three smallest have been refurbished. An annexe room was 'a very good size, with modern furnishings'. Room 10 has 'lovely gold-coloured fabrics, bedspread and curtains, comfortable bed, good lighting but no bedside table'. Some courtyard bedrooms, good for dog-owners and walkers, open on to the car park. A 'suite' at the top was thought 'overpriced'. In the restaurant, Christopher Davy and Andrew Lee offer a four-course dinner menu of 'regional dishes with a modern influence', eg, baked smoked salmon soufflé; char-grilled entrecôte of beef with garlic mushrooms. But one visitor would have liked 'more imaginative' vegetarian dishes. Breakfasts are admired. Bread, marmalade, jams and chutneys are home made. The Davys have written a 'very useful' guidebook to local attractions. (*Felicity Shenton, Guy Kitchen, Christopher Hay, Zara Elliott, Gill Holden, and others*)

12 bedrooms. 5 in rear courtyard. Some on ground floor. Village centre. Closed 24–26 Dec. Residents' lounge, lounge bar, Crown Room (bar meals), restaurant. No background music. Fishing, grouse shooting, birdwatching nearby. No smoking. Dogs allowed in bar; not unattended in bedrooms. MasterCard, Visa accepted. B&B [2007] £65–£110 per person; D,B&B £93–£138. Bar lunches. Set lunch £16.75, dinner £28. New Year package. 1-night bookings refused Sat 'except quiet periods'. ***V*** (Nov–Mar)

> The ***V*** sign at the end of an entry indicates a hotel that has agreed to take part in our Voucher scheme and to give *Guide* readers a 25% discount on their room rates for a one-night stay, subject to the conditions explained in *How to use the Good Hotel Guide*, and given on the back of the vouchers.

ROSS-ON-WYE Herefordshire — Map 3:D5

The Bridge at Wilton NEW

Wilton
Ross-on-Wye HR9 6AA

Tel 01989-562655
Fax 01989-567652
Email info@bridge-house-hotel.com
Website www.thebridgeatwilton.com

'Conveniently near the Welsh end of the M50', Michael and Jane Pritchard's restaurant-with-rooms sits quietly in a hamlet, overlooking an ancient crossing of the River Wye. 'Service is friendly and the menu is imaginative, justifying the 2006 Herefordshire Restaurant of the Year award,' writes the nominator. Local ingredients are used by chef James Arbourne in dishes like venison with root vegetable tarte Tatin, caraway caramel and bitter chocolate jus. 'My room, generously sized, with a capacious four-poster, had a balcony where it would be ideal to sit, glass in hand, taking in the view to the opposite bank and the market town of Ross. Its shower room was well appointed.' The gardens run down to the river. Breakfast can be full English or continental. (*Robert Gower*)

9 bedrooms. Centre of village. NW of Ross-on-Wye, towards Hereford. Lounges, bar, restaurant; background music. 2-acre garden. Unsuitable for ♿. No smoking. No children under 10. No dogs. All major credit cards accepted. B&B: single £70, double £96–£110. Full alc £42. 3-night D,B&B rates.

Wilton Court

Wilton Lane, Ross-on-Wye
HR9 6AQ

Tel 01989-562569
Fax 01989-768460
Email info@wiltoncourthotel.com
Website www.wiltoncourthotel.com

'As good as ever; admirable food and service.' Praise from a returning visitor this year for this 'very pleasant place to stay', on a country lane near the centre of town. Helen and Roger Wynn are 'welcoming hosts'; their staff are 'efficient and pleasant'. 'A relaxed, generous atmosphere.' Refurbishment continues, while respecting the building's 16th-century origins: ancient beams, leaded windows, uneven floors, a huge fireplace with its original iron grate. There is a 'comfortable sitting room, interestingly furnished', and a good conservatory area. Bedrooms vary in size: 'Ours, gorgeous, spacious, overlooked the river and had very comfortable beds,' said an earlier visitor. 'Spotless bathroom, large bottles of toiletries.' Bath sheets are now available on request, we are told, in response to a comment last year. The conservatory-style *Mulberry* restaurant (named after the 300-year-old tree in the garden, which it faces) has Lloyd Loom tables and chairs. Chef Hans Peter Hulsman serves modern cooking, eg, supreme of chicken on parsnip mash with truffle and red wine sauce. Breakfasts were 'really good, delicious fruit salad and excellent cooked dishes'. The garden is in 'country' style; with mature shrubs. (*John Borron, and others*)

10 bedrooms. ¼ mile from centre. Restaurant closed Sun night, and weekdays off-season (full menu served in bar). Sitting room, bar, restaurant; background music at mealtimes; private dining room. 2-acre grounds: riverside garden, fishing. Civil wedding licence. Unsuitable for ♿. No smoking. No dogs in restaurant. Amex, MasterCard, Visa accepted. B&B £45–£140 per person. Full alc £35. Special breaks. Christmas/New Year packages. 1-night bookings occasionally refused Sat in season. *V* (not weekends)

See also SHORTLIST

ROWSLEY Derbyshire — Map 3:A6

East Lodge
Rowsley DE4 2EF

Tel 01629-734474
Fax 01629-733949
Email info@eastlodge.com
Website www.eastlodge.com

In an area of outstanding natural beauty, David and Joan Hardman's elegant 17th-century country house stands up a long, tree-lined drive in large grounds, well back from the busy A6 which passes through this Derbyshire village. Visitors this year liked the ambience and the fact that 'many of the Hardman family were around', which gave it a personal touch. Earlier inspectors found it 'a very pleasant hotel in a beautiful location'; the public rooms and bedrooms are 'user-friendly' and 'the staff are charming'. The best bedrooms face the garden (with pond). 'We were shown a very small room which we didn't like, and were transferred to a much better (more expensive) one. It had a recently refurbished bathroom, very large, with separate walk-in shower and even a TV facing the bath.' The conservatory bar, where light meals are served, has 'plants galore'. In the restaurant a six-strong kitchen brigade serves main courses like pan-roasted salmon fillet with herb risotto and shellfish bisque. Breakfast is liked: 'Generous selection of cereals, juices, etc; well-cooked, ample "country house breakfast"; toast and tea promptly brought.' Reduced-rate tickets to nearby Chatsworth House can be provided. (*HJ Martin Tucker, and others*)

12 bedrooms. Some on ground floor. Village centre. Ramps. Reception/lounge, Garden Room bar, 3 dining rooms; conference/function facilities; background music in public areas 8 am–11 pm. 10-acre grounds. Civil wedding licence. No smoking. No children under 12. No dogs. Amex, MasterCard, Visa accepted. B&B £55–£140 per person; D,B&B £90–£175. Set dinner £35. Special breaks. *V*

The Peacock at Rowsley

Bakewell Road
Rowsley DE4 2EB
Tel 01629-733518
Fax 01629-732671
Email reception@thepeacockatrowsley.com
Website www.thepeacockatrowsley.com

In grounds that run down to the River Derwent, this 'very attractive' building, once the dower house for Haddon Hall, has a Derbyshire stone exterior, with mullioned windows and leaded lights. Owned by Lord Edward Manners, it is managed by Ian and Jenni MacKenzie; their staff are found 'efficient and courteous'. The interior combines 'modern simplicity' with 'country antiques and original features such as beams and stone fireplaces'. Upstairs, bedrooms are around a series of corridors, with short flights of steps between different levels. 'Nice but not luxurious,' is one comment, but some 'lovely old wooden furniture' was liked. Rooms overlooking the garden are quiet; those at the front may hear traffic on the busy Bakewell road. Comments on the cooking of Matthew Ruston, who trained with Gordon Ramsay, vary from 'a triumph' to 'good if not exceptional', 'the dinner menu on both evenings was the same'. The bar serves lunches and suppers. 'Breakfast was a routine buffet.' Guests can shoot on the estate, and visit Haddon Hall (50% discount), and anglers come to stay while fishing on the Derwent and the Wye. (*Monica Williams, and others*)

16 bedrooms. Village centre. Closed 1 week Jan. Restaurant closed 26 Dec evening. Lounge (live guitar music Fri), bar, dining room; conference rooms. Garden on river: fishing Apr–Oct. Civil wedding licence. Unsuitable for ♿. No smoking. No children under 12. No dogs in public rooms. All major credit cards accepted. B&B £72.50–£100 per person; D,B&B £102.50–£140. Cooked breakfast £6.50. Full alc £49.50. Sunday specials. New Year packages. 1-night bookings refused Sat.

> When you make a booking you enter into a contract with a hotel. Most hotels explain their cancellation policies, which vary widely, in a letter of confirmation. You may lose your deposit or be charged at the full rate for the room if you cancel at short notice. A travel insurance policy can provide protection.

RUSHLAKE GREEN East Sussex Map 2:E4

Stone House

Rushlake Green
Heathfield TN21 9QJ

Tel 01435-830553
Fax 01435-830726
Website www.stonehousesussex.co.uk

'It continues to be terrific; everything is delightful,' says a regular visitor to Jane and Peter Dunn's much-loved 'beautiful, comfortable' family home. 'The welcome and charm of the owners and their staff make it very special.' They offer 'a quintessentially English country experience'. Built in 1495, with 18th-century modifications, the house has been owned by the family for over 500 years. There are plenty of sporting activities in its huge grounds (see below), and it is popular with opera-goers (20 minutes' drive from Glyndebourne; a picnic can be provided, with table and chairs). A grand double staircase rises from the black-and-white marble floor of the entrance hall. The largest bedrooms are in the Georgian section: two large rooms have a four-poster ('hugely comfortable') and lavish furnishings. Rooms in the Tudor wing have less space but 'lots of character' (beams, sloping ceilings, antiques, old china). The walled garden has an ornamental lake, gazebos and a 100-foot herbaceous border. Jane Dunn has a *Michelin Bib Gourmand* for her 'French- and Thai-influenced cooking', eg, spicy crab cakes; rack of Pevensey lamb with a mint and walnut crust. Continental breakfast can be taken in the bedroom; a traditional one comes with a 'superb buffet'. (*Catrin Treadwell*)

6 bedrooms. 4 miles SE of Heathfield, by village green. Open 3 Jan–23 Dec. Hall, drawing room, library, dining room; billiard room. No background music. 1,000-acre estate: 5½-acre garden, farm, woodland, croquet, shooting, pheasant/clay-pigeon shooting, 2 lakes, rowing, fishing. Unsuitable for ♿. No smoking. No children under 9. No dogs in public rooms. MasterCard, Visa accepted. B&B [2007] £62.50–£245 per person. Set meals (advance booking for lunch necessary) £24.95; Glyndebourne hamper (*no VAT*) £32. Weekend house parties, winter breaks. Cookery courses. 1-night bookings sometimes refused Sat. *V* (1 Nov–31 Mar; not Fri/Sat)

RYE East Sussex Map 2:E5

The George in Rye NEW

98 High Street
Rye TN31 7JT

Tel 01797-222114
Fax 01797-224065
Email stay@thegeorgeinrye.com
Website www.thegeorgeinrye.com

Oak beams, wood panelling and old fireplaces were retained by Alex and Katie Clarke (film set designer) when renovating this 16th-century inn in the centre of Rye. Their manager is Andy Rogers. The 'quirky' decor includes tapestries, corduroy sofas, *chaises longues*, antique mirrors, roll-top baths, psychedelic prints and 'funky lighting'. Inspectors in 2007 thought it 'comfortable, well designed without being over stylish; high marks for friendliness'. It has 'little sunlit courtyards hidden behind unfrequented stairs; rooms tucked in behind gables, a pleasant open terrace'. There is a 'rather grand' oak-panelled lounge, and a large, lively bar, frequented by locals (noise from this could be a problem for residents). In the bistro-style restaurant (brown walls, plain wooden tables), the cooking of chef Rod Grossman is 'modern British with Mediterranean influence'. 'Some dishes excellent (eg, belly of pork), others less interesting.' Some English wines are on the list. 'With one exception, staff were charming, and kind to our small children: no baby-listening, but they took pains over their supper.' Some bedrooms are in the main building, others across a courtyard. 'Superb bed, very nice sheets; cashmere-covered hot-water bottle. At breakfast the pains au chocolat were unexciting, but cooked dishes excellent.' Functions are held in the 'magnificent' ballroom with its minstrels' gallery.

24 bedrooms. 6 in annexe. Town centre. Pay-and-display car park nearby. Sitting room, lounge/bar (background music), restaurant; ballroom; terrace; courtyard garden. Civil wedding licence. Unsuitable for ♿. No smoking. No dogs: bedrooms, restaurant. All major credit cards accepted. B&B £62.50–£95 per person. Set lunch from £13, dinner £26–£30. Special breaks (gardening, foodies, wine). Christmas/New Year packages. 1-night bookings refused Sat.

Jeake's House

Mermaid Street
Rye TN31 7ET

Tel 01797-222828
Fax 01797-222623
Email stay@jeakeshouse.com
Website www.jeakeshouse.com

César award in 1992

Rye's cobbled streets and ancient buildings 'make a perfect setting' for Jenny Hadfield's 'lovely old B&B'. She is 'efficient and gracious', says a reader this year, 'and was well assisted by a charming man who helped us negotiate our bags up the steep stairs to our room'. An earlier comment: 'Like a proper hotel; nice lounge and help-yourself bar.' The American novelist Conrad Aiken lived in this old wool store (built in 1689) and was visited here by TS Eliot, Malcolm Lowry and others. Mrs Hadfield has filled the building with antiques, pictures and samplers; the galleried, red-walled breakfast room (with high windows, good china, and plants) was once a Quaker meeting house. The Conrad Aiken suite is 'an enormous top-floor room, with four-poster bed and big window seat with views over the garden to fields of sheep and the salt marsh'. This year, there is a new double room which has an inglenook fireplace. In the book-lined bar, furnished with old chapel pews, evening drinks are served, and there is a folder of sample menus from nearby restaurants. Breakfast has a buffet with fresh fruit; full English or vegetarian options cooked to order. (*Carolyn Mathiasen, WS*)

11 bedrooms. Central. Car park (£3 per 24 hours; advance booking needed). Parlour, bar/library, breakfast room (classical background music). Unsuitable for ♿. Smoking allowed in 3 bedrooms. No children under 8. No dogs in breakfast room. MasterCard, Visa accepted. B&B £46–£79 per person. Christmas/New Year packages. 1-night bookings sometimes refused weekends.

See also SHORTLIST

ST ALBANS Hertfordshire — Map 2:C3

St Michael's Manor

Fishpool Street
St Albans AL3 4RY

Tel 01727-864444
Fax 01727-848909
Email reservations@stmichaelsmanor.com
Website www.stmichaelsmanor.com

The Newling Ward family has owned and run this old manor house, 16th-century in origin, for over 40 years. It stands in 'pretty gardens with a lake' in a 'surprisingly peaceful' corner of the old town, below the cathedral. The bedrooms in the main building, named after trees in the grounds (which many overlook) are done in period style. Rooms in a modern wing have a Japanese feel: 'Comfy bed; stylish, modern "wet" bathroom; spotlessly clean.' Another comment: 'Beautiful hotel, very friendly staff; good food and service in the evening. In the conservatory restaurant, with great views over the garden, we shared an excellent chateaubriand, perfectly cooked medium rare.' Other main courses include breast of duck with roasted beetroot and apple with mead jus. 'Excellent wine list.' Breakfast on a Sunday morning was 'a bit haphazard'. Children are welcomed: they have a special menu, snacks all day, cots and babysitting (but there are no interconnecting or family rooms). Weddings, conferences and functions are often held. To avoid them you could visit one of the 'five attractive pubs down the road at Verulamium', or the family's restaurant, *Darcy's*, 15 minutes' walk away. (*Mrs PS Dickson, William Bailey*)

30 bedrooms. 8 in garden wing. In old St Albans, near abbey. Ramps. 2 lounges, bar, restaurant, conservatory; classical background music; private dining room. 5-acre gardens: croquet, lake. Civil wedding licence. Smoking allowed in some bedrooms. Guide dogs only. All major credit cards accepted. B&B [2007] £90–£260 per person. Set menu £30; full alc £50. Weekend breaks. Christmas/New Year packages.

ST HILARY Cornwall — Map 1:E1

Ennys
Trewhella Lane, St Hilary
nr Penzance TR20 9BZ

Tel 01736-740262
Fax 01736-740055
Email ennys@ennys.co.uk
Website www.ennys.co.uk

Travel writer Gill Charlton provides 'farmhouse accommodation with country house style' at her creeper-covered Grade II listed 17th-century manor house. She writes: 'At night, it is truly dark here, and the only sound you will hear is the hooting of owls in the woods.' Reached by a long, narrow drive, *Ennys* is surrounded by fields that lead down to the River Hayle. It has a pretty garden with exotic planting and a swimming pool (available to visitors in the morning and late afternoon). The bright reception rooms contain interesting artwork and souvenirs of the owner's travels. The three bedrooms in the house are decorated in 'modern' style ('no antiques now'); their renovated bathrooms have 'latest shower and bath technology'. In converted barns that open on to a courtyard are two family suites and three self-catering apartments. Complimentary afternoon tea with home-baked cakes is laid out in the kitchen. Wireless Internet access is free. Breakfast has 'eggs from our own hens'. There is an extensive listing of local pubs and restaurants. More reports, please.

5 bedrooms. 2 in barns. 3 self-catering apartments (can be B&B off-season). 5 miles E of Penzance. Open 15 Mar–15 Nov, 20 Dec–3 Jan. Sitting room, breakfast room. No background music. 3-acre grounds: 40-ft heated swimming pool (not available to residents 1–4 pm), tennis. Unsuitable for ♿. No smoking. No children under 3 (except in self-catering accommodation). No dogs. MasterCard, Visa accepted. B&B [2007] £40–£110 per person. 1-night bookings refused high season, bank holidays.

> Don't trust out-of-date editions of the *Guide*. Hotels change hands, deteriorate or go out of business. Every year, we add about 80 entries and drop an equal number.

ST IVES Cornwall — Map 1:D1

Primrose Valley Hotel
Primrose Valley, Porthminster Beach
St Ives TR26 2ED
Tel/Fax 01736-794939
Email info@primroseonline.co.uk
Website www.primroseonline.co.uk

An easy walk from the centre, this Edwardian villa, with a striking modern interior, stands just above the Blue Flag Porthminster Beach. The owners, Andrew and Sue Biss and Rose Clegg, follow a sustainable agenda, recycling waste, supporting conservation initiatives, and using local or Fairtrade food. The public areas have polished wooden floors, leather sofas, specially made walnut and oak tables; bright staircase carpets. Mr Biss 'was a friendly presence, bringing us tea with cake on arrival and presiding over the excellent breakfast'. The bedrooms are on the first and second floors: two have a balcony; inspectors loved their sea view, 'though our room, smartly decorated in white, was very small'. A suite has a 'ridiculously comfortable, beautiful' freestanding bath. A range of Cornish platters (smoked salmon, cheese, salami, etc) is served during the day, and in the evening the bar offers Cornish beers, and more than 50 wines. Breakfast (8 to 10 am) has a buffet with fresh fruit salad, fresh juices, yogurts, loose-leaf teas, a range of cooked dishes, and it can be accompanied by champagne. An optional £1 charge is added to the bill to go towards marine conservation initiatives. A little scenic railway runs by the beach, 'but the single-carriage train trundles in and out with very little noise'.

10 bedrooms. Private road 2 mins from station. Parking (£3). Open Feb–Nov. Lounge, bar ('appropriate' background music), dining room; patio. Porthminster Beach 4 mins' walk. Unsuitable for ♿. No smoking. No dogs. MasterCard, Visa accepted. B&B £42.50–£117.50 per person.

See also SHORTLIST

ST LEONARDS-ON-SEA East Sussex — Map 2:E4

Zanzibar International Hotel
9 Eversfield Place
St Leonards-on-Sea
TN37 6BY
Tel/Fax 01424-460109
Email max@zanzibarhotel.co.uk
Website www.zanzibarhotel.co.uk

Overlooking the promenade in this South Coast seaside resort, this Victorian town house has been turned into an exotic small B&B hotel by owner Max O'Rourke. Bedrooms are themed, reflecting his travels and interests, and described in detail on the website. Antarctica, on the second floor (floor-to-ceiling bay windows facing the sea; white, glass and chrome, varnished wooden floors), was found by an inspector 'very relaxing. Its large bathroom had a sauna and shower unit with every combination of jets and sprinklers imaginable. Good lighting.' Morocco has deep-coloured fabrics, spiral staircase, huge mezzanine bed; Japan has a spa bath. This year a penthouse suite, Manhattan, has been added; also an honesty bar and a conservatory. Breakfast, ordered by 9 pm the night before, is served in the bedroom or at a large table in the Grand Salon, which has sofas, newspapers and 'extravagant flowers'. It includes Buck's Fizz, freshly squeezed juices, fruit, cereals, full English and vegetarian. 'Butter and jams in pots. Excellent coffee and tea.' Help is given with reservations at local restaurants.

9 bedrooms. 1 on ground floor. Seafront. 650 yds W of Hastings pier. Free parking vouchers issued. Lounge ('chilled world music'), bar, breakfast room, conservatory. Small garden. Beach across road. No smoking. Dogs must never be left unattended. MasterCard, Visa accepted (*5% commission charge*). Room with breakfast [2007] £80–£170. Supplements for weekend bookings. 1-night bookings refused Sat.

ST MARTIN'S Isles of Scilly — Map 1:C1

St Martin's on the Isle
Lower Town, St Martin's
Isles of Scilly, Cornwall
TR25 0QW

Tel 01720-422092
Fax 01720-422298
Email stay@stmartinshotel.co.uk
Website www.stmartinshotel.co.uk

'Warmly endorsed' this year, this Pride of Britain member is the only hotel on this 'charming' little island, known for its bulb fields and excellent beaches. Visitors arrive by boat from St Mary's, to be met at a small quay. The manager for many years, Keith Bradford, creates 'a happy blend of efficiency with friendliness', say guests. 'Staff remembered our names; every care for our well-being. No pretentiousness.' But one couple, who had a 'thoroughly enjoyable time', reported muddles over travel arrangements. Bedrooms vary; many have sea views. 'Ours was comfortable, spacious, with all necessary facilities.' The decor 'has a 1980s air: lots of carpets and upholstery'. Tables are changed nightly in the first-floor *Teän* restaurant, so guests share the 'marvellous views'. Chef Kenny Atkinson is tipped by *Michelin* as a rising star: his style is 'modern, elegant; good to look at, good to taste, too', eg, organic salmon with crab risotto. 'Portions not too large, but adequate.' Simpler meals are served in the bar and the bistro (where children have high tea). 'Breakfasts excellent, almost everything one could want (hot and cold) on a buffet; other dishes cooked to order.' 'Lots of families in August.' (*Pam Service, Richard and Catriona Smith*)

30 bedrooms. Some on ground floor. N end of island. Boat/helicopter to St Mary's from Penzance, or fixed-wing aircraft from several local airports in SW England; then boat to St Martin's. Open Apr–Oct. Ramps. Lounge, lounge bar, restaurant; 33-ft indoor swimming pool. No background music. 2½-acre grounds: garden on beach, jetty, boating, diving, water sports. Civil wedding licence. Unsuitable for ♿ (because of transport). No smoking. No children under 9 in restaurant. All major credit cards accepted. D,B&B [2007] £138–£275 per person. 10% discount for pre-paid 5-night or longer bookings.

ST MARY'S Isles of Scilly — Map 1:C1

Star Castle
The Garrison, St Mary's
Isles of Scilly
Cornwall TR21 0JA

Tel 01720-422317
Fax 01720-422343
Email info@star-castle.co.uk
Website www.star-castle.co.uk

'Wonderful position. Fascinating building.' With 'excellent views of harbour and ocean' ('splendid sunsets'), this Tudor fortress, shaped like an eight-pointed star, was built as a defence against the Spanish Armada. Since taking over four years ago, owner Robert Francis has supervised a major refurbishment (his wife, Theresa, is responsible for the decor). His son, James, is co-manager. Families go for the child-friendly, dog-friendly ambience; older visitors enjoy the peace off-season. Guests are met off the ferry or at the airport and are given help with outings (boating, snorkelling with seals, etc). There is a 'cosy' bar (the former dungeon), a beamed dining room with thick stone walls and open fire, and, in summer, a conservatory restaurant (noted for its large grapevine). Two modern blocks in the grounds contain large bedrooms (some with private garden or veranda). More characterful rooms are in the main house, and three small ones are the former guardrooms. 'Water and fresh milk provided, bed turned down. Good power shower.' Gareth Stafford is now chef, serving a daily-changing menu (main courses like John Dory with crushed potatoes, spinach and pesto oil). Bar lunches and picnics are available. 'Good fish and organic juice at breakfast.' There are suntrap lawns enclosed by high hedges and a covered swimming pool (given a 'thorough make-over' in 2007) in the subtropical gardens. (*PM Scott, and others*)

38 bedrooms. 29 in wings. ½ mile from town centre. Boat (2½ hours)/helicopter (20 mins) from Penzance. Air links from Newquay, Exeter, Bristol. Open 10 Feb–30 Nov, Christmas/New Year. Lounge, games room, bar, 2 restaurants. No background music. 4-acre grounds: covered swimming pool (40 by 12 ft), tennis. Beach nearby. Golf, bicycle hire, riding, sailing, diving, fishing available. Unsuitable for ♿. No smoking. Amex, MasterCard, Visa accepted. No children under 5 in restaurants at night. No dogs in restaurants. D,B&B [2007] £60–£127 per person. Special breaks. Christmas/New Year packages.

ST MAWES Cornwall — Map 1:E2

Idle Rocks
Harbourside
St Mawes TR2 5AN

Tel 01326-270771
Fax 01326-270062
Email reservations@idlerocks.co.uk
Website www.idlerocks.co.uk

'Splendidly set' on the harbour (its long terrace forms part of the sea wall, and public rooms, with large picture windows, front the building), this is one of Keith Richardson's small group of hotels. Chris Skidmore became manager in 2007. Inspectors reported 'an exemplary welcome from the receptionist who insisted on carrying the heavier of our bags: "You are on holiday," she said.' Other visitors found the staff helpful, and enjoyed the 'very good Cornish tea' with scones and leaf tea, served on the terrace. The décor may be 'dated' (red sofas and patterned carpets in the lounge), but chef Damian Broom's cooking, served by young, mainly European, waiters, was much admired. 'Superb fish, excellent desserts', eg, cod fillet with parsnip purée, garlic gnocchi and thyme jus gras; lemon and pine parfait with black pepper ice cream. The restaurant is on three levels, 'like a cruise ship', allowing everyone to enjoy the view. 'Breakfast kept up the pace: home-made muesli, fresh croissants, good cooked dishes, fine toast.' Some bedrooms may have an old-fashioned decor, but refurbished ones have a more contemporary look. 'Our room had a fine sea view and a modern bathroom (with window).' (*S and JS, and others*)

27 bedrooms. 4 in annexe. Some on ground floor. Village centre (harbour wall). Parking for 4 cars. Lounge, restaurant; background 'mood' music at night. Waterside terrace. Sandy beach adjacent. Unsuitable for ♿. No smoking. No dogs in restaurant. All major credit cards accepted. B&B [2007] £54–£149 per person; D,B&B £78–£173. Set dinner £29. Christmas/New Year packages.

Hotels will often try to persuade you to stay for two nights at the weekend. Resist this pressure if you want to stay only one night.

The Rising Sun
The Square
St Mawes TR2 5DJ

Tel 01326-270233
Fax 01326-270198
Email info@risingsunstmawes.co.uk
Website www.risingsunstmawes.com

'Highly recommended' by a visitor returning after 15 years, this old inn, overlooking the harbour, is owned by a group, Inns of Cornwall, and licensed to John Milan. 'Very friendly. Good food; a particularly delicious breakfast,' is this year's praise. The 'elegant' restaurant, with a lounge alongside, has a conservatory extension to the front with views across the harbour to the headland. The chef, Ann Long, serves modern English dishes, eg, mini-kedgeree cake with a quail's egg; pork with a cinnamon and chilli sauce. 'The cooking is excellent, the service professional.' The simpler meals in the bar ('well patronised without detracting from the calm') are also liked. The best bedrooms face the harbour (others may be dark). 'We liked the basket-weave furniture and decor of our double.' All the rooms have been repainted this year. Breakfast includes freshly squeezed orange and grapefruit juice, and scrambled eggs with smoked salmon. 'Staff are efficient and cheerful.' (*Barbara Hill, and others*)

8 bedrooms. Village centre, by harbour. Lounge, bar, restaurant. No background music. Terrace. Only restaurant suitable for ♿. No smoking. No dogs in restaurant. MasterCard, Visa accepted. B&B £65–£85 per person. Set dinner £29.50–£33.50.

Hotel Tresanton
27 Lower Castle Road
St Mawes TR2 5DR

Tel 01326-270055
Fax 01326-270053
Email info@tresanton.com
Website www.tresanton.com

'We loved it so much we didn't want to leave,' say a mother and her teenage daughter about Olga Polizzi's hotel on the edge of this seaside village. 'We particularly appreciated the informality, being able to turn up for dinner dressed casually.' The cluster of old houses in terraced subtropical gardens ('lots of places to catch the sun') looks across a narrow promenade to the Fal estuary. Inside, 'subtle marine shades give it its special character'. Other comments: 'High prices, high standards.' 'Fabulous cream teas.' Federica Bertolini, the 'lively manager', supervises a 'capable young staff'. Children have a games room, special menu, etc. Most bedrooms have sea views; the best ones are big; one above the bar can be noisy. 'Ours, in the Nook (a cottage next door), had a balcony but no view.' In the restaurant ('wonderful white mosaic floor', white-clothed tables close together, large white plates, 'top-notch service'), Paul Wadham serves an 'excellent' short daily-changing menu with much fish, eg, 'plump John Dory fillets on a bed of perfectly cooked spinach'. 'Good breakfast: fruit, croissants, cooked dishes.' *Tresanton* has a cinema, a film library, and a 48-foot racing yacht. Mrs Polizzi also owns *Hotel Endsleigh*, Milton Abbot (*qv*). (*Susan Kinder, and others*)

29 bedrooms. Some in 3 annexes. On seafront. Train: Truro; plane: Newquay. 2 lounges, bar, restaurant; cinema; conference facilities; playroom. No background music. Terrace. ¼-acre garden. By sea: shingle beach, safe bathing, 48-ft yacht. Unsuitable for ♿. Civil wedding licence. Smoking allowed in all bedrooms. No children under 6 at dinner. Dogs allowed in 2 bedrooms, not in public rooms. Amex, MasterCard, Visa accepted. B&B £87.50–£207 per person. Set dinner £40. Bridge/yoga weeks, poker weekends. Christmas/New Year packages. 1-night bookings sometimes refused winter weekends.

SALCOMBE Devon — Map 1:E4

The Tides Reach

South Sands
Salcombe TQ8 8LJ

Tel 01548-843466
Fax 01548-843954
Email enquire@tidesreach.com
Website www.tidesreach.com

Facing a sandy cove on the South Devon coast, the Edwards family's seaside hotel (they have run it for two generations) is well placed for safe bathing and water sports. The 'functional' 1960s building has angular balconies, bright blue awnings against white-painted walls, and south-facing views across Salcombe estuary. Most bedrooms have big windows that face the sheltered garden with its large carp and duck pond beside which summer visitors take snack lunches (soups, sandwiches, kedgeree, etc). Colours are bright. The best rooms have a balcony. There is a large sea-water aquarium in the bar. In the dining room (sea views from some tables) the chef, Finn Ibsen, serves modern and traditional dishes, eg, chargrilled local scallops; duck leg confit with a pink peppercorn sauce. Dress for dinner is 'smart casual'. The lack of piped music is appreciated. The swimming pool is in an 'exotic conservatory' which opens to the outside on fine days. The centre of Salcombe can be reached by a winding road, but pedestrians may prefer the South Sands ferry. There is easy access to the Coastal Path. More reports, please.

32 bedrooms. On Salcombe estuary, 1 mile from town. Open Feb–Nov. Lift, ramps. 3 lounges, 2 bars, restaurant; leisure centre: indoor swimming pool (40 by 20 ft), gym, games room; beauty treatments. No background music. ½-acre grounds: pond. Sandy beach 10 yds. Unsuitable for ♿. Smoking allowed in 10 bedrooms. No children under 8. No dogs in 2 lounges. All major credit cards accepted. B&B [2007] £50–£123 per person; D,B&B £62–£143. Set dinner £38.50. 1-night bookings sometimes refused. Bargain breaks. *V*

SALISBURY Wiltshire *See SHORTLIST* Map 2:D2

SANDWICH Kent Map 2:D5

The Bell NEW

Tel 01304-613388
The Quay *Fax* 01304-615308
Sandwich CT13 9EF *Email* reservations@sandwich.theplacehotels.co.uk
Website www.bellhotelsandwich.co.uk

On the quay of this ancient port, overlooking the River Stour, this 19th-century listed building has been given a smart, modern refurbishment by Matthew Wolfman, owner of *The Place*, Camber, and *The Ship*, Chichester (see Shortlist). Matt Collins is manager. James Sallows is the chef, serving modern English dishes with an emphasis on local fish and seafood, salt marsh lamb, and vegetables from nearby farms. Some bedrooms have a balcony facing the river. 'Ask for directions: Sandwich is a maze of one-way streets,' advises our inspector. 'Check-in was friendly, but no assistance was offered with baggage to our first-floor room (no lift). It was furnished with good taste and had a restful feel. French doors opened on to a small balcony facing a road and the river.' Downstairs, a bright conservatory has been added to the brasserie. A few steps lead down to a long bar which opens to a street-side terrace where meals can be served. 'Staff were young, charming, though some were new to the hospitality business. The menu was interesting and had an emphasis on seafood. We endorse the brochure's description: "Unstuffy but stylish."'

34 bedrooms. By Barbican Gate and Toll. Closed Christmas. 2 bars, brasserie; conference/function facilities. Terrace. No background music. Civil wedding licence. Unsuitable for ♿. No smoking. Dogs on terrace only. Amex, MasterCard, Visa accepted. B&B: single £80, double £109, suite £195; D,B&B £79.95–£105 per person. Full alc £37.50. 2-night weekend break. New Year package. *V*

SCARBOROUGH North Yorkshire Map 4:C5
See SHORTLIST

SCOTBY Cumbria — Map 4:B2

Willowbeck Lodge NEW
Lambley Bank
Scotby, nr Carlisle CA4 8BX

Tel 01228-513607
Fax 01228-501053
Email info@willowbeck-lodge.com
Website www.willowbeck-lodge.com

Set amid woodland with birdlife, this four-year-old guest house stands by a large pond in a village near Carlisle, only a mile from the M6 (junction 43), but peaceful. Architect-designed, in bright, modern Scandinavian style, it has a large lounge with soaring ceiling, huge window, gallery and wood-burning stove. The owners, John and Liz McGrillis, are 'welcoming and very helpful', say visitors this year. 'They taxied us into Carlisle each day. We had their last room, a small double, but it had all necessities and comforts, good-quality bedlinen, efficient shower. Excellent dinner.' This is available by arrangement, menu agreed in consultation: the main course could be chicken with mustard seed, spring onions and sun-dried tomatoes. 'Good breakfast, apart from supermarket sliced toast' (7–9.30; you order the night before). There are flat-screen televisions in the bedrooms, and 'high-speed Internet connections throughout'. (*Nick and Rosemary Wright*)

6 bedrooms. 2 in annexe. Closed 21–28 Dec. 2½ miles E of Carlisle. Parking. Lounge, lounge/dining room; conference facilities. Background music 'if guests want; type agreed with them'. 1½-acre garden: stream. No smoking. No children under 12. No pets. Amex, MasterCard, Visa accepted. B&B: single £85–£105, double £95–£115. Evening meal £25.

SEAHAM Co. Durham — Map 4:B4

Seaham Hall
Lord Byron's Walk
Seaham SR7 7AG

Tel 0191-516 1400
Fax 0191-516 1410
Email reservations@seaham-hall.com
Website www.seaham-hall.com

'Beautifully restored' as a spa hotel by Tom and Jocelyn Maxfield, this impressive 17th/19th-century building stands on a headland above the North Sea. 'It combines luxury, style and character,' said one visitor. 'We had a warm welcome for our family group, and our rooms were spacious, harmoniously decorated and generously supplied with everything you could want.' Bedrooms range from 'classic' to 'penthouse', and have 'the latest technology'. Thirty-five more are to be created in a conversion of a disused hall nearby. 'The spa is world class, large, airy, atmospheric; lovely pool; relaxing pool area. Eastern statues and fountains give the feel of a fairy-tale world.' Chef Steven Smith presides over *The White Room*, which gained a *Michelin* star in 2007 for dishes such as crab ravioli with crab consommé; poached and roasted chicken with mushroom purée and truffle gnocchi. The less formal *Ozone* has 'a wonderful menu of Asian tapas; Thai curries; home-made ice creams and sorbets'. The 'most enjoyable' breakfast can be brought to the bedroom. It includes 'scrambled eggs with smoked salmon, in an elegant pyramid'. Popular for weddings and conferences, the house has historical associations with Lord Byron, who married Lady Annabella Milbanke here in 1815. (*MM*)

19 bedrooms. 1½ miles N of Seaham, which is 5 miles S of Sunderland, by B1287. Lift. Lounge, bar, 2 restaurants; constant soft background music in public areas; ballroom; meeting/conference facilities; spa (with lift and ramps): 65-ft swimming pool. 37-acre grounds: pebble beach 5 mins' walk. Civil wedding licence. No smoking. Children under 12 have limited access to spa. Guide dogs only. All major credit cards accepted. Room with breakfast [2007] £225–£575 (includes use of spa, excluding treatments). Set lunch £17.50; full alc £55. Christmas/New Year packages. 1-night bookings refused weekends.

SEAVIEW Isle of Wight — Map 2:E3

Seaview Hotel & Restaurant
High Street
Seaview PO34 5EX

Tel 01983-612711
Fax 01983-613729
Email reception@seaviewhotel.co.uk
Website www.seaviewhotel.co.uk

Inspectors in 2007 enjoyed this hotel/restaurant in this 'charming' seaside village. Owner (for four years) Brian Gardener has redecorated, revamped, and created seven new bedrooms. Filled with nautical memorabilia, it is managed by the 'courteous' Andrew Morgan. 'He and his helpful deputies were around much of the time. When there were problems, they took immediate action. We liked the flexible eating arrangements and the friendly local waitresses.' Graham Walker, head chef, serves sophisticated dishes in the *à la carte* restaurant in two areas: one intimate, the other with conservatory area and a wide mirror wall. 'Delicious crab risotto; pretty desserts.' Simpler meals (eg, fish pie; haddock with mushy peas and chips) are served in the two bars. 'Very busy with locals and visiting yachties.' One couple liked their 'small, modernised room with Solent views over rooftops'. A large ground-floor room was 'spacious, quiet, light. It had flat-screen TV/DVD-player but awkward lighting; table and chairs on a terrace by the pretty garden'. At breakfast, 'a helpful lady presided, pouring lashings of fresh orange juice. Good buffet (cereals, fruit, etc). Porridge and succulent kippers on the menu. Nothing packaged.' Children are welcomed. There is free Wi-Fi in the lounge. 'You can walk for miles by the seashore: the path starts at the bottom of the road.'

24 bedrooms. 2, with balcony, in annexe. 3 on ground floor. 2 self-catering cottages. Village centre. Restaurant closed midday in winter. Lift, ramps. Lounge, 2 bars, 2 dining rooms; function room; patio. No background music. Access to local sports club (swimming pool, gym, tennis, etc). No smoking. No dogs in restaurant. Amex, MasterCard, Visa accepted. B&B [2007] £60–£197.50 per person; D,B&B £90–£227.50. Set Sun lunch £16.95; full alc from £43. 1-night bookings refused some weekends April–Oct. Christmas/New Year packages.

SHANKLIN Isle of Wight — Map 2:E2

Rylstone Manor
Rylstone Gardens
Popham Road
Shanklin PO37 6RG

Tel/Fax 01983-862806
Email rylstonemanor@btinternet.com
Website www.rylstone-manor.co.uk

New owners, Mike (the chef) and Carole Hailston, took over this Victorian country house in May 2006, but they have made no significant changes. 'They are friendly hosts,' says a 2007 report. Set in lovely parkland gardens, the building is a blend of Gothic, Tudor and Georgian styles. Nearby is the Chine, a ravine with woodland walks, a waterfall and rare plants; the view from the house is of lawns and well-tended flowerbeds, with glimpses of the sea. The green-walled lounge has books and ornaments; there is a 'nice Victorian-style covered patio', with basket chairs and magazines. In the lemon-walled, candlelit dining room, 'dinner was very simple food, which I like', says another visitor. Three choices of starter and course are offered (eg, fillet of plaice meunière; supreme of chicken in a sweet-and-sour sauce). The simple wine list is 'fairly priced'. The bedrooms, named after English trees, vary in size. A four-poster has 'beautiful lacy linen and attractive bedding', but a 'tiny' single room was not liked. From the garden, guests have direct access to beaches via steep cliff steps. (*Laurie Brooks, and others*)

9 bedrooms. ½ mile SE of village. Closed Jan. Drawing room, bar lounge, dining room; 'easy listening' background music all day. Terrace. 1-acre garden in 4-acre public gardens. Direct access to sand/shingle beach. Unsuitable for ♿. No smoking. No children under 16. No dogs. All major credit cards accepted. B&B [2007] £52 per person; D,B&B £69. Set dinner £23. Christmas/New Year packages. *V*

SHEPTON MALLET Somerset — Map 1:B6
See SHORTLIST

SHIPTON GORGE Dorset — Map 1:C6

Innsacre Farmhouse
Shipton Gorge
nr Bridport DT6 4LJ

Tel 01308-456137
Email innsacre.farmhouse@btinternet.com
Website www.innsacre.com

'Excellent, with really good attention to detail,' say visitors this year to this 17th-century farmhouse in a 'fantastic' setting in a small valley of fields, orchard and woodland. The 'infallibly friendly' owners, Sydney and Jayne Davies, are committed to using local produce, organic where possible. 'But hair shirts are entirely absent,' said earlier visitors. The Davieses say their aim is 'a mixture of French rustic and English comfort'. 'He is an interesting and interested host with a wry sense of humour. She is welcoming without being intrusive, and a sound cook.' Bedrooms are small, furnished in French country style; there are duvets, oak beds, and simple bathrooms. 'Lots of hot water and bath luxuries including a head rest; blissful after a day tramping the hills.' A three-course no-choice dinner is served, by arrangement, at 8 pm. The style is modern, eg, bruschetta with cured ham sausage; chilli and mint roasted chicken. 'Wonderful food; excellent wine cellar.' The 'brilliant' breakfast has a 'daily goody', and 'superb fruit compote'. Dogs are welcomed (£10 per stay). The nature trail around a hill in the grounds has been extended to two miles. (*Robert Pritchett, Derek Oswald, and others*)

4 bedrooms. 1½ miles SE of Bridport. Closed Christmas/New Year, mid-Sept–mid-Oct. Dining room closed midday, and Sat. Lounge/bar, dining area. No background music. 22-acre grounds: nature trail. Fishing, shingle/sand beach nearby. Unsuitable for ♿. No smoking. No children under 9. No dogs in dining room. MasterCard, Visa accepted. B&B [2007] £42.50–£57.50 per person. Evening meal (by arrangement) £22.50. 1-night bookings refused weekends/bank holidays.

SHREWSBURY Shropshire *See SHORTLIST* — Map 3:B4

Report forms (Freepost in UK) are at the end of the *Guide.* If you need more, please ask. We welcome email reports, too: send these to Goodhotel@aol.com or Goodhotel@btinternet.com.

SIDMOUTH Devon Map 1:C5

Hotel Riviera
The Esplanade
Sidmouth EX10 8AY

Tel 01395-515201
Fax 01395-577775
Email enquiries@hotelriviera.co.uk
Website www.hotelriviera.co.uk

A fashionable watering place in Regency times, when it attracted 'people of quality', this east Devon resort has retained much Georgian architecture. In a prime position on the seafront, opposite a pebble/sand beach (safe bathing), stands the Wharton family's long-established, white, bay-windowed hotel. 'From the moment we arrived, we felt cosseted,' says one enthusiastic visitor in 2007. Others write of 'a warm welcome', 'faultless service' from long-serving staff, 'superb' breakfasts ('real orange juice, excellent porridge, no self-service'), good bedroom lighting. Food is 'of a high quality', 'reasonable choice, portions not excessive', 'not pretentiously elaborate'. 'Excellent bar lunch.' The chef, Matthew Weaver, serves main courses like seared spiced salmon with pepper couscous; rib-eye steak with tomato, shallot and mushroom compote. In summer, alfresco meals are taken under blue-and-white parasols on the large terrace, which faces Lyme Bay. 'Lovely sea view. We heard the waves from our bed.' There are flowers in the bedrooms, afternoon cream teas, and 'good-value breaks'. The *Riviera* has arrangements with Sidmouth Golf Club, and can organise pheasant and duck shooting on seven nearby estates. There could be traffic noise in summer. (*Becky Goldsmith, Richard Creed, EP, and others*)

26 bedrooms. 2 mins' walk from centre. Parking. Lift, ramp. Lounge, bar (pianist at weekends), restaurant; background music; function facilities; terrace. No smoking. No dogs: public rooms, some bedrooms. All major credit cards accepted. B&B [2007] £94–£160 per person; D,B&B £109–£175. Set lunch £25, dinner £36; full alc £50. 3-day/weekend breaks. Christmas/New Year packages.

See also SHORTLIST

How to contact the *Guide*
By mail: From anywhere in the UK, write to Freepost PAM 2931, London W11 4BR (no stamp is needed)
From outside the UK: *Good Hotel Guide*, 50 Addison Avenue, London W11 4QP, England
By telephone or fax: 020-7602 4182
By email: Goodhotel@aol.com or Goodhotel@btinternet.com
Via our website: www.goodhotelguide.com

SNETTISHAM Norfolk — Map 2:A4

The Rose & Crown
Old Church Road, Snettisham
nr King's Lynn PE31 7LX

Tel 01485-541382
Fax 01485-543172
Email info@roseandcrownsnettisham.co.uk
Website www.roseandcrownsnettisham.co.uk

Opposite the cricket pitch in a Norfolk village, Jeannette and Anthony Goodrich's 14th-century village inn has twisting passages, hidden corners, low ceilings and old beams. 'Very much a pub (a good one)', it attracts many locals. The young staff are 'outstanding, efficient and congenial'; reception is 'second to none'. A lounge was due to be completed as we went to press to give guests 'a quieter area away from the main bustle'. Older bedrooms have been upgraded in the contemporary style of the five newer rooms ('well appointed, smaller than some of the others, but comfortable: first-class bed and linen'). Two rooms are suitable for guests with mobility problems. In a heatwave, a visitor, who otherwise rated his experience as 'ten out of ten', found his room above the kitchen uncomfortably hot. Head chef Andy Bruce serves his award-winning menu in the three dining areas. Mrs Goodrich writes: 'All our suppliers come from within a 15-mile radius.' There is free wireless broadband access throughout. The walled garden, once the village bowling green, has herbaceous borders and two large willow trees. (*Patrick Forman, and others*)

16 bedrooms. 2 suitable for ♿. 4 miles S of Hunstanton. Garden Room with guests' seating area, lounge, 3 bars, 3 dining areas. No background music. Large walled garden: play fort, barbecue, heat lamps. Beaches 5 and 10 mins' drive. Golf, birdwatching nearby. Eating areas suitable for ♿. No smoking. Visa accepted. B&B [2007] £42.50–£80 per person. Full alc £30. Christmas/New Year package. ***V***

SOAR MILL COVE Devon — Map 1:E4

Soar Mill Cove Hotel
Soar Mill Cove
nr Salcombe TQ7 3DS

Tel 01548-561566
Fax 01548-561223
Email info@soarmillcove.co.uk
Website www.soarmillcove.co.uk

The setting for Keith Makepeace's single-storey hotel amid National Trust land is 'spectacular', above an isolated cove in grounds that slope down to a beach. Retired people frequent it in low season. Children are well looked after (high teas, high chairs, play areas). 'Our dog was happy too.' The stone and slate building is 'no beauty', and decor may be 'dated', apart from a 'smart new champagne bar' (black velvet, gold walls, black and red leather seats), which a visitor in 2007 thought highlighted 'an identity crisis'. But regulars appreciate the 'warm welcome', the 'enthusiastic, well-trained staff' and 'immaculate housekeeping'. The formal *Serendipity* restaurant, with a picture window, has a 'spectacular view'. Chef Ian MacDonald's cooking was rated 'average' by some, 'as good as ever' by others, and there were grumbles about surcharges for 'special treats', eg, hand-picked white crab. *Castaways*, a coffee bar, is 'for muddy paws and boots, and younger guests'. Bedrooms vary in size; all open on to the terrace. Breakfast has good choice, including fruit salad and 'beautiful' marmalade. 'The garden was colourful; deer and pheasants came to the field nearby.' 'Glorious walks' from the door. There is a sister hotel, the *Rosevine*, Portscatho (*qv*). (*Wendy Brooks, David RW Jervois, Margaret Box, and others*)

22 bedrooms. All on ground floor. 3 miles W of Salcombe. Open 9 Feb–1 Jan. Lounge, 2 bars, restaurant (background/live music), coffee shop. Indoor swimming pool (30 by 18 ft); treatment room (hairdressing, reflexology, aromatherapy, etc), free Internet access. 10-acre grounds: swimming pool (30 by 21 ft), tennis, putting, donkey, miniature pony, children's play area, jogging trail. Sea, sandy beach, 600 yds. No smoking. No dogs in public rooms. MasterCard, Visa accepted. B&B [2007] £94–£229.50 per person. Set dinner £39; full alc £50. Christmas/New Year packages. 1-night bookings sometimes refused Sat. ***V***

SOMERTON Somerset — Map 1:C6

The Lynch Country House
4 Behind Berry
Somerton TA11 7PD

Tel 01458-272316
Fax 01458-272590
Email the_lynch@talk21.com
Website www.thelynchcountryhouse.co.uk

'Perfect setting. Breakfast a delight: no struggles with butter papers, no fingernails broken when opening foil covers.' An accolade in 2007 for this 'superior, stylish B&B', a Grade II listed Regency house in a small town above the Cary valley. It is run by the 'interested and interesting' owner, Roy Copeland (former jazz musician). In his absence, visitors were 'welcomed with quiet, unassuming friendliness by his deputy'. The 'delightful' grounds contain a lake with fish, black swans and exotic ducks. 'We were encouraged to explore, and could have picnicked there had we wished. Our good-sized room in the main house had a high ceiling, practical but pleasant furniture, a restful colour scheme, beautiful views.' There are smaller bedrooms under the eaves, and four others are in the single-storey coach house. Breakfast has a small buffet, pots of marmalade, 'toast of the right thickness', a 'wonderful cooked breakfast'. It is served in the 'attractive, bright' orangery with tall windows overlooking the lake, and a small sitting area for residents. At the top of the house, a little observatory (with telescope) gives wide views. Advice is given, with menus, on where to dine. 'Our little pug dog was made most welcome.' Somerton's church is worth visiting. (*PK, NM*)

9 bedrooms. 4 in coach house. 4 on ground floor. N edge of village. Breakfast room, small sitting area. No background music. 2½-acre grounds: lake. Unsuitable for ♿. No smoking. No dogs in public rooms; in bedrooms by arrangement. All major credit cards accepted. B&B £35–£70 per person. 2-night stays preferred at weekends in high season.

SOUTHWOLD Suffolk *See SHORTLIST* Map 2:B6

STAMFORD Lincolnshire Map 2:B3

The George
71 St Martins
Stamford PE9 2LB

Tel 01780-750750
Fax 01780-750701
Email reservations@georgehotelofstamford.com
Website www.georgehotelofstamford.com

César award in 1986

'Well run. It takes trouble with its guests. Good value.' In the centre of this unspoiled market town, Lawrence Hoskins's 16th-century coaching inn was liked by an inspector in 2007: 'Good booking procedure; good welcome (offer of a porter).' Other visitors wrote of 'spoiling qualities and excellent staff'. There is a 'nice courtyard with plants, chairs and tables [meal service on warm days]; a pretty walled garden'. The busy public rooms have mullioned windows, antique panelling, creaking floorboards ('poor mobile phone reception – thick walls'). 'Flower arrangements the best I have seen anywhere.' 'A good range of sandwiches promptly served, with excellent coffee in the bar. My courtyard bedroom, nicely furnished, modern, clean, comfortable, had space for everything, well-equipped bathroom with power shower *and* bath. Morning tea came on time, with freshly squeezed orange juice.' This self-styled 'old-fashioned hotel' provides an evening turn-down service and nocturnal shoe shining. In the formal, oak-panelled restaurant, men must wear jacket and tie while eating traditional dishes like duck with sage and onion stuffing and apple sauce. Some visitors have been disappointed by their meal. The *Garden Lounge* serves less formal meals and breakfast ('good service and choice; good cooked dishes'). (*Frances Storey Mendler, Joanna Russell, and others*)

47 bedrooms. ½ mile from centre (front windows double glazed). Large car park. Railway station 500 yds. Ramps. 2 lounges, 2 bars, 2 restaurants; 4 private dining rooms; business centre. No background music. 2-acre grounds: courtyard, herb garden, monastery garden, croquet. Unsuitable for ♿. Civil wedding licence. No smoking. No dogs unattended in bedrooms; only guide dogs in restaurant. All major credit cards accepted. B&B [2007] £62.50–£130 per person. Set lunch £18.95; full alc £55. Sunday night rates. Special breaks.

STANSTED Essex *See SHORTLIST* Map 2:C4

STANTON WICK Somerset Map 1:B6

The Carpenters Arms NEW
Stanton Wick, nr Pensford
BS39 4BX
Tel 01761-490202
Fax 01761-490763
Email carpenters@buccaneer.co.uk
Website www.the-carpenters-arms.co.uk

'We had an excellent night's stay in this small hotel/pub,' writes a regular *Guide* reader in 2007. In a hamlet overlooking the Chew valley, it is surrounded by rolling countryside. 'There is a friendly public bar and a busy restaurant. The bedrooms are newly decorated and modern, with dimmers on lights, large TV, well-equipped bathroom. Food was good and plentiful, with a traditional menu, eg, whitebait followed by steak. Wines were reasonably priced and very acceptable.' Generous breakfasts include fresh orange juice, fruit, full English. The manager, Simon Pledge, is 'most attentive'. Meals are served on the large patio in fine weather. Guests' cars are locked in a yard at night, 'though it hardly seems necessary on such a quiet country road'. Children under 12 stay free in their parents' room. (*Janet Walker*)

12 bedrooms. 7 miles S of Bristol, 8 miles W of Bath. Closed nights of 25 and 26 Dec. Bar, 2 dining rooms; function room. Patio. No background music. Unsuitable for ♿. No smoking. Dogs allowed in bar. Amex, MasterCard, Visa accepted. B&B [2007] £42.50–£67 per person. Full alc £30. Weekend breaks.

STOKE CANON Devon *See SHORTLIST* Map 1:C5

STOKE FLEMING Devon — Map 1:D4

Stoke Lodge NEW

Stoke Fleming
TQ6 0RA

Tel 01803-770523
Fax 01803-770851
Email mail@stokelodge.co.uk
Website www.stokelodge.co.uk

South-east of Totnes, on the coast, the Mayer family's traditional hotel is friendly and good value, says its nominator in 2007. 'Pleasant greeting. Everywhere is warm, clean and cosy. Our good-sized bedroom with sea view (extra charge) was in excellent decorative order, with ample storage space, good beds (one made with duvet, the other with blankets, as we had requested).' The lounges, recently refurbished, have 'plenty of squashy sofas and chairs, plus tables for bridge, etc'. The bar is 'very elegant', in dark green. In the attractive grounds are a pond with ducks, a swimming pool surrounded by loungers, and a tennis court. The four-course *table d'hôte* dinner, cooked by chef Steven Wood, is 'very good'. Ample choice (main courses include fried lemon sole with asparagus; grilled sea bass with parsley butter). Portions are generous; 'each dish is perfectly cooked'. Breakfasts, 'equally good', have a good buffet of fruits, cereals, etc. 'Inviting cooked dishes with high-quality ingredients. Possibly the best scrambled eggs we have had anywhere. Butter in small wrapped portions.' 'The owners are kindly and helpful; their staff are cheerful and anxious to please. High standards.' Cream teas are served, on the lawn in fine weather. (*Mary Woods*)

26 bedrooms. 2 miles E of Stoke Fleming, on coast, 2 miles S of Dartmouth. Guests can be met at Totnes railway station (12 miles). 2 lounges, bar, restaurant (background music at night); games room; indoor swimming pool; snooker room. 3-acre garden: heated swimming pool (16 by 32 ft), tennis. Unsuitable for ♿. No smoking. No dogs in public rooms. Amex, MasterCard, Visa accepted. B&B £47.50–£70 per person; D,B&B: single from £85, double from £135. Set menu £25; full alc £34. *V*

****

Traveller's tale The building was stiflingly hot. On the ground floor there is no opening of any kind to create a current of air. The bar and restaurant have been added in a glass-roofed area which retains heat and reflects it up to the bedrooms. We had to prop our window open on a drawer, and discovered (on our last day) that the hot pipes from the kitchen were boxed in between our bedroom and bathroom, which explained why our room was even hotter than the already hot air temperature. (*Hotel in the Midlands*)

****

STOURTON Wiltshire Map 2:D1

Spread Eagle Inn
Stourton, nr Warminster
BA12 6QE

Tel 01747-840587
Fax 01747-840954
Email enquiries@spreadeagleinn.com
Website www.spreadeagleinn.com

Run by Stephen Ross (as a National Trust tenant), this traditional British inn stands in the middle of Stourhead, one of the great gardens of England. 'The view from the back is of a magnificent lake, lined with grottos and classical temples.' 'A bonus of staying here,' said inspectors, 'is that you get free entry to the gardens and can enjoy them after closing time.' A regular visitor reports: 'It is consistently comfortable, and friendly. Totally quiet, though only five minutes from the busy A303.' Jason Lindley is the new manager this year. There is a smallish, red-walled sitting room. The large dining room has chandeliers, ornate mirrors and Victorian paintings 'in keeping with the house style'. The cooking, by chef Tom Bridgeman, is liked: 'Excellent guineafowl terrine.' The bar, with simple wooden tables and chairs, has a blackboard menu (soups, salads, 'robust pies and stews') and serves local beers. 'Our bedroom was spacious, well proportioned, with large sash windows, big, comfortable bed, and some nice antiques (some rather worn).' 'Breakfast had excellent porridge; piping hot toast', and, encouragingly, 'no little pots of preserve, but good big jars'. (*Mark Purcell, Penny Simpson, and others*)

5 bedrooms. 3 miles NW of Mere. Lounge, bar, restaurant (occasional background jazz in early evening). On 2,650-acre National Trust estate which has civil wedding licence. Unsuitable for ♿. No smoking. Guide dogs only. MasterCard, Visa accepted. B&B [2007] £47.50–£90 per person. Full alc £35. Christmas package. 1-night bookings sometimes refused weekends.

STRATFORD-UPON-AVON Warwickshire Map 3:D6

See SHORTLIST

****

Traveller's tale We spent a ghastly night in the suite in the basement of the —— *Hotel.* There was the constant sound of gushing water throughout the night (though it was not raining), humming and hissing from the boiler and kitchen in the room next door. No hot water in the morning. No manager on site. The manager did not return any later telephone calls. (*Hotel in London*)

****

STUCKTON Hampshire — Map 2:E2

The Three Lions Inn NEW

Stuckton, nr Fordingbridge
SP6 2HF

Tel 01425-652489
Fax 01425-656144
Email the3lions@btinternet.com
Website www.thethreelionsrestaurant.co.uk

Quietly set on the edge of the New Forest, this restaurant-with-rooms offers 'excellent if rather expensive food, good bedrooms, attractive gardens', wrote an inspector in 2007. 'Clad in his whites, owner/chef Mike Womersley gave a friendly welcome and carried our case to our annexe room. His wife, Jayne, is charming, very switched on.' They write: 'This is a family business, and we warmly invite guests to bring their children.' A chalet-style room, 'high-ceilinged, light, fresh', had creamy yellow walls, sand-coloured carpet, shot silk patterned curtains in orange and gold. 'A French door opened on to the attractive rear garden (with hot tub and sauna). Everything looked loved and cared for.' Some ground-floor rooms 'provide easy access for the less mobile'. The main building has a bar, a small lounge area, and further seating in a conservatory. No printed menus; you order from a portable blackboard. 'Tables gleamed with good glassware and cutlery. The food was exceptional, notably starters (fresh asparagus and wild mushrooms; smoked haddock galette); and desserts (intensely flavoured sorbets). We could not fault the quality of any dish.' Main courses include casseroled partridge; wild turbot with saffron sauce. The continental breakfast, included in the price was 'first class: fruit, cereals, good croissants, delicious coffee'. Full English breakfast costs £7.50.

7 bedrooms. 4 on ground floor. 3 in courtyard block. 1½ miles E of Fordingbridge. Restaurant closed Sun night/Mon. Ramps. Conservatory, meeting/sitting room, public bar, restaurant; varied background music. 2½-acre garden: sauna, whirlpool. No smoking. No dogs in public rooms. MasterCard, Visa accepted. B&B: single £65–£95, double £75–£115. Set menu £18.75; full alc £40.

STUDLAND Dorset *See SHORTLIST* — Map 2:E1

The 'New' label indicates hotels which are appearing in the *Guide* for the first time or which have been readmitted after an absence.

STURMINSTER NEWTON Dorset — Map 2:E1

Plumber Manor
Sturminster Newton DT10 2AF

Tel 01258-472507
Fax 01258-473370
Email book@plumbermanor.com
Website www.plumbermanor.com

César award in 1987

A tributary of the River Stour runs through the secluded grounds of the Prideaux-Brune family home in unspoilt Dorset countryside. The early 17th-century manor house (Pride of Britain) is run as a restaurant-with-rooms ('homely and comfortable') by Richard Prideaux-Brune, his wife, Alison, and brother, Brian (the chef). Around it are manicured lawns and herbaceous borders, and two Labradors provide 'a warm welcome'. Readers enjoy the 'efficient yet relaxed service'. One commented on the 'house-party atmosphere: most of the other guests had been here before and were engaged in friendly conversation with the owner'. There are open fires in the main bar and dining rooms in winter. Bedrooms in the main house lead off a gallery hung with family portraits. The best rooms are in a converted barn: 'Plenty of space, comfortable window seat, well-equipped bathroom; immaculate housekeeping.' 'Food was excellent,' says a regular correspondent this year. 'Portion control just right for us "oldies" who dislike overloaded plates,' was another comment. The dinner menu has a choice of seven dishes for each of the first two courses. At breakfast, 'top-class ingredients are used'. Complimentary tea with home-made fruit cake is served in the lounge or alfresco, and there is tea-making equipment in the bedroom. (*Rodney Bourne, and others*)

16 bedrooms. 10 on ground floor, in courtyard. 2 miles SW of Sturminster Newton. Closed Feb. Restaurant closed midday, except Sun. Lounge, bar, 3 dining rooms, gallery. No background music. 3-acre grounds: garden, tennis, croquet, stream. No smoking. Dogs allowed in 2 bedrooms only. All major credit cards accepted. B&B [2007] £55–£110 per person. Set dinner £23–£26; full alc £36. Special breaks Nov–April.

SUTTON COLDFIELD Warwickshire — Map 3:C6

See SHORTLIST

Most hotels have reduced rates out of season, and offer breaks throughout the year. It is always worth checking for special deals on the hotel's website or by telephone.

SWAFFHAM Norfolk — Map 2:B5

Strattons
4 Ash Close
Swaffham PE37 7NH

Tel 01760-723845
Fax 01760-720458
Email enquiries@strattonshotel.com
Website www.strattonshotel.com

César award in 2003

Visitors who arrive by public transport at Vanessa and Les Scott's Grade II listed Palladian-style villa ('a small but perfect hotel,' is one comment) get a ten per cent discount on the bed and breakfast rate. This is part of a comprehensive environmental policy embracing waste management, recycling, local sourcing of organic food, the choice of toiletries, etc. This doesn't mean any loss of excitement, says a visitor this year: 'The description of this substantial building as a green hotel has a Spartan feel to it, but *Strattons* is at the opposite end of the scale to Spartan. The furnishing, artworks and knick-knacks littered around have a touch of excess about them and should appeal to the most hedonistic person.' *Strattons* is filled with original paintings, sculptures and ornaments, and noted for its exotic themed bedrooms (Venetian, Red, Opium, etc). A suite, and a double room with balcony, are new this year. And piped music has been introduced. 'I asked for it to be turned off,' one visitor wrote, 'but on the third occasion, in the breakfast room, I gave up.' Sam Bryant has joined Mrs Scott in the kitchen; they produce modern English dishes on a monthly-changing menu (eg, slow-cooked leg of lamb; brown shrimp risotto). Breakfast has freshly squeezed juices, free-range eggs, home-made breads. The Scotts' daughter, Hannah, shares the manager's role with Dominic Hughes. (*John Rowlands, and others*)

10 bedrooms. 2 in annexe. 2 on ground floor. Central. Parking. Closed 1 week Christmas. Drawing room, TV room, restaurant; 'funky' background music all day in public rooms. Terrace. 1-acre garden. Unsuitable for ♿. No smoking. No dogs: restaurant, or unaccompanied in bedrooms (£6.50 per day). MasterCard, Visa accepted. B&B [2007] £75–£175 per person. Set dinner £40. Special breaks. 1-night bookings sometimes refused weekends/holidays. New Year package.

Every year we give a free copy of the *Guide* to each of the 12 readers who send us the best reports. Every report received is considered in this competition.

SWAY Hampshire Map 2:E2

The Nurse's Cottage
Station Road
Sway, nr Lymington
SO41 6BA

Tel/Fax 01590-683402
Email nurses.cottage@lineone.net
Website www.nursescottage.co.uk

Approaching its centenary year, this small house, once the home of successive district nurses, is now a restaurant-with-rooms run in very personal style by owner Tony Barnfield ('a man of strong opinions'). The bedrooms, all on the ground floor, are small, but 'a lot is fitted into a small space'. 'Our room was genteel, immaculate, well thought out,' wrote an inspector. 'Unusual items included a blank video cassette in case we wanted to record a programme while dining. There were shoe-cleaning kit; fresh milk and juice in a fridge; fruit and flowers; sheets and blankets on the bed; a good bathroom. The comprehensive information pack included dire warnings about the consequences of being caught smoking.' Rates are for half board, as 'our main clientele is elderly and seeks out places where dinner is included'. In the attractive blue-and-white conservatory restaurant, the menu changes four or five times a year (but there usually are daily dishes). House specialities include breast of guineafowl in a tarragon, white wine and cream sauce; bananas flambées. The cooking is thought 'very good'. The 'enjoyable' breakfast has a buffet, and standard cooked dishes. (*WC, and others*)

5 bedrooms. All on ground floor. Closed 2 weeks Nov, 3 weeks Feb/March. Village centre. 4 miles NW of Lymington. Train: Sway. Small sitting area, restaurant (background music, 'generally nostalgic'). Small garden. No smoking. No children under 10. No dogs in public rooms. Amex, MasterCard, Visa accepted. D,B&B [2007] £75–£85 per person. Set dinner £20–£23. Bargain breaks. Christmas package.

SYMONDS YAT EAST Herefordshire Map 3:D5

The Saracens Head Inn
Symonds Yat East
Ross-on-Wye HR9 6JL

Tel 01600-890435
Fax 01600-890034
Email contact@saracensheadinn.co.uk
Website www.saracensheadinn.co.uk

In wooded valley in area of outstanding natural beauty, often busy with tourists: 'very helpful' Rollinson family's old inn, part of a string of white buildings on E bank of River Wye near Welsh border. 'Jolly, relaxed, unpretentious; lively bar with red telephone box, fruit machines, billiard table. Children would have a ball.'

Restaurant, with rustic decor, 'very friendly young staff'. Ambitious dishes on long menu: generous portions. 'Good breakfast in pleasant room.' Car park. Closed Christmas/New Year. Lounge, TV room. Background music most of the time. Unsuitable for ♿. 2 riverside terraces: free fishing. No smoking. Dogs allowed in bar. MasterCard, Visa accepted. 10 bedrooms (best ones in Boathouse *annexe; 1 on ground floor). B&B [2007] £37–£65 per person. Full alc £35. More reports, please.*

TALLAND-BY-LOOE Cornwall — Map 1:D3

Talland Bay Hotel NEW
Talland-by-Looe PL13 2JB

Tel 01503-272667
Fax 01503-272940
Email info@tallandbayhotel.co.uk
Website www.tallandbayhotel.co.uk

'A very fine family-run hotel', 'wonderfully situated' in subtropical gardens, 150 feet above the bay. Visitors this year praise the owners, George and Mary Granville, their staff ('courteous, efficient') and the 'outstanding' food. In the wood-panelled dining room, with small-paned windows, antique china in alcoves, flowers and log fire, the best tables have good views. 'Delicious combinations,' said inspectors. 'Modern presentation; mullet with crab crust; perfect pink rack of lamb.' There is 'a wide selection of Cornish cheeses'. Another comment: 'Decor pleasingly country house. Some rooms a little faded, but we like this.' Bedrooms vary greatly; the best have 'smart draperies and great views'. Some have walls three feet thick, some a private garden. Some are small. 'Ours (not one of the refurbished rooms) was comfortable if old-fashioned.' Five rooms are in cottages – one, near car park and kitchen, can be noisy. 'Delicious' breakfasts, accompanied by the weather forecast, have toasted home-made bread, freshly squeezed juices, 'very good' cooked dishes. Light lunches are served in the bar or on the terrace. Afternoon tea, with 'luscious cakes', is included in the price. Children are welcomed (child-listening, high teas for under-fives, small portions for children who dine with their parents). (*Malcolm and Jane Levitt, and others*)

23 bedrooms. 2½ miles SW of Looe; off Looe–Polperro road. Lounge, library, bar, restaurant; patio. No background music. 2½-acre garden: heated swimming pool (May–Sept), badminton, putting, croquet. Beach 5 mins' walk. Golf nearby. Unsuitable for ♿. No smoking. No children under 5 at dinner (high tea at 6 pm). No dogs in public rooms. MasterCard, Visa accepted. B&B £47.50–£105 per person. Set dinner £32.50. Min. 2-night bookings at weekends. Winter, spring, Easter breaks. Christmas/New Year packages.

TAUNTON Somerset — Map 1:C5

The Castle at Taunton

Castle Green
Taunton TA1 1NF

Tel 01823-272671
Fax 01823-336066
Email reception@the-castle-hotel.com
Website www.the-castle-hotel.com

César award in 1987

Wisteria-covered and castellated, Kit and Louise Chapman's hotel attracts many returning guests. One writes: 'My grandfather entertained his sons here, my father took me to lunch when I boarded nearby. When we celebrated our granddaughter's sixth birthday, it was the kindness, skill and care shown by all the staff that impressed us above all.' Another report also mentions the staff: 'Helpful, caring, personable.' The 'elegant' public rooms have old oak furniture, tapestries and paintings, 'lovely flowers'. A fine wrought iron staircase leads to bedrooms of varying size and style: 'Our quiet room had a comfortable, large bed, a settee, plenty of cupboard space.' 'My pleasant single was well equipped; spotless bathroom.' 'Our suite was a delight, bright and colourful.' Some walls may be thin. In the L-shaped restaurant, predominantly red and white, the modern British *Michelin*-starred cooking of chef Richard Guest (eg, turbot with gnocchi and broad beans) was variously thought 'delicious'; 'good, but lacking the "wow" factor'. 'Cheeseboard very good. Local producers named on menus.' 'Excellent wines.' Salads, grills, omelettes, etc, are served in *Brazz,* the lively café/bistro adjacent. 'Breakfast was fine: dishes under domes good and freshly cooked; home-made jams and marmalade.' (*Carol Jackson, Christopher Evans, and others*)

44 bedrooms. Central. Main restaurant closed Sun night. Lift, ramps. Lounge, bar, restaurant, brasserie (background music); private dining/meeting rooms. 1-acre garden: shop. Civil wedding licence. No smoking. Small, 'well-behaved' dogs only; not in public rooms. All major credit cards accepted. B&B [2007] £69.50–£132.50 per person. Set lunch/dinner from £22.50; full alc £60. Christmas/New Year packages.

TAVISTOCK Devon *See SHORTLIST* — Map 1:D4

The *Guide* welcomes recommendations from readers for new entries. Please write or send us an email about any hotel, inn or B&B that you feel should be included.

TEFFONT EVIAS Wiltshire — Map 2:D1

Howard's House

Teffont Evias
nr Salisbury SP3 5RJ

Tel 01722-716392
Fax 01722-716820
Email enq@howardshousehotel.co.uk
Website www.howardshousehotel.co.uk

'Delightful; peaceful, welcoming. We sat in the garden for hours.' 'Lovely, relaxing. A personal air and excellent food.' 'Real value for money.' Praise for this 'romantic' 17th-century dower house in a 'delightful, unspoilt hamlet' near Salisbury. A reader who visited while manager Noële Thompson was away found 'a welcoming young major-domo and courteous staff'. 'Once checked in, we never had to identify ourselves,' was another comment. The 'charming, well-proportioned' lounge has an old stone fireplace, yellow walls, bright fabrics and exposed beams. Tea and home-made biscuits are served here and on the terrace. Bedrooms have pastel colours and floral prints, 'what one might find in a non-designer home'. 'Our spacious room had an idyllic view of the hillside garden and church.' But most rooms are smallish, and beds may be on the small side too. The modern cooking of chef Nick Wentworth includes fillet of sea bass, herb risotto, red wine jus. 'Good wine by the glass.' At breakfast, served at table, 'toast and croissants wrapped in a serviette are brought with the cooked course, so are warm when you eat them'. In the gardens are ancient box hedges. Children and dogs are welcomed. (*Elizabeth Pratt, Anthony Fisher, Michael Blanchard*)

9 bedrooms. Off B3089, 10 miles W of Salisbury. Car park. Closed 5 days at Christmas. Lounge, restaurant. No background music. 2-acre grounds: croquet. River, fishing nearby. Unsuitable for ♿. Smoking allowed in 2 bedrooms. Amex, MasterCard, Visa accepted. B&B [2007]: single £100, double £155. Set dinner £26.95; full alc £52.50. 2-night breaks. New Year package. *V*

TEIGNMOUTH Devon — Map 1:D5

Thomas Luny House *Tel* 01626-772976
Teign Street *Email* alisonandjohn@thomas-luny-house.co.uk
Teignmouth TQ14 8EG *Website* www.thomas-luny-house.co.uk

Built by the marine artist Thomas Luny in 1808, when the town was favoured by admirals and captains, this 'beautiful house' is reached via an archway ('a bit of thought needed before you drive through') in a high whitewashed wall. Owners John and Alison Allan are 'consummate professionals, with a charming, low-key, friendly manner', says a returning visitor this year. The house is 'attractive, fresh and clean'; the spacious double drawing room and breakfast room, each with an open fire and furnished with antiques, lead through French windows on to the 'pretty patio suntrap garden'. 'It is very pleasant to sit outside in summer and drink John's excellent tea and eat Alison's delicious cake.' Upstairs, three of the bedrooms are spacious, the fourth is small. All have flowers, Malvern water, books and magazines, tea-making facilities and bathrobes. The 'splendid' breakfast, taken at separate tables, includes 'good leaf tea', 'freshly baked bread, fresh fruits, perfect scrambled eggs'. 'Excellent value for money.' (*Marilyn Frampton*)

4 bedrooms. Central. 2 lounges, breakfast room. No background music. Small walled garden. Sea, sandy beach 5 mins' walk. Unsuitable for ♿. No smoking. No children under 12. No dogs. MasterCard, Visa accepted. B&B [2007] £42–£73 per person. 1-night bookings sometimes refused.

See also SHORTLIST

TEMPLE SOWERBY Cumbria — Map 4: inset C3

Temple Sowerby House *Tel* 017683-61578
Temple Sowerby *Fax* 017683-61958
nr Penrith CA10 1RZ *Email* stay@templesowerby.com
Website www.templesowerby.com

Originally the principal residence in this conservation village, this Grade II listed house, with thick walls and a Georgian wing, has views of Cross Fell, the highest peak in the Pennines. A bypass was due to open as the *Guide* went to press, 'returning the village to a peaceful, rural setting', say owner/managers Paul and Julie Evans. 'The view from front rooms will be across the green to fields and fells beyond.' Visitors returning for the fifth time found 'hotel, rooms and food all excellent'. The owners 'seem to be on hand to meet visitors' needs at all times'. Refurbishment of bedrooms will be completed early in 2008. The conservatory-style restaurant, which faces the walled garden with its terrace, is the 'perfect spot for a glass of local beer in the late afternoon sun'. Chef Ashley Whittaker serves modern British dishes like poached breast of guinea fowl with confit potatoes. 'The food is very good; wine list good too, and reasonable value.' 'The lounges are cosy,' says another report. Breakfast has 'delicious bread and rolls', 'nice jam and butter, unwrapped'. Meetings, seminars and 'discreet gatherings' are catered for. Ullswater is 15 minutes' drive away. (*CB, ER*)

12 bedrooms. 2 on ground floor. 4 in coach house (20 yds). Centre of village. 6 miles NW of Appleby (front windows double glazed). Closed 1 week at Christmas. 2 lounges, bar, restaurant (varied background music); conference/function facilities. 2-acre garden: croquet. Civil wedding licence. No smoking. No children under 12. Dogs allowed in some bedrooms by prior arrangement; not in public rooms. MasterCard, Visa accepted. B&B [until April 2008] £60–£90 per person. Full alc £45. 2-night breaks. New Year package. 1-night bookings occasionally refused. *V*

TETBURY Gloucestershire — Map 3:E5

Calcot Manor
nr Tetbury GL8 8YJ

Tel 01666-890391
Fax 01666-890394
Email reception@calcotmanor.co.uk
Website www.calcotmanor.co.uk

César award in 2001

A large family party (three years old to 70) found 'something for everyone' this year at Richard and Cathy Ball's child-friendly Cotswold hotel, a conversion of a 14th-century farmhouse, cottages and outbuildings. 'The children were so well catered for that we hardly saw them.' 'The best holiday I have had as a parent,' was another comment. Mrs Ball runs the spa: 'a real bonus in winter', it provides a retreat for adults (children may use the swimming pool at specified times). For the young there is an Ofsted-registered crèche, and a Playzone in a converted tithe barn. 'Everything so well arranged for families that we did not feel we were interfering with other guests' enjoyment.' The suites, in the courtyard, have a double bedroom for parents, and a sitting room with bunks or sofa bed for children; also video, TV, small fridge, baby-listening. In the *Conservatory Restaurant*, Michael Croft's modern cooking was thought 'excellent' (eg, sea bass with truffle glaze). The informal

Gumstool pub (*Michelin Bib Gourmand*) serves 'inexpensive good food', and children's high teas. Breakfasts have fresh orange juice, local Duchy sausages. 'Not cheap, but worth the expense for a trouble-free family get-together.' (*Jennifer Smye, ZE, and others*)

34 bedrooms. 10 (family) in cottage. 11 around courtyard, on ground floor. 3 miles W of Tetbury. Train: Kemble, 10 miles; taxi. Ramps. Lounge, 2 restaurants, 2 bars; background music at mealtimes; private dining room; cinema; conference facilities; children's playroom with nanny (4 hrs daily). 220-acre grounds: tennis, heated outdoor 24-ft swimming pool, children's play area, croquet; bicycles; spa: 48-ft swimming pool, sauna, treatments, etc. Civil wedding licence. Smoking allowed in all bedrooms. Dogs by arrangement, not in public rooms. All major credit cards accepted. B&B [2007]: single £180, double £205–£245, suite £260–£380; D,B&B £132.25–£230 per person. Set dinner £19–£23. 2-day breaks. Christmas/New Year packages. 1-night bookings refused Sat in season.

See also SHORTLIST

THIRSK North Yorkshire *See SHORTLIST* Map 4:C4

THORPE ST ANDREW Norfolk Map 2:B5

The Old Rectory
103 Yarmouth Road
Thorpe St Andrew
nr Norwich NR7 0HF

Tel 01603-700772
Fax 01603-300772
Email enquiries@oldrectorynorwich.com
Website www.oldrectorynorwich.com

In mature gardens looking over the Yare valley, this creeper-clad Grade II listed Georgian rectory (built in 1754) is the family home of Chris and Sally Entwistle, their son, James, and their Birman cats, Rolo and Milli. It is small but has 'all the necessary facilities', one enthusiastic visitor wrote. Women on their own feel comfortable here: 'They come to stay somewhere quiet,' the Entwistles tell us. One wrote: 'My bedroom and bathroom were spacious.' All rooms have Wi-Fi Internet access. Duvets on beds, but you can ask for blankets and sheets. Pre-dinner drinks are taken in the drawing room, where a log fire, big mirrors, decorative plates and family photographs create a 'pleasant atmosphere'. James Perry is the chef: his dishes might include saffron and dill organic salmon gravadlax; roasted marinated medallions of Attleborough sirloin. The conservatory overlooks a terrace (where drinks are served in summer) with a small kidney-shaped swimming pool. The house stands well back from the road, and buses to Norwich city centre (two miles) stop outside. The Norfolk Broads national park is a short drive away.

8 bedrooms. 3 in coach house (20 yds). Also self-catering cottage. 2 miles E of Norwich. Closed 22 Dec–3 Jan. Restaurant closed Sun/Mon. Drawing room, conservatory, dining room; background jazz/classical music at night; meeting/function facilities. 1-acre garden: heated swimming pool, open May–Sept (40 by 12 ft). River Yare 450 yds. Unsuitable for ♿. No smoking. No dogs in public rooms; allowed in 1 bedroom. Amex, MasterCard, Visa accepted. B&B £57.50–£110 per person. Set dinner £27. Special breaks. 1-night bookings refused weekends Easter–Sept.

TISBURY Wiltshire *See SHORTLIST* Map 2:D1

TITCHWELL Norfolk Map 2:A5

Titchwell Manor
Titchwell, nr Brancaster
PE31 8BB

Tel 01485-210221
Fax 01485-210104
Email margaret@titchwellmanor.com
Website www.titchwellmanor.com

Once a Victorian gentlemen's club, Margaret and Ian Snaith's small hotel/restaurant/bar has 'a pleasant split personality', says a visitor in 2007, 'part Chelsea by the sea, but also popular with walkers, bird-watchers, etc'. The building faces dunes and salt marshes, though one couple 'needed a telescope to enjoy the sea view from our room in the main house'. This room had a 'large, comfortable bed', a small but new bathroom. There are 'excellent' rooms around an old herb garden: 'light and airy, with extras like flowers, books and CDs'. Some bedrooms may be small. Public rooms have mosaic tiled floors, dark woodwork, Lloyd Loom furniture, potted plants ('a fusion of modernity and the traditional values of a Victorian house', says the brochure). Seafood is the speciality of the chef, the Snaiths' son Eric, whose cooking using local produce has 'well-balanced flavours and textures' (eg, rack of lamb with celeriac fondant and braised pancetta). The dessert menu 'is a masterpiece'. The bar, with its 'feel of a gastropub', serves light meals all day. Children under 12 have their own menu. Breakfast includes local kippers, smoked salmon and scrambled eggs. One visitor complained of long waits at Reception, and in the lounge before breakfast. The Titchwell nature reserve is close by. (*Mrs CL Hodgkins, Ken and Mildred Edwards, Anne and Chris Martin, and others*)

26 bedrooms. 17 on ground floor, in barn annexe. 2 suitable for ♿. 5 miles E of Hunstanton. 2 lounges, bar, restaurant; background 'relaxing' music in bar and restaurant at night. ½-acre garden. Beaches, golf nearby. No smoking. No children over Christmas/New Year. Dogs allowed in 5 bedrooms, bar and lounge. All major credit cards accepted. B&B £45–£110 per person; D,B&B £15 added. Full alc £35. Christmas/New Year packages. 1-night bookings sometimes refused Sat.

TITLEY Herefordshire — Map 3:C4

The Stagg Inn
Titley, nr Kington
HR5 3RL

Tel 01544-230221
Email reservations@thestagg.co.uk
Website www.thestagg.co.uk

'A lovely place to stay.' Praise in 2007 for Steve and Nicola Reynolds's old pub by the road in a small, straggling village in rolling countryside. Inspectors wrote earlier that 'this must be the most unpretentious and laid-back *Michelin*-starred establishment in Europe'. The restaurant areas are spread around, 'all higgledy-piggledy', some up a few steps, some down. They have 'country-style plain wooden tables and simple upholstered chairs'. The candlelit dinner is based on 'excellent local ingredients', eg, pigeon breast on pearl barley; herb-stuffed free-range chicken. 'All good value, as was the wine list.' Three bedrooms are above the pub. 'We were impressed by ours: bright, tastefully decorated, reasonably sized, heavily beamed. Good lighting and storage, not a lot of furniture, interesting photos and pictures. Bright, clean bathroom. A garden-facing window: some passing traffic.' Three other rooms are down the road in a listed Georgian vicarage, backed by a garden, with stream, chickens, 'a friendly Labrador, and cats'. 'Our splendid room here had two large beds, effective heating, fresh milk in a refrigerator.' Breakfast includes fresh fruit, porridge with honey, 'excellent scrambled eggs, toast made from lovely bread, a large chunk of butter'. (*Frances Rathbone, Gordon Murray, and others*)

6 bedrooms. 3 at *Old Vicarage* (300 yds). On B4355 between Kington (3½ miles) and Presteigne. Closed 25–27 Dec, Sun night/Mon, 10 days end Jan and early Nov. Sitting room and 3-acre garden at *Old Vicarage*. Pub has bar, restaurant areas, small garden. No background music. Unsuitable for ♿. No smoking. Dogs allowed in pub rooms. MasterCard, Visa accepted. B&B £42.50–£65 per person. Full alc £35.

> Hotels do not pay to be included in the *Guide*.

TORQUAY Devon *See SHORTLIST* Map 1:D5

TORVER Cumbria Map 4: inset C2

The Old Rectory
Torver, nr Coniston
LA21 8AX

Tel 015394-41353
Fax 015394-41156
Email enquiries@theoldrectoryhotel.com
Website www.theoldrectoryhotel.com

Liked for the 'excellent hospitality', 'good value' and 'outstanding home-cooked food', Paul and Elizabeth Mitchell's unpretentious 19th-century white-painted house stands in gardens and woods in farmland beneath the peaks of Coniston Old Man. 'Warm and comfortable; offers relaxation and nourishment after a long day's walking or sailing,' is one recent comment. The bedrooms are individually designed: 'Our bright superior room, with modern bathroom, was well furnished, spotlessly clean.' A four-course dinner (no choice until dessert) is served in the conservatory dining room. The Mitchells call the food 'adventurous traditional', eg, butternut squash and coconut soup; Moroccan spiced slow-roasted lamb. Puddings include plum crumble; lemon curd Romanoff. Vegetarians are catered for, given notice. 'Breakfasts were consistently good' (a large buffet and 'plenty of choices from a cooked-to-order menu'). Children are welcomed; high tea, cots and baby monitors available. Coniston Water is reached by a 20-minute stroll along a tarmac lane. Good walking and climbing. *The Old Rectory* was on the market as we went to press, but an early sale was not expected. Please check the position when booking. (*PK*)

9 bedrooms. 1 in annexe. 1 on ground floor. 2½ miles SW of Coniston on A593. Open Feb–Nov. Dining room closed to non-residents. Lounge, dining room. No background music. ½-acre garden plus 2-acre woodland. ¾ mile from Coniston Water. No smoking. No dogs in public rooms. MasterCard, Visa accepted. B&B £33–£49.50 per person; D,B&B £58–£74.50. Set menu £25. 1-night bookings refused bank holidays, half-term.

TOTNES Devon *See SHORTLIST* Map 1:D4

Please always send a report if you stay at a *Guide* hotel, even if it's only to endorse the existing entry.

TRESCO Isles of Scilly **Map 1:C1**

The Island Hotel
Old Grimsby, Tresco
Isles of Scilly
Cornwall TR24 0PU

Tel 01720-422883
Fax 01720-423008
Email islandhotel@tresco.co.uk
Website www.tresco.co.uk

Arriving visitors are ferried by tractor and trailer to this sprawling one-storey building (managed by Euan Rodger) on Robert Dorrien-Smith's tiny private island, which is famed for its subtropical Abbey Gardens (to which hotel residents have unlimited access). 'Running a high-class hotel at the end of a long, tenuous supply line must be difficult, but everything worked,' says a visitor in 2007. 'Our superior room was spotless, well planned, spacious. Staff were charming. No music of any kind, a profound relief.' Others add: 'We thought it wonderful.' 'There is nothing stuffy about it. Magnificent location [by a large sandy beach]. Our rooms were lovely.' Most bedrooms have a sea view; some have a balcony. The public rooms reflect the colours of the sea and beach. There is contemporary artwork throughout. Tables are rotated in the restaurant so everyone can enjoy the view; in good weather dinner may be alfresco. The new chef, Peter Marshall, serves 'adventurous' dishes, 'mostly excellent'. Breakfast is 'excellent, too', though one visitor said: 'It suffered from premature toast, but a quiet word produced results.' 'Lunch menu just right.' There are bar meals and cream teas. The hotel is popular with families in the school holidays (buckets, spades, pushchairs, high teas provided). (*Robert Long, Elizabeth Ryan, Mrs MT Smith*)

48 bedrooms. 8 in 2 annexes. 3 on ground floor. NE side of island. Boat/helicopter from Penzance. Hotel will make travel arrangements and meet guests. Open Feb–Nov. Lounge, TV room, games room, bar, 2 dining rooms. No background music. 2-acre grounds: terrace, tennis, croquet, bowls, heated 75-ft swimming pool (May–30 Sept); beach: safe bathing, diving, snorkelling. Bicycle hire (book in advance). Golf buggies and wheelchairs for ♿. No smoking. No dogs allowed on Tresco. MasterCard, Visa accepted. D,B&B £135–£325 per person. Set dinner £42. Snacks/packed lunches £5–£15. 5% discount for 5 or more days. *V*

TROUTBECK Cumbria *See SHORTLIST* Map 4: inset C2

> Smaller hotels, especially those in remote areas, may close at short notice off-season. Check before travelling that a hotel is open.

TRURO Cornwall — Map 1:D2

Royal Hotel
Lemon Street
Truro TR1 2QB

Tel 01872-270345
Fax 01872-242453
Email reception@royalhotelcornwall.co.uk
Website www.royalhotelcornwall.co.uk

'The lively young staff treated us like real humans,' say visitors this year to Lynn Manning's 200-year-old Grade II listed inn (where Prince Albert stayed in 1846) in the centre of this cathedral city. 'Pleasant welcome; help with luggage.' An earlier visitor wrote of the 'good attitude, pleasant, light decor with abstract prints, and relaxed atmosphere'. The 'mix of background music' was less liked; 'not overly loud but some, in my view, rubbish'. Modern brasserie-style food ('eclectic, with a Thai or American twist') is served from 11 am to 10 pm in the restaurant, where wooden tables are 'reasonably far apart' (some on a platform). Starters include chicken and saffron broth; main courses include tempura fish. 'Good service; generous helpings.' 'Because I was eating alone, I was offered a selection of newspapers and magazines to read, which was nice. At breakfast there were newspapers, a buffet with a large choice, and the food was good.' The third floor has been refurbished, and given air conditioning; Wi-Fi is available throughout. 'My bedroom at the rear was quiet, with good-quality fittings; housekeeping was good and the bed was comfortable.' The bar, open until midnight, serves 'funky cocktails'.

43 bedrooms. 9 apartments (1 suitable for ♿). Central. Closed Christmas. Ramp. Lounge, bar, restaurant; background 'light jazz' all day; boardroom. No smoking. Guide dogs only. All major credit cards accepted. B&B [2007] £47.50–£75 per person. Full alc £56. Weekend breaks off-season. *V*

TUNBRIDGE WELLS Kent — Map 2:D4

Hotel du Vin Tunbridge Wells
Crescent Road
Tunbridge Wells
TN1 2LY

Tel 01892-526455
Fax 01892-512044
Email info@tunbridgewells.hotelduvin.com
Website www.hotelduvin.com

In the centre of the historic spa town, this 18th-century Grade II listed sandstone building was extended in the 1830s by Decimus Burton, known for the Palm House at Kew Gardens. In the 20th century it was turned into a hotel by the Hotel du Vin group (now owned by Marylebone Warwick Balfour). Andy Roger is manager. One recent visitor commented on the 'aura of French chic, from the unusual Reception to the decor of the bedrooms'. The quietest rooms overlook Calverley Park. Even standard rooms are well appointed, 'though not fantastically large'. An inspector's room, though 'cupboard-size', 'had all the latest gadgets: large flat-screen TV, DVD-player, smart tea-making gizmos'. Another room was 'spacious, with an enormous bathroom (the largest shower cubicle I've ever seen)'. Reservations are necessary for the 'lively' bistro where 'at peak times it is necessary to forget about the bustle'. It has a serious wine list (many available by the glass), and chef Paul Nixon offers daily specials, in addition to the seasonally changing *carte* (dishes like pan-fried turbot with cauliflower and chorizo risotto). Staff (many are French) are 'courteous, attentive, well trained'. Wedding receptions and other functions are held. (*Peter Mueller, CA*)

34 bedrooms. 4 in adjacent cottage. Central, opposite Assembly Hall. Lift. 2 lounges, bar, snooker room, bistro; private dining/meeting rooms. No background music. 1-acre grounds: cigar shack; *boules*, small vineyard. Civil wedding licence. No smoking. No dogs in bistro. All major credit cards accepted. Room [2007] £105–£325. Breakfast £9.95–£13.50. Full alc £50.

See also SHORTLIST

TWO BRIDGES Devon — Map 1:D4

Prince Hall Hotel
Dartmoor PL20 6SA

Tel 01822-890403
Fax 01822-890676
Email info@princehall.co.uk
Website www.princehall.co.uk

With panoramic views over the West Dart valley, this small hotel is in the middle of Dartmoor. 'The position is very special, easily a mile from the nearest public road, facing south into a gentle valley,' said one visitor. 'I was made to feel welcome by owners [John and Anne Grove] and staff.' 'What a lovely place.' 'Blissfully quiet at night.' 'Excellent service and delicious food,' said others. The house is 'well maintained, nicely proportioned, decor in keeping, not over fancy'. Head chef Marc Slater (trained by Michel Roux) has won a bronze medal in the 'Taste of the West' awards (main courses on the *table d'hôte* menu include roast monkfish fillet with mussels and tarragon-scented tagliatelle). Dinner can be leisurely. 'Breakfast had warm toast and good cooked dishes (excellent sausages).' 'The ingredients are mostly from local farms, and it shows.' The best bedrooms, like the public areas, face the moor; standard ones are above a courtyard (you might hear an extractor fan). Some were due to be modernised in 2007. Cream teas are served, in the garden in summer. This is a genuinely dog-friendly hotel, say the Groves. You can walk straight from the grounds on to the moor. (*Sara Price, Colette Mather, Trevor Lockwood*)

9 bedrooms. 1 mile E of Two Bridges, on B3357 towards Ashburton. Train: Plymouth/Newton Abbot. Open early Feb–2 Jan. Sitting room, bar, restaurant; jazz/classical background music at night. 5-acre grounds. River Dart, fishing, 5 mins' walk; riding, shooting, golf nearby. Only restaurant and bar suitable for ♿. No smoking. No children under 10. Amex, MasterCard, Visa accepted. B&B [2007] £60–£90 per person; D,B&B £95–£125. Set dinner £40. 3-day breaks. Christmas/New Year packages. 1-night bookings occasionally refused Fri/Sat in season. *V*

ULLSWATER Cumbria — Map 4: inset C2

Howtown Hotel

Tel 01768-486514

Ullswater, nr Penrith CA10 2ND

César award in 1991

On the eastern shore of Lake Ullswater, this 'easy-going' guest house stands up a narrow lane leading to the end of the valley. With gardens on one side, wooded hills on the other, it is run 'in quiet, laid-back style' by Jacquie Baldry ('very professional'), with her son, David (the family have owned it for over a century). Their staff are 'very pleasant, efficient' (some are Polish). They offer 'real rest, and convivial companionship between guests', says a report this year. Visitors returning after 20 years were 'delighted to find it essentially as we remembered; still no TV/radio/telephone in the bedrooms; on the plus side, an attractive bathroom had been added'. All rooms have lake views; some have their bathroom across the corridor. In the main building, early morning tea is brought to the room, and there is an evening turn-down service. A traditional four-course menu is served in the dining room (tables close together) at 7 pm: 'Memorable roast duck; lamb very good, too.' Sunday has a set lunch and a cold supper. Breakfasts are generous. A substantial picnic can be provided. 'Very good value'; popular with walkers: 'The hills and dales around are delightful.' (*Brian Pullee, PE Carter*)

13 bedrooms. 4 in annexe. 4 self-catering cottages for weekly rent. E shore of lake, 4 miles S of Pooley Bridge. Bus from Penrith station, 9 miles. Open Mar–1 Nov. 3 lounges, TV room, 2 bars, dining room. No background music. 2-acre grounds. 200 yds from lake: private foreshore, fishing. Walking, sailing, climbing, riding, golf nearby. Unsuitable for ♿. No smoking. No children under 7. Dogs by arrangement; not in public rooms. No credit cards. D,B&B [2007] £62–£70 per person. Set dinner from £20. 1-night bookings sometimes refused.

Sharrow Bay

Ullswater
nr Penrith CA10 2LZ

Tel 01768-486301
Fax 01768-486349
Email info@sharrowbay.co.uk
Website www.sharrowbay.co.uk

On the eastern shore of Ullswater, looking to jagged Lakeland fells, this famous country house hotel (Relais & Châteaux) 'oozes a certain confidence', according to a visitor this year. Owned by von Essen hotels, it is managed by Andrew King. Recent comments: 'Rooms exceptionally comfortable; thoughtful provision of books and games.' 'Bedrooms chintzy, cosy, if dated. Fantastic views.' The long-serving chef, Colin Akrigg, has for ten years held a *Michelin* star for his 'refined classical cooking'. 'Superb spinach and Parmesan soufflé; tender fillet steak in Burgundy sauce; best-ever icky sticky toffee pudding. The staff, mostly young and foreign, were helpful without going over the top. Our table, in an alcove, overlooked the lake. The wine list, which resembled a small encyclopaedia, even included wine from India (we didn't try it).' The sitting rooms 'are beautifully furnished and decorated; it hasn't been all done up, so everything matches'. The bedrooms in the main building are small, but there are spacious rooms in the garden and in *Bank House*, up the hill (transport provided). 'Breakfast is wonderful.' But another visitor disliked the 'fixed mealtimes, breakfast at 9, dinner at 8; at these prices there should be more flexibility'. (*Gill Holden, and others*)

24 bedrooms. 6 in garden, 4 in lodge, 6 at *Bank House* (1¼ miles). 1 on ground floor (ramp, wide doors). E shore of Ullswater, 2 miles S of Pooley Bridge. 3 lounges, 2 dining rooms in main house; 2 lounges, breakfast room in *Bank House*. No background music. 12-acre grounds: gardens, woodland; ½-mile lake shore, safe (cold) bathing, pier. Civil wedding licence. No smoking. No children under 13. No dogs. Amex, MasterCard, Visa accepted. B&B [2007] £144–£210 per person. Set dinner £54. Christmas/New Year packages. 1-night bookings refused weekends in high season.

See also SHORTLIST

All our inspections are paid for, and carried out anonymously.

ULVERSTON Cumbria — Map 4: inset C2

The Bay Horse

Canal Foot
Ulverston LA12 9EL

Tel 01229-583972
Fax 01229-580502
Email reservations@thebayhorsehotel.co.uk
Website www.thebayhorsehotel.co.uk

'A lovely, restful place; one of the most glorious views anywhere,' writes a fan of this whitewashed 18th-century building. Once a staging post for coaches crossing the sands of Morecambe Bay, it stands at the water's edge of the Leven estuary. The hard-working owner, Robert Lyons, and manager, Lesley Wheeler, who have been here for 20 years, 'seem to enjoy what they do', and 'keep everything up to scratch'. This is 'more of an inn than a hotel' (no residents' lounge), but 'the staff's helpfulness is unmatched in my experience'. Bedrooms are 'small but well equipped'. 'Mine had been repainted, and had new curtains, bedding, lamps and mirror.' Front rooms have a balcony, binoculars and a bird-watching guide. 'At night there is only the sound of seabirds, and the most exciting thing to do is watch the tide dramatically come in.' In the conservatory restaurant overlooking the estuary, dinner is at 7.30 for 8. Robert Lyons 'delivers sound cooking with the accent on flavour'. 'Food is a major draw: we had tender salt marsh lamb and firm grilled salmon steak.' 'Impressive' breakfasts have fresh orange juice, 'proper tea'; 'excellent fried platter: white and black pudding, eggs with good yellowy yolks'; 'superb home-made raspberry jam'. (*Lynn Wildgoose*)

9 bedrooms. 8 miles NE of Barrow-in-Furness. Restaurant closed Mon midday. Bar lounge, restaurant; mixed/classical background music. Picnic area. Unsuitable for ♿. No smoking. No children under 12. Only guide dogs in restaurant. Amex, MasterCard, Visa accepted. B&B £43.75–£80 per person. Bar meals. Full alc £39–£45. Christmas/New Year packages.

VENTNOR Isle of Wight — Map 2:E2

The Hambrough

Hambrough Road
Ventnor PO38 1SQ

Tel 01983-856333
Fax 01983-857260
Email info@thehambrough.com
Website www.thehambrough.com

In 'fantastic' position, on quiet road above harbour, and by Ventnor's cascade gardens: small hotel, run by 'managing partner', Jo dos Santos. Contemporary decor. 'Good welcome, nice bedroom, excellent dinner, good, inexpensive wine list,' say visitors in 2007. Others wrote of 'spacious, quiet rooms; good linen; cheerful service; superb breakfast, with home-baked bread'. Bar lounge, restaurant (closed Tues); terrace; background music all day. Parking. Unsuitable for ♿. No smoking. No dogs. MasterCard, Visa accepted. 7 bedrooms. B&B double [2007] £99–£200. Set menus £30–£38.50. Christmas/New Year packages. *V*

The Wellington Hotel
Belgrave Road
Ventnor PO38 1JH

Tel 01983-856600
Fax 01983-856611
Email enquiries@thewellingtonhotel.net
Website www.thewellingtonhotel.net

'Stunningly located', built into cliffs above a safe, sandy beach, this hotel has 'grandstand views of waves' from its terraces and large sun deck. The decor is contemporary (bare floorboards in public areas). Visitors who arrived shortly after a total redecoration in early 2007 'were impressed by the smart interior' and their 'elegantly decorated, if smallish' bedroom. 'It was a delight to sit on our balcony in the sun, and take in the magnificent view' (all but two rooms face the sea). In the 'equally elegant', spacious dining room (two floors below the bedrooms; no lift), chef Rumen Gigov serves dishes like charred rib-eye steak; roasted rump of lamb. 'The menu didn't change during our stay, but the kitchen was flexible, adapting dishes to our preferences. An excellent base for a civilised break. An example of their willingness to put guests first: their positive response about replacing the duvet with sheets and blankets.' The manager, Marios Porfiropoullos, writes: 'Guests are the bosses. If someone wants a lie-in, late breakfast is arranged' (the breakfast is full English). 'Only criticisms: spasmodic service in the bar; shortage of parking (a few cramped spaces between hotel and road, otherwise the municipal car park, 200 yards away, £6 for 24 hours).' (*John Bickerdike*)

28 bedrooms. Some on ground floor. 5 mins' walk from centre. Limited off-street parking. Reception lounge, bar, restaurant (background music). Sun deck: steps to beach. Unsuitable for ♿. Smoking allowed in 10 bedrooms. No dogs. Amex, MasterCard, Visa accepted. B&B [2007] £59–£100 per person. Set dinner £20; full alc £28. Ferry-inclusive packages. Christmas/New Year packages. 1-night bookings refused Sat in season.

See also ***SHORTLIST***

If you are recommending a B&B and know of a good restaurant nearby, please mention it in your report.

VERYAN-IN-ROSELAND Cornwall Map 1:D2

The Nare
Carne Beach
Veryan
nr Truro TR2 5PF

Tel 01872-501111
Fax 01872-501856
Email office@narehotel.co.uk
Website www.narehotel.co.uk

César award in 2003

'Brilliant. Exceptional staff: many have been there for longer than we can remember; we always get a welcome. An amazing location.' Returning fans in 2007 still loved this unashamedly old-fashioned family hotel. It stands amid trim lawns and flowerbeds above a safe, sandy beach in the Roseland peninsula. Toby Ashworth, the owner/manager, entertains guests at a weekly cocktail party. Other praise: 'Hugely comfortable. A wonderful stay.' Two previous enthusiasts reported problems in summer 2006, leading one to decide not to go back. But the other returned later and found 'everything excellent, room, food, service'. *The Nare* appeals to a mature clientele but has no age restrictions on the young: 'Nice to see children of all ages, and family parties.' Bedrooms vary in the rambling building: 'Our deluxe double had big windows, patio with wonderful views, all comforts and a decanter of sherry.' Sound insulation may not always be perfect. Dinner in the main restaurant is an 'event'; jacket and tie 'preferred' for men. 'The atmosphere was British Landed Gentry *en masse*.' One diner was unhappy with supplements on lobster and fish dishes, and thought the mark-ups on wine 'too high'. Suppers and light lunches are served in the less formal *Quarterdeck* restaurant (alfresco in summer). (*Joanna Russell, Ann H Edwards, John and Sarah Leathes, and others*)

39 bedrooms. Some on ground floor. 1 suitable for ♿. S of Veryan, on coast. Lift, ramps. Lounge, drawing room, sun lounge, bar, billiard room, light lunch/supper room, 2 restaurants, conservatory; indoor swimming pool, spa bath, sauna, gym. No background music. 5-acre grounds: garden, heated swimming pool, tennis, croquet, children's play area, safe sandy beach, fishing. Concessionary golf at Truro golf club. No smoking. No dogs in public rooms. Amex, MasterCard, Visa accepted. B&B [2007] £95–£292 per person; D,B&B (min. 3 nights) £110–£307. Set dinner £41. Christmas/New Year packages.

'Set menu' indicates a fixed-price meal, with ample, limited or no choice. 'Full alc' is the hotel's estimated price per person of a three-course *à la carte* meal, with a half bottle of house wine. 'Alc' is the price of an *à la carte* meal excluding the cost of wine.

WAREHAM Dorset — Map 2:E1

The Priory

Church Green
Wareham BH20 4ND

Tel 01929-551666
Fax 01929-554519
Email reservations@theprioryhotel.co.uk
Website www.theprioryhotel.co.uk

César award in 1996

'Excellent as always, service cannot be faulted. Our favourite haven from a busy life,' writes a returning visitor. Owned by Anne Turner with brother-in-law, Stuart, and managed by her son, Jeremy Merchant, the former Priory of Lady St Mary (16th-century) stands by the River Frome. It is approached across a green with coloured Georgian houses, and a flagstoned courtyard. Earlier praise: 'Meets all my criteria for a really good hotel: proper orange juice; no muzak; staff address you by name; good lighting for reading in bed; room serviced while you dine.' The bedrooms vary greatly in size and aspect; some have a four-poster. 'We loved our Boathouse suite: lots of space and a big spa bath, such a treat after a long walk over the Purbeck hills.' Public rooms are in 'country house style'. An upstairs lounge faces garden, river and meadows. Drinks in the beamed drawing room precede dinner in the stone-vaulted Abbots' Cellar. Lunch is served in the Garden Room or alfresco in fine weather. Christopher Lee's 'modern English' cooking was enjoyed (eg, sea bass with basil mashed potatoes, spaghetti vegetables, tomato and aniseed coulis). The Turner family also own *The Casterbridge*, Dorchester (*qv*). (*Elizabeth Pratt, and others*)

18 bedrooms. 4 in Boathouse. Some on ground floor (in courtyard). Central. Ramps. 2 lounges (1 with pianist Sat night), bar, 2 dining rooms. 4-acre gardens: croquet; river frontage: moorings, fishing; bicycle hire. Unsuitable for ♿. No smoking. No children under 14. Guide dogs only. All major credit cards accepted. B&B [to 31 March 2008] £107.50–£172.50 per person; D,B&B £122.50–£187.50. Set dinner £38.50. Off-season breaks. Christmas/New Year packages. 1-night bookings refused weekends.

WARMINSTER Wiltshire — Map 2:D1

Crockerton House NEW

Crockerton Green
Warminster BA12 8AY

Tel 01985-216631
Email stay@crockertonhouse.co.uk
Website www.crockertonhouse.co.uk

Formerly the owners of *The Old Rectory*, Martinhoe, on Exmoor, Christopher and Enid Richmond have 'painstakingly restored' this 'gorgeous' Georgian house. 'Their taste cannot be faulted,' says an inspector in 2007. 'All is fresh and clean. Inherited antiques and new furnishings are in keeping; old features have been judiciously preserved. Chris is a pleasant front-of-house. Our large, light room, with king-size bed and big windows overlooking the gardens, was a pleasant place to sit and read.' Two bedrooms have a bathroom *en suite*; the third has a bathroom adjacent. All have flat-screen TV and Wi-Fi. An Aga-cooked dinner, at 8, is served by arrangement ('pleasant mushroom risotto, pork a bit overcooked; home-made meringues with strawberries'). No licence; bring your own wine. 'Breakfast was elegantly presented. Excellent bread, home-made preserves'; also freshly squeezed juice, organic cereals, eggs, bacon, etc, and a dish of the day, eg, pancakes. Visitors who arrive before 5 pm are served free tea, at a large table under a tree in the garden if weather permits. The grounds, with hedges, herbaceous borders, an orchard and a kitchen garden, face meadows that lead down to the River Wylye, in a designated area of outstanding natural beauty.

3 bedrooms. 2 miles S of Warminster. Closed Christmas. Dining room closed Sun night. Drawing room, dining room. No background music. 1¼-acre garden. Unsuitable for ♿. No smoking. No children under 12. No pets. MasterCard, Visa accepted. B&B [2007] £36–£97 per person. Set dinner £28.

WARTLING East Sussex — Map 2:E4

Wartling Place

Wartling, Herstmonceux
nr Eastbourne
BN27 1RY

Tel 01323-832590
Fax 01323-832558
Email accom@wartlingplace.prestel.co.uk
Website www.countryhouseaccommodation.co.uk

On a hill near the 13th-century church in a hamlet overlooking Pevensey Levels, this early 18th-century Grade II listed ex-rectory is now an upmarket B&B, run by its owners, Barry and Rowena Gittoes. They tell us that Wi-Fi is now available. The 'beautifully finished', spacious bedrooms have cream carpet, Egyptian cotton bedlinen, large, fluffy towels, flat-screen TV and DVD-player. The two best rooms have an antique four-poster bed. There is 'amazingly generous' storage space. Some guests have noticed slight road noise, but this is mitigated by padded blinds and thick curtains. Staircases in this former rest home have short, wide flights. There are comfortable settees and chairs, antiques, an honesty bar in the elegant lounge, and a long, polished breakfast table by the windows. The 'exceptional' breakfast, served between 8.30 and 9 am (9.30 at weekends), includes fruit, kedgeree, omelettes, waffles with maple syrup, full English, freshly baked rolls. The garden has paths and a patio with fountain. An evening meal is available by arrangement; for dining out, *The Lamb*, an 'excellent' gastropub, almost opposite, is recommended, and there is a list of other eating places. Returning guests get a 'one-off package: three nights for the price of two'. (*MI, and others*)

4 bedrooms. Also self-catering cottage. 3 miles N of Pevensey. Lounge/dining room with honesty bar and CD-player (classical background music all day). 3-acre garden. Unsuitable for ♿, except ground floor of cottage. No smoking. No dogs. Amex, MasterCard, Visa accepted. B&B £57.50–£135 per person. Evening meal by advance arrangement £37.50. Golf, Christmas/New Year packages. 1-night bookings occasionally refused weekends in season.

WARWICK Warwickshire *See SHORTLIST* Map 3:C6

WASDALE HEAD Cumbria Map 4: inset C2

Wasdale Head Inn
Wasdale Head
nr Gosforth CA20 1EX

Tel 019467-26229
Fax 019467-26334
Email wasdaleheadinn@msn.com
Website www.wasdale.com

A returning visitor still loved this informal three-gabled inn, popular with climbers and hikers. Long run by Howard and Kate Christie, it stands in a garden with stream and woodpeckers, seven miles up a dead-end road. 'Stunning setting [at the head of remote, unspoiled Wasdale, which has England's deepest lake, highest mountain and smallest church]. Welcome as warm, breakfasts as tasty, value as good as ever. A cosy, companionable atmosphere.' A dissenter, however, complained of poor maintenance and 'loud, thumping music from the staff quarters' when Mr Christie was away. The decor is traditional: solid old furniture, wood panelling, climbing photographs; books and games in the residents' lounge. Bedrooms are 'comfortable, if dated'. In the hotel's *Abraham's Restaurant*, Roy Sewell (new this year) serves fairly traditional dishes, eg, pork fillet with savoury baked apple, brandy cream and prune sauce. Or you can eat in *Ritson's Bar* (named after the inn's first landlord, a famous liar). The inn's micro-brewery produces 'excellent' beers. Breakfast has a buffet (cereals, fruit, yogurt, local honey and preserves); 'an enormous fry-up', or 'ham and haddie'. Packed lunches and cream teas are available. The 'Bah Humbug' Christmas package has 'no crackers, no silly hats, no Santas', instead a picnic lunch (sandwiches, Mars bars, crisps) to be eaten in the hills. (*Trevor Lockwood, and others*)

15 bedrooms. 2 on ground floor. 3 in adjacent barn. 6 self-catering apartments. 10 miles NE of Gosforth. Restaurant may close midweek in winter. No TV (poor reception). Ramps. Lounge, residents' bar, public bar, dining room; drying room. No background music. 3-acre grounds: beer garden, stream, pond, fitness trail. Unsuitable for ♿. No smoking. No dogs. B&B £59 per person. Bar meals, picnic lunches. Set dinner £28. Christmas/New Year packages. 1-night bookings sometimes refused weekends.

WATERMILLOCK Cumbria — Map 4: inset C2

Rampsbeck

Watermillock on Ullswater
nr Penrith CA11 0LP

Tel 01768-486442
Fax 01768-486688
Email enquiries@rampsbeck.co.uk
Website www.rampsbeck.co.uk

'You couldn't have a better setting' for this white-fronted 18th-century house built by a Victorian industrialist. It stands in large grounds on the shores of Lake Ullswater in 'lovely gardens with unusual plants and well-tended lawns'. The 'hands-on' owners, Tom and Marion Gibb, run it with her mother, Mrs MacDowall. 'Mrs Gibb exudes hospitality, and has a cheerful countenance from dawn till well after dusk,' says a trusted *Guide* correspondent. 'She is ubiquitous and has the knack of selecting first-class staff.' Public rooms 'retain their original feel: rich colours, reproduction lamps and furniture, large fireplaces'. The best bedrooms have lake views and a balcony where a continental breakfast can be taken. 'Ours was spacious, well fitted but not very well lit; old-fashioned but right for the house. The comfortable bed had quality blankets. Bathrooms are modern, with excellent lighting and plumbing. Good housekeeping.' The cooking of Andrew McGeorge, the long-serving chef, is a major draw. 'We enjoyed roasted pigeon breast on rösti; a splendid roasted beef fillet with chicken and mushroom tortellini; well-presented cold desserts. Not cheap, but value for money.' Breakfast, fully served, 'has comprehensive choice; extra helpings of juice'. (*Zara Elliott, Ian and Francine Walsh, John Chute*)

19 bedrooms. 5½ miles SW of Penrith. Open mid-Feb–4 Jan. 2 lounges, bar, restaurant. No background music. 19-acre grounds: croquet; lake frontage: fishing, sailing, windsurfing, etc. Unsuitable for ♿. Civil wedding licence. No smoking. No young children in restaurant at night. Dogs allowed in 3 bedrooms; not in public rooms, except hall. MasterCard, Visa accepted. B&B [2007] £65–£135 per person; D,B&B £105–£175. Set menus £39.50–£47. Christmas/New Year packages. 1-night bookings occasionally refused.

WATH-IN-NIDDERDALE North Yorkshire Map 4:D3

The Sportsman's Arms
Wath-in-Nidderdale, Pateley Bridge
nr Harrogate HG3 5PP

Tel 01423-711306
Fax 01423-712524
Email info@sportsmansarms.fsnet.co.uk
Website www.sportsmans-arms.co.uk

Popular with sporting visitors and walkers (and, with one exception, *Guide* readers), this unpretentious but smart Dales pub has been run by Ray and Jane Carter for almost 30 years. 'The accommodation, ambience, food and wine can only be described as outstanding,' said visitors in 2007. Others agreed: 'A very well-run operation; the staff, Turkish, Thai and Yorkshire, were charming, helpful.' The 'wonderful location', close to an old packhorse bridge on the River Nidd, and 'splendidly varied' clientele 'made a weekend fun'. Locally, there is good shooting, walking, birdwatching and fishing (rights on the Nidd). Mr Carter works in the kitchen with his head chef, Seth Marsland, and his son, Jamie. They serve an English menu 'with a French flavour' in both bar and restaurant: 'We enjoyed local pheasant and rib-eye steak; rhubarb sticky date pudding; more than enough fresh vegetables.' The 'first-class' breakfast is served at 9 am ('unless you would like it earlier'); 'proper butter, blackberry jam, honey and marmalade, decent coffee and excellent cooked dishes'. Some of the bedrooms are in a converted barn and stables around the courtyard. 'Our room was smallish but adequate; no bath but a super shower. With silence all round, we slept well.' (*Gwyn Morgan, Roger Perrin, David and Joan Marston*)

11 bedrooms. 6 in barns and stables (25 yds). 1 on ground floor. 1½ miles NW of Pateley Bridge. Closed 25 Dec. 2 lounges, public bar (background music 'when quiet'), restaurant; private dining/meeting room. 1-acre garden. River 150 yds (fishing). Unsuitable for ♿. No smoking. No dogs: restaurant, bedrooms. MasterCard, Visa accepted. B&B £60–£65 per person. Full alc £28–£38. Midweek breaks.

WELLS Somerset Map 1:B6

Canon Grange
Cathedral Green
BA5 2UB

Tel 01749-671800
Email canongrange@email.com
Website www.canongrange.co.uk

Annette Sowden's friendly B&B in 15th-century listed house, facing cathedral's magnificent west front (floodlit at night). Ask for a room (No. 3 or No. 4) with that view (it is also seen from the breakfast table). Cathedral wall runs through the 5-acre garden. Exposed beams, walnut furniture. Sitting room, dining room (church music). Breakfast English, vegetarian or 'lighter' (for dieters); evening meal by arrangement (£18–£20). No smoking. No dogs. MasterCard, Visa accepted. 5 bedrooms with period decor (1 family, 1 on ground floor). B&B [2007] £31.50–£50 per person. 1-night bookings sometimes refused Sat. More reports, please.

WEST STOKE West Sussex — Map 2:E3

West Stoke House
West Stoke, nr Chichester
PO18 9BN

Tel 01243-575226
Fax 01243-574655
Email info@weststokehouse.co.uk
Website www.weststokehouse.co.uk

César award: Restaurant-with-rooms of the year

Once a dower house to the Goodwood estate, this beautiful white-painted Georgian mansion stands in large grounds, in glorious country on the edge of the South Downs. Rowland and Mary Leach run it informally with their 'supremely professional' manager, Richard Macadam, and 'first-class' staff. 'The charmingly eccentric owner with out-of-control hair wears shorts all year round. An affable man, he loves his house, and delights in showing guests around.' A 'masterpiece of idiosyncratic chic', it has antiques on polished floorboards in the public rooms. 'An interesting collection of mismatched, comfortable chairs', plenty of art on display, most of it by local artists and for sale. An extra bedroom has been added this year. 'Our large room had comfortable bed, good carpet, garden views through large sash windows. It was thoughtfully furnished (some nice antiques). Trendy fittings. Bathroom with powerful shower. Everything exuded quality.' Drinks are served in a spacious lounge (which also serves as the reception area). The blue-walled dining room, with views over the grounds, was originally the ballroom ('pure Jane Austen'). It has tables 'properly laid with white tablecloths, good cutlery and glass', a large chandelier and a musician's alcove. Chef Darren Brown's cooking 'gets better and better'; dishes include fillet of bream, creamed potatoes, garlic palette, mussel cream reduction. The 'equally good' English breakfast, served until 10 am, includes free-range eggs from the West Stoke hens. Weddings and other celebrations are held. (*BB*)

6 bedrooms. 3 miles NW of Chichester. Closed Christmas. Restaurant closed Sun evening/Mon/Tues. Lounge, restaurant; background music; ballroom. 5-acre grounds: garden games. Unsuitable for ♿. Civil wedding licence. No smoking. 'Small, well-behaved' dogs only, not in restaurant. Amex, MasterCard, Visa accepted. B&B [2007] £75–£95 per person; D,B&B £114–£134. Set menus £22.50–£49.50. New Year package. 1-night bookings refused weekends.

WESTON-SUPER-MARE Somerset — Map 1:B6

See SHORTLIST

WHITBY North Yorkshire *See SHORTLIST* — Map 4:C5

WHITEWELL Lancashire — Map 4:D3

The Inn at Whitewell NEW

Forest of Bowland
nr Clitheroe BB7 3AT

Tel 01200-448222
Fax 01200-448298
Email reception@innatwhitewell.com
Website www.innatwhitewell.com

Owned by the Duchy of Lancaster, managed by Charles Bowman, this quirky inn has a lovely setting above the River Hodder, deep in the Forest of Bowland (good walking). Family antiques and old paintings are everywhere, and there is an art gallery. Some bathrooms have antique plumbing. Log fires warm the public rooms. The inn was omitted from the *Guide* last year, but new reports urge its reinstatement, despite some reservations. Staff are generally thought 'exceptionally friendly', 'really helpful', but some visitors found Reception 'brusque', meal service disorganised, and a room in the annexe unappealing. Others wrote: 'Our bedroom, one of the newest, was huge, beautifully furnished, with river view, but in the lovely bathroom, the fittings seemed more designer-led than practical.' 'Delightful rooms, individually designed. Food consistently delicious, served in relaxed manner.' 'Rare, tender local beef and lamb; interesting starters. Good breakfasts: freshly squeezed orange juice, good fruit, porridge with cream and honey, full English.' 'The spacious bars have a different, also excellent, menu.' There is a 'pleasant suntrap garden'. The inn owns seven miles of fishing for salmon, trout, etc. Children are welcomed, and 'many dogs are regular customers'. (*Mary Milne-Day, Sara Price, Mrs GS Wolstenholme, and others*)

23 bedrooms. 4 (2 on ground floor) in coach house, 150 yds. 6 miles NW of Clitheroe. 3 bars, restaurant, board room, orangery. No background music. 5-acre garden: riverside lawn, 7 miles fishing (ghillie available). Unsuitable for ♿. Civil wedding licence. No smoking. MasterCard, Visa accepted. B&B £81–£120 per person. Full alc £33.70.

WHITSTABLE Kent — Map 2:D5

Windy Ridge
Wraik Hill
Whitstable CT5 3BY

Tel 01227-263506
Email scott@windyridgewhitstable.co.uk
Website www.windyridgewhitstable.co.uk

'How comfortable it felt.' Visitors in 2007 to Hugh and Lynda Scott's B&B wrote of the 'welcome and help given to our three toddlers, which would not be found in upmarket hotels'. The Scotts 'offer great value', and 'remember guests' names'. 'They could not have been kinder to me and my dog (no extra charge),' said an earlier report (they have two retrievers of their own). This characterful conversion of two former farm cottages stands by a small country road uphill from the town centre, and has panoramic views of town and sea. There are beamed ceilings, a wood-burning stove in the 'cosy' lounge, and cast iron fireplaces. The bedrooms 'have been refurbished to a very high standard': four were upgraded in 2007. One has a four-poster bed, and there are two two-room family suites (one with a living area, the other with private access from the garden). 'Great value.' 'The dining room, facing the estuary, is lovely.' Breakfast, 'done superbly', has healthy and vegetarian options and meat from local butchers. An evening meal is available by arrangement, and the Scotts 'went out of their way to help with restaurant bookings'. (*Nigel Grunberg, VH*)

10 bedrooms. 3 on ground floor. 1 suitable for ♿. 1½ miles from centre, off A299. Parking. Closed part of Nov. Lounge, bar, dining room (low background music); meeting/conference facilities. ½-acre garden: gazebo. Civil wedding licence. No smoking. Dogs allowed in 1 bedroom. MasterCard, Visa accepted. B&B £40–£50 per person. Christmas/New Year packages. 1-night bookings refused weekends in season. *V*

WICKHAM Hampshire — Map 2:E2

The Old House
The Square
Wickham PO17 5JG

Tel 01329-833049
Fax 01329-833672
Email oldhousehotel@aol.com
Website www.oldhousehotel.co.uk

On the huge main square (quiet at night) of this delightful old village in the Meon valley, this red brick, creeper-covered, Grade II listed early Georgian town house is owned and managed by Paul and Lesley Scott. It has some characterful rooms in main house (some have sloping beams). 'Nice bathroom, shame about the liquid soap,' wrote a returning visitor, who had 'a comfortable room over the restaurant' and found the hotel 'as good as we remembered'. Four contemporary rooms (with king-size or super-king-size bed) are in the newly refurbished annexe, a self-contained block outside the walled garden area, down a steep gravel drive. 'Ours was comfortable, well equipped,' says a visitor who stayed for three nights in 2007. 'A large, superb bathroom, though we found the "wet room" layout awkward: water went everywhere. The espresso machine for tea- and coffee-making was stylish. The excellent flat-screen television worked perfectly, a rarity in many hotels.' Everyone agrees about the 'friendly, efficient' service and the 'very good' cooking of chef Ben Streak ('classic with a contemporary influence'). 'Ample selection of wines by the glass.' Breakfast has a 'lavish' buffet and a good choice of cooked dishes to order (they cost extra). (*Sara Price, John Griffith*)

15 bedrooms. 4 in annexe. Also self-catering cottage. 3 miles N of Fareham. Closed 26–30 Dec. Restaurant closed Sun evening. Lounge (large fireplace), bar, restaurant; background music; private dining/conference room; function room. ¼-acre walled garden. Civil wedding licence. Unsuitable for ♿. No smoking. No dogs. Amex, MasterCard, Visa accepted. B&B £42.50–£75 per person. English breakfast £10. Full alc £36.50.

WILLINGTON Cheshire *See SHORTLIST* Map 3:A5

WILMINGTON East Sussex Map 2:E4

Crossways Hotel

Lewes Road
Wilmington BN26 5SG

Tel 01323-482455
Fax 01323-487811
Email stay@crosswayshotel.co.uk
Website www.crosswayshotel.co.uk

In an affluent village in the Cuckmere valley, this pretty country house is 'ideally placed for Glyndebourne'. The hosts, David Stott (the chef) and Clive James, whose 'welcome gets warmer' every year, are 'well attuned to the particular requirements of the opera set'. No guest lounge, but bedrooms contain 'every appliance imaginable: fridge, TV, clock, knick-knacks galore'. 'Something of a time warp: furnishings from the 1960s.' Some rooms have a sofa; one has a balcony. The four-course dinner menu, served in an intimate dining room, changes monthly; local produce is used where possible, eg, organic guineafowl, lentils with bacon and garlic. 'Quality was good, but we would have liked the option of fewer courses,' one visitor wrote. Breakfast is 'fresh, delicious, copious'. Other praise: 'No heavy weather is made of a two- or three-night single booking. No exorbitant supplement charged.' 'They uncomplainingly chilled wine for a picnic.' The large garden, with a pond, rabbits and a herb garden, runs down to a main road which is 'relentlessly busy', even at night. (*RP, and others*)

7 bedrooms. Also self-catering cottage. 6 miles NW of Eastbourne on A27. Closed 24 Dec–24 Jan. Restaurant closed midday, and Sun/Mon. Breakfast room, restaurant (light classical background music). 2-acre grounds: duck pond. Unsuitable for ♿. No smoking. No children under 12. No dogs. Amex, MasterCard, Visa accepted. B&B £52.50–£70 per person. Set dinner £36.95.

WINCHCOMBE Gloucestershire Map 3:D5

Wesley House

High Street
Winchcombe GL54 5LJ

Tel 01242-602366
Fax 01242-609046
Email enquiries@wesleyhouse.co.uk
Website www.wesleyhouse.co.uk

Named after John Wesley, who stayed here twice, Matthew Brown's 'quirky' restaurant-with-rooms is liked for its balance between the medieval and the modern. On the main street of an attractive town on the North Cotswold Edge, the 15th-century half-timbered building has old beams, inglenook fireplaces, comfortable seating. The restaurant is on two tiers, with an atrium where drinks and breakfast are served; there is a separate wine bar and bistro. The stylish bedrooms, up a steep staircase, have good lighting and storage, a Thermos flask of milk; all but one are small, as are some bathrooms. Some get street noise, and one faces the kitchen of the pub next door, lively until late. One room has a private terrace. The modern dishes of chef Martin Dunn are enjoyed (eg, breast of duck with sweet and sour cabbage). The 'excellent' breakfast has waiter service. More reports, please.

5 bedrooms. Central. Closed 25/26 Dec. Restaurant closed Sun evening, except bank holidays. Lounge/bar ('easy listening' background music in bar area), bar/bistro, restaurant, atrium dining room; function facilities. Unsuitable for ♿. Civil wedding licence. No smoking. Babies in cots or 'children old enough to have their own room' welcome. No dogs. Amex, MasterCard, Visa accepted. B&B [2007] £40–£65 per person; D,B&B £90–£130. Set dinner £29.50–£38. New Year package. 1-night bookings sometimes refused bank holidays and race week. ***V*** (not Sat)

Always discuss accommodation in detail when making a booking, and don't hesitate to ask for an upgrade on arrival if a hotel is clearly not full.

WINCHELSEA East Sussex — Map 2:E5

The Strand House
Tanyard's Lane
Winchelsea TN36 4JT

Tel 01797-226276
Fax 01797-224806
Email info@thestrandhouse.co.uk
Website www.thestrandhouse.co.uk

Backed by a green lawn and old trees, this Grade II listed half-timbered 15th-century malt house stands beneath Winchelsea's 13th-century Strand Gate. It has been 'beautifully renovated' by owner/managers, Janet and Peter Clarke, retaining ancient beams and inglenook fireplaces. It is liked for the warmth of the welcome and the excellent breakfast. *Michelin* awards a blue bib for quality combined with a reasonable price. 'Our room was comfortable, though low beams must be avoided,' said a recent visitor. One room has a four-poster; one is good for a family. There is a 'nice lounge' with log fire, and a garden with tall trees. The Clarkes will advise on nearby eating places. 'Though the house stands on a main road, it is far enough back for even our sensitive ears to be undisturbed.' A working National Trust farm is adjacent. Rye, Battle, Hastings, and Hever and Bodiam castles are near. More reports, please.

10 bedrooms. 1 on ground floor. 2 miles SW of Rye. 300 yds from centre. Parking. Reception, lounge, bar, breakfast room. 1-acre garden. Unsuitable for ♿. Sea 1 mile (safe bathing). No smoking. No children under 5. No dogs. Diners, MasterCard, Visa accepted. B&B [2007] £30–£50 per person. Christmas/New Year packages. 1-night bookings refused some weekends.

WINCHESTER Hampshire — Map 2:D2

Hotel du Vin Winchester
14 Southgate Street
Winchester SO23 9EF

Tel 01962-841414
Fax 01962-842458
Email info@winchester.hotelduvin.com
Website www.hotelduvin.com

Near the cathedral, this Grade II listed Queen Anne town house was converted in 1994 by Robin Hutson and Gerard Basset as the first in their small group of contemporary hotels dedicated to wine. In 2004, they sold the group to Marylebone Warwick Balfour which owns the Malmaison chain. We sent an inspector in 2007 to check progress. 'We enjoyed our stay with one reservation; the price of our double room was significantly more than last year. The room itself was spacious, well thought out: fluffy robes, good shower, large, comfy bed; fresh milk in fridge; bright lighting, lots of wardrobe space, marred only by captive hangers.' Another room was 'small, with nowhere to put clothes, a poor outlook, and noise from a fan'. In the bistro, 'a delightful, bright room with small but well-spaced tables', dinner was 'a success': 'Both fish dishes (sole and brill) met with acclaim; excellent loin of venison; vegetables (a side order) were generous and good. Worth keeping space for the puds, especially the crème brûlée. The wine list is a thing of wonder, as are the mark-ups. A welcome innovation, a "tasting flight" of three different glasses.' Breakfast had 'a good fruit selection, excellent eggs Benedict, poor kippers, tea-bag tea, hovering French staff'. 'Go for a garden room' (others hear traffic).

24 bedrooms. 4 in garden. 2 in cottage. 1 on ground floor. Central (rear rooms quietest). Car park. Station 10 mins' walk. Ramp. Lounge, bar, restaurant. No background music. Small walled garden: cigar shack; *boules*. Civil wedding licence. No smoking. Dogs allowed in garden rooms. All major credit cards accepted. Room [2007] £130–£220. Breakfast £9.95–£13.50. Full alc £55. Christmas/New Year packages.

See also SHORTLIST

WINDERMERE Cumbria — Map 4: inset C2

Gilpin Lodge
Crook Road
nr Windermere LA23 3NE

Tel 015394-88818
Fax 015394-88058
Email hotel@gilpinlodge.co.uk
Website www.gilpinlodge.co.uk

César award in 2000

'Superbly run; smoothness of service now even more impressive.' Praise in 2007 from regular visitors to the Cunliffe family's classic Edwardian country house hotel (Relais & Châteaux). Others agree: 'Everything exceptional.' 'Quietly and understatedly perfect.' 'Helpful, hands-on owners.' Set well back from the road, surrounded by moors, woodlands and gardens, it is run informally (no reception area, no bar). The Cunliffes say: 'No weddings or conferences, just the art of relaxation.' Each bedroom is named after a local beauty spot; some have a four-poster, some a whirlpool bath; many are spacious, with sitting area and good views. Six new garden suites were liked: 'Ours was decorated in contemporary style in neutral tones of browns, rusts and creams. Sliding patio doors opened on to a decking area with a hot tub.' In the four dining rooms, the cooking of chef Chris Meredith (*Michelin* star) 'was beautifully presented without being fussy; portions nicely judged' (eg, sausage of pike with watercress and crayfish). Lunches can be a full meal in the restaurant to a light one in the lounge. Afternoon teas are 'a work of art'. 'Sumptuous breakfast.' (*Wolfgang Stroebe, Bridget and David Reed, Virginia Murphy, Anne and Denis Tate*)

20 bedrooms. 6 in orchard wing. On B5284, 2 miles SE of Windermere. Ramps. 2 lounges, 4 dining rooms. No background music. 22-acre grounds: ponds, croquet. Free access to nearby country club: swimming pool, sauna, squash. Golf course opposite. Unsuitable for ♿. No smoking. No children under 7. No dogs (kennels at nearby farm). All major credit cards accepted. D,B&B [2007] £125–£180 per person. Set lunch £20–£25, dinner £47. Special breaks. Christmas/New Year packages. 1-night bookings sometimes refused weekends.

Holbeck Ghyll

Holbeck Lane
Windermere LA23 1LU

Tel 015394-32375
Fax 015394-34743
Email stay@holbeckghyll.com
Website www.holbeckghyll.com

'As good as we remembered. If you like a country house feel, this is for you,' says a returning visitor to David and Patricia Nicholson's luxurious hotel (Pride of Britain). Its large grounds, with streams, wildlife, tennis, slope down to the lake. There is a small spa. 'We were greeted by name, and helped with luggage. All the staff were friendly.' Other praise: 'A wonderful place, amazing service, sublime food.' 'Impeccable' public rooms have 'a baronial feel': stained glass, open fires, wood panelling, antiques; also free Internet access. This year a new suite, Miss Potter, opened (Renée Zellweger stayed here while making that film); *Madison House*, with three bedrooms, is also new.

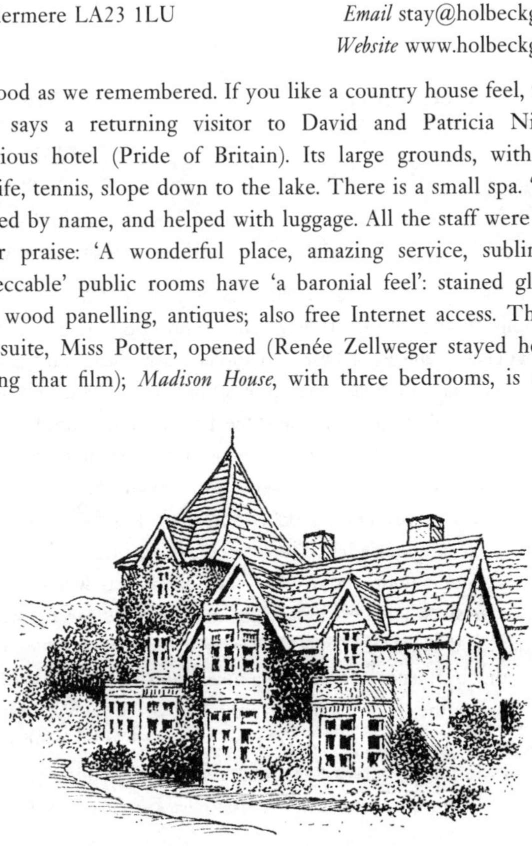

There are two dining rooms, one oak-panelled, the other with French windows that lead on to a terrace (with fountain) for alfresco meals. Chef David McLaughlin has a *Michelin* star: 'Tasty lamb with roasted garlic; steak so tender it could have been eaten with a fork; cherry clafoutis so good I had it again on the second night.' Breakfast has a large buffet, good cooked dishes. Some bedrooms (with balcony or patio) are in a lodge. 'One of the most relaxing breaks we have had.' (*Shirley Tennent, Samantha Taccy*)

23 bedrooms. 6 (1 with kitchenette) in lodge. 1 suitable for ♿. 3 miles N of Windermere off road to Ambleside. Closed 2–18 Jan. Ramp. 2 lounges (1 with background music), bar, restaurant; function facilities; small spa: sauna, steam room, massage, etc. 7-acre grounds: streams, ponds, woods to lake shore (800 yds), tennis, putting, croquet, jogging track. Civil wedding licence. No smoking. No children under 8 in restaurant. No dogs in public rooms. Amex, MasterCard, Visa accepted. B&B £100–£225 per person; D,B&B £120–£275. Set dinner £55. Off-season, Christmas/New Year packages. 1-night bookings sometimes refused Sat. *V*

WINSTER Derbyshire — Map 3:B6

The Dower House

Main Street
Winster, nr Matlock
DE4 2DH

Tel 01629-650931
Fax 01629-650932
Email fosterbig@aol.com
Website www.thedowerhousewinster.com

A visitor in 2007 had a 'most enjoyable stay' at John and Marsha Biggin's 'country house B&B', a Grade II listed 16th-century building in this conservation village in the Peak District national park. Last year's praise is endorsed. 'Bedrooms are generously proportioned and beautifully warm.' All have been redecorated this year. One has window seats facing the main street, another a stone fireplace and views through mullioned windows of the 'lovely walled garden'. Two rooms have an *en suite* bathroom, one a shower. The guests' sitting room has sofas and 'lots of pictures'; there is an honesty bar. The dining hall has original beams, sash windows, part stone floor and a wood fire. Breakfast, which includes home-made muesli, wholemeal bread, 'sausages from our award-winning farm butcher', and preserves from Chatsworth's farm shop, is 'delicious, particularly the local oatcake cushioning nicely yolked eggs'. A gate gives private access to the village churchyard. The driveway's entrance is 'rather narrow: be careful if you have a large car'. The 'cheerful' *Bowling Green* pub in the village serves 'generous, reasonable' food. The 'plague village' of Eyam, close by, is worth a visit. (*John Knighton, P and DE*)

4 bedrooms. 3 miles W of Matlock. Closed Christmas/New Year. Sitting room, bar, dining room ('subdued' classical background music sometimes at breakfast). ⅓-acre walled garden: pond. Unsuitable for ♿. No smoking. No children under 12. No dogs. No credit cards. B&B [2007] £47.50–£75 per person. 1-night bookings refused Fri/Sat in season.

WOBURN Bedfordshire *See SHORTLIST* Map 2:C3

WOLD NEWTON East Yorkshire Map 4:D5

The Wold Cottage
Wold Newton, nr Driffield
YO25 3HL

Tel/Fax 01262-470696
Email katrina@woldcottage.com
Website www.woldcottage.com

'Quite delightful', this 'grand and lovingly restored' red brick Georgian manor house in Yorkshire countryside was once a gentleman's retreat. 'Outstandingly peaceful,' says a visitor this year. Owners Katrina and Derek Gray are 'friendly, informative and most helpful'. With a neighbouring family, the Mellors, they run the Wold Top Brewery, using pure, chalk-filtered water from the farm to produce Mars Magic, Falling Stone and Wold Top Bitter (available by draught at their pub, *The Falling Stone*, two miles away, or sold here in bottles). Guests are welcomed with tea and cake. 'My room in the converted barn was spacious and well equipped.' Extras include dressing gowns, hot-water bottle, fresh milk in a flask. Dinner (arrange when booking) is served by candlelight, communally or at separate tables. 'Two choices of starter and dessert, home-made bread. Main course one night was salmon with hollandaise sauce, next night roast loin of pork. Fresh veg from the garden.' 'Like the best home cooking on dinner-party days. Very good value.' 'Breakfast was excellent, plenty of cereals, fresh fruit and yogurt, variations of full English or a variety of fish dishes, home-made bread and preserves.' (*Roger Perrin, Joan and David Marston*)

5 bedrooms. 2 in converted barn. 1 on ground floor. Just outside village. Lounge, dining room (background music at mealtimes). 3-acre grounds in 300-acre farmland: croquet. No smoking. No dogs. MasterCard, Visa accepted. B&B [2007] £35–£55 per person; D,B&B £51–£73.50. Set dinner £18.50.

Hotels will often try to persuade you to stay for two nights at the weekend. Resist this pressure if you want to stay only one night.

WOLTERTON Norfolk Map 2:A5

The Saracen's Head
Wolterton, nr Erpingham
NR11 7LX

Tel 01263-768909
Fax 01263-768993
Email saracenshead@wolterton.freeserve.co.uk
Website www.saracenshead-norfolk.co.uk

'As always the welcome is warm: polite inquiries about my family,' remarks a regular visitor to Robert Dawson-Smith's 'lost inn' (directions given when you book) in a quiet, rural setting. The 'hands-on' owner/ chef might be 'resplendent in cravat, chinos, checked shirt and denim apron'. It is a 'genuine family affair' – his daughter, Rachel, runs the Shed, a workshop selling retro furniture, pictures, etc. It won't suit all comers: 'too much of a pub' for some. Fans like the 'real bedrooms', with their iron bedsteads and patchwork quilts, though there is one complaint of poor lighting and feeble shower attachments. Three bedrooms, up steep steps, are in the roof; they have rounded dormer windows, sloping ceilings. 'Ours was fair-sized, done in bold colours.' All rooms have been redecorated this year. The public areas are 'cosy, candlelit, filled with paintings and bric-a-brac (a stuffed fox's head, etc)'. Everyone finds the cooking 'wonderful'; up to ten choices for each course are displayed on a daily-changing blackboard menu, eg, grilled halloumi on a lavender croûte; wok-sizzled sirloin with anchovy and tomato. In summer, meals are served alfresco. Breakfast ('especially good') includes freshly squeezed orange juice, fruit, fresh bread, good kippers. (*Tony Betts, RK*)

6 bedrooms. 5 miles from Aylsham. Closed 25/evening of 26 Dec. Lounge, 3 dining rooms. No background music. Courtyard. 1-acre garden: shop. Accommodation unsuitable for ♿. No smoking. No dogs in public rooms. Amex, MasterCard, Visa accepted. B&B £45–£50 per person. Full alc £32. Off-season rates. D,B&B packages. New Year package. 1-night bookings refused weekends.

WOODSTOCK Oxfordshire *See SHORTLIST* Map 2:C2

How to contact the *Guide*
By mail: From anywhere in the UK, write to Freepost PAM 2931, London W11 4BR (no stamp is needed)
From outside the UK: *Good Hotel Guide*, 50 Addison Avenue, London W11 4QP, England
By telephone or fax: 020-7602 4182
By email: Goodhotel@aol.com or Goodhotel@btinternet.com
Via our website: www.goodhotelguide.com

WORFIELD Shropshire — Map 3:C5

The Old Vicarage

Worfield
nr Bridgnorth WV15 5JZ

Tel 01746-716497
Fax 01746-716552
Email admin@the-old-vicarage.demon.co.uk
Website www.oldvicarageworfield.com

'Friendly owners and fine food,' say visitors this year about David and Sarah Blakstad's gabled, red brick Edwardian former parsonage in rural Shropshire. The large grounds contain a granite terrace and a manicured lawn, with statues and seats around venerable elms 'giving a continental air'. Most bedrooms have antique furniture; one has a Victorian four-poster, another a walnut half-tester bed. Three have been redecorated this year. Four luxury rooms are in a converted coach house. Pre-dinner drinks are taken on the patio in fine weather. In the *Orangery* restaurant (good views, bright and airy), the dress code is 'smart casual, no jeans please'. The chef, Simon Diprose, serves dishes like roast Gloucester Old Spot pork with truffled haricot beans, chestnut-spiked potato cake and port sauce. Breakfast has 'very good' sausages, smoked haddock with poached egg, kippers. 'Fruit included passion fruit and figs.' The Blakstads, parents themselves, write: 'While we have limited facilities for children, we actively encourage them to stay.' (*Francine and Ian Walsh, Conrad Barnard*)

14 bedrooms. 4 in coach house. 2 on ground floor. 2 suitable for ♿. 3 miles NE of Bridgnorth. Hotel closed Christmas/New Year. Restaurant closed Sat midday. Ramps. Lounge, bar, restaurant; occasional background music; 2 private dining rooms; small conference facilities. 2-acre grounds: patio, croquet. Civil wedding licence. No smoking. Only guide dogs in public rooms. Diners, MasterCard, Visa accepted. B&B [2007] £49.75–£80 per person; D,B&B £69.75–£110. Set dinner £33.50–£39.50.

WYE Kent *See SHORTLIST* — Map 2:D5

YARCOMBE Devon *See SHORTLIST* — Map 1:C5

> The *Guide* has hotels to meet most tastes and budgets. We are as pleased to hear about simple, cheaper hotels as we are about the better-known, expensive ones.

YARM North Yorkshire Map 4:C4

Judges
Kirklevington Hall
Yarm TS15 9LW

Tel 01642-789000
Fax 01642-782878
Email enquiries@judgeshotel.co.uk
Website www.judgeshotel.co.uk

In large, peaceful, wooded grounds, with stream, birds and 'lovely, well-kept landscaped gardens' (floodlit at night), the Downs family's Victorian house was once a residence for circuit judges. Tim Howard is the manager. 'A little old fashioned, but the comfortable bedroom had nice touches,' say visitors this year. 'Unusual extras' include a goldfish in a bowl and a request to feed it. Another guest 'was kept awake by the noisy fish' and added: 'The rooms have everything one might need, but my son found his bed too soft and slept instead on the floor.' Some rooms have a spa bath. Beds are turned down at night and shoes are shined. In the conservatory restaurant, with green-upholstered chairs and green carpet, chef John Schwarz serves 'modern French' dishes like cumin-spiced turbot; ox cheek with wild mushroom cannelloni. 'Portions not too large.' The extensive wine list includes some 'good buys'. Light meals can be taken during the day in the panelled bar or the lounge, with its antiques, fire and flowers. 'Breakfast a little unexciting, but cheerfully served.' 'Staff friendly and helpful throughout.' Tickets for York races can be arranged. Weddings are held. (*Michael and Eithne Dandy, Philippa and Stephen Parker*)

21 bedrooms. Some on ground floor. 1½ miles S of centre. Ramps. Lounge, bar, restaurant; private dining room; function facilities; business centre. No background music. 36-acre grounds: paths, running routes. Access to local spa and sports club. Civil wedding licence. Smoking allowed in 2 bedrooms. Guide dogs only. All major credit cards accepted. B&B [2007] £89.50–£163 per person; D,B&B £125–£197. Set dinner £44. Christmas/New Year packages. *V*

YEOVIL Somerset *See SHORTLIST* Map 1:C6

The *V* sign at the end of an entry indicates a hotel that has agreed to take part in our Voucher scheme and to give *Guide* readers a 25% discount on their room rates for a one-night stay, subject to the conditions explained in *How to use the Good Hotel Guide*, and given on the back of the vouchers.

YORK North Yorkshire — Map 4:D4

Middlethorpe Hall
Bishopthorpe Road
York YO23 2GB

Tel 01904-641241
Fax 01904-620176
Email info@middlethorpe.com
Website www.middlethorpe.com

The building is a major draw at this luxury hotel: a 'stunning' red brick William III house in a large park with a small lake and old trees and, inside, much panelling, carved wood, stuccoed ceilings, historic paintings, etc. It stands near York racecourse, and a drawback is the noise from traffic on the city's ring road, audible in the grounds and parts of the house. A Pride of Britain member, managed by Lionel Chatard, it has been restored by Historic House Hotels Ltd (see also *Hartwell House*, Aylesbury, *Bodysgallen Hall and Spa*, Llandudno). A report this year: 'I enjoyed my stay very much. We were given a beautiful suite in the annexe. Staff were charming, and the food was delicious.' The best bedrooms, some enormous with a sitting room and gas coal fire, are in the main house. Men are expected to wear jacket and tie in the formal dining room, in interlinked rooms facing the 'delightful' walled garden. Nicholas Evans is the new chef; his modern British dishes, served by candlelight, include honey-glazed pork belly with black pudding and red cabbage. There is also a simpler grill room. Breakfast disappointed: 'A meagre fruit salad and tired pastries; tea and cold toast took 25 minutes to arrive.' There is an 'inviting and stylish' spa in a converted coach house. (*Sue Kinder, and others*)

29 bedrooms. 2 in garden. 1 suitable for ♿. 17 in courtyard. 1½ miles S of centre, by racecourse. Drawing room, sitting rooms, library, bar, restaurant, grill room; private dining rooms; function facilities. No background music. 20-acre grounds: walled garden, white garden, croquet, lake; spa: health and beauty facilities, heated indoor 40 by 20-ft swimming pool. Civil wedding licence. No smoking. No children under 6. Guide dogs only. Amex, MasterCard, Visa accepted. B&B (continental) £92.50–£215 per person; English breakfast £6.95 extra. Set dinner £41.50–£55. Christmas/New Year packages.

See also SHORTLIST

> Inevitably, some hotels change hands or close after we have gone to press. You should always check the ownership when booking, particularly in the case of small establishments.

ZENNOR Cornwall — Map 1:D1

The Gurnard's Head NEW

Treen, nr Zennor
St Ives TR26 3DE

Tel 01736-796928
Email enquiries@gurnardshead.co.uk
Website www.gurnardshead.co.uk

In March 2006, Charles and Edmund Inkin, owners of the *Felin Fach Griffin* inn, in Wales (*qv*), bought this building in rundown condition. Painted lemon yellow, it stands on a coastal road in a hamlet surrounded by 'beautiful coastal moorland', with Atlantic views. They tell us: 'Without losing its spirit of a community pub, we have overhauled the dining room and bar.' Bedroom refurbishment is continuing: there are comfortable beds, Welsh blankets, Roberts radios, local art and photography, and a 'rustic' feel. Andrew Wood and Matthew Williamson have come from *Felin Fach* to be manager and chef. Visitors who knew the place of old 'were staggered to see the changes. Lovely up-to-date decor, light and airy, Mediterranean in feel. Bleached floorboards, large, squashy sofas, newspapers, books, all very relaxed. Feel of a gastropub. Quite remote, with beautiful sea views and a great walk down to a cove. Sunday lunch was one of the best we have had; huge ribs of beef.' On the dinner menu are fish stew; oxtail ravioli. The 'delicious' cooked breakfast is served between 8 and 10 am; packed lunches are available. Children of all ages are welcomed (cots, high chairs). Dogs are welcomed too (no charge): they can sit with their owners in the bar. (*Felicity and Susannah Wilson, and others*)

7 bedrooms. 6 miles SW of St Ives, on B3306. Bar area (background CDs), small room with sofas, dining room (radio by breakfast table for guests' use). 1-acre garden. Unsuitable for ♿. No smoking. MasterCard, Visa accepted. B&B £36.25–£60. Full alc £24. *V*

****

Traveller's tale Perhaps the scaffolding over the door and workmen in action everywhere should have warned me that the hotel was, to put it politely, in a state of flux. I rang for service. A healthy young man appeared, we registered, and he gave us keys, telling us that our rooms were on the first floor, and pointing at a staircase. He presumably thought my 86-year-old mother enjoyed carrying her cases up stairs, through stiff fire doors and along narrow corridors. The bedrooms were adequately equipped, but stifling hot and immediately above the noisy public bar. (*Hotel in Scotland*)

****

Scotland

Hotels in Scotland are flourishing thanks to rising standards of hospitality and cooking, and to the continuing expansion of low-cost flights in the United Kingdom. This year we welcome no fewer than 16 new entries to our Scottish chapter. Some are interesting discoveries: a lighthouse conversion near Stranraer, and a small inn in a remote setting on the Kintyre peninsula. Others, like *The Peat Inn*, in Fife, and *Cleaton House*, on Orkney, are old favourites returning under hospitable new ownership.

The Dower House, Muir of Ord

ABERDEEN *See SHORTLIST* Map 5:C3

ACHILTIBUIE Highland Map 5:B1

Summer Isles Hotel
Achiltibuie
by Ullapool IV26 2YG

Tel 01854-622282
Fax 01854-622251
Email info@summerisleshotel.co.uk
Website www.summerisleshotel.co.uk

César award in 1993

Up a single-track road north of Ullapool, this popular 'croft-style' hotel/restaurant has 'wonderful views' over the sea to the Summer Isles and the Hebrides. 'It is extremely comfortable, run to the highest standards,' says a report in 2007. All bedrooms are 'full of personal touches'. Three rooms are in the house; other bedrooms are in an annexe; log cabin-style rooms are 'very comfortable'; the *Boat House* suite (a new bathroom this year) is in a stone cottage by the road. 'The restaurant runs like a well-oiled machine: superb food and service.' Chef Chris Firth-Bernard has a *Michelin* star for his five-course menus (no choice; dietary requirements accommodated): typical dishes, eg, filo parcel of monkfish tails; haunch of venison with pancetta and juniper. 'Superb cooking. You are encouraged to have both sweet and cheese trolleys. Extensive wine list; they suggested acceptable, reasonably priced wines to go with the main course.' The bar, a friendly local, serves meals with a bias towards fish until 8.30 pm. Breakfasts have home-made bread and rolls, muesli, fruit; cooked dishes include 'outstanding smoked haddock'. 'There is a marvellous amount of nothing to do,' write the hotel's owners, Mark and Gerry Irvine. As we went to press, *Summer Isles* was put on the market. An early sale is not anticipated, but prospective visitors should check the position before booking. (*Richard and Catriona Smith; also Peter and Audrey Hutchinson*)

13 bedrooms. Some in annexe and cottages. NW of Ullapool. Open 25 Mar–16 Oct. Sitting room, sun lounge, cocktail bar, public bar, restaurant. No background music. Small garden. Sea 100 yds. Unsuitable for ♿. No smoking. No children under 8. Dogs by arrangement; not in public rooms. MasterCard, Visa accepted. B&B £62.50–£150 per person. Bar lunches. Set dinner £52.

ALYTH Perth and Kinross *See SHORTLIST* Map 5:D2

ARDUAINE Argyll and Bute *See SHORTLIST* Map 5:D1

ARISAIG Highland *See SHORTLIST* Map 5:C1

ASCOG Argyll and Bute *See SHORTLIST* Map 5:D1

AVIEMORE Highland Map 5:C2

Corrour House
Inverdruie, Rothiemurchus
by Aviemore
PH22 1QH

Tel 01479-810220
Fax 01479-811500
Email enquiries@corrourhousehotel.co.uk
Website www.corrourhousehotel.co.uk

In a lovely rural setting of woodland and gardens, Robert Still's bay-windowed former dower house of the Rothiemurchus estate has 'outstanding' views across to the Lairig Ghru pass and the Cairngorms. Recent visitors thought it a 'house of real antique character, scrupulously maintained. Immense trouble is taken to make sure guests have all they need, and to give them information about the neighbourhood.' There are open fires in the traditionally furnished lounges; bedrooms are 'chintzy'. Dinner is now served by arrangement, as there is not always sufficient demand, and plenty of eating places are nearby. Paul Waters, the 'seasonal' chef, uses 'local produce in a French style', eg, venison with a bitter chocolate sauce. At night, you might see deer cross the lawn. (*R and PC*)

8 bedrooms. ¾ mile S of Aviemore. Open New Year–mid-Nov. Dinner by arrangement. Lounge, cocktail bar (background music when guest numbers are small), dining room. 4-acre gardens and woodland. Unsuitable for ♿. No smoking. No dogs: public rooms or unsupervised in bedrooms. MasterCard, Visa accepted. B&B £35–£55 per person; D,B&B £68.50–£78.50. Set dinner £29.50. Reductions for 3 or more nights. New Year package. 1-night bookings refused in season. *V*

AYR South Ayrshire *See SHORTLIST* Map 5:E1

For details of the Voucher scheme see page 62.

BALLATER Aberdeenshire — Map 5:C3

Balgonie Country House
Braemar Place
Ballater AB35 5NQ

Tel 013397-55482
Fax 013397-55497
Email balgoniech@aol.com
Website www.balgonie-hotel.co.uk

'We cannot fault it,' says a visitor in 2007 to this creeper-clad Edwardian country house. In a 'super position' near the River Dee, overlooking Ballater golf course, it has fine views of the hills of Glen Muick. 'No passing traffic, so very quiet,' say John and Priscilla Finnie, the resident owners. Their manager, Moira McDougall, is 'brilliant, so welcoming and attentive without being obtrusive. Bedrooms, bedlinen immaculate. On a fine day, we sat in the very pretty woodland garden. Food excellent.' John Finnie uses local game, and seafood from the East Coast and Orkney, for his four-course 'modern British with French touch' dinners (eg, breast of guineafowl with chive-and-bacon mash and grain mustard sauce). The light, comfortable interior is 'tastefully furnished'; the elegant dining room and lounge look on to the 'lovely' tree-lined grounds, and a sun terrace leads off the 'cosy' bar. Each bedroom is named after a fishing pool on the Dee. During the 'excellent' breakfast 'young pheasants tapped on the dining room windows'. Local attractions include the Royal Highland Games at Braemar. (*Kathleen Craddock, and others*)

9 bedrooms. W outskirts of Ballater. Open 16 Mar–4 Jan. Lounge, bar, dining room. No background music. 3-acre garden: croquet. Bedrooms unsuitable for ♿. No smoking. No dogs. Amex, MasterCard, Visa accepted. B&B £40–£80 per person; D,B&B £75–£115. Set dinner £37.50–£42.50. 1-night bookings refused New Year, 1st week Sept. *V*

Darroch Learg NEW
Braemar Road
Ballater AB35 5UX

Tel 013397-55443
Fax 013397-55252
Email info@darrochlearg.co.uk
Website www.darrochlearg.co.uk

Named in Gaelic 'an oak wood on a sunny hillside', this pink and granite Victorian listed building, owned by the Franks family for over 40 years, stands on the slopes of Craigendarroch above the Royal Deeside village (great views). 'It has a feel of a well-heeled country house,' says a report this year. 'All very attractive', it is richly furnished and tastefully decorated, with antiques, comfortable seating, watercolours and open fire in the lounge. 'Nigel and Fiona are accomplished, relaxing and welcoming hosts.' The best bedrooms are in the main house; the nearby baronial and turreted *Oakhall*, with cheaper rooms and its own sitting room, is suitable for a group. Most rooms have good views; they have bathrobes, flowers and fruit; some have a four-poster or half-tester bed, some a terrace. In the candlelit conservatory restaurant, the chef of 11 years, David Mutter, serving modern dishes like halibut with mussels and cèpe velouté, 'continues to delight', and staff 'manage, without being starchy, to complement his efforts'. The wide-ranging wine list includes plenty of half bottles, and a fixed mark-up per bottle means that the better wines seem reasonably priced. 'Breakfasts are great (delicious porridge).' Children are welcomed. (*Jane Smith*)

17 bedrooms. 5 in *Oakhall*. 1 on ground floor. On A93, ½ mile W of Ballater. Open Feb–Dec; closed Christmas. Ramp. 2 lounges, dining room. No background music. 4½-acre grounds. River Dee, fishing ¼ mile (prior notice needed), walking, climbing, riding, golf nearby. No smoking. No dogs in public rooms. All major credit cards accepted. B&B [2007] £55–£120 per person. Set menu £41–£46. Autumn, spring breaks, discounts for 2 or more nights. New Year package. 1-night bookings refused Easter, Braemar Gathering.

Deeside Hotel NEW

45 Braemar Road
Ballater AB35 5RQ

Tel 013397-755420
Fax 0871 989 5933
Email mail@deeside.co.uk
Website www.deesidehotel.co.uk

'Heartily recommended': in 'delightful mountainous countryside' near the River Dee, Gordon Waddell and Penella Price's Victorian 'home from home' is on the road to Braemar, a short walk from the village centre. 'The welcome is warm, we could find no fault with the food, both at breakfast and dinner,' says the nominator. 'A good wine list, reasonably priced.' There are log fires in the 'comfortable small lounge' and 'well-stocked bar' (over 40 whiskies). The conservatory restaurant serves main courses like roast crown of partridge with confit leg, rowan jelly and game sauce. Soups and ice cream are home made; many herbs and vegetables are home grown; breads, seafood and meat come from local suppliers. Breakfast options include The Haddock and The Highlander. There are king-size beds and a two-room family suite. Pets are welcomed by arrangement. Red squirrels can be seen in the walled garden. Good for walkers ('both ambling and serious hill walking'). A member of the Green Tourism Business Scheme. 'Very reasonable rates.' (*Derek Ward*)

10 bedrooms. 2 on ground floor. Village outskirts, on road to Braemar. Ramp. Lounge/bar (background Mozart), library, conservatory restaurant. 1-acre garden. No smoking. No dogs: upstairs bedrooms, public rooms. MasterCard, Visa accepted. B&B [2007] £40–£90 per person; D,B&B £60–£110. Full alc £35. New Year package. 1-night bookings refused Sat in season.

BALLYGRANT Argyll and Bute — Map 5:D1

Kilmeny Country House
Ballygrant, Isle of Islay
PA45 7QW

Tel/Fax 01496-840668
Email info@kilmeny.co.uk
Website www.kilmeny.co.uk

On the lovely Isle of Islay, which has eight of the best – and smokiest – whiskies in the world, this traditional, white-painted 19th-century farmhouse has an elevated position with 'spectacular views' over countryside and moorland. The owners (for 21 years), Margaret and Blair Rozga, have added two new bedrooms, one a suite. 'Everything is immaculate' in the house, with its antique furniture and chintzes; *en suite* bathrooms have quality toiletries; bedrooms have home-made biscuits. Guests sit together around one large mahogany dining table, and can bring their own wine (no licence) to accompany the 'absolutely delicious' five-course dinners cooked by the 'sparkling and friendly' hostess. Served on weekdays only, they have two choices for each course, and use local ingredients, eg, roast Colonsay lamb with bramble sauce; scallops poached in white wine and cream. Breakfasts are generous. The house, with beautiful gardens, is on a working beef farm. Islay, though small, is home to a range of wildlife, including the geese who feed on *Kilmeny*'s grasslands. More reports, please.

5 bedrooms. 3 on ground floor. ½ mile south of Ballygrant village. Open Mar–Nov. Dining room closed midday and Sat/Sun. Sitting room, dining room. No background music. 1-acre garden in 300-acre farm. No smoking. No children under 8. No dogs. No credit cards. B&B [2007] £50–£75 per person. Set dinner £35. 1-night bookings sometimes refused.

BALQUHIDDER Stirling — Map 5:D2

Monachyle Mhor
Balquhidder
Lochearnhead FK19 8PQ

Tel 01877-384622
Fax 01877-384305
Email info@monachylemhor.com
Website www.monachylemhor.com

The cooking of owner/chef Tom Lewis is a major draw at this conversion of a pale-pink 18th-century farmhouse and its outbuildings in a 'lovely, remote setting'. It stands in a huge estate at the end of a single-lane track, 'best negotiated in daylight', by Loch Voil, in Scotland's first national park. Public rooms have open fires, antiques and modern furnishings. 'The small sitting room and bar can get crowded.' The bedrooms vary: some have a fire, some have a flat-screen TV; all have a

DVD-player. 'Our small room had an excellent shower in the large *en suite* bathroom.' In the conservatory dining room (with views of loch and mountains), local produce and vegetables and herbs from the organic walled garden are used in dishes like salmon and scallop with peas, courgettes, cherry tomatoes and a light pea cream. There are inventive vegetarian dishes and good bar meals. 'We have never tasted soup as good as this.' Breakfast includes haggis with mixed grill along with more traditional fare. 'Charming staff from around the world.' No age limit for children and 'this is a wonderful place for dogs; pets are most welcome by arrangement', says the website. (*Paul Powell-Jackson, and others*)

13 bedrooms. 1 on ground floor. 5 in courtyard. 17 miles NW of Callander. Sitting room, bar (classical background music), conservatory restaurant. 2,000-acre estate: garden, *pétanque* pitch. Wedding facilities. No smoking. Dogs allowed in 2 bedrooms, not in public rooms. MasterCard, Visa accepted. B&B [2007] double £95–£220; D,B&B double £183–£308. Set dinner £44. 1-night bookings refused Sat in season.

BLAIRGOWRIE Perth and Kinross — Map 5:D2

Kinloch House
Dunkeld Road
by Blairgowrie PH10 6SG

Tel 01250-884237
Fax 01250-884333
Email reception@kinlochhouse.com
Website www.kinlochhouse.com

On a sloping hillside facing a wide valley, the Allen family's grand 19th-century Scottish mansion (Relais & Châteaux) stands peacefully in large grounds with a Victorian walled garden. With its oak-panelled hall, *objets d'art*, log fires, portrait gallery and ornate glass ceiling, it provides 'comfort and quality'. Decor is traditional. 'It feels nothing like a hotel,' according to recent visitors. 'The impression is of an elegant country house with pastoral views.' Graeme Allen presides 'affably but not intrusively', supported by 'superbly trained' staff. The chef, Andrew May, 'has flair and dedication', producing dishes like saddle of rabbit with beans, truffle gnocchi and a rosemary sauce. The extensive wine list includes some expensive bottles as well as 'a good selection of fairly priced quality house wines'. Male guests are asked to wear a jacket at dinner. Most bedrooms are spacious; they are 'tastefully furnished, without being fussy or twee'. Some have a four-poster bed and a large Victorian bath. Most showers are hand-held. The health centre (see below) is an attraction. (*T and MD*)

18 bedrooms. 4 on ground floor. 3 miles W of Blairgowrie, on A923 towards Dunkeld. Closed 12–28 Dec. Ramp. Drawing room, lounge, conservatory, bar, dining room; private dining room; health centre (35 by 16-ft swimming pool, sauna, etc). No background music. 25-acre grounds: walled garden, field with Highland cattle and horses. No smoking. No children under 7 in dining room at night. Dogs by arrangement (dog units available). Wedding facilities. Amex, MasterCard, Visa accepted. B&B £90–£160 per person; D,B&B £135–£205. Set lunch £19.50–£28.50, dinner £48. New Year package. 1-night bookings sometimes refused in peak season.

BOWMORE Argyll and Bute *See SHORTLIST* Map 5:D1

BRODICK North Ayrshire Map 5:E1

Kilmichael Country House NEW

Glen Cloy, by Brodick
Isle of Arran KA27 8BY

Tel 01770-302219
Fax 01770-302068
Email enquiries@kilmichael.com
Website www.kilmichael.com

Said to be the oldest house on Arran, *Kilmichael* sits at the end of an unmade road in grounds patrolled by ducks and 'noisy' peacocks. It has spectacular views of mountains. 'Very special', 'extremely well appointed', visitors tell us this year. But one couple thought 'attention to detail' was lacking. Owners Geoffrey Botterill and Antony Butterworth ('who insists he is the cook, not the chef') offer B&B with the option of dining in (residents must book a table). 'In the comfortable drawing rooms, we enjoyed excellent canapés with pre-dinner drinks. The furniture, pictures, etc, collected with care around the world, contribute to the private house atmosphere.' In the conservatory dining room (open to non-residents), 'superb' meals are served with fine silver and crystal. Main courses include rack of lamb with rosemary, redcurrants and red pepper marmalade. There is always a vegetarian dish, and a light meal can be brought to the bedroom. 'Service first class. Staff quickly learned our quirks and fancies. Only drawback: other local venues suffer by comparison when the dining room is closed.' Two suites are in the main house, as are two bedrooms (one with four-poster and 'bath big enough for two'). The others are in converted stables. All have flowers, fruit, a map, an iron, and 'a wee dram of whisky to welcome you'. Bathrooms have 'wonderfully peaty brown water'. (*Iain M Robertson, Angela and Barbara Dixon, and others*)

7 bedrooms. 3 in converted stables. 6 on ground floor. 4 self-catering cottages. 1 mile SW of village. Open Mar–Oct. Restaurant closed midday and Tues. 2 drawing rooms, dining room (jazz/light classical background music during meals). 4½-acre grounds: burn. Sea 1 mile; sailing, golf, walking nearby. No smoking. No children under 12. No dogs in public rooms. MasterCard, Visa accepted. B&B £60–£95 per person. Set dinner £38.50. Discounts for 3–7 nights; ferry-inclusive packages. 1-night bookings occasionally refused Sat.

CALLANDER Stirling — Map 5:D2

The Roman Camp
off Main Street
Callander FK17 8BG

Tel 01877-330003
Fax 01877-331533
Email mail@romancamphotel.co.uk
Website www.romancamphotel.co.uk

A Roman fort is said to have stood on the site of Eric and Marion Brown's luxury hotel, a much-extended, pink, turreted hunting lodge, just off the main street of this old town east of the Trossachs. It has a 'lovely setting' in large grounds on the banks of the River Teith. Visitors like the country house atmosphere. The 'very nice' bar/lounge area has log fires and oak beams. There is a stone-flagged entrance, a wood-panelled library with a tiny 'secret chapel', and a silk-lined drawing room. The bedrooms in the old house vary in size and style: 'Ours was spacious, nicely decorated, with a wonderful bathroom.' Some rooms, in a modern wing, have a door leading on to the garden. In the oval dining room, with its tapestries, large fireplace, garden views, silver and crystal, the long-serving chef, Ian McNaught, serves a modern four-course menu, eg, a main course of roast loin of hare with sage and onion tapioca, truffle-marinated tomatoes. One visitor thought it 'good, but slightly pretentious'. Breakfast is 'impressive'; there are 'excellent' afternoon teas (sandwiches, scones and cakes). Guests have access to the golf course nearby. More reports, please.

14 bedrooms. 7 on ground floor, 1 suitable for ♿. E end of Main Street. 2 lounges, library with chapel, bar, 2 dining rooms; conference/function facilities. No background music. 17-acre grounds: ¾-mile river, fishing. Golf nearby. Wedding facilities. No smoking. No dogs in public rooms. All major credit cards accepted. B&B £62.50–£112.50 per person. Set menu £48; full alc £70. 2-night midweek breaks. Christmas/New Year packages. *V*

Many hotels increase their prices in the spring. The tariffs we quote are subject to change, especially from April/May 2008. You should always check when booking.

CHIRNSIDE Borders Map 5:E3

Chirnside Hall
Chirnside, nr Duns
TD11 3LD

Tel 01890-818219
Fax 01890-818231
Email reception@chirnsidehallhotel.com
Website www.chirnsidehallhotel.com

'Beautifully restored and elegantly decorated', Christian and Tessa Korsten's distinctive Borders mansion (built as a family home in 1830) has 'inspiring' views from its lounge and dining room across fields to the Cheviot Hills, says a returning visitor. 'The welcome is warm and extremely friendly, with just the correct amount of personal attention.' The comfortable public rooms are 'well decorated', with bold colours and rich fabrics; open fires in marble fireplaces. The bedrooms, each of different shape and size, have 'all the amenities that one expects'. One has a four-poster bed and a sofa. 'Lots of hot water' in the bathrooms. 'Unusually, the bath was suitable for even the tallest person.' Some top rooms may be 'a little dark'. In the handsome small dining room, with its big tables and upholstered chairs, Gary Imlach serves a daily-changing four-course menu of modern dishes, eg, sea bass grilled with sea salt and lime on basil crushed potatoes: 'Generous portions, well presented, met expectations. Breakfast of the same high standard; wonderful to see real kippers.' Hunting and fishing parties make the hotel lively in winter; it is often quieter in summer. (*Conrad Barnard*)

10 bedrooms. 6 miles NE of Duns. Closed Mar. 2 lounges, dining room ('easy listening' background music); billiard room; fitness room; library/conference room. 6-acre grounds. Unsuitable for ♿. Wedding facilities. No smoking. No dogs in public rooms. All major credit cards accepted. B&B [2007] £75–£185 per person; D,B&B £97.50–£105. Set dinner £30. Short breaks. Christmas package.

CLACHAN SEIL Argyll and Bute Map 5:D1

Willowburn Hotel
Clachan Seil, Isle of Seil
by Oban PA34 4TJ

Tel 01852-300276
Email willowburn.hotel@virgin.net
Website www.willowburn.co.uk

'Peace and comfort.' 'Five-star treatment plus family atmosphere.' Warm endorsements for this unpretentious small hotel and its 'kind owners', Jan and Chris Wolfe. Long, low and narrow, it stands on the little island of Seil (reached across a short, 18th-century, semi-circular stone bridge over the Atlantic). The lounge (with fire) and restaurant have picture windows facing the quiet waters of Clachan Sound. The bar, and all bedrooms but one, share this 'delightful' view. Decor is homely. Neat rooms, 'like a ship's cabin', have 'good toiletries', 'comfortable bed, excellent reading lights', 'very good information pack'. Most are small, but one 'was spacious with six-foot bed'. Guests come down at 7 pm to view the menu. Local fishermen and the hotel's garden supply Chris Wolfe's four-course dinners, 'served at a comfortable pace, cooked to perfection'. 'Loch Etive mussels in tomato and herb sauce; langoustines on mint and pea risotto.' 'A surprisingly extensive wine list; very good value.' 'Lots of chat between tables.' 'Delicious bread' appears at dinner and breakfast. Prospective canine guests get a letter from the resident dogs and cat. Two swans, Mr and Mrs D52, often visit *Willowburn*; so do many birds. (*Margaret and Marc Wall, EB Woodsford, John S Millar*)

7 bedrooms. 16 miles S of Oban. Bus from Oban. Open Mar–Nov. Lounge, bar, dining room (quiet background music at night). 1½-acre grounds. Shore 100 yds. No smoking. No children under 8. No dogs: lounge, dining room. MasterCard, Visa accepted. D,B&B £85 per person. Set dinner £37. Reductions for 3 or more nights. 1-night bookings occasionally refused.

COLONSAY Argyll and Bute — Map 5:D1

The Colonsay
Isle of Colonsay
PA61 7YP

Tel 01951-200316
Fax 01951-200353
Email reception@thecolonsay.com
Website www.thecolonsay.com

An unpretentious old inn has been turned into a 'cool, stylish' hotel by the local laird and his wife, Alex and Jane Howard; it is now managed by Scott Omar. They promise 'simple rooms, luxurious beds, sea views, whisky galore'. 'It provides a luxurious nest,' says its nominator, 'where to be pampered is a real treat.' The 'intimate character' is liked. The bar, in pastel colours, serves 'a healthy and delicious lunch' and has 'a buzz of cheerfulness most of the day'. 'For peace and quiet there is a comfortable library.' There are 'plenty of other public areas, lots of log fires, deep sofas and chairs'. 'Vibrant abstract paintings' hang on walls. In the contemporary-style restaurant (with harbour views, wood-burning stove and white linen tablecloths), the cooking is modern, with a strong local accent: shellfish, lamb and game ('our philosophy is to buy the very best and cook it simply'). Children (who stay free in their parents' room) have their own menu. On this 'idyllic' Hebridean island, you can 'explore wildlife and archaeological remains, bask on a splendid golden beach', play golf and tennis and go fishing. (*JR*)

9 bedrooms. 400 yds W of harbour. Closed 5 Jan–28 Feb. Lounge, library, log room, conservatory, bar, restaurant. No background music. 1-acre garden. Beach 5 miles. Unsuitable for ♿. Wedding facilities. No smoking. MasterCard, Visa accepted. B&B £42.50–£70 per person. Full alc £25. 1 free night for a 3-night stay Mar, Apr, Oct. Christmas/New Year packages.

CONTIN Highland — Map 5:C2

Coul House
Contin
IV14 9ES

Tel 01997-421487
Fax 01997-421945
Email stay@coulhousehotel.com
Website www.coulhousehotel.com

Victorian hunting lodge with striking demi-octagonal porch, ½ mile outside village. Extensively refurbished by owners Stuart and Susannah Macpherson in 2006/7; Chris McLeod manages. 'Stunning' views of Strathconon valley and mountains beyond. 'Comfy' drawing room; ornate plaster ceilings and log fires in lounge bar; dining room with 18-foot ceiling, full-height windows. 'Enjoyable' 3-course dinner by chef Garry Kenley; vegetarian menu. 'Friendly staff.' Children and pets welcomed. Background music. 24 bedrooms, individually decorated, 'clean, comfortable; good pillows'. Some on ground floor. Stone terrace (drinks served); 8-acre grounds: 9-hole pitch and putt. Closed Christmas. Wedding facilities. No smoking. No dogs in restaurant. Amex, MasterCard, Visa accepted. B&B [2007] £49.50–£94.50 per person; D,B&B £72–£117. Full alc £35.50. New Year package; off-season breaks. More reports, please.

CRINAN Argyll and Bute — Map 5:D1

Crinan Hotel
Crinan
by Lochgilphead PA31 8SR

Tel 01546-830261
Fax 01546-830292
Email reception@crinanhotel.com
Website www.crinanhotel.com

'The situation is fantastic, the atmosphere relaxed. Staff are charming, and it is beautifully peaceful (no background music),' writes a visitor this year to this white-painted hotel, overlooking the Crinan Canal basin, in a tiny village. It has been owned for 37 years by Nick and Frances Ryan (the artist Frances Macdonald). He is 'very much in evidence, involved and caring'; her large seascapes hang in the public rooms. An earlier report: 'Luggage was carried to our most agreeable bedroom, more like private house than hotel: spacious, with large bed, armchairs from which to admire the view. Small touches abounded, like fresh flowers and ornaments; the bathroom was bright, clean, with robes.' In the 'well-proportioned' *Westward* restaurant, with candles and linen cloths, chef Scott Kennedy's dinners are thought 'excellent'. 'Locally sourced fish: mussels, sole, salmon, scallops, huge prawns, beautifully cooked. Also local venison, lamb and beef. Service quick, efficient, but not rushed.' 'Impressive breakfast: fresh juice, just-right fruit salad, superb cooked dishes, proper toast, attentive service.' Children and dogs are welcomed. An art gallery and a health and beauty treatment room are new this year. But one couple thought the building in need of some external maintenance. (*ABG Guest, and others*)

20 bedrooms. Village centre. Closed Christmas, last 3 weeks Jan. Lift, ramps. 2 lounges, cocktail bar, rooftop bar, public bar, restaurant, coffee shop; art gallery; treatment room (health and beauty). No background music. ½-acre garden. Safe, sandy beaches nearby; fishing. Boat trips. Wedding facilities. No smoking. No dogs in restaurant. MasterCard, Visa accepted. D,B&B £95–£150 per person. Full alc £47.50. Winter/spring rates. New Year package.

DORNOCH Highland — Map 5:B2

2 Quail
Castle Street
Dornoch IV25 3SD

Tel 01862-811811
Email goodhotel@2quail.com
Website www.2quail.com

In a Victorian town house on the main street of this 'lovely town with mellow stone houses and a long sandy beach', a hard-working couple, Michael and Kerensa Carr, run their restaurant-with-rooms without assistance. 'We don't even have a washer-up,' they say. He, *Ritz*-trained, is the chef ('first rate'), she ('a strong personality, cheerful, amusing') is front-of-house, also wine waiter, bartender, housekeeper and bookkeeper. Visitors are asked about likes/dislikes and allergies on booking; the four-course set menu was much admired again this year. 'We enjoyed quail with pan-fried foie gras and roasted fig; turbot with an orange crust; lamb noisettes with Provençal vegetables. Kerensa's service was efficient, well timed.' Residents need to book a table in the popular, book-lined restaurant, which has only 12 covers. It is 'appreciated' if they dine in once during their stay, but this is not obligatory. The lounge, with its large bookcase, is small; it may feel crowded at busy times. Breakfast, served at 8.30 am, was 'excellent: home-made yogurts and muesli, good croissants and fry-up', if 'a bit rushed'. Bedrooms are 'clean, comfortable' and well proportioned. Housekeeping is 'exemplary'. 'We are undoubtedly the smallest golf hotel and restaurant in Scotland,' say the Carrs, keen members of Royal Dornoch. (*Janet and Dennis Allom, and others*)

3 bedrooms. Central. Street parking. Closed Christmas. Limited opening in winter. Restaurant closed midday, and Sun/Mon. Lounge, restaurant; occasional background music. Unsuitable for ♿. No smoking. No children under 10. Guide dogs only. Amex, MasterCard, Visa accepted. B&B [2007] double £100. Set dinner £38.

Dornoch Castle Hotel NEW

Castle Street
Dornoch 1V25 3SD

Tel 01862-810216
Fax 01862-810981
Email enquiries@dornochcastlehotel.com
Website www.dornochcastlehotel.com

Opposite 12th-century cathedral: 15th-century building, recently refurbished, managed by owner Colin Thompson. 'Very enjoyable. Comfortable, cosy rooms, though showers could have been better. Great location, very friendly staff. Good beer, good lunch menu, good dinners' (local ingredients used by chef Grant MacNicol). Weddings a speciality. 24 bedrooms. 2 suitable for ♿. 3 in garden chalets. Closed 24–26 Dec. Lounge, bar, restaurant; light background music all the time. Large grounds. No smoking. No dogs. Amex, MasterCard, Visa accepted. B&B [2007] £41–£165 per person; D,B&B £61–£190. Full alc £35. New Year package.

DUNDEE *See SHORTLIST* Map 5:D3

DUNKELD Perth and Kinross Map 5:D2

Kinnaird

Kinnaird Estate
by Dunkeld PH8 0LB

Tel 01796-482440
Fax 01796-482289
Email enquiry@kinnairdestate.com
Website www.kinnairdestate.com

'The service at this well-appointed country house is friendly, without being overbearing; also extremely efficient' – a 2007 comment on this creeper-covered Grade B listed mansion (Relais & Châteaux). It stands in woodland in a vast Perthshire estate where guests may fish for salmon and trout in the River Tay, and for trout in several lochs. Sumptuously furnished, it has family portraits, grand piano, antiques, flowers, billiards. 'Log fires seemingly ablaze in every room make this a visit to a home, while the art (principally wildlife, especially birds) is worth the trip in itself.' The owner, Constance Ward, is American, as are many guests. Her manager is James Payne. Most bedrooms are large, with a view of the valley. Three are in cottages. 'Each morning a chambermaid brings tea on a tray, and lights the gas log fire.' Men wear a jacket at dinner in the elegant restaurant (frescoes and ornate ceiling), where chef Trevor Brooks serves a much-admired three-course set dinner using home-produced or local ingredients; *Kinnaird* has its own smokehouse and a walled kitchen garden. The wine list has many half bottles. Good breakfasts have freshly squeezed juice, and porridge can come laced with whisky. (*Robert Gower*)

9 bedrooms. 1 on ground floor. 3 in cottages in courtyard. 6 miles NW of Dunkeld. Lift, ramp. 2 lounges, billiard room, restaurant, dining room; function facilities; beauty/therapy room. No background music. 7,000-acre estate: gardens, tennis, croquet, shooting, walking, birdwatching, salmon fishing on Tay, 3 trout lochs. Wedding facilities. No smoking. No children under 10. No dogs in house (heated kennels available). Amex, MasterCard, Visa accepted. B&B [2007] double £295–£375; D,B&B double £395–£475. Set dinner £55. Christmas/New Year packages.

DUNOON Argyll and Bute — Map 5:D1

The Enmore

111 Marine Parade, Kirn
Dunoon PA23 8HH

Tel 01369-702230
Fax 01369-702148
Email enmorehotel@btinternet.com
Website www.enmorehotel.co.uk

With lovely views over the Firth of Clyde, this 18th-century 'gentleman's retreat' on a seafront road is handy for car ferries to the West Highlands. The owners, Robert and Wendy Thomson, are 'charming and obliging', say recent visitors. The well-proportioned lounge, 'uncluttered and airy, with a large period fireplace with a log fire', looks over the water to Gourock. Bedrooms are smart and comfortable. 'Ours had an enchanting seating area overlooking the firth, and a well-appointed bathroom.' The traditional Scottish meals cooked by chef Michael Patton are thought 'entirely satisfactory', and generous, eg, pan-fried duck breast with port. 'They were very obliging about serving us an early breakfast to allow us to catch a ferry.' *The Enmore* owns two squash courts (the only ones in this part of Argyll), free for guests' use. (*AM, and others*)

10 bedrooms. 1 on ground floor. Seafront, 1 mile E of centre. Parking. Ramp. Reception lounge, sitting room, restaurant (background music), bar; meeting room; 2 squash courts. 1¼-acre garden. Shingle beach. Wedding facilities. No smoking. Dogs by arrangement. Diners, MasterCard, Visa accepted. B&B £45–£95 per person; D,B&B £22.50 added. Bar lunches. Set dinner £25. Special breaks. Christmas/New Year packages.

DUNVEGAN Highland — Map 5:C1

The Three Chimneys and The House Over-By
Colbost, Dunvegan
Isle of Skye IV55 8ZT

Tel 01470-511258
Fax 01470-511358
Email eatandstay@threechimneys.co.uk
Website www.threechimneys.co.uk

César award in 2001

'Still excellent in every respect,' says a regular visitor over seven years to Eddie and Shirley Spear's award-winning restaurant-with-rooms in north-west Skye (she is chef/*patronne*). Standing across a single-track road (some day traffic, quiet at night) from Loch Dunvegan, the white-painted crofter's cottage (the restaurant) and the traditionally built adjoining house 'over-by' have a beautiful location. The split-level bedrooms, all with sea views, have a contemporary, stylish decor; there are comfortable beds, large, luxurious bathrooms, flat-screen TV and DVD-player. First-time visitors were 'impressed with the room' but thought it expensive, and that 'privacy was sacrificed when curtains were opened to enjoy the view'. All admire Michael Smith's cooking, served in the two-room restaurant with its candles, dark beams, stone walls. The three- or four-course menu features much fish and local game, eg, carpaccio of Skye smoked salmon and monkfish; Highland venison, skirlie potato cakes. 'Simple fresh ingredients, perfectly cooked and presented. Wonderful home-made breads.' The 'excellent' breakfast has croissants, freshly squeezed orange juice, fruit salad; cheeses, porridge, smoked salmon, smoked venison. Young children are welcomed: cots, children's tea, baby-listening. There is a wide choice of DVDs, CDs, books and maps. (*Elisabeth Smith, and others*)

6 bedrooms. All on ground floor in separate building, 1 suitable for ♿. 5 miles W of Dunvegan. Closed 6–25 Jan. Restaurant closed lunchtime in winter, Sun lunch all year. Ramps. Reception/morning/breakfast room, bar, restaurant. No background music. Garden on loch. No smoking. No children under 8 at dinner. Guide dogs only. Amex, MasterCard, Visa accepted. B&B [to 1 May 2008] £127.50 per person; D,B&B (off-season) £140. Set 3-course lunch £30, dinner (3/4 courses) £50–£55. Autumn/winter/spring breaks. Christmas/New Year packages. 1-night bookings refused Sat.

'Set menu' indicates a fixed-price meal, with ample, limited or no choice. 'Full alc' is the hotel's estimated price per person of a three-course *à la carte* meal, with a half bottle of house wine. 'Alc' is the price of an *à la carte* meal excluding the cost of wine.

DUROR Argyll and Bute — Map 5:D1

Bealach House
Salachan Glen, Duror
Appin PA38 4BW

Tel 01631-740298
Email info@bealach-house.co.uk
Website www.bealach-house.co.uk

Again this year, visitors to Jim and Hilary McFadyen's small guest house were enthusiastic. 'Can't fault it. There is nothing they haven't thought of to make their guests welcome.' 'We loved it. One of the best places we have ever stayed.' Originally a shepherd's croft, then a farmhouse, this is the only dwelling in the Salachan Glen, 'one-and-a-half miles up a forestry track, but well worth the ride'. Surrounded by woods and mountains, it stands in large grounds, and has lovely views; wild birds visit a bird table, and golden eagles and deer are sometimes seen. Inside, it is 'beautifully decorated': muted colours and tasteful furnishings. The lounge has a fire, plenty of books and games. Bedrooms, not large, are 'warmly furnished, immaculate and extremely comfortable'. Bathrooms have a power shower (one also has a bath). The 'superb' dinner, in the communal dining room, is three courses, each with three alternatives (eg, monkfish with sun-dried tomato and basil parcel), including a vegetarian option. Hilary McFadyen's mantra is 'if it can be made on the premises, it is', including the cake with the arrival cup of tea, breads, jams and ice creams. A complimentary glass or two of wine is offered with dinner (the McFadyens have no licence; guests may bring their own). Breakfasts are 'innovative', and include freshly pressed juices of the day. (*Edward and Sarah Gosnell, Michael and Jean Clunas, Richard and Caroline Faircliff*)

3 bedrooms. 2 miles S of Duror. Off A828 between Oban and Fort William. Open Mar–Nov. Lounge, conservatory, dining room; occasional classical background music. 8-acre grounds. Unsuitable for ♿. No smoking. No children under 14. No dogs. MasterCard, Visa accepted. B&B £40–£55 per person. Set dinner £25. 1-night bookings refused bank holidays.

EDINBANE Highland — Map 5:C1

Greshornish House
Edinbane, by Portree
Isle of Skye IV51 9PN

Tel 01470-582266
Fax 01470-582345
Email info@greshornishhouse.com
Website www.greshornishhouse.com

'Nicely refurbished' by owners (since 2004) Neil and Rosemary Colquhoun, this handsome, listed, white manor house, 18th-century with Victorian additions, is 'wonderfully set' by beautiful Loch Greshornish.

It stands secluded in wooded grounds, and has lovely views across the loch to Trotternish. 'Very pleasing on all counts,' says an American visitor this year. An earlier comment: 'Very comfortable, with friendly management.' In the candlelit dining room (open to non-residents), chef Richard Carlton serves a three-course *table d'hôte* dinner of 'traditional Scottish/European' dishes based on local ingredients, eg, medallion of Lochaber venison, skirly mash, roasted vegetables and a juniper berry jus. Log fires burn in the public rooms. For after-dinner entertainment there are billiards, chess, or 'a book with a malt whisky' in the drawing room. Bedrooms are well furnished: one is the former music room, another was a drawing room; two have a four-poster; some are spacious, some are under the eaves and have a sloping ceiling; some look over the loch, some over the Victorian walled garden. For children there are reduced rates, high chairs, cots, etc. (*Stephen Holman, JP*)

9 bedrooms. 12 miles NW of Portree. Closed 2 weeks Nov, Christmas, 2 weeks Feb, occasional midwinter Mon/Tues/Wed. Drawing room, lounge/cocktail bar, billiard room, dining room (usually no background music), conservatory. 10-acre grounds: croquet, tennis; sea loch. Unsuitable for ♿. No smoking. No dogs: public rooms, or unaccompanied in bedrooms. Amex, MasterCard, Visa accepted. B&B £60–£85 per person. Set dinner from £34. Seasonal and 3-day breaks. *V*

EDINBURGH — Map 5:D2

The Scotsman
20 North Bridge
Edinburgh
EH1 1YT

Tel 0131-556 5565
Fax 0131-652 3652
Email reservations@thescotsmanhotel.co.uk
Website www.thescotsmanhotel.co.uk

Once the offices of the *Scotsman* newspaper, this striking ten-storey Edwardian building has been smartly converted into a luxury city hotel. Many original features have been retained, including a 'wonderful' black-and-white marble staircase and intricate stained-glass windows. It is now owned by MBI International, which has 42 hotels in Europe and the Middle East (see also *42 The Calls*, Leeds). 'There is much to enjoy,' says a visitor this year. 'Big comfortable beds, sound systems in the bathrooms, lovely toiletries.' The downsides are a 'fiendishly complicated TV system (even the porter found it difficult)', 'adult' films, and – for rooms on the second floor overlooking Waverley station – loud noise late at night from a sports bar. Features that are liked include hatches for room service (you don't have to open the door), the Edinburgh Monopoly board, and the Cowshed spa with its stainless-steel swimming pool. There are two restaurants: *Vermilion*, with a rich red decor and fine dining, and the slightly brasher *North Bridge* brasserie. The breakfast buffet is 'good, if ridiculously expensive; but I will return for the comfort and the excellent location'. One tip: 'Approach on foot from the Market Street side of Waverley, not the Princes Street exit.' (*SK*)

69 bedrooms. 2 suitable for ♿. Central, by Waverley station. *Vermilion* restaurant closed Mon/Tues. Ramps, lifts. Drawing room, breakfast room, brasserie, restaurant; background music; cinema; health spa: 55-ft swimming pool, sauna, gym, treatments rooms, juice bar, café. Wedding facilities. Smoking allowed in 19 bedrooms. Dogs by arrangement; not in public rooms. All major credit cards accepted. B&B [2007]: double £200–£350, suite £380–£1,200; D,B&B £122–£620 per person. Breakfast £17.50. Full alc: brasserie £35, restaurant £55. Weekend rates and packages on website. 1-night bookings often refused Fri/Sat, rugby weekends, New Year.

Seven Danube Street

7 Danube Street
Edinburgh EH4 1NN

Tel 0131-332 2755
Fax 0131-343 3648
Email seven.danubestreet@virgin.net
Website www.aboutedinburgh.com/danube.html

César award in 2002

Ever popular, this B&B is a handsome Georgian terrace house in a curved, cobbled street near the Water of Leith, and within walking distance of Princes Street. 'Fiona Mitchell-Rose and her husband, Colin, are excellent hosts,' wrote an American visitor this year. 'They take an interest in their guests in warm, personal style, and are a mine of information on local attractions and where to eat.' Their dogs, George, a black pug, and Doris, a Staffordshire bull terrier, 'are an entertainment in themselves'. The house has inherited pictures, good furniture, a lovely cupolaed staircase; 'the feeling of a real home'. Bedrooms on the lower floor (guests have their own front door and key) are 'beautifully furnished', and well equipped, even the small single. 'Ours catered for every conceivable need.' Beds have an electric blanket; 'luxurious' bathrooms have a power shower. Breakfast, 'a wonderful start to the day', is served around one big table. It includes home-made bread, croissants, freshly squeezed orange juice, 'four delightful fresh fruit salads', fruit compote, and cooked dishes. There are also two bedrooms in a flat around the corner (usually self-catering). 'Very helpful restaurant recommendations.' (*Patricia Higgins, Susan and John Wilson*)

3 bedrooms. Also 1 self-catering flat for 4–6 people, 50 yds. Stockbridge. Meter parking. Closed Christmas. Breakfast room. No background music. Small rear garden. Unsuitable for ♿. No smoking. Dogs by arrangement. MasterCard, Visa accepted. B&B [2007] £60–£85 per person. 1-night bookings refused New Year.

Windmill House
Coltbridge Gardens
Edinburgh EH12 6AQ

Tel/Fax 0131-346 0024
Email windmillhouse@btinternet.com

'Super if sometimes a bit disorganised. The place is beautiful.' 'Wonderful. Incredible value.' Though only a mile from Princes Street, Vivien and Michael Scott's imposing Georgian-style house (a Wolsey Lodge, offering 'luxury B&B') has a peaceful, rural hilltop setting, by a waterfall, weir and historic 17th-century windmill. Overlooking the valley of the Water of Leith, it has lovely views to the Pentlands. The stylish interior has antiques, open fires and flowers. Double doors open on to a pillared hall with atrium, wide staircase and galleried landing. The drawing room leads on to a wide terrace where breakfast is sometimes served. Bedrooms are large, and tastefully furnished, and have sherry and mineral water, but no tea- or coffee-making equipment, and no door lock. Breakfast, in the handsome dining room, has a good choice of cereals, 'delicious fruit, generous cooked dishes'. The Scotts are 'helpful and full of information'. The secure parking is appreciated. Badgers visit at twilight. The Scottish National Gallery of Modern Art, in its wooded grounds, is a neighbour. (*Gill Holden, Michael Crick*)

3 bedrooms. 1 mile W of centre. Closed Christmas/New Year. Drawing room, dining room. No background music. Terrace. 2-acre garden, riverside walks. Unsuitable for ♿. No smoking. No dogs. No credit cards. B&B £55–£75 per person. 1-night bookings sometimes refused Aug.

The Witchery by the Castle
Castlehill
The Royal Mile
Edinburgh EH1 2NF

Tel 0131-225 5613
Fax 0131-220 4392
Email mail@thewitchery.com
Website www.thewitchery.com

Film stars and other famous names are regular visitors to this opulent 'restaurant-with-suites'. Owned by restaurateur James Thomson, managed by Jacquie Sutherland, it is in two adjacent 16th-century buildings at the top of the Royal Mile, by the castle. The huge suites (Vestry, Inner Sanctum, etc), in Gothic style, have ornate paintwork, antiques, oak panelling, original fireplaces. Enormous four-poster beds are draped with tapestries and velvet hangings; there are French gilded sofas, a complimentary bottle of Pol Roger, and a roll-top bath big enough for two in each marble-floored bathroom. Twenty-first-century extras include CD/DVD-player. Best of all, 'staff are so friendly, service is brilliant – so is the food'. This is served in the original *Witchery*, with its

17th-century oak panelling, tapestries, gilding, red leather upholstery, antique church candlesticks, and the *Secret Garden*, with its painted ceiling. A two-course light menu is offered at lunch and at pre- and post-theatre times. Breakfast included in the price (cereals, jams, fruit salad, etc) is delivered to the bedroom in a basket, or you can pay £13 for a cooked breakfast in the dining room. More suites, one with a roof terrace, are planned for 2008. More reports, please.

7 suites. In 2 buildings. By Edinburgh Castle. Closed Christmas/New Year. 2 restaurants (background music). Small terrace. Unsuitable for ♿. Wedding facilities. No smoking. No dogs. All major credit cards accepted. B&B suite £295. Set lunch/theatre supper £12.50; full alc £50.

See also SHORTLIST

ELGIN Moray *See SHORTLIST* Map 5:C2

ERISKA Argyll and Bute Map 5:D1

Isle of Eriska
Benderloch, Eriska
by Oban PA37 1SD

Tel 01631-720371
Fax 01631-720531
Email office@eriska-hotel.co.uk
Website www.eriska-hotel.co.uk

César award in 2007

'Near perfect.' 'As good as ever.' 'What sets it apart, other than its beautiful, peaceful location and genuine comfort, is the outstanding service and attention to detail.' This 19th-century baronial mansion (Pride of Britain) is on a 300-acre private island, reached by a wrought iron vehicle bridge. 'More resort than hotel' (see below), it is run by brothers Beppo and Chay Buchanan-Smith, with a 'well-trained, young, mainly Polish staff'. There are wellington boots by the entrance, large sofas, a year-round log fire, panelled lounges. 'Housekeeping standards are awesome.' Bedrooms vary: 'All are immaculate.' 'Ours had sofa, decent-sized TV, huge bed (made while we breakfasted).' 'Large, comfortable Rhum faces the back gardens. Lilac Cottage is excellent.' Each of the suites in the grounds has a conservatory and a private garden with hot tub. Robert MacPherson's six-course dinner (male guests wear jacket and tie) is praised: 'Reliable as ever: outstanding soups; venison, turkey, beef carved from the trolley; amazing selection of cheeses.' 'Lots of vegetables, offer of a salad with the main course; fancy puds (savoury alternative); impeccable, formal waiting.' Light meals are served on a veranda. Breakfasts have 'limitless fresh orange juice'; 'wonderful haddock and kippers'. 'Our dog thoroughly approved.' The spa's changing rooms have been upgraded this year. (*David Jervois, Joanna Russell, David Innes, RC*)

23 bedrooms. 2 on ground floor. 12 miles N of Oban. Closed Jan. Hall, drawing room, bar/library, dining room; leisure centre: swimming pool (55 by 20 ft), gym, sauna; massage, beauty treatments, bar, restaurant. No background music. 350-acre island: tennis, croquet, 6-hole par 22 golf course, marked walks, clay-pigeon shooting. Wedding facilities. No children under 5 in swimming pool; under-16s allowed 10 am–5 pm only. No dogs in public rooms, unaccompanied in bedrooms. Amex, MasterCard, Visa accepted. B&B (*min. advance reservation 2 nights*): single £220, double £360, suite £420. Set dinner £40. Weekly rates. Off-season breaks. Christmas/New Year packages. 1-night bookings sometimes refused.

FETTERCAIRN Grampian *See SHORTLIST* Map 5:C3

FORT WILLIAM Highland Map 5:C1

The Grange
Grange Road
Fort William PH33 6JF

Tel 01397-705516
Email info@thegrange-scotland.co.uk
Website www.thegrange-scotland.co.uk

On a hill, in attractive grounds, this white-painted Victorian Gothic B&B has wonderful views over Loch Linnhe and beyond to the hills above Treslaig. 'Immaculately' and tastefully furnished, and with large windows, it is light and airy. There are log fires, antiques, fresh flowers and crystal. Tea is served to arriving guests in the lounge. Background music is no longer played. Each bedroom is different. The Garden Room ('the most peaceful') has been refurbished and given a 'more minimal' feel. West-facing Rob Roy, where Jessica Lange stayed while making that film, has a colonial-style bed; the Terrace Room has its own terrace, a king-size antique bed and a Victorian slipper bath; the Turret Room faces the garden and loch, and has a Louis XV king-size bed. All rooms have fresh flowers and complimentary sherry. The 'welcoming, helpful' owners, John and Joan Campbell, show 'superb attention to detail', say their fans. Breakfast, ordered the night before, includes fruit compote, smoked haddock and potato pancakes, and is 'excellent value'. More reports, please.

4 bedrooms. 1 on ground floor. Outskirts of town. Open Mar–Oct. Lounge, breakfast room. No background music. 1-acre garden. Unsuitable for ♿. No smoking. No children under 12. No dogs. MasterCard, Visa accepted. B&B double £110. 1-night bookings sometimes refused.

See also SHORTLIST

FORTROSE Highland *See SHORTLIST* Map 5:C2

GATEHOUSE OF FLEET Dumfries and Galloway *See SHORTLIST* Map 5:E2

GATESIDE Fife Map 5:D2

Edenshead Stables

Gateside, by Cupar
KY14 7ST

Tel/Fax 01337-868500
Email info@edensheadstables.com
Website www.edensheadstables.com

The River Eden flows past the foot of the garden of John and Gill Donald's 'luxury B&B': a ruined stable on the edge of the village has been turned into this modern one-storey building. It has fine views of open countryside and the Lomond hills. The nominator loved the 'air of relaxed comfort', adding: 'The interior is immaculate. Beautiful furnishings, lovely paintings.' The best bedroom has a four-poster. The dining room is 'formal and elegant', with antiques and Spode china. The large sitting room, which leads on to a courtyard, is 'comfortable, and full of inviting books and local information'. Breakfast, 7.45–8.45, or earlier by arrangement, is communally served round one large table. It includes local kippers, Arbroath smokies, oatmeal porridge, black pudding, home-made preserves and much else. The 'charming hosts', who own two Hungarian Vizslas, Rosa and Zeta, write: 'As the house is all on one floor, we can offer accommodation to physically disabled, but not wheelchair-bound, guests.' Dinner may be available for groups of four to six. 'A wonderful selection of golf courses' is nearby. (*B and JG*)

3 bedrooms. All on ground floor. Outside village 12 miles SE of Perth. Parking. Train: Ladybank/Cupar. Open 1 Mar–30 Nov. Lounge, dining room; courtyard.

No background music. 3-acre grounds on River Eden. Unsuitable for ♿. No smoking. No children under 12. No pets. MasterCard, Visa accepted. B&B £35–£60 per person. Set dinner £25. 1-night bookings occasionally refused July/Aug. *V* (only for 1 night of a stay of min. 2 nights)

GLAMIS Angus — Map 5:D2

Castleton House
by Glamis
DD8 1SJ

Tel 01307 840340
Fax 01307-840506
Email hotel@castletonglamis.co.uk
Website www.castletonglamis.co.uk

'Every country house hotel should be like this. Wonderful food, well-trained staff, beautifully furnished.' Comments this year back up earlier praise of this Edwardian stone country house, now a popular small hotel. Built on the site of a medieval fortress, it is surrounded by a dry moat (grown over with trees and flowers). Owner/managers David and Verity Webster are 'warmly welcoming', service is 'friendly and unobtrusive'. In the public rooms are tasteful colour schemes, antiques, large log fires. The 'most attractive' conservatory has under-floor heating for winter. Chef Andrew Wilkie's two- or three-course dinners are served here or in the formal dining room. Main courses might include roast loin of venison with confit plum, fennel and star anise sauce. Spacious bedrooms have antiques, good artwork, lots of towels, home-grown flowers, mineral water, coffee and tea. For children there are special meals, a climbing frame in the garden, also ducks and chickens (they provide eggs for the 'excellent' breakfasts), two Tamworth pigs, croquet, and 'space for golf and throwing frisbees'. Dogs are welcomed. The house is on a busy road, though screened by trees. (*Jessica Blossom, and others*)

6 bedrooms. On A94 Perth–Forfar, S of Glamis. Drawing room, library/bar, conservatory/dining room, dining room; conference facilities; background jazz afternoon and evening. 10-acre grounds: stream; climbing frame, croquet, putting. Only dining room suitable for ♿. Wedding facilities. Smoking allowed in 3 bedrooms. Amex, MasterCard, Visa accepted. B&B £110–£160 per person; D,B&B £135–£185. Set dinner £35–£40; full alc £52. Discounts for 2 or more nights. Gourmet events. Christmas/New Year packages.

When we quote the range of prices per person, the lowest is for one person sharing a double room out of season, the highest for a single room in high season.

GLASGOW Map 5:D2

Malmaison Glasgow
278 West George Street
Glasgow G2 4LL

Tel 0141-572 1000
Fax 0141-572 1002
Email glasgow@malmaison.com
Website www.malmaison.com

In the city's financial district, this branch of the Malmaison chain is a chic conversion of a Greek Orthodox church whose central feature is a magnificent Art Nouveau central staircase. A returning visitor was impressed by the 'incredibly helpful, gracious staff; a wonderful experience'. There are bold colours and stripes, prints and black-and-white photographs in the bedrooms. A suite, with a well-furnished sitting room, was liked for 'all the usual goodies one associates with Malmaison' (CD-player, minibar, big bed, etc). The Big Yin suite, named in honour of Glaswegian comedian Billy Connolly, has a scroll-top tartan-painted double bath on a platform of pebbles in the living area. The early set menu in the brasserie in the vaulted basement is devoted to 'home-grown and local food'; later the *carte* has classic French bistro dishes, eg, steak frites; confit belly of pork. Light meals, tea and coffee are served in the champagne bar in the atrium, open to the glass roof of the first floor. (*SH*)

72 bedrooms. Some on ground floor. 4 suitable for ♿. Central (windows double glazed). NCP nearby. Lift. Champagne bar, brasserie/bar; fitness room; meeting room. 'Cool, funky' music in public areas all day. No smoking. All major credit cards accepted. Room [2007] £129–£345. Breakfast £11.95–£13.95. Set menu (5–7.30 pm) £15.50; full alc £40. 2-day weekend breaks. Christmas/New Year packages.

See also SHORTLIST

GLENFINNAN Highland Map 5:C1

Glenfinnan House
Glenfinnan, by Fort William
PH37 4LT

Tel/Fax 01397-722235
Email availability@glenfinnanhouse.com
Website www.glenfinnanhouse.com

'Warm and welcoming.' 'Staff helpful.' 'A beautiful setting.' Praise again for Jane MacFarlane-Glasgow's handsome Victorian mansion with 18th-century origins. Managed by Duncan and Manja Gibson, it stands on the shores of Loch Shiel, looking across the water to Ben Nevis and the Glenfinnan Monument (where Bonnie Prince Charlie raised the standard at the start of the 1745 Jacobite Rebellion). Fans of the *Harry Potter* movies will recognise the Glenfinnan Viaduct. The hotel is well furnished, with traditional decor and wood panelling. All the front bedrooms have 'superb views'; one has a four-poster. One couple were unhappy with their attic room, next to staff quarters ('not conducive to peace and quiet: but our complaint was handled brilliantly, and we were given a discount'). In the 'relaxing dining room', Duncan Gibson ('we do not serve fast food') provides continental-influenced traditional Scottish dishes, eg, venison with braised red cabbage and celeriac mash. 'Good meals' are served in the bar; a popular local, it also has fine views. Breakfast includes smoked salmon, haddock, kippers, but one visitor wrote of 'sliced bread toast and carton orange juice' and added: 'We had to listen to the same Scottish music CD at all meals.' Children are welcomed (under-twelves accommodated free) and have their own short menu. There is Wi-Fi access; and loch cruises can be arranged. 'A focus for village activities' and a popular Saturday wedding venue. (*John Munro, David Fowler, and others*)

13 bedrooms. 15 miles NW of Fort William. Open Mar–mid-Nov. Hall, drawing room, playroom, bar, restaurant; background music; function/conference facilities. 2-acre grounds: children's playground. Unsuitable for ♿. Wedding facilities. No smoking. No dogs in restaurant. All major credit cards accepted. B&B [2007] £40–£65 per person; D,B&B £68–£93. Full alc £41.25. Bar meals/packed lunches. Special breaks (see website). *V*

Prince's House NEW

Glenfinnan, by Fort William
PH37 4LT

Tel 01397-722246
Fax 01397-722323
Email princeshouse@glenfinnan.co.uk
Website www.glenfinnan.co.uk

'From outside it is not particularly impressive', but inside you receive the warmest of welcomes from co-owner Ina Kelly, says the nominator of this white-painted, gabled former coaching inn. 'She was most attentive throughout our ten-day stay.' Her 'very pleasant' husband, Kieron, is chef. They hold a Green Tourism Silver award for their eco-friendly ways. 'The atmosphere is friendly and homely, enhanced by the Kellys' two sons, much in evidence, who sometimes provide entertainment on their violins in the bar.' The bedrooms are on the first floor; best ones at the front. 'Ours was of reasonable size, well appointed. Its bathroom contained some unusual toiletries.' Dinner is a three-course meal in the spacious dining room (at quiet times opened for pre-booked meals only) or a blackboard menu in the bar or lounge/bar. 'We always chose the latter. Much emphasis on locally caught seafood. Bread home baked. Sweets include some interesting ice creams. Breakfast has porridge, fresh fruit and a cooked main course.' Though the building is on the road to Mallaig, 'traffic at night is minimal and no noise is heard inside. A fine base for exploring the spectacular scenery of the most westerly part of the British mainland.' (*AJ Gillingwater*)

9 bedrooms. 15 miles NW of Fort William. Open Mar–Dec and New Year. Closed 2 weeks Oct, Christmas. Lounge/bar, bar, dining room; background music. Small front lawn. Unsuitable for ♿. No smoking indoors (designated area outside). No dogs: restaurant, some bedrooms. MasterCard, Visa accepted. B&B [2007] £42.50–£65 per person; D,B&B £67.50–£90. Set menu £30. Bar meals. New Year package.

GLENLIVET Moray — Map 5:C2

Minmore House
Glenlivet
AB37 9DB

Tel 01807-590378
Fax 01807-590472
Email enquiries@minmorehousehotel.com
Website www.minmorehousehotel.com

Formerly the home of the founder of the famous distillery, this handsome, white-painted, stone-built country house has wonderful views of the hills of the surrounding Crown-owned Glenlivet Estate in the Cairngorms national park. Owned by David and Jill Pethick, it is managed by Victor and Lynne Janssen (he is the chef with his son, Marcus). Elegantly furnished, it has open fires in the entrance hall, the spacious, 'light and airy' drawing room and the wood-panelled bar, which stocks over 100 malt whiskies. Bedrooms are comfortable (one has a four-poster), though bathrooms can be small (but four of them have now been upgraded). The four-course dinner (no-choice but preferences accommodated) is liked, eg, rack of Highland lamb, grilled with a crust of rosemary and garlic. After-dinner coffee comes with home-made fudge. The lavish tea (£12.50), served on a lace tablecloth, includes sausage rolls, sandwiches, tarts, scones, home-made jam, 'sparkling silver teapots, fine china'. *Minmore* has one-and-a-half miles of fishing on the River Avon (pronounced 'aarn'). Tutored whisky evenings are held, and 'corporate packages with team-building activities' can be arranged. More reports, please.

9 bedrooms. 1 on ground floor, in coach house. By Glenlivet distillery; 8 miles N of Tomintoul. Open 29 Dec–end Nov. Drawing room, whisky bar, dining room; soft background music. 8-acre grounds. Fly-fishing. No smoking. No children under 6 in dining room at night (early supper provided). Dogs by arrangement; not in public rooms. Amex, MasterCard, Visa accepted. B&B [2007] £52–£86 per person; D,B&B £91–£135. Set dinner £40. New Year package. 1-night bookings sometimes refused at high season weekends. ***V***

GRANTOWN-ON-SPEY Highland — Map 5:C2

Culdearn House NEW

Woodlands Terrace
Grantown-on-Spey PH26 3JU

Tel 01479-872106
Fax 01479-873641
Email enquiries@culdearn.com
Website www.culdearn.com

Returning to the *Guide* with new owners, William and Sonia Marshall (she is the chef), this 100-year-old granite house is on the edge of a picturesque market town/resort in the Spey valley. A major refurbishment has decreased the number of bedrooms, creating 'luxury bathrooms'. 'Delightful, tiny and unassuming, exceptionally comfortable, I cannot praise it too highly,' says this year's report. 'Friendly welcome with offer of tea in the drawing room. Bedrooms are charming and thoughtfully done; bath/shower rooms immaculate.' As to the food, served in a candle-lit room with log fire: depending on local suppliers, it is 'exquisitely fresh and beautifully cooked' (eg, breast of chicken stuffed with haggis, with a whisky sauce). 'A useful stopping-off point, but also a place to rest in, like staying with old friends without the slightest pressure to be sociable.' Some rooms are spacious (some beds are king-size); extras include flowers and chocolates. The lounge has 'lots of easy armchairs and sofas', the original wood panelling, watercolours, antique maps. Salmon and sea-trout fishing on the Spey, as well as private beats with ghillie services, can be arranged. Anagach Woods adjoin the garden. (*Jane Ackroyd*)

6 bedrooms. 1 on ground floor. Edge of town, by Anagach Woods. Lounge (occasional classical background music), dining room. 1-acre garden. Unsuitable for ♿. No smoking. No children under 10. Guide dogs only. MasterCard, Visa accepted. B&B [2007] double £116–£150. Set dinner £32; full alc £40. Spring/autumn breaks. Reduced rates for 4–7 nights.

See also SHORTLIST

Traveller's tale We paid £175 for a double room. A four-foot-six bed had been stuck against the wall because the room was too small for a double bed; I had to climb over my wife to get in. This was a single room pretending to be a double. There was only one chair and only one towel. The water from the cold tap smelled nasty; the wallpaper in the bathroom was coming off the wall. Breakfast was badly cooked. And at night the piped muzak reminded us of a mediocre transport caff. (*Hotel in Co. Durham*)

GRULINE Argyll and Bute — Map 5:D1

Gruline Home Farm
Gruline, Isle of Mull
PA71 6HR

Tel 01680-300581
Email boo@gruline.com
Website www.gruline.com

'A warm welcome on a rainy day', with afternoon tea in the conservatory, was accorded to visitors this year by Colin (the cook) and Angela Boocock. On a remote peninsula of 'exceptional wild beauty', their 'handsomely converted' Georgian/Victorian farmhouse and outbuildings have views of the foothills of Ben More and the surrounding countryside. Access is along a long, rough drive which also leads to the Macquarie Mausoleum where lies the 'father of Australia'. The house is well decorated, with good antique and modern crafted furniture. Improvements this year include the installation of a 'fantastic' chandelier from Prague. In the dining room, 'most attractive, with Crown Derby china and crystal glasses', the 'excellent' four-course dinner (two choices of starter and main course, sorbet in between) might include partridge breast with a cognac sauce. No licence (bring your own wine; no corkage), but you are offered complimentary sherry and introduced to other guests before eating (a dinner-party atmosphere is encouraged). Breakfast, with 'outstanding' warm fruit compote, and lots of cooked dishes (including, sometimes, duck eggs with asparagus spears), is served, like dinner, on stylish crockery. 'Angela is meticulous with presentation and service.' The garden is midge-free, she promises. (*Joan and David Marston*)

3 bedrooms. 1, on ground floor, 5 yds from main house. 2½ miles from Salen village; 14 miles S of Tobermory. Open May–Oct. Lounge, conservatory, dining room; light classical background music all day. 2½-acre garden: stream. No smoking. No children under 16. Dogs in annexe only. MasterCard, Visa accepted. D,B&B (min. 2 nights) [2007] £85–£137.50 per person. Set dinner £34. 1-night bookings sometimes refused.

GULLANE East Lothian — Map 5:D3

Greywalls
Muirfield, Gullane
EH31 2EG

Tel 01620-842144
Fax 01620-842241
Email hotel@greywalls.co.uk
Website www.greywalls.co.uk

'A house by [Sir Edwin] Lutyens and a garden by [Gertrude] Jekyll are a good start, but *Greywalls* is no museum piece; it is a quite exceptionally well-run hotel.' Praise from a correspondent on his third visit to this elegant building which was commissioned by a golfer who wanted to be within a mashie niblick shot of the 18th green at Muirfield. It has belonged to the family of owners Giles and Ros Weaver since 1924: Sue Prime manages. Staff are 'plentiful, obliging; always an immediate offer of help with luggage'. The interior is richly furnished 'with restrained good taste'. The drawing rooms, conservatory and panelled library provide 'cosy areas to sit'; the 'intimate' bar offers 'an interesting gin with a slice of cucumber'. Chef David Williams's 'spectacularly good' modern British cooking is served in two airy dining rooms overlooking Muirfield's 10th tee. 'Starter with three different presentations of oyster; main course of slow-roasted pork: both outstanding. Sensible portion sizes. Interesting wine list with well-chosen section at lower end of price range.' Spacious bedrooms are furnished with antiques. Fellow guests might include American golfers 'fretting noisily about the late arrival of their helicopter to St Andrews'. (*Peter Jowitt*)

23 bedrooms. 6 in lodges. 4 on ground floor. Off A198, near Gullane village. Open Mar–Dec, 'possibly' Christmas. 2 lounges, conservatory, library, bar, 2 dining rooms. No background music. 7-acre grounds: walled garden, croquet, tennis, putting. No smoking. No dogs in public rooms. Amex, MasterCard, Visa accepted. B&B £110–£150 per person. Set dinner £45. Spring/autumn breaks. *V*

HEITON Borders — Map 5:E3

The Roxburghe Hotel & Golf Course

Heiton, by Kelso
TD5 8JZ

Tel 01573-450331
Fax 01573-450611
Email hotel@roxburghe.net
Website www.roxburghe.net

'The perfect retreat for anyone who likes an active country break', the Duke and Duchess of Roxburghe's castellated Scots baronial mansion has been managed since October 2006 by George Mack. It stands by the River Teviot on their huge estate, which has mature woodland, rolling parkland and the only championship course in the Scottish Borders, designed by Ryder Cup star Dave Thomas. Guests can fish in the duke's private beats on the River Tweed or in the stocked trout pond, and many other outdoor activities are available (see below). The 'particularly comfortable public rooms' have rich furnishings, ancestral portraits and fresh flowers. 'We spent our first day relaxing by the log fire.' Bedrooms (feature, deluxe and standard) are designed by the duchess. 'Ours was spacious and well equipped, with comfortable beds and a large bathroom.' Some rooms have a four-poster bed and a sofa; two have a log fire. The chef, Keith Short, serves 'scrumptious' dinners in the red-walled, candlelit dining room. A simpler lunch menu is available in the library bar. For breakfast, you can choose between 'light' (with pastries, fresh fruit and yogurt), and full Scottish. (*Rowana Grant, and others*)

22 bedrooms. 6 across courtyard. Some on ground floor. 3 miles S of Kelso. Ramps. Drawing room, library bar (soft background music), dining room, conservatory; function facilities; health and beauty suite. 500-acre grounds: woodland walks, golf course, fishing, clay-pigeon shooting, falconry, archery, horse riding, croquet, mountain bikes. Wedding facilities. No smoking. No dogs. All major credit cards accepted. B&B [2007] £89–£148 per person. Set dinner £32–£37. Seasonal packages, midweek breaks, golfing breaks.

INVERGARRY Highland — Map 5:C2

Tomdoun Sporting Lodge
Invergarry
PH35 4HS

Tel 01809-511218
Email enquiries@tomdoun.com
Website www.tomdoun.com

Overlooking the Upper Garry river on the old drovers' road to Skye, this simple sporting hotel, owned and run by Mike Pearson and Sheila Condie, offers a 'house-party atmosphere' for sportsmen and women. 'No TV, phone or fax in the bedrooms,' they promise. A reader enjoyed 'an authentic Highland lodge experience: it is furnished with old bits and pieces; ancient leather luggage in the hall. Four or five dogs wandered about. Everything was clean. There was a welcome buzz in the bar, a cosy fire burning in the grate.' Front bedrooms have views of Glengarry; simpler, cheaper rooms share a bathroom. Guests can eat in the bar (popular with locals and holidaymakers), or in the dining room. Jason Wilson's menus feature mainly seafood from across the north-west of Scotland, eg, squat lobster with garlic and ginger; cod in a Bloody Mary sauce. Simpler accommodation is available in the *Bunkhouse*, next to the lodge. Sporting pursuits include excellent fishing, and walking (from the door or to 30 Munros near at hand). (*ER*)

10 bedrooms. 5 with facilities *en suite.* 10 miles W of Invergarry; 6 miles off A87. Drawing room, bar (background music sometimes), dining room. 80-acre grounds. Fishing, walking, stalking, shooting, mountain biking. No smoking. MasterCard, Visa accepted. B&B [2007] £40–£55 per person. Packed lunch £5.95. Full alc £30. 1-night bookings sometimes refused. *V*

IONA Argyll and Bute — Map 5:D1

Argyll Hotel

Isle of Iona PA76 6SJ

Tel 01681-700334
Fax 01681-700510
Email reception@argyllhoteliona.co.uk
Website www.argyllhoteliona.co.uk

In a row of 19th-century houses in the centre of Iona village, this is the smaller of the two hotels on this mystical Hebridean island. It is a short walk from the jetty where the ferry from Mull docks. Owners Daniel Morgan and Claire Bachellerie are committed to 'minimising our impact on the environment'. They and six of their staff are locals. 'Whenever possible, produce and resources are acquired locally'; waste is recycled or composted. There are 'idyllic views' from the book-filled lounges; one has an open fire. The conservatory is 'a haven on sunny days'. Some bedrooms may be small, but they have 'good storage, pleasant watercolours, paperback books and a well-planned bathroom'. The hotel's organic garden supplies vegetables and herbs for the kitchen; the food is thought 'extremely good'. The wine list is 'firmly rooted in the deep and spiritual appreciation of the small French château'. Light lunches (soups and pies) are served; picnics are provided. Children are welcomed (they can have an early supper), and so are dogs, 'but local crofters insist they be exercised on a lead'. John Smith, a former leader of the Labour Party, is buried among the early kings of Scotland in Iona's 11th-century abbey. More reports, please.

16 bedrooms. 7 in annexe. Centre of village. Open 1 Mar–15 Nov. 2 lounges, conservatory, TV/computer room, restaurant (background music). Large organic garden. Unsuitable for ♿. No smoking. No dogs in dining room. MasterCard, Visa accepted. B&B £35–£85 per person; D,B&B £48–£102. Full alc £22. 1-night bookings sometimes refused.

KELSO Borders *See SHORTLIST* — Map 5:E3

KILBERRY Bute and Argyll — Map 5:D1

Kilberry Inn NEW
Kilberry, by Tarbert
PA29 6YD
Tel 01880-770223
Email relax@kilberryinn.com
Website www.kilberryinn.com

'Personally run, supremely likeable, with a touch of sophistication yet modest', this restaurant-with-rooms in a 'tiny, red-roofed building', red telephone box in front, has a 'beautiful if slightly remote' position on the Kintyre peninsula, on the scenic single-track road between Lochgilphead and Tarbert. 'A haven of good food and wine, plus some unusual beers,' writes the nominator. Owners for the past two years, Clare Johnson and David Wilson, have extensively renovated. He 'runs front-of-house with friendly efficiency'; she presides over the tiny kitchen: *Michelin* awards a *Bib Gourmand* for good food at moderate prices. 'There are two dining areas: beams and bare stone walls with interesting artworks give it plenty of character. Tables are impeccably laid with crisp white tablecloths, and the sensibly short menu offers such delicacies as potted Kilberry crab with lemon and toasted sourdough bread; spiced monkfish pan-fried with herby couscous.' Bread is home made. Breakfast includes smoothies, scrambled eggs with smoked salmon, home-made marmalade. The 'stylish, modern bedrooms' (with shower, and each with its own entrance) are in adjacent buildings. 'Ours was cheerful and impeccably clean.' Around are good walks, sailing, plenty of wildlife and 'fabulous sunsets'. (*John Rowlands*)

4 bedrooms. All on ground floor. 16 miles SW of Tarbert, on B8024. Open Mar–Nov Tues–Sun, weekends only Nov, Dec, also New Year. Bar/restaurant, smaller dining room; gentle background music during meals. No smoking. No children under 12 in bedrooms (any age in small dining room). No dogs: public rooms, 3 bedrooms. MasterCard, Visa accepted. B&B double £90. Full alc £32. Short breaks. 3-night New Year package.

KILCHRENAN Argyll and Bute — Map 5:D1

Ardanaiseig
Kilchrenan
by Taynuilt PA35 1HE
Tel 01866-833333
Fax 01866-833222
Email ardanaiseig@clara.net
Website www.ardanaiseig-hotel.com

Remotely set in a beautiful garden on Loch Awe, this grey stone baronial mansion has been filled by its owner Bennie Gray, of Gray's Antiques Market in London, with antiques, and given bold colour schemes, tapestries and rich furnishings. The long drawing room has panelled walls painted in mottled gold. Open fires burn here and in the 'cosier' library bar. One bedroom has apple-green walls, one has Chinese-style lacquered furnishings and an open-plan 'bathing room' with a central bath big enough for two. Beds are large: some four-posters. A boat house has been converted into a 'romantic' suite with modern decor, double-height windows and a glass balustrade giving an uninterrupted view of the loch. In the candlelit dining room, Gary Goldie's 'excellent' no-choice four-course dinners use local produce in dishes like best end of lamb with aubergine caviar, garlic nuggets, olive and caper jus. Breakfast has brown toast, honey and preserves in jars. Home-made scones appear at afternoon tea. Guests can watch activities on the loch through a telescope, and go in the hotel's boats to its own island. In a small amphitheatre in the garden, performances of song and dance are sometimes held. Peter Webster is the 'hands-on' manager.

17 bedrooms. Some on ground floor. 1 in boat house. 2 self-catering cottages. 3 miles E of Kilchrenan, by Loch Awe. Open 8 Feb–2 Jan. Drawing room, library/bar, restaurant (background CDs). 160-acre grounds on loch: gardens, open-air theatre, tennis, croquet, safe bathing, fishing, boating. Wedding facilities. No smoking. No children under 12 at dinner. No dogs in public rooms. All major credit cards accepted. B&B £58–£124 per person. Set dinner £45. Spring/autumn reductions: 3 nights for the price of 2. Special breaks: Valentine, autumn gold, etc. Christmas/New Year packages. *V*

KILDRUMMY Aberdeenshire — Map 5:C3

Kildrummy Castle Hotel NEW

Kildrummy
by Alford AB33 8RA

Tel 01975-571288
Fax 01975-571345
Email bookings@kildrummycastlehotel.co.uk
Website www.kildrummycastlehotel.co.uk

An impressive gabled and castellated house, now a 'stylish and comfortable' country hotel. Set in manicured lawns, by the romantic ruins of a 13th-century castle and Kildrummy Castle gardens, it has been run for 25 years by Thomas and Mary Hanna. 'The staff are exceptionally nice,' says a visitor this year. 'The meals were all of high quality. Admirable wine list.' Earlier reports told of the 'warm welcome and excellent housekeeping'. The spacious public rooms, which include a small library, have ornate panelled walls and ceilings, open fires, a magnificent carved oak staircase and original tapestries commissioned in 1900 by Colonel 'Soapy' Ogston, who built the house after selling his detergent business in Aberdeen to a then unknown entrepreneur named Lever. The bedrooms vary greatly in shape, size and outlook; some have antique furniture and a four-poster, others are modern in style. Chef Alan Greatbatch serves traditional dishes on a four-course menu, eg, grilled breast of pheasant with a horseradish scented mash and cider cream sauce. The beautifully kept gardens have a large collection of rare alpine plants, shrubs and specimen trees. The Hannas own a private stretch of fishing on the River Don two miles away. (*John RE Borron*)

16 bedrooms. 35 miles W of Aberdeen, NE of Ballater off A97. Open 8 Feb–3 Jan. Drawing room, library, lounge bar, restaurant; snooker room. No background music. 3-acre grounds: ruined castle, gardens. Private trout/salmon fishing on River Don, 2 miles. Unsuitable for ♿. No smoking. No dogs in public rooms. MasterCard, Visa accepted. B&B £82.50–£95 per person. Set dinner £36.50. Short breaks. Christmas/New Year packages.

KILLIN Perth and Kinross — Map 5:D2

Ardeonaig Hotel

South Loch Tay Side
by Killin FK21 8SU

Tel 01567-820400
Fax 01567-820282
Email info@ardeonaighotel.co.uk
Website www.ardeonaighotel.co.uk

César award in 2007

'Three splendid nights.' 'Delightful. We were very impressed.' Almost all visitors this year enjoyed their stay at Pete and Sara Gottgens's white-painted old inn. Reached up a narrow road in an isolated situation, it has majestic views over Loch Tay and Ben Lawers. 'A warm welcome from Sara; the staff were equally helpful.' 'Charming, knowledgeable, unstuffy.' 'Our favourite Scottish hotel,' were other comments. The 'elegant yet unfussy' public areas have a 'Cape-colonial' feel, with floorboards, rugs, prints from the host's native South Africa. The white lounge has generous sofas; the brown snug is 'cosy'; the library, with books and board games, has the best views. At night, candles line the route to the dining room where the 'forthright' Pete Gottgens, a renowned chef, offers a *table d'hôte* menu and a seasonal *carte*. 'Astonishingly good.' The exclusively South African wine list is 'a star feature'. Breakfast has a 'long and interesting' menu and freshly squeezed orange juice. 'Simple but comfortable' bedrooms have no TV, but fresh milk, good bedlinen and toiletries, towelling bathrobes. Some bathrooms are 'cramped' and there is little storage in some smaller rooms. Major building work is planned for early 2008: seven more bedrooms, two new dining rooms (the current small one is often crowded), a new kitchen. (*Gordon Murray, Gordon Franklin, Iain Elliott, Charles Gorer, and others*)

20 bedrooms. 2 in courtyard. S shore of Loch Tay. Lounge, library, snug, bar, restaurant; background music. 13-acre grounds on loch. Wedding facilities. No smoking. Dogs by arrangement, in snug and bar only; not unattended in bedrooms. MasterCard, Visa accepted. B&B [2007] £48.50–£123.50 per person; D,B&B £75–£150. Set dinner £26.50; full alc £48. Midweek breaks. Christmas/New Year packages. 1-night weekend bookings in high season accepted only close to date. *V*

KINCLAVEN Perth and Kinross — Map 5:D2

Ballathie House

Kinclaven
Stanley
nr Perth PH1 4QN

Tel 01250-883268
Fax 01250-883396
Email email@ballathiehousehotel.com
Website www.ballathiehousehotel.com

On a vast estate, with 'wonderful trees', a Victorian garden and lawns that sweep down to the broad River Tay (one of Scotland's finest salmon rivers), this large 19th-century house is managed by the long-serving Christopher Longden. It has creeper-covered turrets and pointed roofs. The main building is traditionally furnished, and has high ceilings, ornate plasterwork, antiques, deep sofas and open fires. 'The very pleasant drawing room overlooks the grounds; the large, bright dining room has a lovely view down to the river.' A grand staircase leads to bedrooms of varying sizes; some have a four-poster. They are well appointed, 'comfortable and well cared for; our suite was an amazing size, and had a large bathroom with gold fittings and a whirlpool bath, but the towels didn't quite live up to this splendour', and a faulty bathplug caused grief to one couple this year ('the plumber commented that most people take a shower nowadays'). A recently added white-painted *Riverside* building has bedrooms, suites and meeting rooms. There was another change of chef this year, following which two visitors were disappointed by the dinners, so we'd like more reports, please.

41 bedrooms. 1 suitable for ♿. 16 in *Riverside* building. 8 miles N of Perth. Ramp. Drawing room, morning room, bar, dining room; conference room. No background music. 100-acre grounds: walks; river (some fishing rights). Wedding facilities. No smoking. No unattended dogs in bedrooms; only guide dogs in public rooms. All major credit cards accepted. B&B [2007] £85–£165 per person. Set dinner £41.50–£45. 2-day breaks. Offers on website. Christmas/New Year packages.

'Set menu' indicates a fixed-price meal, with ample, limited or no choice. 'Full alc' is the hotel's estimated price per person of a three-course *à la carte* meal, with a half bottle of house wine. 'Alc' is the price of an *à la carte* meal excluding the cost of wine.

KINGUSSIE Highland Map 5:C2

The Cross at Kingussie
Tweed Mill Brae, Ardbroilach Road
Kingussie PH21 1LB

Tel 01540-661166
Fax 01540-661080
Email relax@thecross.co.uk
Website www.thecross.co.uk

'We keep going back,' say fans of David and Katie Young's restaurant-with-rooms, drawn by the 'quality of personal attention and the exceptional food'. In 2007 it won a Scottish 'Good for the Soul' award, and *Michelin* bestows two red crossed spoon-and-forks. A handsome, stone-built, 19th-century tweed mill, it stands in wooded grounds by the River Gynack in the Cairngorm national park. The millstream and gardens border a pretty terrace where drinks are served in summer. Interiors are 'light and bright', with 'appropriate Scottish art'. An earlier comment: 'Our spacious room, thoughtfully prepared, had a selection of books and music, ample lighting, large, comfortable bed and the restful noise of the river running by.' There are 'top-quality toiletries'. David Young, a former AA hotel inspector, shares the cooking with Becca Henderson and Simon Wallwork. He describes the food as 'modern Scottish, using seasonal and local ingredients in an educated manner' (eg, roast fillet of Glenfeshie hind with spiced red cabbage). It is 'beautifully cooked and presented'. 'High-grade' breakfasts have 'excellent juice, fruit, croissants, etc' and a daily-changing hot dish of the day, and 'the light breakfast really hits the mark'. (*Tony and Marlene Hall, Jo Dickson, and others*)

8 bedrooms. Tea-making facilities on request. 440 yds from village centre. Open mid-Feb–mid-Dec, New Year. Closed Sun and Mon evenings. 2 lounges, restaurant. No background music. 4-acre grounds: woodland, river (no bathing/fishing), *pétanque*. Wedding facilities possible by 2008. Only restaurant suitable for ♿. No smoking. 'We welcome babies and older children. Most guests are here to escape their own children, so we're not keen on toddlers.' No dogs. Amex, MasterCard, Visa accepted. B&B [2007] £45–£130 per person; D,B&B £80–£165. Set dinner £43–£45. New Year package. Website packages.

KINROSS Perth and Kinross *See SHORTLIST* Map 5:D2

KIRKBEAN Dumfries and Galloway Map 5:E2

Cavens
Kirkbean, by Dumfries
DG2 8AA

Tel 01387-880234
Fax 01387-880467
Email enquiries@cavens.com
Website www.cavens.com

Built by a tobacco baron in 1752, this handsome 18th-century bow-windowed, white-painted country house stands in landscaped grounds near the Solway coast. The hosts, Jane and Angus Fordyce, are 'visible and friendly', readers tell us; their staff are 'all very pleasant'. Interiors are elegant and well furnished; fires burn in the large sitting rooms, which open on to a terrace. 'Our bedroom, large and well decorated, overlooked the large back garden.' Decor is 'a blend of traditional and modern'. The host's cooking is 'beautifully prepared and a joy to eat'; his three-course dinner menu has two choices for each course of 'locally grown or reared produce'. The main course could be platter of Kirkcudbright scallops and prawns, or Galloway beef in a cream and pepper sauce. 'Breakfasts very good, including gorgeous muesli – the best I've eaten.' (*AD*)

7 bedrooms. 12 miles S of Dumfries. Open Mar–Nov, also New Year. 2 sitting rooms, dining room; computer room. No background music. 6-acre grounds. Unsuitable for ♿. No smoking. No children under 12. No dogs in public rooms. Diners, MasterCard, Visa accepted. B&B £40–£150 per person. Set dinner £30. *V*

KIRKCOLM Dumfries and Galloway Map 5:E1

Corsewall Lighthouse NEW
Corsewall Point
Kirkcolm, Stranraer DG9 0QG

Tel 01776-853220
Fax 01776-854231
Email info@lighthousehotel.co.uk
Website www.lighthousehotel.co.uk

This 'splendid place', on a windy promontory north of Stranraer, on Loch Ryan, was discovered by a regular *Guide* reader ('I loved it'). A 200-year-old 'A' listed working lighthouse has been sympathetically turned by owner/manager Gordon Ward into a 'truly unique' hotel. Some small bedrooms, with shower, are in the main building. 'Our suite, in a separate building, had an average-size bedroom and a large conservatory lounge with panoramic views of coast and lighthouse.' In the restaurant (with black beams and seascapes), chef Andrew Downie's daily-changing five-course dinner 'was spot on for cooking and service; meat and fish of excellent quality; locally smoked salmon, chicken and duck, wild salmon, rack of lamb, venison; everything freshly cooked and hot. You could tell from the attention to detail and non-fussy but thoughtful presentation that the kitchen was manned by people who took pride in the product. Good choice at breakfast too, including Buck's Fizz. Warm welcome. Helpful staff seemed to enjoy what they were doing. We never had to say which room we were in: they knew, though the hotel was full. Quite remote and not for those who want bright lights. The last mile or so is down a roughish track, so not for the nervous driver.' (*Lynn Wildgoose*)

11 bedrooms. 1 suitable for ♿. 5 suites in separate buildings. 5 miles N of Stranraer. 2 small lounges, restaurant; background CDs/radio; function/conference facilities. 20-acre grounds. Wedding facilities. Golf, pony trekking, birdwatching, walking nearby. No smoking. No dogs in hotel (allowed in some suites). All major credit cards accepted. D,B&B [2007] £70–£130 per person. Set menu £32.50; full alc £44. 3-night midweek breaks. Christmas/New Year packages. 1-night bookings refused Sat in high season.

KIRKCUDBRIGHT Dumfries and Galloway Map 5:E2

Gladstone House

48 High Street
Kirkcudbright DG6 4JX

Tel/Fax 01557-331734
Email hilarygladstone@aol.com
Website www.kirkcudbrightgladstone.com

In a 'pleasant little town [pronounced "Kurcoobrie"], which most people rush past on the A75', Gordon and Hilary Cowan's Georgian town house 'merits its entry as a value-for-money guest house', say visitors this year. The light, elegant building, Grade II listed, is 'beautifully decorated'; the 'fine drawing room with comfortable seating takes up most of the first floor'. Guests may use the secluded garden. 'Gordon welcomed us with tea, cake and a chat.' Evening meals are served by arrangement in a pretty dining room (no licence; bring your own wine). 'Delicious cream of celery soup; roast gammon and Cumberland sauce with seasonal salad and vegetables; delightful walnut tart. Served and presented in a professional manner.' The 'excellent' breakfast has fresh fruit, 'any cooked dish you fancy', home-made rolls and jam. Bedrooms are cosy, well furnished, with a good if 'old-fashioned' bathroom. The best is a double whose window seats overlook the impressive architecture of the high street and the maze of gardens running to the river. (*David and Joan Marston*)

3 bedrooms. Town centre. Closed Christmas/New Year. Occasional closures for owners' holidays. Lounge, dining room. No background music. ½-acre garden.

Unsuitable for ♿. No smoking. No children under 14 ('or at owners' discretion'). No dogs. MasterCard, Visa accepted. B&B [2007] £32–£41 per person. Set dinner £19.50. 3-night breaks or longer.

See also SHORTLIST

KIRKTON Dumfries and Galloway — Map 5:E2

Wallamhill House
Kirkton
Dumfries DG1 1SL

Tel/Fax 01387-248249
Email wallamhill@aol.com
Website www.wallamhill.co.uk

In a peaceful farming village north of Dumfries, Gordon and Margaret Hood's single-storey B&B was found 'better than many five-star hotels' by one admiring visitor. A report this year talks of 'huge, comfortable rooms, stunning setting, excellent hosts'. 'Everything comes on a very grand scale.' There is a large, well-furnished drawing room with a writing desk, and a big garden with croquet. All four bedrooms are on the ground floor: They have 'magnificent country views – cows grazing in the next field'; also king-size bed, power shower, large TV, video, CD-player, sherry, biscuits, chocolates and a fridge with water and fresh milk. 'Our enormous room had a small shower room.' The generous breakfast (last orders taken at 8.30 am) has choice of fruit and cereals; freshly cooked dishes. 'Gordon did the honours, padding around in his chef's overalls and socks.' There are fitness facilities upstairs, and plenty of outdoor activities available locally. (*Stuart Turner, Caroline and Richard Faircliff*)

4 bedrooms. All on ground floor. 3 miles N of Dumfries. Safe parking. Closed Christmas. Lounge, breakfast room; fitness room, sauna, steam room. 1½-acre garden; croquet. Walking, cycling, fishing, golf, beaches, mountain biking nearby. No smoking. No dogs. MasterCard, Visa accepted. B&B [2007] £28–£38 per person.

KIRKWALL Orkney — Map 5:A3

Lynnfield Hotel NEW
Holm Road
Kirkwall KW15 1SU

Tel 01856-872505
Fax 01856-870038
Email office@lynnfield.co.uk
Website www.lynnfieldhotel.com

Malcolm Stout and Lorna Reid, who previously ran the popular *Cleaton House*, Westray, have now moved to Orkney's capital. They are still upgrading their hotel, which stands adjacent to the Highland Park Distillery, facing the town and beyond. Visitors in late 2006 enjoyed their stay: 'Spacious rooms overlooking the town, very comfortable.' The restaurant faces the bay. 'From an extensive menu we enjoyed tender local lamb; excellent steak; strudel; clootie dumpling. The varied wine list had some inexpensive bottles.' There is a small bar, and a 'comfortable' residents' lounge with 'lovely squashy seating'. Mr Stout has a 'gentle, laid-back manner' and, with his Orcadian staff, runs the hotel in a 'relaxed manner'. (*Shirley Tennent*)

10 bedrooms. 1 suitable for ♿. ½ mile from centre, by Highland Park Distillery. Ample parking. Closed Christmas/New Year. Residents' lounge, bar lounge, restaurant (background Scottish music). Small garden. Wedding facilities. No smoking. No children under 12. No dogs in public rooms. MasterCard, Visa accepted. B&B [2007] £45–£75 per person. Full alc £35. *V*

KYLESKU Highland — Map 5:B2

Kylesku Hotel
Kylesku
by Lairg IV27 4HW

Tel 01971-502231
Fax 01971-502313
Email info@kyleskuhotel.co.uk
Website www.kyleskuhotel.co.uk

In 'breathtaking' north-west Sutherland ('purple mountains, huge white beaches, incredible rock formations'), this white-painted 17th-century former coaching inn stands on the shoreline where lochs Glendhu and Glencoul meet. The 'hands-on young owners', Louise and Struan Lothian (he is the chef), have completed a two-year make-over of the public rooms. The lounge, 'cosy with comfy sofas and a wood-burning stove', faces the water, as does the dining room. 'Good views', too, from the 'simple but warm and comfortable' bedrooms. 'Our room had cream walls (we hate flouncy curtains and chintz) and a pine-clad bathroom.' The bar is busy all day with visitors, and with locals eating in the early evening; the menus here and in the restaurant are similar. 'Generous portions of huge langoustines, haddock, scallops, lobster fresh from the sea lochs, or perhaps duck with dark cherry sauce; a light bread-and-butter pudding. First-rate fry-up at breakfast and the best ever Achiltibuie kippers. The service from the well-trained and cheerful young staff was faultless, and really made a difference to our stay.' Children are welcomed. (*Janet and Dennis Allom, GC*)

8 bedrooms. 1 in annexe. 10 miles S of Scourie. Open 1 Mar–mid-Oct. Restaurant closed Mon. Lounge, bar (stove, background music), restaurant. Small garden (tables for outside eating). Unsuitable for ♿. No smoking. No dogs: bar, restaurant. MasterCard, Visa accepted. 8 bedrooms. 1 in annexe. B&B [2007] £44–£60 per person. Set dinner £25–£29; full alc (bar) £26.

LANARK South Lanarkshire — Map 5:E2

New Lanark Mill

Mill 1, New Lanark Mills
Lanark ML11 9DB

Tel 01555-667200
Fax 01555-667222
Email hotel@newlanark.org
Website www.newlanark.org

In a steep wooded valley just below the Falls of Clyde, this restored 18th-century cotton mill is not a typical *Guide* hotel. Owned by New Lanark Conservation Trust, it is part of a World Heritage Site, a regeneration of a village and mill developed by the philanthropic socialist, Robert Owen. The 'attractive' complex includes a visitor centre, shops, self-catering accommodation and a youth hostel. Original features of the cotton mill, such as the Georgian windows and barrel-vaulted ceilings, have been kept. The decor is light, simple, modern (one couple thought it 'bland'); the spacious bedrooms have views of the Clyde or the surrounding conservation area. 'Our room was well furnished and clean, with an absolutely acceptable bathroom.' Five bedrooms are equipped for disabled visitors. Mike Hudson is the new chef this year: his 'Scottish/international' cooking is considered 'ok; rather routine vegetables'. Breakfast is a 'standard' buffet. The bar is busy with non-residents, and the village is popular for weddings (check when booking whether your stay coincides with a wedding party). Ceilidhs and party nights are held in winter. One visitor disliked the piped music. The accessible Clyde walkway leads to the Falls of Clyde wildlife reserve. (*Angela and Barbara Dixon, Tony and Marlene Hall, and others*)

38 bedrooms. 5 suitable for ♿. 1 mile S of Lanark. Lounge, bar, restaurant; varied background music. Heated indoor swimming pool (40 by 20 ft). Wedding facilities. Smoking allowed in 10 bedrooms. Dogs allowed in allocated bedrooms, not in public rooms. All major credit cards accepted. B&B £45–£74.50 per person. Set dinner £25.50. Christmas/New Year packages. 1-night bookings sometimes refused. *V*

> The terms printed in the *Guide* are only a rough indication of the size of the bill to be expected at the end of your stay. Always check the tariffs when booking.

LARGOWARD Fife — Map 5:D3

The Inn at Lathones NEW
by Largoward, nr St Andrews
KY9 1JE

Tel 01334-840494
Fax 01334-840694
Email lathones@theinn.co.uk
Website www.theinn.co.uk

In a hamlet near St Andrews, Nick White, 'a friendly owner', has modernised this 400-year-old single-storey coaching inn and added bedrooms in adjacent buildings. 'The reception desk at the back may be unimpressive, but the welcome from a man called Simon could not have been warmer,' say inspectors. 'He took us to our room in a former smithy: recently revamped in modern style, it had laminated floors, attractive light wooden Italian furniture, ultra-comfortable bed, TV, DVD-player, etc, a decent-sized bathroom.' The bar ('where you can mix with locals') stocks a wide range of whiskies. In a 'cosy' lounge, 'loud background music' was an unwelcome accompaniment to pre-dinner drinks. But 'dinner was first class and well presented. Not cheap (around £22 for a main course). Langoustine bisque, rich yet delicate, preceded the freshest of sea bass and tender loin of lamb; a magnificent dessert of berries with the lightest of white chocolate sauces. Good home-baked rolls.' Breakfast, no menu, served at table, had 'excellent fresh orange juice but thin sliced toast, cooked dishes but no mention of muesli or fruit'. Children under 12 are accommodated free. Functions and parties are often held. A winner of 'Best small golfing hotel in Scotland'.

13 bedrooms. All outside main building. Some on ground floor. 5 miles S of St Andrews. Closed Christmas, 2 weeks Jan. Ramps. Lounge, cocktail bar, restaurant; background jazz; function room. 1-acre grounds. No smoking. No dogs in public rooms. All major credit cards accepted. B&B £60–£130 per person; D,B&B (min. 2 nights) £90–£160. New Year package. 1-night bookings refused Sat. *V*

LOCHARNON Western Isles — Map 5: inset A1

See SHORTLIST

When you make a booking you enter into a contract with a hotel. Most hotels explain their cancellation policies, which vary widely, in a letter of confirmation. You may lose your deposit or be charged at the full rate for the room if you cancel at short notice. A travel insurance policy can provide protection.

LOCHINVER Highland Map 5:B1

The Albannach

Baddidarroch
Lochinver IV27 4LP

Tel 01571-844407
Fax 01571-844285
Email info@thealbannach.co.uk
Website www.thealbannach.co.uk

'We loved it. Food and atmosphere terrific.' Sheltered by trees and a walled garden on a hill above Lochinver's working harbour, Colin Craig and Lesley Crosfield's handsome, white-painted 19th-century house wins praise again this year for the 'considerate' service and imaginative cooking. The windows in the dining room have been enlarged to maximise the views over the deep sea loch to the dome of Suilven and, beyond, the mountains of Assynt; all but one of the bedrooms and all the public rooms have the views. 'Nice bedrooms, great meals, great staff – owners and non-owners alike – unpretentious and easy,' said one visitor. 'Expensive but terrific,' is another comment. Two small rooms have been converted into a new suite this year; a penthouse suite up steep steps is 'large and luxurious'. The owner/chefs serve 'light Scottish/French' dishes (eg, saddle of wild roe deer on croft beetroot, truffled squash) on a five-course menu: no choice, but the menu is discussed in advance and alternatives are available. The fish and shellfish are landed at the harbour below, and the meat, game and vegetables are all local. 'Good breakfasts.' (*Richard and Trisha Bright, IM*)

5 bedrooms. 1 in byre, with private patio. ½ mile from village. Open April–Nov, and 'festive season', except Mon. Snug, conservatory, dining room. No background music. 1-acre garden; 6 acres croftland. Unsuitable for ♿. No smoking. No children under 12. No dogs. MasterCard, Visa accepted. D,B&B [2007] £120–£190 per person. Set dinner £48.

Inver Lodge

Iolaire Road
Lochinver IV27 4LU

Tel 01571-844496
Fax 01571-844395
Email stay@inverlodge.com
Website www.inverlodge.com

Purpose-built in 1989, Edmund Vestey's hotel, on a hill above Lochinver's harbour, is surrounded by the dramatically beautiful mountains of Assynt. Bedrooms may be 'predictable, well fitted, with good furnishings but little character', and public rooms 'undistinguished' (comfortable furniture, stags' heads, patterned carpets) but everyone admires the 'stunning' setting, the warm welcome, the 'excellent, cosmopolitan staff', led by 'hands-on' manager Nicholas Gorton. 'Assistance with luggage at the double. They don't keep asking who you are when you order drinks, etc.' The interior is light: picture windows everywhere. The view from the dining room is 'breathtakingly beautiful': tables reallocated daily ensure that it is enjoyed by all. Peter Cullen 'produces ambitious dinner menus of up to six courses in modern British style. Emphasis is on local meat and fish. Timing of some fish dishes was erratic but venison was a particularly strong suit. The wine list covers the world at fair prices; half bottles more than usually numerous.' Breakfasts have freshly squeezed juice, good cooked dishes, but 'mediocre toast and preserves'. 'A nice touch – the bed is made whilst you breakfast, so the room is tidy when you return; the rest of the servicing is done later.' (*Andrew Wardrop, YH, and others*)

20 bedrooms. ½ mile from village. Open 11 Apr–2 Nov. 2 lounges, bar, restaurant; sauna, solarium; gift shop. No background music. ½-acre garden. Unsuitable for ♿. Wedding facilities. No smoking. No children under 10. No dogs in public rooms except foyer lounge. All major credit cards accepted. B&B [2007] £100–£155 per person; D,B&B £130–£185. Set dinner £47.

LOCHRANZA North Ayrshire — Map 5:D1

Apple Lodge

Lochranza
Isle of Arran KA27 8HJ

Tel/Fax 01770-830229

César award in 2000

Once the village manse, John and Jeannie Boyd's white-painted, grey-roofed guest house has a homely atmosphere (handmade artefacts, family photographs, books, a plethora of teddy bears), and a loyal clientele. Close to the sea (and the small ferry to Kintyre), it has wonderful views. Mrs Boyd's three-course, no-choice menus are discussed in the morning; she describes her cooking as 'best of British', perhaps smoked haddock and mushroom vol-au-vents; roast chicken with celery, almond and apple stuffing. 'Excellent quality, well presented,' say visitors returning in 2007. 'Main courses were first class over four days. Desserts this year were lighter (last year there were many "comfort" puddings).' Meals are served with candlelight, crystal and flowers. No licence. Bring your own wine. The bedrooms are warm and comfortable, supplied with books and local information; bathrooms are 'beautifully fitted'. You can walk to the hills from the doorstep. In the surrounding countryside, deer and eagles are often sighted. The Boyds tell us that they are 'winding down a little', so will no longer serve an evening meal in July and

August: 'Most of our regulars come in spring and autumn, and like to eat in after a busy day.' (*Joan and David Marston*)

4 bedrooms. 1 on ground floor. Outside village on N side of island. Closed Christmas/New Year. Dining room closed midday, and for dinner Tues, and July/Aug. No telephone (payphone available). Lounge, dining room. No background music. ¼-acre garden. Unsuitable for ♿. No smoking. No children. No dogs. No credit cards. B&B £37–£52 per person. Set dinner £24. Usually min. 3-night booking.

LOCKERBIE Dumfries and Galloway — Map 5:E2

See SHORTLIST

LYBSTER Highland *See SHORTLIST* — Map 5:B3

MAYBOLE South Ayrshire — Map 5:E1

Ladyburn

by Maybole KA19 7SG

Tel 01655-740585
Fax 01655-740580
Email jh@ladyburn.co.uk
Website www.ladyburn.co.uk

'An excellent retreat in a beautiful part of Scotland.' In an Ayrshire valley, surrounded by woods and fields, this 17th-century white former dower house is run by owners Jane Hepburn and her daughter, Catriona, like a friendly family home. 'The warm welcome and attention to detail made our stay a delight,' says a visitor this year. 'A luxurious feel.' The interior is comfortable, well furnished, with family antiques; the 'inviting' drawing room is light and airy, the library has a wood fire. Some bedrooms have a four-poster. There is additional accommodation in the 'Granny Flat', accessible from the main house but with its own entrance. Dinner (or supper) is now served by arrangement only: 'good traditional Scottish home cooking, with French overtones', eg, roast duck breast with caramelised pears and red cabbage. Mrs Hepburn still holds her alcohol licence. A picnic can be supplied. In spring, rhododendrons, azaleas and bluebells grow in the large garden: part of Scotland's gardens scheme, it has three national rose collections. *Ladyburn*'s guests may walk in the grounds of the magnificent adjacent Kilkerran estate. Shooting parties, weddings and functions are catered for. The golf courses of Turnberry are a short drive away, and salmon fishing can be arranged. (*Bernard Allen*)

5 bedrooms. 2 more in adjoining apartment. 14 miles S of Ayr. Restricted opening Nov–Mar. Drawing room, library, dining room. No background music. 5-acre garden: croquet. Limited access for ♿. Wedding/function facilities. No smoking. No children under 16. Guide dogs only. MasterCard, Visa accepted. B&B £35–£60 per person. Supper (2 courses) £17.50, dinner £26.50.

MELROSE Borders — Map 5:E3

Burts
Market Square
Melrose TD6 9PL

Tel 01896 822285
Fax 01896 822870
Email burtshotel@aol.com
Website www.burtshotel.co.uk

The Henderson family are 'very hands-on, always around' at their listed 18th-century building (with black and white facade and window boxes) on the market square of this charming border town. 'Good food; lovely, homely hotel,' said one visitor. The residents' lounges are small, 'but the large bar, with live fire, is friendly and much used by locals'. Bedrooms are 'acceptable, not luxurious'. In the restaurant, 'a favourite eating place' for a long-time *Guide* reader, Alistair Stewart serves modern Scottish dishes, eg, cauliflower velouté with white truffle oil; duo of red mullet and sea bream with langoustine risotto. The cheaper bar menu is also liked: 'Good value.' 'Breakfast was excellent.' A dissenter wrote of a disappointing dinner, and a dark bedroom. The family also own *The Townhouse*, opposite (see Shortlist). A good base for touring the Borders. (*CB, Evelyn Schaffer, and others*)

20 bedrooms. Central. Closed 24–26 Dec, 2–3 Jan. 2 lounges, bar, 2 dining rooms; private dining/conference facilities. No background music. ⅓-acre garden. Unsuitable for ♿. No smoking. No children. No dogs in public rooms. MasterCard, Visa accepted. B&B £56–£60 per person; D,B&B £82–£85. Set dinner £32.75. 2-day breaks.

See also SHORTLIST

We asked hotels to quote their 2008 tariffs. Many hadn't yet fixed these rates as we went to press. Prices should always be checked on booking.

MUIR OF ORD Highland — Map 5:C2

The Dower House
Highfield
Muir of Ord IV6 7XN

Tel/Fax 01463-870090
Email info@thedowerhouse.co.uk
Website www.thedowerhouse.co.uk

César award: Scottish guest house of the year

'Interesting, relaxing, comfortable.' 'Like staying in a family home.' 'I felt totally pampered.' So say visitors to Robyn and Mena Aitchison's gabled, one-storey *cottage-orné*. 'They are friendly but don't interfere. He is an excellent self-taught cook, and will play golf with guests if he has time.' She describes herself as 'owner, waitress, cleaner'. Visitors this year were 'warmly welcomed on a cold afternoon'. The pretty house stands in a 'large, beautiful' wooded garden bordered by the rivers Beauly and Conon. Inside are antiques, chintzy wallpaper, flowery fabrics. The small lounge has potted plants, open fire, ornaments, books, and a bar cupboard full of malt whiskies. 'An excellent, large bedroom.' Some rooms are small, but all have large bed, well-equipped bathroom: 'Ours had Edwardian-style fittings.' Three rooms are in a gatehouse (also let as self-catering). Guests are expected to take dinner in the 'most attractive' dining room with its 'gleaming mahogany tables'. The host describes his no-choice menu as 'gutsy modern British' cooking, eg, breast of pheasant with cabbage, bacon and puy lentils. 'Magnificent puddings.' 'Dietary requests speedily dealt with.' Generous breakfasts include fresh fruit salad, local honey, home-laid eggs. Children are welcomed: under-fives have high tea. (*Mike and Shirley Stratton, Gordon Murray, ER*)

4 bedrooms. 3 more in lodge (also let as self-catering unit). 14 miles NW of Inverness. Closed Christmas. Lounge, dining room. No background music. 4-acre grounds: small formal garden, swings, tree house. No smoking. No children under 5 at dinner. No dogs in public rooms. MasterCard, Visa accepted. B&B [2007] £60–£85 per person. Set dinner £38.

NEWTON STEWART Dumfries and Galloway — Map 5:E1

Kirroughtree House
Newton Stewart DG8 6AN

Tel 01671-402141
Fax 01671-402425
Email info@kirroughtreehouse.co.uk
Website www.kirroughtreehouse.co.uk

César award in 2003

'As good as ever, maybe even better,' says its greatest fan, returning to the McMillan group's imposing, white, bow-windowed mansion in large grounds by the Galloway Forest Park. Jim Stirling is the able manager: 'There may be changes in staff but somehow they always collect a delightful lot.' There are three oak-panelled lounges, hung with oil paintings, and a wooden 'modesty staircase' (panels prevent glimpses of a lady's ankles). Bedrooms are supplied with sweet sherry and fruit. 'Our usual room on the ground floor was not available, but the installation of a lift allowed us to see more of the hotel; we were given a huge room on the second floor; well furnished, all the usual extras; marvellous views and a great bath.' Men are required to wear a jacket at dinner. 'Charming' chef Rolf Mueller's modern British menus, served with white linen, crystal and bone china, have three courses (with 'pre-starter') and might include scallops wrapped in pancetta; breast of pigeon on a lentil and pumpkin purée. 'Breakfast is really good.' 'Our preferences are carefully recorded; our drinks appear as soon as we go for dinner.' (*Evelyn Schaffer, and others*)

17 bedrooms. 1½ miles NE of Newton Stewart. Open 9 Feb–2 Jan. Lift. 2 lounges, 2 dining rooms. No background music. 8-acre grounds: gardens, tennis, croquet, pitch and putt. No smoking. No children. No dogs: some bedrooms, public rooms. Amex, MasterCard, Visa accepted. B&B £80–£110 per person. Set dinner £32.50. 2-night breaks or longer. Christmas/New Year packages. 1-night bookings sometimes refused.

OBAN Argyll and Bute — Map 5:D1

Lerags House
Lerags, by Oban
PA34 4SE

Tel 01631-563381
Email stay@leragshouse.com
Website www.leragshouse.com

The atmosphere is informal and home-like at this handsome grey stone house in a mature garden by Loch Feochan. The owners, Charlie and Bella Miller (she is the cook), and their two Hungarian Vizsla dogs, Libby and Rex, 'offer a warm welcome'. It is a 'really lovely place, and excellent value', one visitor wrote. The Millers, from Perth, Western Australia, came here in 1993 'for a summer', and kept coming back; they have run *Lerags* since 2001. Guests stay on half-board terms only: the three-course dinners ('Scottish with Australian flair') provide 'delicious food, imaginatively prepared', eg, monkfish in pancetta with caper Béarnaise. No choice, but 'Bella is very flexible to guests' preferences'. Public rooms and bedrooms are comfortably furnished and elegantly decorated in white with a few stylish touches of colour. 'Our spacious suite had lovely views. The bed was one of the best ever, beautifully made, with crisp, white linen.' The breakfast menu includes waffles, kippers, porridge and 'full Scottish'. Charlie Miller says: 'We are a hybrid, not really a hotel, not really a guest house (horrid word); here it is just Bella and me to look after people.' Guests with 'limited disability' can be accommodated. (*TM*)

6 bedrooms. 4 miles S of Oban, by Loch Feochan. Closed Christmas. Sitting room, dining room ('appropriate' background music). 2-acre grounds. Wedding facilities. No smoking. No children under 12. No dogs. MasterCard, Visa accepted. D,B&B [2007] £82–£102 per person. New Year package by arrangement. 1-night bookings sometimes refused holiday weekends.

The Manor House

Gallanach Road
Oban PA34 4LS

Tel 01631-562087
Fax 01631-563053
Email info@manorhouseoban.com
Website www.manorhouseoban.com

On a rocky headland half a mile from the town centre, Leslie and Margaret Crane's listed Georgian stone house continues to please. Built as the principal residence of the Duke of Argyll's estate in 1780, it has spectacular views over Oban's busy harbour and bay to the Morvern hills and the Isle of Mull. Binoculars are provided in each 'well-appointed' and 'cosy' bedroom – also Wi-Fi. 'Our room was spotless,' say returning visitors, 'and service is very good; the Polish waitress who looked after us last year said she was happy to be back, a good sign.' In the candlelit dining room, chef Patrick Freytag serves a five-course menu: 'Up to standard, though maybe too substantial for those who haven't had much exercise. Puddings less good than the rest.' Main courses include supreme of corn-fed chicken stuffed with brie and spinach, with herb risotto. The admired breakfasts have fresh orange juice, 'excellent scrambled eggs and smoked salmon'. The bar (a popular local, with 'good lunches, nicely served') has 'good views across the water; so does the little lounge'. In fine weather, lunch and drinks are served on a panoramic terrace. (*David and Joan Marston, and others*)

11 bedrooms. ½ mile from centre. Closed Christmas. 2 lounges, bar, restaurant; 'easy listening' background music. ½-acre grounds. Unsuitable for ♿. Wedding facilities. No smoking. No children under 12. No dogs in public rooms. Amex, MasterCard, Visa accepted. B&B [2007] £47.50–£145 per person; D,B&B £76.50–£173. Set dinner £34; full alc £40–£45. New Year package.

> If you are recommending a B&B and know of a good restaurant nearby, please mention it in your report.

ONICH Highland Map 5:C1

Cuilcheanna House NEW *Tel* 01855-821226
Onich, by Fort William *Email* relax@cuilcheanna.freeserve.co.uk
PH33 6SD *Website* www.smoothhound.co.uk/hotels/cuilcheanna

Surrounded by beautiful mountain scenery, Russell and Linda Scott's white-painted, gabled country house stands in peaceful grounds above Loch Linnhe. There are 'wonderful views' across to the hills of Mull, and 'a nice waterfront walk to the village'. In this 'unpretentious, honest little hotel', which offers 'excellent value', the well-furnished bedrooms are compact but comfortable. The small lounge has a log fire, books and TV. Mrs Scott's cooking, based on local produce, is enjoyed: 'Our favourites were the rolled beef and the bread and butter pudding.' The four-course (including cheese) menu offers no choice, but 'they went out of their way to provide alternatives if I was not keen on something'. The wine and whisky lists are 'extensive'. 'Everywhere was spotless. Our lovely room faced the loch.' Local wildlife includes roe deer, red squirrels, seals and otters. Fort William and Glencoe are within easy reach. So is Corran ferry, making day-trips possible to Morvern, the Isle of Mull and the lovely Ardnamurchan peninsula. The hotel went on the market as the *Guide* went to press. (*Paul and Jenny Tucker, Gordon Murray, Mr and Mrs JT Mills*)

5 bedrooms. 10 miles SW of Fort William, off A82. Open late Apr–early Oct. Lounge with TV, dining room. No background music. ½-acre garden. Near Loch Linnhe: shingle beach. Unsuitable for ♿. No smoking. No children under 12. Dogs by arrangement; not in public rooms. MasterCard, Visa accepted. D,B&B £60–£80 per person.

PEAT INN Fife Map 5:D3

The Peat Inn NEW *Tel* 01334-840206
Peat Inn, by Cupar *Fax* 01334-840530
KY15 5LH *Email* stay@thepeatinn.co.uk
Website www.thepeatinn.co.uk

New owners, Katherine and Geoffrey Smeddle, now preside over this famous old coaching inn at the crossroads of this tiny village near St Andrews. He is the chef (formerly head chef of Terence Conran's *étain* restaurant, Glasgow), she the 'particularly friendly' front-of-house. Many staff have remained from the previous regime. 'It was busy on a Tuesday evening in October,' inspectors tell us. 'No wonder, for food and service were exceptional, the rooms most relaxing.' Overnight guests stay in suites at the side of the inn. Most are split-level. 'Ours was traditionally furnished, well lit, with plenty of storage. Upstairs was a sitting room; downstairs were the bedroom (with large, comfy bed) and a terrific marble bathroom (fluffy white towels, bathrobes, plenty of shelf space).' Guests gather in a lounge (with log fire) before dinner, which is served in three 'discreet rooms', with big windows and widely spaced tables. 'Highlights were a starter of wild cèpes with beetroot; halibut on puy lentils. Cooking of the highest order, not cheap, but good value, especially the no-choice menu of the day (£32). A splendid breakfast, delivered to the room by two cheerful local women, included fresh juice, boiled eggs, toast and croissants.' Refurbishment began in 2007.

8 suites. All on ground floor, in annexe. 2 family. 6 miles SW of St Andrews. Closed Sun/Mon, 25/26 Dec, 1/2 Jan. Ramp. Lounge, restaurant. No background music. 1-acre garden. No smoking. Amex, MasterCard, Visa accepted. B&B [2007] £72.50–£125 per person. Set lunch £22, dinner £32; full alc £40–£45. Special breaks all year.

PEEBLES Borders — Map 5:E2

Castle Venlaw
Edinburgh Road
Peebles EH45 8QG

Tel 01721-720384
Fax 01721-724066
Email stay@venlaw.co.uk
Website www.venlaw.co.uk

In mature grounds and woodland on the slopes of the Moorfoot hills, John and Shirley Sloggie's handsome 18th-century Scots baronial mansion overlooks this attractive Borders town. 'Splendid; we were warmly welcomed,' says a visitor this year. Bedrooms, each named after a malt whisky, are comfortable and have good views. 'Our lovely room was large, with a good sitting area.' Two 'romantic' suites have an antique four-poster and a second bathroom with a double bath, heated floor tiles, fibre-optic lighting, music system and champagne cooler. The family suite, in a tower, has a children's 'den' with bunk beds, games and books. In the light dining room, with a parquet floor and elegant furnishings, the 'very enjoyable' daily-changing menu might include terrine of rabbit and chicken; rack of lamb with char-grilled Mediterranean vegetables. *Castle Venlaw* is on the market, but an early sale is not expected. (*Gordon Murray*)

12 bedrooms. 1 mile NE of Peebles. Library/bar (background music at lunch and dinner), restaurant. 4-acre garden: woodlands. Unsuitable for ♿. Wedding facilities. No smoking. No children under 5 in restaurant at night. No dogs in public rooms. MasterCard, Visa accepted. B&B [2007] £63–£115 per person; D,B&B £83–£105. Set dinner £26.50–£30. Short breaks. Christmas/New Year packages. 1-night bookings occasionally refused.

See also SHORTLIST

PERTH *See SHORTLIST* Map 5:D2

PITLOCHRY Perth and Kinross Map 5:D2
See SHORTLIST

PLOCKTON Highland Map 5:C1

Plockton Hotel
Harbour Street
Plockton IV52 8TN

Tel 01599-544274
Fax 01599-544475
Email info@plocktonhotel.co.uk
Website www.plocktonhotel.co.uk

'A great three-night stay. Owners and staff very friendly. Two comfortable, quiet rooms. Very good breakfasts (smoked salmon the best I've had). Good dinners too. Beers well kept.' This year's endorsement for the Pearson family's award-winning inn. 'Beautifully situated' on the palm-fringed waterfront of one of the prettiest villages in Scotland (National Trust), it has spectacular views over Loch Carron to the Applecross hills beyond. Part of a terrace of mainly white-painted, stone-built houses, the hotel is in one building, the bar – a popular local – and small dining room are in an adjoining one; a cottage annexe is a few doors along. Bedrooms are stylishly and individually furnished: 'Mackintosh-inspired fabrics, lighting and furniture' and 'good, large bathroom'. But a back room in the annexe faces a wall, so is dark. 'The chintzy lounge bar, very welcoming, and dining room, also have echoes of Mackintosh.' But one couple regretted the 'lack of a proper sitting room', and found service 'a bit casual' at times. Chef Alan Pearson's cooking is 'simple traditional Scottish', eg, local salmon poached with lime leaves, with lime crème fraîche. There is a garden in front across a small road, above the beach, and a rear terraced garden with waterfall.

This lively place has weekly bar entertainments, and the restaurant has a ceilidh dance floor. The hotel was put on the market as we went to press: prospective guests should check the position before booking. (*Jeffrey Taylor, and others*)

15 bedrooms. 1 suitable for ♿. 4 in cottage annexe. Village waterfront. Closed 25 Dec. Small lounge, lounge bar, public bar, snug, restaurant; soft background CDs. Front and rear gardens. Wedding facilities. No smoking. Dogs allowed in public bar. Amex, MasterCard, Visa accepted. B&B £35–£65 per person. Full alc £25–£30. Off-season discounts.

PORT APPIN Argyll and Bute — Map 5:D1

The Airds Hotel
Port Appin PA38 4DF

Tel 01631-730236
Fax 01631-730535
Email airds@airds-hotel.com
Website www.airds-hotel.com

At the edge of the village, this white-painted former ferry inn is now Shaun and Jenny McKivragan's small luxury hotel; Martin Walls is manager. This year they have created two new suites by combining existing bedrooms, and upgraded six bathrooms; Wi-Fi is available. The rooms have floral fabrics, antiques; flat-screen TV and DVD-player. 'Staff are punctilious; the male receptionist was scrupulously polite,' says a visitor this year. Other comments: 'Not cheap, but good value.' 'Our room at the back was nicely decorated. Two built-in cupboards, gleaming bathroom with power shower, never-ending hot water.' 'Our suite had a wonderful view over Loch Linnhe.' 'We liked the assortment of wellies by the door.' The lounges have 'squashy, comfy seating'; the conservatory at the front, where pre-dinner drinks are served, is 'light and airy'. Award-winning chef, Paul Burns, serves modern French dishes ('with a hint of Scottish'). 'We enjoyed langoustine and sea bream; delicious prune and Armagnac soufflé. Service was leisurely. Female staff, mainly East European, kilted at night.' Breakfasts are 'excellent' (fresh juice; home-made jams; 'very good kippers'), as are packed lunches and afternoon tea. Dogs are welcomed. A small paved area and lawn are across the road. (*Shirley Tennent, Margaret and David Mallett, P and AH*)

11 bedrooms. Also self-catering cottage. 25 miles N of Oban. Closed 13–31 Jan. 2 lounges, conservatory, restaurant. No background music. 1-acre garden: croquet, putting. Unsuitable for ♿. Wedding facilities. No smoking. No children under 8 in dining room in evening. Dogs by prior agreement; not in public rooms. MasterCard, Visa accepted. D,B&B [2007] £122.50–£260 per person. Set dinner £49.50. Off-season/winter breaks. Christmas/New Year packages.

PORT CHARLOTTE Argyll and Bute — Map 5:D1

Port Charlotte Hotel
Main Street
Port Charlotte
Isle of Islay PA48 7TU

Tel 01496-850360
Fax 01496-850361
Email info@portcharlottehotel.co.uk
Website www.portcharlottehotel.co.uk

With views across Loch Indaal (the distinctive Paps of Jura form a backdrop), Grahame and Isabelle Allison's small hotel stands on the waterfront of this pretty conservation village of white-washed cottages. A recent visitor praised its 'friendly staff, who looked after us very well'. It is attractively furnished, with oriental rugs, polished wood floors, 'nice antique furniture' and contemporary Scottish art. Live traditional music is a feature in the bar, popular with locals. It stocks 118 single malts, and serves evening meals. Hotel guests are advised to book a table at the busy restaurant, where the chef, Rangasamy Dhamodharan, serves a three-course menu with much local produce, eg, Loch Gruinart oysters; saddle of venison with a blackberry jus. The bedrooms are 'fine, if a little on the small side'; nine of them have sea views. You can reach a sandy beach from the small garden that leads from the conservatory. As well as peaty malt whiskies, Islay, warmed by the Gulf Stream, has many deserted beaches, and is a paradise for birdwatchers. (*IGCF, and others*)

10 bedrooms. 2 on ground floor. Village centre. Parking. Closed 24–26 Dec. Lounge, conservatory, bar, restaurant; traditional background/live music. Small garden (bar meal service). Wedding facilities. No smoking. No dogs in public rooms. Diners, MasterCard, Visa accepted. B&B £65–£85 per person. Full alc £42. 3 nights for the price of 2, Oct–Mar.

PORTPATRICK Dumfries and Galloway — Map 5:E1

Knockinaam Lodge
Portpatrick
DG9 9AD

Tel 01776-810471
Fax 01776-810435
Email reservations@knockinaamlodge.com
Website www.knockinaamlodge.com

Shielded by cliffs and thickly wooded hills, this grey stone 19th-century hunting lodge, up a long drive, is now a luxury hotel owned by the 'genial but unobtrusive' David and Sian Ibbotson. 'Beautifully decorated', the house has rich fabrics, antiques, oak panelling and open fires. Churchill met Eisenhower secretly here during the Second World War: you can stay in his comfortable bedroom, the largest, with its enormous bath ('stool provided so you can climb in'). There are some fine single malts in the bar. In the formal, candlelit dining room ('we prefer gentlemen to wear a jacket in the evening,' say the room notes), chef Tony Pierce's four-course, no-choice (except for dessert or cheese) dinner is much admired (*Michelin* star). The style is classical/modern Scottish, eg, baked scallop with champagne sauce; cannon of Galloway lamb with thyme pomme purée, garlic beignet. Vegetarians are well catered for. Portions are 'small but satisfying'; 'the full Scottish breakfast more than makes up in quantity'. In fine weather there are tea, drinks and barbecues on the lawn. There is a tree house for children, who are welcomed here. *Knockinaam* has its own sandy cove. Good walking and country pursuits. (*SC, and others*)

9 bedrooms. 2 miles S of Portpatrick. 2 lounges, bar, restaurant (classical background music). 30-acre grounds. Sand/rock beach 50 yds; fishing. Only restaurant suitable for ♿. Wedding facilities. No smoking. No children under 12 in dining room after 7 pm (high tea at 6). No dogs: public rooms, some bedrooms. Amex, MasterCard, Visa accepted. D,B&B [to April 2008] £135–£300 per person. Set meals £50. Reductions for 3 or more nights off-season. Christmas/New Year packages. *V*

PORTREE Highland — Map 5:C1

Cuillin Hills Hotel

Portree, Isle of Skye
IV51 9QU

Tel 01478-612003
Fax 01478-613092
Email info@cuillinhills-hotel-skye.co.uk
Website www.cuillinhills-hotel-skye.co.uk

In wooded grounds overlooking Portree Bay, this white-walled, gabled traditional hotel (a former Victorian hunting lodge) is owned by the small Wickham group; Murray McPhee is its new manager. 'Commanding an outstanding view to the Cuillin Hills', it is liked for the 'sense of space', and the staff, 'local, and characteristically friendly and helpful'. But one visitor found meal service 'amateurish'. In the candlelit restaurant, chef Robert MacAskill serves a daily-changing dinner menu with 'a good choice and high standards'. Typical dishes: peppered loin of venison; darne of salmon, risotto rice cake, saffron cream sauce. Less formal meals are served in the bar/conservatory. Breakfast also has a wide choice. There are bright tartans and stripes in the bedrooms: a premier room was 'spacious, warm and sparklingly clean; serviced twice daily; fruit and shortbread replenished'. In summer, you can take a drink on the lawn while watching the activities in the harbour. (*J and TS, and others*)

27 bedrooms. 7 in annexe. 3 on ground floor. 1 suitable for ♿. 10 mins' walk from town. Lounge, bar, restaurant; background music; function rooms. 15-acre grounds. Wedding facilities. No smoking. No dogs. Amex, MasterCard, Visa accepted. B&B [2007] £60–£120 per person. Set menus £32.50–£35. Christmas/New Year packages.

Viewfield House

Portree
Isle of Skye IV51 9EU

Tel 01478-612217
Fax 01478-613517
Email info@viewfieldhouse.com
Website www.viewfieldhouse.com

César award in 1993

The 'affable' Hugh Macdonald welcomes guests to this 'magnificent' baronial pile, his family's ancestral home for over two centuries. The public rooms may be 'a bit shabby', but they are 'interesting and comfortable', say visitors this year. They have a 'Gothic air' (the house is Georgian with Victorian additions). There are family pictures, Indian brass and other Imperial relics; Persian carpets on polished wood floors. 'Our huge bedroom had four windows overlooking the gardens and bay. It was furnished with antiques, books, two writing desks; the vast, slightly chilly bathroom had a new walk-in power shower as well as a claw-footed bath and two washstands.' The 'absence of hotel-type notices' is liked, and there is no hotel-style reception or bar – but drinks are served more or less on request. Mr Macdonald no longer provides dinner ('most of our guests do not wish to be tied down,' he says). Simple hot dishes and salads are available throughout the evening (home-made soups, cheese platter, etc). 'Breakfast has plenty of fresh and dried fruit, Mallaig kippers, fresh juices.' Don't miss the ground-floor cloakroom, 'a unique "antique" experience'. There is Wi-Fi Internet access throughout, and a small office for guests' use. Children are welcomed. (*Janet and Dennis Allom, and others*)

11 bedrooms. 1 on ground floor suitable for ♿. S side of Portree. Open Mar–mid-Oct. Ramp. Drawing room, morning/TV room, dining room. No background music. 20-acre grounds: croquet, swings. No smoking. No dogs in public rooms. MasterCard, Visa accepted. B&B £45–£60 per person. 3- to 5-day rates. 1-night group bookings sometimes refused. *V*

RODEL Western Isles *See SHORTLIST* Map 5:B1

For details of the Voucher scheme see page 62.

ST ANDREWS Fife — Map 5:D3

Rufflets
Strathkinness Low Road
St Andrews
KY16 9TX

Tel 01334-472594
Fax 01334-478703
Email reservations@rufflets.co.uk
Website www.rufflets.co.uk

In her family's ownership for over 50 years, Ann Murray-Smith's turreted, white, baronial style mansion (built in the 1920s) stands in award-winning gardens just outside the 'home of golf'. 'Everything was of the highest standard,' one visitor wrote. 'We loved it; the welcome was warm.' 'Lovely and comfortable' bedrooms are individually furnished, and have a smart bathroom, a teddy bear and a supply of shortbread. Public rooms have rich interiors; there is an Adam fireplace in the elegant drawing room. In the *Garden Restaurant*, the chef, Mark Nixon, serves modern dishes, using fresh Scottish produce, eg, boneless quail on game boudin; seared monkfish and smoked bacon with wild mushroom risotto croquette. Light lunches are served in the split-level music room, with its antique fireplace and curved, intricately carved bar. 'A wonderful breakfast.' This is the first official carbon-neutral hotel in Scotland. (*SK*)

24 bedrooms. 4 in lodges in grounds. 1 mile W of St Andrews. Drawing room, music room/bar, restaurant; background music. 10-acre grounds. Golf nearby. Wedding facilities. No smoking. No dogs. All major cards accepted. B&B [2007] £65–£150 per person; D,B&B £100–£185. Set dinner £40. 3-day breaks. Christmas/New Year packages.

ST OLA Orkney — Map 5:A3

Foveran
St Ola
Kirkwall KW15 1SF

Tel 01856-872389
Fax 01856-876430
Email foveranhotel@aol.com
Website www.foveranhotel.co.uk

Overlooking Scapa Flow, this simple, single-storey hotel (owned by the Doull family) 'has a relaxed feel but is very professionally run'. 'Such a warm welcome from Helen Doull, with an instant tray of tea – the beginning of a lovely week,' said one visitor. The well-equipped bedrooms, decorated in blond woods, and with simple designs, are 'small but immaculate and comfortable'. In the lounge, pre-dinner drinks are served by a fire. In the restaurant, 'large, light and airy', with well-spaced tables, Paul Doull's 'consistently good' cooking is enjoyed by 'a constant flow of locals' as well as visitors. The emphasis is on local produce: 'Scallops, monkfish, lamb were all delicious.' The service from 'a splendid team of youngsters' is praised: 'They really care about their guests.' 'Breakfast was excellent.' A fine base for exploring Orkney, its abundant wildlife and fascinating archaeological sites. (*RP, MW*)

8 bedrooms. All on ground floor. 3 miles SW of Kirkwall. Open mid-April–early Oct; by arrangement at other times. Restaurant closed Sun evening end Sept–early June. Lounge, restaurant (Scottish background music in evening). 12-acre grounds; private rock beach. Wedding facilities. No smoking. No dogs. MasterCard, Visa accepted. B&B [2007] £49.50–£59.50 per person; D,B&B £72–£82. Full alc £32. 1-night bookings sometimes refused.

SCARISTA Western Isles *See SHORTLIST* Map 5:B1

SCOURIE Highland *See SHORTLIST* Map 5:B2

SHAPINSAY Orkney Map 5:A3

Balfour Castle
Shapinsay
KW17 2DY

Tel 01856-711282
Fax 01856-711283
Email info@balfourcastle.co.uk
Website www.balfourcastle.co.uk

'A fascinating place', this 'magnificent' turreted 19th-century castle, 'a Victorian time warp', stands on a small hill outside Shapinsay harbour. It has been the home of the Zawadski family since Captain Tadeusz Zawadski, a Polish cavalry officer, bought it in 1961; his daughter, Mrs Patricia Lidderdale, is now in charge. 'We loved it,' say visitors in 2007. The handsome drawing room has views over the water to St Magnus Cathedral and Kirkwall; French doors lead to a conservatory; there is a small bar in the oak-panelled library, and a small chapel where weddings are held. The no-choice (with vegetarian options) three-course communal dinners are 'simple and fresh' (eg, wild duck breasts with plum sauce). Fiona Firth, the chef, 'is a mine of information; we learnt a lot as she chatted through the main course'. Most bedrooms are large; one has a four-poster bed with carved coat of arms of the Balfour family; another has a small turret and a large brass bed. Bathrooms have 'lashings of hot water'. In the 'beautiful grounds' are a wood, and a walled garden which produces 'particularly good' fruit and vegetables. Shapinsay has a wealth of birds, seals, wild flowers, good walks. (*Richard and Trisha Bright*)

6 bedrooms. 5 mins' walk from harbour. Ferry (20 mins) to Shapinsay from Kirkwall; they will meet. Closed Christmas/New Year/Jan–Apr. Drawing room, library, dining room, breakfast room, conservatory; billiard room; chapel. No background music. 70-acre grounds: beaches, fishing, wildlife walks. Unsuitable for ♿. Wedding facilities. No smoking. No dogs in house. MasterCard, Visa accepted. D,B&B £100–£125 per person. 10% discount for 3 or more nights.

SHIELDAIG Highland — Map 5:C1

Tigh an Eilean
Shieldaig, Loch Torridon
IV54 8XN

Tel 01520-755251
Fax 01520-755321
Email tighaneilean@keme.co.uk

César award in 2005

With 'glorious' views across the sea to Shieldaig Island (a sanctuary for ancient pines), Christopher and Cathryn Field's 'unpretentious' and 'friendly' small hotel is 'highly recommended' by a family this year. 'The owners are delightful, helpful. Our children were well catered for.' A returning visitor identifies the 'easy way' the Fields run the hotel as the main attraction: 'You don't come for posh comfort, but for good food and to be looked after. Our room had loch views; ample-sized bathroom.' A rare dissenting note came from visitors who thought the decor 'shabby', and the bedrooms poorly insulated: but a 'rolling' redecoration programme is in progress. In two 'comfortable lounges', the honour bar is 'a nice touch', and 'tasty' canapés come with pre-dinner drinks. Christopher Field cooks a three-course menu: 'We enjoyed juicy scallops, langoustines, tender rabbit; portions are generous (our dog benefited from a doggy bag); particularly good breads. Cooked breakfasts were equally generous: freshly squeezed juice, excellent yogurt, smoked haddock, various breads.' Free Wi-Fi Internet access is now available throughout. The Fields also own the adjacent village pub, where you can be 'inexpensively and well fed'. Around are 'lovely scenery, peace, quiet and good walks'. (*Wendy Brooks, Shirley Tennent, and others*)

11 bedrooms. Village centre. Open mid-Mar–end Oct. 2 lounges (1 with TV and wood-burning stove), bar/library, village bar (separate entrance), dining room; drying room. No background music. Small front courtyard, small rear garden. Unsuitable for ♿. Wedding facilities. No smoking. No dogs in public rooms. Amex, MasterCard, Visa accepted. B&B [2007] £70–£75 per person; D,B&B £110–£115. Bar meals. Set dinner £42.50 (non-residents). Reductions for 5 or more nights (3 in Mar/Apr and Oct). *V*

SKIRLING Borders

Map 5:E2

Skirling House

Skirling, by Biggar ML12 6HD

Tel 01899-860274
Fax 01899-860255
Email enquiry@skirlinghouse.com
Website www.skirlinghouse.com

César award in 2004

'The whole experience remains delightful,' says one fan of this fine Arts and Crafts house (Wolsey Lodge) on the green of a tiny village amid lovely Borders countryside. Built in 1908 as the summer retreat of a Scottish art connoisseur, it contains 'a stunning collection of artworks', lots of books, fresh flowers. And many other visitors wrote to praise Bob and Isobel Hunter in their 'unique home'. 'Gets better and better.' 'We felt spoilt in every way.' 'A beautiful bedroom, with everything one could want; toiletries to die for.' 'One of the most relaxing places we know. Good food, congenial company.' The drawing room has a 16th-century carved wood ceiling, full-height windows, a log fire and a baby grand piano. 'Excellent breakfasts' have fresh orange juice, French toast with caramelised apples and black pudding, home-made jams and marmalades. 'A late-afternoon request for tea in the garden was met without demur.' The host's 'ever more adventurous' four-course dinners (no choice; preferences discussed), served by his wife, are much admired: 'Roasted rib-eye beef was gorgeously succulent.' Game casserole is another speciality. Vegetarians get 'an interesting meal'. 'Good wine list.' Children are welcomed. (*Gordon Murray, Harry and Annette Medcalf, Margaret Kershaw, Dr M Tannahill*)

5 bedrooms (plus 1 single available if let with a double). 1 on ground floor, suitable for ♿. 2 miles E of Biggar, by village green. Closed Jan/Feb, 1 week in winter. Ramps. Drawing room, library, conservatory, dining room. 'No background music at present.' 3½-acre garden (tennis, croquet) in 115-acre estate with woodland. No smoking. Dogs by arrangement, not in public rooms or unattended in bedrooms. MasterCard, Visa accepted. B&B [2007] £50–£60 per person. Set dinner £30. ***V***

The ***V*** sign at the end of an entry indicates a hotel that has agreed to take part in our Voucher scheme and to give *Guide* readers a 25% discount on their room rates for a one-night stay, subject to the conditions explained in *How to use the Good Hotel Guide*, and given on the back of the vouchers.

SLEAT Highland — Map 5:C1

Toravaig House NEW

Knock Bay, Sleat
Isle of Skye
IV44 8RE
Tel 01471-820200
Fax 01471-833231
Email info@skyehotel.co.uk
Website www.skyehotel.co.uk

In a 'beautiful setting' on the coast road, close to the Armadale ferry, this handsome, white-painted building has been renovated by Anne Gracie and Kenneth Gunn (a former captain of the *Hebridean Princess* cruise ship). 'They are much in evidence, hands on,' say inspectors in 2007. 'They work hard, greeting guests, making small talk, serving at table.' The interior is decorated 'in strong, but not intimidating' colours; 'handsome lighting; the drawing room has a log fire, comfortable seating. In the pleasing dining room (though it has only two windows), the menu uses flowery language (sea bass is "set over a cushion of braised fennel"), but the cooking of chef Peter Woods is accomplished. We enjoyed a salad of ham and apricots; tender Skye venison; flavoursome guineafowl; excellent vegetables. Background muzak was fortunately subdued. Disappointingly, our bedroom faced the car park; nicely decorated, it had comfortable bed, effective reading lights, armchairs, good fabrics; spotless, compact bathroom.' Breakfast had an 'underwhelming buffet; good marmalade and butter in proper pots; excellent bacon but poor toast'. The staff, in neat black uniforms, were 'agreeable and professional; a shame no one offered help with our bags'. Captain Gunn takes guests on trips on his yacht. (*RMH, and others*)

9 bedrooms. 3 miles N of Armadale. Lounge, dining room (Celtic 'ambience' background music). 1-acre grounds. Unsuitable for ♿. No smoking. No children. No dogs. MasterCard, Visa accepted. B&B [2007] £69.50–£85 per person; D,B&B £102–£120. Set dinner £32.50. Christmas/New Year packages.

STRATHYRE Stirling — Map 5:D2

Ardoch Lodge

Strathyre
FK18 8NF
Tel/Fax 01877-384666
Email ardoch@btinternet.com
Website www.ardochlodge.co.uk

César award in 2006

'Simple, friendly and relaxed', John and Yvonne Howes's white-painted early Victorian country house has many fans. 'Perfect; this couple really does think of everything,' say returning visitors. The setting, in the Loch Lomond and Trossachs national park, is enjoyed for its 'sheer tranquillity'. 'My son wrote down 40 bird types we had seen in four days; also red squirrels.' The large bedrooms have easy chairs, plenty of space, good tea, coffee and shortbread. 'Our bathroom was immaculate with good toiletries.' Mr Howes, who has a 'dry sense of humour', serves dinner in the elegant dining room. 'Yvonne keeps a low profile, producing her straightforward but excellent menus. We enjoyed venison liver with red onion marmalade; roast chicken with haggis.' Guests are asked to decide in advance from a choice of two dishes for each of three courses, but alternatives are willingly supplied. A vegetarian was delighted that her preferences were remembered. A lighter supper tray can be taken 'in your room, the conservatory or outside'. Unlicensed, but guests can bring their own drinks (no corkage charge). Breakfast has 'the best porridge, creamy scrambled eggs'. Dogs are welcomed. (*J and F Waters, Janet and Dennis Allom, Janette Brown, Kathleen Craddock*)

3 bedrooms. No telephone/TV. 3 self-catering cabins/cottages in grounds. W of Strathyre. Open 20 Mar–mid-Nov. Drawing room (with TV), conservatory, dining room (classical background music at night). 12-acre grounds: walled garden, wildflower meadow, riverside walk. Fishing. Unsuitable for ♿. No smoking. No dogs in dining room. MasterCard, Visa accepted. B&B £41–£70 per person. Set dinner £29.50; supper tray £15. Special breaks.

STRONTIAN Highland — Map 5:C1

Kilcamb Lodge
Strontian
PH36 4HY

Tel 01967-402257
Fax 01967-402041
Email enquiries@kilcamblodge.co.uk
Website www.kilcamblodge.co.uk

Liked again this year ('expensively excellent'; 'tremendous atmosphere'), this Georgian building (one of the oldest stone houses in Scotland, with sympathetic Victorian additions) has a splendid setting, surrounded by woodland and hills, and with its own beach, on the shores of Loch Sunart. David and Sally Ruthven-Fox are the 'friendly', 'hands-on' owners. Their staff are 'all excellent', say visitors in 2007, 'though the house-keeping was sometimes relaxed'. The 'beautifully furnished' house has open fires, fresh flowers and 'spacious, comfortable period lounges'. 'The food is much better': Gordon Smillie, who took over the kitchen in 2007, serves a short four-course menu of modern dishes, eg, goat's cheese beignet; Ardnamurchan venison with confit potatoes. The bedrooms have 'excellent linen and towels'; the best are large, with 'enormous bed, window seat and loch view'. Breakfast has newly baked croissants, a good selection of cereals, free-range eggs. Dogs are welcomed: 'no flowerbeds or ornamental gardens to worry about', and you might find some 'doggy treats' in your bedroom. Much wildlife can be seen on the Ardnamurchan peninsula (most easily reached by a short ferry crossing), with red deer, otters, eagles and whale-watching trips.

10 bedrooms. On edge of village. Open Feb–end Dec; closed 2 days a week Feb, Nov. Drawing room, lounge bar, dining room (background music: jazz/classical, piano). 22-acre grounds: loch frontage: beach (safe bathing), fishing, boating. Unsuitable for ♿. Wedding facilities. No smoking. No children under 12. No dogs in public rooms. MasterCard, Visa accepted. B&B [2007] £60–£112.50 per person. Set dinner £45. Off-season breaks. Christmas/New Year packages.

SWINTON Scottish Borders — Map 5:E3

The Wheatsheaf at Swinton NEW
Main Street
Swinton, nr Duns
TD11 3JJ

Tel 01890-860257
Fax 01890-860283
Email reception@wheatsheaf-swinton.co.uk
Website www.wheatsheaf-swinton.co.uk

Owned since 2005 by 'very friendly' Chris and Jan Winson: old stone-built inn opposite green of pretty village in rolling countryside. 10 miles SW of Berwick-upon-Tweed; on B6462 to Kelso. 'A very pleasant stop-over en route home from Scotland. Delightful, large, well-appointed bedroom; good modern bathroom; first-class restaurant.' John Keir serves 'well-prepared and -presented' modern dishes using local produce. Good breakfast in conservatory. Traditional decor. Cots, camp beds, special menu for children. 10 bedrooms. 1 suitable for ♿. 3 are 15 yds away. Roadside rooms hear traffic. Closed 25/26 and 31 Dec. 2 lounges, bar, 2 dining rooms, conservatory; background jazz/'mood music'. ½-acre garden. No smoking. No dogs. MasterCard, Visa accepted. B&B £54–£71 per person; D,B&B £28 added.

TAYNUILT Argyll and Bute *See SHORTLIST* Map 5:D1

How to contact the *Guide*
By mail: From anywhere in the UK, write to Freepost PAM 2931, London W11 4BR (no stamp is needed)
From outside the UK: *Good Hotel Guide*, 50 Addison Avenue, London W11 4QP, England
By telephone or fax: 020-7602 4182
By email: Goodhotel@aol.com or Goodhotel@btinternet.com
Via our website: www.goodhotelguide.com

TIGHNABRUAICH Argyll and Bute — Map 5:D1

An Lochan
Shore Road
Tighnabruaich PA21 2BE

Tel 01700-811239
Fax 01700-811300
Email info@anlochan.co.uk
Website www.anlochan.co.uk

In October 2006, Roger and Bea McKie renamed their white, bay-windowed seafront hotel (formerly *The Royal*). Its new name is Gaelic for 'by the small loch'. It stands across a small road from the shore in an attractive fishing village on the Kyles of Bute; both dining rooms and all but three of the bedrooms have the view across the sea to Bute. Praise this year: 'First class, from the very beginning; warm, friendly staff; fantastic room; superb food.' 'We are foodies and love to be pampered. This is the place.' James Stocks, who joined as head chef in March 2007 (he is assisted in the kitchen by the McKies' daughter, Louise), has reorganised the menus. In the wooden-floored *Deck* brasserie, and the more formal *Crustacean* restaurant, guests can choose between a *Local Food Heroes* menu, or a more extensive *carte*. The former features only produce supplied locally, perhaps 'scallops caught by Mary, or salmon smoked by Guido'. Bold colours are used in the 'attractive and comfortable' public rooms, which have local paintings and sculptures, books and family memorabilia, and also in the 'tastefully decorated' bedrooms. The *Shinty* bar is popular with locals. (*James Ralston, Rhona Ferguson*)

11 bedrooms. On shore road. Closed 16–21 Dec, 7–12 Jan. 2 lounges, bar, 2 restaurants; background music in bar in evening. ½-acre grounds; 100 yards from sea: shingle beach. Only restaurant and bar suitable for ♿. No smoking. Dogs by arrangement (£3 a night). MasterCard, Visa accepted. B&B £50–£95 per person. Set menus £35–£48. Special breaks. New Year package. 1-night bookings sometimes refused July/Aug.

TIRORAN Argyll and Bute — Map 5:D1

Tiroran House
Tiroran, Isle of Mull
PA69 6ES

Tel 01681-705232
Fax 01681-705240
Email tiroran-house@btinternet.com
Website www.tiroran.com

A couple who bought the *Guide* to find a special hotel for their wedding were 'not disappointed' by Laurence Mackay and Katie Munro's attractive, white-fronted Victorian house in extensive grounds on the shores of Loch Scridain. 'The exceptional hosts did their utmost to ensure our day was special.' Another visitor wrote of the 'wonderful surroundings', the 'warm welcome', and a 'well-appointed room with excellent views'. The house has been refurbished throughout. Each bedroom has an individual decor (with a colour theme); 'Ours was spacious; very peaceful.' Both sitting rooms have a log fire, fresh flowers; one has a polished wooden floor. In the small dining room, or the adjacent conservatory (shaded by an indoor vine), Katie Munro serves 'wonderful' food; three courses (with three options each) using fresh local produce, eg, lobster salad with Glengorm leaves; loin of pork with honey and black pepper crust. Children are welcome: under-12s can have an early supper or, 'by negotiation', dinner. Breakfast, in a conservatory, has home-made muesli, breads, marmalade and preserves, and free-range eggs. A burn with waterfalls runs through the secluded gardens; otters and eagles can be seen. (*Graham and Tracy Hoggarth, FW*)

7 bedrooms. 1 annexed to self-catering cottage. 2 on ground floor. N side of Loch Scridain. Drawing room (traditional/'easy listening' background music at night), sitting room, dining room, conservatory. 17½-acre grounds: burn; beach front (mooring). Wedding facilities. No smoking. 'Usually' no children under 12 in dining room. Dogs allowed in 1 bedroom, not in public rooms. MasterCard, Visa accepted. B&B £67–£72 per person. Set dinner £37. 1-night bookings sometimes refused. *V*

TORRIDON Highland — Map 5:C1

The Torridon Hotel
Torridon, by Achnasheen
IV22 2EY

Tel 01445-791242
Fax 01445-712253
Email info@thetorridon.com
Website www.thetorridon.com

A sense of Victorian grandeur is retained at this turreted former shooting lodge in a remote and beautiful setting at the foot of Ben Damph on the shores of Loch Torridon. Now a luxury hotel (Pride of Britain), it is owned by Rohaise and Daniel Rose-Bristow and managed by Robert Ince. They tell us that the public rooms have been refurbished this year; many original features, including decoratively patterned ceilings, have been retained. Furnishings are traditional; wood panelling, big open fireplaces. Bedrooms are warm and well furnished; some have a king-size bed and a claw-footed freestanding bath; one has a four-poster. 'Comfortable room with superb housekeeping,' said one visitor. Another guest had a 'good view of the loch' from his attic room, which had 'an irritating sloping mirror'. The chef, Kevin John Broome, serves three-course dinners in the panelled dining room: 'The best we had in Scotland, an excellent dish of scallops.' The 'first-class' breakfast has porridge with whisky, kippers, haggis, highly praised raspberry jam. 'Everyone very friendly, from the owners downwards; extremely helpful.' A popular wedding venue. (*Dr Alec Frank, David Innes*)

19 bedrooms. 1, on ground floor, suitable for ♿. 1 suite in cottage. On W coast, 10 miles SW of Kinlochewe. Closed Jan, Mon/Tues Nov–Mar. Lift. Drawing room, library, whisky bar, dining room (classical background music at night). 58-acre grounds: croquet, kitchen garden, river, nature walk, loch. Wedding facilities. No smoking. No children under 10 in dining room in evening. Dogs allowed in cottage. Amex, MasterCard, Visa accepted. B&B £52.50–£192.50 per person; D,B&B £92.50–£232.50. Set dinner £40. Special breaks. Christmas/New Year packages.

ULLAPOOL Highland — Map 5:B2

The Ceilidh Place NEW
14 West Argyle Street
Ullapool IV26 2TY

Tel 01854-612103
Fax 01854-613773
Email info@theceilidhplace.com
Website www.theceilidhplace.com

Jean Urquhart has for many years presided over this unusual bookshop/café/pub/restaurant/hotel, winner of a 'Good for the Soul' award in 2005. Ceilidhs are often held in summer at this 'joyous place, full of character and originality'. It includes a wholefood shop and an arts centre with plays, poetry readings and exhibitions by Scottish artists. 'The bookstore is a real one, with serious titles and genuine literature,' writes a visitor this year. He found the accommodation 'eminently satisfactory. Obviously recently refurbished. Simple, spacious room, functionally laid out. Surprising touches: thick bathrobes, hot-water bottles. Pleasant younger staff; reasonable restaurant.' Earlier visitors wrote of the 'relaxed atmosphere' and 'genuine friendliness'. The 'Scottish eclectic' menu, which 'changes according to what the fishermen catch and what is ripe in the garden', includes char-grilled steak with whisky and peppercorn sauce; local smoked haddock baked with Parmesan and cream. Vegetarian dishes are a speciality. The lounge has games, books, a small pantry with free tea and coffee, and an honesty bar, and the furniture is crafted from local materials. Ullapool, a pleasant fishing port and holiday resort near the mouth of Loch Broom, was laid out in a grid pattern in the 18th century. (*Stephen Holman, and others*)

13 bedrooms. 10 with facilities *en suite*. Village centre. Large car park. Public bar, parlour bar, café; background music; restaurant, bookshop; conference/function/wedding facilities. ½-acre garden. Rocky beach, sea angling, waterskiing, loch fishing, pony trekking nearby. Only public areas suitable for ♿. No smoking. No dogs in public rooms. All major credit cards accepted. B&B £63 per person. Full alc £30. New Year package.

See also SHORTLIST

WALKERBURN Borders Map 5:E2

Windlestraw Lodge NEW
Tweed Valley
Galashiels Road
Walkerburn EH43 6AA

Tel 01896-870636
Email reception@windlestraw.co.uk
Website www.windlestraw.co.uk

In an elevated position, looking down the Tweed valley and over the Elibank Forest, this 'stunning' Edwardian building is now the home of chef Alan Reid and his wife, Julie, formerly of the popular *Wheatsheaf*, Swinton (*qv*). 'Our third two-night stay, even more impressive than the earlier occasions,' writes a visitor in 2007. 'Romantic and elegant candle-lit open-plan public rooms. Tasteful decor (*objets d'art*, family photos). Lovely open fires. Smart, comfortable bedrooms. Superb food.' Local ingredients are used in dishes like sea bream with cockles and fresh asparagus, served in the wood-panelled dining area ('breathtaking views'). Seasonal venison is another speciality. The Mackintosh master bedroom has a king-size brass bed and original bathtub. At breakfast, the continental version has smoked venison, cheese and fruit, and cooked dishes include porridge with honey and cream; boiled eggs with 'soldiers'; smoked haddock and poached eggs. 'The Reids achieve the perfect balance of friendly interest with efficiency.' (*Agnes M Campbell*)

6 bedrooms. All on first floor. On outskirts of village, 2 miles E of Innerleithen. Closed Christmas/New Year, Feb. Lounge, sun lounge, drawing room, dining room; function/wedding facilities. No background music. 2-acre grounds. Unsuitable for ♿. No smoking. No dogs: public rooms, some bedrooms. B&B £60–£90 per person; D,B&B from £95. Set menus £40. *V*

'Set menu' indicates a fixed-price meal, with ample, limited or no choice. 'Full alc' is the hotel's estimated price per person of a three-course *à la carte* meal, with a half bottle of house wine. 'Alc' is the price of an *à la carte* meal excluding the cost of wine.

WESTRAY Orkney — Map 5:A3

Cleaton House NEW

Pierowall
Westray KW17 2DB

Tel 01857-677508
Fax 01857-677442
Email info@cleatonhouse.co.uk
Website www.cleatonhouse.co.uk

Alone on a promontory on one of the most northerly Orkney isles, this white mansion faces the little island of Papa Westray. Both small hotel and local pub, it has been owned since February 2006 by the 'hospitable' Lynne and Tony Thorpe. 'They have maintained previous high standards. Accommodation is luxurious. Lynne's cooking is out of this world,' says one visitor. 'She presents local produce, such as the great Orkney beef and freshly caught clams and crayfish, to perfection.' Seafood comes with 'delicately flavoured sauces'. The 'elegant' dining room has linen tablecloths, cut-glass goblets, coat of arms and pictures of the Stewart family, who built the house in 1850. The bar serves simple meals. The 'comfortable, well-furnished' lounge has board games and a collection of Orcadian literature. 'Our excellent bedroom had all mod cons (very fancy TV) and good views.' Shutters keep out the light of the long summer nights. Guests can be met at the ferry or airstrip; and can be driven to remote parts of the island so they can walk back. The island has miles of sandy beaches, and the second-largest breeding seabird colony in the UK (puffins between May and August). (*JL Craven, CJR Thorne*)

6 bedrooms. 1 on ground floor. 2 miles SE of Pierowall village. Ferry/small plane from Kirkwall; they will meet. Closed Nov. Ramps. Residents' lounge, lounge bar (background music if required), restaurant. 2-acre garden: *pétanque*; sandy bay, sea ¼ mile. No smoking. Dogs allowed in lounge only. MasterCard, Visa accepted. B&B [2007] £40–£55 per person; D,B&B £54–£83. Set dinner £28. Special breaks. Christmas/New Year packages.

WHITHORN Dumfries and Galloway — Map 5:E2

The Steam Packet Inn

Harbour Row
Isle of Whithorn
Newton Stewart DG8 8LL

Tel 01988-500334
Fax 01988-500627
Email steampacketinn@btconnect.com
Website www.steampacketinn.com

The Isle of Whithorn is not an island, but the name given to the tip of the Machars peninsula; on the quayside of a pretty fishing village stands this inn, managed by the 'helpful' Alastair Scoular, whose family has owned it for 25 years. Calum Harvey is the new chef for a restaurant that is popular with locals; his blackboard menus (changed twice daily) are served in the bars and in the dining room and conservatory. They use fish from the harbour (a 'kettle of fish' has langoustines, mussels, clams, prawns and squid), steaks from Inverurie. 'Substantial dishes designed for hearty appetites.' Tea and coffee are served all day. A visitor liked her bedroom with 'two enormous picture windows (with window seats and cushions) looking over the harbour, large coffee table, two comfortable armchairs, big bed and clean bathroom'. Children and dogs are welcomed. The area has interesting archaeological remains, 'wonderful coastal walks along springy turf, and some beautiful gardens'. (*ER*)

7 bedrooms. Village centre. 9 miles S of Wigtown. Closed Christmas. 2 bars, 2 restaurant areas. No background music. Small garden. Unsuitable for ♿. Smoking allowed in bedrooms. No dogs in restaurant. MasterCard, Visa accepted. B&B [2007] £30–£35 per person. Full alc £29.

Wales

Many of our Welsh hotels take considerable pride in their national identity. Menus are often written in Welsh as well as English, as visitors are encouraged to embrace the local culture. We have recognised this tradition of hospitality by giving two *César* awards to Welsh hotels this year: *Y Goeden Eirin*, a small guest house near Caernarfon with a committed green philosophy; and *Plas Tan-Yr-Allt*, a villa on the Glaslyn estuary which is run in informal house-party style.

Y Goeden Eirin, Dolydd

ABERAERON Ceredigion — Map 3:C2

Harbourmaster Hotel
Pen Cei, Aberaeron
SA46 0BA

Tel 01545-570755
Fax 01545-570762
Email info@harbour-master.com
Website www.harbour-master.com

César award in 2005

This picturesque quayside hotel 'has real buzz, combining local pub with restaurant and rooms', says a 2007 visitor. The Georgian building has been 'brilliantly updated' in modern yet locally sympathetic fashion. Other comments: 'We liked the bilingual atmosphere.' 'Service relaxed, seemingly effortless.' 'The delightful owners [Glenn and Menna Heulyn] and their young staff gave every assistance.' But one correspondent agreed with last year's comment: 'The busy bar, which opens directly on to the dining room, has priority over residents', and reported delays at dinner; another thought prices 'a bit high'. In the small dining room (tables close together) chef Steven Evans serves 'modern Welsh' dishes like smoked haddock and Penclawdd cockle chowder. 'Our lovely room was filled with things that were a pleasure to use.' The top bedroom has a small lounge and views of harbour and sea. The cottage two doors down (where children under five are welcome) is 'well furnished and equipped'. 'Its bathroom was huge; the bath tub needed a grab handle even for the able-bodied.' The Heulyns have bought the adjacent grain warehouse; they plan to create a separate bar, larger restaurant and four more bedrooms (due for completion in early 2008). (*Tony and Marlene Hall, Frances Rathbone, Peter and Sarah Adam, Michael Nugent, Mr and Mrs HC Medcalf, and others*)

9 bedrooms. 2 in cottage. 4 more planned for 2008. Central, on harbour. Closed 25 Dec. Restaurant closed Mon midday. Bar, restaurant; background music. Pebble beach, safe bathing nearby. Unsuitable for ♿. No smoking. No children under 5 except in cottage. No dogs. MasterCard, Visa accepted. B&B [2007]: single £60, double £110–£130, suite £140–£150. Full alc £36. 1-night bookings refused Fri and Sat.

When you make a booking you enter into a contract with a hotel. Most hotels explain their cancellation policies, which vary widely, in a letter of confirmation. You may lose your deposit or be charged at the full rate for the room if you cancel at short notice. A travel insurance policy can provide protection.

ABERDYFI Gwynedd — Map 3:C3

Penhelig Arms

Terrace Road
Aberdyfi LL35 0LT

Tel 01654-767215
Fax 01654-767690
Email info@penheligarms.com
Website www.penheligarms.com

'Cheerful atmosphere, good food, accommodating staff.' An inspector reports on Robert and Sally Hughes's handsome former fishermen's inn by the harbour, overlooking the Dyfi estuary. Other comments: 'Wonderful; the presence of the owner gave a great buzz.' 'Our room was well designed and equipped, but small (so was the shower room). The view from its window must be one of the best in the world.' All bedrooms but one face the estuary; some have flat-screen TV and DVD-player. *Pen House*, suitable for a family, is a 'delightful' loft-style apartment with its own terrace. The building is filled with flowers, original artwork ('more rewarding than many an art gallery'), and family photographs. Log fires burn in the public rooms. 'Blissful absence of canned music.' There are two 'pubby' bars. In the 'attractive, simple' dining room, 'robust, generally straightforward' food is served by 'charming Welsh girls'. The emphasis is on fresh fish, eg, grilled sardines; hake and mussel stew. Meals are also served in the beamed bar. The tiny car park has seats where you can have a drink and enjoy the view. 'The inn is set into a rock, where a colourful rock garden has been created.' The drawback: the position, on a busy coast road; annexe rooms are the quietest. (*Gwyn Morgan, Jelly Williams, Brian Pullee*)

16 bedrooms. Central, by harbour. Closed 25/26 Dec. Lounge, public bar, small cocktail bar, restaurant. No background music. Concessionary fees at nearby championship golf course. Unsuitable for ♿, but 'please telephone for advice'. No smoking. MasterCard, Visa accepted. B&B £45–£65 per person; D,B&B £72–£97. Set menu £29. 1-night bookings refused Sat 'except at last minute'.

Trefeddian Hotel

Tywyn Road
Aberdyfi LL35 0SB

Tel 01654-767213
Fax 01654-767777
Email info@trefwales.com
Website www.trefwales.com

'Beautifully situated' on a bluff above a links golf course on Cardigan Bay, this unpretentious, large, white Edwardian hotel has been run by the Cave family for three generations. It remains equally popular with families and retired couples. 'Having brought my children, I'm now back with the grandchildren,' said one devotee. During a packed half-term week, another guest reported that the hotel 'somehow absorbed all the children and kept cool'. 'It manages, by having three lounges, to keep the whole spectrum of visitors happy': one is reserved for adults; there is another 'large and airy' one for families; dogs are allowed in a third one. Playrooms are 'well equipped, yet noise does not impinge'. Bedrooms, some with balcony, are 'well furnished'; bathrooms 'cleaned to a high standard'. 'Very comfortable beds.' The dining room has been refurbished. 'The food is excellent', if 'fairly traditional'. 'Sunday lunch provided succulent beef with Yorkshire pudding, and a hearty pudding to follow.' Disabled guests are 'marvellously catered for'. For children there are reduced rates, a supper menu and baby monitoring. 'Great walking from the door; the four-mile beach is fantastic.' (*MBB, DB, and others*)

59 bedrooms. ½ mile N of village. Lift. 3 lounges, bar lounge, restaurant; fitness centre: indoor swimming pool (40 by 20 ft), beauty salon. No background music. 15-acre grounds: tennis, 9-hole pitch and putt, children's playground. No smoking. Dogs allowed in one lounge, some bedrooms. MasterCard, Visa accepted. D,B&B [2007] £73–£99 per person. Set lunch £16.95, dinner £27. Christmas/New Year packages. 1-night bookings sometimes refused.

ABERGAVENNY Monmouthshire — Map 3:D4

The Angel Hotel NEW

15 Cross Street
Abergavenny NP7 5EN

Tel 01873-857121
Fax 01873-858059
Email mail@angelhotelabergavenny.com
Website www.angelhotelabergavenny.com

This 'lively town hotel', managed by William and Charlotte Griffiths, is 'unquestionably Abergavenny's social hub', write inspectors. 'Its function rooms are often busy with weddings and other events. It is not perfect, and certainly not the place for a quiet weekend, but we feel it deserves a *Guide* entry.' There is a 'lovely drawing room with good armchairs and sofas', where afternoon teas, with fine china, 'proper linen' and fresh-baked pastries are served from 3 to 5 pm. The *Foxhunter* bar is '*the* gathering place, big log fire, very busy at night'. In the dining room, 'with old-fashioned feel, large helpings of good comfort food were served at a nice pace. Good rump of lamb with gratin potatoes. Delicious home-made ice creams.' No lift in this old coaching inn, and sloping corridor floors. Renovation is ongoing. 'Go for a refurbished room. Our superior double had modern, neutral colours, flat-screen TV, smallish double bed, excellent bathroom.' Front rooms could be affected by street noise. For families there are interconnecting rooms. 'Breakfast was a basic buffet with packaged juices, OK cooked dishes; could try harder.'

30 bedrooms. Town centre. Closed 25 Dec. Ramps. Lounge, bar (background music sometimes); conference/wedding/function facilities. Courtyard. Disabled accommodation planned. No smoking. No dogs in restaurant; £10 per dog per night in bedrooms. Amex, MasterCard, Visa accepted. B&B [2007]: single from £60, double from £85; D,B&B: single from £85, double from £135. Full alc £35.

ABERSOCH Gwynedd — Map 3:B2

Porth Tocyn Hotel
Bwlch Tocyn
Abersoch LL53 7BU

Tel 01758-713303
Fax 01758-713538
Email bookings@porthtocyn.fsnet.co.uk
Website www.porth-tocyn-hotel.co.uk

César award in 1984

'Definitely our favourite hotel, even if the hot water came out of the cold tap and vice versa,' says one of many fans of this family-friendly hotel which the Fletcher-Brewer family have run for five decades. With 'breathtaking' views of Cardigan Bay and the mountains of Snowdonia, it is five minutes' walk from some excellent beaches with opportunities for water sports. 'Our children enjoyed their stay, making new friends and exploring the hotel and its grounds.' In the latter are a heated swimming pool and sun loungers. Nick and Louise Fletcher-Brewer tell us that they have now introduced new beds, Egyptian cotton sheets, curtains and towels, as well as off-season walking holidays. The 'rambling' structure of former lead miners' cottages has 'grown organically' over the years; some rooms are interconnected. A conservatory and many sitting rooms provide space to relax inside. Jonathan Bell has been promoted to run the kitchen with Louise Fletcher-Brewer: 'The food really is superb,' all agree (a *Good Food Guide* entry for 50 years). (*Derek Lambert, and others*)

17 bedrooms. 2 miles outside village. Open 2 weeks before Easter–early Nov. Sitting rooms, children's rooms, bar, dining room, conservatory. No background music. 25-acre grounds: swimming pool (30 by 18 ft; heated May–Sept), tennis. Beach (5 mins' walk), sailing, fishing, golf, riding nearby. Telephone to discuss disabled access. No smoking. No tiny children at dinner (high tea at 5.30 pm). Dogs by arrangement; not in public rooms. MasterCard, Visa accepted. B&B [2007] £45–£87 per person. Cooked breakfast £6. Set dinner £32.50–£39.50. 1-night bookings sometimes refused. *V*

We ask for more reports on a hotel if we haven't received feedback from readers for some time. Please send an endorsement if you think a hotel should remain in the *Guide*.

BEAUMARIS Anglesey — Map 3:A3

Ye Olde Bulls Head
Castle Street
Beaumaris, Anglesey
LL58 8AP

Tel 01248-810329
Fax 01248-811294
Email info@bullsheadinn.co.uk
Website www.bullsheadinn.co.uk

Originally a medieval staging inn for coaches to Ireland, this 500-year-old house has old beams and creaking staircases. 'A good atmosphere with friendly service,' says a reader this year. It 'feels like a Dickensian inn', and Dickens once stayed here. Bedrooms, named after his characters, are small and 'smartly cosy'. The owner/managers, Keith Rothwell and David Robertson, have begun refurbishment of six bedrooms, and as we went to press, work was due to begin on an adjacent property to provide 13 more rooms. There is a 'very comfortable' residents' lounge. The bar, popular with locals, has a rare 17th-century brass water clock, antique weapons and the town's oak ducking seat; a huge coal fire in winter. Its traditional feel is balanced by the 'more contemporary' styling of the *Loft* restaurant (where chef Craig Yardley serves dishes like fillet of Anglesey Black beef with spinach, pancetta and Madeira jus), and the clean lines of the brasserie in the converted stables (where Simon Doyle is the chef). A visitor this year ate 'scallops followed by pinky venison and local brill, both very tasty'. Service at breakfast 'was a little erratic, more than compensated for by an excellent kipper'. (*David Willis, and others*)

13 bedrooms. 2 on ground floor. Main street. Closed 25/26 Dec, for food 1 Jan evening. Lounge, bar, brasserie (background music), restaurant. Sea 200 yds. No smoking. No children under 7 in restaurant or bedroom suites. No dogs. Amex, MasterCard, Visa accepted. B&B [2007] £50–£80 per person. Set dinner (*Loft* restaurant) £38.

See also SHORTLIST

BODUAN Gwynedd — Map 3:B2

The Old Rectory
Boduan
nr Pwllheli LL53 6DT

Tel/Fax 01758-721519
Email thepollards@theoldrectory.net
Website www.theoldrectory.net

An 'elegant, comfortable, well-loved home in a quiet location'. Standing in woodland in a village in the Lleyn peninsula, this small, pale yellow B&B is run by 'very kind hosts', Roger and Gabrielle Pollard. The 'beautifully restored' former Georgian rectory ('they obviously enjoy sharing it with visitors,' say visitors in 2007) has 'large, elegant' public rooms, with antique family furniture and paintings by contemporary artists. A fire is lit in the drawing room on cold days. 'Spacious, well-equipped' bedrooms are individually styled: 'Ours, shining clean, had tea-making facilities, complimentary sherry, and fine views over fields.' Some bathrooms have a roll-top bath. Breakfast includes porridge, compotes made from home-grown fruit, smoked salmon, home-made breads, jam and marmalade. Dinner is no longer served: reservations can be made for guests at local restaurants. Babies under one stay free; cots and high chairs are provided. Nearby are three golf courses, Bodnant Gardens, coastal footpaths, and splendid sandy beaches. (*Mr and Mrs MC Wilson*)

3 bedrooms. Also self-catering cottage. 4 miles NW of Pwllheli. Closed 24/25 Dec. Drawing room, dining room. No background music. 3½-acre grounds. Unsuitable for ♿. No smoking. No dogs. No credit cards. B&B [2007] £42.50–£85 per person. 1-night bookings refused bank holidays.

BRECHFA Carmarthenshire — Map 3:D2

Tŷ Mawr
Brechfa SA32 7RA

Tel 01267-202332
Email info@wales-country-hotel.co.uk
Website www.wales-country-hotel.co.uk
www.flockinnbrewery.co.uk

On the edge of the Brechfa forest, by the 'gently bubbling' River Marlais, this 'welcoming' 17th-century farmhouse is 'extremely good value', say visitors this year. 'A very relaxed stay.' The 'friendly but not pushy' owners, Annabel Viney ('intelligent, responsive and helpful') and Stephen Thomas (the chef) have 'done an exemplary job in making the house and grounds attractive', said our inspector. They have added a micro-brewery and tap room (*The Flock Inn*) serving real ales, 'including a beer called "Tup of the Morning"'. Visitors can take part in a 'brewing day'. 'Our room was fairly plain, but very comfortable. It had two chairs (so often a double has only one). In perfect weather, we sat on its patio with our drinks, watching the river.' The food ('modern, with an emphasis on local ingredients') is admired: 'We particularly enjoyed scallops with a lime crust; Welsh lamb chops with leeks and chestnuts; strawberries and water buffalo ice cream in a brandy snap basket. Main courses came with chunky fresh veg and a different potato dish every day. Breakfasts were good too.' Portia, the 'soft and gorgeous' Turkish rescue dog, may take guests for a walk. *Tŷ Mawr* was up for sale as we went to press; please check the situation before booking. (*GC, and others*)

5 bedrooms. Village centre. Sitting room, bar, breakfast room, restaurant; brewery and tap room; background music. 1-acre grounds: croquet, *boules*. Unsuitable for ♿. No smoking. No children under 12. No dogs in restaurant. Amex, MasterCard, Visa accepted. B&B: single £65, double £95; D,B&B £70 per person. Set menu £29. Christmas/New Year packages. *V*

BRECON Powys *See SHORTLIST* Map 3:D3

BRIDGEND *See SHORTLIST* Map 3:E3

BROADHAVEN Pembrokeshire Map 3:D1

The Druidstone
nr Broadhaven
Haverfordwest SA62 3NE

Tel 01437-781221
Fax 01437-781133
Email jane@druidstone.co.uk
Website www.druidstone.co.uk

Jane Bell is the owner ('still managing after 35 years') with her husband, Rod, and son, Angus, of this unusual 'family holiday centre' in a 'stunning cliff-top position, above a huge, almost deserted beach'. 'An institution to many, it is a fantastic family-friendly establishment with bags of character,' says a fan. 'Extremely hospitable. The slightly rough-around-the-edges feel only adds to the welcome eccentricity. The perfect antidote to over-priced designer hotels.' Mrs Bell writes: 'Folk coming in from the beach do not want to worry about buckets of sand.' The two 'rather luxurious' penthouse bedrooms each have a balcony facing the bay; other rooms are less smart: only four have a private bathroom. The cottages in the grounds include the tiny Roundhouse, an 'Eco Hut', which derives its energy from the sun. Meals are served in the 'cosy' bar, used by locals, and the dining room; both open on to a sea-facing terrace and garden. 'The bar food is unpretentious, the restaurant excellent [a *Good Food Guide* entry for many years] and the children's high tea is always interesting (no chicken nuggets).' Pets are welcomed, so long as they get on with Jake, the donkey. Popular for weddings and parties. (*MG*)

11 bedrooms. 5 cottages. 7 miles W of Haverfordwest. Sitting room, TV room, bar (background music/occasional live music), restaurant; small conference/function facilities. 22-acre grounds. Sandy beach, safe bathing 200 yds. Civil wedding licence. No smoking. No dogs in restaurant. Amex, MasterCard, Visa accepted. B&B £45–£75 per person. Full alc £31. Courses, conferences. Christmas, New Year and midweek packages. 1-night advance bookings refused for Sat.

CAPEL GARMON Conwy — Map 3:A3

Tan-y-Foel Country House

Capel Garmon
nr Betws-y-Coed LL26 0RE

Tel 01690-710507
Fax 01690-710681
Email enquiries@tyfhotel.co.uk
Website www.tyfhotel.co.uk

'High marks all round' this year for this 17th-century stone guest house in a 'lovely location', high on wooded hills in the Snowdonia national park. The name means 'house under the hillside'; it is popular with walkers. 'The hosts are charming, very professional; the food is excellent.' 'Must be almost unique in that there are no staff apart from the owners. Mrs Pitman cooks, Mr Pitman wields a screwdriver, their charming daughter, Kelly, is front-of-house, serving meals etc.' The building, rescued from near dereliction, has a contemporary interior, with understated earth tones, lavish fabrics. 'For a country house the decor is esoteric, but it worked for us.' Three bedrooms have been refurbished, in muted shades, and now have flat-screen TV, DVD- and CD-player. Some rooms have a 'magnificent view' of the valley; some have a four-poster bed; two have their own entrance. Bathrooms are 'spacious and well equipped'. As to the 'modern fusion' cooking, which uses organic ingredients when possible: 'The quality of materials, cooking and presentation were exceptional; different dishes on each night of our stay. Breakfast scrambled eggs were perfect – rare indeed.' 'Car essential,' the Pitmans warn. (*John Chute, Peter and Sarah Adam*)

6 bedrooms. 1½ miles off A470 (N), E of Betws-y-Coed. Closed Dec & Jan. Lounge, breakfast room, restaurant. No background music. 6-acre grounds. Unsuitable for ♿. No smoking. No children under 12. Guide dogs only. MasterCard, Visa accepted. B&B £62.50–£155 per person. Set dinner £40–£42. 1-night bookings refused weekends, bank holidays.

CARDIFF Map 3:E4

Jolyon's

5 Bute Crescent
Cardiff CF10 5AN

Tel/Fax 029-2048 8775
Email info@jolyons.co.uk
Website www.jolyons.co.uk

'Greatly enjoyed' in 2007 by former *Guide* hoteliers, Jolyon Joseph's 'intriguing' boutique hotel is a converted Georgian town house opposite the New Millennium Centre, home of the Welsh National Opera. He is 'laid back' and 'very personable'; Barbie Gerami is the manager. Bedrooms (some with views of Cardiff Bay) have 'contemporary touches enhanced by antiques', says an earlier report. 'A large wardrobe had Art Nouveau designs; a massive Jacobean mirror was hung behind the bed, which was large enough to sleep three. The large chrome-fitted bathroom was a joy, modern yet cosy; a leaf-shaped bath, fluffy towels, lots of hot water.' Some rooms have a whirlpool bath; one has a wet room. Downstairs the 'friendly' *Bar Cwtch* (Welsh for 'cuddly') has an eclectic wine list. A wood-burning oven in the lounge/restaurant cooks a Mediterranean/Welsh fusion menu, named 'Cwtchas' ('cuddly tapas'). Full cooked breakfasts are now included, and a continental buffet is available. Mr Joseph plans to add 14 rooms in 2008. (*Gordon and Magdalene Ashman-Marr, and others*)

6 bedrooms. 1, on ground floor, suitable for ♿. Cardiff Bay waterfront. Residents' lounge, bar (varied background music). Terrace. No smoking. No children under 16. No dogs. All major credit cards accepted. B&B £44.50–£75 per person. Full alc £25.

See also SHORTLIST

CONWY *See SHORTLIST* Map 3:A3

****

Traveller's tale Our bedroom was beautiful. The bed had stacks of pillows and was invitingly soft. But the radiators were all turned off. The bathroom was also freezing. We decided to make tea and get into bed to keep warm. When we came down for a drink before dinner, the fire in the lounge was not lit, and the room felt unwelcoming. (*Hotel in Yorkshire*)

****

CRICKHOWELL Powys — Map 3:D4

Glangrwyney Court

Glangrwyney, Crickhowell
NP8 1ES

Tel 01873-811288
Fax 01873-810317
Email info@glancourt.co.uk
Website www.glancourt.co.uk

'Very upmarket, comfortable, indeed opulent.' 'One of the best B&Bs we have stayed in, considering the people, the setting, and the accommodation.' Praise in 2007 for Christina and Warwick Jackson's grade II listed family home on the edge of the Brecon Beacons national park. It stands in 'beautiful, peaceful' grounds with gardens (ancient magnolias and Japanese Acer trees a feature) and parkland. 'Christina and her two daughters were excellent hosts,' said other visitors this year. The Georgian house has a cantilevered staircase of architectural significance, and an arched window with views of the Black Mountains. There are log fires, a 'well-stocked' honesty bar, 'lots of comfy sofas'. The bedrooms in the house (all facing the garden and recently redecorated) are 'spacious and attractively furnished in country house style'. The master suite has a steam shower; one twin room has a spa bath. Some beds are king-size. 'We stayed in a self-catering cottage on B&B terms; very good value.' Mrs Jackson serves an evening meal by arrangement for groups only. 'Very good, all local produce' (eg, lamb tagine with seasonal vegetables). There is 'ample scope for eating nearby'. (*Mrs M Kershaw, Stephen and Jane Savery, BR*)

5 bedrooms. Also 2 in self-catering lodge. 2 miles SE of Crickhowell, off A40. Sitting room, library with honesty bar, dining room (background music at dinner if requested). 4-acre garden: croquet, *boules*, tennis. River 500 yds: fishing by arrangement. Unsuitable for ♿. Civil wedding licence. No smoking. No dogs. MasterCard, Visa accepted. B&B [2007] £32.50–£85 per person. Set dinner (by arrangement, for groups only) £30. Off-season discounts. 1-night bookings sometimes refused weekends in the summer. *V*

Gliffaes

Crickhowell
NP8 1RH

Tel 01874-730371
Fax 01874-730463
Email calls@gliffaeshotel.com
Website www.gliffaeshotel.com

'The four generations of the Brabner and Suter family have worked steadily to improve what was always a happy and enjoyable place.' Guests on their 34th visit praise this smart sporting hotel run by Susie (née Brabner) and James Suter. Their staff, 'a well-established mix of locals and young people from around the world', provide 'attentive service'. The 19th-century Italianate building stands in large wooded grounds on a private stretch of the trout- and salmon-laden River Usk (fishing courses arranged). 'Lovely gardens. Good walks from the door.' There are attractive sitting areas, particularly the conservatory. 'Bedrooms are comfortable,' says a visitor this year. Most are large; the best have balcony and river view. *Gliffaes* subscribes to the Slow Food Movement, dedicated to sourcing 65 per cent of ingredients from within 75 miles. Chef Stephan Trinci 'has raised the standard to new heights; it looks good and tastes even better'. Typical dishes: tartare of crab with crostini; tournedo of pork with black pudding, honey and grain mustard jus. Breakfasts are copious. Children are welcomed: 'The owners treated ours as if they were their own, and always accommodated their requests.' (*Col AJW and Mrs HM Harvey, RMJ Kenber, and others*)

23 bedrooms. 1 on ground floor, suitable for ♿, in annexe. 3 miles W of Crickhowell, off the A40. Closed Jan. Ramp. Sitting rooms, conservatory, bar (background jazz in evening), dining room. 33-acre garden: tennis, croquet, fishing (ghillie available). Civil wedding licence. No smoking. No dogs indoors. All major credit cards accepted. B&B [to 30 Mar 2008] £44–£105 per person. Set dinner £33. Website deals. Christmas/New Year packages. 1-night bookings refused weekends.

CWMBACH Powys — Map 3:C3

The Drawing Room

Cwmbach, Newbridge-on-Wye
Builth Wells LD2 3RT

Tel 01982-552493
Email post@the-drawing-room.co.uk
Website www.the-drawing-room.co.uk

César award in 2007

'Exceeded expectations in every way,' says a visitor to Colin and Melanie Dawson's 'delightful' restaurant-with-rooms. 'The brilliant hosts deserve every accolade that comes their way.' A reporter left 'with such a warm feeling' because of their 'sheer likeability'. The Georgian building has 'fixtures and fittings of a high standard'. Bedrooms have a '1920s feel' with 'top-quality Laura Ashley fabrics, simple, classic-style furniture, ample storage space, TV/DVD-player, Internet connection'. Other visitors 'had the smallest of the three rooms, but it was very comfortable, perfectly kitted out'. More traditionally styled lounges have comfortable sofas, armchairs, log fire and *objets d'art*. Colin Dawson is the chef, his wife is *sous-chef*, responsible for desserts, breads and pastry, and also front-of-house. In the small restaurant overlooking the garden, 'the food was exquisite without being fussy. Hot banana soufflé one of the most fantastic puddings I have ever eaten.' The Dawsons tell us that the menus have been 'slightly reduced to ensure quality and freshness'. 'Breakfast was a civilised delight: beautifully set tables, appetising menu; really fresh orange juice, toast made from super bread.' Only drawback: the location on a main road, 'but there is little traffic at night, and windows are double glazed'. (*Sue Cooper, Gordon Franklin, and others*)

3 bedrooms. On A470, 3 miles N of Builth Wells. Closed Christmas/New Year, Sun/Mon, except bank holidays. 2 lounges, restaurant; private dining room; background music. Small garden. Only restaurant suitable for ♿. No smoking. No children under 12. Guide dogs only. MasterCard, Visa accepted. D,B&B £105–£120 per person. Set menu £32–£40. 1-night bookings sometimes refused weekends.

DOLYDD Gwynedd — Map 3:A2

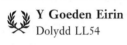

Y Goeden Eirin NEW
Dolydd LL54

Tel 01286-830942
Email john_rowlands@tiscali.co.uk
Website www.ygoedeneirin.co.uk

César award: Green guest house of the year

'We are a far cry from a conventional hotel,' write the owners of this small guest house, very Welsh (bilingual menus and wine list) and very green (solar panels, recycling and composting policies; organic food; Fairtrade tea and coffee). Guests wishing to arrive by train can be collected from Bangor, and advice is given about the 'excellent local transport'. The nominator wrote: 'A winning formula of husband-and-wife team [John and Eluned Rowlands] running it on very personal lines.' Inspectors found it 'wonderful'. The renovated farm buildings (local granite, slates, beams; decor a mixture of traditional and modern) stand amid rough pasture with views of mountains and sea. There is under-floor heating, books, 'beautiful objects, fine paintings', a grand piano and Wi-Fi. In the dining room, open to the public, 'wholesome, innovative' Aga-cooked food, eg, roast pork with apple; coq au Riesling, uses local and home-grown ingredients ('one of us is an award-winning cook, the other a restaurant critic'). 'Excellent' breakfasts have locally cured bacon, lamb's kidneys, home-baked bread, home-made preserves. 'Our room, large and bright, had glorious views, large TV, a good-sized bathroom.' One bedroom has a collection of books; another a Welsh dresser. (*Owain Peredur, and others*)

3 bedrooms. 2 in annexe. 3 miles S of Caernarfon. Closed Christmas/New Year. Lounge, dining room; occasional live piano music; Wi-Fi access. In 20-acre pastureland. Unsuitable for ♿. No smoking. No children under 12. No credit cards; cash payment requested on arrival. B&B £30–£50. Set dinner £25. *V*

FELIN FACH Powys — Map 3:D4

The Felin Fach Griffin

Felin Fach, nr Brecon
LD3 0UB
Tel 01874-620111
Fax 01874-620120
Email enquiries@felinfachgriffin.co.uk
Website www.felinfachgriffin.co.uk

'Service can be a bit dippy but we love it for meals,' writes one regular visitor to Charles and Edmund Inkin's 'civilised' terracotta-coloured inn between the Brecon Beacons and the Black Mountains. It is on a main road, with a large car park in front. Julie Bell is the manager. 'An attractive pub with rooms' was another comment, from visitors who felt the 'hotel side of things' lacked a 'personal touch' and who had a 'very small' twin-bedded room. But other bedrooms ('decor a mix of old and new') are thought 'simple but comfortable'; they have 'luxurious bedlinen'. Everyone admires the cooking of the Dutch chef, Ricardo Van Ede, using home-grown organic ingredients. 'The restaurant was full every evening. We drooled over scallops with morels and asparagus. Probably our best risotto ever. We enjoyed the evening buzz and the welcoming bar': no residents' lounge, but comfortable leather sofas round a fireplace and a big table with newspapers. The simple breakfast has boiled eggs or a fry-up, and you make your own toast, from 'excellent bread', on the Aga. The 'relaxed atmosphere' is liked. Dogs are welcomed (usually no charge). There is excellent walking nearby. The Inkins now also own the *Gurnard's Head*, near Zennor, Cornwall (*qv*). (*Frances Rathbone, JH, and others*)

7 bedrooms. 4 miles NE of Brecon, in village on A470. Closed 24–26 Dec; restaurant closed Mon lunch. Bar area, dining room, breakfast room; background CDs/radio most of the time (*Today* programme at breakfast); private dining room. 1½-acre garden: croquet, stream, kitchen garden. No smoking. MasterCard, Visa accepted. B&B £41.25–£60 per person. Full alc £36. Wine, fishing, shooting packages. 1-night Sat bookings occasionally refused. *V*

FISHGUARD Pembrokeshire — Map 3:D1

The Manor Town House

Main Street
Fishguard SA65 9HG
Tel/Fax 01348-873260
Email enquiries@manortownhouse.com
Website www.manortownhouse.com

'This is a hotel I would like to return to,' said a visitor to Gail and James Stewart's Georgian Grade II listed town house. 'They were warm, friendly and helpful, and gave lots of useful advice.' This year the Stewarts have redecorated the hall, landing and stairs, and three of the bedrooms; the garden and terrace have been improved. The restaurant is in a 'homely' basement; in summer, a patio and gazebo facing the sea double as a dining/drinks area. 'Gail's cooking was excellent (her soups are particularly fine). The wines were reasonably priced.' 'Only two choices for each course, but everything was meticulously prepared.' Local, organic ingredients are used where possible for dishes such as Cyw iar gyda eirin (chicken in a plum sauce). Antiques 'give character' to the public rooms. Most of the bedrooms have a sea view. 'Ours was a comfortable size, with nice furniture, though the bathroom, carved out of the wall, was small.' Another guest 'had a stunning view of the old harbour, one of the most comfortable beds we have ever had, furniture of the "whatever comes to hand" variety. Above all, it was quiet.' Nearest parking is 150 yards away. (*CG, and others*)

6 bedrooms. Near town square. Closed Christmas, 'occasionally off-season for owners' holidays'. Restaurant closed Wed in off-season. 2 lounges, bar/restaurant (classical background music at mealtimes). Walled garden: terrace, gazebo. Sea, safe bathing 2 miles. Unsuitable for ♿. No smoking. No dogs (kennels nearby). MasterCard, Visa accepted. B&B [2007] £32.50–£37.50 per person. Set dinner £20; full alc £25. New Year package. 1-night bookings occasionally refused.

HARLECH Gwynedd *See SHORTLIST* Map 3:B3

HAVERFORDWEST Pembrokeshire *See SHORTLIST* Map 3:D1

KNIGHTON Powys Map 3:C4

Milebrook House

Milebrook
Knighton
Powys LD7 1LT

Tel 01547-528632
Fax 01547-520509
Email hotel@milebrook.kc3ltd.co.uk
Website www.milebrookhouse.co.uk

Covered in Virginia creeper, Beryl and Rodney Marsden's hotel/ restaurant stands amid 'very special' gardens facing the Shropshire hills, an area of natural beauty. The gardens are 'overlooked by the dining room' and provide for croquet on warm summer evenings – as well as the vegetables on the dinner table. Otters and kingfishers are to be found in and by the River Teme next to the building, and walkers are spoilt for choice in the surrounding Welsh Marshes. 'The quintessential country hotel run by lovely people in a lovely house,' said a devoted guest on his fourth visit. But for some visitors the noise from the nearby road is a drawback. 'We are sensitive sleepers and were aware of the traffic in our pleasant, spacious room at the back.' 'Our room was comfortable but the squeaking from the wrought iron bed was a real passion killer,' said other guests. Robert Henshaw and Chris Marsden are the new chefs, serving a three-course *table d'hôte* menu (main courses like halibut with wild mushrooms and pancetta stew). 'An excellent wine list: especially by the glass.' The 18th-century house was once owned by Wilfred Thesiger and visited by Emperor Haile Selassie. (*RC, and others*)

10 bedrooms. 2 on ground floor. On A4113, 2 miles E of Knighton. Restaurant closed Mon midday. Lounge, bar, 2 dining rooms (soft background music in the evening). 3-acre grounds on river: terraces, pond, croquet, fishing. No smoking. No children under 8. No dogs. MasterCard, Visa accepted. B&B [2007]: single £64–£68.50, double £99.50–£105.50. Set menu £31.50. Christmas/New Year packages. 1-night bookings refused weekends.

LAMPETER Ceredigion *See SHORTLIST* Map 3:D3

****

Traveller's tale From the brochure photograph and the written description, *The* —— seemed not too bad, so on booking by phone I chose a superior room. When I walked in, I knew I had made a mistake. The reception area, basically a large hole in the wall surrounded by chipped timber, was dirty; layers of dust on a faded patterned carpet bore witness to the lack of any real cleaning. Having called for the receptionist several times in vain, I went for assistance. I found the manager in the bar, enjoying a smoke and a beer. He explained that the room I had requested was no longer available due to a plumbing problem. He offered a standard room instead. I asked to see it before deciding. The door was opened to disclose a small, dark room with purple carpet, a matching purple counterpane, and furniture that matched the woodwork in Reception. I didn't bother to look at the bathroom. I would have preferred sleeping in my car to staying here. While in the car park, phoning to make other arrangements, I saw a couple who had been behind me at Reception return to their car with their bags. (*Hotel in Yorkshire*)

****

LLANARMON DYFFRYN CEIRIOG Denbighshire

Map 3:B4

The Hand at Llanarmon
Ceiriog Valley
Llanarmon Dyffryn Ceiriog
LL20 7LD

Tel 01691-600666
Fax 01691-600262
Email reception@thehandhotel.co.uk
Website www.thehandhotel.co.uk

'Roaring log fires at all hours and flickering candles on all the tables' set the scene for chef Grant Mulholland's 'straightforward, hearty fare' in this down-to-earth and 'charming' inn beneath the Berwyn mountains. 'Local pork and lamb were excellent; chicken liver pâté and trout perfect. We never had room for pudding,' said visitors this year. 'Popular with local farmers exchanging gossip' and tourists alike ('all were warmly welcomed'), the 16th-century building is in the Ceiriog valley, described by Lloyd George as 'a little bit of heaven on earth', with many sites of interest and unlimited walking potential. 'You can step out of the front door and walk for miles in any direction and probably not see another soul.' 'We can arrange for you almost any country pursuit, even white-water rafting,' say the owners, Gaynor and Martin De Luchi. The 'excellent' breakfast (apart from 'disappointing toast') has good cooked choice, and is served until 10 am. 'Our double-aspect room (No. 3) was warm, comfortable, tastefully decorated and well equipped. Owners and staff all so friendly. No mobile phone signal here, just peace and tranquillity.' (*Janet and Dennis Allom, and others*)

Note Not to be confused with the *Hand Hotel* at Chirk.

13 bedrooms. 4 on ground floor. 10 miles W of Oswestry. Accommodation closed at Christmas. Lounge, bar, restaurant, games/TV room (pool, darts). No background music. 2-acre grounds. Civil wedding licence. No smoking. No dogs in public rooms, except bar. MasterCard, Visa accepted. B&B [2007] £40–£65 per person. Full alc £30. New Year package. *V*

See also SHORTLIST

The *V* sign at the end of an entry indicates a hotel that has agreed to take part in our Voucher scheme and to give *Guide* readers a 25% discount on their room rates for a one-night stay, subject to the conditions explained in *How to use the Good Hotel Guide*, and given on the back of the vouchers.

LLANDRILLO Denbighshire — Map 3:B4

Tyddyn Llan
Llandrillo
nr Corwen LL21 0ST

Tel 01490-440264
Fax 01490-440414
Email tyddynllan@compuserve.com
Website www.tyddynllan.co.uk

César award in 2006

Once a shooting lodge for the dukes of Westminster, Bryan and Susan Webb's restaurant-with-rooms is an 'elegant Georgian house in manicured grounds', in the vale of Edeyrnion, facing the Berwyn Mountains. There is praise (and one dissenting report, on a Monday-night visit) this year. The plaudits: 'Truly excellent; wonderful rooms – so peaceful.' 'Lovely. Outstanding food. Very good service.' 'Any misgivings after an initial cool welcome were quelled by Susan Webb's delightful greeting, and an excellent dinner' (dishes like roast pigeon with girolles; calf's liver with wild garlic bubble and squeak). 'Comfortable' lounges have 'elegant drapes, soft lighting, a piano in case you need to burst into song'. The bedrooms are 'thoughtfully furnished'. 'Nicely framed paintings, masses of glossies, bathroom with beautifully tiled floor and large walk-in shower.' Some rooms have 'views across stunning scenery in two directions'. All now have flat-screen TV, and DVD-player; six have a new bathroom. There is a covered terrace, 'lots of nice seating areas' and a pond in the 'immaculate' garden. Breakfast 'was excellent; good compote, freshly segmented pink grapefruit; delicious porridge; good undyed smoked haddock; perfect poached eggs'. (*Tessa Royal, Frances Rathbone, John and Jane Holland, and others*)

13 bedrooms. 1 suitable for ♿. 5 miles SW of Corwen. Closed last 2 weeks Jan. Restaurant closed midday Mon–Thurs (check during Nov and Feb). 2 lounges, bar, 2 dining rooms; occasional background music at mealtimes. 3-acre grounds. Fishing, riding, golf, sailing, walking nearby. Civil wedding licence. No smoking. No dogs in public rooms; allowed in some rooms at £5 a night. MasterCard, Visa accepted. D,B&B £60–£95 per person. Set meals £45; full alc £53. Christmas/New Year house parties. *V*

How to contact the *Guide*
By mail: From anywhere in the UK, write to Freepost PAM 2931, London W11 4BR (no stamp is needed)
From outside the UK: *Good Hotel Guide*, 50 Addison Avenue, London W11 4QP, England
By telephone or fax: 020-7602 4182
By email: Goodhotel@aol.com or Goodhotel@btinternet.com
Via our website: www.goodhotelguide.com

LLANDUDNO Conwy — Map 3:A3

Bodysgallen Hall and Spa

Llandudno LL30 1RS

Tel 01492-584466
Fax 01492-582519
Email info@bodysgallen.com
Website www.bodysgallen.com

César award in 1988

Owned by Richard Broyd's Historic House Hotels, and managed by Matthew Johnson, this Grade 1 listed, 17th-century mansion has fine panelled public rooms, ancestral portraits, antiques, splendid fireplaces and stone mullioned windows; lots of places to sit, many with log fire. It is liked for the 'great old-fashioned luxury; room-service breakfast in bed', and for its 'well-equipped' spa. 'Beautifully situated' in parkland, it has a knot garden, follies, and views of Snowdonia and Conwy Castle. The best bedrooms are 'large and elegant', traditionally furnished; some have a four-poster. The cottage suites (Pineapple Lodge, Gingerbread House) suit families, but only those with children over six (and the under-eights may not use the swimming pool). In the formal restaurant (ask for a window table), male guests are asked to wear a jacket and tie, except in summer. The chef, John Williams, serves modern dishes, eg, contrast of scallop and mullet; cannon of lamb with a little shepherd's pie. The afternoon teas are much admired. More reports, please.

33 bedrooms. 16 in cottages, 1 suitable for ♿. 2 miles S of Llandudno. Hall, drawing room, library, bar, dining room; conference centre. No background music. 220-acre park: gardens, tennis, croquet; spa: 50-ft swimming pool, gym, sauna, beauty treatments. Riding, shooting, fishing, sandy beaches nearby. Civil wedding/partnership licence. No smoking. No children under 6 in hotel, under 8 in spa. No dogs. Amex, MasterCard, Visa accepted. B&B [2007] £87.50–£197.50 per person. Set menu £41.50. Special breaks. Christmas/New Year packages.

St Tudno Hotel

The Promenade
Llandudno LL30 2LP

Tel 01492-874411
Fax 01492-860407
Email sttudnohotel@btinternet.com
Website www.st-tudno.co.uk

César award in 1987

Once frequented during childhood holidays by Alice Liddell who inspired Lewis Carroll (it has an Alice in Wonderland suite), this grade II listed building is opposite the town's Victorian pier, gardens and beach. Martin Bland, the owner, is 'much in evidence, helpful, charming. His staff, a good mix of seasonal workers and youthful professionals from around the world, are friendly, quietly efficient,' say visitors this year. Bedrooms are brightly decorated with colourful wallpaper and furnishings (lots of primary colours). 'Our small second-floor room had sea view; a comfortable bed (extra pillows came as soon as we asked), lots of hanging space; delicious shortbread and fresh milk with the tea tray; wonderful use of space in the small bathroom.' The housekeeping team keeps the rooms 'top rate'. Public rooms have patterned wallpaper, swagged drapery, potted plants. *The Terrace* restaurant is Italianate, with murals of Lake Como, stone fountains, tented ceiling, and chandeliers. Stephen Duffy has returned as head chef; his style is 'modern, with a twist', eg, butter-poached chicken, tomato couscous. The wine list has 'some impressive choices at impressive prices'. The indoor swimming pool is 'an unexpected treat'. Phone for special offers. (*Stephen and Pauline Glover, PG Knowles*)

18 bedrooms. Central, on promenade opposite pier. Lift. Sitting room, coffee lounge, lounge bar; restaurant; indoor 25-ft swimming pool; 'secret garden'. No background music. Secure car park, garaging. No smoking. Dogs by arrangement (£10 per night); not in public rooms or unattended in bedrooms. All major credit cards accepted. B&B £42.50–£155 per person. Full alc £45. Christmas/New Year packages. Special breaks. 1-night bookings occasionally refused. *V*

See also SHORTLIST

LLANDWROG Gwynedd — Map 3:A2

Rhiwafallen NEW

LLANDWROG, nr Caernarfon
LL54 5SW

Tel 01286-830172
Email ktandrobjohn@aol.com
Website www.rhiwafallen.co.uk

Opened in September 2006, this restaurant-with-rooms stands well away from the Caernarfon–Pwllheli road. Kate John, the 'cheerful front-of-house', and her husband, Rob, the chef, 'do almost everything themselves', says the nominator. 'Thoroughly renovated to a high standard', this traditional granite farmhouse, 'despite its feel of a modern city house', has a 'welcoming atmosphere'. The spacious lounge, in two areas, is furnished in contemporary style. Emphasis is on natural materials, slate, wood, subdued colours. 'Everything blends perfectly. Lots of candles, even by day (it is a bit dark).' Dining is in a smallish but light conservatory, and outdoors in fine weather. 'Slate floors and blond wood, bistro-style, but tables smartly laid. The food is a cut above the ordinary: genuine without unnecessary flourishes. Natural flavours shine through; innovative pairings of texture, colour and flavouring. Raw materials from the best local suppliers. Home-baked bread.' 'One of the best meals we've eaten in this decade,' write inspectors. At breakfast, juices are freshly squeezed and there is plenty of choice (American pancakes; locally smoked salmon with organic scrambled eggs; full Welsh). Afternoon tea is included in the price. The bedrooms have oak flooring, goose-feather duvet, Egyptian cotton bedlinen. 'Sleek *en suite* bathrooms.'

5 bedrooms. 1 on ground floor. 6 miles S of Caernarfon. Restaurant closed Mon, Christmas. Ramp. Lounge, restaurant; modern 'chill-out' background music. 1½-acre garden. No smoking. No children under 12 (must have own room; standard rates). No dogs. Amex, MasterCard, Visa accepted. B&B double [2007] £100–£150. 20% discount for single occupancy. Set menu £29.50. New Year package.

LLANGAMMARCH WELLS Powys — Map 3:D3

The Lake
Llangammarch Wells
LD4 4BS

Tel 01591-620202
Fax 01591-620457
Email info@lakecountryhouse.co.uk
Website www.lakecountryhouse.co.uk

César award in 1992

'It filled our requirements: good ambience, golf, fishing and leisure facilities.' 'Wonderful.' Comments this year on Jean-Pierre Mifsud's mock-Tudor, purpose-built Edwardian hotel. It stands amid 'superb scenery', in 'magnificent' grounds: its lawns slope down to the River Irfon. There are daffodils and lambs in spring, and sightings of red kites and red-breasted mergansers. The large lounge has log fire, paintings, grand piano. The spa, which overlooks the lake, 'is quite the best I have come across', says a regular visitor. 'A really good-sized pool', a 'small but well-equipped gym'; also health and beauty treatments. The suites in the new wing are also liked: 'Very comfortable, big bedroom, big bathroom with separate shower.' The older rooms, though well equipped, may feel 'somewhat dated': 'four different patterns'. The 'modern British' food is generally enjoyed, and the young staff are 'helpful and friendly', though one couple reported 'no offer of help with luggage'. Men are asked to wear a jacket after 7 pm. Breakfast is 'everything you'd expect at a country house hotel'. Mr Mifsud 'likes to circulate the dining room chatting to guests'. (*Graciela Holbutt, John Barnes, Gordon Hands, and others*)

30 bedrooms. 12 in adjacent lodge. 8 miles SW of Builth Wells. 2 lounges, bar, billiard room, restaurant; spa: 50-ft swimming pool, sauna, gym. No background music. 50-acre grounds: lake (fishing), river, tennis, croquet, 9-hole par 3 golf course, clay-pigeon shooting, archery. Civil wedding licence. No smoking. No children under 8 in spa, or in dining room after 7 pm (high tea provided). Dogs allowed in some bedrooms (£6 a day); only guide dogs in public rooms. MasterCard, Visa accepted. B&B [2007] £85–£180 per person; D,B&B (min. 2 nights) £110–£205. Set menus £39.50. Christmas/New Year packages.

LLANGOLLEN Denbighshire *See SHORTLIST* Map 3:B4

LLANWRTYD WELLS Powys Map 3:D3

Carlton Riverside

Irfon Crescent
Llanwrtyd Wells LD5 4ST

Tel 01591-610248
Email info@carltonrestaurant.co.uk
Website www.carltonrestaurant.co.uk

César award in 1998

Big changes here: Mary Ann and Alan Gilchrist have renamed their unpretentious restaurant-with-rooms and moved it to another building in this old spa town. They now have a larger dining room and 'more modern' decor. Unchanged are the hostess's 'extrovert personality', which 'adds to the charm', and her 'excellent cooking'. 'Every meal a delight,' one visitor wrote. Others appreciated the 'very good vegetarian options, efficient meal service', 'relaxed atmosphere'. Only problem: 'Checking in and out a bit of a problem as the Gilchrists live about 175 yards away and are not always easy to contact.' The building, painted strong blue, 'is hard to miss'. Its interior is 'tasteful in brown and cream'. 'Our bedroom was large, well furnished, with modern fittings, good attention to detail.' The L-shaped lounge (with bar and small library) is 'a little tight on space, but comfortable enough, well lit (large windows)'. In the 'simple but elegant' dining room, best tables face the River Irfon. There are two fixed-price menus, one with limited choice: main courses include seared fillet of salmon with avocado salsa. The wine list has many half bottles. 'Breakfast had fresh orange juice, very good scrambled eggs.' Noise 'can be a problem at night (traffic and youths who congregate nearby)'. (*John and Kay Patterson, and others*)

4 bedrooms. Town centre. No private parking. Closed 4 Dec–1 Jan, restaurant closed Sun. Reception, bar/lounge, restaurant; classical background music.

Unsuitable for ♿. No smoking. No dogs in public rooms. MasterCard, Visa accepted. B&B £35–£50 per person. Set menu £35; full alc £42.50. Gourmet breaks. New Year package. 1-night bookings occasionally refused. *V*

See also SHORTLIST

LLYSWEN Powys — Map 3:D4

Llangoed Hall
Llyswen
nr Brecon LD3 0YP

Tel 01874-754525
Fax 01874-754545
Email enquiries@llangoedhall.com
Website www.llangoedhall.com

Beneath the Cambrian and Black mountains, this fine 17th-century manor house stands amid lovely countryside beside the River Wye. It was redesigned by Clough Williams-Ellis in 1919, and turned into a hotel by Sir Bernard Ashley in 1990. There are pictures, antiques and Ashley fabrics in the public rooms; the Great Hall has log fires, the morning room a piano, the library a snooker table. The spacious bedrooms have floral fabrics: 'Ours had sitting areas, a grand Victorian mirror.' 'Staff mainly Polish, with some Welsh: very polite, good sense of humour.' Dining is a formal affair (men are asked to wear a jacket and tie). Visitors from the neighbourhood to 'our local hotel de posh' in 2007 were 'pleased to note that the service had become more friendly and relaxed, less starched and stiff than it used to be. A superb, though expensive, meal.' The cooking of chef Sean Ballington is 'modern European with a traditional twist', eg, fillet of Welsh Black beef on a sweet potato rösti. 'But the menu doesn't change for quite a time.' *Llangoed Hall* is the hotel of choice for literary bigwigs attending the Hay-on-Wye book festival. Good local walking and fishing. (*Frances Rathbone, JT, and others*)

23 bedrooms. 11 miles NE of Brecon. 4 lounges (1 with pianist at weekends), restaurant, billiard room; private dining room; classical background music; function rooms. 17-acre grounds: tennis, croquet, maze; helipad; River Wye (200 yds), fishing. Riding, golf, gliding, clay-pigeon shooting, canoeing nearby. Civil wedding licence. Unsuitable for ♿. No smoking. No children under 8. Only guide dogs in house (heated kennels in grounds). All major credit cards accepted. B&B [2007] £105–£350 per person. Set dinner £45. 2-night and Christmas/New Year/Easter packages. 1-night bookings refused in high season.

MUMBLES Swansea *See SHORTLIST* Map 3:E3

NANT GWYNANT Gwynedd Map 3:A3

Pen-y-Gwryd Hotel
Nant Gwynant
LL55 4NT

Tel 01286-870211
Website www.pyg.co.uk

César award in 1995

'Spectacularly located' among the peaks of Snowdonia, this old climbing inn 'oozes atmosphere'. Hillary and his team stayed here before climbing Everest (their signatures are scrawled on the ceiling of a bar). The 'warm-hearted' owners, Brian and Jane Pullee (now supported by sons Rupert and Nicolas), 'hold the secret of *PyG*'s success', says a TV director who first came in the 1960s to film a documentary on the Everest team's training. 'Fifty years later, I'm still an appreciative guest.' Visitors are 'immediately put at ease' and 'soon settled in the wood-panelled snug, absorbing the atmosphere'. 'The hotel is utterly charming, spotlessly clean, never twee. Flowers in lounge and dining room. Jane Pullee makes sure that children enjoy themselves. She organises a rota for the popular role of banging the gong for breakfast and dinner, and holds a touching ceremony when children have climbed Snowdon.' Bedrooms have 'Edwardian charm', old-fashioned furniture, 'masses of bedding'. Only five have facilities *en suite*. 'Sliding into a Victorian bath after a marvellous day in the hills sums up a stay in this unique hotel.' Meals, eaten in house-party style, are 'hearty and very acceptable fare'. 'Scrumptious' packed lunches. The 'lovely garden' with pond and stream 'has an undersigned appearance but is well kept and blends with the surrounding scenery'. (*John Hefin, Sir Roland and Lady Jackson, Jelly Williams*)

16 bedrooms. 1 on ground floor. Between Beddgelert and Capel Curig. Closed Nov–Feb, except New Year. Lounge, bar, games room, dining room; chapel. No background music. 2-acre grounds: natural swimming pool, sauna. No smoking. Dogs welcome. Master Card, Visa accepted. B&B [2007] £38–£48 per person. Set dinner £26. 3-night rates. 1-night bookings sometimes refused weekends.

Deadlines: nominations for the 2009 edition of this volume should reach us not later than 15 May 2008. Latest date for comments on existing entries: 1 June 2008.

NEWPORT Pembrokeshire — Map 3:D1

Cnapan
East Street, Newport
nr Fishguard SA42 0SY

Tel 01239-820575
Fax 01239-820878
Email enquiry@cnapan.co.uk
Website www.cnapan.co.uk

On the fairly quiet main street of this Pembrokeshire seaside town (the larger Newport is in Gwent), this pink-painted, listed Georgian restaurant-with-rooms has been run by the Lloyd and Cooper families for more than 20 years. Michael and Judith Cooper (née Lloyd, the chef), and their son Oliver (the third generation), are now in charge: founding partner John Lloyd died in late 2006 aged 92. The house is crammed with family treasures, books and games; there's a Welsh dresser in the entrance hall, a wood-burning stove in the lounge. 'On arrival one is greeted with a blast of "hellos", there is much hustling and bustling,' said one visitor. The small bedrooms have pine furniture, bright colours, tea/coffee-making facilities. The family room has an adjoining bunk bedroom for children. There is much fresh fish on the menu, eg, spicy sea food chowder with green-lipped mussels; smoked haddock fish cakes. Puddings, a speciality, include some unusual ones like damson sorbet. 'We were very well fed, vegetables especially good. Service was brisk and attentive, everyone showed kindness.' Huge breakfasts include home-made marmalade, free-range eggs and kippers. Beaches and scenic coastal paths are close by. (*DS, and others*)

5 bedrooms. Town centre. Closed early Jan–mid-Mar, Christmas. Restaurant closed Tues. Lounge, bar, restaurant (jazz/classical background music). Small garden. Unsuitable for ♿. No smoking. Guide dogs only. MasterCard, Visa accepted. B&B £40-£47 per person; D,B&B £53.50–£74. Set meals £28. 1-night bookings occasionally refused peak season, Sat.

PENMYNYDD Anglesey — Map 3:A3

Neuadd Lwyd
Penmynydd, nr Llanfairpwllgwyngyll
Anglesey LL61 5BX

Tel/Fax 01248-715005
Email post@neuaddlwyd.co.uk
Website www.neuaddlwyd.co.uk

'An enchanting home,' says a 2007 endorsement of inspectors' earlier comment: 'A lovely house, warm and welcoming, beautifully furnished, spotlessly clean. Superb food.' This early Victorian rectory, set amid farmland and with 'wonderful' views of Snowdonia, is run as a small, upmarket guest house by owners Susannah and Peter Woods (they prefer to call it a country house). Welsh speakers, they are 'enthusiastic about Anglesey and promote local produce in their meals'. Susannah Woods and Delyth Gwynedd, who met while training at Ballymaloe cookery school in Ireland, serve a no-choice, four-course dinner at 'beautifully laid tables'; perhaps salad of warm smoked goose breast; braised shoulder of lamb. 'Delicious home-baked breads; farmhouse butter; wonderful cheeses. Personal dislikes are discussed, but exact dishes remain a surprise.' The 'extremely comfortable' lounge has high-backed wooden chairs on each side of bay windows (binoculars provided). 'Lots of pictures everywhere; attractive chandeliers.' 'Our lovely bedroom had white-painted cast iron bedstead and furniture, pink-and-white wallpaper, original black slate fireplace'; also flat-screen TV/DVD/CD-player. 'Lovely' bathrooms, tastefully done: slipper baths, painted floors and expensive soaps. 'First-class breakfast: fresh orange juice, home-made compotes and cereals, creamy scrambled eggs, Welsh rarebit. When we left, everyone came out to say goodbye.' (*Gordon Franklin, and others*)

4 bedrooms. 3 miles W of Menai Bridge. Train: Bangor. Closed Sun/Mon (except bank holidays). Drawing room, lounge, dining room; background music in evening 'only if requested'. 6-acre grounds. Unsuitable for ♿. No smoking. No children under 12. No dogs. MasterCard, Visa accepted. B&B [2007] £82.50–£135. Set dinner £37.50. Christmas/New Year packages. See website for mid-week rates.

'Set menu' indicates a fixed-price meal, with ample, limited or no choice. 'Full alc' is the hotel's estimated price per person of a three-course *à la carte* meal, with a half bottle of house wine. 'Alc' is the price of an *à la carte* meal excluding the cost of wine.

PORTHKERRY Vale of Glamorgan Map 3:E3

Egerton Grey
Porthkerry, nr Cardiff CF62 3BZ

Tel 01446-711666
Fax 01446-711690
Email info@egertongrey.co.uk
Website www.egertongrey.co.uk

'A very relaxing couple of days' (a comment this year). This grey stone former Victorian rectory has a beautiful setting in a wooded valley with views through an impressive viaduct to the Bristol Channel. Its pretty terraced gardens are bordered by mature woodland creating an air of tranquillity tempered only by aircraft heading to and from Cardiff airport ten miles away (but the hotel stands in its own valley, and most guests have not been bothered by this). 'We were well looked after by everyone we met: receptionist, waiters, etc.' Earlier guests praised the welcoming co-owner (with Huw Thomas), Richard Morgan-Price: 'He carried our bags and led us upstairs to our room.' Most bedrooms are spacious, and have colourful wallpaper, and fabrics, thick carpet and antique or repro furniture. There are antiques, interesting objects and squashy sofas in the lounges. Dinner (modern British cooking by Mark Parry) is served by candlelight in the former billiard room. 'Excellent' is this year's verdict (main courses like pan-fried sea bass with red pepper risotto; duck breast with fondant potato, pine nut and orange glaze). Breakfast 'has a nice choice of well-cooked classics'. Children are welcomed. Small weddings and functions are held. (*Gwen Griffiths, Rodney Burges, and others*)

10 bedrooms. 10 miles SW of Cardiff. 2 lounges, drawing room, library, bar, restaurant; classical background music; conservatory; private dining room; function facilities. 7-acre garden: croquet. Rock beach 400 yds; golf nearby. Only restaurant suitable for ♿. Civil wedding licence. No smoking. No dogs in public rooms. Amex, MasterCard, Visa accepted. B&B £65–£130 per person. Set menus £30. Christmas/New Year packages. 1-night bookings occasionally refused. *V*

PORTMEIRION Gwynedd Map 3:B3

Portmeirion Hotel
Portmeirion LL48 6ET

Tel 01766-770000
Fax 01766-770300
Email hotel@portmeirion-village.com
Website www.portmeirion-village.com

'A favourite place, consistently good, very friendly, with long-established staff who make one feel most welcome.' Praise from a *Guide* hotelier for Sir Clough Williams-Ellis's 'enchanting' creation of castles and cottages, Italianate villas and towers on a private, 'magical', wooded peninsula on the Snowdonia coast. Another comment: 'Unique location. Comfort provided by both facilities and service.' There are three areas of accommodation: the Victorian hotel/restaurant on the shore; *Castell Deudraeth*, an 1850s folly with mock Tudor towers and ramparts, which overlooks the estuary; and 17 cottages and villas scattered about the hillside. The hotel has bright fabrics, furniture and ornaments from Rajasthan, and a 'Mughal-style' bar. Its luxurious bedrooms include the Peacock suite (where Edward VIII once stayed), with 'vast marble fireplace' and 'bed so high you need a footstool to climb into it'. *Castell Deudraeth*, the 'boutique' option, has striking modern interiors. Rooms in the village, each different, should be chosen carefully, as 'a ground-floor one can leave you vulnerable to curious eyes of day visitors'. In the hotel's restaurant, menus are bilingual and the food was 'very good; a mini shepherd's pie as a garnish to a main course was creative and enjoyable'. 'No lift. Elderly or infirm guests should insist on a ground-floor room, and be aware that there is a lot of climbing to get anywhere on the estate.' (*Brian Pullee, Deborah Starbuck-Edwards, and others*)

14 bedrooms in hotel, 28 in village, 11 in *Castell Deudraeth*. Between Penrhyndeudraeth and Porthmadog. Closed 6–17 Jan. Free minibus service from Minffordd station. Hall, 2 lounges, 2 bars, restaurant (harpist sometimes), children's supper room; function room; beauty salon. Babysitters available. No background music. 170-acre grounds: garden, heated swimming pool (25 by 50 ft; May–Sept); spa, tennis, lakes, sandy beach. Free golf nearby. Civil wedding licence. No smoking. Guide dogs only. All major credit cards accepted. B&B [2007]: single £132–£242, double £167–£209, suite £225–£277. Set dinner £35.50; alc £41. Winter breaks. Christmas/New Year packages.

PWLLHELI Gwynedd — Map 3:B2

Plas Bodegroes
Nefyn Road
Pwllheli LL53 5TH

Tel 01758-612363
Fax 01758-701247
Email gunna@bodegroes.co.uk
Website www.bodegroes.co.uk

César award in 1992

'Just the place for a special occasion; a beautiful house in lovely grounds; intelligently prepared food.' A *Guide* hotelier leads the praise for Chris and Gunna Chown's restaurant-with-rooms, a white Georgian manor house in wooded grounds on the Lleyn peninsula. Mr Chown tells us that five of the bedrooms have been 'trendied up with a Shaker oak look', and all rooms now have flat-screen TV. Guests are advised that two smaller rooms at the top are not suitable for stays of longer than one night, but visitors this year thought them 'cleverly designed' and well equipped. 'We enjoyed the view from the window seat.' Two rooms are in a cottage at the rear, facing a tranquil courtyard garden. The 'gorgeous' dining room has 'delightful illuminated display cabinets, polished wood floors, a wealth of serious works of art', 'perfect lighting'. Chris Chown's 'culinary wizardry' has long held a *Michelin* star for dishes like grilled breast of Goosnargh duck with confit leg and morel sauce. The 'enjoyable breakfast' includes fresh orange juice, 'perfectly cooked hot dishes, very good toast'. 'Smoked haddock the best I have been served.' (*Brian Pullee, Deborah Starbuck-Edwards, and others*)

11 bedrooms. 2 in courtyard annexe. 1 mile W of Pwllheli. Open mid-Mar–mid-Nov. Closed Sun night/Mon. Lounge, bar, breakfast room, restaurant (occasional background music). 5-acre grounds. Unsuitable for ♿. No smoking. No dogs in public rooms. MasterCard, Visa accepted. B&B £50–£85 per person. Set dinner £40. Midweek breaks. 1-night bookings refused bank holidays, summer weekends.

RUTHIN Denbighshire *See SHORTLIST* Map 3:A4

ST DAVID'S Pembrokeshire *See SHORTLIST* Map 3:D1

SKENFRITH Monmouthshire Map 3:D4

The Bell at Skenfrith
Skenfrith NP7 8UH

Tel 01600-750235
Fax 01600-750525
Email enquiries@skenfrith.co.uk
Website www.skenfrith.co.uk

With its flagstone floors, huge inglenook fireplace and 'simple yet sophisticated' bedrooms, Janet and William Hutchings's 17th-century coaching inn has a 'wonderfully quiet setting' deep in the Welsh Marshes, beside an old stone bridge across the River Monnow. 'One of the best gastro-pubs I've visited,' says a report in 2007. Other readers had reservations: 'Can't make up its mind whether it is a foodie restaurant-with-rooms, a fishing pub or a hotel.' And some were unhappy about the welcome. The chef, David Hill, serves elaborate modern dishes, eg, fillet of Brecon beef, wild mushroom glaze, fondant potato, feuillette of snails. The 'splendid, if pricey' wine list has a wide selection of half bottles, and 14 wines by the glass. 'My magnificent suite had views over the bridge; comfortable bed, huge stylish bathroom.' All bedrooms have DVD- and CD-player and Internet access. 'Bed turned down at night, and made up during breakfast' (the latter includes eggs Florentine; French toast; boiled egg with soldiers). The owners' quarters on the first floor are to be turned in early 2008 into three new bedrooms. (*Mark Purcell, and others*)

8 bedrooms. 3 more planned for 2008. 9 miles W of Ross-on-Wye. Closed Jan–mid-Feb 2008 for building work; also Mon Nov–Mar. 2 bars, 2 dining rooms. No background music. 1-acre grounds. River opposite. Quad biking; archery, go-karting, clay-pigeon shooting, fishing nearby. Unsuitable for ♿. No smoking. No children under 8 in restaurant in evening. No dogs in restaurant. Amex, MasterCard, Visa accepted. B&B [2007] £52.50–£120 per person. Full alc £37. Christmas package. 1-night bookings refused Sat.

SWANSEA *See SHORTLIST* — Map 3:E3

TALSARNAU Gwynedd — Map 3:B3

Maes-y-Neuadd

Talsarnau LL47 6YA

Tel 01766-780200
Fax 01766-780211
Email maes@neuadd.com
Website www.neuadd.com

César award in 2003

'A wonderful old house in a stunning setting', this 'mansion in the meadow' (as the Welsh name translates) stands peacefully in 'well-kept and interesting grounds', with 'unforgettable views' over Snowdonia and Cardigan Bay. 'The site is beautiful, rooms are comfortable, and the bar and restaurant staff are friendly,' says a 2007 visitor. 'Lovely and bright' lounge areas have oak beams, antique and modern furniture, an inglenook fireplace and 'caged canaries in the seating area'. The bedrooms vary in size and style; many have been refurbished, though a visitor this year was unhappy with a room yet to be improved. Peter Jackson's cooking, using local and organic produce (vegetables and herbs from the garden), is thought 'excellent' by fans, but some guests find it 'overcomplicated'. Dishes include noisettes of lamb with a leek mousse; a parcel of braised shoulder, root vegetables, fondant potatoes. A 'well-chosen' wine list has a 'good range of prices'. Breakfast has 'a good selection of dishes both hot and cold'. One visitor this year acknowledged that 'the hotel was full of people obviously having a good time', but was uncomfortable with 'the variety of little forms and notes, and things to be signed for'. (*Gordon Hands, John A Tyzack, and others*)

16 bedrooms. 3 ground-floor rooms. 3 miles NE of Harlech. Lift. 2 lounges, bar, conservatory, restaurant; business facilities; terrace. No background music. 80-acre grounds. Civil wedding licence. Unsuitable for ♿. No smoking. Dogs in coach house only. Diners, MasterCard, Visa accepted. B&B [2007] £55–£90 per person. Set dinner £33–£37. 2/3-night breaks. Murder, fireworks weekends. Christmas/New Year packages.

TALYLLYN Gwynedd — Map 3:B3

Tynycornel

Talyllyn, Tywyn
LL36 9AJ

Tel 01654-782282
Fax 01654-782679
Email reception@tynycornel.co.uk
Website www.tynycornel.co.uk

In a 'most beautiful valley, with a lake for fishermen that takes some beating', this is a 'solid, traditional' inn. It stands on the shore of Talyllyn Lake (which it owns), beneath Cader Idris, the mountain that marks the end of the Snowdonia range. 'A lot of money has been spent on it, and it looks good and works well,' says a visitor this year. 'Most helpful staff, both local and Eastern European.' There is a new manager, Mair Eleri Jones, and a new chef, and six new bedrooms have recently been added. The lounge faces the lake and has paintings by the local bird artist Terence Lambert ('for the real thing you can sit in the window seats and watch the bird life on the lake'). The restaurant serves 'modern' cuisine, eg, baked salmon, with Welsh rarebit, saffron sauce. The lake has one of the few remaining natural brown trout fisheries south of Scotland. (*Brian Pullee, and others*)

22 bedrooms. 9 in annexe. Some on ground floor. 9 miles SW of Dolgellau. Train: Machynlleth, 10 miles. Ramp. Lounge, bar, restaurant, conservatory restaurant; background music in restaurant; live Welsh music sometimes; conference facilities; drying room. ½-acre grounds. Civil wedding licence. No smoking. Dogs in annexe rooms only. MasterCard, Visa accepted. B&B [2007] £40–£65 per person; D,B&B £60–£85. Set dinner £22.50. New Year package. *V*

The *V* sign at the end of an entry indicates a hotel that has agreed to take part in our Voucher scheme and to give *Guide* readers a 25% discount on their room rates for a one-night stay, subject to the conditions explained in *How to use the Good Hotel Guide*, and given on the back of the vouchers.

TREDUNNOCK Monmouthshire — Map 3:E4

The Newbridge
Tredunnock, nr Usk
NP15 1LY

Tel 01633-451000
Fax 01633 451001
Email eatandsleep@thenewbridge.co.uk
Website www.thenewbridge.co.uk

'Excellent. The surroundings are peaceful and bucolic, the atmosphere is relaxing,' said the nominators of Annie and Dave Davies's restaurant-with-rooms. Managed by Iain Sampson (also the chef) and Gethin Owen, it stands by a bend in the picturesque River Usk. Inside are 'many different seating areas, comfy sofas, wooden chairs and tables'. The decor is 'slightly rural Italian': terracotta walls, flagstone and wooden floors. 'Interesting art work everywhere. Our first-floor room in the discreet annexe was light and spacious, with beams, solid oak furniture, polished floors, two metal chandeliers. The [handmade] bed was large and firm; the huge bathroom had roll-top bath and separate shower. The dinner menu was interesting, too, with local ingredients; the fish specials listed on a blackboard came from Cornwall. Cooking was excellent [eg, fish cake with sweet chilli sauce]; the wine list also a winner, and reasonably priced.' We dined at a table overlooking the river.' Breakfast has a huge platter of cheese, meat, fresh fruit, home-made bread and pastries. Children of all ages are welcomed. (*P and JT*)

6 bedrooms. All in annexe, 20 yds. Some on ground floor. 5 miles S of Usk. Closed 26 Dec, 1 week early Jan. Lounge, bar, restaurant ('easy listening' background music). Civil wedding licence. No smoking. No dogs. All major credit cards accepted. B&B [2007] £55–£95 per person; D,B&B £80–£90. Full alc £35. *V*

TREMADOG Gwynedd — Map 3:B3

Plas Tan-Yr-Allt
Tremadog, nr Porthmadog
LL49 9RG

Tel 01766-514545
Email info@tanyrallt.co.uk
Website www.tanyrallt.co.uk

César award: Welsh country house of the year

'A delightful place to unwind,' says a 2007 visitor to this Grade II listed house, overlooking the Glaslyn estuary. Known as 'Tanny', it is run in informal house-party style by Michael Bewick and Nick Golding (the chef). The poet Shelley, who spent a year here, described the building as 'tasty enough for the villa of an Italian prince'. 'We were warmly welcomed by Michael and Nick and offered tea, which was elegantly served in the garden. In the entrance hall, bright red with Philippe

Starck "ghost" chairs, you can talk to Percy the parrot; a real ice-breaker. 'Our lovely bedroom, Shelley's Theatre, had a beautifully dressed four-poster bed, window seat, huge bathroom.' Each bedroom has its own style: Madocks has a domed ceiling, white paintwork, huge modern chandelier, metal-framed bed ('very comfortable') and 'wonderful sea views'. Guests dine together at a huge refectory table in the pretty dining room. 'A glorious affair. The company was good. Our three-course meal was delicious; emphasis on locally sourced food, first-rate asparagus.' Breakfast, 'another social affair', was 'excellent, good coffee, fruit salad, cooked dishes, lashings of toast with local jams'. No children under 16, unless you rent the entire house. (*Wendy Ashworth*)

6 bedrooms. 1 mile N of Porthmadog. Closed Christmas, Jan, Mon/Tues Oct–Mar. Drawing room with log fire, library, dining room. No background music. 47-acre grounds. Unsuitable for ♿. No smoking. No children under 16. No dogs. Amex, MasterCard, Visa accepted. B&B £57.50–£125 per person. Set dinner £35. New Year package. 1-night bookings refused weekends Apr–Oct.

WHITEBROOK Monmouthshire — Map 3:D4

The Crown at Whitebrook
Whitebrook, nr Monmouth
NP25 4TX

Tel 01600-860254
Fax 01600-860607
Email info@crownatwhitebrook.co.uk
Website www.crownatwhitebrook.co.uk

Surrounded by woods in the Wye valley, this 17th-century inn, in a small village near Monmouth, is now a restaurant-with-rooms managed by Michael Obray. The chef, James Sommerin, won a *Michelin* star in 2007 for his modern British 'with French flair' cooking, eg, confit of pig's trotter with seared foie gras; crown of partridge, haricot blanc, chanterelle mushrooms and truffle/garlic emulsion. 'Outstandingly good,' said a recent *Guide* reporter. There are 250 wines to choose from. Public rooms have log fires; bedrooms, in a modern extension, have under-floor heating, 'the latest technological advancements' (Internet facilities, flat-screen TV, etc). Some rooms have a power shower, and two have a double-ended bath. The decor is 'light and simple'; the views are extensive. 'We were well treated in a comfortable environment.' Breakfast is a 'sumptuous Welsh' affair. Guests may take part in a complimentary round at a local golf club. More reports, please.

8 bedrooms. 6 miles S of Monmouth. Closed Christmas/New Year and Mon. Lounge/bar, restaurant; soft background music (jazz/soul); business facilities. 5-acre garden. River Wye 2 miles, fishing. Unsuitable for ♿. No smoking. No dogs. MasterCard, Visa accepted. B&B [2007] £50–£85. Set menu £39.95.

Channel Islands

Close to Normandy, these *Îles Anglo-Normandes*, as the French call them, have a distinct French flavour, notably in their cooking of lunch and dinner (breakfast tends to be boldly British). The hotels vary greatly. Two of our entries (one a former *César* winner) are long-time favourites on car-free Sark; a third is on the tiny island of Herm. On the opposite end of the scale is the sumptuous *Longueville Manor*, in St Saviour, with its *Michelin*-starred restaurant.

La Sablonnerie, Sark

CASTEL Guernsey — Map 1:D5

Cobo Bay Hotel
Cobo Coast Road
Castel
GY5 7HB

Tel 01481-257102
Fax 01481-254542
Email reservations@cobobayhotel.com
Website www.cobobayhotel.com

Good for families, 'spectacular' Cobo Beach is on Guernsey's west coast. Here, the Nussbaumer family's modern hotel has 'welcoming and helpful' staff, said a recent visitor. Fourteen of the bedrooms have sea views; some have a balcony. 'Our room, though not large, had all one expects nowadays: lovely bathroom, comfortable beds with duvets, etc'; also satellite TV and baby-listening. Pre-dinner drinks are taken in a big lounge with dark red leather settees. In the 'large, attractive' sea-facing restaurant ('views of sunsets'), 'dinners were highly enjoyable'. Plenty of choice for each of three courses. 'Main courses tended towards fussiness in presentation but were of excellent quality. Two or three fish dishes; also steak, Aylesbury duck, rack of lamb. Unpretentious wine list; house wine at £9.95 a bottle. Breakfast well up to standard. A comprehensive and well-organised bus service, which stops close by the hotel, enabled us to see much of this charming island.' Visitors to Guernsey can split their holiday and also stay at *The Farmhouse Country Hotel*, under the same ownership. Three golf courses are within three miles. (*DJB*)

36 bedrooms. 3 miles NW of St Peter Port, on main W coast road. Closed 1 Jan–28 Feb. Lift. Lounge with bar, TV room, restaurant; classical background music; function room; health suite: whirlpool, sauna, etc. Front outdoor sitting area. Unsuitable for ♿. No smoking. Guide dogs only. Amex, MasterCard, Visa accepted. B&B £38.50–£79 per person; D,B&B £20 added per person. Set menus £23. Special break: 6 nights for the price of 7. Christmas/New Year packages.

HERM — Map 1:D6

The White House
Herm, via Guernsey GY1 3HR

Tel 01481-722159
Fax 01481-710066
Email hotel@herm-island.com
Website www.herm-island.com

César award in 1987

'Escapism and relaxation are the order of the day', at Adrian and Pennie Heyworth's much-loved hotel, the only one on this beautiful, tiny island, which is 'extremely peaceful, particularly when the day-trippers have left'. Set by a beach, it is managed by Jonathan Watson with an 'efficient staff from around the world'. Guests (many regulars) are met at the boat. 'The best family holiday we've had,' one visitor wrote. 'Children treated like VIPs: amazing high tea buffet, good baby-listening.' Family suites have second room with a bunk bed. Spacious cottage rooms have small garden and balcony. The 'old-timey' quality is liked (eg, jacket required of male diners). Neil Southgate's cooking 'is outstanding, beautifully served'. 'Excellent wine list.' 'As you dine, the sun sets over Guernsey.' 'Ample and good light lunch.' 'Exceptional value.' The bedrooms lack 'upmarket extras' (minibar, Wi-Fi, etc) but have good storage and an evening turn-down service. Neighbouring islands are visible from the lounge (with board games and free self-help tea and coffee). Herm (no cars, no TV) has high cliffs, a little harbour, pastel-painted cottages, three shops, an inn, a 10th-century chapel, birdwatching, shell gathering, bathing, fishing. (*Andrew Rockett, Stephen Holman, Nigel and Jennifer Jee*)

40 bedrooms. 23 in 3 cottages. Some on ground floor. By harbour. Air/sea to Guernsey; ferry to Guernsey (20 mins). Open 28 Mar–5 Oct. 3 lounges, 2 bars, carvery, restaurant; conference room. No background music. 1-acre garden: tennis, croquet, 20-ft solar-heated swimming pool; beach 200 yds. On 300-acre island: boating, fishing, snorkelling. Herm unsuitable for ♿. No smoking. No children under 9 in restaurant at night (high teas provided). Guide dogs only. Amex, MasterCard, Visa accepted. D,B&B [2007] £76–£114 per person. Set menu £25.

ST BRELADE Jersey — Map 1:E6

St Brelade's Bay Hotel

St Brelade JE3 8EF

Tel 01534-746141
Fax 01534-747278
Email info@stbreladesbayhotel.com
Website www.stbreladesbayhotel.com

'Peaceful and idyllic,' says a devotee who has known this 'large, glamorous' place for 51 years. 'A wonderful family hotel,' says another guest, visiting with a 17-strong three-generation group. 'Luxurious throughout', it is run by the 'hands-on' Robert Colley (fifth-generation owner/managing director), with manager Claire Frost. 'Staff are friendly, helpful without being obtrusive. Marvellous situation and grounds.' The long, white, modern building faces Jersey's loveliest bay: the 'beautiful beach' is across a road. Elegant public rooms have parquet floors, moulded ceilings, chandeliers, oriental rugs, formal flower arrangements, 'a wonderful collection of paintings'. Loungers stand on lawns near the freshwater swimming pools. In summer, alfresco lunches are served, and 'afternoon tea is automatically brought while you laze in the shade'.

Bedrooms are spacious; front ones have a balcony and 'fantastic' views; second-floor ones above the kitchen might be noisy; there are communicating family rooms, cots, high chairs, etc (see below), and tea for small children at 5.15–6 pm. Five penthouses are new this year. Chef Franz Hacker serves 'fantastic' six-course dinners. 'Wonderful crab and lobster specialities.' 'Superb English breakfast.' 'Smart casual' clothing is expected in the restaurant, and mobile phones are 'not welcome' in public areas. (*PM Turner, Alan Parsons*)

85 bedrooms. 5 miles W of St Helier. Bus from St Helier. Open end Apr–beginning Oct. Lift, ramps. Lounge, cocktail bar (evening entertainment: singers disco, magician, etc, daily except Sun); restaurant; toddlers' room, games room, snooker room; sun veranda. 7-acre grounds: outdoor restaurant, 2 heated 80 by 30-ft swimming pools (1 for children) with bar and grill; sauna, mini-gym; tennis, croquet, putting, *boules*, children's play area. Beach across road. Golf nearby. Unsuitable for ♿. Smoking on terrace only. No children in restaurant after 7 pm. No dogs. All major credit cards accepted. B&B [2007] £60–£152 per person; D,B&B £25 added. Set menus £25; full alc £35. Weekend breaks.

ST MARTIN'S Guernsey *See SHORTLIST* Map 1:E5

ST PETER PORT Guernsey *See SHORTLIST* Map 1:E5

ST SAVIOUR Jersey Map 1:E6

Longueville Manor
Longueville Road
St Saviour JE2 7WF

Tel 01534-725501
Fax 01534-731613
Email info@longuevillemanor.com
Website www.longuevillemanor.com

This is Jersey's most sumptuous hotel (Relais & Châteaux). Exuding 'a pleasant air of confidence' (a recent comment), the 'beautifully kept', extended 13th-century manor house stands inland from St Helier, in wide grounds by a lovely wooded valley. Malcolm Lewis is the 'attentive' third-generation owner, Andrew Baird the executive head chef. His main courses include oven-roast duck with foie gras ballottine, braised savoy cabbage and glazed grapes, and he offers 'wonderful vegetarian dishes'. Some ingredients come from the garden. 'A superb cheese trolley.' There is a 400-strong wine list. Meals are served in a large, light room facing the garden, or a darker panelled one. The decor is smart –

swagged curtains, oriental rugs, original paintings, antiques, repro furniture, but the atmosphere is 'unstuffy'. 'Guests share the reception rooms with the house cats and dogs.' 'Obliging staff dealt with everything with military precision but no loss of approachability. Our bedroom was richly decorated: comfortable chair in front of fireplace, just like home.' Breakfast, 'a relaxed affair', has a wide choice of cooked dishes, 'proper tea'. Lunches and afternoon teas are served by the swimming pool. The Royal Jersey Golf Club is near. Day-trips to France can be arranged. (*JW*)

31 bedrooms. 8 on ground floor. 2 in cottage. 1½ miles E of St Helier by A3. Double-glazed windows throughout. Lift. 2 lounges, cocktail bar, 2 dining rooms; function/conference facilities. No background music. 15-acre grounds: woodland, croquet, tennis, heated swimming pool. Golf, bowls, squash nearby; sea 1 mile. Wedding facilities. Smoking allowed in bedrooms. All major credit cards accepted. B&B [2007] £100–£400 per person; D,B&B £150–£550. Set menus £47.50–£70; full alc £65. Winter weekend breaks. Christmas/New Year packages.

SARK — Map 1:E6

Hotel Petit Champ

Sark
via Guernsey GY9 0SF

Tel 01481-832046
Fax 01481-832469
Email info@hotelpetitchamp.co.uk
Website www.hotelpetitchamp.co.uk

César award in 2007

On little Sark's west coast, facing Guernsey, Caroline and Chris Robins's 'delightful' small hotel, a low, late Victorian granite building, stands alone on a headland (superb views, spectacular sunsets). It is much loved. 'The perfect place to relax. Warm, attentive hospitality,' one returning visitor wrote. There is regular praise for the 'most welcoming' owners, the 'old-fashioned values', and the housekeeping: 'Rooms done during breakfast, beds turned down at night.' The cooking is thought 'excellent value', and 'consistently successful'. Chef Tony Atkins specialises in local lobster and crab. 'Interesting menus, good-quality ingredients'; 'portions never too big'; 'top-notch wines at low-notch prices'. The 'scrummy' breakfast has ample choice and a weather forecast on each table. The decor is traditional, and 'rooms are given an annual face-lift: everything seems freshly minted'. 'Our bedroom with balcony had generous storage and a lovely view.' 'Plenty of lounges where one can lose oneself.' Games, puzzles, etc, are supplied for children. Tips are not expected. A secluded beach, sandy at low tide, is a steep walk down from the hotel; many other safe beaches are near. No cars on Sark: bicycles can be hired, and the hotel's visitors can be met by a horse and carriage. (*Chris Handley, HJ Martin Tucker; also Mr and Mrs T Weight*)

10 bedrooms. 15 mins' walk from village. Open Apr–early Oct. 3 sun lounges, library lounge, TV room, cocktail bar (background CDs), restaurant. 1-acre garden: solar-heated swimming pool (40 by 15 ft), putting, croquet. Sark unsuitable for ♿. Smoking allowed in 1 lounge, all bedrooms. 'Children must be old enough to sit with parents at dinner (approx. 7 yrs).' Guide dogs welcomed, otherwise no dogs in bedrooms or restaurant. All major credit cards accepted. B&B £45–£56.50 per person; D,B&B £61.75–£63.75. Set lunch (Sun) £12.50, set dinner £21.50; full alc £31. *V*

La Sablonnerie

Little Sark
Sark, via Guernsey GY9 0SD

Tel 01481-832061
Fax 01481-832408
Email lasablonnerie@cwgsy.net
Website www.lasablonnerie.com

This 'wonderful little hotel with wonderful food' (a comment this year) is 'run with gusto' by its 'gorgeous' owner, Elizabeth Perrée. 'Stylish, idiosyncratic', it stands in 'lovely' grounds, in a quiet southern corner of the island, reached by an isthmus; cows graze in an adjacent field. Its white walls are fronted by flowers; indoors are low ceilings, oak beams, a bar with log fire. Standards are 'consistently high'. 'The enthusiastic, young, multi-ethnic staff all seemed to want us to have fun.' Canapés at the bar precede dinner in the candlelit restaurant. Chef Colin Day's dishes include savarin of red mullet filled with creamed potato, with a chive tapenade sauce. There is a separate lobster menu. Many ingredients come from the home farm. Breakfasts can start with champagne, and they include freshly cooked 'Sark Breakfast' (porridge with cream; eggs, kippers, etc). The tea room serves 'very good lunches'. The bedrooms are 'charming but not luxurious': some are reached through a tiny door in the bar; some spacious ones are in cottages. You should pack rubber-soled shoes for bathing from rocks or shingle, a torch for caving, a dress or tie for dinner. Nearby are the natural pools of Venus and Adonis, cliffs, coves, sandy beaches. (*John Barnes, and others*)

22 bedrooms. Some in cottages. S part of island. Boat from Guernsey; hotel will meet. Open Easter–Oct. 3 lounges, 2 bars (classical background music/piano), restaurant. 1-acre garden: tea garden/bar, croquet; wedding facilities. Smoking allowed in some bedrooms. Sark unsuitable for ♿. Dogs at hotel's discretion; not in public rooms. MasterCard, Visa accepted. B&B (*excluding 10% service charge*) £40–£80 per person; D,B&B £55.50–£97.50. Set menu £25.80; full alc £39.50.

IRELAND

The twin arts of conversation and hospitality remain very much alive in Ireland, which is why some of the *Guide*'s favourite hotels can be found in this chapter. Ireland is fruitful ground for the kind of small, family-run hotels that we support. These days, some of the staff may be recruited from all corners of Europe, but the warmth of the welcome remains truly Irish. In many of the smaller places, you will be received as a friend of the family, and given an insight into the Irish way of life.

Cashel House, Cashel Bay

ADARE Co. Limerick — Map 6:D5

Dunraven Arms

Tel 00 353 61-396633
Fax 00 353 61-396541
Email reservations@dunravenhotel.com
Website www.dunravenhotel.com

In a pretty village near Limerick, this much-expanded, yellow-fronted old coaching inn is liked for its lively atmosphere and 'charming' location. The owners, Brian and Louis Murphy, 'have their hands very much on the tiller'; they maintain a 'personal touch' while continuing to expand the facilities (ten new rooms this year). 'A cracking hotel; if you play golf, hunt or fish, this is the place for you,' says one enthusiastic visitor. Bedrooms are in several wings, along 'long corridors hung with hunting and equestrian prints'. 'Our spacious suite lacked charm but had everything the traveller could need' (lots of storage space, apples, whiskey; slippers provided with the evening turn-down). The bar and the 'splendidly old-fashioned' *Maigue* restaurant are busy with locals; a silver trolley with roast rib of beef was a happy reminder 'of the days before the bistro'. 'Hot chocolate pudding, equally pleasing. All the staff (mainly French or Polish) were well trained. Proprietor on hand at breakfast' (this was 'fine, with proper butter and jam, linen serviettes'). There are small lounges 'for quiet reading', and a leisure centre. Guests can hunt with the famous local packs. Free Wi-Fi access throughout. (*MH, and others*)

86 bedrooms. In village, 10 miles SW of Limerick. Private parking. Lift. Lounge, writing room, TV room, residents' bar (pianist at weekends), public bar, restaurant, conservatory; conference/function facilities; leisure centre: 50-ft swimming pool, steam room, gym. 3-acre gardens. River, fishing, golf, riding, fox-hunting nearby. No smoking. No dogs. Amex, MasterCard, Visa accepted. (*Excluding 12½% service charge.*) Room [2007] €77.50–€180 per person. Breakfast €20. Full alc €50–€60.

ARTHURSTOWN Co. Wexford — Map 6:D6

Dunbrody Country House NEW

Arthurstown, New Ross

Tel 00 353 51-389600
Fax 00 353 51-389601
Email dunbrody@indigo.ie
Website www.dunbrodyhouse.com

'It deserves a warm commendation,' says a report this year, restoring to the *Guide* this elegant Georgian mansion. Converted into a hotel by Kevin and Catherine Dundon, it formerly belonged to the Marquess of

Donegal, who still lives on the estate. 'Excellent in every way; one of the nicest country house hotels we have stayed in. We arrived bruised and battered after a car crash 30 miles away. The Dundons sent a car to pick us up; over three days they and their marvellously helpful staff did everything possible to make us comfortable, and we were able to enjoy the large and tranquil grounds.' A magnificent foyer has a grand piano and splendid chandelier. All the furniture is antique or 'good repro'. The bedrooms, up three attractive staircases, have fine carpets and curtains, good furnishing; dressing gowns, flowers and apples. The large red dining room is impressive. Kevin Dundon, chef/*patron*, serves 'splendid dinners' on a seasonal menu, or a daily-changing tasting menu. Typical dishes: open ravioli of red mullet and broad beans; fillet of Wexford beef with an oxtail cottage pie. There is also an informal seafood bar and a spa. Breakfasts are thought 'delicious'. (*Sir Patrick Cormack*)

22 bedrooms. 4 (1 suitable for ♿) on ground floor. 10 miles S of New Ross. Closed Christmas. Ramps. Lounge, bar, seafood bar, restaurant; background jazz. Terrace. 20-acre gardens in 300-acre grounds. Golf, fishing, sailing, hunting, nearby. No smoking. No dogs. All major credit cards accepted. B&B [2007] €117.50–€215 per person. Set dinner €65. Special breaks. New Year package. 1-night bookings refused winter weekends. ***V***

AUGHRIM Co. Wicklow — Map 6:C6

Clone House

Tel 00 353 402-36121
Fax 00 353 402-36029
Email stay@clonehouse.com
Website www.clonehouse.com

'An individual experience in a beautiful part of Ireland,' say visitors this year to this ochre-coloured converted farmhouse in the Wicklow Hills. It is run as a guest house by Carla Edigati from Florence with her Californian husband, Jeff Watson. 'Carla welcomed us, offering tea or coffee and choice of bedroom. We picked a lovely, simply furnished room with open fireplace, white armchair, and comfortable four-poster bed. Our spacious wooden-floored bathroom, across the hall (robes provided), had a wonderful claw-footed bath.' Most bedrooms have a fire; all have views of the surrounding mountains. The rambling house has period furnishings, strong colours, wooden floors, a reading room, a small bar, a large 'snug' with old Irish artefacts. 'Dinner is a real event, Carla's cooking is amazing.' She serves Tuscan dishes on a three- or five-course no-choice menu. 'She created two main courses for us, one vegetarian. Tasty home-made breads; spinach and ricotta tortellini; baked salmon with abundant side dishes; tiramisu. Breakfast had home-made breads and cakes, wonderful sausages.' In the gardens are a pond, a creek, stone walls, 'thousands of flowers'. 'We enjoyed a stroll, followed by the outdoor cats.' Children are welcomed. (*Olivia Howes and Patrick Smith*)

7 bedrooms. 2 miles SW of Aughrim. Train: Rathdrum/Arklow; taxi. Drawing room, library, music room, dining room (background music: classical/jazz); function facilities; gym, sauna. 1½ acre grounds. Riding, fishing, golf nearby. Unsuitable for ♿. No smoking. No dogs. MasterCard, Visa accepted. B&B [2007] €70–€110 per person. Set dinner €55–€65. Seasonal discounts. 1-night advance bookings refused bank holiday Sat.

BAGENALSTOWN Co. Carlow — Map 6:D6

Lorum Old Rectory
Kilgreaney

Tel 00 353 59-977 5282
Fax 00 353 59-977 5455
Email bobbie@lorum.com
Website www.lorum.com

'Worth making a detour for', this granite Victorian ex-rectory has a 'beautiful setting, mountain views all round' in large grounds in the rolling land at the foot of Mount Leinster. Fresh endorsements come from visitors this year: 'No fall in standards here. Welcome, catering and comfort cannot be faulted.' 'The owner [Bobbie Smith] is delightful and a wonderful cook.' She 'knows every inch of land and, it seems, every inhabitant', said earlier visitors. 'Each of the bedrooms is perfectly proportioned, and has a spacious *en suite* bathroom, cleverly added. She has an eye for colour, and our four-poster bed was artfully draped without being fussy.' 'Our room was spacious, pretty and comfortable. Shower, no bath.' Bobbie Smith is a member of Euro-Toques, dedicated to using local and organic produce. The six-course dinner menu (including sorbet and cheese), served at a large mahogany table in the red dining room, might include pork stuffed with prunes and apricots, Irish Mist and apple sauce. The 'wonderful' breakfast has a 'good full Irish, home-baked breads, much fruit – and the feeling that you have all day to enjoy it'. Nearby are the gardens at Kilfane, Woodstock and Altamont. (*R Bell, Mrs AE Mathews*)

5 bedrooms. 4 miles S of Bagenalstown on R705 to Borris. Open Mar–Nov. Drawing room, bar, study, dining room. No background music. 1-acre garden: croquet. Unsuitable for ♿. No smoking. Children by arrangement. No dogs. Amex, MasterCard, Visa accepted. B&B €75–€85 per person. Set dinner €45. 10% discount for stays of more than 2 nights.

BALLYCASTLE Co. Mayo — Map 6:B4

Stella Maris

Tel 00 353 96-43322
Fax 00 353 96-43965
Email info@stellamarisireland.com
Website www.stellamarisireland.com

On the coast of north Mayo, 'one of the wildest and emptiest counties in Ireland', this 19th-century coastguard station has been rescued from near ruin by Frances Kelly, a local who has lived in the United States, and her American husband, Terence McSweeney. He works for the US PGA during the winter, and can advise on nearby golf courses. 'A terrific find', it was admired this year by a trusted correspondent, apart from 'a major quibble: overloud piped music'. 'Redecoration of the public and private rooms is of the highest standard. The welcome, on first-name terms, is warm. They are attentive to guests throughout.' Bedrooms, each named after a golf course, are not large. An earlier visitor had a 'plainish but comfortable' room; 'lots of hot water in the bathroom'. Drinks are served in a hundred-foot conservatory, 'full of books, many on golf', along the front of the building. Frances Kelly's cooking is 'a real bonus, on a suitably limited menu. Excellent cod, lamb, prawns; I enjoyed starters of tian of crabmeat; devilled kidneys. A brief but carefully chosen wine list.' Breakfast has fresh grapefruit, home-made preserves, 'the usual cooked things attractively presented'. (*Richard Parish, and others*)

11 bedrooms. 1 on ground floor, suitable for ♿. 1½ miles W of village, 16½ miles NW of Ballina. Open Easter–Oct. Restaurant closed to non-residents on Mon. Ramps. Lounge, bar, restaurant, conservatory; background music throughout. 2-acre grounds. Golf, sea/freshwater fishing, sandy beach nearby. No smoking. No dogs. MasterCard, Visa accepted. B&B [2007] €100–€185 per person. Full alc €57.

BALLYCOTTON Co. Cork — Map 6:D5

Bayview Hotel

Tel 00 353 21-464 6746
Fax 00 353 21-464 6075
Email res@thebayviewhotel.com
Website www.thebayviewhotel.com

On the edge of cliffs above a pretty fishing harbour, Carmel and John O'Brien's holiday hotel stands in well-tended gardens. The large, low, white house looks Georgian/Victorian but was massively rebuilt in 1991. Steps lead down to the sea from the pretty terraced gardens. The bedrooms, all redecorated this year, have sea views; the better ones are spacious, with full-length windows, a small balcony; smaller, 'attic-style' rooms on the second floor have dormer windows. Visitors like the evening bedroom turn-down and the 'classy' toiletries; less liked is the 'intrusive' piped music. And one reporter who stayed for four nights 'saw neither owner nor manager', and felt that 'staff did not always get things right'. In the hotel's elegant *Capricho* restaurant, the 'talented chef', Ciaran Scully, cooks 'elaborate' modern dishes, eg, roast rack and loin of pork, apple and celeriac purée, chartreuse of spring cabbage. The breakfast menu lists the local suppliers of the ingredients; it has 'good fresh bread, scones, compote of rhubarb; high-quality bacon, sausages, fish options', but 'poor toast and coffee'. 'A useful base for exploring the interesting east Cork coast.' More reports, please.

35 bedrooms. 4 on ground floor. Village centre, near harbour. 20 miles SE of Cork city. Open 20 Mar–27 Oct. Lift. 2 lounges, bar, restaurant; Irish and classical background music; 2 meeting rooms. 1-acre grounds. Access to public (rock) beach. Smoking allowed in 10 bedrooms. No dogs. All major credit cards accepted. B&B [2007] €85–€127 per person; D,B&B €115–€167. Full alc €70. 2- and 3-night rates.

BALLYLICKEY Co. Cork — Map 6:D4

Seaview House

Ballylickey, Bantry Bay

Tel 00 353 27-50073
Fax 00 353 27-51555
Email info@seaviewhousehotel.com
Website www.seaviewhousehotel.com

Overlooking Bantry Bay in a quiet West Cork village, Kathleen O'Sullivan's extended, white, bay-windowed Victorian house stands back from the road in large grounds. 'I cannot praise this family hotel too highly,' says a visitor who stayed for a week with three generations of his family. 'Miss O'Sullivan and her excellent staff could not have been kinder. My young granddaughters were given delicious high teas in the library and were made to feel special.' Earlier visitors wrote of the owner's dedication: 'She runs it with loving care. A serene environment. Staff have been there for many years. Our bedroom in the main house was not particularly smart; the bathroom was old-fashioned. But it had style and a homely feel.' A large bedroom in the new wing, with under-floor heating in the bathroom, was also enjoyed. From some upper rooms there are sea glimpses. Several rooms have been redecorated this year. Eleanor O'Donovan's daily-changing five-course dinner menu has extensive choice (main courses like roast duckling with port and orange sauce; roast quail with honey and mustard seed dressing): 'The food was excellent, and the wine list sensibly priced.' 'No music: bliss.' Breakfast also has a wide choice. There is a library with books in mahogany cases, and a lounge with an open fire. (*Sir Patrick Cormack, David and Gail Crabb, PP*)

25 bedrooms. 2, on ground floor, suitable for ♿. 3 miles N of Bantry. Open 15 Mar–15 Nov. Lounge bar, library/TV room, restaurant/conservatory. No background music. 3-acre grounds on waterfront: fishing, boating; riding, golf nearby. Smoking allowed in 4 bedrooms. No dogs in public rooms. All major credit cards accepted. B&B €70–€120 per person; D,B&B €95–€130. Set dinner €45; full alc €50. Special breaks. *V* (only on bookings at full rack rate)

BELFAST — Map 6:B6

Ash-Rowan
12 Windsor Avenue
Belfast BT9 6EE

Tel 028-9066 1758
Fax 028-9066 3227

In a tree-lined avenue near Queen's University, Evelyn and Sam Hazlett's Victorian house is 'an extraordinary place'. Public areas 'are happily cluttered in Edwardian style'. 'It's like living in an upmarket antiques shop,' said an inspector. 'Minimalists would be horrified.' The best bedrooms are the two 'magnificent' doubles on the top floor (rooms 7 and 8); one has a power shower, the other a bath. The small singles are not so well liked; beds are comfortable, with linen sheets and lace-trimmed pillowcases; but the plumbing may be noisy. The conservatory/sitting room has newspapers, as well as old copies of *Picture Post.* Everyone agrees that the breakfast is 'excellent', with a wide choice (made the night before): 'Yummy porridge with Drambuie, a delicious lemon-lime drink, home-made wheaten bread, and an individual cafetière.' 'The kedgeree set me up for the day.' The Hazletts no longer serve evening meals: 'We are surrounded by excellent restaurants.' Popular with university visitors and musicians. (*SP, and others*)

5 bedrooms. Just off Lisburn road, 1½ miles SW of centre. Car park, buses. Closed Christmas. Lounge, dining room, conservatory. No background music. ⅓-acre garden. Unsuitable for ♿. No smoking. No children under 12. No dogs. MasterCard, Visa accepted. (*5% service charge added.*) B&B [2007]: single £59–£66, double £96.

****

Traveller's gripe Far too many hotels spend money on facilities like TV in the bedrooms while failing to provide the absolute essential: a comfortable bed.

****

Ravenhill House NEW

690 Ravenhill Road
Belfast BT6 0BZ

Tel 028-9020 7444
Fax 028-9028 2590
Email info@ravenhillhouse.com
Website www.ravenhillhouse.com

In a leafy suburb with good bus links to the city centre, Roger and Olive Nicholson's detached Victorian house is a 'convenient, well-run, friendly place', says an inspector in 2007. 'My small single bedroom was clean, well equipped and well lit; comfortable bed, with good pillows and sheets, blankets not a duvet; a clean bathroom with a good shower; just enough storage space. Although the road is busy, I was not disturbed by traffic noise.' Fresh coffee is provided on the landing, and a payphone. The sitting room has a piano, an open fire and a computer with Internet access. Guests are asked to make their choices for breakfast in the evening; it had 'home-made bread, excellent fruit compote, a good buffet selection with fresh fruit'; cooked dishes include a traditional Ulster fry or a vegetarian option. 'Mr Nicholson was most helpful, providing a map and other information. Good value for money in a newly thriving city.' Many eating places are nearby.

5 bedrooms. 2 miles S of centre. Closed Christmas/New Year, 2 weeks in summer. Sitting room, dining room. No background music. Unsuitable for ♿. No smoking. No dogs. MasterCard, Visa accepted. (*3% surcharge.*) B&B [2007] £35–£45 per person.

See also SHORTLIST

BLACKLION Co. Cavan — Map 6:B5

MacNean House

Main Street

Tel 00 353 7198 53022
Fax 00 353 7198 53404

Ireland's best-known celebrity chef, Neven Maguire, runs a celebrated restaurant in his family home, a plain town house on the main street of this unremarkable border village. He is a 'modest and charming host', say visitors in 2007, and his cooking 'is really special'. In the refurbished restaurant ('elegant, tables not too close, discreet lighting'), he serves several set menus, including one for vegetarians: 'We enjoyed a feast, with an *amuse-bouche* of sweet potato and bacon soup; an assembly of four styles of seafood; a generous portion of organic salad leaves to prepare us for a divine turbot fillet stuffed with beef cheek; a wonderfully presented sweet selection. With lovely bread, water and digestifs, it was a bargain at €60; reasonably low mark-ups on the excellent wine list. A shame about the loud, repetitive muzak (repeated at breakfast).' Four bedrooms have been added this year. 'Our simple room at the back, away from the busy road, had a tasteful decor. Breakfast had warm fruit (apricot, prunes, with yogurt, yum yum); successful scrambled egg with smoked salmon; an emasculated kipper.' No lounge, so 'not for an extended stay', was an earlier comment. (*Simon and Pearl Willbourn, and others*)

10 bedrooms. Centre of village on N16 Belfast–Sligo. Closed Christmas, Jan, Mon–Wed (off-season), Mon/Tues (high season). 2 dining rooms; background music. Unsuitable for ♿. No smoking. Pets by arrangement. MasterCard, Visa accepted. D,B&B [2007] €120 per person. Set lunch (Sun) €30, dinner €60.

BLARNEY Co. Cork *See SHORTLIST* Map 6:D5

BUSHMILLS Co. Antrim Map 6:A6

Bushmills Inn
9 Dunluce Road
Bushmills BT57 8QG

Tel 028-2073 3000
Fax 028-2073 2048
Email mail@bushmillsinn.com
Website www.bushmillsinn.com

Traditionally the last stop for visitors to the Giant's Causeway, this 'very cosy' coaching inn is in the centre of a village that gave its name to the world's oldest distillery (Old Bushmills was first licensed in 1608). The building was rescued from disrepair in the late 1980s; a decade later 22 bedrooms were added in an adjoining mill house on the banks of the River Bush. The public areas, a series of rooms leading into each other, 'would be ideal for hide and seek'; they have a 'relaxing atmosphere' with old furniture, pictures, bits and pieces, and 'comfortable sitting areas'. There are peat fires and a 'secret library'. The smaller bedrooms in the original inn are to be replaced during 2008 by 12 new larger rooms and three suites on the river side. A standard room in the *Mill House* was 'spacious, traditionally furnished, with a small dressing room; nice extras included bathrobes'. The staff are found 'consistently welcoming and helpful'. 'We liked the hotel's atmosphere, but the town was dilapidated,' say visitors in 2007. 'The food was good, as was the service.' Donna Thompson cooks 'New Irish' dishes, eg, onion soup with Guinness; blackened tenderloin of pork. Breakfast has a buffet table with freshly squeezed juice, fruit and cheese, and cooked specials, like Ballymoney ham on soda bread, with a poached egg. (*Margaret and Patrick Filsell, JE*)

32 bedrooms. 1, on ground floor, suitable for ♿. 200 yards from centre. Car park. Closed 25 Dec. Hall, drawing room, library, loft; 2 bars, restaurant in 4 sections; classical background music all day; private dining room; conference room. 3-acre grounds. No smoking. Dogs by arrangement, not in restaurant. MasterCard, Visa accepted. B&B [2007] £49–£134 per person. Full alc £40. Short breaks. New Year package. 1-night bookings refused Sat in winter.

CAHERLISTRANE Co. Galway — Map 6:C5

Lisdonagh Manor House

Caherlistrane, nr Headford

Tel 00 353 93-31163
Fax 00 353 93-31528
Email cooke@lisdonagh.com
Website www.lisdonagh.com

'Expertly restored' from a run-down state, John and Finola Cooke's white Georgian manor house stands on a large estate, with ancient trees and a lake, in remote country north of Galway city. 'She is charming, interested and interesting,' said inspectors who were 'graciously' welcomed. The house 'is worth visiting alone' for the fine spiral staircase and the frescoes in the courtyard, painted by John Ryan in 1790. 'No shabby chic here, more like a hotel (smart new doors).' The drawing room has a log fire and comfortable chairs. In the high-ceilinged dining room, with lake views, the South African head chef, Craig Goivea, serves a set evening meal (vegetarian option available): portions are generous. Local fish, beef and lamb are used. 'Intrusive background music, alas.' Many other staff are South African, too (the Cookes live in Cape Town off-season). First-floor bedrooms have views of lake or garden. 'Ours, the Yeats suite, had plenty of storage, chairs, dressing table, bright lights, a well-integrated bathroom.' Four rooms at garden level are 'less dark than you would expect'. The highlight at breakfast was a platter of mixed fruits and berries; 'good croissants, well-presented poached egg'. Children are welcomed. House parties and weddings are catered for.

10 bedrooms. 4 at garden level. 2 self-catering apartments in courtyard. Open May–Oct. 20 miles N of Galway city, off R333. Drawing room, library with honesty bar, dining room; background CDs. 200-acre estate: walled garden, kitchen garden; lake (fishing); woodland walks; horses. No smoking. No dogs in house. Amex, MasterCard, Visa accepted. B&B €90–€140 per person. Set dinner €49.

CAPPOQUIN Co. Waterford Map 6:D5

Richmond House

Tel 00 353 58-54278
Fax 00 353 58-54988
Email info@richmondhouse.net
Website www.richmondhouse.net

In parkland in the Blackwater valley, Paul and Claire Deevy's small hotel/restaurant is liked for its 'lived-in feel, highly conducive to relaxation', and 'good value'. He is the award-winning chef, she the hostess 'who keeps her eye on the ball'. Built by the Earl of Cork in 1704, the substantial Georgian house retains its original feel: 'Our second-floor bedroom was impressively large, with king-size bed, wardrobe, chest of drawers and other antique furniture; the bathroom was well proportioned and equipped,' said a recent visitor. The cooking is modern, with a French influence, eg, braised shank of lamb, celeriac mash, rosemary and garlic jus. Vegetarians have their own menu. The traditional breakfast includes freshly squeezed juice and crisp, hot toast. More reports, please.

9 bedrooms. ½ mile E of Cappoquin on N72. Closed 23 Dec–15 Jan. Restaurant closed Sun/Mon in winter. Lounge, restaurant; 'easy listening' background music. 12-acre grounds. Fishing, golf, pony trekking nearby. Unsuitable for ♿. No smoking. No dogs. All major credit cards accepted. B&B [2007] €75–€110 per person. Set dinner €56. *V*

CARAGH LAKE Co. Kerry Map 6:D4

Carrig House

Caragh Lake
Killorglin

Tel 00 353 66-976 9100
Fax 00 353 66-976 9166
Email info@carrighouse.com
Website www.carrighouse.com

Once a hunting lodge, Mary and Frank Slattery's attractive yellow 1850s house, with a recent extension, stands in large grounds with camellias and azaleas. The setting is 'sublime', in a lakeside dell facing the MacGillycuddy Reeks and near the Ring of Kerry. An inspector was 'greeted warmly' by the 'large, dapper' host. 'Our pleasant ground-floor room had doors leading on to a patio with the most beautiful view (the equal, on a sunny day, of anything in the Italian lake district). It had all you could need for a comfortable stay; so did the bathroom.' Pre-dinner drinks are taken in the 'cosy, handsome' drawing room with its open fire; the Slatterys take dinner orders from an extensive menu of modern dishes cooked by John Luke, eg, risotto of smoked haddock; fillet of pork with cinnamon roasted plums. A pianist sometimes accompanies the meal. Breakfast has 'all the usual dishes, and proper butter and conserves'. One couple were unhappy about the background music. In the grounds are 950 species of trees, rare flowers and shrubs; also marked walks, a stream and waterfalls.

17 bedrooms. Some on ground floor. 22 miles W of Killarney. Open Mar–Nov. Lunch not served. 2 lounges, snug, library, TV room, dining room (classical background music or pianist). 4-acre garden on lake: croquet; private jetty, boat, fishing; walks. 10 golf courses locally. Smoking allowed in 4 bedrooms. No children under 8 (except infants under 12 months). No dogs. Diners, MasterCard accepted. B&B €75–€195 per person. Full alc €55. *V*

CARRICK-ON-SHANNON Co. Leitrim — Map 6:B5

Hollywell Country House
Liberty Hill

Tel/Fax 00 353 71-962 1124
Email hollywell@esatbiz.com

'Welcoming and comfortable', Tom and Rosaleen Maher's rambling Georgian home has large gardens running down to the River Shannon. Inside, it may be 'slightly faded', but it is 'awash with fascinating antiques, *objets d'art*, and books'. 'In her parents' absence, Claire Maher looked after us very well,' say visitors (see below: no relation) this year. Two bedrooms at the back overlook the river: 'Ours was interestingly furnished, exceptionally large, and with a good view.' Earlier guests liked their 'large front bedroom, comfy and friendly, with a lived-in look, artefacts, table and chairs, tea- and coffee-making facilities'. Visitors can sit by an open fire in the large drawing room: seating is 'cleverly arranged so that groups of guests do not have to eyeball each other'. 'Breakfasts were spectacular: a tremendous range of well-presented food'; fresh orange juice, cereals, fresh fruit, porridge, an Irish fry or smoked salmon and scrambled eggs. *Hollywell* is just outside a pretty town famed for its angling; the Mahers' two sons run an 'excellent' restaurant here, *The Oarsman*, a short walk away (dinner served Thursday to Saturday). (*Ann and Michael Maher*)

4 bedrooms. 500 yds NW of Carrick-on-Shannon. Open late Feb–early Nov. Drawing room, dining room. No background music. 2½-acre grounds. Fishing. Unsuitable for ♿. No smoking. No children under 12. No dogs. Amex, MasterCard, Visa accepted. B&B €55–€75 per person. Midweek breaks.

Hotels do not pay to be included in the *Guide*.

CARRIGBYRNE Co. Wexford — Map 6:D6

Cedar Lodge
Carrigbyrne, Newbawn

Tel 00 353 51-428386
Fax 00 353 51-428222
Email cedarlodge@eircom.net
Website www.prideofeirehotels.com

In award-winning gardens below the slopes of Carrigbyrne forest, Tom and Ailish Martin's low, white, modern hotel provides an 'unexpected treat' for travellers on the road from the ferry port of Rosslare to Cork. It has long been a popular stopping point for motorists on their way in and out of Ireland. 'Beautifully appointed', it has 'a happy, homely atmosphere'; bedrooms are 'extremely comfortable, quiet and well equipped'; windows facing the main road are triple glazed. Mr Martin is a 'charming and ebullient' host, says a visitor this year; his staff are 'courteous and well trained'. In the dining room 'of great character', with its large canopied log fire, Mrs Martin serves 'excellent' traditional dishes, eg, sirloin steak with black pepper sauce. The wine list is 'well researched'. (*John Holloway, JFR*)

28 bedrooms. Some ground-floor rooms. On N25, 14 miles W of Wexford. Open 1 Feb–20 Dec. Ramp. Lounge, lounge bar, restaurant; varied background music; occasional pianist. 1½-acre garden. No smoking. Dogs by arrangement. All major credit cards accepted. B&B €75–€135 per person. Set dinner €52.50.

CASHEL BAY Co. Galway — Map 6:C4

Cashel House

Tel 00 353 95-31001
Fax 00 353 95-31077
Email res@cashel-house-hotel.com
Website www.cashel-house-hotel.com

César award: Country house hotel of the year

'Long may the McEvillys continue,' says one of many enthusiastic visitors to this civilised 19th-century manor house (Relais & Châteaux), owned and run by the McEvilly family, Kay, Dermot, Frank and Lucy. 'One of the best hotels we have been in. Kay and Dermot do everything right, and work very hard. She seems to be in the dining room every evening; during the day she is gardening and welcoming people.' An inspector in 2007 agreed: 'A warm, lived-in place, in a lovely, sheltered bay. I have rarely felt so relaxed in a hotel.' There is a 'welcoming', comfortable lounge ('full of beautiful things'), with antiques and fresh flowers, a library, and a big, modern bar. Bedrooms vary in size; not all face the sea. In the dining room, with its conservatory extension, the cooking of Arturo Amit and Arturo Tillo is much admired: modern dishes like quail and smoked duck parcel; gratin of cod with bacon, dill and tomato. 'The fish, caught daily by local fishermen, is particularly good.' Breakfasts are 'copious'. The house, designed by Dermot McEvilly's great-great-grandfather, stands in 'rambling gardens, full of surprises', which run down to the beach. Cashel is a small village on the Atlantic coast; deep-sea fishing can be arranged. 'A wonderful walking area.' (*Gill Holden, and others*)

32 bedrooms. 42 miles NW of Galway. Open 4 Feb–4 Jan. 2 lounges, bar, library, dining room/conservatory. No background music. 50-acre grounds: tennis, riding; small private beach. Smoking allowed in 8 bedrooms. No dogs in public rooms. Amex, MasterCard, Visa accepted. B&B €85–€175 per person; D,B&B €120–€215. Set dinner €55; full alc €70 (*12½% service charge added*). Winter breaks. Christmas/ New Year packages. *V* (not July/Aug, Christmas/New Year)

CASTLEBALDWIN Co. Sligo — Map 6:B5

Cromleach Lodge NEW

Castlebaldwin, via Boyle

Tel 00 353 71-916 5155
Fax 00 353 71-916 5455
Email info@cromleach.com
Website www.cromleach.com

César award in 1999

'Big changes are taking place at *Cromleach* [which is why it was dropped from the *Guide* for a year], but the superb service, wonderful food, and luxurious comfort remain.' Visitors this year welcomed the changes to the public areas made by Moira and Christy Tighe at their purpose-built hotel on a low hillside above Lough Arrow. 'Guests are made to feel genuinely welcome by the owners and their young, enthusiastic staff. The cooking continues to be full of flavour and light in texture; even our vegetarian was impressed. Service well balanced.' The two dining rooms have been replaced by 'a large, light room with panoramic views over the lough'; at the rear is the glass-fronted kitchen. Fifteen new bedrooms and a small spa, to the side of the main building, were due to be completed as the *Guide* went to press. And 21 more bedrooms will be added to the side and back during 2008; these will be linked to a separate function area for weddings. The existing bedrooms are 'spotless, well appointed, with plenty of storage space'; all have 'fantastic views'. The new rooms will be 'more contemporary in style'; some standard rooms will not have the view; three will be equipped for disabled guests.

Children of all ages are welcome (babysitting, special menus). (*Andy Aitken and Carole Sheppard*)

25 bedrooms. 21 more planned for 2008. 3 miles E of Castlebaldwin. Lounge, bar, dining room; function room; classical background music; spa (sauna, steam room); function rooms. 30-acre grounds: forest walks; private access to Lough Arrow: fishing, boating, surfing; walking, hill climbing. No smoking. No dogs in public rooms. Amex, MasterCard, Visa accepted. B&B €75–€200. Set menu €65. Internet offers. *V*

CASTLEHILL Co. Mayo — Map 6:B4

Enniscoe House
Castlehill, nr Ballina

Tel 00 353 96-31112
Fax 00 353 96-31773
Email mail@enniscoe.com
Website www.enniscoe.com

On a large country estate, Susan Kellett runs her Georgian manor house ('one of the most beautiful country houses in Ireland') as a small private hotel. She is now supported by her son, Donald John ('everybody calls me DJ'), 'quiet-spoken and humorous', say inspectors in 2007. A descendant of the family that settled on the land in the 17th century, she operates a heritage centre on the large estate, helping returning emigrants trace their Irish roots. The house has 18th-century plasterwork, and a 'magnificent staircase, one of the great sights in County Mayo'. The large sitting rooms have original furniture and are 'packed with books on Irish art and history'. There are polished wood floors with rugs, and plenty of family memorabilia. All the bedrooms have recently been restored; some have a four-poster, three overlook the loch. Ms Kellett cooks a five-course dinner in Irish country style ('very appetising', eg, roast goose with orange sauce; salmon with lemon cream sauce). In the grounds are a 19th-century ornamental garden, a Victorian walled garden with a tea room, and an organic vegetable garden which supplies the kitchen. There is a resident fishing manager – brown trout can be caught in the lough. Nearby are the great cliffs of north Mayo, and three golf courses. 'Heartily recommended.' (*Franz Kuhlmann, and others*)

6 bedrooms. Self-catering units, behind house. On R315, 2 miles S of Crossmolina. Open 1 Apr–31 Oct. Only groups at New Year. 2 sitting rooms, dining room. No background music. 150-acre estate: garden, tea room, farm, heritage centre, conference centre, forge, fishing (tuition, ghillie). Golf, riding, cycling, shooting nearby. Unsuitable for ♿. No smoking. No dogs in public rooms. MasterCard, Visa accepted. B&B €90–€136 per person. Set dinner €50. New Year package. 10% discount for 3 nights or more. 1-night bookings refused bank holiday Sat.

CASTLELYONS Co. Cork — Map 6:D5

Ballyvolane House

Tel 00 353 25-36349
Fax 00 353 25-36781
Email info@ballyvolanehouse.ie
Website www.ballyvolanehouse.ie

'I cannot recommend a better family or house to typify the warmth for which the Irish are so well known. We were enthralled from the moment we drove up the impressive driveway.' Praise in 2007 for Justin and Jenny Green who run their Georgian house, modified in Italianate style, 'not as a B&B, guest house or hotel', but as a 'family heritage home'. 'It is beautiful without being pretentious. The hospitable owners treated us with generosity.' Wi-Fi is available throughout (guests have use of a laptop). Large, comfortable bedrooms, with family souvenirs and antiques, have 'breathtaking views of the wonderful gardens'. Guests are encouraged to eat communally around the main dining table (two tables are available for those who prefer to sit separately). Lorraine McSweeney serves a four-course menu of country house dishes, eg, asparagus with three dipping sauces; grilled black sole with lemon caper butter sauce. Breakfast is served until noon. The Greens hope to complete five stand-alone 'pod' bedrooms in the walled garden by December 2007; they will have a large bedroom, a sunken bath, a sitting room upstairs. There are three trout lakes in the grounds; *Ballyvolane* has six miles of fishing on the River Blackwater. (*DC Atwell*)

6 bedrooms. 5 'pod' rooms due to open Dec 2007. 22 miles NE of Cork. Closed 24 Dec–1 Jan. Hall, drawing room, honesty bar, dining room. No background music. 15-acre grounds: garden, croquet; 3 trout lakes. No smoking. No dogs in bedrooms: outhouse provided. All major credit cards accepted. B&B €105–€150 per person. Set dinner €55.

CLIFDEN Co. Galway — Map 6:C4

The Quay House
Beach Road

Tel 00 353 95-21369
Fax 00 353 95-21608
Email thequay@iol.ie
Website www.thequayhouse.com

César award in 2003

On the waterfront, a short walk from this interesting little town, Paddy and Julia Foyle's B&B, a cluster of three buildings, was once the harbourmaster's house. 'They are wonderful hosts,' says an American visitor this year. In the Irish manner, 'they manage to make you feel as if you have known them all their lives. He helped us change a punctured tyre in the rain.' The decor is 'amusingly eccentric', with Irish paintings and antiques, and Napoleonic mementos. The 'cosy' drawing room has gilt-framed family portraits, a peat fire at night, large sofas, some draped with animal skins. There are seven studios, some with balcony overlooking the estuary. 'Our quiet, spacious room on the top floor had a kitchenette and huge bath.' Breakfast in the conservatory has fresh juice, good coffee. 'Paddy and Julia were there to greet us each evening on return from exploring; on our last night we were invited into their kitchen for drinks and conversation.' The town has 'great pubs and shops; we enjoyed our meal at *Foyle's* (yes, a relation)'. (*Elizabeth Summers*)

14 bedrooms. 1 on ground floor. 7 studios (6 with kitchenette) in annexe. Harbour; 8 mins' walk from centre. Open mid-Mar–early Nov. Ramps. 2 sitting rooms, breakfast conservatory. No background music. ½-acre garden. Fishing, sailing, golf, riding nearby. No smoking. No dogs. MasterCard, Visa accepted. B&B €70–€120 per person. 1-night bookings refused bank holiday Sat.

CONG Co. Mayo — Map 6:C4

Ballywarren House
Cross

Tel/Fax 00 353 9495-46989
Email ballywarrenhouse@gmail.com
Website www.ballywarrenhouse.com

In farming country between Lough Corrib and Lough Mask, David and Diane Skelton's creeper-covered replica Georgian home has open peat fires, an oak staircase and a galleried landing. There are books and magazines in the sitting room where tea and home-made cake are taken; bowls of chocolates and walnuts throughout, and more chocolates, sherry and glossy magazines in the bedrooms. 'Our four-poster bed,' one couple wrote, 'had good white linen; the huge bath was deep and double-ended, and there was a pile of lovely thick towels.' Mrs Skelton's no-choice *table d'hôte* menu is posted on a blackboard (allergies and likes are discussed in advance). Her Aga-cooked dishes, with a French bias, served in a pretty garden room, include, eg, peppered fillet steak on a crouton, with Mediterranean vegetables. The wine list is entirely French. The Skeltons sometimes join guests for after-dinner drinks. Breakfast has a 'brilliant buffet spread', a choice of six cooked dishes, home-made bread, jams and marmalades; eggs come from the hens which roam the grounds with Rodney, the cockerel. Good fishing nearby. More reports, please.

3 bedrooms. On R346, 2 miles E of Cong. Reception hall, 2 sitting rooms, dining room. No background music. 6-acre grounds: 1-acre garden. Lake, fishing nearby. Unsuitable for ♿. No smoking. No children under 12. No dogs: bedrooms, public rooms. Amex, MasterCard, Visa accepted. B&B: single €98–€136, double €136–€148. Set dinner €38.

DINGLE Co. Kerry *See SHORTLIST* Map 6:D4

DONEGAL Co. Donegal Map 6:B5

St Ernan's House

St Ernan's Island

Tel 00 353 74-97 21065
Fax 00 353 74-97 22098
Email res@sainternans.com
Website www.sainternans.com

Inspectors enjoyed a day 'of calm' at Brian O'Dowd's 'tranquil' and historic house (built in 1826 by a nephew of the Duke of Wellington). It stands on a wooded tidal island reached by a single-track causeway. The white two-storey building has 'astonishingly high' ceilings, and 'high standards of decoration'. 'Well-preserved but functional period furnishings, appropriate modern luxury carpets and radiators.' One lounge has a grand piano, good seating, a log fire. 'We were given a suite at the "superior" price: large and comfortable bed, good lighting, plenty of storage space. A large, bright, warm bathroom; limited water pressure.' In the 'gorgeous' dining room, whose high windows overlook the causeway, chef Gabrielle Doyle serves a short traditional menu on three nights each week. 'Good goat's cheese and tomato tart; slightly bland fillet of beef on leek mustard mash; highlights were the raspberry and crumble tart and the artisan cheeses. Breakfast had freshly squeezed grapefruit and orange juice, yogurt, fruit; excellent smoked salmon and scrambled egg; lovely scones, but white toast and a dull fry-up.' There are paths on two levels around the island 'through a profusion of wild garlic'. Donegal town 'is a short, cheap taxi ride away'. Nearby is Donegal's fine golf course.

8 bedrooms. On R267, 2 miles S of Donegal town. Open end Apr–early Oct. Hall, 2 lounges, dining room open Tues, Fri, Sat evenings. No background music. 8-acre grounds. Unsuitable for ♿. No smoking. No children under 6. No dogs. MasterCard, Visa accepted. B&B [2007] €120–€165 per person. Set dinner €52.

See also SHORTLIST

DUBLIN Map 6:C6

Aberdeen Lodge
53–55 Park Avenue,
Ballsbridge, Dublin 4

Tel 00 353 1-283 8155
Fax 00 353 1-283 7877
Email aberdeen@iol.ie
Website www.halpinsprivatehotels.com

In a leafy residential area of south Dublin, Pat Halpin's small hotel is again commended for providing 'good accommodation without city-centre prices'. 'What a wonderful find,' says a visitor in 2007. 'We were warmly welcomed out of pouring rain, with tea and scones. The staff, of varying nationalities, were charming. Once we had dried out, we were taken to our room where our bags were already installed; it was comfortable with goodies in bathroom and masses of hot water. When we paid we were delighted that there were no extras.' A room at the back, though 'impeccable', heard noise from the DART trains (which along with buses give good connections to the city centre). There is free Wi-Fi Internet access, antiques, and a garden. Breakfast, in the 'attractive' dining room, has 'a table full of fruit, yogurt, cereals, freshly squeezed orange juice and a tasty cooked selection', eg, scrambled eggs with smoked salmon and chives. 'Pity about the piped music.' A limited drawing room/room-service menu is available. Ten minutes' walk away is booming Sandymount village with good restaurants (*Browne's* and *Mario's* are recommended). The Halpin family owns three other hotels in Dublin, and one in Kilkee, County Clare (see Shortlist and website). (*David Uren, Sara Price, and others*)

17 bedrooms. S of city, close to DART station. Ramps. Drawing room, dining room; background music. ½-acre garden. Beach nearby. No smoking. Guide dogs only. All major credit cards accepted. B&B €69.50–€170 per person. Set meals €25–€35; full alc €45. Christmas/New Year packages. *V*

Belcamp Hutchinson
Carrs Lane, Malahide Road
Balgriffin, Dublin 17

Tel 00 353 1-846 0843
Fax 00 353 1-848 5703
Email belcamphutchinson@eircom.net
Website www.belcamphutchinson.com

Named after Francis Hely-Hutchinson, third Earl of Donoughmore, who built his mansion just outside Dublin in 1786, this 'beautifully restored' house is run as a B&B by co-owners Count Karl Waldburg and Doreen Gleeson. It is close to Dublin airport; a popular base for travellers catching an early or late flight. 'We continue to be very happy staying here,' say returning visitors this year. Doreen Gleeson is 'charming and a good hostess'; she provides guides for restaurants, timetables and change for the bus (only the correct fare is accepted). The elegant building has two 'large, wonderful' fanlights, high ceilings, smart furnishings, moulded fireplaces; 'comfortable sofas, log fire, guidebooks and an honesty bar in the drawing room'. Bedrooms are themed to a colour or material. 'We stayed in the Blue Room, as beautifully decorated as the others. Standards are extremely high.' Breakfast is a communal affair, around a long table: fruit compote, creamy porridge, home-made soda bread, jams, 'excellent coffee'. In the gardens are a wildflower meadow, a privet maze ('great fun'), neat lawns, abundant flowers, herbs, soft fruit. Inevitably, there is aircraft noise. Malahide, an interesting old village, is nearby. (*Jeanette Bloor*)

8 bedrooms. 3 miles NE of centre. Parking. Buses. Closed 20 Dec–1 Feb. Drawing room with TV, breakfast room. No background music. 4-acre garden. Golf, riding, horse racing nearby. Unsuitable for ♿. Smoking allowed in 2 bedrooms. No children under 11. No dogs in breakfast room. MasterCard, Visa accepted. B&B [2007] €75 per person.

The Clarence

6–8 Wellington Quay
Dublin 2

Tel 00 353 1-407 0800
Fax 00 353 1-407 0820
Email reservations@theclarence.ie
Website www.theclarence.ie

On Temple Bar, Dublin's lively cultural quarter on the south bank of the River Liffey, this handsome 19th-century warehouse was restored with 'minimalist designer chic' by Bono and The Edge, of the rock group U2. The situation is a strength – the area is where old Dublin meets youth culture – but also a weakness: noise was reported this year from heavy traffic at the front, overlooking the Liffey, and revellers leaving late-night bars at the back. First-time visitors enjoyed the *Clarence*: 'The decor is fresh, uncluttered, much use of wood; service by the European staff was extremely good.' Other guests were 'underwhelmed by the scale and grandeur', and thought that the famous *Octagon* bar, where upwardly mobile young Dubliners gather, 'lacked atmosphere'. Residents can retreat to *The Study*, a large, 'pleasant' lounge. Bedrooms have Egyptian cotton sheets, huge pillows, good wardrobe space; but some rooms are small. Simple meals are provided from 11 am to 5.30 pm in the *Octagon* bar; French/Irish cooking is served in the formal *Tea Room*. An *à la carte* breakfast is also taken here: 'Everything delicious; attentive waiters.' There is Wi-Fi Internet access in all public areas. (*Jill and Mike Bennett, and others*)

49 bedrooms. Central: in Temple Bar on S bank of Liffey. Valet parking. Closed Christmas. *Tea Room* closed Sat lunch. Lounge, bar, restaurant (*Tea Room*); varied background music all day. Smoking allowed in 10 bedrooms. No dogs. All major credit cards accepted. Room [2007]: single/double €350–€400, suite €720–€2,600. Breakfast €27.50. Bar meals. Full alc €65. Special breaks, midweek packages, courses. New Year package. 1-night bookings refused weekends.

See also SHORTLIST

DUNFANAGHY Co. Donegal — Map 6:A5

The Mill
Figart

Tel/Fax 00 353 74-913 6985
Email themillrestaurant@oceanfree.net
Website www.themillrestaurant.com

César award in 2007

Overlooking a lake just outside a small coastal village, Susan and Derek Alcorn (he is the chef) run their restaurant-with-rooms in a modest, white, late 19th-century house, once the home of her grandfather, Frank Egginton, a watercolour artist. She is a 'vivacious hostess', said our inspector, 'welcoming us with pleasing informality, carrying our bags to the room, and offering tea and coffee'. Bedrooms vary: an earlier visitor had a 'spacious, well-lit room facing the lake; large sleigh bed, antiques'. 'Ours, smallish but light, had a mix of old and new furnishings; good-sized bathroom.' Dinner, the main event, is ordered over drinks and canapés in the cosy lounge; always busy, tables need to be booked a long time ahead. The food 'is the whole point of coming here', says another report. 'Wonderful local ingredients, and an enormous talent for combining flavours; mackerel, with crisp skin but moist flesh, was served on a bed of couscous, flavoured with cumin, coriander and ginger. Wow.' Breakfast has 'an above-average buffet with treats like rhubarb compote, carrageen milk mousse; lovely home-made breads and preserves; super bacon and sausage'. 'Remarkable value.' All rooms are hung with paintings by Egginton and his nephew, Robert.

6 bedrooms. At Figart, ½ mile W of Dunfanaghy. Open mid-Mar–mid-Dec. Weekends only Mar, Nov/Dec, except Christmas/New Year. Restaurant closed Mon. Sitting room, conservatory, restaurant (background music). 1-acre grounds. Lake. Beach ½ mile. Only restaurant suitable for ♿. No smoking. No dogs. Amex, MasterCard, Visa accepted. B&B [2007] €47.50–€65. Set dinner €40–€42.

DUNGARVAN Co. Waterford Map 6:D5

The Tannery Restaurant and Townhouse NEW
10 Quay Street

Tel 00 353 58-45420
Fax 00 353 58-45814
Email info@tannery.ie
Website www.tannery.ie

Chef/*patron* Paul Flynn (with his wife, Maire, as front-of-house) has put this small seaside town on the culinary map by attracting visitors to his restaurant, *The Tannery*, in a converted leather warehouse. They can stay in 'ultra-modern, well-thought-out' bedrooms in the *Townhouse*, in nearby Church Street. Our inspector enjoyed 'some fine cooking from a good kitchen' in the first-floor restaurant (the open kitchen can be seen behind glass on the ground floor). 'We were brought excellent bread with olives and pesto; as starter we had wood pigeon on a tasty parsnip pudding; then came delicious, melt-in-the-mouth, slow-cooked beef and appealing quail and foie gras pie. A jug of iced water was provided; a good wine list. The delightful Latvian waitress was attentive without being intrusive. Our bedroom was compact but comfortable. The bed, probably the biggest I have seen, could have held four people. Louvred window shutters can be set at whatever level you like. Spacious shower room.' Breakfast is a 'DIY affair' in your room: yogurt, fruit purée and fresh fruit in a fridge; a bag with bread and pastries is hung on the door last thing at night. 'Very good value, but don't expect a sea view.' Children are welcomed.

7 bedrooms. Town centre. Closed 2 weeks end Jan, 1 week Sept, Sun (except evening July/Aug), Mon. Restaurant ('appropriate' background CDs); private dining room. Unsuitable for ♿. No smoking. All major credit cards accepted. B&B [2007] €50–€80 per person. Early bird menu €28; full alc €110.

See also SHORTLIST

****

Traveller's tale Management was unfriendly and distinctly monosyllabic. None of the staff gave us their name, and no one appeared to be in charge. When I queried an item on my bill the girl had to scuttle off to telephone her manager 'because I'm not authorised to make any changes'. There was nobody with whom we could discuss our problems, and no sense at all of being looked after. (*Hotel in Oxfordshire*)

****

DUNKINEELY Co. Donegal — Map 6:B5

Castle Murray House NEW

St John's Point

Tel 00 353 74-973 7022
Fax 00 353 74-973 7330
Email info@castlemurray.com
Website www.castlemurray.com

In an elevated position above McSwyne's Bay, Marguerite Howley's small hotel/restaurant has a fine view over St John's Point and the ruined castle from which the bay takes its name. It is commended in 2007 by an inspector: 'Good value for such a fine location; fine food; we felt comfortable.' Dinner orders are taken in a 'splendid long narrow seating area' facing the sea. 'The efficient young man remembered my email request about our dietary requirements.' The chef, Remy Dupuy, serves French dishes with a modern twist on a lengthy menu; seafood is a speciality. 'Delicious starter of prawn and monkfish baked in garlic butter; generous helpings of good grilled sea bass; excellent lamb and pigeon; jugs of iced water were supplied. The staff, all non-Irish, were attentive if a little too quick. Breakfast was a slower affair; fresh orange juice, nice muesli, porridge and fresh fruit salad; proper coffee, preserves and butter; a substantial fry. The awful piped music was the only let-down.' The themed bedrooms (African, Oriental, etc) on the first and second floors (no lift) are generally thought 'comfortable', but a family room was 'disappointing (pine-effect dressing table, harsh lighting)'.

10 bedrooms. 1 mile SW of village. Open mid-Feb–mid-Jan, New Year. Bar, restaurant ('easy listening' background music). Unsuitable for ♿. No smoking. Only small dogs allowed, not in bar/restaurant after 6 pm. MasterCard, Visa accepted. B&B €60–€90 per person; D,B&B €108–€138. Set dinner €49. New Year package. 1-night bookings refused bank holiday weekends.

DURROW Co. Laois — Map 6:C5

Castle Durrow NEW

Tel 00 353 57-873 6555
Fax 00 353 57-873 6559
Email reservations@castledurrow.com
Website www.castledurrow.com

In a village in the Irish midlands, this early 18th-century house, built in fortified style in local grey stone by the Flower family, has been restored by Peter and Shelly Stokes, owners since 1998. It stands in large grounds with manicured lawns, formal, herb and vegetable gardens. Inside 'the space and elegance is married with quality furnishings and carefully chosen antiques', says the nominator. 'Attention to detail under the expert eye of a designer is obvious; modern rugs on wooden and stone floors.' Mrs Stokes has designed the bedrooms, each different. 'My room, Captain Flower, was large, with a four-poster bed, quality period furniture and fabrics; it overlooked the immaculate formal gardens and open countryside. The evening turn-down included a goodnight message left on the pillow.' In the restaurant, with its high, ornate ceiling and chandeliers, *chef de cuisine* David Rouse serves a menu of modern country house cooking. 'Excellent and well presented; ever-present background music, alas.' Breakfast ('a pleasure') has proper toast and freshly squeezed juice. 'All the staff were pleasant and charming in the Irish way.' A crèche is provided for young children. (*Conrad Barnard*)

26 bedrooms. Village centre, 12 miles S of Portlaoise. Closed Christmas/New Year. Restaurant closed 24 Dec–17 Jan. Ramp. Drawing room, library, bar, restaurant (background music); 2 private dining rooms; wedding/conference facilities. 30-acre estate: herb garden; tennis; clay-pigeon shooting, golf nearby. No smoking. No dogs in house. Amex, MasterCard, Visa accepted. B&B [2007] €100–€140 per person. Set dinner €50. Midweek breaks.

ENNISCORTHY Co. Wexford — Map 6:D6

Salville House
Salville

Tel/Fax 00 353 92-35252
Email info@salvillehouse.com
Website www.salvillehouse.com

On a hilltop near this cathedral town, this Victorian country house overlooks the River Slaney and the Blackstairs mountains; mature beech trees stand on the lawn. The owners, Jane and Gordon Parker, 'do an excellent job', says a regular visitor. Fans love the 'home from home' atmosphere. Three bedrooms (Pink, Yellow, Blue) are in the main house; there is also a two-bedroom apartment. Most rooms are spacious. 'Ours was lovely, bright, with large bed, plenty of facilities, excellent bathroom'; another was 'warm, comfortable, elegant'. Dinner, 'the very best cuisine', must be booked the evening before. Likes and dislikes are taken into account for the four-course no-choice menu served at 8 pm. 'Over four nights we enjoyed a great selection of dishes using local meat, poultry and fish; many ingredients are organic, from the garden. Desserts out of this world. To end, coffee by a fire in the lounge.' Early suppers are provided for guests attending the Wexford opera festival. No liquor licence; no corkage charge. Breakfast has fresh orange juice, fruit compote, toasted oats and honey; full Irish or smoked haddock with rösti and poached egg. The grass tennis court in the garden is 'definitely not Wimbledon standard', write the Parkers. (*DAR, SW*)

5 bedrooms. 2 in apartment at rear. 2 miles S of town. Closed Christmas. Dining room closed Sun. Drawing room, dining room. No background music. 4-acre grounds: 'rough' tennis, badminton, croquet. Golf nearby; beach, bird sanctuary 10 miles. Unsuitable for ♿. No smoking. Dogs by arrangement; not in public rooms, bedrooms. No credit cards. B&B €55–€65 per person. Dinner €40. Weekend house-party package. New Year package.

GALWAY Co. Galway — Map 6:C5

Killeen House
Bushypark

Tel 00 353 91-524179
Fax 00 353 91-528065
Email killeenhouse@ireland.com
Website www.killeenhousegalway.com

'How special it is,' says the greatest fan of Catherine Doyle's attractive 1840s building, after a return visit in 2007. Long, low and white, it stands in large grounds on the shores of Lough Corrib. First-time visitors were equally enthusiastic: 'As near to perfection as a guest house could be. The little touches make all the difference; tea and home-made scones on a silver service on arrival; TV listings magazine left open on the correct page.' Each of the four front bedrooms is in a different style – Art Nouveau, Regency, Edwardian, Victorian. A room at the side is 'massive and magnificent, with king-size bed, beautiful furnishings, wide-screen TV, lovely bathroom, a third single bed in an annexe'. 'Our supremely comfortable suite overlooked the fine garden.' The drawing rooms have antique furniture, china in cabinets, a fine octagonal rug on a parquet floor; all 'a delight to look at'. 'Breakfasts are, like everything else, a throwback to a more relaxed and stylish age.' 'Prunes on the menu; not just ordinary ones but Agen prunes; porridge made with pinhead oats, the best oatmeal in Ireland. The sort of place the *Guide* exists for.' (*Esler Crawford, Ann and Michael Maher*)

6 bedrooms. On N59, 3 miles NW of Galway city. Closed Christmas week. 2 drawing rooms, breakfast room. No background music. 25-acre grounds, by lake. Unsuitable for ♿. Smoking allowed in 2 bedrooms. No children under 12. No dogs. All major credit cards accepted. B&B €70–€150 per person. *V*

See also SHORTLIST

GLIN Co. Limerick — Map 6:D4

Glin Castle

Tel 00 353 68-34173
Fax 00 353 68-34364
Email knight@iol.ie
Website www.glincastle.com

'It is a delight to stay in this warm, elegant, welcoming place.' This year's praise for the country seat of Desmond and Olda FitzGerald; he is the 29th Knight of Glin (his forebears have owned the land for 800 years). 'We spent a whole day in the hotel and its delightful grounds; a wonderful switch-off.' Earlier visitors judged it the 'most relaxing place in all Ireland'. 'More historic house than hotel', the Georgian Gothic castle, beautifully set on the Shannon estuary, has secret doorways, Corinthian pillars, an unusual flying staircase. The drawing room has an Adam-influenced plaster ceiling; huge windows face the garden. The Knight, as he is formally titled, is sometimes in residence: he sometimes dines with visitors. His manager, Bob Duff, 'welcoming and entertaining', runs everything with 'great attention to detail'; staff are 'efficient, courteous'. The chefs, Eddie Bagio and Seamus Hogan, serve 'modern Irish' dishes, eg, fried foie gras with fig compote; magret of duck with honey and thyme sauce. Breakfasts are thought 'excellent'. The bedrooms are lavish: there are four-poster beds, *chaises longues*, river or garden views. Not everyone likes the background music. (*Sir Patrick Cormack, and others*)

15 bedrooms. Edge of village, 32 miles W of Limerick. Open 1 Mar–30 Nov. Hall (traditional music twice weekly), drawing room, sitting room, library, dining room (background music). 500-acre estate: 5-acre garden, tennis, croquet, tea/craft shop, parkland, dairy farm, clay-pigeon shooting. On Shannon estuary: boating, fishing; golf nearby. Unsuitable for ♿. No smoking. No children under 10. No dogs in house (kennels available). All major credit cards accepted. B&B €155–€254 per person. Set dinner €58. Off-season rates. House parties (max. 25). *V*

GOREY Co Wexford — Map 6:D6

Marlfield House NEW
Courtown Road

Tel 00 353 53-942 1124
Fax 00 353 53-942 1572
Email info@marlfieldhouse.ie
Website www.marlfieldhouse.com

Set in fine gardens, this Regency building (once the principal Irish home of the earls of Courtown) is now a luxury hotel (Relais & Châteaux), run by Ray and Mary Bowe with daughters Margaret and Laura. 'Faultless; one of the best hotels I have visited; wonderful care and attention from the family,' says a reader this year restoring it to the *Guide* after a time without reports. It has a grand marble hall, a lounge with open fire, smart antique furniture, spectacular flower displays. The bedrooms ranged from 'Mews' to 'State': the best ones have antiques, too, and dramatic wallpapers and curtains, hand-embroidered sheets, choice of pillows (real lace pillowcases), marble bathroom. In the 'glorious' dining room (with frescoes and a large domed conservatory), the chef, Colin Byrne, serves classic dishes with modern influences, eg, slow-cooked crispy pork belly, fondant potato, braised red cabbage and caramelised onion. Many ingredients are home grown. 'The food is delicious, the wine well chosen.' Breakfast has a generous buffet. In the wooded grounds are a lake with ducks, geese and swans, and a wildfowl reserve. Nearby are sandy beaches and golf. (*JS Rutter*)

20 bedrooms. 1 mile E of Gorey. Closed mid-Dec–1 Feb. Reception hall, drawing room, library/bar (background music all day), restaurant with conservatory; function/conference facilities. 36-acre grounds: gardens, tennis, croquet, wildfowl reserve, lake. Sea, sandy beaches, safe bathing 2 miles. Fishing, golf, horse riding nearby. No smoking. Dogs by arrangement only. All major credit cards accepted. B&B €120–€280 per person. Set dinner €66. *V* (not Sat)

HOLYWOOD Co. Down — Map 6:B6

Rayanne House
60 Demesne Road
Holywood BT18 9EX

Tel/Fax 028-9042 5859
Email rayannehouse@hotmail.com
Website www.rayannehouse.co.uk

In an elevated position above this attractive small town on the Belfast Lough, this lovely old Victorian building is run as a guest house by Conor and Bernadette McClelland. It has wide landings, sweeping stairs, 'display cabinets, bookshelves and ornamental bits and pieces everywhere; a wonderful Art Deco theme'. A ground-floor room equipped for disabled visitors has been added in a recent extension. A *Guide* inspector gave a 'ringing endorsement for the high standards of comfort and food', and ambience of 'cheerful luxury'. Many of the bedrooms look over the town and across the lough to the Antrim hills. 'Ours, on the top floor, was enormous; pretty blue and primrose yellow decor; an electric blanket had been switched on; the huge bathroom under the eaves had lots of fluffy towels and toiletries.' Conor McClelland, who has worked as a chef in New York, serves meals by arrangement: 'Cooking of the highest standard: wonderful confit of duck; large scallops and prawns with a sizzling dauphinoise gratin. He knows his wines, too.' The award-winning breakfast, ordered the evening before, has home-made wheaten bread, and an array of interesting choices (eg, prune soufflé; French toast with black and white pudding).

10 bedrooms. 1, on ground floor, suitable for ♿. ¾ mile from town centre, 6 miles E of Belfast. Parking. Train: Holywood. Restaurant closed 23 Dec–2 Jan. 2 lounges, dining room (jazz/classical background music). 1-acre grounds. No smoking. No dogs. MasterCard, Visa accepted. B&B: single £70–£75, double £90–£110. Set menu £42.

KENMARE Co. Kerry — Map 6:D4

Shelburne Lodge

Cork Road

Tel 00 353 64-41013
Fax 00 353 64-42135
Email shelburnekenmare@eircom.net
Website www.shelburnelodge.com

Standing in a large garden on the eastern edge of this charming little town, this handsome, half-timbered 1740s farmhouse has long been a favourite with *Guide* readers. The owner/managers, Tom and Maura Foley, are 'generous and professional hosts': a returning visitor was 'treated' (ie, free of charge) to coffee and home-baked cake on arrival. Another guest, who had to leave before breakfast, had €15 deducted from the bill. The house, filled with antiques and modern art, is 'elegant, spacious and extremely comfortable'; there are log fires and good seating in the drawing room and library. The landings have striking colour schemes; one bedroom has 'stripped pine, a cosy alcove, attractive repro furniture; a small bathroom'. An 'even nicer' room at the front has a large bathroom. In the grounds are a grass tennis court, a small orchard and a pretty herb garden. At breakfast, Tom Foley explains an interesting menu, which might contain fish. The Foleys own *Packies*, a popular pub/restaurant in the town, which is also noted for its fine fish. More reports, please.

8 bedrooms. On R569 to Cork, ½ mile E of town centre. Open mid-Mar–30 Nov. Drawing room, library, breakfast room. No background music. 3-acre garden: tennis. Golf adjacent. Unsuitable for ♿. No smoking. No dogs. MasterCard, Visa accepted. B&B €60–€120 per person.

Virginia's Guesthouse
36 Henry Street

Tel 00 353 64-41021
Fax 00 353 64-42415
Email virginias@eircom.net
Website www.virginias-kenmare.com

In the centre of Kenmare, the gateway to the Iveragh peninsula and the Ring of Kerry, Neil and Noreen Harrington's small guest house is found above *Mulcahy's*, a popular restaurant. 'They are an engaging, helpful couple,' said an inspector. 'The library is a nice little room, with reading, and tea- and coffee-making. Our bedroom, in pretty, cheerful colours, was spacious, though it looked out over a back yard. Rooms at the front have a good view of Henry Street, a lively thoroughfare with pubs, wine and food shops and restaurants.' No baths, but power showers. Breakfast, ordered the evening before (when a time is agreed), is 'very good', with an interesting range of cooked choices, including 'Noreen's blue cheese, pears and bacon', and poached seasonal fruits. 'Pleasant accommodation at budget prices.'

8 bedrooms. Central. Train: Killarney; bus. Closed 24–25 Dec. Library, breakfast room; classical background music. Unsuitable for ♿. No smoking. No children under 12. No dogs. MasterCard, Visa accepted. B&B €45–€85 per person. 3-night off-season breaks. New Year package. 1-night bookings refused bank holidays.

See also SHORTLIST

KILCONNELL Co. Galway — Map 6:C5

Ballinderry Park NEW
Kilconnell
nr Ballinasloe

Tel/Fax 00 353 90-968 6796
Email info@ballinderrypark.com
Website www.ballinderrypark.com

In 'glorious isolation in the eerily desolate countryside of east Galway', this 'beautifully proportioned Georgian building' has been restored from ruin by George and Susie Gossip, 'a charming couple'. The Gossips, who established a following among *Guide* readers in the 1990s at *Tullanisk*, near Birr, receive guests in Irish country house style, with an honesty bar, 'disguised as a cupboard', and communal dining. They are assisted by a 'pleasant young Polish couple'. 'The restoration owes much to George's good taste,' says an inspector in 2007. 'The drawing room, with a roaring log fire, is cosy on a chilly day. Our bedroom was not large, but warm (electric blanket in the bed); a cleverly installed bathroom.' Mr Gossip, who lectures on cooking game at the cookery school at *Ballymaloe House* (*qv*) in the off-season, serves a set 'but flexible' four-course dinner (tastes are discussed, and vegetarians catered for). 'I had expressed an interest in game and was served with woodcock, shot on the land by the man himself; my wife had delicious John Dory.' Breakfast has good ingredients; freshly squeezed orange juice, wheaten bread (baked by the Polish lady!). A fine stopping place for any aficionado of the Irish country house.'

4 bedrooms. 7 miles W of Ballinasloe. Open Apr–Oct. Groups by arrangement at other times. Dining room 'not guaranteed' to open Sun/Mon. Hall, drawing room, dining room. No background music. 40-acre garden. Fishing, horse riding nearby. Unsuitable for ♿. No smoking. 'Well-behaved' dogs allowed; 'prefer not in bedrooms'. MasterCard, Visa accepted. B&B €80–€115 per person. Set dinner €50. ***V***

KILLARNEY Co. Kerry — Map 6:D4

Aghadoe Heights
Aghadoe

Tel 00 353 64-31766
Fax 00 353 64-31345
Email info@aghadoeheights.com
Website www.aghadoeheights.com

With fine views of lakes and fells, this luxury hotel and spa has an ugly concrete exterior ('like a food-processing factory') that belies the 'beautifully conceived' interior, where a large marble foyer with open fire creates a 'feeling of well-being'. It is large for the *Guide* but is family owned (by Jerry and Anne O'Reilly), and managed by a married couple, Pat and Marie Chawke. Our inspector praised the staff ('professional, cheerful, chatty'), and liked his spacious room, which had a hall with a built-in wardrobe, a sitting area, a sleeping area through an archway, a well-fitted bathroom with twin sinks and separate shower. In the *Lake Room* restaurant, on two levels to allow every table to enjoy the view, an 'eclectic European' menu is served, eg, confit belly of pork and milk-fed veal. A resident pianist plays during dinner. Breakfast has 'a huge array of fruit and fruit juices, cereals, cheese and breads; a mountainous Irish Fry; thoughtful touches, like a tea strainer. More reports, please.

74 bedrooms. 1 suitable for ♿. Off N22, 3 miles NW of Killarney. Open mid-Feb–31 Dec, Christmas for hotel guests only. Lounge, 2 bars, restaurant (pianist at night); background music; function facilities; leisure centre: 50-ft indoor swimming pool, fitness room, sauna, spa. 8½-acre grounds: river, fishing. Golf, sea/lake fishing, riding nearby. No smoking. No dogs. All major credit cards accepted. B&B [2007] €125–€325 per person. Set dinner €65; full alc €100. Special breaks. Christmas package.

Cahernane House

Muckross Road

Tel 00 353 64-31895
Fax 00 353 64-34340
Email info@cahernane.com
Website www.cahernane.com

One of Killarney's oldest hotels, once the residence of the Earls of Pembroke, Jimmy and Sara Browne's 19th-century house has a 'tranquil' setting facing the lakes and mountains. In the old section, a foyer with a fine staircase leads to the 'mainly charming' public rooms, which have burnished wooden floors, 'nice furniture and pictures' and an open fire in the 'cosy' lounge. In the 'slightly dingy' dining room, the chef, Pat Kearney, serves a modern European menu, eg, scallops and smoked pancetta; fillet of beef, spring onion champ. 'All very satisfactory, served by smartly dressed staff.' Breakfast, 'also satisfactory', has proper preserves, a tea-strainer, 'perfect poached eggs'. Most bedrooms are in a modern wing: 'Our ground-floor room, with little veranda, had huge bed, writing desk, comfortable chairs, good lighting.' Some rooms have a spa bath. A 'magnificent' suite had 'every accessory one could need', a bathroom with under-floor heating, and a balcony with a bucolic view. The atmosphere is generally found 'soothing', but things can change when a wedding is held.

38 bedrooms. 27 in new wing. Edge of national park, 1 mile from centre. Open 1 Feb–1 Dec. Lifts. Drawing room, library, cellar bar (jazz/classical background music all day), restaurant (background music during meals), conservatory; snooker room. 20-acre grounds: croquet. Smoking allowed in 12 bedrooms. No dogs. All major credit cards accepted. B&B €112–€255 per person. Set dinner €60. *V*

Killarney Royal

College Street

Tel 00 353 64-31853
Fax 00 353 64-34001
Email info@killarneyroyal.ie
Website www.killarneyroyal.ie

Near the railway station of this popular resort town, Margaret and Joe Scally's hotel is 'excellent for business or pleasure'. It has been in her family's hands since 1961. 'They seem to know what travellers want, and have hired a most professional and cheerful staff,' said an inspector. This year the bar and lounge have been redecorated, and the restaurant has new furnishings. 'Our large bedroom had no view but good lighting, restful colours, even a walking stick and umbrella; and a large bathroom.' Two dining options: generous portions from a 'bill of fayre' in the bar; modern Irish cooking in the restaurant, eg, seafood and shellfish cakes; pavé of salmon on leek fondue. 'We took coffee in the lounge (which has a real coal fire): a most comfortable place for watching the world go by.' 'Breakfast was excellent (proper conserves and butter).' More reports, please.

29 bedrooms. Central. Closed 23–27 Dec. Lift. Lobby, bar/bistro (live music Sat), lounge, restaurant; background music; massage room; meeting room. No smoking. All major credit cards accepted. B&B €80–€205 per person. Set dinner €35; alc €55. 2- and 3-night breaks. New Year package. 1-night bookings sometimes refused. *V*

See also SHORTLIST

KILLEAGH Co. Cork — Map 6:D5

Ballymakeigh House
Killeagh, nr Youghal

Tel 00 353 24-95184
Fax 00 353 24-95370
Email ballymakeigh@eircom.net
Website www.ballymakeighhouse.com

César award in 2006

'Effortlessly excellent', this small guest house on the family dairy farm stands in green countryside close to the estuary town of Youghal. The owner, Margaret Browne, describes its bedrooms as having 'bags of old-fashioned comfort'. She has 'a wonderful presence', say fans, and is 'full of local knowledge'. She is 'very much in evidence', as are her husband, Michael, and daughter, Kate. Mrs Browne, who has written a cookbook and runs cookery courses in winter, serves 'farmhouse helpings' of Irish dishes 'with a twist', eg, John Dory with a light citrus sauce. 'Each meal was made special by her manner and outstanding cooking.' An 'excellent', leisurely breakfast has fresh juices, porridge, and six cooked choices. The dining room is a spacious, south-facing conservatory 'with nice views of the pastures and flowers surrounding the house'. Children are welcomed. Mrs Browne's nearby equestrian centre offers riding courses and treks to sandy beaches.

6 bedrooms. 6 miles W of Youghal. Open 1 Feb–1 Nov. Drawing room, conservatory, restaurant (classical background music). 400-acre farm: 4-acre garden, tennis, play area. Unsuitable for ♿. No smoking. Guide dogs only. MasterCard, Visa accepted. B&B €65–€75 per person. Set dinner €45. Cookery courses. New Year package. *V*

KILLYBEGS Co. Donegal *See SHORTLIST* Map 6:B5

KILMALLOCK Co. Limerick Map 6:D5

Flemingstown House

Kilmallock

Tel 00 353 63-98093
Fax 00 353 63-98546
Email info@flemingstown.com
Website www.flemingstown.com

César award in 2005

'Superb. Imelda Sheedy-King is the perfect hostess. Top-quality dining at a reasonable price.' A tribute in 2007 to this 'flawless' guest house on a working dairy farm near an important medieval town. The 18th-century building, 'comfortable rather than luxurious', has a 'cosy lounge with mostly 19th-century pieces'. The 'energetic' hostess, 'the heart and soul of the place', welcomed returning visitors 'with extraordinary warmth, and insisted on helping with our luggage'. 'Attention to every detail makes your stay special.' Bedrooms are spacious: 'Our well-lit room had a cheerful air, a crystal chandelier, superb views across fields to the Ballyhoura mountains.' Dinner, in a room with big stained-glass windows, is 'the highlight of a stay'; 'scrumptious and plentiful', Mrs Sheedy-King's five-course menu (up to four choices for each course) features traditional dishes, eg, leg of Irish lamb with mint sauce. Her sister's own Cheddar cheese might be offered. 'Give plenty of notice that you wish to dine, and bring your own wine.' Breakfast has home-made breads, cheeses, jams and cakes; fresh juices and a range of cooked dishes including pancakes with banana and grapes. Families are accommodated. They can explore the farm and watch the cows being milked. The local pub has live music at weekends. (*Paul Humphreys, J and JM*)

5 bedrooms. On R512, 2 miles SE of Kilmallock. Closed 2 Nov–31 Jan. Lounge, dining room (classical background music). 2-acre garden in 100-acre farm. Golf, riding, fishing, cycling nearby. Unsuitable for ♿. No smoking. No children under 3. No dogs. MasterCard, Visa accepted. B&B €60–€75 per person. Set dinner €40–€45.

KINSALE Co. Cork — Map 6:D5

The Old Presbytery

43 Cork Street

Tel 00 353 21-477 2027
Fax 00 353 21-477 2166
Email info@oldpres.com
Website www.oldpres.com

In a quiet street near the centre of this lovely old fishing and holiday town, Philip and Noreen McEvoy's red-doored Georgian house has long been liked by *Guide* readers for the warmth of welcome: they are a 'friendly, chatty couple'. The rambling old house, once the home of priests at the nearby church of St John the Baptist, is 'all ups and downs'; the sitting room is 'Victorian in every detail'. A penthouse suite has its own kitchen and splendid views over the harbour. There is old pine furniture in the bedrooms; three have a spa bath. Fresh orange juice and fruit salad appear at breakfast; cooked dishes include fruit-filled crepes; there is black and white pudding with the full Irish. Kinsale, a short drive from Cork airport and harbour, has an annual gourmet festival. More reports, please.

7 bedrooms. Some on ground floor. Also 3 self-catering apartments. Central; near parish church. Car park. Open 1 Mar–30 Nov. Lounge with TV, conservatory, breakfast room (classical/Irish background music). Sea/river fishing, water sports, golf nearby. Unsuitable for ♿. No smoking. No dogs. MasterCard, Visa accepted. B&B €55–€140 per person.

See also SHORTLIST

LAHINCH Co. Clare — Map 6:C4

Moy House

Tel 00 353 65-708 2800
Fax 00 353 65-708 2500
Email moyhouse@eircom.net
Website www.moyhouse.com

Built in the 18th century for Sir Augustine Fitzgerald, this flat, white, tower-topped building has been converted 'with panache' into a hotel by the owner, Antoin O'Looney. With its Gothic look, the building is an 'architectural oddity'; two floors are on one elevation, one on the other. Readers find it 'warm and welcoming'; the 'charming' Brid O'Meara is the general manager. In the conservatory restaurant, the chef, Verry

Samudra, serves a daily-changing menu of modern Irish/French dishes, eg, warm salad of duck breast; salmon and sea bass with a prawn and spring onion dressing. 'Our bedroom, down a spiral staircase, was tastefully lavish; a king-size bed with a canopy of gold brocade; excellent reading lights; generous supplies of lotions and potions in the bathroom.' Breakfast has fresh orange juice; home-made muesli; cooked dishes include eggs Benedict; warm pancakes with maple syrup. *Moy House* is popular with golfers: Lahinch has a renowned championship course. More reports, please.

9 bedrooms. 4 on ground floor. 1 mile S of Lahinch. Open Feb–Dec; closed Christmas. Ramp. Drawing room with honesty bar, library, dining room (background music during meals). 15-acre grounds; access to beach. No smoking. Unsuitable for young children. Guide dogs only. Amex, MasterCard, Visa accepted. B&B [2007] €105–€165 per person. Set dinner €55. Special breaks. New Year package.

LETTERFRACK Co. Galway — Map 6:C4

Rosleague Manor

Tel 00 353 95-41101
Fax 00 353 95-41168
Email info@rosleague.com
Website www.rosleague.com

'The easy informality' of this Georgian manor on Connemara's Atlantic coast again wins much praise from visitors this year. Owned by Edmund Foyle, and managed by his son, Mark, it has 'a really lovely setting' with views across 'exquisite' gardens to sea and mountains. 'Outstanding; ten out of ten,' is one comment. Mark Foyle 'heads a helpful and kind staff'. The two elegant lounges have log and turf fires, an extensive collection of paintings, antiques and *objets d'art.* 'The bed in our room was set to take in the view; a separate sitting and dressing area; a corner bath to make best use of space in a narrow bathroom.' A recently refurbished downstairs suite is 'vast'. Pre-dinner drinks are served in the conservatory set in an internal courtyard with trees and shrubs. In the 'handsome' dining room, with fine furniture and silverware, the French chef, Pascal Marinot, serves a daily-changing four-course dinner menu. 'Straightforward, often classic, treatment of top-quality ingredients.' 'Do not miss the delicious fish options at breakfast and dinner.' Breakfast has freshly squeezed juice, good toast and coffee, excellent brown bread and scones, fresh fish of the day. Popular with wedding parties. (*Andrew Wardrop, Ann and Michael Maher, Geoffrey Garsten*)

20 bedrooms. 2 on ground floor. 7 miles NE of Clifden. Open 15 Mar–mid-Nov. 2 drawing rooms, conservatory/bar, dining room. No background music. 30-acre grounds: tennis. Unsuitable for ♿. Smoking allowed in 10 bedrooms. Only 'well-behaved dogs' in public rooms; with own bedding in bedrooms. Amex, MasterCard, Visa accepted. B&B €80–€145 per person. Set dinner €48. 1-night bookings refused Aug bank hols. *V*

LISDOONVARNA Co. Clare — Map 6:C4

Sheedy's

Tel 00 353 65-707 4026
Fax 00 353 65-707 4555
Email info@sheedys.com
Website www.sheedys.com

'Fully lived up to its outstanding reputation,' write visitors to this small hotel this year. 'John and Martina Sheedy run a very friendly but efficient ship.' Earlier, an inspector wrote of their 'personal approach'. The yellow building, in neat grounds, has been owned by John Sheedy's family since the 18th century. He is an 'accomplished' cook; his wife, Martina, is the 'hands-on, charming' manager. Bedrooms, in the main house and a modern extension, are 'well cared for': 'Ours was spacious, cool, decorated in excellent taste.' Pre-dinner drinks are taken in a bright sun lounge. The modern cooking (eg, seared scallops with coriander and lentil sauce), served in a 'pleasant, light' dining room, is 'of a very high standard'. Bar meals might include crab claws in garlic, chilli and ginger butter. Breakfast, served at table, has 'real' juice, home-made preserves, good teas, interesting cooked dishes. The spa resort is famed for its annual match-matching festival in September. Nearby are the Cliffs of Moher where a new 'eco-friendly' visitor centre has been controversial: 'The Sheedys provided us with a refreshing haven in which to recover from the concreting ravages being committed at the cliffs.' (*Ann and Michael Maher*)

11 bedrooms. Some on ground floor. 1 suitable for ♿. Village centre, 20 miles SW of Galway. Open mid-Mar–mid-Oct. Restaurant closed Tues Mar/Apr. Ramp. Sitting room/library, sun lounge, bar, restaurant (background jazz). 1½-acre garden: rose garden. No smoking. Restaurant 'not suitable for children under 10'. Guide dogs only. MasterCard, Visa accepted. B&B [2007] €68.50–€105 per person. Full alc €60. 1-night bookings refused Sept.

Please always send a report if you stay at a *Guide* hotel, even if it's only to endorse the existing entry.

LONGFORD Co. Longford *See SHORTLIST* Map 6:C5

MALIN Co. Donegal Map 6:A6

Malin Hotel

Tel 00 353 74-937 0606
Fax 00 353 74-937 0770
Email info@malinhotel.ie
Website www.malinhotel.ie

In 'pretty little village' 10 miles from Malin Head, Ireland's most northerly point ('magnificent coastal scenery'): Patrick Loughrey's small hotel with 'warm welcome'. 'Small but comfy' lounge; popular Green's *bar (bar meals; regular live music). 'Atmospherically lit'* Jack Yeats's *restaurant: 'straightforward food, good quality, plenty of it; decent wine list'. Wedding receptions, entertainment; management centre; golf packages. 'Easy listening' background music in all public areas during opening hours. Children's supervised play area on Sun, 4–9 pm. Blue Flag beach nearby. Closed 24/25 Dec. No smoking. No dogs. 18 bedrooms (4 added this year), ranging from 'quaint and cosy village rooms' to 'tranquil countryside' ones. MasterCard, Visa accepted. B&B [2007] €55–€75 per person. Set dinner from €20; full alc €55–€60. More reports, please.*

MILLSTREET Co. Waterford Map 6:D5

The Castle Country House

Millstreet
Cappagh

Tel 00 353 58-68049
Fax 00 353 58-68099
Email castlefm@iol.ie
Website www.castlecountryhouse.com

The River Finisk runs through Joan and Emmett Nugent's family farm, and they give visitors 'the best welcome' in their unusual farmhouse, a restored wing of a 15th-century tower house built to protect livestock. There are 'fresh flowers through the house, not a speck of dust', said one visitor. 'Our room had a wonderful view down the valley; the biggest bed and a lovely hot tub.' Mrs Nugent serves traditional country dishes (with meat from the local butcher, organic eggs from neighbours) in the original castle dining room (with five-foot walls). Breakfast ('at a time of your convenience') has fresh fruit, porridge, home-baked breads, and an unusual cooked selection (eg, French toast with stewed apple and black pudding). There is good fishing on the Finisk and on the nearby Blackwater. Guests are encouraged to 'lend a hand' on the family dairy farm. (*EO'B*)

Note There are two villages called Millstreet in County Waterford and one in neighbouring County Cork. This is the one closest to the estuary town of Dungarvan.

5 bedrooms. In village, 10 miles NW of Dungarvan. Open Mar–Nov. Drawing room, dining room (classical background music). Unsuitable for ♿. No smoking. Amex, MasterCard, Visa accepted. B&B €50–€65 per person. Set dinner €30.

MILTOWN MALBAY Co. Clare — Map 6:C4

Admiralty Lodge
Spanish Point

Tel 00 353 65-708 5007
Fax 00 353 65-708 5030
Email info@admiralty.ie
Website www.admiralty.ie

On a flat stretch of the Clare coast, but close to the dramatic Cliffs of Moher and some fine golf courses, this much-extended Georgian country house has been transformed into a small hotel by owner/managers Pat and Aoife O'Malley. 'They are much in evidence, and their multi-national staff are well drilled; a very good hotel,' says a visitor this year. 'The lounges have leather furniture and a clubby look; the dining room, with a centrepiece baby grand piano, is bright and pleasant. The dinner menus were imaginatively conceived and skilfully executed; we were pleased with various treatments of notably fresh fish. Service was friendly and efficient. On Saturday evening the pianist played with determination. Breakfast had a well-cooked traditional grill or smoked salmon and scrambled eggs; a dirge-like version of "The Wild Colonial Boy" would not be our choice of accompaniment.' The bedrooms have flat-screen TV, CD-player and air conditioning. 'Our ground-floor room had adequate storage space and a comfortable bed; very well-equipped bathroom. A high standard of housekeeping, with turn-down. Reasonable prices.' (*Ann Walden, and others*)

11 bedrooms. 1 mile SW of village. Closed Jan–7 Feb. Restaurant closed Mon/Tues in winter. Ramps. 3 lounges, bar, restaurant (resident pianist/background music). ½-acre grounds. Helipad. Beach 2 mins' walk. Golf, fishing nearby. No smoking. No children under 2 in restaurant. No dogs. Amex, MasterCard, Visa accepted. B&B [2007]: single €120–€165, double €140–€230, suite €200–€300. Set dinner €45; full alc €50. Special breaks. *V*

Hotels will often try to persuade you to stay for two nights at the weekend. Resist this pressure if you want to stay only one night.

MOUNTRATH Co. Laois — Map 6:C5

Roundwood House
Mountrath

Tel 00 353 57-873 2120
Fax 00 353 57-873 2711
Email roundwood@eircom.net
Website www.roundwoodhouse.com

César award in 1990

The 'gracious and unaffected' hosts, Rosemarie and Frank Kennan, may join guests after dinner for whiskey and coffee, when 'good company and conversation abound', at their 18th-century Palladian villa below the Slieve Bloom mountains. They continue with restoration of the house, which they bought from the Georgian Society in 1983; this year they tell us of 'the beginnings of a library called "the history of civilisation" in the playroom'. *Roundwood* has a two-storeyed hall, creaking floorboards and an eclectic collection of books, furniture and ornaments. Visitors find it 'warm and comfortable', and enjoy the 'slightly shabby Irish charm'. The first-floor Blue bedroom, large and high-ceilinged, is 'very comfortable'. Mrs Kennan serves an 'excellent' no-choice menu, 'based on what is in the market', eg, cream of cucumber soup; butterfly leg of lamb. Children are welcomed (there is a 'wet day' nursery with toys) and encouraged to feed the donkeys, ducks, horses, etc. Around are 'shimmering trees and meadows, bluebells and blackberries'. A coach house, forge and cottage have been turned into self-catering units. More reports, please.

10 bedrooms. 4 in garden annexe. 3 miles N of village. Closed 25 Dec, 1 Jan–1 Feb. Drawing room, study/library, dining room; playroom, table tennis room. No background music. 20-acre grounds: garden, woodland. Golf, walking, river fishing nearby. Unsuitable for ♿. Smoking allowed in 4 bedrooms. No dogs: public rooms, bedrooms. All major credit cards accepted. B&B €90–€115 per person. Set dinner €55. 3-night breaks. *V*

MULTYFARNHAM Co. Westmeath — Map 6:C5

Mornington House

Tel 00 353 44-937 2191
Fax 00 353 44-937 2338
Email stay@mornington.ie
Website www.mornington.ie

In large grounds with ancient trees near Lough Derravaragh, this old Anglo-Irish house, 'grand yet homely', has been in one family since 1858. Much original furniture and many portraits remain. There are red walls, elaborate wallpapers, stags' antlers, oriental rugs. 'Absolutely delightful,' say recent visitors. The owners, Warwick and Anne O'Hara, are 'wonderful, welcoming hosts, great conversationalists'. Guests, entertained on house-party lines, help themselves to pre-dinner drinks in the 'pleasant, light' drawing room where a turf or log fire burns in cold weather. At 8 pm, Mrs O'Hara's 'very good' four-course meal (no choice for the first two courses) is served at a large table in the candlelit dining room. 'Salmon was delicious, as was the steak in Guinness; the cheesecake sublime, like a soufflé.' Vegetarians are 'particularly welcome', but should give advance notice. Much produce comes from the walled garden. Mr O'Hara cooks the 'very good' breakfast: fresh orange juice; 'superb home-made muesli and brown bread; a full Irish Fry'; linen napkins. Bedrooms are 'a bit idiosyncratic': 'Ours was large, quiet, with plenty of light.' Two dogs, Caspar and Cleo, accompany guests on walks. The nearby lake has trout, pike, eel, canoes and boats. (*MJW*)

5 bedrooms. 9 miles NW of Mullingar. Open 1 Apr–31 Oct. Drawing room, dining room. No background music. 50-acre grounds: bicycle hire. Unsuitable for ♿. No smoking. No dogs in house. All major credit cards accepted. B&B €65–€75 per person. Set dinner €45.

NEWPORT Co. Mayo — Map 6:B4

Newport House

Tel 00 353 98-41222
Fax 00 353 98-41613
Email info@newporthouse.ie
Website www.newporthouse.ie

Run like 'a large private home', Thelma and Kieran Thompson's creeper-covered Georgian mansion (Relais & Châteaux) is on an estuary facing Achill Island, in a village on lovely Clew Bay. Catherine Flynn is the manager; most of the 'friendly, helpful' staff are local. *Guide* readers find the house 'delightful'. 'It feels like every country house hotel should but rarely does,' was one comment. There are fine plasterwork and chandeliers; cheerful fires burn in the public rooms; a grand staircase has a lantern and dome. Some bedrooms are in self-contained units, good for a family; others are in two houses near the courtyard. In the formal dining room the cooking of John Gavin is thought 'very good indeed'; the style is 'country house/French', eg, chicken liver parfait with gooseberry chutney; steamed fillet of brill with champagne sauce. 'We use only fresh wild fish.' The wine list and the *sommelier* are much admired. 'Breakfast was our best in Ireland, thanks largely to the incomparable eggs Benedict.' It also has fresh orange juice. 'Not cheap, but good value.' (*ADLM, and others*)

18 bedrooms. 5 in courtyard. 4 on ground floor. In village, 7 miles N of Westport. Open 19 Mar–10 Oct. Dining room, sitting room, bar, restaurant; billiard/TV room, table-tennis room. No background music. 15-acre grounds: walled garden. Private fishing on Newport river; golf, riding, walking, shooting, hang-gliding nearby. Unsuitable for ♿. Smoking allowed in 9 bedrooms. Dogs allowed in courtyard bedrooms. Amex, MasterCard, Visa accepted. B&B €114–€190 per person. Set dinner €65.

OUGHTERARD Co. Galway — Map 6:C4

Currarevagh House
Oughterard

Tel 00 353 91-552312
Fax 00 353 91-552731
Email rooms@currarevagh.com
Website www.currarevagh.com

César award in 1992

The Hodgson family have taken guests at their early Victorian manor house, on parkland and woodland on Lough Corrib, for over a century; Harry, June and son Henry are the present hosts. Their 'easy Irish charm' has long been liked by *Guide* readers (an entry in every edition). A regular listed the 'delights': the absence of room keys; 'the warmth of the rooms on early autumn days; the changing light on Lough Corrib'. 'Quality of welcome, atmosphere and food remain unchanged.' There is much to do in the area, 'but you can just spend the day in the house and gardens'. Free afternoon tea with scones and cakes awaits arriving guests. A gong announces dinner, cooked by mother and son: a five-course menu of 'simple Irish country house cooking', perhaps roasted red pepper soup, followed by guineafowl with sausage meat stuffing. Coffee afterwards, in the lounge, is 'a sociable affair'. An 'Edwardian' buffet breakfast includes kedgeree, black pudding. Bedrooms have fresh flowers, hot-water bottles; many have 'wonderful views'. And 'no single-occupancy-of-a-double-room supplement'. *Currarevagh* has its own boats and ghillies for fishing on Lough Corrib ('probably the best wild brown trout lake in Europe'); also good swimming and boating. (*Richard Parish*)

15 bedrooms. 2, on ground floor, in mews. 4 miles NW of Oughterard. Open Easter–mid-Oct. Sitting room/hall, drawing room, library/bar with TV, dining room. No background music. 170-acre grounds: lake, fishing (ghillies available), boating, swimming, tennis, croquet. Golf, riding nearby. Unsuitable for ♿. Smoking allowed in 4 bedrooms. Not suitable for very young children. 'Well-behaved' dogs by arrangement. MasterCard, Visa accepted. B&B [2007] €75–€99 per person; D,B&B €120–€140. Snack/picnic lunch available. Set dinner €45. 3-day/weekly rates. Winter house parties. 1-night bookings sometimes refused 'if too far ahead'.

RAMELTON Co. Donegal — Map 6:B5

Frewin

Rectory Road

Tel/Fax 00 353 74-915 1246
Email flaxmill@indigo.ie
Website www.frewinhouse.com

Outside a 'heritage' Georgian port at the mouth of the River Lennon, this 'small, stylish' Victorian rectory in mature wooded grounds has an elegant staircase, stained glass and a library. Regina and Thomas Coyle have renovated their home 'with flair', said our inspector, 'retaining the period features'. The largest bedroom, on a corner at the front, has views to both sides, and its own sitting room, 'a lovely little nook'. In the 'atmospheric' dining room, Mrs Coyle ('a charming hostess') serves dinner by request: 'Simple but satisfactory', and 'a couple of reasonable restaurants are within walking distance'. Breakfast, taken communally, was good, with home-made muesli, fresh fruit, home-baked bread and freshly squeezed juice; proper butter and conserves; good tea and coffee; also a full fry-up.' There is a small shop in the courtyard. (*Franz Kuhlmann, and others*)

4 bedrooms. Outskirts of town. Closed Christmas. Dinner by arrangement. Sitting room, library, dining room. No background music. 2-acre garden. Golf, horse riding, beaches nearby. Unsuitable for ♿. No smoking. 'Not suitable for very young children.' No dogs. MasterCard, Visa accepted. B&B €60–€90 per person. Set dinner €45.

RATHMULLAN Co. Donegal — Map 6:B5

Fort Royal

Tel 00 353 74-915 8100
Fax 00 353 74-915 8103
Email fortroyal@eircom.net
Website www.fortroyalhotel.com

Owner/chef Tim Fletcher is the third generation of his family to run this rambling white house with 'magnificent grounds' and fine views over Lough Swilly. *Fort Royal* may stand in the shadows of the neighbouring *Rathmullan House* (see next entry), which is larger and grander, but our inspector recommended it for those looking for a less expensive option in this popular holiday village. 'The foyer, which like the drawing room and bar has an open fire, is a welcoming place. Our bedroom, in the eaves, was plainly furnished but comfortable.' Mr Fletcher serves a three-course dinner menu featuring fish, eg, smoked trout mousse; Killybegs plaice meunière. Breakfast has fresh juice, 'proper conserves and good bacon and sausages'. More reports, please.

15 bedrooms. 4 in annexe. ¼ mile N of village. Open Apr–mid-Oct. Drawing room, bar, dining room. No background music. 17-acre grounds: tennis, pitch-and-putt golf. Unsuitable for ♿. Smoking allowed in bedrooms. No dogs in public rooms. All major credit cards accepted. B&B [2007] €85–€95 per person; D,B&B €120–€129. Set dinner €50. 1-night bookings refused at busy weekends.

Rathmullan House

Tel 00 353 74-915 8188
Fax 00 353 74-915 8200
Email info@rathmullanhouse.com
Website www.rathmullanhouse.com

'Thoroughly well managed', this informal country hotel has long been popular with *Guide* readers. The Wheeler family owners are 'much in evidence', says a visitor this year. Mark Wheeler is manager. 'Everything runs smoothly in a supremely comfortable and cosseting environment.' The handsome, white 1800s mansion stands in well-maintained gardens on a long sandy beach on Lough Swilly (an inlet of the sea). Its public rooms are spacious, with high ceilings, chandeliers, antiques, marble fireplaces, log fires, oil paintings, lots of books. Bedrooms come in various styles; older rooms are 'classic country house', some with a lough view, some with a balcony. Ten newer rooms are spacious and have restful colours and under-floor heating. Families are welcomed; one bedroom has a 'room' for a dog. In *The Weeping Elm*, the conservatory-style dining room, with its tented ceiling, Tommi Tuhkanen's cooking is thought 'beyond reproach'. Typical dishes: crispy tartlet of poached quail; assiette of lamb with aubergine and Parmesan gratin. Breakfast, with its wide choice and unusual alternatives, eg, carrageen (seaweed) moss with fruit compote, and 'daily choice of Donegal-landed fish', 'sets standards for other hotels'. There's a large indoor swimming pool and a pretty ornamental garden. (*Esler Crawford, and others*)

32 bedrooms. Some on ground floor. 2 suitable for ♿. ½ mile N of village. Bus: Letterkenny; hotel will meet. Open 9 Feb–7 Jan. Ramps. 4 lounges, library, TV room, cellar bar/bistro, restaurant; 50-ft indoor swimming pool, steam room; small conference centre. No background music. 7-acre grounds: tennis, croquet; direct access to sandy beach, safe bathing. Golf, boating, riding, hill walking nearby. No smoking. 1 dog-friendly bedroom; no dogs in public rooms. Amex, MasterCard, Visa accepted. B&B €99–€154 per person. Set dinner €45–€50; full alc €85. 1-night bookings refused weekends, bank holidays.

The *Guide* welcomes recommendations from readers for new entries. Please write or send us an email about any hotel, inn or B&B that you feel should be included.

RIVERSTOWN Co. Sligo — Map 6:B5

Coopershill

Tel 00 353 71-916 5108
Fax 00 353 71-916 5466
Email ohara@coopershill.com
Website www.coopershill.com

César award in 1987

On a large estate traversed by the River Arrow, this fine Palladian mansion has been owned by seven generations of the O'Hara family. This year, Simon O'Hara, of the eighth generation, has joined his parents, Brian and Lindy, as manager. They are an 'engaging' family: 'Lindy, along with her three dogs, warmly welcomed us with afternoon tea,' said visitors in 2007. The house is, 'unlike some of its Irish peers', in 'pristine condition'. The bedrooms retain their original dimensions; many have four-poster or canopied bed; some have a freestanding Victorian bath. 'The house was full, and our bathroom was down the corridor; bathrobes and slippers were provided.' Dinner, by candlelight, with family silver and glass, starts at 8.30 or so and is leisurely: guests dine at separate tables, but are served each course at the same time. Mrs O'Hara, with 'an able kitchen staff', cooks traditional dishes, eg, baked cod with tomato and lemon. The 'fine breakfast' has fresh orange juice, leaf tea with a strainer. Children are welcomed. The O'Haras run a sizeable farm; deer and sheep roam the estate. Fishing is available. (*Florence and Russell Birch, EC*)

8 bedrooms. 11 miles SE of Sligo. Open Apr–Oct. Off-season house parties by arrangement. 2 halls, drawing room, TV room, dining room; snooker room. No background music. 500-acre estate: garden, tennis, croquet, woods, farmland, river (trout fishing). Unsuitable for ♿. No smoking. No dogs in house. All major credit cards accepted. B&B €117–€165 per person; D,B&B €176–€224. Set dinner €59. Discounts for 3 or more nights.

ROSSLARE Co. Wexford — Map 6:D6

Churchtown House

Tagoat

Tel 00 353 53-913 2555
Fax 00 353 53-913 2577
Email info@churchtownhouse.com
Website www.churchtownhouse.com

'Big house, very well run. Good food.' In a hamlet south of Rosslare, Austin and Patricia Cody's handsome white Georgian house has long been liked for its 'beautiful location and calm atmosphere'. 'Comfortable, quiet and spotless.' 'It stands out over other places by virtue of the extensive grounds, both cultivated and wild, and the interior space,' say visitors in 2007. The 'delightful' Codys, 'open and approachable', cater 'kindly and sensibly' for children. There are 'tasteful modern *objets d'art*' in rooms and passages, and Irish paintings hang on the walls. Guests meet for sherry before the four-course dinner, which is served at separate tables. The country cooking is based on 'what is in season in our locality', perhaps seafood from Kilmore Quay, lamb from the county; vegetables and fruit are from the garden. There is no wine list; appropriate wines are offered for each meal. The Codys serve an early supper for guests staying for the Wexford opera festival; and the 'superb' breakfast can even be provided for those catching an early ferry from Rosslare. (*Margaret and Patrick Filsell, Simon and Pearl Willbourn*)

12 bedrooms. 5 on ground floor. On R736, 2½ miles S of Rosslare. Open 22 Mar–31 Oct. Restaurant closed Sun and Mon. 2 lounges, 2 dining rooms; private dining room. No background music. 8-acre grounds. Golf, fishing, riding, beaches nearby. No smoking. No dogs in house. Amex, MasterCard, Visa accepted. B&B [2007] €60–€95 per person. Set dinner €40.

SCHULL Co. Cork — Map 6:D4

Rock Cottage
Barnatonicane

Tel/Fax 00 353 28-35538
Email rockcottage@eircom.net
Website www.rockcottage.ie

César award in 2004

A couple who discovered Barbara Klötzer's slate-sided Georgian hunting lodge 'by happy chance' felt 'thoroughly cared for', adding: 'The best dinner and breakfast we had in Ireland.' Another guest, in 2007, praised 'the friendly service, fantastic food and lovingly decorated rooms'. The house, now entirely redecorated in 'more sophisticated' style, has fine furnishings and an eclectic collection of paintings, prints, ornaments and flowers. It stands in large grounds among grassy hillocks, one of which has 'stunning' views of Dunmanus Bay. Two bedrooms are 'spacious and airy'; all rooms now have facilities *en suite.* Ms Klötzer has introduced new dishes to her three-course menu based on fresh local produce, eg, coriander-crusted monkfish with saffron oil, crispy noodles. No choice: 'Let me know your preferences, otherwise it is a surprise.' Vegetarians are catered for. Breakfast, in the dining room with new cream table linen, has fresh orange juice, a variety of cooked dishes, cheeses, etc. Hens, dogs and cats roam on the working farm next door, but the horse and donkey have died ('after 21 happy years'). (*Josephine and Angus Irvine, Christina Vaughan Buckley*)

3 bedrooms. Also 1 self-catering cottage. 8 miles NW of Schull. Dining room closed Sun night in summer. Lounge (background music 'when guests want it'), dining room. 17-acre grounds. Unsuitable for ♿. No smoking. No children under 10. Guide dogs only. MasterCard, Visa accepted. B&B €65–€95 per person. Set dinner €45. 1-night bookings refused bank holidays.

SHANAGARRY Co. Cork — Map 6:D5

Ballymaloe House

Tel 00 353 21-465 2531
Fax 00 353 21-465 2021
Email res@ballymaloe.ie
Website www.ballymaloe.ie

César award in 1984

The 'fantastic, faultless food' is just one of the charms of the Allen family's hotel/restaurant, a favourite since the first edition of the *Guide*. The veteran Myrtle Allen ('what a star') still presides, 'carving for the magnificent Sunday buffet'. One daughter-in-law, Hazel, is manager; another daughter-in-law, Darina, the food writer, runs the nearby cookery school, with its famous *potager*. Set in large grounds (with sculptures, ponds with duck and geese, a swimming pool and much else, see below), the ivy-clad Georgian house is filled with paintings and books. Guests love its 'feel of a cultured private home'. The surrounding farm supplies the kitchen. Jason Fahey's five-course dinner, served in a series of small dining rooms, has main courses like roast duck with port and orange sauce; roast lamb with redcurrant jelly. Breakfast includes fresh juices, porridge, 'delicious marmalade'. Afternoon tea has 'fluffy scones' and home-made jams. Staff are 'excellent, especially the lady in charge of breakfast'. 'You feel cherished.' Some bedrooms are in a Norman keep; those in the main house are largest; some open straight on to the garden through French windows. Some rooms may be a bit cramped. (*Mike Hutton, and others*)

34 bedrooms. 9 in adjacent building. 4 on ground floor. 4 self-catering apartments. On L35 Ballycotton road, 20 miles E of Cork. Closed 24–26 Dec, 2 weeks mid-Jan. Drawing room, 2 small sitting rooms, conservatory, 7 dining rooms; conference facilities. No background music. Irish entertainment weekly in summer. 40-acre grounds: farm; gardens, tennis, swimming pool (heated in summer), 6-hole golf course, croquet, children's play area; craft shop. Cookery school nearby. Sea 3 miles: sand and rock beaches; fishing, riding by arrangement. Unsuitable for ♿. No smoking. No dogs. All major credit cards accepted. B&B €110–€190 per person; D,B&B €180–€260. Set dinner €70. Special breaks. New Year package.

STRANGFORD Co. Down *See SHORTLIST* Map 6:B6

THURLES Co. Tipperary Map 6:C5

Inch House
Inch, Thurles

Tel 00 353 504-51348
Fax 00 353 504-51754
Email mairin@inchhouse.ie
Website www.inchhouse.ie

The 'magnificent public rooms' of John and Nora Egan's Georgian mansion, which they run as a 'country house and restaurant', are mostly decorated in Adam style. But the drawing room has William Morris decor, 'country house furniture', and a huge stained-glass window. The dining room, elegant in red and green, has a log fire. 'It was like staying with a family; we were sorry to leave,' said one visitor. 'We were welcomed by daughter Mairin, who runs front-of-house with efficiency, and invited to relax in the drawing room while a tray of tea was brought with delicious home-made profiteroles and caramel sauce.' Another correspondent liked the feel of 'old-style living'. The bedrooms, with their 'quirky charm', are large and comfortable: 'Ours, the biggest, had a sofa by the fireplace.' The chef, Michael Galvin, serves 'European dishes with an Irish influence', eg, chicken with smoked bacon and chorizo. 'The food was excellent, the service efficient but not intrusive. A well-stocked wine cellar.' Breakfast has fruit, yogurt, home-made jams and soda bread. (*NW*)

5 bedrooms. On R498, 4 miles W of Thurles. Closed Christmas/New Year. Dining room closed midday, Sun night, Mon night. Drawing room, bar, restaurant (Irish background music); chapel; conference/function facilities. 2-acre garden on 250-acre farm. Golf, riding, fishing nearby. Unsuitable for ♿. No smoking. No children under 12 in the restaurant. Guide dogs only. MasterCard, Visa accepted. B&B €60–€80 per person. Set dinner €50–€55.

WATERFORD Co. Waterford Map 6:D5

Foxmount Country House
Passage East Road

Tel 00 353 51-874308
Fax 00 353 51-854906
Email info@foxmountcountryhouse.com
Website www.foxmountcountryhouse.com

On a working dairy farm, 'though you would hardly know it', David and Margaret Kent's creeper-covered 17th-century house B&B stands up a tree-lined drive. It is 'a most relaxed place', said an enthusiastic report. Mrs Kent, 'friendly without being imposing', cooks an award-winning breakfast, with home-made scones, preserves and bread; 'her scrambled eggs passed the test, as good as it gets'. Guests can take tea in front of the log fire, and bring their own pre-dinner drinks. 'When we phoned to say our ferry was late, they booked a table for us at a restaurant in Waterford to ensure that our evening was not spoiled.' 'Our bedroom was clean and homely, with fresh fruit, pretty view, lovely towels in the huge bathroom.' (*NS*)

5 bedrooms. 2 miles W of Waterford. Open Mar–Nov. Sitting room, dining room (background music). 3-acre grounds. No smoking. No dogs. No credit cards. B&B €55–€65 per person.

See also SHORTLIST

****

Traveller's tale On arrival we were shown to the guest bedrooms in what can only be described as the servants' quarters. On the lower ground floor, they were cold and faced the dustbins. Our room had not been properly cleaned. Hair on the bathroom floor had not been removed; the grouting was poor; the shower screen was black. Preparing for bed at night, we realised there were no loo rolls and had to go in search of them. At breakfast, the owners were inhospitable. They served me the smallest cooked breakfast I have seen. No choice of eggs: they came scrambled. Toast was stale and inedible. When we left, no one asked if we had enjoyed our stay. (*Hotel in Wales*)

****

SHORTLIST

This Shortlist is designed mainly to fill gaps in our maps. Because our selection of hotels for main entries in the *Guide* is based on quality and character rather than on location, we have a limited choice in some towns and cities (in some cases no hotels at all). In this section we identify hotels, guest houses and B&Bs which we believe provide reasonable accommodation in these areas. Some are more business-oriented than the places that we include in the main section. We also feature establishments that may qualify for a full entry in later editions of the *Guide*. They include new nominations that we have not yet checked, recent openings on which as yet we have no reports, and hotels which have had a full entry in the past but have no recent reports, or mixed reviews. We welcome readers' comments on all the hotels on the Shortlist. Those places which do not also have a full entry in the *Guide* are indicated on the map by a triangle.

LONDON **Map 2:D4**

Apex City of London, 1 Seething Lane, EC3N 4AX. *Tel* 0845-365 0000, www.apexhotel.co.uk. Near Tower of London, hi-tech, contemporary hotel. Panoramic views. *Addendum* restaurant and brasserie, chic bar; background music; business facilities; gym, sauna, steam room. 130 bedrooms. B&B from £90 per person. (Underground: Tower Hill.)

base2stay, 25 Courtfield Gardens, SW5 0PG. *Tel* 0845-262 8000, www.base2stay.com. In pillared, white stucco town house: smart, modern rooms. No frills, but kitchenettes and state-of-the-art equipment. Reception, lobby (background music). 67 bedrooms (some on ground floor): single £89, double £119, suite £189. Breakfast £4.50. (Underground: Earls Court, Gloucester Road.)

B+B Belgravia, 64–66 Ebury Street, SW1W 9QD. *Tel* 020-7259 8570, www.bb-belgravia.com. Posh town house address, with sleek contemporary interior. Helpful staff. Lounge with open fire, free Internet, complimentary tea/coffee. No background music. Small garden. 17 bedrooms (2 family; 1 suitable for ♿): single £97, double £107. (Underground: Victoria.)

City Inn Westminster, 30 John Islip Street, SW1P 4DD. *Tel* 020-7630 1000, www.cityinn.com. Large, contemporary hotel (City Inn group) by Tate Britain. 'Excellent value, we really enjoyed our stay.' Lounge (background music); modern art, ruby-red decor in *Millbank* cocktail bar; *City* café ('food very good and reasonably priced'); gym. 460 bedrooms: double from £129 (excluding breakfast). Weekend breaks. (Underground: Pimlico.)

The Colonnade, 2 Warrington Crescent, Little Venice, W9 1ER. *Tel* 020-7286 1052, www.theetoncollection.com. Near Regent's Canal: 2 Victorian town houses converted into lavishly decorated, luxury boutique hotel (Eton Collection). Lounge, bar, restaurant (background music). Wedgwood fireplace; Art Deco lift. Terrace. Conference facilities. 43 bedrooms (some split-level). B&B double from £185. (Underground: Warwick Avenue, Paddington.)

County Hall Premier Travel Inn, Belvedere Road, SE1 7PB. *Tel* 0870-238 3300, www.premiertravelinn.com. 'Basic, but has all you need': budget hotel, in old County Hall building on river by London Eye, opposite Houses of Parliament. Lift. Lobby, bar, restaurant; background music. 'Helpful staff.' 314 uniform bedrooms. B&B double £99. (Underground: Waterloo.)

Covent Garden Hotel, 10 Monmouth Street, WC2H 9HB. *Tel* 020-7806 1000, www.coventgardenhotel.co.uk. Suitably dramatic interior for theatreland location (Royal Opera House nearby): part of Firmdale Hotels group, managed by Helle Jensen. Drawing room, library, bar, *Brasserie Max*; screening room; gym; beauty treatments. No background music. 58 bedrooms [to 29 Feb 2008]: single £225, double £275–£320, suite £375–£995. Breakfast £19.50. (Underground: Covent Garden.)

Dorset Square Hotel, 39 Dorset Square, NW1 6QN. *Tel* 020-7723 7874, www.dorsetsquare.co.uk. Regency residence facing garden square, site of Thomas Lord's first cricket ground, near Regent's Park. Grand country house interior. Dorset country produce in *The Potting Shed* restaurant. Lounge, bar. No background music. Leisure centre nearby. 37 bedrooms: double £230–£270, suite £350. Breakfast £13.50–£15.75. (Underground: Baker Street, Marylebone.)

Dukes Hotel, 35 St James's Place, SW1A 1NY. *Tel* 020-7491 4840, www.dukeshotel.com. In quiet side street: discreet hotel, now part of Gordon Campbell Gray's group (see also *One Aldwych*, main entry). Michael Voight is manager. Relaunched in spring 2007 after complete renovation: traditional English style combined with latest technology (Wi-Fi, etc). Lounge, restaurant ('classic British'), bar (famed for martinis); 24-hour room service; health club; courtyard garden. No background music. 90 bedrooms: single £185–£295, double £225–£420, suite £340–£1,050. Breakfast £14.95. (Underground: Green Park.)

Elizabeth Hotel, 37 Eccleston Square, SW1V 1PB. *Tel* 020-7828 6812, www.elizabethhotel.com. Overlooking garden square: imposing 19th-century town house, with traditional English character. Privately owned. Lounge, breakfast room; lift. No background music. Garden with tennis court. 40 bedrooms. B&B double from £79. (Underground: Victoria.)

Haymarket Hotel, 1 Suffolk Place, SW1Y 4BP. *Tel* 020-7470 4000, www.haymarkethotel.com. Brightly coloured contemporary interior in 3 Georgian houses, next to Theatre Royal; the latest (May 2007) of Tim and Kit Kemp's boutique hotels (Firmdale group). Lift, drawing room, library; restaurant, bar; background music. Indoor swimming pool, gym. 50 bedrooms: single £245, double £275–£385, suite £385–£2,250. Breakfast £20. (Underground: Green Park, Piccadilly.)

High Road House, 162 Chiswick High Road, W4Y 1PR. *Tel* 020-8742 1717, www.highroadhouse.co.uk. Private members' club and (Soho House group) hotel in Chiswick. Bar, brasserie; 'Playroom' (red leather sofas, pool table, football table, board games, plasma screens, DVDs, Wi-Fi); background music. 14 (small, white wood-panelled) bedrooms: double £140–£160. (Underground: Turnham Green.)

The Hoxton, 81 Great Eastern Street, EC2A 3HU. *Tel* 020-7750 1000, www.hoxtonhotels.com. 'Urban living meets country lodge lounging': buzzy hotel owned by Sinclair Beecham (co-founder of Pret A Manger), with radical preferential early booking system, inexpensive phone calls, free Internet/Wi-Fi. Lift. Huge lobby, sitting area, bar, brasserie *Hoxton Grille*;

background music; business facilities; shop. Courtyard. 205 bedrooms. B&B double (Lite Pret breakfast) £59–£149. (Underground: Old Street.)

Kensington House, 15–16 Prince of Wales Terrace, W8 5PQ. *Tel* 020-7937 2345, www.kenhouse.com. In quiet street near Kensington Gardens: 19th-century stucco-fronted town house, with contemporary interior. Informal dining or drinks in *Tiger Bar*, 24-hour room service. No background music. 41 bedrooms. B&B (continental): single £150, double £175–£195, suite £215. Weekend offers. (Underground: High St Kensington.)

Knightsbridge Hotel, 10 Beaufort Gardens, SW3 1PT. *Tel* 020-7584 6300, www.knightsbridgehotel.com. Chic yet homely B&B hotel (Firmdale group) in peaceful, tree-lined cul-de-sac near shops. Lounge, library, bar. No background music. Room service. 44 bedrooms: single £160–£175, double £195–£280, suite £330–£550. Breakfast £16.50. (Underground: Knightsbridge.)

The Lennox, 32 Pembridge Gardens, W2 4DX. *Tel* 0870-850 3317, www.thelennox.com. Refurbished Notting Hill town house hotel (formerly *Pembridge Court*). Lounge/*Lennox* bar; background music. Preferential rates for ballroom and Latin dance classes at nearby dance studio. 20 bedrooms: well equipped, decorated in earth shades (cream, brown and taupe); most are spacious. B&B: single £100, double £125–£185, suite £220. (Underground: Notting Hill Gate.)

The Levin, 28 Basil Street, SW3 1AT. *Tel* 020-7589 6286, www.thelevinhotel.co.uk. Metamorphosis of David Levin's former *L'Hotel* into glamorous boutique hotel with mirrored entrance, fireplaces, oak floors, *Le Metro* restaurant (background music). 12 bedrooms. B&B: single/double £195–£265, suite £325. (Underground: Knightsbridge.)

Malmaison, Charterhouse Square, EC1M 6AH. *Tel* 020-7012 3700, www.malmaison.com. Former nurses' hostel, in quiet Clerkenwell square. Informal style. Small rooms (greys or earth tones, bright splashes of colour; amusing touches). Bar, brasserie; background music; gymtonic. Dogs welcome (£10 charge). 97 bedrooms: from £245. Breakfast £16.95. (Underground: Farringdon, Barbican.)

The Mayflower, 26–28 Trebovir Road, SW5 9NJ. *Tel* 020-7370 0991, www.mayflowerhotel.co.uk. Town house hotel with 'funky' ethnic style: hand-carved wooden beds, oriental antiques, bright colours. Lounge/juice bar, attractive breakfast room. Tropical garden. 48 bedrooms (some are small; all have Wi-Fi). B&B (continental buffet): single from £75, double from £89. (Underground: Earl's Court.)

Miller's Residence, 111A Westbourne Grove, W2 4UW. *Tel* 020-7243 1024, www.millersuk.com. Antiques aplenty and sumptuous embellishment by owner Martin Miller (of *Miller's Antiques* guides). Large candlelit drawing room/breakfast room/bar (complimentary drinks; classical background music). 8 bedrooms, named after British poets. B&B (continental, *excluding VAT*): double £150–£185, suite £230. (Underground: Notting Hill Gate, Bayswater, Queensway.)

Montagu Place, 2 Montagu Place, W1N 2ER. *Tel* 020-7467 2777, www.montagu-place.co.uk. Intimate Grade II listed Georgian town house with modern brown/beige interior retaining some original features (eg, fireplaces). Lounge, bar, breakfast room. No background music. 16 bedrooms ('Comfy', 'Swanky', 'Fancy'; free Internet access): double (*excluding VAT*) £149–£195. Breakfast £12.95. (Underground: Marylebone, Baker Street.)

Number Sixteen, 16 Sumner Place, SW7 3EG. *Tel* 020-7589 5232, www.numbersixteenhotel.co.uk. White stucco, mid-Victorian, terraced building in 'great location with a neighbourhood feel'. Part of Firmdale Hotels group. Lift. Drawing room, library, conservatory (background music). Courtyard garden with fountain. 42 bedrooms (some smoking): single £110–£150, double £185–£210. Breakfast £16.50. (Underground: South Kensington.)

Portobello Gold, 95–97 Portobello Road, W11 2QB. *Tel* 020-7460 4910, www.portobellogold.com. Quirky restaurant-with-rooms on street famed for Saturday market. Monthly photographic/art exhibitions in Gold Gallery. Live music on Sun. Bar, conservatory restaurant with sliding roof (mainly seafood); Internet café; function facilities. 8 bedrooms: double £70–£170. (Underground: Notting Hill Gate.)

Royal Park Hotel, 3 Westbourne Terrace, W2 3UL. *Tel* 020-7479 6600, www.theroyalpark.com. At Lancaster Gate, near Hyde Park: elegant conversion of 3 listed Georgian town houses. Victorian and Georgian antiques; plain-painted walls in Regency colours. Four-poster and half-tester beds. Drawing room. Background music. Small room-service menu. 48 bedrooms (*excluding VAT*): single £190, double £215–£250, suite £290–£300 (includes glass of champagne). (Underground: Paddington.)

Searcy's Roof Garden Rooms, 30 Pavilion Road, SW1X 0HJ. *Tel* 020-7584 4921, www.30pavilionroad.co.uk. Stylish, quirky Knightsbridge B&B in Georgian town house off Sloane St. Owned by Searcy's catering group, managed by Dimitrios Neofitidis. No public rooms. Large roof garden. Function facilities. 10 bedrooms. B&B: double £120–£180, suite £140–£200. (Underground: Sloane Sq.)

Shaftesbury Hotel, 65–73 Shaftesbury Avenue, W1D 6EX. *Tel* 020-7871 6000, www.shaftesburyhotellondon.co.uk. In theatreland, Best Western hotel with ultra-modern interior: mood lighting, TV in bathrooms, air conditioning. Wi-Fi. Lift. Lounge, *Premier* bar, restaurants; background music;

fitness room; conference facilities. 67 bedrooms (some small). B&B double £119–£229. (Underground: Piccadilly Circus, Leicester Sq.)

Sleep Inn City of London, 22–24 Prescot Street, E1 8BB. *Tel* 020-7977 5450, www.hotels-city-of-london.com. Opened April 2007, 'premium economy' hotel (CHE group) near Tower of London. Sleek, shiny decor; spacious; large beds. Bar, restaurant, coffee shop; background TV. Wi-Fi. 163 bedrooms (some suitable for ♿). B&B £63.60 per person. (Underground: Tower Hill, Aldgate East.)

The Soho Hotel, 4 Richmond Mews, off Dean Street, W1D 3DH. *Tel* 020-7559 3000, www.sohohotel.com. Stylish luxury hotel (part of Tim and Kit Kemp's Firmdale Hotels group). Granite, oak, and glass bathrooms. Lift. Drawing room, library, *Refuel* bar/restaurant; background music; 4 private dining rooms; 2 screening rooms. 85 bedrooms (some suitable for ♿): single £230–£255, double £255–£315, suite £305–£2,500. Breakfast from £18.50. (Underground: Leicester Sq.)

The Stafford, 16–18 St James's Place, SW1A 1NJ. *Tel* 020-7493 0111, www.thestaffordhotel.co.uk. In quiet backwater off St James's St: luxury hotel (Shire Hotels Ltd). Lounge, American bar (food served), restaurant. No background music. Children welcomed. Access to nearby fitness studio. 105 bedrooms (26 in mews; 3 suitable for ♿) (*excluding VAT*): single £250, double £260–£370, suite £425–£1,200. Breakfast £22.50. (Underground: Green Park.)

Threadneedles, 5 Threadneedle Street, EC2R 8AY. *Tel* 020-7657 8164, www.theetoncollection.com. Near Bank of England: 1856 banking hall strikingly converted into 'luxury boutique hotel'. Part of Eton Collection (see also *The Colonnade*). Original stained-glass dome towers over reception lounge (background music). Bar, *Bonds* restaurant (closed weekends); 3 meeting rooms; health/fitness club; conference facilities. 69 bedrooms (some suitable for ♿): double £125–£280, suite £265–£480. Breakfast £16.40. (Underground: Bank.)

Twenty Nevern Square, 20 Nevern Square, SW5 9PD. *Tel* 020-7565 9555, www.twentynevernsquare.co.uk. Red brick Victorian town house, overlooking garden square. Emphasis on natural materials; hand-carved furniture. 'Excellent reception staff. Good continental breakfast.' Lounge, *Café Twenty*; background music. 20 bedrooms. B&B: single £79–£140, double £175–£195, suite £250. (Underground: Earl's Court.)

ENGLAND

ALDEBURGH Suffolk — Map 2:C6

White Lion, Market Cross Place, IP15 5BJ. *Tel* 01728-452720, www.whitelion.co.uk. Central, opposite beach, Aldeburgh's oldest hotel (16th-century; Best Western). Oak panelling, beams, inglenook fireplace. 2 lounges, 2 bars, restaurant (local produce; sea views); background music. Parking. 38 bedrooms (some with sea view). B&B £47–£102.50 per person; D,B&B (min. 2 nights) £52.50–£109.50.

BATH Somerset **Map 2:D1**

Aquae Sulis, 174–176 Newbridge Road, BA1 3LE. *Tel* 01225-420061, www.aquaesulishotel.co.uk. Peaceful family-run hotel in Edwardian house, traditionally furnished. 30-min. riverside stroll or short bus trip from abbey (Park & Ride close by). 2 lounges (1 with bar); background music. Wi-Fi. Patio garden. Parking. 14 bedrooms (some family). B&B £50–£79 per person.

The Ayrlington, 24–25 Pulteney Road, BA2 4EZ. *Tel* 01225-425495, www.ayrlington.com. A blend of Asian and English antiques at Simon and Mee-Ling Roper's elegant listed Victorian house near centre. Lounge/bar, breakfast room; background music sometimes. Lovely Oriental-style walled garden with views of city. Parking. Spa breaks. 14 bedrooms. B&B £75–£175 per person.

Dorian House, 1 Upper Oldfield Park, BA2 3JX. *Tel* 01225-426336, www.dorianhouse.co.uk. Cellist Tim Hugh and wife Kathryn's characterful Victorian stone house, 10 mins' walk from centre. Bedrooms (some with four-poster) named after musicians. Lounge (open fire), breakfast room/music library; classical background music. Wi-Fi. Garden. Parking. 7 bedrooms. B&B £40–£77.50 per person.

Dukes Hotel, Great Pulteney Road, BA2 4DN. *Tel* 01225-787960, www.dukesbath.co.uk. Elegant Grade 1 Palladian-style townhouse (lots of stairs) with colourful bedrooms. Lounge, bar, *Cavendish* restaurant (modern organic food; background music). Patio garden. 17 bedrooms. B&B £62.50–£115 per person; D,B&B £100–£150.

Haydon House, 9 Bloomfield Park, BA2 2BY. *Tel* 01225-444919, www.haydonhouse.co.uk. Now owned by John and Alison Criddle: semi-detached Edwardian house (fronted by dovecote) on hill above centre; ample parking. 2 sitting rooms, breakfast room; background music (classical/jazz). Garden. 5 'flouncily romantic' bedrooms (2 on ground floor). B&B £37.50–£95 per person.

Kennard, 11 Henrietta Street, BA2 6LL. *Tel* 01225-310472, www.kennard.co.uk. Giovanni and Mary Baiano's 18th-century 'very clean, very comfortable' town house, 'perfect' (just across Pulteney Bridge) for exploring Bath. 'We came away feeling indulged.' 2 sitting areas, breakfast room. No background music. 'Georgian' garden. 10 bedrooms (2 on ground floor). B&B £48–£65 per person.

BATTLE East Sussex **Map 2:E4**

The PowderMills, Powdermill Lane, TN33 0SP. *Tel* 01424-775511, www.powdermillshotel.com. A mile from town: Douglas and Julie Cowpland's 18th-century building with elegant interior, on site of former gunpowder works. 'Excellent.' Drawing room, library, *Orangery* restaurant, conservatory; background music; function/wedding facilities. 150-acre grounds: unheated swimming pool, 7-acre fishing lake, woods. 41 bedrooms (12 in *Pavilion*; some suitable for ♿). B&B £65–£105 per person. Dinner £30.

BEAULIEU Hampshire **Map 2:E2**

The Master Builder's House, Buckler's Hard, SO42 7XB. *Tel* 01590-616253, www.themasterbuilders.co.uk. Rambling building in 2-acre garden leading to river; direct sailing to Solent from pontoon. Near Maritime Museum. Lounge, *Yachtsman's* bar, *Riverview* restaurant; background music; conference facilities. Garden. Parking. 25 bedrooms. B&B £90–£154 per person. Full alc £41.

Montagu Arms, Palace Lane, SO42 7ZL. *Tel* 01590-612324, www.montaguarmshotel.co.uk. In New Forest riverside village: sprawling, elegantly restored, 1930s building. 'Food good, varied and interesting.' Lounge, library/bar, conservatory, *Monty's* bar/brasserie, *Terrace* restaurant; quiet CDs played when required; conference/function facilities. Garden; croquet. Parking. 22 bedrooms. B&B £92.50–£142.50 per person.

BERWICK-UPON-TWEED Northumberland **Map 4:A3**

Marshall Meadows, TD15 1UT. *Tel* 01289-331133, www.marshallmeadows.co.uk. England's most northerly hotel, 400 yds from Scottish border and 2 miles from Berwick-upon-Tweed. Georgian building in 15-acre gardens and woodland. Lounge, bar, two-tiered restaurant with oak-panelled gallery; soft background music; conference/function facilities. 19 bedrooms (farmland or garden views). B&B £60–£85 per person; D,B&B from £86.

BEVERLEY East Yorkshire **Map 4:D5**

Tickton Grange, Main Street, Tickton, HU17 9SH. *Tel* 01964-543666, www.ticktongrange.co.uk. Whymant family's Georgian house in formal gardens, 5 miles NE of Beverley (Hull and York within easy reach). On A1035 (some traffic noise). Traditional furnishing. Restaurant specialising in Yorkshire produce ('good food; noteworthy cheeseboard'); background music; function/wedding facilities. Parking. 17 bedrooms. D,B&B £90–£120 per person.

BIDDENDEN Kent **Map 2:D5**

Tudor Cottage, 25 High Street, nr Tenterden, TN27 8AL. *Tel* 01580-291913, www.tudorcottagebiddenden.co.uk. 'Excellent-value' B&B in timber-framed cottage with beams and 'cat-slide' roof. Breakfast room. No background music. Garden. 2 restaurants and a pub nearby. 3 bedrooms. B&B £30–£55 per person.

BIRMINGHAM West Midlands **Map 2:B2**

Malmaison, The Mailbox, 1 Wharfside Street, B1 1RD. *Tel* 0121-246 5000, www.malmaison.com. In Mailbox complex: converted 1960s Royal Mail sorting office, short walk from station. Funky design; hi-tech facilities. Bar, brasserie; background music; 'gymtonic'; meeting/function facilities. Dogs welcome (£10 per night). 184 bedrooms: double £170–£190, suite £240–£295.

BLACKBURN Lancashire **Map 4:D3**

The Millstone at Mellor, Church Lane, Mellor, BB2 7JR. *Tel* 01254-813333, www.millstonehotel.co.uk. 3 miles NW of Blackburn: stone-built former coaching inn retaining quaint style, owned by Shire Hotels, run by chef Anson Bolton. 2 lounges, bar, *Millers* restaurant (emphasis on Lancashire produce); background music. Parking. 23 bedrooms (6 in courtyard; 1 suitable for ♿). B&B £62.50–£149.50 per person. Full alc £36.50.

Stanley House, Mellor, BB2 7NP. *Tel* 01254-769200, www.stanleyhouse.co.uk. 17th-century manor house (former dairy farm) in 54-acre parkland, 3 miles NW of Blackburn. Lavish interior, beams, stone fireplaces, mullioned windows. Lounge, bar, restaurant; background music. 12 bedrooms (in separate listed building). B&B £97.50–£112.50 per person. Dinner £32.50.

BLACKPOOL Lancashire **Map 4:D2**

Number One, 1 St Lukes Road, South Shore, FY4 2EL. *Tel* 01253-343901, www.numberoneblackpool.com. Stylish B&B in period house on regenerated South Shore, run by welcoming hosts, Mark and Claire Smith. Modern bathrooms; state-of-the-art gadgetry. Red-walled dining room. No background music. Large garden. Ample parking. 3 bedrooms (plasma TV, DVD-player, etc). B&B from £60 per person.

Raffles Hotel & Tea Room, 73–77 Hornby Road, FY1 4QJ. *Tel* 01253-294713, www.raffleshotelblackpool.co.uk. Within walking distance of all the sights: small, flower-fronted, bay-windowed hotel, run by chef/proprietor Ian Balmforth and Graham Poole. 2 lounges, bar, traditional English tea room (open 11 am to 6 pm); background music. Free parking. 20 bedrooms. B&B £31–£72 per person.

BONCHURCH Isle of Wight **Map 2:E2**

Winterbourne Country House, Bonchurch Village Road, PO38 1RQ. *Tel* 01983-852535, www.winterbournehouse.co.uk. In tranquil sea-facing gardens: house where Charles Dickens wrote *David Copperfield*. 2 lounges, breakfast room, snug; classical background music; secluded terrace. Garden: swimming pool, stream, private path to small beach. 7 bedrooms. B&B £50–£85 per person.

BORROWDALE Cumbria **Map 4: inset C2**

The Borrowdale Hotel, CA12 5UY. *Tel* 017687-77224, www.theborrowdalehotel.co.uk. Run by Fidrmuc family owners: traditional Lakeland hotel at head of Derwentwater, below Shepherd's Crag. 2 lounges, bar (background music), dining room, restaurant (6-course dinner). Four-poster beds. Dogs welcome. 36 bedrooms (some family; 2 suitable for ♿). B&B £66–£97 per person.

BOSCASTLE Cornwall **Map 1:C3**

Bottreaux Hotel, Camelford Road, PL35 0BG. *Tel* 01840-250231, www.boscastlecornwall.co.uk. Now owned by John Annerley: 19th-century building 10 mins' walk down steep hill to harbour, overlooking wooded valley and Atlantic Ocean. Sea-grass flooring, teak furniture, large beds. Lounge, bar, restaurant (background music). Parking. 7 bedrooms. B&B from £47.50 per person; D,B&B from £72.50.

Trerosewill Farmhouse, Paradise, PL35 0BL. *Tel* 01840-250545, www.trerosewill.co.uk. Steve and Cheryl Nicholls's B&B on 40-acre of farmland (with badger sett). Member of Green Tourism Business Scheme. Coastline views, north to Hartland Point and Lundy Island, and southwest to Tintagel and the Rumps. Local produce at breakfast. 2 lounges, conservatory dining room; video library. No background music. 1-acre garden; summer house; hot tub on terrace overlooking coastline. 8 bedrooms. B&B £40–£62 per person.

BOWNESS-ON-WINDERMERE Cumbria **Map 4: inset C2**

Lindeth Howe, Lindeth Drive, Longtail Hill, LA23 3JF. *Tel* 015394-45759, www.lindeth-howe.co.uk. Imposing country house, built 1897 as holiday home for wealthy mill owner, owned by Potter family 1902–1913 (Beatrix Potter wrote tales of Timmy Tiptoes and Pigling Bland here). Traditional interior; views of lake and fells. 3 lounges, library, bar, restaurant (classical background music); sun terrace; leisure centre (swimming pool, sauna, fitness room). 6-acre garden. 36 bedrooms. B&B £42.50–£65 per person. Dinner £38.50.

BRIGHTON East Sussex **Map 2:E4**

Fivehotel, 5 New Steine, BN2 1PB. *Tel* 01273-686547, www.fivehotel.com. Near The Lanes, Caroline and Simon Heath's crisp, contemporary B&B in period townhouse in Kemp Town Regency square. 2 public rooms. No background music. Organic breakfasts; free Wi-Fi; sea views. 10 bedrooms. B&B £35–70 per person.

Paskins Town House, 18–19 Charlotte Street, BN2 1AG. *Tel* 01273-601203, www.paskins.co.uk. 100 yds from sea, 10 mins' walk to centre: Susan and Roger Marlowe's eco-friendly (Green Tourism Business Scheme) town house. Organic/locally produced ingredients at breakfast; vegetarian/vegan dishes a speciality. Art Nouveau reception, 2 lounges, bar, Art Deco breakfast room. No background music. 19 bedrooms (modern Japanese/imaginative colours). B&B £40–£62.50 per person.

Hotel Seattle, Brighton Marina, BN2 5WA. *Tel* 01273-679799, www.aliashotels.com. In waterfront development 1 mile E of centre: owned by Alias Hotels. Contemporary style (nautical undertones), amusing touches. 'Exceptionally friendly' reception staff. Black-and-white cocktail bar; saloon lounge with decking; sea-facing *Café Paradiso* bistro (Mediterranean food; special events); background music; meeting/function facilities. Large, free car park. 71 bedrooms (1 suitable for ♿): £115–£170. Breakfast £9.95–£13.50.

Square, 4 New Steine, BN2 1PB. *Tel* 01273-691777, www.squarebrighton.com. Off seafront, Keith Allison's Regency town house in Kemp Town garden square. Glamorous interior: suede sofas, fur throws, deep baths. 'Reverse penthouse' in basement. Cocktail bar (background music). Health and beauty therapies. No children. 10 bedrooms (some with sea view). B&B: single £110–£160, double £120–£210, penthouse £380.

BRISTOL **Map 1:B6**

The Berkeley Square Hotel, 15 Berkeley Square, Clifton, BS8 1HB. *Tel* 0117-925 4000, www.cliftonhotels.com. On Georgian square, part of small group of hotels in Clifton. Lounge (bright, airy; dashing decor; artwork), *Lower Deck* for light meals; dining room; light background music; basement bar/club. Parking. 43 bedrooms (Wi-Fi, DVD/CD-player, etc): single £129, double £140–£149. Breakfast £7.50–£11.50. Dinner from £16.95.

BROMSGROVE Worcestershire **Map 3:C5**

Ladybird Lodge, 2 Finstall Road, Aston Fields, B60 2DZ. *Tel* 01527-889900, www.ladybirdlodge.co.uk. Near Bromsgrove station and handy for Birmingham (15 miles) and NEC (23 miles): modern extension to

Ladybird Inn, overlooking countryside. 'Airy rooms; friendly staff.' Lift. Lounge, pub, *Rosado's* restaurant (Italian; background music); conference facilities. Parking. 43 bedrooms (3 suitable for ♿), some family), with DVD-player, modem point. B&B £30–£65 per person.

BUNGAY Suffolk **Map 2:B6**

Earsham Park Farm, Old Railway Road, Earsham, NR35 2AQ. *Tel* 01986-892180, www.earsham-parkfarm.co.uk. Three miles NW of town, up ½-mile drive off A143: 'top-notch' Victorian farmhouse on 600-acre working farm (arable crops, free-range outdoor pig-breeding herd), sweeping views over Waveney valley. Informally run by Mrs Bobbie Watchorn. 'Fabulous breakfasts.' Lounge, dining room; background music. Garden. 3 bedrooms. B&B £35–£42.50 per person.

BURY ST EDMUNDS Suffolk **Map 2:B5**

Ravenwood Hall, Rougham, IP30 9JA. *Tel* 01359-270345, www.ravenwoodhall.co.uk. Historic home (Tudor origins; inglenook fireplaces) of Craig Jarvis, in 7-acre garden (croquet, heated swimming pool) and woodland. Child-friendly (toys, games, colouring books, goats, geese). Off A14 (some traffic noise), 3 miles SE of Bury. Lounge (inglenook fireplace), bar (informal meals); 'easy listening'/classical background music; restaurant, garden dining room; Edwardian pavilion and summer house for conferences/weddings. 14 bedrooms (7 in mews, some on ground floor). B&B £60–£97.50 per person.

BUXTON Derbyshire **Map 3:A6**

Grendon, Bishops Lane, SK17 6UN. *Tel* 01298-78831, www.grendonguesthouse.co.uk. Hilary and Colin Parker's welcoming guest house, ½ mile NE of centre, on quiet country lane leading to Goyt valley hills. Lounge, breakfast room (background music); terrace, 1-acre garden overlooking golf course. Parking. 5 bedrooms. B&B £32–£45 per person. Dinner £17.

CAMBER East Sussex **Map 2:E5**

The Place, Camber Sands, New Lydd Road, nr Rye, TN31 7RB. *Tel* 01797-227003, www.theplacecambersands.co.uk. Opposite sandy beach: red-roofed, white, single-storey building with seasidey fresh, light interior; managed by Morné Potgieter. Glass-fronted brasserie (local, seasonal produce; soft background jazz); conference facilities. Terrace. 'Exceptionally pleasant staff.' 18 bedrooms (all on ground floor; 1 suitable for ♿). B&B £40–£92.50 per person.

CAMBRIDGE Cambridgeshire **Map 2:B4**

Hotel Felix, Whitehouse Lane, Huntingdon Road, CB3 0LX. *Tel* 01223-277977, www.hotelfelix.co.uk. Extended, late Victorian, yellow brick mansion, 1½ miles from centre, on edge of city: business people's hotel, managed by Shara Ross. 'Clean-cut, style-conscious' decor; 'excellent bathrooms, comfortable beds'. Small lounge, bar, *Graffiti* restaurant (modern Mediterranean cooking; background music); function facilities. Garden, terrace. Parking. 52 bedrooms (4 suitable for ♿). B&B (continental) £87.50–£160 per person.

Hotel du Vin Cambridge, Trumpington Street, CB2 1QA. *Tel* 01223-352646, www.hotelduvin.com. Chic luxury, with interesting architectural features, in central medieval building: 9th hotel in Hotel du Vin group (opened 2007). Managed by Denis Frucot. Library, vaulted cellar bar, bistro (open-style kitchen); terrace. No background music. 41 bedrooms: £67.50–£97.50.

Wallis Farmhouse, 98 Main Street, Hardwick, CB3 7QU. *Tel* 01954-210347, www.wallisfarmhouse.co.uk. Late Georgian farmhouse B&B in village 5 miles W of Cambridge. Communal breakfast. No background music. *Blue Lion Inn* nearby for evening meal. Large garden and meadows adjoining woodland. Parking. 6 bedrooms (all on ground floor, in barn conversion across courtyard from farmhouse, 1 suitable for ♿). B&B £32.50–£50 per person.

CANTERBURY Kent **Map 2:D5**

ABode Canterbury, 30–33 High Street, CT1 2RX. *Tel* 01227-766266, www.abodehotels.co.uk. In pedestrian precinct (directions needed), near cathedral, part of small group of chic hotels developed by chef Michael Caines and Andrew Brownsword. Champagne bar, restaurant, traditional tavern (background music). 77 bedrooms, contemporary, well equipped (LCD TV, DVD-player, broadband; wet room; tuck box); choice of 'comfortable', 'desirable', 'enviable', 'fabulous': £109–£155.

Ebury Hotel, 65–67 New Dover Road, CT1 3DX. *Tel* 01227-768433, www.ebury-hotel.co.uk. Henry Mason's solid Victorian house (*c.* 1840) with original features, near cathedral. Lounge, restaurant (French cuisine); indoor swimming pool. No background music. 2-acre grounds: 1-acre garden. Charlie the labradoodle has his own web page. 15 bedrooms, 2 self-catering cottages. B&B £42.50–£80 per person; D,B&B £52.50–£95.

Magnolia House, 36 St Dunstan's Terrace, CT2 8AX. *Tel* 01227-765121, www.magnoliahousecanterbury.co.uk. Isobelle Leggett's late Georgian guest house in residential street ½ mile from centre. Dinner by arrangement (Nov–Feb). Sitting room, dining room (background music). Walled garden.

Parking. 7 bedrooms (some four-poster beds). B&B £47.50–£77.50 per person. Dinner £35.

CASTLE COMBE Wiltshire **Map 2:D1**

Goulters Mill, Nettleton, GL52 2BD. *Tel* 01249-782555, *email* alison@harvey3512.freeserve.co.uk. Secluded 17th-century mill cottage, in 25-acre wooded valley with stream, ¾ mile W of village. 2 sitting rooms (open fire), dining room (evening meal by arrangement, £25). No background music. Charming English cottage garden. 3 bedrooms. B&B £35–£40 per person.

CHELTENHAM Gloucestershire **Map 3:D5**

The Big Sleep, Wellington Street, GL50 1XZ. *Tel* 01242-696999, www.thebigsleephotel.com. Bright, shiny, low-cost accommodation in former Inland Revenue building in centre (sister hotel of *The Big Sleep*, Cardiff, *qv*). Lobby with seating (background music); breakfast room. Parking. 62 bedrooms (some suitable for ♿). B&B (continental) £42.50–£60 per person.

The Townhouse, 12–14 Pittville Lawn, GL52 2BD. *Tel* 01242-221922, www.cheltenhamtownhouse.com. Adam and Jayne Lillywhite's smart, modern B&B, decorated in cream, caramel and coffee shades. 10 mins' walk from Pump Rooms. 'Good location; comfortable, quiet.' Lift. Lounge, bar, dining room (background music); sun deck. Parking. 22 rooms (5 serviced apartments opposite). B&B £39–£70 per person.

CHICHESTER West Sussex **Map 2:E3**

Abelands Barn, Bognor Road, Merston, PO20 1DY. *Tel* 01243-533826, www.abelandsbarn.co.uk. Converted flint barn (1859), 2 miles S of town. Living room, photographic gallery, dining room. No background music. Lavish breakfast. Large garden. 'Comfortable bed, corner bath; amazing views over farmland and South Downs.' Justin Geri and Angela Jarvis also own the *King's Head* pub (¼ mile). 5 bedrooms. B&B £30–£70 per person.

The Ship, North Street, PO19 1NH. *Tel* 01243-778000, www.shiphotelchichester.co.uk. Only hotel within old city walls: Grade II listed. Refurbishment under way by new owner Matthew Wolfman (see also *The Place*, Camber, Shortlist, *The Bell*, Sandwich, main entry). Lift. Lounge, bar, brasserie; background music; conference/wedding facilities. 37 bedrooms (on 3 floors; 1 family). B&B £57.50–£89 per person. Set menu from £12.50.

CHRISTCHURCH Dorset **Map 2:E2**

Waterford Lodge, 87 Bure Lane, Friars Cliff, Mudeford, BH23 4DN. *Tel* 01425-272948, www.bw-waterfordlodge.co.uk. Family-owned, a 4-min stroll from natural coastline, 2 miles SE of Christchurch: 'Perfect example of how to run a small hotel' (Best Western). Lounge, bar (light meals; background music), 'fantastic', garden-facing restaurant; free Wi-Fi; conference facilities; free swimming at local leisure centre. 18 bedrooms (3 on ground floor). B&B £47–£70 per person.

COOKHAM DEAN Berkshire **Map 2:D3**

The Inn on the Green, The Old Cricket Common, SL6 9NZ. *Tel* 01628-482638, www.theinnonthegreen.com. Chef Garry Hollihead and Mark Fuller's restaurant-with-rooms, in 1-acre grounds, 3 miles NW of Maidenhead. Stylish mix of sparse modern with plush. Lounge/bar, 3 dining rooms (background music); alfresco dining in courtyard in summer. Food 'excellent and well presented'. Hot tub. Parking. 9 bedrooms (4 on ground floor). B&B £55–£80 per person.

COVENTRY Warwickshire **Map 2:B2**

Coombe Abbey, Brinklow Road, Binley, CV3 2AB. *Tel* 02476-450450, www.coombeabbey.com. Just outside city, in Coombe Country Park: 16th-century Cistercian abbey turned into 'out-of-the-ordinary' hotel. 'Eccentric collections'; ecclesiastical architecture, bishop's tomb; sculptures; ornate furniture. Gothic reception, bar, restaurant; banqueting hall; background music; function/wedding facilities. 500-acre park: moat, formal gardens. 83 'bedchambers'. B&B from £80 per person.

CUCKFIELD West Sussex **Map 2:E4**

Ockenden Manor, Ockenden Lane, RH17 5LD. *Tel* 01444-416111, www.hshotels.co.uk. 'Blissfully quiet' manor house (Elizabethan, with Victorian additions), 20 mins' drive from Gatwick airport. 'Nice atmosphere; a good hotel all round.' Bar, wood-panelled restaurant with stained-glass windows, stone fireplace. No background music. Conference/wedding facilities. 9-acre garden. 22 bedrooms (some with four-poster). B&B £82.50–£170 per person.

DARLINGTON Co. Durham **Map 4:C4**

Headlam Hall, nr Gainford, DL2 3HA. *Tel* 01325-730238, www.headlamhall.co.uk. In lower Teesdale hamlet, in 200-acre farmland: Robinson family's 'welcoming, excellent-value' hotel: rambling building, half Jacobean, half 18th-century. 3 lounges, bar, restaurant (background music in evening). Spa (pool, sauna, gym, treatment rooms); billiard room; conference/function facilities. Terraces; 4-acre walled garden: lake, tennis, 9-hole golf course, croquet. 40 bedrooms (in mews or coach house; some on ground floor). B&B £55–£85 per person.

DARTMOUTH Devon **Map 1:D4**

Browns, 27–29 Victoria Road, TQ6 9RT. *Tel* 01803-832572, www.brownshoteldartmouth.co.uk. Formerly *The Little Admiral*, informal town house hotel, refurbished in modern style by Clare and James Brown. Sitting area, bar, *Tapas* restaurant (Tues–Sat; background music). 10 bedrooms. B&B £42.50–£85 per person.

Dart Marina, Sandquay Road, TQ6 9PH. *Tel* 01803-832580, www.dartmarina.com. Stylish hotel on waterfront overlooking marina. Contemporary decor. Lift. 2 lounges, 2 bars, *River* restaurant (terrace: alfresco dining), *Wildfire* bistro; background 'chill-out' music. Spa (pool, gym, treatments). Parking. Pebble beach. 49 bedrooms (all with river view, some with balcony or French window; 1 suitable for ♿). B&B £77.50–£145 per person; D,B&B from £100.

DEDHAM Essex **Map 2:C5**

Dedham Hall, Brook Street, CO7 6AD. *Tel* 01206-323027, www.dedhamhall.demon.co.uk. Cluster of old buildings (15th-century cottage, 18th-century house, Dutch barn) run as guest house/restaurant/art school by Wendy and Jim Sarton. 2 lounges, 2 bars, restaurant. No background music. 18 bedrooms (13 in annexe for painting holidays). B&B £47.50–£55 per person; D,B&B £75–£82.50.

Maison Talbooth, Stratford Road, CO7 6HN. *Tel* 01206-322367, www.milsomhotels.com. Paul Milsom's Victorian mansion, in tranquil location overlooking Stour valley, provides accommodation for his restaurant *Le Talbooth*, and hotel/brasserie, *milsom's*, both nearby. 'Attractive' large drawing room, breakfast room. No background music. 'Efficient, unobtrusive staff.' 3-acre grounds. 13 bedrooms. B&B £85–£250 per person. Closed Oct 2007–Apr 2008 for development (3 new suites, breakfast room, treatment room, swimming pool).

The Sun Inn, High Street, CO7 6DF. *Tel* 01206-323351, www.thesuninndedham.com. Piers Baker's yellow-painted old coaching inn with modern enhancements; informal atmosphere. Seasonal, locally produced food; picnics provided; on-site fruit-and-veg shop, *Victoria's Plums*. Lounge, bar, dining room; background music. Covered terrace; walled garden. 5 bedrooms. B&B (continental) £42.50–£65 per person.

DERBY Derbyshire **Map 3:B6**

Mickleover Court, Etwall Road, Mickleover, DE3 0XX. *Tel* 01332-521234, www.menzies-hotels.co.uk. Large, modern hotel (Menzies group), 4 miles from centre. Designed around central atrium. Glass lift. 2 bars, brasserie; indoor leisure facilities (pool, gym, etc); background music sometimes; extensive conference/function facilities. Good access throughout for ♿. 99 bedrooms. B&B £77–£144 per person.

The Stuart, 119 London Road, DE1 2QR. *Tel* 01332-340633, www.thestuart.com. Near centre and station: large, privately owned commercial hotel, renovated in contemporary style: dark wood, designer fabrics. Bar, *XS* restaurant; background music; conference/wedding facilities. Parking. 90 bedrooms: double £89–£109, suite £119. Breakfast from £9.95.

DOVER Kent **Map 2:D5**

Loddington House, 14 East Cliff, CT16 1LX. *Tel* 01304-201947, www.loddingtonhousehotel.co.uk. Seafront Regency Grade II listed guest house, run by owners Kathy and Robert Cupper. Harbour views; convenient for ferry terminals; 10 mins' walk from centre. Lounge (balcony sea view), dining room (evening meal by arrangement, £25). No background music. Small garden. 6 bedrooms (rear ones quietest). B&B £32.50–£55 per person. Dinner £25.

DURHAM Co. Durham **Map 4:B4**

Cathedral View, 212 Gilesgate, DH1 1QN. *Tel* 0191-386 9566, www.cathedralview.co.uk. 'Small, unpretentious' Georgian town house, 10 mins' riverside walk from cathedral and castle. 'Lovely view from the back.' Breakfast room. No background music. Garden. Good restaurants nearby. 6 bedrooms (all redecorated in 2007). B&B £30–£60 per person.

DUXFORD Cambridgeshire **Map 2:C4**

Duxford Lodge, Ickleton Road, CB2 4RT. *Tel* 01223-836444, www.duxfordlodgehotel.co.uk. Off M11, near Imperial War Museum: 1900s red brick house (some motorway noise). Cambridge 20 mins' drive N, Stansted 20 mins' drive S. Traditional decor. Lounge, bar (pictures of aeroplanes and fighter pilots), *Le Paradis* restaurant; function/wedding facilities. No background music. Garden. 15 bedrooms (4 in garden annexe). B&B £64–£88 per person.

EASTBOURNE East Sussex **Map 2:E4**

Grand Hotel, King Edwards Parade, BN21 4EQ. *Tel* 01323-412345, www.grandeastbourne.com. Traditional 5-star, 19th-century seafront 'white palace'. 'Vast public rooms; high-ceilinged bedrooms; general air of pampering.' Live band on Sat; monthly teatime Palm Court quartet; no background music. Children welcomed (playroom, carers, high teas). 3 lounges, bar, 'excellent' *Mirabelle* and *Garden* restaurants; conference/function facilities; health spa; indoor and outdoor swimming pools; garden:

putting, etc. Parking. 152 bedrooms (many with sea view). B&B £90–£165 per person.

EXETER Devon **Map 1:C5**

ABode Exeter (formerly *The Royal Clarence*), Cathedral Yard, EX1 1HD. *Tel* 01392-319955, www.abodehotels.co.uk. Boutique hotel in city centre, first in the ABode group (Andrew Brownsword and Exeter-born chef Michael Caines). Imaginative styling. 2 bars, restaurant; background music; fitness spa. 53 bedrooms. B&B £62.50–£125 per person.

Hotel Barcelona, Magdalen Street, EX2 4HY. *Tel* 01392-281000, www.aliashotels.com. Former Victorian eye hospital near cathedral green, imaginatively converted by Alias Hotels group. Youthful style. Lounge, 2 private dining rooms, *Kino* cocktail bar, conservatory-style *Café Paradiso* (Mediterranean menu), terrace; background jazz. Walled 1-acre garden. 46 bedrooms ('very clean; water very hot'), some suitable for ♿): £95–£115. Breakfast £11.95.

FALMOUTH Cornwall **Map 1:E2**

Green Lawns, Western Terrace, TR11 4QJ. *Tel* 01326-312734, www.greenlawnshotel.com. Ivy-clad, privately owned hotel in style of small French château, near centre. Views across Falmouth Bay. 3 lounges, 2 bars, *Garras* restaurant (background music); leisure/conference/function facilities (indoor swimming pool, sauna, whirlpool). Award-winning garden: patio area. 39 bedrooms (11 on ground floor). B&B £55–£115 per person.

The Greenbank, Harbourside, TR11 2SR. *Tel* 01326-312440, www.greenbank-hotel.com. 10 mins' walk from centre: white hotel (said to be first in this Cornish port) by water's edge. 'Excellent room, small balcony, great harbour views.' Lounge, bar, *Harbourside* restaurant; background swing/jazz. Private quay, decking area. 58 bedrooms ('tastefully refurbished'). B&B £52.50–£130 per person; D,B&B £78–£157.

Penmere Manor, Mongleath Road, TR11 4PN. *Tel* 01326-211411, www.penmere.co.uk. In subtropical gardens and woodland, 1 mile from sandy beaches and port: white-painted seaside hotel (Best Western). Lounge, bar, restaurant (background music); conference facilities; gym, solarium, beauty treatments; indoor and outdoor swimming pools. 37 bedrooms. B&B £69.50–£94.50 per person; D,B&B from £94.50. On the market as the *Guide* went to press.

FOLKESTONE Kent **Map 2:E5**

Hotel Relish, 4 Augusta Gardens, CT20 2RR. *Tel* 01303-850952, www.hotelrelish.co.uk. Now owned by Sarah and Chris van Dyke: B&B 'that

successfully combines modern design with a Victorian building', in West End, ¼ mile from centre. Lounge, breakfast room (Radio 2 played); Wi-Fi, broadband; unlimited coffee/tea with cake; small terrace. Direct access to Augusta Gardens. Parking. 10 bedrooms. B&B £42.50–£60 per person.
Sandgate Hotel, 8–9 Wellington Terrace, The Esplanade, CT20 3DY. *Tel* 01303-220444, www.sandgatehotel.com. Owned by Lois McKinnon and Peter Slade, opposite pebble beach ('great sea views'), between Hythe and Folkestone, 10 mins' drive from Eurotunnel terminal. 19th-century facade; modern interior. Lounge, bar (music on Sun), restaurant; floodlit terrace. 15 rooms. B&B (continental) £47.50–£80 per person. English breakfast £9.95.

GATWICK West Sussex — Map 2:D4

Langshott Manor, Langshott, RH6 9LN. *Tel* 01293-786680, www.alexanderhotels.co.uk. Classic timber-framed Tudor house, now luxury hotel, in 3-acre garden (ancient moat). 5 mins' drive from airport. Lounge, *Mulberry* restaurant (background music); conference/wedding facilities. 22 bedrooms (some in mews). B&B £115–£320 per person.
Latchetts Cottage, Norwood Hill, nr Horley, RH16 0ET. *Tel* 01293-862831, www.latchettscottage.co.uk. In rural setting 3 miles from Gatwick but off flight path: David Lees's small B&B, 2 converted 1820s farmworkers' cottages. Residents' lounge. Wi-Fi. No background music. Cottage-style garden. Local pub for meals, 200 yds. Parking. Free one-way airport transfer (by arrangement). 3 bedrooms (plain; pine furniture). B&B £27.50–£35 per person.
Lawn Guest House, 30 Massetts Road, Horley, RH6 7DF. *Tel* 01293-775751, www.lawnguesthouse.co.uk. Carole and Adrian Grinsted's B&B: large Victorian house, 1½ miles from airport, 2 mins' walk from Horley centre. Lounge, breakfast room. No background music. Secluded garden. Long-term parking (£3.50 per night)/transfer service. 12 bedrooms (some family). B&B £30–£50 per person.

GLASTONBURY Somerset — Map 1:B6

Number Three, 3 Magdalene Street, BA6 9EW. *Tel* 01458-832129, www.numberthree.co.uk. Patricia Redmond's Georgian town house B&B, in 1-acre walled garden by abbey ruins. Breakfast room. No background music. Parking. 5 bedrooms (1 on ground floor; 3 in *Garden House*). B&B £55–£95 per person.

GRANTHAM Lincolnshire — Map 2:A3

Allington Manor, Bottesford Road, NG32 2DH. *Tel* 01400-282574, www.allingtonmanor.co.uk. Grand Jacobean house (Grade II listed).

Impressive red hall (2 large fireplaces), galleried landing (grand piano), drawing room, dining/breakfast room; display of arms and armour; background music. Wedding facilities. 1-acre garden. 3 bedrooms. B&B £55–£95 per person. Dinner £27.50.

Angel and Royal, High Street, NG31 6PN. *Tel* 01476-565816, www.angelandroyal.co.uk. Ancient inn (1203), once hostel for Brotherhood of Knights Templar, and visited by royalty including King John, Richard III and Charles I (as well as Cromwell). Lounge, *Angel* bar (background jazz), *King's Room* restaurant, *Simply Bertie's* bistro; conference/function/wedding facilities. 29 bedrooms (1 on ground floor). B&B £40–£68 per person. Dinner £26.95.

GREAT BIRCHAM Norfolk — Map 2:A5

The King's Head, Lynn Road, PE31 6RJ. *Tel* 01485-578265, www.the-kings-head-bircham.co.uk. Handsome Victorian inn, extended and refurbished, with contemporary interior, 'welcoming staff'. 8 miles to Brancaster Beach; Sandringham close by. Lounge, bar, restaurant (brasserie and *à la carte* menu); background music; function facilities; courtyard. 12 bedrooms (king-size beds, play station, CD- and DVD-player, Internet). B&B £62.50–£100 per person; D,B&B from £82.50 per person.

GREAT CHESTERFORD Essex — Map 2:C4

The Crown House, London Road, CB10 1NY. *Tel* 01799-530515, www.crownhousehotel.com. Grade II listed building in large garden, 5 mins' walk from village station; 11 miles N of Cambridge. 'Kind staff.' Lounge, bar, restaurant; background music; weddings/functions held. 22 bedrooms (10 in stable block; some on ground floor): single £74.50, double £99.50, suite £120–£145. Breakfast £5. Dinner £25.

HARROGATE North Yorkshire — Map 4:D4

Ascot House, 53 Kings Road, HG1 5HG. *Tel* 01423-531005, www.ascothouse.com. In handsome Victorian building an easy walk from centre, Stephen Johnson's personally run hotel: 'comfortable; attentive staff and management'. Lounge, bar, restaurant (background music); function facilities; themed dinners: *Fawlty Towers*, etc. 18 bedrooms. B&B £47.50–£75 per person; D,B&B £74–£95.50.

Grants, Swan Road, HG1 2SS. *Tel* 01423-560666, www.grantshotel-harrogate.com. Pam Grant's central, 'notably good-value' hotel in Victorian terrace. Lift. Lounge, *Harry Grant's* bar, *Chimney Pots* bistro (background music); business/function facilities. Patio garden. Leisure club affiliation. Parking. 42 bedrooms. B&B £47.50–£130 per person.

HELMSLEY North Yorkshire **Map 4:C4**

No. 54, 54 Bondgate, YO62 5EZ. *Tel* 01439-771533, www.no54.co.uk. Near North Yorkshire Moors national park: Lizzie Would's town house B&B. Simple decor: crisp white linen, pine furniture, York stone floors; open fires. No background music. Good breakfasts (continental can be delivered to bedroom in a hamper). Dinners (from £28) and picnics available. 4 bedrooms (around sunny courtyard). B&B £30–£45 per person.

HEXHAM Northumberland **Map 4:B3**

The Hermitage, Swinburne, NE48 4DG. *Tel* 01434-681248, *email* katie.stewart@themeet.co.uk. Approached through grand arch and up long drive: B&B with 'true country house atmosphere', Katie and Simon Stewart's rural family home, 7½ miles N of Hexham. Drawing room, dining room. No background music. 4-acre grounds: terrace, tennis. 3 bedrooms. B&B £45 per person.

HOARWITHY Herefordshire **Map 3:D4**

Aspen House, HR2 6QP. *Tel* 01432-840353, www.aspenhouse.net. In Wye valley village 4 miles NW of Ross-on-Wye: guest accommodation in Sally Lawrence and Rob Elliott's 18th-century farmhouse. Emphasis on local, seasonal produce (some Polish influence). 'If only all things could be this good. A true find.' Lounge, decked area. No background music. ¾-acre garden. 4 bedrooms. B&B £35–£40 per person; D,B&B £62.50–£67.50.

HOLKHAM Norfolk **Map 2:A5**

The Victoria at Holkham, Park Road, NR23 1RG. *Tel* 01328-711008, www.victoriaatholkham.co.uk. On Earl of Leicester's Holkham estate, 2 miles W of Wells-next-the-Sea: former pub refurbished in colonial style. Ornate Indian furniture, vibrant colours. 'Well placed for walks and drives to some of the best bird places in the country.' Lounge area, 3 bars, restaurant; background music. 3-acre grounds: children's play area, barbecue. 10 bedrooms plus further accommodation in 3 'follies'. B&B £60–£130 per person.

HOLMFIRTH West Yorkshire **Map 4:E3**

Sunnybank, 78 Upperthong Lane, HD9 3BQ. *Tel* 01484-684857, www.sunnybankguesthouse.co.uk. Peter and Anne White's 'welcoming' B&B in Victorian gentleman's residence on hillside: views over Holme valley. 'Very good breakfast with excellent fresh local produce' in oak-panelled room (fire in winter; background music if requested). 2-acre wooded gardens. 3 bedrooms. B&B £32.50–£70 per person.

HOVE East Sussex **Map 2:E4**

The Claremont, 13 Second Avenue, BN3 2LL. *Tel* 01273-735161, www.theclaremont.eu. Boutique hotel in Victorian villa just off seafront. Black-and-white checked entrance floor, high ceilings, chandeliers, bright colours (lots of red); exhibitions by local artists. Drawing room, study, breakfast room (full English or vegetarian breakfast; Radio 2 played); conference/wedding facilities. ½-acre walled garden. 11 bedrooms (2 with four-poster). B&B £55–£90 per person.

HUDDERSFIELD West Yorkshire **Map 4:E3**

Three Acres Inn & Restaurant, Roydhouse, Shelley, HD8 8LR. *Tel* 01484-602606, www.3acres.com. In Pennine countryside, 5 miles SE of centre: Neil Truelove and Brian Orme's smart old roadside drovers' inn. *Seafood Bar*, 2 dining rooms; live/occasional background music. Small garden: dining terrace. Grocery. 20 bedrooms (10 in adjacent cottages). B&B £50–£70 per person. Dinner £34.95.

HULL East Yorkshire **Map 4:D5**

Willerby Manor, Well Lane, Willerby, HU10 6ER. *Tel* 01482-652616, www.willerbymanor.co.uk. In rural setting 4 miles NW of centre: Alexandra Townend's Edwardian mansion (Best Western). *Everglades* brasserie, *Icon* restaurant; health club (swimming pool, gym, etc), crèche; extensive business/function facilities (5 function rooms can have background music). 3-acre gardens. Parking. 63 bedrooms. B&B £59–£92.50 per person. Dinner £35.

HUNSTANTON Norfolk **Map 2:A5**

The Neptune Inn, 85 Old Hunstanton Road, PE36 6HZ. *Tel* 01485-532122, www.theneptune.co.uk. Paul and Hilary Berriff's 'welcoming' 19th-century coaching inn on A149, revamped with 'New England' interior and nautical touches. 'Clean, comfortable; good food.' Lounge, bar; background jazz; restaurant (daily fresh local produce). 7 bedrooms (small). B&B £35–£50 per person; D,B&B £50–£80.

HUNTINGDON Cambridgeshire **Map 2:B4**

The Old Bridge, 1 High Street, PE29 3TQ. *Tel* 01480-424300, www.huntsbridge.com. Ivy-clad 18th-century building overlooking River Ouse: part of John Hoskins's small Huntsbridge group of inns. 'Elegant reception areas; lovely, restful restaurant with oval skylight' (popular with locals); patio (outside dining); business centre. No background music. Garden. Parking. Busy roads nearby. 24 bedrooms (2 on ground floor). B&B £62.50–£120 per person. Full alc £30.

KESWICK Cumbria **Map 4: inset C2**

Dalegarth House, Portinscale, CA12 5RQ. *Tel* 017687-72817, www.dalegarth-house.co.uk. Bruce and Pauline Jackson are chef/proprietors of this 'pristine' country hotel: Edwardian house in village 1 mile W of Keswick. 'Out-of-this-world views. Excellent food and service.' 'Standards never drop.' Generous Cumbrian breakfast. Traditional decor. Lounge, bar (quiet background music), dining room. Garden. Parking. 10 bedrooms. B&B £37–£40 per person; D,B&B £52–£55.

Lyzzick Hall, Underskiddaw, CA12 4PY. *Tel* 017687-72277, www.lyzzickhall.co.uk. Former home of textile merchant, now country hotel with Spanish owner, Mr Fernandez. 'Glorious setting' (views of mountains) on lower slopes of Skiddaw, 1½ miles N of town. 'Good food, professional staff.' 2 lounges, bar, restaurant (traditional English/Spanish); background music; small indoor swimming pool, whirlpool, sauna. 'Very pretty garden.' 31 bedrooms (sound insulation not always perfect). B&B £58–£73 per person; D,B&B £85–£90.

KING'S LYNN Norfolk **Map 2:A4**

Congham Hall, Lynn Road, Grimston, PE32 1AH. *Tel* 01485-600250, www.conghamhallhotel.co.uk. Georgian country house (von Essen hotels), on large estate 6½ miles E of King's Lynn: 'exceptionally peaceful situation'. Front rooms face walled garden and cricket pitch; back ones overlook lawns and parkland. Lounge, *Orangery* restaurant; terrace. No background music. Herb garden (over 700 varieties); clay-pigeon shooting. 14 bedrooms. B&B £80–£182.50 per person; D,B&B £122.50–£225.

KINGSBRIDGE Devon **Map 1:D4**

Buckland Tout-Saints, Goveton, TQ7 2DS. *Tel* 01548-853055, www.tout-saints.co.uk. Luxurious William and Mary manor house in 'glorious' rural setting 2½ miles NE of Kingsbridge. Wood-panelled public rooms, open fires; traditional bedrooms, contemporary bathrooms. 4½-acre garden. Lounge, bar, 2 attractive dining rooms; background music; function/wedding facilities. 16 bedrooms. B&B £67.50–£147.50 per person.

Thurlestone Hotel, Thurlestone, TQ7 3NN. *Tel* 01548-560382, www.thurlestone.co.uk. Large, 'well-organised', family-friendly hotel 4 miles SW of Kingsbridge in 19-acre subtropical gardens. 9-hole golf course adjacent. 'Good dinners; breakfasts exceptionally good.' Lounges, bar, *Margaret Amelia* restaurant; function facilities; leisure complex and beauty spa (indoor and outdoor heated swimming pools, tennis, squash, badminton). No background music. Coastal walks close by. 64 bedrooms. B&B £87–£148 per person.

KNUTSFORD Cheshire — Map 4:E3

Belle Epoque, 60 King Street, WA16 6DT. *Tel* 01565-633060, www.thebelleepoque.com. Owned and run by Mooney family for over 30 years: brasserie-with-rooms in commuter town 18 miles SW of Manchester. Bar, Art Nouveau dining room (original Venetian glass floor, marble-pillared alcoves, statuary, lavish drapes, tall glass vases, cosy recesses); background music ('easy listening'/jazz) throughout. Mediterranean roof garden. 6 bedrooms. B&B from £88 per person. Dinner £35.

Longview, 51 and 55 Manchester Road, WA16 0LX. *Tel* 01565-632119, www.longviewhotel.com. In two Victorian houses: Lulu Ahooie's popular hotel looking across busy road to heath. Cellar bar, *Stuffed Olive* restaurant, recently smartly redecorated: 'enjoyable' menu (eastern Mediterranean dishes and 'British standbys'); background music. 32 bedrooms (suites have lounge and private garden). B&B £49.50–£149 per person.

LEEDS West Yorkshire — Map 4:D4

Malmaison, 1 Swinegate, LS1 4AG. *Tel* 0113-398 1000, www.malmaison.com. Former bus/train administration building on River Aire, in Calls district, now buzzy city-centre hotel. Bedrooms in aubergine and plum tones; brown hues, wood and leather downstairs. Bar with cosy alcoves, brasserie (vaulted ceiling; 'good food'); background music; meeting rooms; wheelchair lift; high-tech gym. 100 bedrooms. B&B £49.50–£99.50 per person.

Quebecs, 9 Quebec Street, LS1 2HA. *Tel* 0113-244 8989, www.theetongroup.com. Luxury town house B&B in Grade II listed Victorian red brick building (former Leeds and County Liberal Club), 2 mins' walk from station. Grand oak staircase, stained-glass window, panelled lounge, library, bright breakfast room, conservatory; 24-hour room service. No background music. 'Attentive staff.' 45 bedrooms (some small). B&B £67.50–£122.50 per person.

Woodlands, Gelderd Road, Gildersome, LS27 7LY. *Tel* 0113-238 1488, www.woodlandsleeds.co.uk. Textile mill owner's residence in landscaped gardens, 6 miles S of centre, now contemporary, 'quality' hotel owned by Rob Foulston and Tom Horsforth (Tomahawk group). Lounge, bar (all-day snack menu), 3 dining rooms; gym, swimming pool; 'chill-out' background music throughout. Terrace. House parties catered for. 17 bedrooms (some on ground floor). B&B £69.50–£139 per person. Full alc £45.

LEOMINSTER Herefordshire — Map 3:C4

Ford Abbey, Pudleston, HR6 0RZ. *Tel* 01568-760700, www.fordabbey.co.uk. Beautiful half-timbered, medieval farmstead, once part of Leominster

Abbey, luxuriously converted by Dr Albert Heijn. Lounge, library/TV room, restaurant; background music; courtyard; heated swimming pool, fitness suite. 320-acre landscaped grounds: large patio areas, duck pond, farm animals, woodland. 9 bedrooms (some suitable for ♿; 4 barn lodges). B&B £65–£99.50 per person.

LEWES East Sussex **Map 2:E4**

Shelleys, High Street, BN7 1XS. *Tel* 01273-472361, www.shelleys-hotel.com. Once owned by poet's family, now company-owned, managed by 'hands-on' Graeme Coles: 16th-century, 'elegant' yellow manor house. Drawing room, writing room, lounge, bar, restaurant; classical background music; function facilities. Terrace ('lovely lunch'). 1-acre secluded garden. Parking. 19 bedrooms. B&B £60–£125 per person; D,B&B £92–£157.

LICHFIELD Staffordshire **Map 2:A2**

Swinfen Hall, Swinfen, WS14 9RE. *Tel* 01543-481494, www.swinfenhallhotel.co.uk. Helen and Victor Wiser's Grade II listed mid-18th-century manor house in 95-acre estate in rolling countryside 2 miles S of Lichfield on A38, 20 mins' drive from Birmingham and NEC. 'Inviting; good food; beautiful furniture; helpful staff.' Period decoration in 1st-floor bedrooms; 2nd-floor rooms more contemporary. Lounge, cocktail lounge, bar, *Four Seasons* restaurant, banqueting hall; conference/wedding facilities; classical background music. 6-acre formal gardens: terrace, walled vegetable garden: croquet, tennis, ornamental ponds; 45-acre deer park. 17 bedrooms. B&B (£5 supplement for cooked breakfast) £72.50–£155 per person.

LINCOLN Lincolnshire **Map 4:E5**

Castle Hotel, Westgate, LN1 3AS. *Tel* 01522-538801, www.castlehotel.net. Near cathedral and castle, in historic centre (ask for directions). 2 small lounges, bar, *Knights* restaurant (background music). Parking. 19 bedrooms, 'modest, but clean and comfortable' (some rooms in attic). B&B £47–£90 per person.

Hillcrest Hotel, 15 Lindum Terrace, LN2 5RT. *Tel* 01522-510182, www.hillcrest-hotel.com. Victorian vicarage with 'lovely views' over parkland; cathedral 7 mins' walk. 'Caring' owner, Jennifer Bennett, and staff, supporters of British Hedgehog Preservation Society. Lounge/bar (background music), conservatory restaurant (Lincolnshire produce; closed Sun); conference facilities. Small, sloping garden. 14 bedrooms. B&B £44.50–£69 per person; D,B&B £59–£89.

LITTLE SHELFORD Cambridgeshire **Map 2:C4**

Purlins, 12 High Street, CB22 5ES. *Tel* 01223-842843, *email* dgallh@-ndirect.co.uk. In picturesque village beside the River Cam, 4½ miles S of Cambridge: Arts and Crafts-style B&B, built 1978 by owners, musician David Hindley and wife, Olga. Conservatory sitting room, vaulted dining room, gallery. No background music. 'Excellent breakfast.' 2-acre mature woodland, meadow, lawn, wildlife. 4 bedrooms. B&B £33-£54 per person.

LIVERPOOL Merseyside **Map 4:E2**

Malmaison, William Jessop Way, Princes Dock, L3 1QW. *Tel* 0151-229 5000, www.malmaison-liverpool.com. In regenerated area of city: ultra-stylish, 11-storey, purpose-built hotel with river views. Black-and-purple decor. *Plum* bar, brasserie; gymtonic; background music; function facilities. 131 bedrooms (wet-room showers; some circular baths). B&B from £72.50 per person.

Thornton Hall, Neston Road, Thornton Hough, Wirral, CH63 1JF. *Tel* 0151-336 3938, www.thorntonhallhotel.com. In hamlet midway between Liverpool (20 mins) and Chester: owned by Thompson family: former home of 19th-century shipping magnate. Many original features. Lounge, bar, restaurant; function/wedding/conference facilities; swimming pool, health club, beauty spa; background music. 7-acre garden. 63 bedrooms (most in modern annexe): £119–£305.

LOOE Cornwall **Map 1:D3**

Fieldhead Hotel, Portuan Road, Hannafore, PL13 2DR. *Tel* 01503-262689, www.fieldheadhotel.co.uk. Built 1896 as private residence, in elevated position 15 mins' walk from centre, now owned by Julian Peek. Traditional ambience. Lounge with huge bow window (views across Looe Bay), bar, *Horizons* restaurant specialising in seafood; 'gentle' classical background music. 1½-acre garden: terrace, swimming pool. 16 bedrooms. B&B £36–£75 per person; D,B&B £60–£96.

LORTON Cumbria **Map 4: inset C2**

Winder Hall, Cockermouth, Low Lorton, CA13 9UP. *Tel* 01900-85107, www.winderhall.co.uk. 15 mins' drive from Keswick: owner/chef Nick Lawler's 17th-century manor house, in grounds sloping down to River Cocker. Lounge, restaurant (oak-panelling, mullioned windows; quiet background music); summer house with sauna, hot tub. 7 bedrooms (fell views). D,B&B £71–£101 per person.

LOWESTOFT Suffolk **Map 2:B6**

Ivy House, Ivy Lane, off Beccles Road, Oulton Broad, NR33 8HY. *Tel* 01502-501353, www.ivyhousecountryhotel.co.uk. Converted farm buildings near Norfolk Broads national park. Lounge, conservatory, 18th-century, thatched, beamed *Crooked Barn* restaurant; background music; function/conference facilities; courtyard. 4-acre garden (2 lily ponds, summer house), surrounded by farmland. 19 bedrooms. B&B £56–£95 per person.

LUDLOW Shropshire **Map 3:C4**

Overton Grange, Hereford Road, SY8 4AD. *Tel* 01584-873500, www.overtongrangehotel.com. Owned by Franck Choblet-Metzo (manager Tracey Flowers), with smart, contemporary interior: Edwardian manor house 1 mile S of Ludlow. 'Comfortable public areas.' 'Smashing views.' Lounge, library, breakfast room, *Plum Room* restaurant. No background music. 2½-acre garden. 14 bedrooms. B&B £70–£105 per person.

LYME REGIS Dorset **Map 1:C6**

Alexandra Hotel, Pound Street, DT7 3HZ. *Tel* 01297-442010, www.hotelalexandra.co.uk. Long-established (built 1735) hotel, 'an institution', in 'excellent' position (fine sea views) above The Cobb. Owned by Haskins family for 25 years; daughter Kathryn Richards now in charge, carrying out total refurbishment. Drawing room, conservatory, bar, restaurant (new chef, Ian Grant; light classical background music). 1½-acre garden. Town 100 yds; beach 300 yds. Parking. 26 bedrooms. B&B £50–£75 per person; D,B&B £60–£75.

LYMINGTON Hampshire **Map 2:E2**

Wistaria House, 32 St Thomas Street, SO41 9NE. *Tel* 01590-688090, www.wistaria.org.uk. In centre: Jonathan Crouch's wistaria-clad Georgian town house (Grade II listed), transformed, after over 60 years as doctor's surgery, into smart, modern restaurant-with-rooms. Bar, restaurant; new terrace for alfresco dining; background music. 3 bedrooms (1st floor). B&B £32.50–£60 per person; D,B&B from £67.50.

LYNMOUTH Devon **Map 1:B4**

Shelley's Hotel, 8 Watersmeet Road, EX35 6EP. *Tel* 01598-753219, www.shelleyshotel.co.uk. Jane Becker and Richard Briden's 18th-century cottage B&B in centre (Percy Bysshe Shelley honeymooned here in summer 1812). Views over Lynmouth Bay. Lounge, bar, conservatory breakfast room. No background music. 11 bedrooms (1 on ground floor). B&B £35–£70 per person.

LYTHAM Lancashire **Map 4:D2**

Clifton Arms, West Beach, FY58 5QJ. *Tel* 01253-739898, www.cliftonarms-lytham.com. Traditional seafront hotel opposite Lytham green. Lounge/cocktail bar, library/TV room, *The West Beach* restaurant, *Churchills* brasserie; background music; conference/banqueting facilities. Small garden. Parking. 48 bedrooms. B&B £67.50–£130 per person.

MAIDENHEAD Berkshire **Map 2:D3**

Fredrick's, Shoppenhangers Road, SL6 2PZ. *Tel* 01628-581000, www.fredricks-hotel.co.uk. Lösel family's lavish hotel with luxury spa, overlooking Maidenhead golf club. Lounge, bar; background music; restaurant; conference/function facilities; terrace. 2½-acre landscaped gardens: swimming pool, sculptures. Parking. 34 bedrooms (chocolates, fruit, 'the latest technology'). B&B £147.50–£215 per person.

MANCHESTER **Map 4:E3**

Bewley's Hotel, Outwood Lane, Manchester Airport, M90 4HL. *Tel* 0161-498 0333, www.bewleyshotels.com. Large, modern chain hotel with triple glazing. 10 mins' walk to Terminal 1, 20 mins to Terminal 2. Sitting area, bar, brasserie; Wi-Fi; business facilities. No background music. 226 bedrooms (some suitable for ♿): £79. Breakfast from £6.95.

Great John Street Hotel, Great John Street, Castlefield, M3 4FD. *Tel* 0161-831 3211, www.greatjohnstreet.co.uk. Converted Victorian schoolhouse on quiet side street off Deansgate: now a hotel, smartly furnished while retaining school origins. Some mezzanine-level rooms. Lounge, *Oyster* bar, *School Yard* terrace; background music. Roof garden; hot tub; small gym; function facilities. 30 bedrooms: double £235–£425. Breakfast £12.40–£14.50.

The Lowry, 50 Dearmans Place, Chapel Wharf, M3 5LH. *Tel* 0161-827 4000, www.thelowryhotel.com. Sleek, luxury hotel owned by Rocco Forte Hotels. On Manchester/Salford boundary. Bar, *River* restaurant; terrace (alfresco dining); spa/fitness suite; background music; function facilities; free PlayStation portables. Car park. 165 spacious bedrooms (all have business equipment, Internet, etc; some overlook River Irwell): £142.50–£265. Buffet breakfast from £17.50.

Malmaison, 1–3 Piccadilly, M1 3AQ. *Tel* 0161-278 1000, www.malmaison.com. 'Stylish, comfortable' hotel by station. Buzzy atmosphere; striking decor; dimly lit public areas. Bar, brasserie; background music;

gym; spa in basement. Conference facilities. Dogs welcomed. 167 bedrooms: £150–£415.

The Midland, Peter Street, M60 2DS. *Tel* 0161-236 3333, www.qhotels.co.uk. Next to G-Mex centre: built for Midland Railway Company (1903), luxuriously ornate hotel with terracotta-tiled exterior (QHotel group). *Octagon* lounge (afternoon tea, light snacks), *Wyvern* bar, *The French* and *The Colony* restaurants; health club (gym, swimming pool, squash); background music. Parking (charge). 312 bedrooms: double from £167. Breakfast from £14.

Old Trafford Lodge, Lancashire County Cricket Club, M16 0PX. *Tel* 0161-874 3333, www.oldtraffordlodgehotel.co.uk. Purpose-built hotel beside Lancashire's test match ground. Photographs of cricketing heroes; pictures of bats, balls, stumps, etc; free match tickets. Lounge, bar (sandwiches). No background music. Parking. 68 bedrooms (36 have balcony overlooking pitch; others face car park). B&B from £34.50 per person.

MARKET DRAYTON Shropshire — Map 3:B5

Goldstone Hall, Goldstone, TF9 2NA. *Tel* 01630-661202, www.goldstonehall.com. Cushing family's sprawling house in 5-acre grounds (interesting plant collections), in hamlet 4½ miles S of Market Drayton on A529. Ramps. 2 lounges; bar, conservatory, Edwardian panelled restaurant (modern cooking); snooker room; function/wedding facilities. No background music. 12 bedrooms (2 on ground floor). B&B £66–£108 per person; D,B&B from £92.50.

MATLOCK Derbyshire — Map 3:B6

The Red House, Old Road, Darley Dale, DE4 2ER. *Tel* 01629-734854, www.theredhousecountryhotel.co.uk. Victorian architect's country home, now David and Kate Gardiner's 'well-run' hotel, on quiet road off A6, 2½ miles NW of centre. Views over Derwent valley. Many original features. 2 sitting rooms, bar, dining room; 'easy listening' background music during dinner. ¾-acre garden. Next to carriage museum (horse riding, carriage driving). Parking. 10 bedrooms (3 on ground floor in coach house). B&B £52.50–£62.50 per person; D,B&B £78.50–£88.50.

MIDHURST Sussex — Map 2:E3

The Spread Eagle, South Street, GU29 9NH. Tel 01730-816911, www.hshotels.co.uk. 15th-century coaching inn (Historic Sussex Hotels group). 'Pleasant, relaxing, with friendly staff; above-average dinner.' Residents' lounge (huge fireplaces, Tudor bread oven), lounge bar, restaurant (inglenook fireplace), conservatory, terrace (alfresco dining); function facilities; spa: swimming pool, gym. No background music. 1-acre garden. 39 bedrooms. B&B from £99 per person.

MOUSEHOLE Cornwall **Map 1:E1**

The Old Coastguard, The Parade, TR19 6PR. *Tel* 01736-731222, www.oldcoastguardhotel.co.uk. Bill Treloar's modern, light hotel with 'warm welcome'. 4 miles W of Penzance, above village, in large subtropical garden leading to sea. Views of Mounts Bay. Lounge, bar, restaurant (emphasis on local fish and seafood); background music (classical/jazz). Terrace. Parking. 22 bedrooms (7 in *Lodge,* by sea). B&B £45–£85 per person.

NAYLAND Suffolk **Map 2:C5**

The White Hart, 11 High Street, CO6 4JF. *Tel* 01206-263382, www.whitehart-nayland.co.uk. 15th-century coaching inn with 'very good food'; good welcome to children; French feel; lots of character (beams, sloping floors; plain walls, brightly checked fabrics). Lounge, bar (background music), restaurant. Owned by Michel Roux; new manager being appointed as the *Guide* went to press. 6 bedrooms. B&B £48–£109 per person.

NEWBURY Berkshire **Map 2:D2**

The Vineyard at Stockcross, RG20 8JU. *Tel* 01635-528770, www.the-vineyard.co.uk. 3 miles NW of centre, Sir Peter Michael's (founder of Classic FM) 'restaurant with room to stay' (Relais & Châteaux): former hunting lodge housing eclectic art collection. 2 *Michelin* stars for chef John Campbell. Lounge, music room, conservatory, bar, restaurant; background music: function facilities; spa: swimming pool, gym. Garden: patio. Parking. 49 bedrooms: £167.50–£645.

NEWCASTLE UPON TYNE Tyne and Wear **Map 4:B4**

Malmaison, The Quayside, NE1 3DX. *Tel* 0191-245 5000, www.malmaison.com. On quayside near Millennium Bridge: former warehouse converted in contemporary style (strong colours, bold prints, modern furniture); managed by Lizzy Kelk. River views. Lift. 2 lounges, café, bar, brasserie (dimly lit); background music. Spa (holistic and beauty treatments). 122 bedrooms (4 suitable for ♿): £95–£380. Breakfast £11.95–£13.95.

NEWMARKET Suffolk **Map 2:B4**

Bedford Lodge, Bury Road, CB8 7BX. *Tel* 01638-663175, www.bedfordlodgehotel.co.uk. Georgian hunting lodge in 3-acre secluded gardens near racecourse. Lounge, bar, *Orangery* restaurant; background music; extensive function/wedding/conference facilities; fitness centre: indoor swimming pool, beauty salon. 55 bedrooms (1 on ground floor). B&B £60–£145 per person.

NEWQUAY Cornwall **Map 1:D2**

The Headland Hotel, Fistral Beach, TR7 1EW. *Tel* 01637-872211, www.headlandhotel.co.uk. Owned 27 years by John and Carolyn Armstrong: grand Victorian edifice; coastal views on three sides; traditional/contemporary decor. Lounges, bar, restaurant, *Sand* brasserie (alfresco dining on terrace); background music; conference/function facilities. Snooker; table tennis; 2 swimming pools, sauna; croquet; tennis; 9-hole golf approach course and putting green; families welcomed (bunk beds, baby-listening, etc). Surf school nearby. 104 bedrooms. B&B £41.50–£131 per person.

NORWICH Norfolk **Map 2:B5**

Annesley House, 6 Newmarket Road, NR2 2LA. *Tel* 01603-624553, www.bw-annesleyhouse.co.uk. In conservation area near centre: Best Western member composed of 3 Grade II listed Georgian houses. Run since 1985 by owners David and Jill Reynolds. Bar/lounge, attractive conservatory restaurant (facing water gardens and koi pond; background music); conference/function facilities. 'Friendly, reasonably priced, good food, adaptable staff.' Garden. Parking. 26 bedrooms (some face main road). B&B £41.50–£118 per person.

Barnham Broom Hotel, Honingham Road, NR9 4DD. *Tel* 01603-759393, www.barnham-broom.co.uk. Sister to *Bedford Lodge*, Newmarket (above): golf hotel (two 18-hole courses) in 250-acre grounds, 10 miles W of Norwich. Lounge, 2 bars, *Flints* restaurant; background music; function facilities; health/fitness club (indoor swimming pool, gym, sauna, etc), tennis, squash. 52 bedrooms. B&B £70–£145 per person.

Beaufort Lodge, 62 Earlham Road, NR2 3DF. *Tel* 01603-627928, www.beaufortlodge.com. Owned since Jan 2007 by Aylwin and Don Shingler, who have redecorated and extended: B&B in Victorian villa, 5 mins' walk from centre. Breakfast room (classical background music). Garden. 7 bedrooms. B&B £32.50–£55 per person.

Catton Old Hall, Lodge Lane, Old Catton, NR6 7HG. *Tel* 01603-419379, www.catton-hall.co.uk. Roger and Anthea Cawdron's characterful small hotel, built 1632, in village 2½ miles NE of centre. Afternoon tea; dinner by arrangement; vegetarian options at breakfast. Lounge, dining room. No background music. Garden. 7 bedrooms. B&B £35–£60 per person.

Norfolk Mead, Church Loke, Coltishall, NR12 7DN. *Tel* 01603-737531, www.norfolkmead.co.uk. Jill and Don Fleming's Georgian manor house in 8-acre grounds by River Bure, 7 miles NE of Norwich, on edge of Norfolk

Broads. Lounge, bar, candlelit restaurant; background music; conference facilities, beauty salon. Walled garden, unheated swimming pool; fishing lake; off-river mooring. 12 attractive bedrooms (beamed ones in cottage suite). B&B £50–£95 per person; D,B&B £80–£125.

NOTTINGHAM Nottinghamshire — Map 2:A3

Dakota, Lakeview Drive, Sherwood Business Park, Annesley, NG15 0DA. *Tel* 0870-442 2727, www.dakotanottingham.co.uk. 'Impressive' new brainchild of Ken McCullough (Malmaison group's founder) and racing driver David Coulthard: 'Cool', value-for-money motorway hotel, just N of city, minutes from junction 27 of M1. 'Well-trained staff. Food well presented, very fresh. Great prices.' Lift. Bar, grill; background music; gym; function facilities. Parking. 101 bedrooms (compact, 'modern but not stark'): £89. Sister hotels in Edinburgh and Glasgow; one planned for Farnborough.

OXFORD Oxfordshire — Map 2:C2

Burlington House, 374 Banbury Road, OX2 7PP. *Tel* 01865-513513, www.burlington-house.co.uk. B&B in 'handsome, well-maintained' Victorian house, run by 'most welcoming' resident manager. In leafy Summertown, 1½ miles from centre on busy road. 'Small, attractive lounge, giving on to paved garden; excellent breakfast served in pleasant room.' No background music. 12 bedrooms (3 on ground floor). Internet access. B&B £42.50–£65 per person.

Cotswold House, 363 Banbury Road, OX2 7PL. *Tel* 01865-310558, www.cotswoldhouse.co.uk. Derek and Hilary Walker's B&B: Cotswold stone house 2 miles N of centre on busy road (reliable bus service). 'Good atmosphere; lovely fresh fruit at breakfast.' Lounge, breakfast room. No background music. Garden. Parking. 8 bedrooms (1 on ground floor). B&B £42.50–£65 per person.

Malmaison, 3 Oxford Castle, New Road, OX1 1AY. *Tel* 01865-268400, www.malmaison.com. Converted Victorian castle prison (Grade I listed) retaining original features: metal walkways, cell doors, keys, spyholes (reversed). *Visitors' Room* lounge, 2 bars, brasserie; background music; broadband; gym; outside seating. No private parking. 94 bedrooms (16 in *House of Correction*, some in *Governor's House*, some suitable for ♿): £150–£440.

The Randolph, Beaumont Street, OX1 2LN. *Tel* 0870-400 8200, www.randolph-hotel.com. Oxford institution, by Ashmolean Museum, now 'spick and span', high-comfort chain hotel (Macdonald group), with 'attentive management'. 'Superb breakfast.' Lounges (pianist on Sat), *Morse* bar, restaurant (background music). Newly opened cellar spa (vaulted ceilings, luxury tiling, candlelight; thermal suite, hydrotherapy bath, relaxation room). 151 bedrooms. B&B £74–£236.50 per person.

PADSTOW Devon **Map 1:D2**

The Seafood Restaurant, Riverside, PL28 8BY. *Tel* 01841-532700, www.rickstein.com. Rick (celebrity chef) and Jill Stein's flagship restaurant-with-rooms on waterfront; other rooms in *St Petroc's House* (reading room, lounge; courtyard; café; background music), *St Edmund's House* (private garden), *Bryn Cottage*, *Prospect House*. 38 bedrooms (best ones light, well designed, with good views). B&B £70–£215 per person.

PENRITH Cumbria **Map 4: inset C2**

The George, Devonshire Street, CA11 7SU. *Tel* 01768-862696, www.georgehotelpenrith.co.uk. 300-year-old coaching inn, 4 miles from Lake Ullswater. Traditional decor. Lounges (background music at night), bar, restaurant; function/wedding facilities. Free use of local leisure facilities. Parking. 32 bedrooms. B&B: £50–£82 per person; D,B&B £67–£99.

Westmorland Hotel, Near Orton, CA10 3SB. *Tel* 01539-624351, www.westmorlandhotel.com. 'Dramatic' moorland and mountain views. Contemporary design blends with traditional materials in secluded modern hotel just off M6 (Tebay Motorway Services, Junction 38). 'Streets ahead of typical motorway stops; well-appointed bedrooms.' Bar (log fires), lounge, split-level dining room; background music; Wi-Fi; function facilities. 51 bedrooms. B&B £45–£90 per person; D,B&B £69–£130.

PENZANCE Cornwall **Map 1:E1**

The Tarbert Hotel, 11–12 Clarence Street, TR18 2NU. *Tel* 01736-363758, www.tarbert-hotel.co.uk. White-painted building in centre. 'Fresh and delightful. Excellent dinners and breakfasts. Young, enthusiastic, friendly staff.' Tropical fish tanks; open fires; Wi-Fi. Bar, lounge, restaurant (open to non-residents); patio; generally no background music. 14 bedrooms (some family). B&B £32.50–£47.50 per person.

PLYMOUTH Devon **Map 1:D4**

Bowling Green Hotel, 9–10 Osborne Place, Lockyer St, The Hoe, PL1 2PU. *Tel* 01752-209090, www.bowlingreenhotel.co.uk. 5 mins' walk from Barbican, Tom Roberts's small B&B in Georgian house facing 'Drake's bowling green'. Lounge, TV room, breakfast room, conservatory. No background music. Parking. 12 bedrooms. B&B £28–£40 per person.

Plantation House, Totnes Road, Ermington, PL21 9NS. *Tel* 01548-831100, www.plantationhousehotel.co.uk. In rural location, on sunny side of River Erme valley, Richard and Magdalena Hendey's cream-painted former rectory (Grade II listed), 10 miles E of Plymouth. Bar, dining room, breakfast room; background music if required. 9 bedrooms. B&B £45–£70 per person.

POOLE Dorset **Map 2:E1**

Hotel du Vin Poole (formerly *The Mansion House*), Thames Street, BH15 1JN. *Tel* 01202-685666, www.hotelduvin.com. Now owned by Hotel du Vin group; reopening after refurbishment, in spring 2008: Georgian town house (1779) near quayside. Bar, bistro; alfresco dining; function facilities; roof garden. No background music. Parking. 38 bedrooms: double from £150.

RAVENGLASS Cumbria **Map 4: inset C2**

The Pennington, Main Street, CA18 1SD. *Tel* 01229-717222, www.thepennington.co.uk. 'Bright, airy' beachfront hotel, former coaching inn. Period features retained in revamp in unpretentious style by Pennington family of nearby Muncaster Castle. Lounge, restaurant ('good ingredients, cooked well; very good breakfast'); background music; Internet access; terrace. 19 bedrooms (1 suitable for ♿). B&B from £75 per person.

READING Berkshire **Map 2:D3**

The Forbury, 26 The Forbury, RG1 3EJ. *Tel* 08000-789789, www.theforburyhotel.co.uk. Civic grandeur meets glamour at 100-year-old County Hall building opposite gardens, now a sumptuous hotel. Up-to-the-minute equipment; artwork by French and British painters and sculptors. Bar, *Cerise* restaurant; background music ('can be turned off if required'); cinema; courtyard garden; function facilities. 24 bedrooms: £140–£245.

ROSS-ON-WYE Herefordshire **Map 3:D5**

The Hill House, Howle Hill, HR9 5ST. *Tel* 01989-562033, www.thehowlinghillhouse.com. Above Forest of Dean: Duncan and Alex Stayton's 17th-century house (views of Black Mountains). Organic local produce: Aga-cooked, vegetarian-friendly breakfasts; packed lunch/evening meal by arrangement. Morning room, lounge; cinema (DVD film library), bar (background music), restaurant; sauna (background music). Garden. 4½-acre woodland. 5 bedrooms. B&B £25–£29 per person; D,B&B £35–£50.

Pencraig Court, Pencraig, HR9 6HR. *Tel* 01989-770306, www.pencraig-court.co.uk. Georgian house in 3½-acre garden and woodlands overlooking River Wye, 4 miles SW of town. Family owned (Liz and Malcolm Dobson and daughter, Katie). Lounge, dining room (background music; home-grown fruit, vegetables, herbs). Croquet. 10 bedrooms. B&B £43–£55 per person.

RYE East Sussex **Map 2:E5**

Durrant House, 2 Market Street, TN31 7LA. *Tel* 01797-223182, www.durranthouse.com. Now owned by Jilly Mitchell and William Bilecki:

in centre, guest house with white-painted Georgian facade, hanging flower baskets. Lounge with bar, breakfast room (background CDs/radio). Small garden: 'exhilarating views' over Romney Marsh to sea. 5 bedrooms. B&B £37.50–£78 per person.

ST IVES Cornwall **Map 1:D1**

Blue Hayes, Trelyon Avenue, TR26 2AD. *Tel* 01736-797129, www.bluehayes.co.uk. Small luxury hotel, managed by owner Malcolm Herring, in 1920s house on Porthminster Point, overlooking bay and harbour. 2 lounges, bar, dining room; terrace (panoramic views). No background music. Garden: gate leading to South West Coastal Path. Parking. 6 bedrooms. B&B £70–£95 per person. Light supper £15.

Boskerris Hotel, Boskerris Road, TR26 2NQ. *Tel* 01736-795295, www.boskerrishotel.co.uk. High above sandy Carbis Bay: Jonathan and Marianne Bassett's newly renovated hotel, with panoramic ocean views and bright white interior. 30 mins' coastal walk in to town; 5 mins by local train. Lounge, bar, small restaurant; large decked terrace. 1½-acre garden. 15 bedrooms (including family suite). B&B £85–£95 per person.

The Garrack, Burthallan Lane, TR26 3AA. *Tel* 01736-796199, www.garrack.com. Creeper-clad stone building on hill above Porthmeor beach, a short, steep walk from town. Owned for over 40 years by Kilby family. 'Food and hospitality as good as ever.' Lounge, restaurant (Cornish produce; background music); leisure centre (gym, sauna, indoor swimming pool). 2-acre garden: sun terrace. Parking. 18 bedrooms (1 suitable for ♿). B&B £72–£95 per person; D,B&B £94–£116.

The Porthminster, TR26 2BN. *Tel* 01736-795221, www.porthminster-hotel.co.uk. Victorian building in subtropical gardens overlooking bay: direct access to Porthminster beach. Traditional interior. Lift. Lounge, bar, cocktail bar, restaurant (seafood/fish specialities); background music; leisure club: indoor/outdoor swimming pool; tennis; function/wedding/business facilities. 43 bedrooms (some family). B&B £60–£110 per person.

SALISBURY Wiltshire **Map 2:D2**

Leena's, 50 Castle Road, SP1 3RL. *Tel* 01722-335419. 15 mins' riverside walk from centre: Leena and Malcolm Street's budget B&B: Edwardian house on busy Amesbury road (double glazing). Lounge, breakfast room. No background music. Garden. Parking. 6 bedrooms (1 on ground floor). B&B £28–£33 per person.

Milford Hall, 206 Castle Street, SP1 3TE. *Tel* 01722-417411, www.milfordhallhotel.com. Georgian mansion with modern extension, owned by Hughes family. Lounge, bar, *brasserie@206*; conference/business/wedding facilities; Masonic festival weekends; Wi-Fi; background music. Parking. 35 bedrooms. B&B £59.50–£109 per person.

Spire House, 84 Exeter Street, SP1 2SE. *Tel* 01722-339213, www.salisbury-bedandbreakfast.com. In 18th-century Grade II listed town house, Lois and John Faulkner's B&B near cathedral. Breakfast full English or healthy. No background music. Walled garden. Ample parking. 4 bedrooms. B&B £35–£55 per person.

SCARBOROUGH North Yorkshire — Map 4:C5

Interludes, 32 Princess Street, YO11 1QR. *Tel* 01723-360513, www.interludeshotel.co.uk. Listed Georgian building in Old Town conservation area. Run by theatre buffs, Ian Grundy and Bob Harris, 'magically attuned to guests' needs'. 'Eccentrically decorated' (thespian memorabilia); 2 resident cats. Lounge, dining room (light classical background music); small patio. 5 bedrooms (4 with sea views). B&B £32–£36 per person. Evening meal ('simple but tasty') £14.

SHEPTON MALLET Somerset — Map 1:B6

Charlton House, Charlton Road, BA4 4PR. *Tel* 01749-342008, www.charltonhouse.com. Owned by Roger and Monty Saul, founders of the Mulberry label: hotel with theatrical decor, 'a romantic backdrop to antiques, paintings, quirky curios'; four-poster beds; open fires. 'Excellent staff.' 2 drawing rooms, bar, restaurant; light jazz/classical background music; Wi-Fi; conference/function facilities; private dining room spa. Garden: tennis. 25 bedrooms. B&B £60–£140 per person.

SHREWSBURY Shropshire — Map 3:B4

Albright Hussey, Ellesmere Road, SY4 3AF. *Tel* 01939-290523, www.albrighthussey.co.uk. 2½ miles N of centre, Subbiani family's hotel/restaurant: much extended Grade II listed Tudor house. Antiques, panelling, open fires, beams. Lounge, bar, *Moat Room* restaurant; function facilities. No background music. 4-acre garden. 26 bedrooms. B&B £60–£135 per person.

SIDMOUTH Devon — Map 1:C5

Victoria Hotel, The Esplanade, EX10 8RY. *Tel* 01395-512651, www.victoriahotel.co.uk. On hill, at western end of esplanade (views across bay), large, majestic hotel (Brend Group) in 5-acre grounds. Long-serving staff; atmosphere of 'general affability, which enhances one's stay'. Families welcomed. Lounges, restaurant (dinner dances Sat eve); background music; snooker; gym; outdoor/indoor swimming pools, whirlpool, sauna, solarium;

tennis, putting. 61 bedrooms (some with sea views, some with balcony). B&B £85–£130 per person.

SOUTHWOLD Suffolk **Map 2:B6**

The Swan, Market Place, IP18 6EG. *Tel* 01502-722186, www.adnamshotels.co.uk. 300-year-old building on market square, managed by Francis Guildea. 'Excellent location and service.' Traditional decor. Lift. 2 lounges, bar, restaurant; function facilities. No background music. Garden. Parking. Beach 200 yds. 42 bedrooms (1 suitable for ♿; 17 dog-friendly garden rooms round old bowling green). B&B £73–£83 per person.

STANSTED Essex **Map 2:C4**

Oak Lodge, Jacks Lane, Smiths Green, Takeley, CM22 6NT. *Tel* 01279-871667, www.oaklodgebb.com. In village 2 miles SE of airport: 'highly recommended' 16th-century B&B, run by owners, Jan and Ron Griffiths. 'Very good breakfast'; evening meal by arrangement. Lounge/TV room, dining room. Oak beams; Wi-Fi. No background music. 2-acre garden. Parking. No credit cards. 3 bedrooms. B&B £30–£50 per person.

STOKE CANON Devon **Map 1:C5**

Barton Cross Hotel, Huxham, EX5 4EJ. *Tel* 01392-841245, *email* bartonxhuxham@aol.com. In quiet location 4 miles N of Exeter, off A396: part-thatched 17th-century house: wooden beams, gallery, inglenook fireplace. 'Superb, considerate host', Brian Hamilton. Lounge, bar, breakfast room, restaurant ('very good cooking' by Paul Bending). No background music. 1-acre garden. Parking. 9 bedrooms. B&B £49–£78 per person; D,B&B £73–£95.

STRATFORD-UPON-AVON Warwickshire **Map 3:D6**

Parkfield, 3 Broad Walk, CV37 6HS. *Tel* 01789-293313, www.parkfieldbandb.co.uk. Roger and Joanna Pettitt's 'homely' B&B in Victorian house near centre. 'Breakfast very good'; vegetarians catered for; help with theatre tickets. No background music. Large car park. 7 bedrooms. B&B £27.50–£30 per person.

STUDLAND Dorset **Map 2:E1**

Manor House Hotel, Studland Bay, BH19 3AU. *Tel* 01929-450288, www.themanorhousehotel.com. 'Lovely old hotel in superb location overooking bay.' 18th-century National Trust property in 20-acre grounds, run by owner Andrew Purkis. Lounges, bar (lunches), restaurant (background music at night); picnic hampers; 2 tennis courts; power boat. 21 bedrooms (sea/garden/country views). D,B&B £88–£134 per person.

SUTTON COLDFIELD Warwickshire **Map 3:C6**

New Hall Hotel, Walmley Rd, B76 1QX. *Tel* 0121-378 2442, www.newhalluk.com. Former hunting lodge for earls of Warwick (Grade I listed): oldest inhabited moated manor house in England, owned by Bridgehouse Hotels. 20 mins' drive from Birmingham. Lounges, bar; background music; oak-panelled *Bridge* restaurant, *Terrace* room; leisure facilities (swimming pool, spa bath, steam room, beauty treatments, fitness room); function facilities. 26-acre grounds: tennis, 9-hole par 3 golf course. 60 bedrooms: double from £145.

TAVISTOCK Devon **Map 1:D4**

Browns Hotel, 80 West Street, PL19 8AQ. *Tel* 01822-618686, www.brownsdevon.co.uk. Now owned by Helena King and Phil Biggin: hotel/wine bar/brasserie in 17th-century coaching inn. Blend of chic modern furnishings with natural materials (stone, brick, slate, wood). Lounge/bar, restaurant, conservatory/orangery; background music ('easy listening') throughout. Courtyard garden. 20 bedrooms (4 in mews; some family; 1 suitable for ♿). B&B £69–£89 per person.

TEIGNMOUTH Devon **Map 1:D5**

Britannia House, 26 Teign Street, TQ14 8EG. *Tel* 01626-770051, www.britanniahouse.org. Reputedly built by 16th-century sea captain: Jennifer and Michael Gillett's 'very welcoming' home, in maze of small streets, 5 mins' walk from seafront. Locally sourced ingredients at breakfast. Sitting room, dining room; soft classical background music. Small walled garden. 3 bedrooms. B&B £30–£60 per person.

TETBURY Gloucestershire **Map 3:E5**

The Close, 8 Long Street, GL8 8AQ. *Tel* 01666-502272, www.theclose-hotel.com. 16th-century yeoman's house in centre, a hotel since 1974, now owned by Greene King group, managed by Colin and Val Holman. Elegant interior: panelled rooms; dramatic touches. Lounge, bar, restaurant (Adam ceiling); background music; function/wedding facilities. Terrace: alfresco meals. Walled garden. Parking. 15 bedrooms. B&B from £50 per person.

THIRSK North Yorkshire **Map 4:C4**

Oswalds, Front Street, YO7 1JF. *Tel* 01845-523655, www.oswaldsrestaurantwithrooms.co.uk. Near North Yorkshire national park and

Yorkshire dales: restaurant-with-rooms on quiet street a short walk from centre of market town. Lounge, bar, restaurant; background music; function room; hot tub (pamper breaks). 16 bedrooms. B&B £42.50–£65 per person.

TISBURY Wiltshire **Map 2:D1**

The Compasses Inn, Lower Chicksgrove, SP3 6NB. *Tel* 01722-714318, www.thecompassesinn.com. Alan and Susie Stoneham's 14th-century pub (thatched roof, stone-paved path; front and back gardens) in rural setting off A30, halfway between Salisbury and Shaftesbury. Sitting room, bar, dining room. No background music. 4 bedrooms (3-bed cottage). B&B £45–£65 per person.

TORQUAY Devon **Map 1:D5**

Mulberry House, 1 Scarborough Road, TQ2 5UJ. *Tel* 01803-213639, www.mulberryhousetorquay.co.uk. Laura and Chris Wood's guest house/restaurant: Victorian house (Grade II listed) on corner, a short stroll to sea and centre. Lounge, restaurant (open fire; soft background music); function facilities. Children welcomed. 3 'fresh, bright' bedrooms. B&B £30–£52 per person. Full alc £24–£32.

Orestone Manor, Rockhouse Lane, Maidencombe, TQ1 4SX. Tel 01803-328098, www.orestonemanor.com. Large Edwardian house overlooking Lyme Bay, 3½ miles N of Torquay. Owned since July 2006 by Alan and Jean May. Ramps. Drawing room with bar, conservatory, restaurant (open fires; background music); private dining/conference room; indoor swimming pool; Wi-Fi. Panoramic terrace. 2½-acre garden. 12 bedrooms. B&B £67.50–£112.50 per person. Dinner £25.

TOTNES Devon **Map 1:D4**

Royal Seven Stars, The Plains, TQ9 5DD. *Tel* 01803-862125, www.royalsevenstars.co.uk. 17th-century coaching inn, renovated 2006 in contemporary style (Wi-Fi, etc). Local watering hole; 'good, basic pub grub'; light meals available all day. 2 bars (background music; log fires in winter); alfresco dining. Business facilities. Parking. 16 bedrooms (quietest at back). B&B £49.50–£110 per person.

TROUTBECK Cumbria **Map 4: inset C2**

Broadoaks, Bridge Lane, LA23 1LA. *Tel* 015394-45566, www.broadoakscountryhouse.co.uk. Trevor and Joan Pavelyn's 'highly recommended' Victorian country house 2 miles N of Windermere. Lounge, music room with barrel-vaulted acoustic ceiling, restaurant; function facilities; background music. 'Welcoming environment. Fantastic food.' 7-acre grounds: bowling, pitch-and-putt, fishing, rifle and clay-pigeon range. Access to leisure club, 1½ miles. 14 bedrooms (1 suitable for ♿; 3 in coach house). B&B £55–£80 per person.

TUNBRIDGE WELLS Kent **Map 2:D4**

Spa Hotel, Mount Ephraim, TN4 8XJ. *Tel* 01892-520331, www.spahotel.co.uk. 'Excellent' old-style hotel with modern facilities, owned by Goring family (see *The Goring Hotel*, London). 18th-century mansion in 14-acre grounds overlooking town. Lounge, dining room; health/leisure centre (sauna, swimming pool); tennis; jogging trail; stables. Wi-Fi access throughout. No background music. 69 bedrooms. B&B £84–£123 per person.

ULLSWATER Cumbria **Map 4: inset C2**

The Inn on the Lake, Glenridding, CA11 0PE. *Tel* 017684-82444, www.lakedistricthotels.net. At rugged end of Lake Ullswater, in 15-acre grounds leading to shore: large, traditional, 3-star hotel (Lake District group). Lounge, 2 bars, *Lake View* restaurant; background music; extensive conference/function/wedding facilities. 46 bedrooms. B&B £69–£97 per person; D,B&B £89–£119.

VENTNOR Isle of Wight **Map 2:E2**

The Royal Hotel, Belgrave Road, PO38 1JJ. *Tel* 01983-852186, www.royalhoteliow.co.uk. Five mins' walk from centre: William Bailey's classic seaside hotel (largest on island), used by Queen Victoria as annexe to Osborne House. 'Well-trained young staff. Food excellent.' 2 lounges, bar, restaurant, conservatory; occasional background music. 2-acre landscaped gardens: terrace, heated swimming pool, children's play area. Sandy beach nearby (hilly walk). Parking. 55 bedrooms. B&B £70–£125 per person; D,B&B £102.50–£157.50.

WARWICK Warwickshire **Map 3:C6**

Northleigh House, Five Ways Road, Hatton, CV35 7HZ. *Tel* 01926-484203, www.northleigh.co.uk. Viv and Fred Morgan's 'very friendly' white-painted B&B in countryside 4 miles N of Warwick. 'When we arrived late at night, they gave us tea and toast.' Children and dogs welcome. Sitting room. Organic breakfasts. No background music. Garden. 7 bedrooms (some on ground floor). B&B £35–£50 per person. Family-style evening meal £7.

WESTON-SUPER-MARE Somerset **Map 1:B6**

Beachlands, 17 Uphill Road North, BS23 4NG. *Tel* 01934-621401, www.beachlandshotel.com. One mile S of centre, owned by Porter and

Baker families: hotel facing sand dunes (300 yds from beach) and 18-hole links golf course. 2 lounges, bar, restaurant; background music. 30-ft indoor swimming pool, sauna; function/business facilities. Children welcome. Garden. Parking. 21 bedrooms. B&B £55–£90 per person; D,B&B £69.50–£111.

WHITBY North Yorkshire — Map 4:C5

Bagdale Hall, 1 Bagdale, YO21 1QL. *Tel* 01947-602958, www.bagdale.co.uk. Central, near harbour: Tudor manor house, 'genuinely olde-worldly' (mullioned windows, beamed ceilings, carved wooden overmantels; four-poster beds). Lounge, bar, restaurant. No background music. 19 bedrooms (12 in Victorian lodge, 8 in annexe nearby; 1 suitable for ♿). B&B from £45 per person.

Dunsley Hall, Dunsley, YO21 3TL. *Tel* 01947-893437, www.dunsleyhall.com. Period features (oak panelling, stained-glass window with seafaring scene, inglenook fireplace) combine with comfort and good food at Victorian mansion built for shipping magnate, in hamlet 2½ miles NW of Whitby. Lounge, bar (background music), 2 restaurants. 4-acre garden: putting, croquet, tennis, peacocks. Sea 1 mile. Parking. 26 bedrooms (8 in new wing; some suitable for ♿). B&B £62.50–£115 per person.

White Horse & Griffin, 87 Church Street, YO22 4BH. *Tel* 01947-604857, www.whitehorseandgriffin.co.uk. In centre of old town: former 17th-century coaching inn, now restaurant-with-rooms run by chef Stewart Perkins. Bright and airy; quirky building. 'Good food. Excellent breakfast; friendly, efficient staff.' Restaurant; background music; open fires. 10 bedrooms. B&B £30–£42.50 per person.

WILLINGTON Cheshire — Map 3:A5

Willington Hall, CW6 0NB. *Tel* 01829-752321, www.willingtonhall.co.uk. Diana and Stuart Begbie's 'beautifully situated' 19th-century building in 17-acre grounds at foot of Willington hills, 3½ miles NW of Tarporley, 10 miles E of Chester. Original features, antiques, family portraits. Lounge, 2 bars, 4 restaurants; terrace; function facilities. No background music. 10 bedrooms. B&B £60–£80 per person.

WINCHESTER Hampshire — Map 2:D2

Lainston House, Sparsholt, SO21 2LT. *Tel* 01962-776088, www.exclusivehotels.co.uk. 17th-century country house managed by Cliff Hasler. 2½ miles NW of city by B3049, in 63-acre park (tennis, croquet). Wood panelling; four-poster beds; smart bathrooms; elegant, traditional style. Drawing room, *Cedar* bar, *Avenue* restaurant; gym; function/wedding facilities. No background music. Children welcomed. 50 bedrooms (4 in courtyard or stables; some suitable for ♿): £125–£625. Breakfast £17–£19.50.

WOBURN Bedfordshire **Map 2:C3**

The Inn at Woburn, George Street, MK17 9PX. *Tel* 01525-290441, www.theinnatwoburn.com. Modern comforts at refurbished 18th-century coaching inn on Woburn estate, 8 miles SE of Milton Keyes, managed by Richard Carr. *Tavistock* bar, *Olivier's* restaurant (background music sometimes); function/wedding facilities. 50 bedrooms (plus 7 cottages): £115–£205. Breakfast £8–£11.

WOODSTOCK Oxfordshire **Map 2:C2**

The King's Arms, 19 Market Street, OX20 1SV. *Tel* 01993-813636, www.kingshotelwoodstock.co.uk. David and Sara Sykes's 'nicely decorated', 'excellent' small hotel made up of converted Georgian houses. 8 miles N of Oxford; some traffic noise from A44. 'Wonderful dinner.' Lounge, 2 bars, bistro; 'easy listening' background music. 15 bedrooms. B&B £70–£95 per person.

WYE Kent **Map 2:D5**

The New Flying Horse Inn, Upper Bridge Street, TN25 5AN. *Tel* 01233-812297, www.newflyinghorsewye.co.uk. Old-style, white-painted pub with updated accommodation in 17th-century roadside posting house off A28 between Canterbury and Ashford. Bar, dining room; patio. Award-winning garden. 9 bedrooms (some in coach house). B&B £42.50–£55 per person.

YARCOMBE Devon **Map 1:C5**

The Belfry, Nr Honiton, EX14 9DB. *Tel* 01404-861234, www.thebelfrycountryhotel.com. Built of flint cob, with stone mullioned windows, Paul and Katie Blake's small hotel converted from 1860s village schoolhouse. 'Everything for a relaxing stay.' Lounge, dining room; light classical background music. Small garden/patio. 6 bedrooms (some on ground floor), named after 19th-century English poets. B&B £40–£55 per person. 'Very good' dinner (order a day in advance) from £28.

YEOVIL Somerset **Map 1:C6**

Yeovil Court, West Coker Road, BA20 2HE. *Tel* 01935-863746, www.yeovilhotel.com. In rolling countryside, 2 miles from centre: spacious white-painted hotel owned by Brian and Carol Devonport. Stylish, modern interior. Lounge, bar, restaurant; conference facilities; background music.

30 bedrooms (1 suitable for ♿). B&B £52.50–£78 per person; D,B&B £82.50–£95.

YORK North Yorkshire **Map 4:D4**

Bar Convent, 17 Blossom Street, YO30 6BL. *Tel* 01904-643238, www.bar-convent.org.uk. Elegant Georgian building near Micklegate: England's oldest active convent (sisters of the Congregation of Jesus), with café, museum, shop, chapel; function facilities. No background music. Garden. Simple accommodation (communal self-catering on each floor). 25 bedrooms (some suitable for ♿) B&B (continental) £28.50–£33 per person. Full English breakfast £3.50.

The Bloomsbury, 127 Clifton, YO30 6BL. *Tel* 01904-634031, www.bloomsburyhotel.co.uk. Paul Andrew's B&B: Victorian house in leafy area, 12 mins' walk from minster. Bright, sunny dining room; vegetarians catered for. No background music. High-speed Internet access. Parking. 9 bedrooms. B&B £30–£60 per person.

Dean Court, Duncombe Place, YO1 7EF. *Tel* 01904-625082, www.deancourt-york.co.uk. 'Comfortable and enjoyable': opposite minster, award-winning Best Western member in contemporary style. 'Delicious food, excellent service.' Children welcomed. 2 lounges, bar, *The Court* café/bistro/bar, *D.C.H.* restaurant; contemporary background music; conference/function facilities. Valet parking. 37 bedrooms (some family; some suitable for ♿). B&B £49.50–£130 per person.

4 High Petergate, 2–4 High Petergate, YO1 7EH. *Tel* 01904-658516, www.fourhighpetergate.co.uk. Adjoining Bootham Bar, 100 yds from minster: compact bistro (local produce; background music) with rooms in 18th-century town house. Owned and managed by a Yorkshire racing family. Stylish decor; teak furniture. Walled garden. 14 bedrooms. B&B £47.50–£88 per person.

The Grange, 1 Clifton, YO30 6AA. *Tel* 01904-644744, www.grangehotel.co.uk. Just outside city walls, on busy road, Jeremy Cassell's Grade II listed Regency town house, managed by Amie Postings: classically furnished hotel. Ramps. Lounge, morning room, 2 bars, *Ivy* brasserie; wedding/function facilities. No background music. Wi-Fi throughout. 30 bedrooms (some on ground floor). B&B £77.50–£265 per person.

SCOTLAND

ABERDEEN **Map 5:C3**

Marcliffe Hotel and Spa, North Deeside Road, Pitfodels, AB15 9YA. *Tel* 01224-861000, www.marcliffe.com. Large, luxury hotel in lower Dee valley, 3 miles W of centre, 20 mins' drive from airport. Country house decor. Drawing room, lounge, bar, conservatory restaurant. No background music. 24-hour room service. Health spa. Function facilities. 11-acre wooded grounds. 42 bedrooms (1 suitable for ♿). B&B £75–£190 per person.

ALYTH Perth and Kinross **Map 5:D2**

Lands of Loyal, Loyal Road, PH11 8JQ. *Tel* 01828-633151, www.landsofloyal.com. Grand country house hotel in 7-acre grounds, overlooking Vale of Strathmore. Run by Howell family owners. Great hall (modelled on lounge of the steamship *Mauritania*), lounge, bar, dining room; background music (classical/'easy listening'). 'Enjoyed a New Year break here: decided to go back for Christmas.' 16 bedrooms (3 in coach house). B&B £62.50–£92.50 per person.

ARDUAINE Argyll and Bute **Map 5:D1**

Loch Melfort Hotel, PA34 4XG. *Tel* 01852-200233, www.lochmelfort.co.uk. 'Lovely situation; food very good; a most enjoyable stay.' Nigel and Kyle Schofield's white-painted hotel overlooking Asknish Bay (views to Jura, Shuna and Scarba). 2 lounges, wood-panelled library, bistro, restaurant; conference facilities. No background music. 26-acre grounds. Arduaine Gardens adjacent. 25 bedrooms (20 in modern wing reached via covered walkway). B&B £40–£89 per person.

ARISAIG Highland **Map 5:C1**

Cnoc-Na-Faíre, Back of Keppoch, PH39 4NS. *Tel* 01687-450249, www.cnoc-na-faire.co.uk. 1 mile from village, on Road to the Isles: small hotel with 'gorgeous views' over the sea to Skye. Lounge/bar/café (Internet, light lunches, suppers), restaurant (Scottish theme); background music; terrace café; wedding facilities (marquee); house parties. Substantial breakfast (can be in bed). 'A happy stop. Good food, obliging staff, beautifully decorated premises.' 6 simple bedrooms (plaid fabrics). B&B from £52 per person.

ASCOG Argyll and Bute **Map 5:D1**

Balmory Hall, PA20 9LL. *Tel* 01700-500669, www.balmoryhall.com. B&B in opulent, secluded Victorian mansion in 10-acre grounds (deer, owls, hawks), overlooking Ascog Bay. 'Wonderful hosts', Tony and Beryl Harrison, aim for house-party atmosphere. Reception hall, drawing room, dining room. No background music. No stiletto heels. 'Fantastic breakfasts.' 5 mins' walk to beach (seal colony). 4 bedrooms (plus self-catering lodge). B&B £65–£85 per person.

AYR South Ayrshire **Map 5:E1**

Fairfield House, 12 Fairfield Road, KA7 2AR. *Tel* 01292-267461, www.fairfieldhotel.co.uk. On seafront (spectacular views across Firth of Clyde to Isle of Arran): luxury hotel, once home of Victorian Glasgow tea merchant. Reception area, *Martin's* bar/bistro, restaurant ('very good cooking; service friendly, prompt, attentive'); leisure club (gym, indoor swimming pool, spa, sauna, steam room); background music throughout; function facilities. 44 bedrooms. B&B £49.50–£109 per person.

BOWMORE Argyll and Bute **Map 5:D1**

Harbour Inn & Restaurant, The Square, Isle of Islay, PA43 7JR. *Tel* 01496-810330, www.harbour-inn.com. Neil and Carol Scott's old whitewashed inn by harbour of village on E side of Loch Indaal. Conservatory lounge, *Schooner* bar, restaurant (local produce; background music). Small garden. Free use of local leisure centre (pool, gym). 7 bedrooms. B&B £52.50–£70 per person.

DUNDEE **Map 5:D3**

Apex City Quay Hotel & Spa, 1 West Victoria Dock Road, DD1 3JP. *Tel* 01382-202404, www.apexhotels.co.uk. Busy, 'well-run', 5-storey modern hotel on dockside (views over River Tay). *Metro* bar/brasserie, *Alchemy* restaurant; spa: gym, sauna, hot tubs, treatments; conference/events centre; background music throughout. 153 'cheerful' bedrooms (Internet, big desk, open-plan shower). B&B £64.50 per person.

Duntrune House, Duntrune, DD4 0PJ. *Tel* 01382-350239, www.duntrunehouse.co.uk. Family history enthusiasts Barrie and Olwyn Jack's B&B in 'amazing', lovingly restored stately home (1846). Part of Green Business Tourism Scheme. 5-acre grounds and woodlands. 5 miles NE of city; views over River Tay. Sitting room, breakfast room. Dinner by arrangement. No background music. Parking. 4 bedrooms. B&B £45–£50 per person.

Invercarse Hotel, 371 Perth Road, DD2 1PG. *Tel* 01382-669231, www.bestwestern.co.uk. In large wooded grounds on hill overlooking River Tay: extended Victorian mansion (Best Western). 3 miles from centre, 1 mile from airport. 2 bars, restaurant; large function facilities. No background music. Parking. 44 bedrooms (some smoking). B&B from £42.50 per person.

EDINBURGH **Map 5:D2**

Acer Lodge, 425 Queensferry Road, EH4 7NB. *Tel* 0131-336 2554, www.acerlodge.co.uk. 'Value for money': Gillian and Terry Poore's B&B in suburban house 3 miles W of centre ('wonderful bus service: 15 mins to

Princes Street'); ample parking. No background music. 5 bedrooms. B&B £25–£75 per person.

Apex City, 61 Grassmarket, EH1 2JF. *Tel* 0131-243 3456, www.apexhotels.co.uk. 'Good facilities, helpful staff' at large, contemporary hotel in Old Town (castle views). *Agua* bar, restaurant; background music; conference facilities. Spa at *Apex International* hotel next door (pool, sauna, gym). Parking. 119 bedrooms (Internet, widescreen TV; power shower). B&B £44.50–£109.50 per person.

Glenora Hotel, 14 Rosebery Crescent, EH12 5JY. *Tel* 0131-337 1186, www.glenorahotel.co.uk. In Haymarket district: Mr and Mrs Rasmusen's Victorian town house with original features enhanced by sophisticated modern furnishing. Morag Thomas is manager. Reception, breakfast room (continental/full Scottish; organic ingredients; background radio). 11 bedrooms. B&B £45–£75 per person.

The Howard, 34 Great King Street, EH3 6QH. *Tel* 0131-557 7402, www.thehoward.com. Dedicated butler, chauffeur, planned itineraries all offered by discreet luxury hotel (Town House Company), created from 3 Georgian houses in cobbled New Town street. Managed by Johanne Falconer. Drawing room, small *Atholl* restaurant ('traditional Scottish fare'); room-service meals. No background music. Parking. 18 bedrooms: £82.50–£197.50 per person.

The Lairg, 11 Coates Gardens, EH12 5LG. *Tel* 0131-337 1050. www.thelairghotel.co.uk. Furnished in traditional Scottish style, Marie Campbell's guest house on quiet street near Haymarket station, 25 mins' walk from Waverley station. Breakfast room (background music; Scottish breakfast). 10 bedrooms (some spacious). B&B £30–£60 per person.

Malmaison, 1 Tower Place, Leith, EH6 7DB. *Tel* 0131-468 5000, www.malmaison.com. Overlooking Leith harbour: stylishly converted 19th-century seamen's mission. Café/bar, brasserie; meeting/function facilities; fitness room; background music. Free parking. 100 bedrooms: £170–£315.

Prestonfield, Priestfield Road, EH16 5UT. *Tel* 0131-225 7800, www.prestonfield.com. Restaurateur James Thomson's romantic 17th-century mansion with opulent interior (see also *The Witchery*, full entry); managed by Alan McCuggan. 1½ miles from centre, views to Arthur's Seat. In 'much enjoyed' 20-acre garden/parkland, surrounded by golf course. 3 drawing rooms, 2 bars, *Rhubarb* restaurant; 3 private dining rooms; e-salon (Internet, etc); function facilities; background music. 'Great staff.' Parking. 22 bedrooms (2 suitable for ♿). B&B: double £225–£275, suite £350.

Rick's, 55a Frederick Street, EH2 1LH. *Tel* 0131-622 7800, www.ricksedinburgh.co.uk. Fashionable bar/restaurant-with-rooms in basement of neo-classical house in Georgian New Town. Eclectic modern cooking;

background 'soul/funk' music. Some street noise. 10 bedrooms (custom-designed furniture, CD, DVD, Wi-Fi), across covered courtyard. B&B double £125.25.

ELGIN Moray **Map 5:C2**

Mansion House Hotel & Country Club, The Haugh, IV30 1AW. *Tel* 01343-548811, www.mansionhousehotel.co.uk. On River Lossie in woodland, 5 mins' walk from centre: David Baker's 19th-century baronial mansion. Period decor. Piano lounge, snooker room, bar, restaurant, bistro; leisure club (indoor swimming pool, gym, snooker, body clinic); function/business facilities; background music. Fishing (permits available). Parking. 23 bedrooms (some interconnecting; some smoking). B&B £97–£143 per person.

FETTERCAIRN Grampian **Map 5:C3**

Ramsay Arms, Burnside Road, AB30 1XX. *Tel* 01561-340334, www.ramsayarmshotel.co.uk. 'Well-run, friendly', family-owned hotel: large white house in village at foot of the Cairn o' Mount. Lounge/bar, restaurant (Scottish dishes); wide selection of malts, real ales, fine wines; small function facilities; background music. Garden. Children welcomed. 12 simply decorated, 'nice, comfortable' bedrooms. B&B (full Scottish breakfast) £42.50–£60 per person.

FORT WILLIAM Highland **Map 5:C1**

Inverlochy Castle, Torlundy, PH33 6SN. *Tel* 01397-702177, www.inverlochycastlehotel.com. Baronial pile (1863) in foothills of Ben Nevis, 3 miles NE of Fort William. Lavish interior: Great Hall (Venetian chandeliers, frescoed ceiling); front hall, drawing room, restaurant (live music at dinner), billiard room; evening entertainment. 500-acre grounds: tennis, loch, fishing. 17 bedrooms. B&B £150–£350 per person.

FORTROSE Highland **Map 5:C2**

The Anderson, Union Street, by Inverness, IV10 8TD. *Tel* 01381-620236, www.theanderson.co.uk. Lively restaurant-with-rooms in 1840s building in seaside village on Black Isle. American owners, Jim and Anne Anderson. Public bar, Whisky bar (*tapas* menu; over 160 single-malt whiskies; live Scottish music in summer), dining room. Beer garden. Sandy beach 1¼ miles. Parking. 9 bedrooms. B&B £37.50–£45 per person.

GATEHOUSE OF FLEET Dumfries and Galloway **Map 5:E2**

The Bank of Fleet, 47 High Street, DG7 2HR. *Tel* 01557-814302, www.bankoffleet.co.uk. Small, family-run hotel on edge of Galloway Forest

Park. Much blue in decor. Bar/restaurant (inglenook fireplace) overlooking walled garden, dining room; small function facilities; background music. 'Excellent value for money.' 6 rooms. B&B £30–£32.50 per person.

GLASGOW **Map 5:D2**

Cathedral House, 28–32 Cathedral Square, G4 0XA. *Tel* 0141-552 3519, www.cathedralhouse.com. In leafy suburb, by cathedral, 1 mile from centre: 19th-century red brick mansion. Bistro/bar (open all day); conference/function facilities; background music. Beer garden. Scottish breakfast (vegetarians catered for). Parking. 8 bedrooms (via spiral staircase). B&B £32.50–£42.50 per person.

Hotel du Vin at One Devonshire Gardens, 1 Devonshire Gardens, G12 0UX. *Tel* 0141-339 2001, www.onedevonshiregardens.com. Formerly *One Devonshire Gardens*, now part of du Vin group: spread over 5 town houses in West End (on busy road; double glazing). Original features (stained glass, grand staircase, oak panelling), with state-of-the-art opulence. Bar, bistro; gym. No background music. Walled garden. 48 bedrooms: £127.50–£305. Breakfast from £12.

GRANTOWN-ON-SPEY Highland **Map 5:C2**

The Pines, Woodside Avenue, PH26 3JR. *Tel* 01479-872092, www.thepinesgrantown.co.uk. On edge of town, down quiet country lane, Michael and Gwen Stewart's small, 'beautifully kept', Victorian Highland home in 1-acre landscaped gardens and woodland. Elegant decor: family portraits, original watercolours, oil paintings, antiques, *objets d'art*. 'Every meal a delight.' 2 lounges, 2 dining rooms, library. No background music. 7 bedrooms (1 on ground floor). B&B £47–£68 per person. Dinner £32.

Ravenscourt House, Seafield Avenue, PH26 3JG. *Tel* 01479-872286, www.ravenscourthouse.co.uk. Former Church of Scotland manse (1905) in quiet location on edge of Cairngorms national park. Owned by Andrew Sheena and Mark Williamson. 2 lounges, conservatory restaurant (classical background music). Small garden. 8 bedrooms. B&B £40–£42.50 per person; D,B&B £60–£67.50.

KELSO Borders **Map 5:E3**

The Cross Keys, The Square, TD5 7HL. *Tel* 01573-223303, www.cross-keys-hotel.co.uk. Family-run hotel ('delightful owners, Marchello Becattelli and son Luca, and staff') on cobbled town square. Lift. Lounge, bar, restaurant; background music. 'Food straightforward, well prepared from local produce.' 28 bedrooms. B&B £33.50–£50 per person; D,B&B £48.50–£65.

KINROSS Perth and Kinross — Map 5:D2

Roxburghe Guest House, 126 High Street, KY13 8DA. *Tel* 01577-862498, www.roxburgheguesthouse.co.uk. Sandy Ferguson and Steve Wrigley's modest guest house on high street of old market town. Traditional Scottish cooking; local produce. 'Great breakfast.' Dining room (background music), patio (barbecue). Award-winning garden. Walkers and cyclists welcome (drying facilities). Off-street parking. 5 bedrooms. B&B £20–£40 per person. Full alc £25.

KIRKCUDBRIGHT Dumfries and Galloway — Map 5:E2

The Marks, DG6 4XR. *Tel* 01557-330854, www.marksfarm.co.uk. 3 miles NE of town: Sheila Watson and Chris Caygill's B&B in 16th-century farmhouse cradled by Galloway hills. Drawing room, study, breakfast room. No background music. Rambling gardens (woods, loch, walks, stabling). Beside working farm with sheep, Limousin cattle, dairy herd, worms (for organic waste management, fishing, composting). 3 bedrooms. B&B £25–£30 per person.

LOCHCARNAN Western Isles — Map 5: inset A1

Orasay Inn, Isle of South Uist, HS8 5PD. *Tel* 01870-610298, www.orasayinn.co.uk. On NE corner of 'fantastic' island ('unequalled birdlife'): Alan and Isobel Graham's low, white, modern inn/local pub. 'Everyone very friendly.' Simple accommodation, good breakfasts. Ramps. Residents' lounge, lounge bar, restaurant with conservatory extension ('outstanding views'); decked area for summer meals; Celtic/'easy-listening' background music on request. ¾-acre grounds. 9 bedrooms. Some on ground floor. Some have private deck area; some a bathroom equipped for ♿. B&B £30–£50 per person.

LOCKERBIE Dumfries and Galloway — Map 5:E2

The Dryfesdale, Dryfebridge, DG11 2SF. *Tel* 01576-202427, www.dryfesdalehotel.co.uk. Useful staging post near the border: family-run former manse, 1 mile from centre, near M74, exit 17. Lounges, bar, *Kirkhill* restaurant; conference/function facilities; background music. 5-acre grounds. 16 bedrooms (5 family; 1 suitable for ♿). B&B £55–£75 per person; D,B&B £82.50–£100.

LYBSTER Highland — Map 5:B3

The Portland Arms, KW3 6BS. *Tel* 01593-721721, www.portlandarms.co.uk. On A99 S of Wick: handsome granite coaching inn (1850s) on outskirts of fishing village, ½ mile from sea. Convenient stop-over for Orkney ferry. Lounge, library bistro/bar, *Kitchen* restaurant (local produce);

function facilities. No background music. Small front garden. 22 rooms. B&B £37.50–£50 per person.

MELROSE Borders **Map 5:E3**

The Townhouse, Market Square, TD6 9PQ. *Tel* 01896-822645, www.thetownhousemelrose.co.uk. Smartly renovated house with white-painted exterior in town square, opposite Henderson family's other hotel, *Burts* (see main entry). Brasserie, restaurant; background music; function facilities. 11 bedrooms. B&B £50–£70 per person. Dinner £28.50.

PEEBLES Borders **Map 5:E2**

Cringletie House, off Edinburgh Road, EH45 8PL. *Tel* 01721-725750, www.cringletie.com. 2 miles N of town, luxury hotel (Pride of Britain): pink stone, turreted Victorian mansion on 28-acre wooded estate. Lounge, library, bar, 'imposing' dining room; background music. 13 bedrooms (1 suitable for ♿). B&B £100–£245 per person; D,B&B £135–£280.

Park Hotel, Innerleithen Road, EH45 8BA. *Tel* 01721-720451, www.parkpeebles.co.uk. Gabled, white building (McMillan group), with views of Peebleshire hills. Lounge, bar (background music available), restaurant. Garden, putting, croquet; access to sports/health facilities at large sister, *Peebles Hotel Hydro* (700 yds: swimming pool, sauna; tennis, etc). 24 bedrooms. B&B £62.50–£92.50 per person; D,B&B £78–£108.

PERTH Perth and Kinross **Map 5:D2**

The Parklands, 2 St Leonard's Banks, PH2 8EB. *Tel* 01738-622451, www.theparklandshotel.com. Scott and Penny Edwards's contemporary hotel overlooking South Inch Park: views across River Tay to Kinnoull Hill. 5 mins' walk to town. Lounge, bar, *Acanthus* restaurant, *Number 1 The Bank* bistro; function facilities; light background music; free Wi-Fi. Terrace, garden. 16 bedrooms. B&B £45–£119 per person; D,B&B £59.50–£149.

Sunbank House, 50 Dundee Road, PH2 7BA. *Tel* 01738-624882, www.sunbankhouse.com. 'Well-looked-after hotel with superb food.' By River Tay, Remigio (chef) and Georgina Zane's Victorian house in landscaped gardens, 2 miles E of centre. 'Friendly service, homely atmosphere.' Italian-influenced dishes using Scottish produce. Lounge/bar, restaurant (light classical background music). Traditional decor. Wi-Fi. 9 bedrooms. B&B £42.50–£79 per person; D,B&B £70–£90.

PITLOCHRY Perth and Kinross **Map 5:D2**

Craigatin House, 165 Atholl Road, PH16 5QL. *Tel* 01796-472478, www.craigatinhouse.co.uk. 'Good overnight stop': B&B with stylish,

contemporary rooms in secluded Victorian house 5 mins' walk from town. Peaceful setting, good views. Lounge, conservatory breakfast room. Garden. 13 bedrooms (some suitable for ♿). B&B £24–£60 per person.
Green Park, Clunie Bridge Road, PH16 5JY. *Tel* 01796-473248, www.thegreenpark.co.uk. McMenemie family's country house, near theatre. 'Superb position' in 3-acre garden on Loch Faskally (putting, fishing, boat hire). 'Excellent value for money.' 3 lounges, library, bar, restaurant. No background music. 51 bedrooms (16 on ground floor; 1 suitable for ♿). B&B £50–£63 per person; D,B&B £56–£87.

RODEL Western Isles — Map 5:B1

Rodel Hotel, Isle of Harris, HS5 3TW. *Tel* 01859-520210, www.rodelhotel.co.uk. Donald and Dena MacDonald 'want guests to enjoy themselves' at their much-extended small hotel on picturesque harbour of tiny, historic village looking across to Skye. Works by local artists on display. 'Lovely modern woodwork.' Bar, restaurant ('good food'); background music. 4 bedrooms. B&B £50–£70 per person.

SCARISTA Western Isles — Map 5:B1

Scarista House, Isle of Harris, HS3 3HX. *Tel* 01859-550238, www.scaristahouse.com. Handsome white Georgian manse, 15 miles SW of Tarbert, above 'glorious' 3-mile sandy beach. Managed by co-owners (with Neil King) Tim and Patricia Martin. 'Very good food.' Children welcomed. 5 bedrooms (3 small ones in house, 2 suites and 2 self-catering units adjacent). Drawing room, library, dining room. No background music. 1-acre garden: trampoline. B&B £85–£97.50 per person. Dinner £41.50.

SCOURIE Highland — Map 5:B2

Eddrachilles Hotel, Badcall Bay, IV27 4TH. *Tel* 01971-502080, www.eddrachilles.com. Mr and Mrs Flannery's white-painted old manse above bay ('spectacular views'), 2 miles S of village. Reception, conservatory, bar, 2 dining rooms; classical background music at night. 4-acre garden; 60-acre grounds. 11 bedrooms. B&B £44–£70 per person; D,B&B £60–£84.
Scourie Hotel, IV27 4SX. *Tel* 01971-502396, www.scourie-hotel.co.uk. Overlooking Scourie Bay: Patrick and Judy Price's fishing hotel (old coaching inn). 2 lounges, 2 bars, *table d'hôte* restaurant. 9-acre grounds leading to sea (5 mins' walk to sandy beach); 25,000 acres of loch, river and hill-loch fishing for brown trout, salmon and sea trout. 20 bedrooms (views of bay or mountains; 2 family rooms in garden). B&B £33–£49 per person; D,B&B £53–£69.

TAYNUILT Argyll and Bute **Map 5:D1**

Roineabhal Country House, Kilchrenan, PA35 1HD. *Tel* 01866-833207, www.roineabhal.com. Roger and Maria Soep's smart guest house near Loch Awe. 'Good home cooking; exceptional accommodation.' Lounge, dining room (5-course dinners: dietary needs catered for; background music at night); veranda. Garden. Afternoon teas. Pick-up service from Oban/Taynuilt. 3 bedrooms (1 on ground floor). B&B £45–£55 per person. Dinner £35 (with wine).

ULLAPOOL Highland **Map 5:B2**

The Sheiling, Garve Road, IV26 2SX. *Tel* 01854-612947, www.thesheilingullapool.co.uk. Now owned by Iain and Lesley MacDonald: 'value-for-money' B&B. Modern, white, low-roofed building 5 mins' walk from town. Light, contemporary interior. Sitting room (log fire), dining room. No background music. 1-acre garden: lochside patio; mountain views across Loch Broom; trout fishing free to guests. *Sportsman's Lodge* in grounds (laundry, drying room; sauna, shower). 6 bedrooms. B&B £30–£35 per person.

WALES

BEAUMARIS Anglesey **Map 3:A3**

Bulkeley Hotel, Castle Street, LL58 8AW. *Tel* 01248-810415, www.bulkeleyhotel.co.uk. In 'magnificent setting' (sweeping views across Menai Straits): seaside hotel (Best Western) near castle. Cocktail lounge, restaurant (background music); wedding/function facilities. 43 bedrooms (some suitable for ♿). B&B £60–£90 per person.

BRECON Powys **Map 3:D3**

Cantre Selyf, 5 Lion Street, LD3 7AU. *Tel* 01874-622904, www.cantreselyf.co.uk. Near St Mary's church: Mr and Mrs Roberts's yellow-painted 17th-century town house. Lounge, dining room (traditional Welsh/continental breakfast; organic produce). No background music. Walled garden: summer house. Parking. 3 bedrooms (moulded, beamed ceilings, Georgian fireplaces, cast iron beds). B&B £31–£74 per person.

BRIDGEND **Map 3:E3**

The Great House, Laleston, CF32 0HP. *Tel* 01656-657644, www.great-house-laleston.co.uk. 2 miles W of Bridgend: 16th-century Grade II* listed hunting lodge, restored by 'hands-on' owners, Stephen and Norma Bond; many historical/architectural features. Lounge, bar, bistro, *Leicester's* restaurant (background music); health suite; conference/wedding facilities. 1-acre walled garden: dovecote. 16 bedrooms (some suitable for ♿). B&B £60–£75 per person.

CARDIFF **Map 3:E4**

The Big Sleep, Bute Terrace, CF10 2FE. *Tel* 029-2063 6363, www.thebigsleephotel.com. Friendly, budget, designer B&B hotel (former British Gas office building), owned by Cosmo Fry with consortium including John Malkovich. ½ mile from station. 'Minimalist kitsch' decor (much formica). Good views over city. Lift. Residents' bar, breakfast room; background music. Limited parking. 81 bedrooms. B&B (continental) £22.50–£75 per person.

CONWY **Map 3:A3**

Sychnant Pass House, Sychnant Pass Road, LL32 8BJ. *Tel* 01492-596868, www.sychnant-pass-house.co.uk. Bre and Graham Carrington-Sykes's 'relaxed' Edwardian home in foothills of Snowdonia national park. Open fires, 'comfy sofas'. Children and dogs welcomed (resident cats and dogs). Sitting room, study, restaurant (background music at night); indoor swimming pool; hot tub; gym. Terrace. 12 bedrooms (named after TS Eliot's 'practical cats'; 3 are small). B&B £47.50–£90 per person; D,B&B £75–£117.50.

HARLECH Gwynedd **Map 3:B3**

Castle Cottage, Y Llech, LL46 2YL. *Tel* 01766-780479, www.castlecottageharlech.co.uk. Just off high street: Jacqueline and Glyn Roberts's informal restaurant with contemporary rooms in 2 adjoining buildings (16th/17th century). Wooden beams, sloping floors; log fires. 'Stone-floored bathrooms, soft towels, lots of storage.' Lounge/bar, dining room (castle views); 'low-key' background music. 'Food a delight; fantastic, yet reasonable, wine list.' 7 bedrooms (4 in annexe; 2 on ground floor). B&B £50–£70 per person.

HAVERFORDWEST Pembrokeshire **Map 3:D1**

Crug-Glas, Abereiddy, Solva, SA62 6XX. *Tel* 01348-831302, www.crug-glas.co.uk. 1½ miles inland from Pembrokeshire coast: Evans family's guest house on 600-acre working farm. Traditional decor (family heirlooms). Lounge (videos, books), bar; dining room (background music). 1-acre garden. 5 bedrooms. B&B £40–£65 per person.

College Guest House, 93 Hill Street, St Thomas Green, SA61 1QL. *Tel* 01437-763710, www.collegeguesthouse.com. Grade II listed former college for Baptist ministers, 5 mins' walk from centre: now B&B run by

Colin Larby and Pauline Good. Lounge, dining room. Welsh breakfast using Pembrokeshire produce. No background music. Beach 6 miles. Parking. 8 bedrooms. B&B £30–£45 per person.

LAMPETER Ceredigion **Map 3:D3**

Tŷ Mawr Mansion, Cilcennin, SA48 8DB. *Tel* 01570-470033, www.tymawrmansion.co.uk. 'A wonderful hideaway', 4 miles SE of Aberaeron: Grade II listed country house restored by Catherine and Martin McAlpine. 'We felt pampered and replete after our visit.' 3 lounges, library, restaurant (local produce, mainly from garden/within 10-mile radius; 'easy listening' background music); panelled snooker room. 12-acre grounds. 9 bedrooms (some on ground floor). B&B £60–£120 per person; D,B&B £79.50–£150.

LLANARMON DYFFRYN CEIRIOG Denbighshire Map 3:B4

The West Arms, LL20 7LD. *Tel* 01691-600665, www.thewestarms.co.uk. In hamlet 7 miles SW of Llangollen: 16th-century building, now Williams family's country hotel, by River Ceiriog. Lounge, 2 bars (meal service), restaurant; 'mellow' background music; conservatory; conference/function facilities. Garden facing Berwyn mountains. 'Loved it. Food and service excellent.' 15 bedrooms. B&B £53.50–£89.50 per person; D,B&B £70–£114.

LLANDUDNO Conwy **Map 3:A3**

The Lighthouse, Marine Drive, Great Orme's Head, LL30 3XD. *Tel* 01492-876819, www.lighthouse-llandudno.co.uk. On cliff top, in Great Orme country park (2 miles from town): disused lighthouse, built in castle style by Mersey Docks and Harbour Co. in 1862. Welcoming hosts, the Kilpatrick family; renowned Welsh breakfast. 3 bedrooms (Lamp Room has panoramic views). B&B £75–£95 per person.

LLANGOLLEN Denbighshire **Map 3:B4**

Gales, 18 Bridge Street, LL20 8PE. *Tel* 01978-860089, www.galesofllangollen.co.uk. Off main street: lively wine bar/brasserie in 18th-century town house, owned 30 years by Gale family. Informal atmosphere. Chunky wood furniture, carved bedheads, beams. Meeting room, restaurant; wine shop adjacent; background music; conference facilities. Wi-Fi. Small patio. 15 bedrooms (7 above shop). B&B £35–£55 per person.

LLANWRTYD WELLS Powys **Map 3:D3**

Lasswade Country House, Station Road, LD5 4RW. *Tel* 01591-610515, www.lasswadehotel.co.uk. In UK's smallest town, in foothills of Cambrian mountains: Roger and Emma Stevens's Edwardian hotel. 'Warm, personal welcome. A good team – he in kitchen, she front-of-house.' Local, organic food. Drawing room; conservatory/function room (panoramic views); restaurant. No background music. Garden: kennels. Parking. 8 bedrooms. B&B £32.50–£65 per person.

MUMBLES Swansea — Map 3:E3

Norton House Hotel, Norton Road, SA3 5TQ. *Tel* 01792-404891, www.nortonhousehotel.co.uk. 3 miles SW of Swansea: 18th-century former mariner's house 100 yds from seafront. Elegant octagonal hall, lounge, bar, restaurant; function facilities; background music. 1-acre grounds. 15 bedrooms (some on ground floor; 8 in stable block). B&B £45–£86 per person.

Patricks with Rooms, 638 Mumbles Road, SA3 4EA. *Tel* 01792-360199, www.patrickswithrooms.com. Restaurant-with-rooms on bay (beautiful views), 5 miles SW of Swansea. Colonial-style lounge/bar; restaurant (fresh fish; vegetarian options); background music. Beach 100 yds. 8 colourful bedrooms (some suitable for ♿). B&B double £110.

RUTHIN Denbighshire — Map 3:A4

Manorhaus, Well Street, LL15 1AH. *Tel* 01824-704830, www.manorhaus.com. Bauhaus-inspired boutique hotel/art gallery owned by Christopher Frost and Gavin Harris: Grade II listed Georgian building off main square. Refurbished in modern style in 2006. Lounge, restaurant, library; 'easy listening' background music; steam room, sauna; fitness room. 8 bedrooms (designed around original works of art). B&B £57.50–£110 per person.

The Wynnstay Arms, Well Street, LL15 1AN. *Tel* 01824-703147, www.wynnstayarms.com. In centre: half-timbered coaching inn (established 1549); contemporary comforts inside. Lounge, bar, café bar, *fusions* brasserie; background music. Parking. 6 bedrooms. B&B (continental) £30–£50 per person; D,B&B £49.50–£70.

ST DAVID'S Pembrokeshire — Map 3:D1

Old Cross Hotel, Cross Square, SA62 6SP. *Tel* 01437-720387, www.oldcrosshotel.co.uk. In centre: 'simple, unspoilt' stone-built hotel, owned by Alex and Julie Babis. 'Friendly, efficient staff; excellent breakfasts, 2 very good dinners.' Lounge, bar (popular with locals; background radio), restaurant. Garden: alfresco meals in summer. Parking. 16 bedrooms ('clean, well appointed'). B&B £34–£62 per person; D,B&B £54–£82.

SWANSEA — Map 3:E3

Morgans Townhouse, Somerset Place, SA1 1RR. *Tel* 01792-484848, www.morganshotel.co.uk. 'Superb' conversion of Regency Port Authority building

(Grade II* listed), owned by Martin and Louisa Morgan. Modernised, with many impressive features. Bar, *Plimsoll* restaurant; background music; gym; function/wedding facilities. Courtyard. Parking. 41 bedrooms (21 in *Morgans Townhouse* opposite; 'daring double showers'). B&B double £80–£250.

CHANNEL ISLANDS

ST MARTIN'S Guernsey — Map 1:E5

Hotel Bella Luce, La Fosse, GY4 6EB. *Tel* 01481-238764, www.bellalucehotel.guernsey.net. Manor house (11th-century origins), 2 miles SW of St Peter Port. Oak-beamed lounge, bar (light meals), restaurant; background music. Garden: solar-heated swimming pool. Rock beach 5 mins' walk. 31 bedrooms (some family, 1 suitable for ♿). B&B from £51 per person.

ST PETER PORT Guernsey — Map 1:E5

La Frégate, Beauregard Lane, GU1 1UT. *Tel* 01481-724624, www.lafregatehotel.com. Recently expanded and refurbished 18th-century manor house: contemporary decor. On hillside (harbour views), 5 mins' walk from centre. Bar, restaurant ('very good dinner; excellent breakfast'); function facilities. No background music. 'Lovely' terrace. Small, secluded garden. 22 bedrooms (some with balcony). B&B £65–£85 per person. Dinner £27.50.

IRELAND

BELFAST — Map 6:B6

Culloden Estate and Spa, Bangor Road, Holywood, BT18 0EX. *Tel* 028-9042 1066, www.hastingshotels.com. Former bishop's palace, with Scottish baronial architecture and modern extension; views over Belfast Lough and Co. Antrim coastline. 5 miles NE of city. Comfortable public areas. Lounges, *Mitre* restaurant; health club, spa; background music. 12-acre grounds: *Cultra Inn.* Conference/function/wedding facilities. 79 bedrooms. B&B £100–£160 per person.

Malmaison, 34–38 Victoria Street, BT1 3GH. *Tel* 028-9022 0200, www.malmaison-belfast.com. Converted 1860s red brick warehouses near River Lagan in Cathedral Quarter (edge of centre). Smartly decorated (sombre tones). Lounges, bar, brasserie; background music; gym; small business centre; free Internet access. 64 bedrooms: £140–£355. Breakfast from £12.

The Merchant Hotel, 35–39 Waring Street, BT1 2DY. *Tel* 028-9023 4888, www.themerchanthotel.com. In Cathedral Quarter, former headquarters of Ulster Bank: extravagant Victorian Italianate interiors; striped carpets. Lifts. 2 bars (*Cloth Ear* the more informal), restaurant (stained-glass domed ceiling); club; background music; function facilities. Bentley car for hire. 26 bedrooms (2 suitable for ♿): £70–£300 per person. Dinner from £30.

Old Inn, Main Street, Crawfordsburn, Co. Down, BT19 1JH. *Tel* 028-9185 3255, www.theoldinn.com. Ancient coaching inn (1640), in village 10 miles E of centre. On edge of wooded country park that sweeps down to sea. Old-world charm: part thatched, beamed ceilings, wood-panelled walls. Gallery lounge, *Parlour* bar, conservatory-style *1614* restaurant; background music; conference/function facilities. Small garden. 30 bedrooms (1 suitable for ♿). B&B £47.50–£100 per person.

BLARNEY Co. Cork **Map 6:D5**

The Muskerry Arms. *Tel* 00 353 21-438 5200, www.muskerryarms.com. Lively public house in village centre, owned by O'Connor family for over 20 years; they have 'a natural talent for hospitality'. Bar ('full of atmosphere'), restaurant; live music. 11 'superb, peaceful' bedrooms (spacious, with wood floor; Wi-Fi). B&B €54–€108 per person.

DINGLE Co. Kerry **Map 6:D4**

Milltown House, *Tel* 00 353 66-915 1372, www.milltownhousedingle.com. Overlooking harbour, on peninsula 3 km W of town: Kerry family's friendly B&B in white, 19th-century gabled house. Lounge, conservatory/breakfast room (light meals available). No background music. 1½-acre garden. Golf driving range, pitch-and-putt behind house. Parking. 10 bedrooms (some with garden or sea views). B&B €65–€130 per person.

DONEGAL Co. Donegal **Map 6:B5**

Harvey's Point, *Tel* 00 353 74-972 2208, www.harveyspoint.com. 4 miles NE of Donegal on Lough Eske, at foot of Blue Stack mountains: much extended country hotel. Spacious accommodation (lavish penthouse suites). Lounge, bar, restaurant; conference/wedding facilities; frequent events. 20-acre grounds. 60 bedrooms. B&B €99–€145 per person. Dinner €55.

DUBLIN **Map 6:C6**

Brownes, 22 St Stephen's Green, Dublin 2. *Tel* 00 353 1-638 3939, www.brownesdublin.com. Elegant hotel in Georgian town house (Stein Group). 'Striking staircase; good period furniture.' Drawing room, restaurant ('dinner thoroughly enjoyable'); background music; function/meeting facilities. 11 bedrooms: €195–€480. Breakfast €12.50–€20.

Leixlip House, Captain's Hill, Leixlip, Co. Kildare. *Tel* 00 353 1-624 2268, www.leixliphouse.com. Overlooking village, 8 miles NW of Dublin (20 mins by motorway to centre/airport): Frank Towey's Georgian house.

Traditional decor. Lounge, bar (background music), *Bradaun* restaurant (modern Irish cuisine); conference/function facilities; Wi-Fi. Golf packages. Parking. 19 bedrooms (4 in coach house). B&B €85–€140 per person.

Longfields, 10 Fitzwilliam Street Lower, Dublin 2. *Tel* 00 353 1-676 1367, www.longfields.ie. Conversion of 2 Georgian terraced houses. Lounge, reading room, bar, *No. 10* restaurant. No background music. 26 bedrooms (quietest at rear). B&B €49.50–€135 per person.

Merrion Hall, 54–56 Merrion Road, Dublin 4. *Tel* 00 353 1-668 1426, www.halpinsprivatehotels.com. Refurbished, creeper-covered Edwardian hotel in Ballsbridge, S of city. Owned by Pat Halpin (see also *Aberdeen Lodge,* main entry). 2 drawing rooms, dining room/conservatory; background music. Free Wi-Fi. Garden. 28 bedrooms (2 suitable for ♿). B&B €74.50–€175 per person.

DUNGARVAN Co. Waterford **Map 6:D5**

Powersfield House, Ballinamuck West. *Tel* 00 353 58-45594, www.powersfield.com. 1 mile outside Dungarvan, on little peninsula: Edmund and Eunice (award-winning cook) Power's B&B in symmetrical white house. Crisp, smart interior. 'Superb food' (dinner by arrangement, €27.50–€35; background CDs/radio if wanted). Wi-Fi. Garden. Cookery courses. 6 bedrooms (1 suitable for ♿). B&B €55–€75 per person.

GALWAY Co. Galway **Map 6:C5**

The g, Wellpark. *Tel* 00 353 91-865200, www.theghotel.ie. Luxury hotel owned by Gerry Barrett, designed by milliner Philip Treacy. Striking colour schemes (pink, cerise, purple; swirling black-and-white striped carpets); 'decadent' furnishings; black marble lobby, champagne-drinking area, restaurant (facing Lough Atalia); spa; function facilities; background music; live pianist at weekends. 101 rooms: €250–€480. Breakfast €26.

KENMARE Co. Kerry **Map 6:D4**

Sheen Falls Lodge. *Tel* 00 353 64-41600, www.sheenfallslodge.ie. Overlooking waterfall: extended manor house in 300-acre mature woodlands. Former summer residence of Marquis of Lansdowne. 2 miles SE of town (off N71). Lift. Lounge, sun lounge, library, study, 2 bars, *La Cascade* restaurant; billiard room; background music. Health and fitness club (pool, whirlpool, sauna, treatments); tennis. 66 bedrooms. B&B €174–€469 per person; D,B&B €239–€534.

KILLARNEY Co. Kerry **Map 6:D4**

Dunloe Castle, Beaufort. *Tel* 00 353 64-71350, www.dunloecastlehotel.com. Modern 5-star hotel facing ruins of medieval keep (views of Gap of

Dunloe and River Laune: salmon fishing). 5 miles SW of town. Lounge, bar, *Oak Room* restaurant; background music/live pianist; indoor swimming pool; conference/wedding facilities. Children welcomed. 64-acre parkland: 20-acre subtropical garden; garden café. 2 indoor tennis courts, putting, croquet, fishing. 102 bedrooms. B&B €105–€300 per person. Dinner from €45.

KILLYBEGS Co. Donegal **Map 6:B5**

Bay View, Main Street. *Tel* 00 353 74-973 1950, www.bayviewhotel.ie. Modern 3-star hotel in centre, by pier and harbour. Lounge (snacks served), *Wheel House* bar/carvery, *Captain's Table* restaurant (overlooking harbour; 'catch of the day'); background music sometimes; leisure centre: swimming pool, gym, sauna. Conference facilities. 40 bedrooms. B&B €60–€120 per person.

KINSALE Co. Cork **Map 6:D5**

Pier House, Main Street. *Tel* 00 353 21-477 4475, www.pierhousekinsale.com. Ann and Pat Hegarty's B&B in family home on waterfront. Simply decorated; natural textures and colours; sleigh beds; under-floor-heated bathrooms. Lounge, breakfast room; background music. Landscaped garden: hot tub, sauna. Children welcomed. 10 bedrooms. B&B €50–€70 per person.

LONGFORD Co. Longford **Map 6:C5**

Viewmount House, Dublin Road. *Tel* 00 353 43-41919, www.viewmounthouse.com. Jim and Beryl Kearney's handsome Georgian house ('welcoming, comforting, homely') in 4-acre gardens adjoining golf course. Sitting room, reception room, library, restaurant; 'easy listening' background music. 4-acre garden. 13 bedrooms (7 new suites in modern extension were due to open as the *Guide* went to press). B&B €60–€150 per person.

STRANGFORD Co. Down **Map 6:B6**

The Cuan, BT30 7ND. *Tel* 028-4488 1222, www.thecuan.com. 'For the price, a very good stop-over.' Family-run (Peter and Caroline McErlean) licensed guest house in conservation village on S tip of Strangford Lough (ferries to Portaferry). Seafood restaurant; food served all day; conference/function facilities. 9 bedrooms. B&B £37–£42.50 per person.

WATERFORD Co. Waterford **Map 6:D5**

Granville Hotel, The Quay. *Tel* 00 353 51-305555, www.granville-hotel.ie. Overlooking waterfront and marina: large, traditionally furnished hotel in Georgian building, run by owners Liam and Ann Cusack. Lounge, bar, *Bianconi* restaurant; conference/wedding facilities; background/live music. 100 bedrooms (penthouse suites have wide views). B&B €47.50–€80 per person.

Alphabetical list of hotels

(S) indicates a Shortlist entry

D

E

F

G

N

Y

Z

[2008]

To: *The Good Hotel Guide*, Freepost PAM 2931, London W11 4BR

NOTE: No stamps needed in UK. Letters posted outside the UK should be addressed to 50 Addison Avenue, London W11 4QP, England, and stamped normally. Unless asked not to, we assume that we may publish your name. If you would like more report forms please tick ☐

Name of Hotel ______________________________

Address ______________________________

____

Date of most recent visit | Duration of visit

☐ New recommendation | ☐ Comment on existing entry

Report:

Please continue overleaf

I am not connected directly or indirectly with the management or proprietors

Signed ____________________

Name (CAPITALS PLEASE)

Address ____________________

____

Email address ____________________

[2008]

To: *The Good Hotel Guide*, Freepost PAM 2931, London W11 4BR

NOTE: No stamps needed in UK. Letters posted outside the UK should be addressed to 50 Addison Avenue, London W11 4QP, England, and stamped normally. Unless asked not to, we assume that we may publish your name. If you would like more report forms please tick ☐

Name of Hotel ______________________________

Address ______________________________

____

Date of most recent visit

Duration of visit

☐ New recommendation

☐ Comment on existing entry

Report:

Please continue overleaf

I am not connected directly or indirectly with the management or proprietors

Signed ______________________________

Name (CAPITALS PLEASE)

Address ______________________________

____

Email address ______________________________

[2008]

To: *The Good Hotel Guide*, Freepost PAM 2931, London W11 4BR

NOTE: No stamps needed in UK. Letters posted outside the UK should be addressed to 50 Addison Avenue, London W11 4QP, England, and stamped normally. Unless asked not to, we assume that we may publish your name. If you would like more report forms please tick ☐

Name of Hotel ______________________________

Address ______________________________

____

Date of most recent visit

Duration of visit

☐ New recommendation

☐ Comment on existing entry

Report:

Please continue overleaf

I am not connected directly or indirectly with the management or proprietors

Signed ______________________________

Name (CAPITALS PLEASE)

Address ______________________________

____

Email address ______________________________